TEXT-SUPPORTING WEB SITES

South-Western's Finance Resource Center. A unique, rich, and robust online resource for finance students, **http://finance.swcollege.com** provides customer service and product information, learning tips and tools, access to all of South-Western's text-supporting Web sites, and other cutting-edge educational resources such as our highly regarded Finance in the News, Finance Interactive, Corporate Finance Online, Investment Analysis Calculator, FinanceLinks Online, and Finance Digital Case Library.

Lasher Support Web Site. The Lasher Web site, **http://lasher.swcollege.com**, provides you with open access to online quizzes with immediate student feedback, the opportunity to communicate with us, direct links to all the Internet addresses and activities mentioned in the text, downloadable learning support tools, and much more.

THIRD EDITION

Practical
Financial
Management

William R. Lasher

NICHOLS COLLEGE

THOMSON

SOUTH-WESTERN

Australia · Canada · Mexico · Singapore · Spain · United Kingdom · United States

THOMSON
SOUTH-WESTERN

Practical Financial Management, 3rd Edition
William R. Lasher

Vice President/Team Director:
Michael P. Roche

Executive Editor:
Michael R. Reynolds

Senior Developmental Editor:
Susanna C. Smart

Senior Marketing Manager:
Charlie Stutesman

Senior Production Editor:
Kara ZumBahlen

Manufacturing Coordinator:
Sandee Milewski

Media Developmental Editor:
John Barans

Media Production Editor:
Mark Sears

Compositor:
Pre-Press Company, Inc.

Printer:
R.R. Donnelley & Sons
Willard Manufacturing Division

Internal and Cover Designer:
Rick Moore

Cover and Internal Illustrations:
©Fred Otnes, Stock Illustration
Source

Library of Congress Cataloging-
in-Publication Data
ISBN: 0-324-07184-1 (Text and
CD)
ISBN: 0-324-17489-6 (Text only)
ISBN: 0-324-14590-X (CD only)

Lasher, William.
    Practical financial management/
    R. Lasher.—3rd ed.
        p. cm.
    ISBN 0-324-07184-1 (alk. paper)
    1. Business enterprises—
    Finance. 2. Corporations.—
    Finance.

HG4026 .L37 2002
658.15—dc21   2001057644

*For the lights of my life,
Donna and our Amanda Noel*

BRIEF CONTENTS

v

CONTENTS

● CHAPTER 3   Cash Flows and Financial Analysis   57

● CHAPTER 8   **Risk and Return**   250

● PART THREE

Business Investment Decisions—Capital Budgeting   295

● CHAPTER 9   **Capital Budgeting**   296

● CHAPTER 10   Cash Flow Estimation   329

● CHAPTER 11   Risk Topics and Real Options in Capital Budgeting   355

● PART FOUR

Long-Term Financing Issues 419

● CHAPTER 14   Dividends   468

● PART FIVE

Operations Issues— Working Capital Management and Planning   491

● CHAPTER 15   The Management of Working Capital   492

● PART SIX

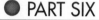

Current Topics in Financial Management   589

● **CHAPTER 17   Corporate Restructuring   590**

● **CHAPTER 18   International Finance   625**

The third edition of *Practical Financial Management* is the latest milestone in a 28-year journey in education that began when I was still a corporate executive teaching finance as an adjunct professor.

Not long after starting down that road I realized that I might be able to improve on the approach taken by most finance texts. It was true then, and it's still true today, that most finance texts are harder for students to understand than they should be. The issue is relatively unique to the field. No other business discipline seems to have finance's reputation for unfathomable reading material.

I eventually came to the conclusion that the problem lies in the fact that textbook presentations are inconsistent with the background knowledge and abilities of typical business students. That isn't to say that the texts are poorly done. By and large, finance texts are good books. They're logical, well written, and comprehensive. But they're consistently off target in several key areas with respect to the students who read them.

The first problem has to do with background. Texts tend to introduce topics using a voice that assumes the student already has some grounding in the area to be studied. Even bright students are confused and intimidated by this practice, because most don't know anything about the subject area when they start a chapter.

Then there is the thorny issue of quantitative material. A great deal of finance is grounded in math and statistics, so students have to take prerequisite courses in those areas. But most business students aren't really comfortable with quantitative methods, even after they've had the courses. This leads to the biggest pedagogical problem we have. Textbooks assume business students are inherently more facile with math than they really are, so most readers can't follow the presentations without an inordinate amount of time and study.

Finally, there is a troubling lack of practicality in much of this literature. For example, texts present financial techniques such as (NPV) and (IRR) in capital budgeting in ways that imply a hair-splitting accuracy that doesn't exist in the real world, where results often depend on biased and uncertain inputs. Textbooks are also silent on the behavioral problems that financial managers deal with every day. For example, the conflict between sales and finance over receivables can tear a company apart, but it is rarely mentioned in textbooks.

The result of all this has been that finance professors don't get much help from textbooks in teaching introductory courses. We develop classroom approaches that get the ideas across, but spend a great deal of time explaining what the text is trying to say rather than using it to support our teaching.

Over a period of years, I developed ways around these problems that eventually evolved into *Practical Financial Management*. I began by writing expositions on subjects that gave students the most trouble, starting with time value and portfolio theory. Those explanations really worked! Time value is a good example. Students have difficulties even though they've generally seen it before. After reading my material students would come in saying, "I never really understood time value when I had it in accounting and math, but now I do!" As you can imagine, that felt pretty good.

Fifteen years later, after serving in a number of corporate financial positions including chief financial officer (CFO), I changed careers, becoming a full-time educator in order to pursue my first loves, teaching and writing. One of the results is *Practical Financial Management (PFM)*, now in its third edition. *PFM* is unique because of its approach to teaching finance. That approach is the result of a combination of classroom and practical experience. The theme is easy to summarize.

We begin every area of study by presenting the heart of the business problem or issue. We start from scratch, assuming students know nothing about the area. That's critical—we bring readers up from absolute zero so there is no confusion and they know exactly where they are going and why. Look at the beginning of Chapter 8 on portfolio theory for an example (pages 250–251). We begin the chapter by explaining why we study "risk and return" in the first place and define the investor's goals right away in terms beginning students can understand. After that key theories are explained clearly and are quickly backed up with practical examples.

Next, wherever math is involved we explain the physical and business relationships between variables before developing or using equations. We discuss what each aspect of a relationship means as we put it together. That gives the equations substance and meaning to students who are less than comfortable in quantitative areas. See the development of IRR in Chapter 9 as an example (pages 305–306).

Then, when we do use math or complex procedures, we carefully explain what we're doing step by step. We assume students have the basic tools of algebra or accounting or statistics, but we don't assume they know that material well. This is another crucial point. Most students aren't really skilled in those areas. But because our systematic presentation recognizes that, students don't get lost or stuck. *PFM* is a resource students can use by themselves as well as under supervision. They can read whole chapters on their own and come to class better prepared than ever before. Look at the first pages in the development of the time value of money in Chapter 5 as an example (page 143). Also see the development of the statement of cash flows in Chapter 3 for the same idea in the context of difficult accounting material rather than math (pages 70–72).

Finally, I've drawn on my years of experience as a financial executive, including time behind the CFO's desk, to present some insights into how things really work. You'll find these explanations throughout the book, identified by a "From the CFO" icon in the margin. A prime example deals with the problems associated with estimating cash flows for capital budgeting projects, which is found in Chapter 10 (see Example 10.2, pages 342–345). *PFM*'s end-of-chapter discussion questions are an important practical feature. A few in each chapter are mini-cases designed to open students' eyes to the realities of applying financial principles in actual business. The questions at the end of Chapter 10 on cash flow estimation provide additional good examples (pages 346–347).

Throughout, I've tried to write this book in a way that's easy to read, enjoyable, and unintimidating. The word that sums that up is "accessible." I think I've been successful, because reviewers have been unanimous in their praise of the work's conversational style and easy readability.

Thank you for using *Practical Financial Management*. I'm absolutely sure you and your students will be pleased with the learning experience they'll have as a result.

Changes to This Edition

We've made a number of exciting changes in the third edition that will please professors and students alike. The following is a brief summary.

Decision Tree Analysis Added to the Treatment of Risk in Capital Budgeting

Our treatment of risk in capital budgeting, which previously included scenario analysis, simulation, and risk adjusted rates, has been expanded to include decision tree analysis. This important addition focuses on enhancing the capital budgeting decision-making process by presenting management with estimated probability distributions for NPV and IRR rather than point estimates for those parameters.

A Treatment of Real Options Has Been Added That's Both Clear and Comprehensive

One of the most exciting new developments in corporate finance is the practice of building options into operating plans that potentially enhance performance. Real options thinking is especially effective in capital budgeting for big-ticket items. In response to heightened interest in academic and business circles, a treatment of real options has been included in the third edition. The exposition is included as a risk issue in capital budgeting, and is a continuation of the new section on decision trees.

Real options is an advanced topic, and contemporary treatments often leave students frustrated and confused. *PFM*'s explanation is detailed and thorough, but guaranteed not to confuse or mystify students.

Capital Budgeting Is Now Covered in Three Chapters

In previous editions, capital budgeting was treated in two chapters, the second of which covered cash flow estimation as well as risk issues. With the addition of decision tree analysis and real options, the second chapter has been split into two. Hence in the third edition, capital budgeting models are covered in Chapter 9, cash flow estimation is treated in Chapter 10, and Chapter 11 deals with risk-related topics including the new material.

Additional End-of-Chapter Problems

New problems have been added at the end of every chapter. The emphasis is on relatively easy exercises that provide a smoother transition into subsequent, more difficult problems.

New INSIGHTS Boxes on Real World Applications Added

A new series of INSIGHTS boxes has been added to the third edition. **INSIGHTS: Real Applications** boxes illustrate the application of chapter material to situations faced by prominent companies.

There are now three separate sets of INSIGHTS boxes. The *ethics* series highlights moral or ethical dilemmas faced by financial executives, the *practical finance* series applies chapter concepts to real and hypothetical problems, and *real applications* now focuses on well-known companies.

Coverage of Spreadsheet Solutions Included

Computer spreadsheets are being used to solve computational problems in virtually all areas of practical finance. However, the more complex functions can be tricky to use. Recognizing this, the third edition includes instruction on using computer spreadsheets to solve time value and capital budgeting problems.

Instruction on Using Financial Calculators Expanded

It's easy to do basic math and simple time value problems with financial calculators. But more advanced calculations involving uneven cash flow streams can be tedious. Unfortunately, calculator manuals are hard to read and easy to forget. Recognizing this, we've added instructions on finding NPVs and IRRs for projects with uneven cash flows in Chapter 9 on capital budgeting. This is in addition to instruction on the use of financial calculators already in the time value material in Chapter 5.

Test Bank and Study Guide Revised

The test bank and study guide have been completely redeveloped. Their content and approach are detailed below under supplements.

New Technology

E-LECTURES. E-Lectures for each chapter are new to this edition. These are available on the Xtra! CD and serve as a review of problems as the student walks through the concepts and mathematical processes being discussed. E-Lectures are a useful learning tool for both the visual and audial learner.

POWERPOINT PRESENTATION UPGRADED. The PowerPoint presentation accompanying the text has been updated and expanded to include animation. The presentation is available in three versions of increasing sophistication. It is described in more detail below under supplements.

ON-LINE QUIZZES UPDATED. On-line quizzes, available for student use at the text's web site, have been updated and expanded.

Continuing Unique and Important Features

The following special features have been retained from earlier editions.

From the CFO

This feature highlights material that's based on the author's experience as a CFO. These comments deal with finance in actual practice, and offer tips and insights that are grounded in real-world experience. "From the CFO" material appears throughout the text and is identified by a logo in the page margin and italicized print.

Margin Notes

PFM's summarizing margin notes are particularly complete and thorough. They provide students with a convenient summary/outline of the textual material rather than just a list of key words.

Internet Notes and Problems

Internet addresses and descriptions are included in the margin material to direct students to web sites that expand upon the material being presented. Internet problems are also included in end of chapter material.

INSIGHTS: Practical Finance

These boxed features provide information, analysis, and commentary on current topics in the real financial world.

INSIGHTS: Ethics

"INSIGHTS: Ethics" boxes delve into ethical issues faced by financial managers in their professional lives. These issues are relevant to the topics being discussed or pertain to high-interest issues.

Supplements

Practical Financial Management comes with a full set of supplements, with many available in print and/or on the text web site.

Study Guide. The study guide, prepared by John A. McDougald of Northern Illinois University, has been expanded in the third edition. It contains learning objectives for each chapter along with chapter summaries, and detailed reviews that encapsulate relevant points and concepts, with important equations highlighted. In addition, each chapter is reinforced with a generous number of self-test questions including true/false, multiple choice, fill-in, and problems. Answers are provided for all.

Product Support Web Site. PFM's web site at http://lasher.swcollege.com contains student resources, instructor resources, Internet updates and links, spreadsheet software, PowerPoint slides, online quizzes, and other useful features. Students can go directly to the text web site to link to the Internet addresses in the text margins and to work the end-of-chapter Internet exercises.

Lasher Xtra! CD-ROM. The Lasher Xtra! CD-ROM, packaged with every new text, provides students and instructors with complimentary access to the robust set of additional online learning tools found at the site. If you don't have the CD, you can purchase access to the online version at http://lasherXtra.swcollege.com. Here is a tour through some of the study support features found there:

- E-Lectures: Difficult concepts from each chapter are explained and illustrated via streaming video and animated tutorials. These video clips and tutorials can be extremely helpful review and clarification tools if you had trouble understanding an in-class lecture or if you are more of a visual learner who sometimes has difficulty grasping concepts as they are presented in the text.

- CNN Video: CNN Video segments bring the "real world" right to your desktop. The accompanying CNN video exercises help to illustrate how finance is an important part of your daily life.

- Xtra! Quizzing: In addition to the open-access chapter-by-chapter quizzes found at the PFM Product Support Web site, Lasher Xtra! offers an opportunity to practice for midterms and finals by taking online quizzes that span multiple chapters.

- The Problem Bank: The Problem Bank: Practice Problems for Financial Management contains over 400 problems in multiple-choice format—with solutions—to help students practice computational skills.

● Enhanced PowerPoint: PowerPoint slides consist of added materials such as links to Internet sites and to spreadsheets, as well as additional figures not included in the text. These are placed on the Xtra! CD to make them more easily accessible to students by avoiding long download times associated with large files.

Instructor's Manual. The *Instructor's Manual*, by the text author, contains chapter-by-chapter focus statements, pedagogical tips, and teaching objectives. All of the discussion questions are answered in detail, and solutions to the problems are fully worked out. The *Instructor's Manual* is also available on the text's Web site, password protected for instructors only.

Spreadsheet Software. PFM contains two types of computer problem in the end-of-chapter material. Some problems use spreadsheet templates, and others require students to create their own spreadsheet software. The templates, developed by the author and Leonard W. Gajewski of Nichols College, are available—on the text web site and the Xtra! CD-ROM—to both students and instructors.

Powerpoint Solutions Slides. The Instructor's Resource CD contains PowerPoint slides with solutions to most numerical problems at the end of each chapter. The slides can be used in class either electronically or printed as transparency masters. These are also available on the text's Web site, password protected for instructors only.

Powerpoint Lecture Slides. Three PowerPoint slide packages have been created for the third edition of *PFM*. Two are available on the text web site at **http://lasher.swcollege.com**, and one is only on the Xtra! CD. These color slides are particularly unique and complete. The slides provide a detailed and highlighted outline that instructors can work from in front of a class, and that can also be downloaded by students for use in note-taking. Each illustrative example is summarized and provides a useful lecture and study tool.

● Version 1: Basic PowerPoint slides provide lecture notes for instructors that can also serve as a study aid for students.

● Version 2: Expanded PowerPoint slides include the basic lecture notes, as well as figures and examples from the text.

● Version 3: Enhanced PowerPoint slides are available on the Xtra! CD-ROM.

Test Bank. Revised and prepared by Lee McClain of Western Washington University, the test bank contains more than a thousand insightful questions categorized by topic area. The questions include multiple choice, true/false, fill-in, and problems.

ExamView. The ExamView computerized testing program contains all of the questions in the printed test bank. ExamView is an easy-to-use test creation software compatible with Microsoft Windows. Instructors can add or edit questions, instructions, and answers, and select questions by previewing them on the screen, selecting them randomly, or selecting them by number. Instructors can also create and administer quizzes on-line, whether over the Internet, a local-area network (LAN), or a wide-area network (WAN).

South-Western Finance Resource Center at **http://finance.swcollege.com**. The South-Western Finance Resource Center provides unique features such as "Finance in the News," "Corporate Finance Online," "FinanceLinks Online," customer service information, and links to book-related web sites. Learn about valuable products and services to help with your finance studies, contact the finance editors, register for Thomson Financial Network, and more.

Thomson Financial Network. This is the leading provider of Internet-based, on-line financial information. A subscription provides individual investors with a wealth of information and the tools needed to make informed investment decisions. A portfolio tracker, live stock quotes, business news, a variety of company and industry reports, market analysis and commentary, and more are available at the site. Contact your Thomson Learning representative for details. Meanwhile, visit http://www.thomsonfn.com for a preview.

Cases. Two resources for cases are available with the text.

- *Casenet* Internet resources takes learning to the next level with the premier series of field cases that explore real business scenarios. Find the best cases for your course, as well as instructions on how to order them, at http://casenet. thomsonlearning.com. Comprehensive teaching packages are available to instructors.

- The *Finance Digital Case Library* includes more than 100 cases from which instructors can create their own course-specific casebook. Contact your Thomson Learning sales representative for details.

ACKNOWLEDGMENTS

We can't say enough in praise of the following reviewers who participated in the writing of each edition of this book. They provided encouragement, criticism, ideas, and enthusiasm, all at the right times.

Ibrahim Affaneh
Indiana University of Pennsylvania

Brian L. Belt
University of Missouri–Kansas City

Sheela Bhagat
Rust College

Gilbert W. Bickum
Eastern Kentucky University

Eric Blazer
Millersville University

Gordon R. Bonner
University of Delaware

Karl Borden
University of Nebraska

G. Michael Boyd
Stetson University

Paul Bursik
St. Norbert College

Haiyang Chen
Youngstown State University

Faye Austin Cook
University of North Carolina
at Charlotte

Ron Cooley
South Suburban College

Louann Hofheins Cummings
Siena Heights University

Maryanne P. Cunningham
University of Rhode Island

Dennis Debrecht
Carroll College

Gary R. Dokes
University of San Diego

R. Stephen Elliott
Northwestern State University

Soga Ewedemi
Clarion University of Pennsylvania

E. Bruce Fredrikson
Syracuse University

Phillip Fuller
Jackson State University

Robert J. Hartwig
Worcester State College

Delvin D. Hawley
University of Mississippi

Marianne Hite
University of Colorado at Denver

Norbert Jerina
Cuyahoga Community College

Jenna J. Johannpeter
Belleville Area CC

Larry Johnson
New Hampshire College

Frederick J. Kelly
Roger Williams University

Robert T. Kleiman
Oakland University

Morris Knapp
Miami-Dade Community College

S. Brooks Marshall
James Madison University

Lee McClain
Western Washington University

John A. McDougald
Northern Illinois University

Stuart Michelson
University of Central Florida

Allen D. Morton
Western Connecticut State University

James M. O'Donnell
Huntington College

Gregory J. Petrakis
University of Missouri–Kansas City

Dennis Proffitt
Grand Canyon University

Michael R. Rouse
University of Massachusetts–Lowell

Frederick P. Schadler
East Carolina University

David Schalow
California State University, San Bernadino

Patricia Setlick
Wm. Rainey Harper College

Sandeep Singh
SUNY Brockport

Elliott P. Smith
Boston College

Edward J. Stendardi
St. John Fisher College

Waymond D. Summers
Oklahoma City Community College

William K. Templeton
Butler University

Clifford F. Thies
Shenandoah University

Bijesh Tolia
Chicago State University

Sanjay B. Varshney
SUNY Institute of Technology at Utica/Rome

Sarah S. Wells
Columbia College

Fran Wolf
Youngstown State University

Shirley Zaragoza
Borough of Manhattan Community College

In addition, I would like to extend my sincere appreciation to the members of the South-Western College Publishing team whose efforts resulted in this third edition and all of its supplements: Mike Mercier and Mike Reynolds, my acquisitions editors, who provided encouragement and guidance; Susanna Smart, my developmental editor, whose ideas and support resulted in many of the new features in this edition; Julie Lindsay and Charlie Stutesman, the marketing managers who enthusiastically contributed to the promotion and new supplements for the text; and Kara ZumBahlen, my production editor, whose attention to detail resulted in this final product.

William R. Lasher

William R. Lasher has a unique background spanning both education and practice in finance. Prior to entering full-time academics, he worked for Texas Instruments, Harris Corporation, and the Pacific Telesis organization. He has held positions as a planner, a controller, and a subsidiary CFO. While working in industry he served as an adjunct professor at the University of Dallas, the University of Texas at Dallas, and Golden Gate University in San Francisco. He moved into education full time in 1988 by joining the faculty at Nichols College.

Professor Lasher has a B.S. and an M.B.A from Columbia University, received his Ph.D. from Southern Methodist University, holds a J.D. from New England School of Law, and is a Certified Public Accountant. He has also published books on business planning, franchising, and the strategic management of small firms.

PART ONE

Introduction to Financial Management

CHAPTER 1

Foundations

Chapter Outline

AN OVERVIEW OF FINANCE

Finance is the art and science of handling money. In the modern world virtually every organization, public and private, runs on money. That includes families, businesses, governments, and nonprofit enterprises. Money touches everything we do. And finance, the management of money, is behind most everything we see each day. We don't physically observe the financing behind a building or a new car or a house, but it's there, and without it most of the things we do see wouldn't exist. That's because without money to pay for resources and a financial system to make trading possible, no one could organize more than a few people to work together at one time.

Our study of finance will be broadly divided into two areas: (1) investments and financial markets and (2) the financial management of companies.[1] These are separate but related. A financial system involves flows of money and paper between them.

To begin our study of finance, we need a few basic terms and ideas. Let's master these before going any further.

http://

Besides stock quotes and other data and information, the NYSE has a financial glossary at

● www.nyse.com

---

1. The banking system, a third sector of the financial world, is generally covered in an economics course on "Money and Banking" or "Financial Institutions."

FINANCIAL ASSETS

● A **real asset** is an object that provides a service. A **financial asset** (or **security**) is a document representing a claim to income.

A **real asset** is an object or thing, such as a car, a house, a factory, or a piece of machinery. Real assets have value because they provide some kind of service, such as transportation, shelter, or the ability to produce something.

Financial assets, on the other hand, are legal documents, pieces of paper. Their value comes from the fact that they give their owners claim to certain future *cash flows.* Most financial assets are either stocks or bonds, and their claim to future income is based on ownership or debt, respectively.

Stock ownership means that the holder of a share owns a piece of the company that issued the stock. As a part owner, he or she is entitled to a share of the firm's profits, which may be paid out in dividends or retained to enhance prospects for growth. The shareholder generally expects to sell the share at some time in the future and will then receive the proceeds of that sale in cash. Thus, the owner of a stock certificate can look for two sources of cash in the future: dividends and the eventual selling price of the share.

● **Stock** represents an **ownership** interest. **Bonds** represent a **debt** relationship.

A bond signifies a debt relationship. When a person buys a bond, he or she is actually lending money to the firm issuing the bond. The terminology seems strange— "buying a bond" meaning "lending money." Nevertheless, a bondholder is actually a lender and as such is entitled to interest on the amount lent and the repayment of principal at the end of the loan period.

Companies issue financial assets to raise money. They generally use that money to buy real assets that are used in running their businesses.

● **Investing** involves buying financial assets in the hope of earning **income.**

Financial assets are purchased by people or other companies to earn income with funds they don't currently need. Buying such an asset is similar to opening a savings account and receiving interest on the money you've put in the bank. In fact, a savings account is another kind of financial asset. Another name for a financial asset like a stock or a bond is a **security.** A person or organization buying a financial asset is said to be **investing** in that asset, and we generally call that buyer an *investor.*

● A **mutual fund** purchases securities with the pooled resources of many investors.

Investments in financial assets can be made directly by buying securities or indirectly by buying shares in a **mutual fund.** A mutual fund pools the contributions of many investors and employs a professional manager to select securities that match a particular set of investment goals.

FINANCIAL MARKETS

● Securities are traded in **financial markets** like the **stock market.**

Both kinds of financial assets are issued by companies and purchased by investors in *financial markets.* A **financial market** isn't exactly a place; rather, it's a framework or organization in which people can buy and sell securities in accordance with well-defined rules and regulations. The best known financial market is the **stock market.** It is centered in several places around the country, called **stock exchanges.** The largest exchange is the New York Stock Exchange.

● A **stockbroker** is licensed to trade securities on behalf of investors.

To participate in the market, you don't have to go to an exchange. You simply establish a relationship with a *stockbroker* in your area and communicate with him or her by phone. A **stockbroker** is a person who is licensed to help investors buy and sell securities for a commission. Local brokers are connected to the various exchanges electronically. The stock market is really the entire network of brokers and exchanges all connected together. Bond markets for trading in debt securities operate similarly.

In summary, financial markets are "places" where investors buy financial assets from companies that issue them. Investors also buy and sell the same financial assets between themselves in the same financial markets. In fact, the vast majority of transactions are between investors. That's because a security is issued by a company only once, but it may be traded among investors many times thereafter.

In practice, the term "market" describes the combined actions of investors acting within the marketplace just described. For example, someone might say that the market has placed a price of $100 on a share of IBM. That would mean the going price among investors buying and selling the stock of the IBM corporation within the structure of the stock market is $100.

Figure 1.1 is a schematic representation of the interaction between companies and the market.

The field of investments involves making decisions about buying stocks and bonds. Decisions about how to raise money and what to do with it are part of the financial management of a firm. These decisions are made on the two sides of Figure 1.1, which represent the two areas in which our study will focus.

Now let's consider the word "finance" itself. Its use can be a little confusing. It's a noun, as in "the field of finance." It's a verb, as in "to finance something." And it also has an adjective form, as in "financial management." Let's explore these variations in meaning.

● RAISING MONEY

The most common application of the term "finance" involves raising money to acquire assets. We've all heard people say they're going to *finance* a car or a house. When they say that, individuals usually mean they're going to borrow money from a bank to buy the item.

● **Financing** means raising money to acquire something.

The word is used similarly in business. Companies *finance assets* when they raise money to acquire those assets. They do that by borrowing, selling stock, or using money they've earned. In recent years, many assets have been acquired through leasing. We say those items are *lease financed*.

A company itself is *financed* when money is raised to get it started or for expansion. Such money can come from borrowing or from selling stock. To the extent the money is borrowed, we say the company is *debt financed*. To the extent it comes from selling stock, we say the firm is *equity financed*. Equity implies financing with an owner's own money.

Looking at Figure 1.1, we see that firms in the box on the right are raising money, financing things. They do that by selling stocks and bonds to investors in the box on the left. The *field of finance* includes both sides of this money-raising transaction. It relates to the concerns of parties raising money and to those of parties providing it. Further, because the money raised flows through financial markets and institutions, their operation is a part of the field as well.

FIGURE 1.1

Simplified Financial System

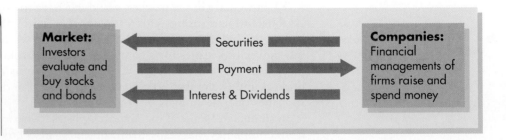

The Changing Focus of Finance

Historically, the field of finance was narrowly limited to activity within financial markets. Today the perspective has expanded in two directions.

First, in modern finance a great deal of attention is given to the goals and activities of the investor. In the early days a complete description of a particular security (stock or bond) was felt to be all an investor needed to make a decision comfortably. Today we've become concerned with the notion of risk in investing and with how investors put together groups of securities called **portfolios** to minimize that risk. We'll examine these concepts at length in Chapter 8.

● A **portfolio** is a collection of securities.

The second direction of expansion involves the role and function of financial management within firms. Historically financial managers were told how much money their companies needed for particular projects, and they went outside in pursuit of those funds. They had little to do with deciding how much was needed or what was done with the money after it was raised. Today financial managers are deeply involved in those related decisions.

●FINANCIAL MANAGEMENT

Financial management means the management and control of money and money-related operations within a business. Companies have finance departments that are responsible for these functions.

● The corporate executive in charge of finance is called the **Chief Financial Officer (CFO).**

The executive in charge of the finance department is the company's **Chief Financial Officer,** abbreviated **CFO.** The title **Vice President of Finance** is sometimes used instead of CFO. In either case, the position usually reports to the president of the company.

The term "financial management" refers to the things the CFO and the finance department do. These activities include keeping records, paying employees and vendors, receiving payments from customers, borrowing, purchasing assets, selling stock, paying dividends, and a number of others.

It's important to notice that accounting is included in this broad definition of finance and that the accounting function is usually found within the finance department.

http://

Wonder what careers in finance are all about? Visit
● www.careers-in-business.com

Business Decisions

Financial management also refers to the financial input that goes into general business decisions. This extremely important concept is best explained by an example.

Suppose a domestic company is contemplating expanding overseas. That's likely to be a big decision discussed by the firm's key executives over a long period of time. Each executive will have opinions and recommendations related to his or her own area of responsibility, such as marketing or manufacturing. The CFO will similarly have opinions on how to set up the finance function in the new venture, how to do its accounting, and what banks to use. In addition, he or she will probably have to secure funding to support the project, either from a bank or by issuing securities.

Beyond that, however, the CFO must form a judgment about the feasibility of the project in terms of whether it will be profitable enough to justify its own cost. In other words, the bottom line for most projects is money, and the responsibility for assessing that bottom line falls to financial management. (We'll study the techniques used to make this kind of decision in Chapters 9, 10, and 11.)

Oversight

Another important aspect of financial management involves the relationship between finance and other departments in the day-to-day management of the firm. It's important to grasp the fact that finance is responsible for its own activities, but has a responsibility for the operation of other departments as well.

Let's look into that idea a little more deeply. Finance is responsible for money, but other departments deal in money too. That's because they have to spend it to do their jobs, and their success is defined in terms of money. For example, manufacturing's task may be to produce some quantity of product, but doing the job properly involves keeping costs low and using a reasonable level of inventory.

The finance department generally has an *oversight responsibility* for the effective management of the money other departments spend. Hence, if manufacturing's costs are too high or if it carries too much inventory, finance is responsible for calling attention to those facts and ensuring that corrective action is taken. In other words, *part of finance's job involves looking over everyone else's shoulder to make sure they're using money effectively.*

● The finance department **oversees** how other departments spend money.

from the CFO

THE PRICE OF SECURITIES—A LINK BETWEEN THE FIRM AND THE MARKET

The two sides of finance, investments and the financial management of the firm, are connected by the fact that companies sell securities to investors in financial markets.

A fundamental truth, which we'll examine in detail later, is that investors buy securities for the future cash flows that come from owning them. Those cash flows depend on the issuing companies' financial performance. Hence, the prices investors are willing to pay for securities depend on their expectations about how well the issuing companies are likely to do in the future in terms of profit. Further, because the future is never guaranteed, the market is also concerned about the risk associated with expected performance. A perception of greater risk tends to lower investor interest and security prices.

The link between company management and investments comes from this relationship between price and expected financial results. Everything firms and their managers do is watched by the market, and has an impact on investors' perceptions of likely future performance and risk. Those perceptions, in turn, have a direct impact on the prices of stocks and bonds.

In other words, the study of investments includes looking at the way companies are managed to estimate future performance. At the same time, the management of companies includes consideration of how business decisions are perceived by investors and the effects those perceptions have on the prices of stocks and bonds.

FINANCE AND ACCOUNTING

In most industrial companies, the majority of the people involved in money-oriented activities are accountants, so people sometimes get the idea that accounting and finance are synonymous. In fact they're not, and it's important to understand how they fit together.

Accounting is a system of record keeping designed to portray a firm's operations to the world in a fair and unbiased way. The records are used periodically to produce financial statements that present the company's results to anyone who reads them.

However, several other financial functions are performed in most companies. These include raising money, analyzing results, and handling relationships with outsiders such as banks, shareholders, and representatives of the investment community. Most of these functions are performed by the *treasury department*.

The *finance department* normally consists of both the *accounting department* headed by the *controller* and the *treasury department* headed by the *treasurer*. Both of these positions report to the *chief financial officer (CFO)*. The typical organization is depicted in Figure 1.2.

○ The **controller** is in charge of accounting while the **treasurer** supervises most other financial functions.

In practice, it's become common to think of accounting as an almost separate field, and to refer to the other financial functions as finance. For the most part this means that the treasury functions are called *finance* and the controller functions are called *accounting*.

People tend to have careers in one side of the department or the other, but crossover is possible. It's generally easier for an accountant to move into treasury than the other way around. That's because of the large number of specialized courses required to be a professional accountant. Either controllers or treasurers can become CFOs.

Companies are organized in different ways, and who does what isn't always clear cut. Many of the activities we'll study in this book are done in the accounting department in one company and in the treasury (finance) department in another. Activities such as financial analysis (Chapter 3), financial planning (Chapter 16), and capital budgeting (Chapters 9, 10, and 11) are generally done wherever the resources are available to do the job best.

Finance majors shouldn't be discouraged by the preponderance of accounting jobs in typical industrial companies. The majority of jobs in the investment industry and in financial institutions such as banks and insurance companies are in finance rather than accounting.

● THE IMPORTANCE OF CASH FLOW

The relative emphasis placed on cash flow is important in conceptually differentiating between accounting and finance. The accounting system attempts to portray a business's financial results in a way that reflects what is physically going on. In finance we're less interested in such a representative portrayal, and tend to concentrate on where cash is coming from and going to. In finance, "cash is king"!

○ In finance, **cash is king.**

This point can be made clear with a simple example. We'll consider how a typical accounting system represents the acquisition and use of a long-lived asset, and contrast that with the way people in finance look at the same event.

Suppose a firm buys a $1,000 asset to be depreciated straight line over five years at $200 per year. The accounting books show the initial addition of the

FIGURE 1.2

Finance Department Organization

$1,000 asset followed by yearly depreciation entries, each of which has two parts. Every year depreciation appears on the income statement to reflect the allocation of $200 to cost. Further, an addition of $200 is made to an accumulated depreciation account on the balance sheet each year to reflect the wearing out of the item. (We'll review fixed asset accounting in more detail in Chapter 2.)

Notice how much information this set of numbers conveys. The asset originally cost $1,000 and results in an expense of $200 each year that reduces profit. At the same time, the balance sheet indicates how worn out the item is by showing the portion of its original value that's left on the books. The accounting representation thus gives us a portrait of the entire life of the asset and its impact on the business in numbers!

from the **CFO**

When people in the finance department think about the same asset, their orientation is very different. They're interested in only two numbers: the $1,000 cash outflow needed to acquire the asset in the first place and the annual tax saving generated by the depreciation deduction. The reason for this emphasis is easy to understand. Finance is responsible for raising the initial $1,000, and the future tax saving affects the amount of cash that will have to be raised for other things later on. In fact, a finance person might react that the accounting representation doesn't display the most important piece of financial information about the asset—where the money to buy it came from.

The point behind the illustration is that in finance the emphasis is on cash. We're not implying that accountants are ignorant of the cash requirements associated with the asset in the example. Their emphasis is simply different, involving a broader portrayal of the business. Finance concentrates on cash flow. We'll keep that in mind throughout our study.

●THE LANGUAGE OF FINANCE

● Accounting is the **language of finance.**

The practice of finance is closely tied to accounting, because financial transactions are recorded within the structure of accounting systems. It's often said that *accounting is the language of finance.* Because of this connection, all finance professionals need some knowledge of accounting. However, the level of knowledge required varies significantly depending on one's job.

A financial analyst, who investigates companies and makes recommendations about their investment value, needs to know quite a bit of accounting. That's because analysts have to decipher complex financial statements without missing any of the detailed implications that may be buried in the notes and numbers. Stockbrokers, on the other hand, generally sell securities on the basis of a broad knowledge of what's going on in various industries and expectations generated by the reports of analysts. They can get by without much more than an ability to read basic financial statements.

FINANCIAL THEORY—THE RELATIONSHIP WITH ECONOMICS

So far we've been examining the practical side of finance and how it fits into the business world. Finance is a field of endeavor in which millions of people find jobs after they've mastered certain skills that are taught in school. As in any other field, success comes with experience and wisdom after you've learned the basics. In this regard, finance is a lot like accounting—you learn the techniques in school and apply them on the job.

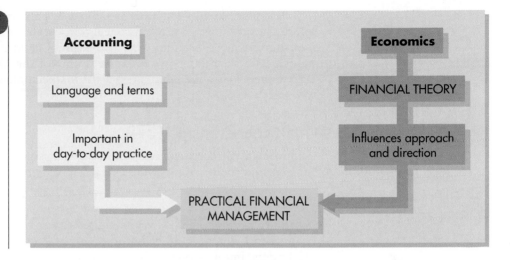

FIGURE 1.3

The Influence of Accounting, Economics, and Financial Theory on Financial Management

● Financial **theory** has grown out of **economics.**

However, there's also a theoretical aspect to finance. Financial theory is a body of thought that is studied and continually developed by highly trained experts, usually professors. In this regard, finance is a lot like economics. Scholars in both fields observe the world of business and government and attempt to model and explain behavior in abstract terms.

In fact, modern financial theory began as a branch of economics during the 1950s. Since that beginning, finance has grown so much that most people now think of it separately, although the term "financial economics" is still used occasionally. The techniques of advanced financial theory are very similar to those of advanced economic theory.

Financial theory has a big impact on practice in some areas and less influence in others. Where the impact is significant, theory influences the direction and approach that people take in practice. As we go forward we'll identify and explain theoretical elements that have had a noticeable influence on the way the world operates. Theory's most significant impact in recent years has been in the area of investments, which we'll cover in Chapter 8.

The ideas and relationships discussed in this and the last section are portrayed graphically in Figure 1.3.

FORMS OF BUSINESS ORGANIZATION AND THEIR FINANCIAL IMPACT

A business can be legally organized in one of three ways: as a sole proprietorship, as a partnership, or as a corporation. Within the third category there are two possibilities, the regular or C-type corporation and the S-type corporation, which is intended for small businesses.

The choice of form is important financially because it can have an impact on raising money, taxation, and financial liability. The issue is really relevant only in the context of smaller businesses, because virtually all large companies are organized as C-type corporations.[2]

---

2. With the exception of personal service organizations such as law or CPA firms, which are generally sole proprietorships or partnerships.

For financial purposes, a partnership is essentially a sole proprietorship with more than one owner, so we'll concentrate on distinguishing between a proprietorship and a corporation. We'll also begin by ignoring S-type corporations, and reintroduce them later. We'll explore some of the ideas behind form through a hypothetical example that stresses the *financial* advantages and disadvantages of each.

● THE PROPRIETORSHIP FORM

Suppose an entrepreneur wants to open a business, has enough money to get started, and chooses to organize as a sole proprietorship.

Getting Started

Starting a proprietorship is very simple. Because the business is indistinguishable from the entrepreneur, all he has to do to get started is obtain a local permit and declare the business open. That's an advantage of the proprietorship form—it's easy to start.

Taxes

Now suppose the entrepreneur operates for a while and makes a profit. That profit will simply be taxed as personal income to the business owner. That's another advantage of the proprietorship form—the business's profits are taxed only once, and that tax is at personal income tax rates. (We'll see why this is an advantage in a moment.)

Raising Money

Next, suppose the business is successful for six months and the entrepreneur wants to expand, but doesn't have enough money to buy the assets required. He therefore looks for outside financing in the form of a loan. Any number of sources are possible, including family, friends, and a bank.

Family and friends might advance some money on the strength of their personal relationship with our entrepreneur, but people who don't know him will always ask two very important questions.

First they'll want to know, "What happens to my money if your business fails?" The honest answer is that the money will be lost.

Next they'll ask, "What happens to me if you're phenomenally successful?" The answer is simply that the lender will get his or her money back with interest.

Now consider the lender's position. Lending to the entrepreneur is a gamble, but not a very good one. The worst possible outcome is a total loss, whereas the best result imaginable is merely getting back the amount loaned with a few dollars of interest. That might be all right if the chance of loss is very small, but in fact the overwhelming majority of small businesses fail. Of course lenders know this, so the loan isn't very attractive to them.

● Assets pledged to guarantee a loan are **collateral**.

For this reason it's almost impossible for a new business to get a loan that isn't fully *collateralized*. A collateralized loan is backed by some asset (the collateral) that the lender can take and sell in the event the borrower defaults on paying off the loan. Many entrepreneurs use their houses as collateral for start-up loans. In the case we're considering, our business owner's expansion plans would be stopped cold if he didn't have enough collateral to guarantee a loan.

This result is a major disadvantage of the sole proprietorship form. The only way a nonowner can advance money to the business is by lending, and that's a

● A major **financial disadvantage** of proprietorship is the difficulty encountered in **raising money.**

very risky proposition. Therefore raising start-up or expansion money is difficult while the business is new.

● THE CORPORATE FORM

Now let's explore what happens when another entrepreneur starts a similar business using the corporate form.

Getting Started

The first thing she'd find is that getting started is somewhat difficult. She must go through the legal process of incorporation and register with the state, probably using a lawyer to file the papers. The whole thing would take some work and cost a bit of money.

Taxes

Once set up, the incorporated business operates in much the same way as the sole proprietorship. When the business makes a profit, however, the tax situation is significantly different.

A corporation is a separate legal entity subject to a *corporate tax* on whatever it earns. What's left over after the corporate tax is paid (earnings after tax or net income) belongs to the corporation.

That's an important point. Even though the entrepreneur owns the business, she doesn't own its earnings directly. The corporation owns them. To get the earnings into her own pocket, the entrepreneur has to declare a dividend that is paid to her as an individual.

However, such a dividend is taxable income to the individual. Hence our entrepreneur will pay individual taxes on the after (corporate) tax earnings of her company.

● **Double taxation of earnings** is the major **financial disadvantage** of the traditional **corporate form.**

In other words, the profits of the business will be taxed twice, once at corporate rates and once at individual rates, before the entrepreneur gets to spend any of the business's earnings. This phenomenon is known as the **double taxation of corporate earnings.** It is the main *financial* disadvantage of the corporate form.[3]

EXAMPLE 1.1

Hazel Gilroy owns a business that earns $100,000 before taxes. She wants to take the earnings home and spend them on herself. Assume a simplified tax system in which the relevant rates are 34% for corporations and 28% for individuals on the entire amounts subject to those taxes. Compare the total tax bills under the sole proprietorship and corporate forms of organization.

Solution: Under the corporate form, the $100,000 is first subject to a 34% corporate income tax of $34,000, leaving earnings of $66,000. If Hazel wants to take that sum home, she has to declare it as a dividend and pay personal tax on it at 28%, an additional tax of (.28 × $66,000 =) $18,480.

In a sole proprietorship, the $100,000 is taxed once at 28% for a total tax bill of $28,000. The calculations are summarized as follows.

---

3. The owner would pay herself a salary, which wouldn't be taxed twice but would have to be reasonable for the value of the work performed. The salary would be part of the business's expenses. Only profit is taxed twice.

	Corporate	Proprietor
Pretax earnings	$100,000	$100,000
Less:		
Corporate tax (34%)	34,000	—
Earnings/dividend	$ 66,000	$100,000
Less:		
Personal tax (28%)	18,480	28,000
Net	$ 47,520	$ 72,000

Notice that the difference is a very significant $24,480. That's almost a quarter of pretax income. In this case the business is paying a great deal for the privilege of being a corporation!

Raising Money

Let's assume that our incorporated entrepreneur's business is successful and that she wants to expand, but needs money to do it. If she tries to borrow as an incorporated business, she'll run into the same problems that face the sole proprietor. Lending to a new business is risky and generally no one will do it. Whether the business is incorporated doesn't make much difference.

However, a corporation has an option that isn't available to a sole proprietor. The incorporated firm can raise money by offering stock to investors. New stockholders will own shares of the business and may have some influence over how it's run. But if less than a 50% interest is sold, effective control can still be maintained by the original owner.

People contemplating buying stock will ask the same two questions that potential lenders ask, "What happens to my investment if the business fails?" and "What happens if it does very well?"

The answer to the first question is the same as it was in the lending case. If the business fails, the stockholder is likely to lose most or all of his or her investment. But the answer to the second question is very different. If the company does extremely well, the stock's price will go up, perhaps multiplying the value of the original investment many times over. In short, the answer to the second question for a stockholder is "You may get rich!"

Now consider the potential stockholder's position. An investment in the new business is still a gamble in which the worst possible outcome is total loss, but the best result is a very substantial gain. This is a much more attractive gamble than the loan, because the potential reward justifies the risk.

What this means in practical terms is that although people will almost never make uncollateralized loans to start-ups or new companies, they'll frequently buy stock in such ventures. That fact leads us to the *most significant financial advantage of the corporate form: ease of raising money.*

● **Ease of raising money** by selling stock is the most significant financial advantage of the corporate form.

● THE TRUTH ABOUT LIMITED LIABILITY

The most frequently cited advantage of the corporate form is limited liability. The concept says that a stockholder cannot be held liable for the debts of the corporation or for damages it may do to others. That in turn implies that all the stockholder can lose is his or her investment in the stock.

Let's state the matter another way. Suppose someone has a valid claim against a business that exceeds its assets. If the business is a proprietorship, the claimant can take the owner's personal property after taking the assets of the business. On the other hand, if the business is a corporation, only the assets of the business can be taken, not the personal assets of the stockholder owners.

The limited liability concept is absolutely true in the context of owning shares in a company that the investor isn't running. But it doesn't usually work when an entrepreneur is operating his or her own incorporated business. Let's explore why.

Companies generally create liabilities that exceed their assets in two ways: by borrowing money they can't repay and by losing a lawsuit. The first situation is very common. It usually occurs when a firm takes out a loan in the expectation of good business in the near future. The plan is to pay off the debt with the profits from the anticipated business. Trouble arises when the expected sales don't materialize and the firm can't make its loan payments. If things get bad enough, the company goes bankrupt and the value of the unpaid loan along with other debts exceeds the value of its assets.

⦿ **Personal guarantees** make entrepreneurs liable for loans made to their businesses.

Theoretically, incorporation protects business owners from having their personal assets seized as a result of such unpaid loans. In practice, however, lenders circumvent this feature of incorporation by demanding **personal guarantees** from small business owners before making loans to their companies.

Personal guarantees are side agreements signed along with loan papers that make owners personally responsible for repayment should their businesses fail to meet loan obligations. This device virtually destroys the value of limited liability where loans to small businesses are concerned.

In the second situation the entrepreneur or an employee damages some outside party. For example, suppose an auto repair shop fixes a customer's brakes negligently and thereby causes an accident. In such a case, the injured party can sue *both* the business and the negligent individuals, bypassing the limited liability of the corporate form.

The limited liability feature of corporations is largely a myth for owner-operated small businesses. However, it is real for stockholders who don't participate in the business themselves.

⦿ S-TYPE CORPORATIONS AND LIMITED LIABILITY COMPANIES

We've seen that the major financial advantage and disadvantage of the corporate form are the ability to raise money through the sale of stock and the double taxation of earnings, respectively. It's difficult to expand a company that's not a corporation, and double taxation makes it hard to accumulate earnings if a company is a corporation.

However, the government generally favors small businesses because of the jobs they create. To encourage the formation and expansion of new businesses, Congress created some devices that give small firms the best of both worlds. These include the S-type corporation and limited liability companies (LLCs).

⦿ The **S-type corporations and LLCs** let small businesses avoid double taxation.

Both are corporations in the sense of limited liability and the ability to sell stock, but their earnings are not subject to corporate income tax. Earnings flow directly to the personal income of the owners, and are taxed only once at personal rates. Essentially, the tax system treats S-type corporations and LLCs as partnerships. That feature makes them a significant incentive to small business formation.

INSIGHTS

Real
Applications

The Limited Liability Company (LLC): An Alternative to the S-Type Corporation

The big advantage of an S-type corporation is that it's treated like a proprietorship with respect to federal income taxes. It allows income to "pass through" to the business's owners before being taxed. Although the S-type is predominantly used by smaller businesses, there isn't really any size limitation. The "S" stands for subchapter S of the Internal Revenue Code, not for small.

S-type corporations sound like a good idea in that they avoid double taxation, but they come with lots of restrictions that make them hard to use in some situations. One of the most significant limitations is that all of the shareholders must be people. That means an S-type corporation can't be owned by another corporation. This makes it impossible to use when two businesses want to form a joint venture to do something together. Until recently companies forming joint ventures had to organize as either traditional corporations (called C-type corporations) or as partnerships. The C-type corporate form usually subjects the earnings of the new business to some double taxation, while the partnership form opens the owing companies up to any liabilities incurred by the joint venture. (Partnerships don't have limited liability, so the debts of the partnership are also the debts of the partners.)

Another business form has been gaining popularity since the late 1970s and is permitted under the law of every state today. The new form is called the limited liability company (LLC), and is more flexible than the S-type in several ways. It can elect to retain the pass–through characteristic of S-type corporations with respect to tax, but doesn't have the restriction that all of its owners must be people. And, as the name implies, it has limited liability. The LLC is rapidly replacing the S-type corporations as the organizational form of choice among small businesses, but is also used by big firms.

For example, two industrial giants, the Dow Chemical Company and Cargill Inc, a large agricultural company, recently formed a joint venture to explore making plastics from crops like corn rather than from petrochemicals. The idea is to make plastics out of renewable resources rather than from oil byproducts. Dow and Cargill choose the LLC form of organization and formed Cargill Dow LLC. The venture is building a $300 million factory in Nebraska, and plans to develop a commercial line of plastics made from corn and other plants. The new product line is aptly named NatureWorks™ PLA.

Source: http://www.cargilldow.com

THE GOALS OF MANAGEMENT

http://

See which companies are on the *Forbes 500* and other lists at
www.forbes.com/lists/

To run a company, management needs a goal or objective against which to measure the implications of its decisions. In the study of economics, theorists assume that the goal of the firm is profit maximization. The concept works in theory, but is unmanageable in the real world. Truly maximizing profit today (in the short run) is likely to cause serious problems tomorrow (in the long run).

For example, the work of most research and development (R&D) departments has little effect on current business, because their efforts are focused on developing products that won't be marketed for years. If a firm fires its R&D staff, today's business won't be affected and profits will increase immediately because of the expenses saved. However, in two or three years the firm won't have any new products to sell and will probably be in trouble. From that example we can deduce that simply maximizing today's profit isn't a very good goal for a real company.

Fortunately, financial markets provide an easy-to-state yet realistic goal for management. Because stockholders own the company and have invested for financial gain, and because management works for those stockholders, the appropriate managerial goal is the *maximization of shareholder wealth*. That's generally taken to be equivalent to *maximizing the price of the company's stock*.

This idea gets around the short-run/long-run problem just described. Remember that stock market investors watch everything the company does and reflect those actions in their expectations about the firm's future performance. Those expectations determine the price of the stock today. Current profits also affect the price of the stock, but only as an indicator of future profit.

● **Shareholder wealth maximization** is a practical goal for corporate management.

If a real company fired its R&D department and thereby increased current profits, its stock price wouldn't go up. The market would recognize the long-run folly of the move, and the stock price would drop like a stone.

As our study of finance proceeds, we will run into situations in which a management decision has an impact on stock price. In such cases we'll assume that the best decision is the one that results in the highest stock price.

STAKEHOLDERS AND CONFLICTS OF INTEREST

In any company, several groups of people have special interests in the way the firm is run. These groups include the following.

Stockholders	Management
Employees	Creditors
Customers	Suppliers
Local community	

Such interested groups can be called *stakeholders* in or *constituencies* of the company. We'll use the term "stakeholder," meaning that each group has a stake or vested interest in the way the firm is operated. Various conflicts of interest are possible between stakeholder groups. A conflict of interest occurs when something that benefits one group takes away from another.

CONFLICTS OF INTEREST—AN ILLUSTRATION

Suppose an employee group at a manufacturing company comes to management with a request. They want the company to build an athletic complex on the factory site so employees can exercise before and after work and during lunch hours. They argue that although this project will cost money, it will lead to a happier employee population that will be more effective on the job.

Management agrees that happy workers are good workers, but also sees a possibility that employees will spend time at the gym at the expense of their jobs or that they will be exhausted on the job after working out. Therefore they aren't sure whether the facility would help or hurt productivity. On balance, management feels the net efficiency effect will be more or less neutral.

It's important to recognize that this situation reflects a conflict of interest between two stakeholder groups, employees and stockholders. If the athletic facility is built, the money will come out of profits that belong to shareholders. Hence, making the employees a little happier entails making shareholders a little

Ethics   Ethics and Ethical Investing

Investors buy stocks and bonds expecting to get back more than they spend. That's called earning a **return** on the investment. People are generally interested in the size of the return and the risk associated with it. But is that all they should be concerned about?

Earlier we said companies sold securities to raise money to finance assets. But suppose the assets are to be used in some project or business that's unethical or immoral. Doesn't that mean the investor is indirectly participating in the unethical activity? Should investors be concerned about that? Should they refuse to invest in companies whose activities they feel are unethical?

Let's be precise about what we mean by *unethical.* It's important not to get ethics mixed up with legality. Most illegal activities are also unethical, so there's no question that we should not participate. Ethics comes up when an activity is morally wrong but is technically legal.

Unethical activities generally involve at least two groups of people. One typically has some power over the other and uses it to gain a benefit at the other's expense.

The tobacco industry provides a good example. People smoke by choice, and the production and sale of cigarettes are legal activities. But the medical community tells us that smoking accounts for 435,000 deaths and drains more than $200 billion per year from the economy.* Further media reports say tobacco companies have allegedly kept sales up by targeting children in advertising and manipulating nicotine levels to promote addiction.

Some people consider the making and selling of tobacco products to be a legal but unethical business activity. Under this view the groups that benefit are the managements and stockholders of tobacco companies who enjoy lucrative jobs and profits. The injured group is smokers who become sick and may die. The power of the benefited group is seen as coming from advertising and the addictive properties of smoking.

On the other hand, some people feel that smokers are aware of the health risks of tobacco and make their own decisions about using it, and that there's nothing morally wrong with providing the product to those who want it.

The question is whether ethics should keep investors who do morally condemn the industry from buying tobacco stocks in pursuit of financial returns. Or should the financial market

*Simon, Harvey B. *Conquering Heart Disease* (New York: Little Brown, 1994).

—continued

poorer and presumably less happy. In this case management is something of an arbitrator, and has to make a decision in favor of one group or the other.

In this hypothetical example, the employees' request is something of a luxury, so the decision doesn't generate a lot of emotion when we read about it. But what if working conditions were really terrible at the plant, and employees were asking for money to create a clean, safe work environment? The conflict of interest would still be there, but we would be more likely to favor the employees on an emotional or ethical basis.

MANAGEMENT—A PRIVILEGED STAKEHOLDER GROUP

● The ownership of a **widely held company** is dispersed so no one has enough control to influence management.

Management often has a special position among stakeholder groups. Although top managers theoretically work for the company's stockholders, they often have little accountability to that group. If ownership is widely dispersed and no one holds more than 1% or 2% of the company, stockholders have limited influence because no one can muster enough power to force a change in the management team.

Ethics **Continued—**

act as a veil that legally and morally separates investors from what is eventually done with their money?

Ethical investing is a growing practice in which people concern themselves with what the companies whose securities they buy do. Also known as socially responsible investing, it generally takes the form of avoiding the securities of firms that engage in activities considered questionable by the investor.

Ethical mutual funds exist which avoid the stocks of companies that engage in certain activities. For example, the Calvert Social Investment Fund describes its objective in a marketing brochure by saying "The Fund systematically avoids investing in companies associated with unhealthy products and practices or poor records on labor relations, human rights, and the environment."

Ethical issues can be hard to analyze. They're usually charged with emotion and involve costs and benefits that are difficult to see. To keep your thinking clear, go through the following steps when analyzing an ethical problem.

1. Clearly identify the unethical practice. Is it all or part of what the firm is doing? In the tobacco illustration is it wrong to make cigarettes at all or just to advertise to children?

2. Separate legal and ethical issues. Something may not be OK just because it's legal.

3. Identify the benefited party or group and describe the benefit.

4. Identify the injured party or group and describe the injury or cost.

5. Identify the nature and source of the power of the benefited group. Do they have the ability to manipulate and preserve their power? How did the power come about? Did they do something to create it?

6. State any alternatives the injured group has. How difficult are they to use?

7. State the opposing view. What argument will someone who doesn't feel there's a problem make?

As we continue with our study we'll highlight ethical issues in finance from time to time.

In such cases, top managers become entrenched in positions controlling vast company resources, and are able to use those resources for their own benefit rather than for the benefit of shareholders.

● THE AGENCY PROBLEM

The special position of management in widely held companies leads to a particularly onerous conflict of interest known as the **agency problem.** The term is derived from the legal concept of agency.

● An **agent** is hired by a principal and given **decision-making** authority.

An *agency relationship* is created when a person hires another and gives him or her decision-making authority over something. For example, if Smith hires Jones to run his business, Jones is the agent of Smith, who is called the *principal.* Conversely, if Smith hires Jones to sweep the floor, no agency relationship is created, because no decision-making authority is involved. The agency relationship creates an opportunity for abuse by the agent who has control over the assets of the principal. In general, corporate managers are the agents of the firm's stockholders.

The Abuse of Agency

The most common example of abuse of the agency relationship is the practice in which companies pay top executives excessive compensation (compensation includes salary, bonuses, and special deals on buying the company's stock called stock options). The conflict is with stockholders because the excess pay would otherwise be profit, which belongs to them.

Executive compensation levels in excess of $200 million in a year have recently been recorded. Stockholders have a right to ask whether anyone can be worth that much. Perhaps even more outrageous is the fact that high levels of compensation for top executives aren't necessarily connected to good performance by the company.

Compensation isn't the only way in which managers can feather their own nests. The use of company-owned assets such as boats, airplanes, and vacation retreats is common, as are such benefits as expense account meals, chauffeur-driven limousines, and paid country club memberships. These benefits are called *perquisites* ("perks" for short) and have become a way of life among top corporate executives.

● Privileges and luxuries provided to executives are called **perquisites** (or "perks").

Controlling the Agency Problem

Efforts to manage the agency problem generally involve monitoring what the agent is doing. For example, principals can employ auditors to periodically review company books to make sure funds aren't being diverted to questionable uses. Such measures involve costs known as *agency costs*.

Another way to manage the agency problem is to pay a good part of managers' compensation in the form of a bonus tied to company profit. This approach reduces the incentive to spend money on company-owned assets that are used by executives. For example, buying a vacation retreat for executive use will reduce profit by the cost of the facility. If the president's bonus goes up or down with the size of profits, he or she will be less inclined to approve the expenditure for the retreat.

The government has gotten into the act by limiting the corporate tax deductibility of certain expenses such as luxurious meals and executive compensation exceeding $1 million per year. However, the effect of these efforts has been minimal, and the agency problem remains a major issue in the efficient functioning of the American economy.

CREDITORS VERSUS STOCKHOLDERS— A FINANCIALLY IMPORTANT CONFLICT OF INTEREST

The conflict of interest between creditors and stockholders is important at this point, because it will begin to develop your concept of risk in finance. Let's explore the idea through an illustration.

Suppose Smith starts a business with $1,000 of his own money and convinces Jones to lend the business another $1,000 without a personal guarantee. The business now has cash of $2,000, which comes from debt of $1,000 and equity of $1,000. Smith is the sole owner and decision maker. Jones is a creditor.

Now suppose Smith decides to use the business to take on some very risky venture. Imagine that the venture has a high probability of total failure, say 50%, in which case all invested funds would be lost. However, if the venture is

● A **creditor** is anyone owed money by a business, including lenders, vendors, employees, or the government.

successful, it will double invested money in a few months. Smith puts the entire $2,000 into the risky enterprise.

It's important to recognize that this is a very unfair deal between Smith and Jones. It is an abuse of the creditor by the stockholder. To see this, consider what happens if the venture fails versus what happens if it is successful.

In the event of failure, both investors lose equally—their entire $1,000 investments. If the venture succeeds, the company will have $4,000 in cash. However, Jones's claim against that sum will still be $1,000, representing the unpaid loan balance (plus a little interest). The remaining $3,000 will belong entirely to Smith.

To put it another way, the venture is a gamble. The losses are shared equally between the stockholder and the creditor, but the profits all belong to the stockholder. That's not a very good deal for the creditor.

This situation occurs in practice when companies that have borrowed money take on ventures that are riskier than those they took on before borrowing. To prevent this from happening, lenders generally put clauses in loan agreements that preclude the borrowing company from becoming more of a risk taker.

DISCUSSION QUESTIONS

1. Companies are generally financed with a mix of debt and equity. How does the riskiness of the company as perceived by the financial market change as the mix shifts from all equity to mostly debt? Why? Would changes in perceived risk induced by changes in the debt–equity mix affect the company's stock price?

2. Diversified companies are made up of divisions, each of which is a separate business. Large companies have divisions spread over the entire country. In such companies *most* treasury functions are centralized whereas *most* accounting functions are carried out in the individual divisions.

   The cash management function controls the collection of revenues and the disbursement of funds from various bank accounts. It makes sure that the company never runs out of cash by monitoring outflows and having lines of bank credit ready in case temporary shortages occur. Today's banking system is linked electronically so that cash can be transferred around the country immediately.

   The credit and collection function decides whether a particular customer can be sold to on credit. After the sale, it is responsible for following up to ensure that the bill is paid. Customers are often reluctant to pay because of problems and misunderstandings with sales or service departments.

   If you were designing the finance department of a diversified company, would you centralize these functions or locate them in the remote divisions? Why? Address each function separately.

3. The company president is reviewing the performance and budget of the marketing department with the vice president of marketing. Should that be a one-on-one meeting or should the CFO be present? Why? If you feel the CFO should be there, what should be his or her role in the meeting?

4. Discuss the differences, similarities, and ties between finance and accounting.

5. Discuss the relationship between finance and economics.

6. How does the activity of investors in financial markets affect the decisions of executives within the firm?

7. What are the significant financial advantages and disadvantages of the sole proprietorship/partnership form in comparison with the corporate form?

8. Is limited liability a meaningful concept? Why? For whom?

9. What conflict(s) of interest can you imagine arising between members of the community in which a company operates and some other stakeholders? (*Hint:* Think about pollution.)

10. Is the agency problem an ethical issue or an economic issue?

 Internet Problem

1. Visit the *Business Job Finder* at http://www.careers-in-business.com to explore a career in finance. Prepare a one-page report profiling one of the positions listed. Include education and skills required and average starting salaries.

CHAPTER 2

Financial Background: A Review of Accounting, Financial Statements, and Taxes

Chapter Outline

Accounting Systems and Financial Statements
    The Nature of Financial Statements
    The Accounting System
The Income Statement
    Presentation
The Balance Sheet
    Presentation
    Assets
    Liabilities
    Equity

The Tax Environment
    Taxing Authorities and Tax Bases
    Income Taxes—The Total Effective Tax Rate
    Progressive Tax Systems, Marginal and
        Average Rates
    Capital Gains and Losses
Income Tax Calculations
    Personal Taxes
    Corporate Taxes

http://

For more help with your review of accounting, go to Accounting Over Easy at

● **www.ezaccounting.com/ previewindex.html**

    Some knowledge of accounting is necessary to appreciate finance. That's because financial transactions are recorded in accounting systems, and financial performance is stated in accounting terms. In other words, if we want to deal with money in business, we have to deal with the system that keeps track of it, and that's accounting. Some knowledge of taxes is also necessary, because tax considerations influence most financial decisions.

    Although accounting is generally a prerequisite, finance students have differing levels of knowledge about the subject. Some are quite expert, while others, who may have taken accounting some time ago, don't remember much.

    This chapter provides a review of what you need to know about accounting and taxes in a condensed form. If you're not strong in the area, reading the chapter carefully will be a lot quicker than digging the ideas out of your old accounting text. If you are up to speed, you can skim the material and move on.

We'll conduct our review as painlessly as possible, keeping in mind that while financial people need to know something about accounting, they don't have to be accountants. In fact, we won't even have to use debits and credits!

ACCOUNTING SYSTEMS AND FINANCIAL STATEMENTS

Virtually everything business enterprises do is recorded as a series of money transactions within the structure of an accounting system. That record and the system itself provide the framework most managements use to control their businesses. Accounting systems produce several fairly standard reports known as financial statements that reflect business performance.

● THE NATURE OF FINANCIAL STATEMENTS

● **Financial statements** are numerical representations of a firm's activities for an accounting period.

A business's **financial statements** are numerical representations of what it is physically doing. Keep that concept firmly in mind as we go forward. The idea behind statements is to give a picture of what's happening within the company and between the company and the rest of the world both physically and financially. This excellent idea creates a problem, however, in that it causes statements to be somewhat counterintuitive. That is, they don't necessarily say what a person untrained in accounting is likely to think they're saying. Here's an example.

Is Income "Income"?

Most people think of income as the money they're paid, which after payroll withholding is what they take home. In other words, income means cash in your pocket or cash paid to Uncle Sam for your taxes.

The income statement is one of the traditional financial statements. It starts with the dollar amount the company has sold, deducts costs, expenses, and taxes, and winds up with a figure called net income (also called earnings after tax, which is abbreviated as EAT). Most people would expect that figure to represent cash in the pocket of the business or its owner, just like a paycheck. However, it doesn't mean that at all. Several accounting concepts get in the way and give net income a character of its own. We'll describe two major differences between net income and cash flowing into the company's pocket.

ACCOUNTS RECEIVABLE   It's customary for many businesses to sell most of their products on credit, receiving a promise of later payment rather than immediate cash. Despite the fact that no money is received, accounting theory says that when a credit sale occurs, the firm has done everything it has to do to earn the related income, and the income therefore should be *recognized* in the financial statements.

In fact, however, the firm has less cash than it would have had if it never made the sale. That's because, although it hasn't collected from the customer, it did supply product and to do so it had to pay for labor and materials.

Uncollected payments for product sold are called *accounts receivable* and represent a big difference between cash and accounting income.

DEPRECIATION   Another idea that seems odd to the uninitiated is the way long-lived assets are handled financially. Suppose a company buys a machine to use in its business, paying $10,000 in cash at the time of purchase. Assume the machine is expected to last five years. How is the cost of the machine recognized as a cost of doing business?

Someone unfamiliar with accounting might think the cost would be recognized along with the outflow of money that pays for the machine—that is, a $10,000 cost in the year of purchase. However, accounting theory says that to properly reflect the workings of the business, we have to match the cost of the machine with the period over which it gives service. Therefore we prorate the $10,000 cost over the five-year life of the asset.

Depreciation is the proration of an asset's cost over its service life.

That's done with a financial device called **depreciation**. If the proration is even over the life of the asset, depreciation allocates $2,000 to cost in the income statement in each of the asset's five years of life. (Evenly prorated depreciation is called *straight line*.)

That convention creates a strange situation in terms of cash in the company's pocket. In the first year the firm spent $10,000, but could declare only $2,000 as a cost of doing business. In other words, it used up a lot more cash than the income statement indicates. In each of the subsequent four years it didn't spend anything, but still got to declare $2,000 in cost. So in those years the income statement indicates that the company used up more money than it actually did.

Clearly these practices indicate that accounting income is conceptually different from paycheck income, and that financial statements are concerned with more than just the flow of money in and out of the business. They do tell us about that, but they also tell us about what's going on in other ways.

The Three Financial Statements

Three financial statements are of interest to us: the income statement, the balance sheet, and the statement of cash flows. There is a fourth that pertains to changes in owner's equity, but we won't be concerned with it here. The income statement and the balance sheet are the *basic* statements that derive from the books of account. The statement of cash flows is developed from them.

We'll consider the income statement and balance sheet in this chapter and the statement of cash flows in Chapter 3. First a little background on accounting in general is in order.

THE ACCOUNTING SYSTEM

A firm's **financial books** are a collection of records in which money transactions are recorded.

An accounting system is an organized set of rules by which every transaction the firm makes is recorded in a set of records. The records are collectively known as the company's "books." Books used to be kept in ledgers that looked like books—hence the name. Today they're more likely to be records in a computer.

The books are separated into a series of "accounts." An account generally holds records of transactions of a particular type or those related to a particular part of the business. For example, a revenue account receives all transactions involving the sale of product to customers, while a fixed asset account receives records related to the acquisition and disposal of heavy machinery.

Transactions include activities like selling product, buying inventory, paying wages, building product, borrowing money, paying taxes, and paying dividends. A business transaction is recorded in the books by an *entry*. An entry generally means that we add or subtract a dollar figure to or from the balance in an account.

The Double Entry System

● In **double entry** accounting, every entry has two sides that must balance.

Most accounting systems use the double entry system of keeping records. Double entry means that each entry has two equal parts, called *sides*. Each side of an entry is made to a different account.

The double entry concept is hard to grasp at first. You can get used to the idea by thinking of certain kinds of entries in which the two sides represent where we get money and what we do with it. For example, suppose we bought a machine on credit for $1,000. That essentially means we bought the machine and took out a loan for the purchase price at the same time. One side of the entry that records this transaction would involve adding $1,000 to the fixed asset account to show that the company now has the machine. The other side would involve adding $1,000 to a payable account to reflect an obligation to pay the money. The asset side of the transaction shows what we did with the money, and the payable side shows where we got it.

The two sides of an entry are called *debits* and *credits*. In any entry the total debit must equal the total credit. (This is the only time we'll mention debits and credits.)

Consider another example, recording a sale. Suppose we sold an item to a customer for $200. One side of the entry would add $200 to the sales account, but what would the other side be?

The answer depends on the terms of the sale. If the customer paid cash, the other side would simply add $200 to the cash account to reflect that the firm now has that additional money. However, if the customer bought on credit, the $200 would be added to a receivable account to reflect the fact that the company is owed the money.

Every entry must have two equal or *balancing* sides. Hence it's common to say that correctly kept books are balanced.

Accounting Periods and Closing the Books

● Books are **closed** by **updating the period's transactions** in the accounting system and **creating financial statements.**

In business, time is divided into accounting periods, usually months, quarters, and years, during which transactions are accumulated. At the end of each period, all the transactions occurring in the period are totaled and the company's books are brought up to date as of the last day of the period. This process, called *closing the books*, usually takes place in the days immediately following the last day of an accounting period.

Certain procedures are applied to the closed books to generate the financial statements with which we began our discussion. It's important to understand that financial statements are associated with particular accounting periods. The balance sheet is associated with the point in time at the end of the period, while the income statement and statement of cash flows are related to the entire period.

Implications

It's important to keep in mind that last year's financial statements don't say anything about what's going on this year or what will happen next year. They refer only to the past.

Statements can, however, be used as an indication of what is likely to happen in subsequent years. Past financial statements are a little like a person's medical history. If you were sick last year, you're more likely to be sick next year than if you were healthy. However, a sick person can get well, and a healthy person can get sick and die. Similarly, a firm that was financially sound last year can fail next year if it's mismanaged or something dramatic happens to its business.

Stocks and Flows

There is a fundamental difference between the two basic financial statements. The income statement reflects *flows* of money *over a period of time*. The balance sheet represents *stocks* of money *at a point in time*.

The income statement shows money flowing in and out of the organization. Revenues flow in while costs and expenses flow out. The difference is profit. The balance sheet makes a statement as of a moment in time. It says at this instant the company owns a particular list of assets and owes a particular list of creditors.

A set of statements includes an income statement that covers an entire accounting period and a balance sheet that can be thought of as a snapshot at the end of that period. The derived statement of cash flows, like the income statement, represents flows over an entire period.

THE INCOME STATEMENT

An income statement shows how much money a company has earned during the accounting period, commonly a year.

PRESENTATION

Most income statements have a form similar to the one shown in Table 2.1. Let's examine each line individually.

Sales

Sales, also called *revenue*, represents the total receipts from selling whatever it is the company is in business to sell. In other words, sales are receipts from normal business operations.

This is an important point. If the company receives money from activities outside its usual form of business, that money should be recorded as other income rather than as sales. For example, a retail business might sell the store in which it operates to move to another. That sale of real estate shouldn't be included in the sales line.

TABLE 2.1

A Conventional Income Statement Format

Sales	$1,000
Cost of goods sold	600
Gross margin	$ 400
Expenses	230
Earnings before interest & taxes	$ 170
Interest expense	20
Earnings before tax	$ 150
Tax	50
Net income	$ 100

Cost and Expense

Cost of goods sold and expenses are subtracted from sales to arrive at earnings before interest and taxes. Both cost and expense represent money spent to do business, but there's an important distinction between the two.

COST OF GOODS SOLD (COGS)   COGS represents spending on things that are closely associated with the production of the product or service being sold. For example, in a retail business COGS is usually just the wholesale cost of product plus incoming freight. In a manufacturing business, however, COGS is much more complex. It includes labor and material directly associated with production as well as any peripheral spending in support of production. The peripheral spending is called *overhead* and can be substantial. It includes the cost of such things as factory management, the factory building itself, and depreciation on machinery.

In a service business COGS includes the wages of the people who provide the services, depreciation on their tools and equipment, travel costs of getting to sites requiring service, and the cost of any facilities housing service operations.

EXPENSE   Expenses represent spending on things that although necessary aren't closely related to production. These include functions like marketing and sales, accounting, personnel, research, and engineering. The money spent in those areas tends to be related to the passage of time rather than to the amount produced.

DEPRECIATION   Although not a separate line on *most* income statements, depreciation is an important item. We'll study the idea in more detail later. For now it's important to note that *both* cost and expense usually include some depreciation.

Gross Margin

Gross margin, sometimes called *gross profit margin*, is simply sales revenue less COGS. It is a fundamental measure of profitability, getting at what it costs to make the product or service before consideration of the costs of selling, distributing, or accounting for it.

Interest and Earnings before Interest and Taxes

Most but not all income statement presentations show interest expense separately and give an earnings figure calculated before interest has been paid.

INTEREST   If the firm has borrowed money, it has to pay interest on those borrowings. It's important to realize that there's a big difference in the amount of interest various companies pay. If a business is completely financed with the owners' money, there's no interest at all. If part of the financing is borrowed, the firm is burdened with debt and the associated interest payments. A company financed with debt is said to be **leveraged.**

● **Leverage** is the use of **debt** financing.

EARNINGS BEFORE INTEREST AND TAXES (EBIT)   Earnings before interest and taxes is an important line on the income statement, because it shows the profitability of the firm's operations before consideration of how it is financed. The line is also called *operating profit.*

● **Operating profit (EBIT)** is a business's profit **before** consideration of **financing charges.**

To understand the concept of EBIT, imagine that we want to compare the performance of two businesses that are identical except for their financing. Assume one business is entirely equity financed and the other has a significant amount of debt.

If we try to judge the two companies on the basis of net income, we won't get a true picture of the relative strengths of business operations, because the second firm will have its profit reduced by the interest it pays on borrowed money. But the amount borrowed has nothing to do with how well the product sells, the cost of making it, or how well operations are managed.

The problem arises because interest is shown on the income statement but dividends are not. Therefore, a company with debt financing will always look weaker at the net income line than an otherwise identical firm that's equity financed.

To get around this problem we create the EBIT line. It shows the profitability of business operations *before* results are muddied by the method of financing.

Earnings before Tax, and Tax

Gross margin less all expenses, including interest, yields earnings before tax. This is conceptually simple, what the business produces before Uncle Sam and the state take out their bites.

TAX   The tax line on the income statement refers to *income* taxes on the amount of earnings before tax. Companies pay other taxes, but those appear as cost or expense items farther up on the income statement.

However, the statutory tax rate applied to earnings before tax doesn't always give the tax shown on the statement. There can be a variety of credits and adjustments behind the final number.

The tax figure also doesn't necessarily reflect the tax actually due, because some items are treated differently for tax and reporting purposes. When the tax due is different from the tax shown, most of the difference is usually taken to a deferred tax account on the balance sheet. Current taxes can be deferred or previously deferred taxes can be due now. Some complicated accounting is generally involved.

Net Income

Net income is calculated by subtracting tax from earnings before tax, and is the proverbial "bottom line." As we've already said, it is not equivalent to cash in the firm's pocket. In some cases it may be close to cash flow, but in others it's significantly different. It takes the statement of cash flows to figure out how much the company is really making in the short run.

Net income, also called *earnings*, belongs to the company's owners. It can either be paid out as dividends or retained in the business. *Retained earnings* become an addition to owner's equity on the balance sheet.

Terminology

The terminology used on the income statement is far from uniform between companies. The words "income," "profit," and "earnings" are generally synonyms, so you may see any of them on the various lines instead of the expressions we've used here. "Profit before tax" and "profit after tax," abbreviated PBT and PAT, are particularly common as are EBT and EAT for "earnings before tax" and "earnings after tax."

http://

Rutgers University provides links to tax and accounting sites at

● http://accounting.rutgers.edu/

● **Retained earnings** are those **not paid** out as dividends.

THE BALANCE SHEET

The balance sheet lists everything a company owns and everything it owes at a moment in time. Stated another way, it shows where all of the business's money has come from and what it's been used for. The fundamental principle is that all the sources of money and all the uses must be equal.

● A **liability** is an amount a firm must eventually pay.

The firm's money comes from creditors and owners. Creditors have loaned money in one form or another, and thereby create *liabilities* for repayment. Owners have invested in the company or let past earnings remain in it rather than drawing them out. In a loose sense, the firm "owes" its owners their equity investments.

A firm uses its money to acquire assets, both tangible and intangible.

● PRESENTATION

A balance sheet has two sides. One lists all of the company's assets, and the other lists all of its liabilities and equity.

The balance sheet can be thought of as an equation,

$$\text{assets} = \text{liabilities} + \text{equity}.$$

On one side we have assets, representing what the company has done with its money. On the other side we have liabilities and equity, representing where the money came from. If everything has been accounted for properly, the two sides must be equal, or "balance"—hence the name balance sheet. The balance sheet is sometimes called the *statement of financial position*.

A typical balance sheet looks like the one shown in Table 2.2. Notice that total assets equals total liabilities plus equity.

This illustration is somewhat simplified, but it will serve to explain the important features of a balance sheet. We'll start on the asset side and work through the entire statement.

● The ease with which an asset **becomes cash** is referred to as **liquidity.**

Both assets and liabilities are arranged in decreasing order of **liquidity**. Liquidity, in this context, means the readiness with which an asset can be turned into cash or a liability will require cash. On the asset side the most liquid asset is cash itself. Next comes accounts receivable because one expects that in the normal course of business receivables will be collected within a few days. Inventory is next because

TABLE 2.2

A Conventional Balance Sheet Format

Assets		Liabilities	
Cash	$1,000	Accounts payable	$1,500
Accounts receivable	3,000	Accruals	500
Inventory	2,000	Current liabilities	$2,000
Current assets	$6,000	Long-term debt	$5,000
Fixed assets		Equity	2,000
Gross	$4,000	Total capital	$7,000
Accumulated depreciation	(1,000)	Total liabilities	
Net	$3,000	and equity	$9,000
Total assets	$9,000		

it is normally sold in short order, generating cash or a receivable. Fixed assets are low on the list because they would generally have to be sold on a used equipment market to be turned into money. Similar logic applies on the liabilities side.

● ASSETS

In what follows, we'll consider each asset and present the important elements of its financial/accounting treatment.

Cash

Cash is defined as money in bank checking accounts plus currency on hand. Currency is usually a minor amount. Companies keep cash balances in bank accounts to pay bills and as a precaution against unforeseen emergencies.

● **Marketable securities** are **liquid** investments that are held **instead of cash.**

Larger companies usually hold a near cash item called **marketable securities** as well as cash itself. Marketable securities are short-term investments that pay a modest return and are very secure. They can be sold almost immediately if the need arises. Thus they fill the precautionary need for cash, but earn a little interest at the same time.

Accounts Receivable

Accounts receivable represent credit sales that have not yet been paid. Under normal conditions, these should be paid in cash within a matter of weeks.

Most companies sell on credit terms of approximately 30 days. Customers often push those terms by taking somewhat longer to pay. That means it isn't unusual for a company to have 45 days of credit sales in receivables. That's (45/360=) 12.5% of a year's revenue.

THE BAD DEBT RESERVE   Receivables are usually stated net of an offsetting account called the *allowance for doubtful accounts* or the *bad debt reserve*. As the name implies, this offset allows for the fact that most businesses make some credit sales that are never paid. These are usually a small percentage of total sales.

The bad debt reserve is created and maintained by adding an amount equal to a small percentage of sales to its balance each month. This amount estimates credit sales that will never be collected even though nobody knows which ones will prove bad when they are made. The amount added is generally based on experience. The other side of the entry which maintains the reserve is an expense, that is, a reduction in profit.

WRITING OFF A RECEIVABLE   When a receivable is known to be uncollectible (perhaps because the customer is bankrupt), it should be *written off*. Writing off a receivable means reducing the balance in accounts receivable by the uncollected amount. The other side of the entry normally reduces the bad debt reserve which has been provided regularly each month for that purpose.

If the lost receivable is unusually large, the other side of the write-off has to go directly to an expense account. That generally represents an unexpected reduction in profit.

from the CFO   OVERSTATED RECEIVABLES   *Profit reductions caused by uncollectible receivables are distasteful, so managements sometimes postpone writing off bad debts beyond the time when they should be recognized. This causes the receivables balance to include amounts that will never be collected. Such an account is said to be* **overstated***.*

Inventory

Inventory is product held for sale in the normal course of business. In a manufacturing company, inventory can be in one of three forms: raw materials, work in process (abbreviated WIP), and finished goods. A retailer has only finished goods inventory.

WORK IN PROCESS INVENTORIES   The nature of raw materials and finished goods is self-explanatory, but WIP needs a little explanation. As raw materials move through the production process, labor is expended to produce product. We think of that labor as being embodied in the inventory. For example, if in a certain production step a piece of wood costing $10 is worked on for one hour by a worker who makes $7 an hour, we would think of the wood as having a value of $17 when it emerges from that process. Thus work in process inventory contains the cost of raw materials and the cost of an increasing amount of labor as it moves toward becoming finished product.

Besides labor, most accounting systems add the cost of factory overhead (the building, equipment, heat, electricity, supervision, etc.) to the value of inventory as labor is added.

THE INVENTORY RESERVE   Inventory on the balance sheet is assumed to be usable but frequently isn't. A number of things can happen to make inventory worth less than the firm paid for it. Items can be damaged, become spoiled, get stolen (called *shrinkage*), and become obsolete.

Firms conduct periodic physical counts to discover shrinkage, but other damage often goes undetected until an attempt is made to use or sell the item.

Balance sheet inventories are generally stated net of an inventory reserve to allow for a normal amount of problem material. The inventory reserve is conceptually similar to the bad debt reserve associated with accounts receivable. It is maintained similarly with an addition each month, the other side of which is an expense.

WRITING OFF BAD INVENTORY   If inventory is discovered to be missing, damaged, or obsolete, the balance sheet inventory account must be reduced to reflect the loss. The other side of the entry that reduces the recorded inventory balance normally reduces the inventory reserve. However, if the loss is large, the reduction may have to be offset directly to an expense account, resulting in a reduction in profit.

from the CFO

OVERSTATED INVENTORY   *Managements usually try to avoid reducing recorded profits. Therefore they're prone to accept any rationalization to the effect that the inventory is holding its original value. This can lead to an overstatement of the inventory balance.*

Overstatements

The overstatement of receivables and inventories can be a significant problem to users of financial statements that purport to reflect the value of a company. To the extent that assets are overstated, the firm's value is less than it is being held out to be. Overstatements can also mean that the company isn't managed effectively. Both of these possibilities are of significant concern in valuing the firm's securities.

Current Assets

● **Current assets** become cash, within **one year.**

The first three assets on our balance sheet are called *current assets*. The term "current" means that in the normal course of business, these items can be expected to become cash within one year. More complex businesses have a few other current items, but they are of minor importance compared with these.

The current concept is important in financial analysis, because it relates to a company's ability to meet its obligations in the short run. All of the money the business receives from normal operations flows in through the current asset accounts. In other words, money that isn't in current assets today may be a long time coming in, whereas money now in current assets can be expected to be realized as cash soon.

Fixed Assets

Longer-lived items are located below the current section of the balance sheet. Although many things can be in this category, the predominant item is usually fixed assets, which can also be called *property, plant, and equipment* (PPE).

The word "fixed" can be a little confusing. It doesn't mean fixed in location, as a truck or a railroad car can be a fixed asset. It simply implies long lived. A fixed asset is something that has a useful life of at least a year. It's important to understand the basics of fixed asset accounting and the associated concept of depreciation.

● According to the **matching principle** recognition of an asset's **cost** should match its **service life.**

DEPRECIATION   Depreciation is an artificial accounting device that spreads the cost of an asset over its estimated useful life regardless of how it is acquired or paid for. If the cost is spread evenly over the life of the asset, we say the depreciation is straight line. The idea behind depreciation is to match the flow of the asset's cost into the income statement with the delivery of its services over time. This *matching principle* is an important accounting concept.

● **Accelerated depreciation** recognizes more of an asset's cost in the **early years** of its life.

In some cases an argument is made that cost flows out of an asset more rapidly in the early years of its life than in the later years. Depreciation can be structured to be greater in the early years to reflect that idea. When the depreciation schedule is front loaded like that, it's called **accelerated depreciation**.

FINANCIAL STATEMENT REPRESENTATION   Depreciation appearing on the income statement reflects an asset's cost. The same depreciation also appears on the balance sheet where its cumulative value helps to reflect the remaining worth of the asset.

Recall that every accounting entry has two sides. The entry posting depreciation expense to the income statement posts the same amount to a balance sheet account called *accumulated depreciation*. Accumulated depreciation is carried as an offset to the value of an asset, so at any time the net value of the asset is the difference between its original cost and its accumulated depreciation. An example should make the idea clear.

Suppose a firm buys a truck for $10,000 and decides to depreciate it over a useful life of four years at $2,500 each year. During that time, the income statement will include a $2,500 expense item each year. During the same period, each year's balance sheet will carry three numbers related to the asset: its gross value, its accumulated depreciation, and its net value.

TABLE 2.3

Fixed Asset Depreciation

Year	Income Statement		Balance Sheet	
1	Depreciation expense	$2,500	Gross	$10,000
			Accumulated depreciation	($ 2,500)
			Net	$ 7,500
2	Depreciation expense	$2,500	Gross	$10,000
			Accumulated depreciation	(5,000)
			Net	$ 5,000
3	Depreciation expense	$2,500	Gross	$10,000
			Accumulated depreciation	(7,500)
			Net	$ 2,500
4	Depreciation expense	$2,500	Gross	$10,000
			Accumulated depreciation	(10,000)
			Net	-0-

It's important to understand the pattern of these numbers over time. The accounts will look like those shown in Table 2.3 at the end of each year. Notice that each year's depreciation expense is the same. That's because the example is using straight line depreciation. If accelerated depreciation were being used, the early years would have larger numbers than the later years. The total depreciation expense, however, would still be equal to the $10,000 cost of the asset.[1] That's an important idea. Total depreciation can never exceed the cost of the asset.

Also notice that accumulated depreciation grows each year by the amount of depreciation expense in that year, but the asset's gross value stays the same. The asset's true value at any point in time is approximated by the net line, which is known as the item's book value or net book value, abbreviated NBV.

DISPOSING OF A USED ASSET   Net book value is not market value. The asset may be salable on the used equipment market for an amount that's more or less than its NBV at any time. It's important to understand the accounting treatment if that occurs.

Suppose the truck in the example is sold after two years for $6,000. The firm would recognize revenue of $6,000 at that time. The cost associated with that revenue, however, would be the truck's NBV at that time, $5,000. The $1,000 difference would be a profit on the disposal of the asset.

Notice that the profit would not be part of operating income, because selling used trucks isn't the company's business. It should be recorded as an item of other income. Such a profit would generally be taxable.

The transaction recording the sale of the truck would remove both its gross value and its accumulated depreciation from the books. The net of these, $5,000, becomes the used asset's cost.

---

1. We're assuming that at the end of its life the asset will have a zero salvage value. If a positive salvage value is assumed, we would depreciate only the difference between the original cost and that value. Otherwise the procedure would be the same.

THE LIFE ESTIMATE Depreciation runs over the estimated useful life of an asset. However, it's quite common for things to last beyond their estimated lives. Assets still in use beyond their life estimates are said to be fully depreciated. Such an asset's gross value remains on the books entirely offset by accumulated depreciation. If it is sold after that time, there is zero cost.

TAX DEPRECIATION AND TAX BOOKS The government provides many incentives to business through the tax system. One of the most prominent involves depreciation, which is a tax-deductible expense.

Deductibility implies that higher depreciation in a given year results in lower tax in that year, because taxable profit is lower. That means accelerated depreciation reduces taxes early in the life of an asset. The savings is given back later in the asset's life when depreciation is lower and taxes are higher, but the net effect is to *defer* taxes if accelerated depreciation is used.

Unfortunately the lower recorded profit in early years caused by accelerated depreciation isn't something management likes to see. It makes the company look less successful in the short run than it would appear if straight line depreciation were used. To get around this conflict, the government allows businesses to use different depreciation schedules for tax purposes and for financial reporting purposes. The term "tax books" is used to mean financial records and statements generated by using the tax rules, and the term "financial books" or just "books" is used to mean the regular statements that we're talking about here. The difference between the two methods results in an account called *deferred tax* on the financial books.

DEPRECIATION IS A NONCASH EXPENSE Depreciation is a financial fiction; it doesn't represent a current flow of money even though it's treated as a cost or expense. It has nothing to do with how an asset is acquired or paid for.

Total Assets

The things we've talked about so far constitute most of the left side of the balance sheet for a majority of companies. Their sum is simply total assets.

● LIABILITIES

Liabilities represent what the company owes to outsiders.

Accounts Payable

● Vendors extend **trade credit** when they deliver product without demanding immediate payment.

Accounts payable arise when firms buy from vendors on credit (called **trade credit**). Payables and receivables are opposite sides of the same coin. When a credit sale is made, the seller records a receivable and the buyer records a payable. In most companies, the bulk of accounts payable arises from the purchase of inventory.

TERMS OF SALE The length of time allowed until payment is due on a credit sale is specified in the *terms of sale*. Common terms involve payment within 30 days and include a discount for prompt payment. Terms of two 10, net 30, written 2/10, n.30, mean that a 2% discount is allowed if payment is received within 10 days or the full amount is due in 30 days. Trade credit is generally free in that no interest is charged if the full amount is paid within the allowed time.

Vendors become upset if their bills aren't paid in the times specified under the terms of sale. Delaying payment of trade payables is called *stretching payables* or *leaning on the trade*. If a customer abuses a vendor's terms, the credit privilege is likely to be revoked, and the seller will subsequently demand cash in advance before shipping goods.

UNDERSTATED PAYABLES   When we discussed accounts receivable and inventory we were concerned about overstatements, conditions in which the balance sheet claims assets the company doesn't have. On the liabilities side we're concerned about understatements, conditions in which the firm has liabilities that are not reflected on its balance sheet. *For example, it's possible to receive goods from a vendor, use them, and simply not recognize the transaction financially. Eventually, the vendor will demand payment and the issue will be raised, but that may take quite a while.*

from the **CFO**

Accruals

● **Accruals** represent **incomplete** transactions.

Accruals are poorly understood by most nonfinancial businesspeople. They are an accounting device used to recognize expenses and liabilities associated with transactions that are not entirely complete.

A PAYROLL ACCRUAL   The best way to understand accruals is to consider a simple example involving payroll. Suppose a company pays its employees every Friday afternoon for work through that day. Then suppose the last day of a particular month falls on a Wednesday, and the books are closed as of that afternoon. Figure 2.1 shows this situation graphically.

As of the close of business on Wednesday, the financial statements have to include two things that aren't reflected by paper transactions. These arise from the fact that employees have worked for three days (Monday, Tuesday, and Wednesday) that are in the first month, but won't be paid for those days until Friday, which is in the second month.

The first issue is that as of the closing date, the firm owes its employees for those days, and the debt (liability) must be reflected on the balance sheet. The second issue is that the work went into the month just closing and should be reflected in that month's costs and expenses.

If we were to simply recognize payroll expense when the cash is paid on Friday, the three days' labor would go into the second month, and there would be

FIGURE 2.1

A Payroll Accrual

no recognition of the liability at month end. The solution is a month-end *accrual* entry in the amount of the three days' wages. One side of the entry increases an accrued wages liability on the balance sheet, while the other side increases wage expense in the closing month. It's important to realize that the liability will be paid in just two days on the next payday.

OTHER ACCRUALS   There are accruals for any number of things. For example, suppose a company is billed in arrears for property tax at the end of a government fiscal year in June. If the firm closes its books at the end of December, it owes the local government for six months of property tax even though it has received no bill and won't until June. A property tax accrual properly reflects this expense in the meantime.

Current Liabilities

● **Current liabilities** require cash within **one year.**

Current liabilities are defined as items requiring payment within one year; hence payables and accruals are classified as current. Other current liabilities include notes payable, short-term loans, and any long-term debt that's within a year of its due date.

Working Capital

● **Net working capital** represents the money required to support **day-to-day** activities.

Current assets are collectively referred to as *gross working capital*, while the difference between current assets and current liabilities is known as net working capital.

Conceptually, net working capital represents the amount of money a firm needs to carry on its routine day-to-day activities. Formally,

$$\text{net working capital} = \text{current assets} - \text{current liabilities}.$$

In practice, people frequently omit the word "net."

Working capital is an important idea to which we'll devote all of Chapter 15.

Long-Term Debt

Typically, the most significant non-current liability is long-term debt. It is common practice to refer to it simply as debt, especially if there isn't much short-term debt. Long-term debt usually consists of bonds and long-term loans.

● A business financed with **debt** is said to be **leveraged.**

LEVERAGE   A business that is financed with debt is said to be leveraged. The word implies that when things are going well, using borrowed money can enhance the return on an entrepreneur's own investment. It works like this.

Suppose a business is started with a total investment of $100,000, and earns an after-tax profit of $15,000 in the first year. First imagine that the invested money is entirely from the entrepreneur's own pocket. The return on his or her invested equity is 15% ($15,000/$100,000).

Now suppose the entrepreneur had borrowed half the money, $50,000, at an interest rate that nets to 10% after tax. In that case profit would be reduced to $10,000 by the $5,000 interest paid (10% of $50,000) on the loan, but the entrepreneur's investment would be only half as much, $50,000. Hence the return on his or her investment would be 20% ($10,000/$50,000). Borrowing money would have levered the return up from 15% to 20%. The figures are shown in the margin.

In general, a business is able to produce a higher return to the owner's invested funds by using borrowed money *if* the return on the *total* amount of invested

	All Equity	Leveraged
Earnings	$ 15,000	$ 15,000
Interest	—	(5,000)
EAT	$ 15,000	$ 10,000
Debt	—	$ 50,000
Equity	$100,000	$ 50,000
Total	$100,000	$100,000
Return	15%	20%

money exceeds the interest rate being paid on the loan. Otherwise, the effect is in the opposite direction and the return is worse with borrowed money.

FIXED FINANCIAL CHARGES   The most significant concern about borrowed money is the interest charge. It's important to keep in mind that interest charges are fixed. That means they must be paid regardless of how the business is doing. You can't go to the bank and say, "Sales are down a little this month, so do you mind if I skip the interest payment?" That can be a real problem in tough times. Many businesses have gone bankrupt because of fixed financial obligations.

●EQUITY

● **Equity** financing is provided by a business's **owners.**

Equity represents funds supplied to businesses by their owners. These funds are in two forms: direct investment and retained earnings. Direct investment occurs when stock is sold or an entrepreneur puts money into his or her business. Retained earnings occur when profits are kept in the business rather than being paid out to the owners.

The Representation of Direct Investment by Owners

If a business is incorporated, its direct equity investments are reflected in two stock accounts. One is entitled **common stock** and represents an arbitrary amount called the *par value* of each share times the number of shares outstanding. The other account is usually called *paid in excess* and represents the amount paid for the stock over its par value. The two together represent the total direct equity investment, that is, the money paid for the stock.

It's important to understand that par value is an arbitrary and largely meaningless number. If the business isn't incorporated, the two separate accounts aren't necessary.

Retained Earnings

● **Retained earnings** are profits that have **not** been distributed to shareholders as dividends.

A company's profit belongs to its owners, who can either pay it to themselves or leave it in the business. Earnings paid out are said to be distributed; those kept in the business are said to be retained. If a business is incorporated, the balance sheet will show retained earnings separately from the directly invested money shown in the stock accounts. This may or may not be so in an unincorporated business.

Money retained or "reinvested" in a business is just as much the contribution of its owners as directly invested money. That's because they could have taken it out and used it elsewhere if they wanted to do so.

The retained earnings account is subject to a common misconception. Probably because of the words in the name, people sometimes get the idea that retained earnings represents a reserve of cash on which the firm can draw in times of need. That isn't so. Just like any other invested funds, retained earnings are generally spent on assets shortly after they become available.

The retained earnings account shows all earnings ever retained by the company just as the stock accounts show all money ever invested directly by owners. Neither is generally available as cash at any point in time, because both tend to have been spent on assets to build the business.

Example: Equity Accounts

We'll summarize these ideas with a brief illustration. Suppose a firm is started with the sale of 20,000 shares of $2 par value stock at $8 per share, and subsequently earns $70,000 of which $15,000 is paid in dividends. The equity accounts will then be as follows.

Common stock ($2 × 20,000)	$ 40,000
Paid in excess ($6 × 20,000)	120,000
Retained earnings ($70,000 − $15,000)	55,000
Total equity	$215,000

The Relationship between Net Income and Retained Earnings

It is very important to understand the interaction between net income and retained earnings in the financial statements.

Net income (or earnings after tax) becomes part of retained earnings and therefore part of equity at the end of the accounting period *if* it is not distributed to the owners. That means that if no new equity investments are made and nothing is paid out to the owners during an accounting period,

$$\text{beginning equity} + \text{net income} = \text{ending equity.}$$

If something is paid out to owners in the form of a dividend, the relation is

$$\text{beginning equity} + \text{net income} - \text{dividends} = \text{ending equity.}$$

If new equity is contributed through the sale of additional stock,

$$\text{beginning equity} + \text{net income} - \text{dividends} + \text{stock} = \text{ending equity.}$$

Beginning balance sheet figures, including equity, are those of the balance sheet dated at the end of the prior accounting period. For example, the beginning balance sheet for 2003 is the ending balance sheet for 2002. Therefore, 2003's beginning equity is 2002's ending equity.

Preferred Stock

Preferred stock is a security issued by some firms that is effectively a cross between debt and common equity. It's thought of as a hybrid, because it has some of the characteristics of each of the more traditional securities. Legally, however, it is classified as equity and is included in the equity section of the balance sheet *above* the common stock accounts. Total equity is the sum of common and preferred equity.

Total Capital

The sum of long-term debt and equity is total capital. These funds are generally used to support long-term assets.

Total Liabilities and Equity

The sum of the right side of the balance sheet reflects where all of the company's funds have come from and the obligations it has to outsiders and owners as a result of those advances. Total liabilities and equity must always equal total assets.

THE TAX ENVIRONMENT

In finance, we're primarily concerned with federal income taxes for both individuals and corporations. We will begin, however, with a little background on taxes in general.

TAXING AUTHORITIES AND TAX BASES

Taxes are imposed by various governmental authorities. In this country we typically think in terms of three taxing levels: federal, state, and local.

Every tax must have a **tax base**, the thing that is taxed. The three common tax bases are income, wealth, and consumption.

● A **tax base** is the item that is taxed, usually income, wealth, or consumption.

Income Tax

The idea of an income tax is straightforward. A taxpayer pays a fraction of income in a designated time period, generally a year, to the taxing authority. The most important income tax is the federal tax, because it typically takes the biggest share of our income. Depending on how much an individual makes, the federal tax can be over 35% of the last dollar earned.[2] Most states have income taxes, but the rates are much lower, typically from 5% to 10%. Several major cities also have income taxes with rates in the neighborhood of 1%. New York City is a prominent example.

Individuals and corporations are both subject to income taxes, but under different sets of rules, which we'll discuss shortly.

http://

Federal tax information and forms can be found at
● **www.irs.treas.gov**

Wealth Tax

Wealth taxes are based on the value of certain types of assets. The most common wealth tax is levied by cities and counties on the value of real estate. The money collected from real estate taxes is typically used to run local school systems and pay for town services such as fire and police. Wealth taxes are also called *ad valorem taxes*.

Consumption Tax

Consumption taxes are based on the amount of certain goods we use. The most common consumption tax is a *sales tax* in which the end user of a product pays a tax on its purchase price. It's important to understand that because the tax is on consumption or use, only the end user pays. Therefore if something is purchased for resale, no sales tax is due.

Sales taxes are imposed by state and local governments. The federal government taxes the consumption of certain items such as alcohol, tobacco, and gasoline. The federal government's consumption taxes are called *excise taxes*.

INCOME TAXES—THE TOTAL EFFECTIVE TAX RATE

Many investment decisions turn on the tax rate that an individual or company will pay on the income from the investment. If there is a state income tax, it should be taken into consideration along with the federal tax. The total effective tax rate is the combined rate to which the taxpayer is subject. It is not simply the sum of the federal and state rates, because state tax is deductible from income in the calculation of federal tax.

For example, suppose a taxpayer is subject to a 30% federal tax and a 10% state tax on income of $100. He or she would pay as follows.

---

2. Legislation passed in 2001 phases the maximum rate down from 39.6% in 2000 to 35% in 2006 and thereafter.

Taxable income for state tax	$100
State tax @ 10%	$ 10
Taxable income for federal tax	$ 90
Federal tax @ 30%	$ 27
Net after tax	$ 63
Total tax	$ 37
Total effective tax rate ($37/$100)	37%

Adding the two rates would give 40%. In general we can calculate the *total effective tax rate* (TETR) by using the formula

(2.1) $$\text{TETR} = T_f + T_s\,(1 - T_f)$$

where T_f is the federal tax rate and T_s is the state tax rate.

● PROGRESSIVE TAX SYSTEMS, MARGINAL AND AVERAGE RATES

● A **progressive tax** system is characterized by **higher tax rates** on incrementally **higher income**.

The U.S. federal income tax system is progressive. In a progressive tax system a taxpayer's tax rate increases as income increases. It's important to distinguish that idea from the simpler notion that taxpayers with higher incomes pay higher taxes. The latter statement would be true if everyone paid the same tax rate regardless of their income.

A progressive system might be one in which everyone earning less than $20,000 pays at a 20% rate, but those who earn over $20,000 pay 30% on earnings over $20,000. Because the rate goes up as income increases past $20,000, the system is progressive.

Notice that taxpayers with income over $20,000 don't pay the higher rate on their entire incomes, but only on the amounts over $20,000. For example, a taxpayer earning $25,000 would calculate taxes as follows.

20% of the first $20,000	=	$4,000
30% of the remaining $5,000	=	$1,500
Total tax		$5,500

Brackets

● A **tax bracket** is a range of income in which the tax rate is constant.

Tax rates in progressive systems don't increase smoothly as income goes up. Rather they remain constant over some range of income and then jump abruptly to a higher level for another range. Ranges of income through which the tax rate is constant are called **tax brackets**. Here's a hypothetical progressive tax system with three brackets.

Bracket	Tax Rate
0–$5,000	10%
$5,000–$15,000	15%
Over $15,000	25%

This representation of the tax structure is called a *tax table* or a *tax schedule*.

Prior to 1986 the actual personal tax system had as many as 14 brackets, and many years ago the top rates were as high as 70%. In the early 2000s, there are six brackets, and the highest rate is being stepped down to 35%. We'll discuss the actual rate structure after we illustrate a few ideas using our simplified example.

A taxpayer is often identified by his or her bracket, which is named by its highest rate. Thus a person earning $10,000 in our example would be said to be in the 15% bracket.

The Marginal and Average Tax Rates

Two tax rate concepts are applicable to every taxpayer. The marginal tax rate is the rate that will be paid on the next dollar of income the person earns. The average tax rate is the percentage of total income the person pays in taxes. The marginal rate is relevant for investment decisions. We'll illustrate why shortly. Now let's calculate some hypothetical taxes as well as some average and marginal rates to get used to the procedure.

Calculations

Using the three-bracket hypothetical tax rate schedule above, we'll calculate the dollar tax and the two rates on incomes of $4,000, $11,000, and $25,000.

At an income of $4,000, a taxpayer is in the lowest bracket and is subject to only one rate. The calculations are very simple. The tax is just 10% of $4,000 or $400, and the average and marginal rates are both clearly 10%.

At $11,000, things are a little more interesting. The tax calculation follows.

$$
\begin{array}{lr}
10\% \text{ of the first } \$5,000 & = \$ \quad 500 \\
15\% \text{ of the next } \$6,000 & = \underline{\quad 900} \\
& \$1,400
\end{array}
$$

The average rate is the total tax bill divided by taxable income.

$$\$1,400/\$11,000 = 12.7\%.$$

The marginal rate is 15% because that's what would be paid on the eleven-thousand-and-first dollar of income.

Notice that the marginal rate is almost always the bracket rate. Only at the very top of a bracket is it the rate of the next bracket.

At $25,000 the calculation is as follows.

$$
\begin{array}{lr}
10\% \text{ of the first } \$5,000 & = \$ \quad 500 \\
15\% \text{ of the next } \$10,000 & = \quad 1,500 \\
25\% \text{ of the last } \$10,000 & = \underline{\quad 2,500} \\
& \$4,500
\end{array}
$$

Notice that each rate is applied to the income within the relevant bracket only. The average tax rate is

$$\$4,500/\$25,000 = 18.0\%.$$

The marginal rate is 25%, because that's what would be paid on an additional dollar of earnings.

An important conceptual point in the system we've illustrated is that high-income taxpayers enjoy lower rates on the first part of their earnings. Notice that the taxpayer with a $25,000 income pays only 10% on his or her first $5,000 even though the rest is taxed at much higher rates. You can think of this as a benefit being retained by the high income taxpayer. In the actual tax system, some of this benefit is taken back as income increases.

In the foregoing examples, we've applied a tax rate schedule to *taxable income*. Taxable income isn't a taxpayer's total or gross income. It must be calculated according to rules within the tax code. We'll cover the basics of those rules shortly.

●CAPITAL GAINS AND LOSSES

The tax system recognizes two major types of income: ordinary and capital gain.

● **Ordinary income** includes wages, business profits, dividends, and interest.

Ordinary income is generally the result of normal money-making activity. Examples include salary earned, the profit from an unincorporated business, or interest and dividends received from investments. Salaries, dividends, and interest can only be positive, but business profits can be positive or negative. Hence ordinary income can also be an ordinary loss.

● **Capital gain/loss income** arises when an asset that's held for investment is sold for more/less than was paid for it.

A **capital gain or loss** arises when someone buys something for a particular price, holds it for a while, and then sells it for a different price. If the price at which the object is sold is higher than the price at which it was purchased, the difference represents a capital gain. If the selling price is lower, we have a capital loss. The item involved can be a real or a financial asset.

The Tax Treatment of Capital Gains and Losses

Historically, capital gains have received favorable tax treatment. That is, they are taxed at lower rates than ordinary income. The reason behind this treatment lies in the use of the tax system as a means to incentivize desirable economic activity. Investment in assets stimulates the economy, and Congress generally views that as favorable. Taxing profits earned through such investment at lower rates makes projects more attractive and more are undertaken.

● The capital gains tax rate is currently **capped at 20%** for long-term gains.

The capital gains system is actually very complicated, requiring many rules and explanations of what qualifies for particular treatments. Further, the rules tend to be changed frequently. The most important distinction is the length of time the taxpayer holds an asset before selling it. Currently, if the *holding period* is less than one year, any capital gain on an asset's sale is classified as short-term and isn't eligible for favorable tax treatment. Gains on assets held for more than a year are classified as long-term and usually qualify for favorable tax treatment. As of 2001, the essence of the system was that *generally* the tax rate on long-term gains was capped at 20% for individuals.

That means a taxpayer in a bracket above 20% with respect to ordinary income generally pays no more than 20% on long-term capital gains income. That can be a considerable saving, since as we'll see shortly the top personal tax bracket rate is over 35%. Corporations don't get favorable rates on capital gains.

Capital losses can be used to offset capital gains. But if gains and losses add up to a net loss, no more than $3,000 of that loss can be used by individual taxpayers to offset ordinary income in any one year. Corporate taxpayers can't use capital losses to offset ordinary income at all. Thus capital losses receive *unfavorable* tax treatment.

If an individual's capital losses exceed capital gains by more than $3,000 in a given year, the excess can be carried forward into future years as a reduction to ordinary income of up to $3,000 per year. Corporate capital losses can be carried forward to offset future capital gains only.

The Significance of the Tax Treatment

It's important to understand why the treatment of capital gains is a financially significant issue. Many investors buy stock in anticipation of an increase in price rather than to receive dividends. The profit derived from an increase in a stock's price is a capital gain. If it is taxed at substantially lower rates than other profits, buying stock becomes a relatively more attractive proposition to the general investing public. Therefore favorable tax treatment of capital gains makes it easier to raise money by selling stock. Hence the idea is enthusiastically supported by the business community.

INCOME TAX CALCULATIONS

Income taxes are paid by both people and corporations according to the same basic tax principles. In each case, the tax is levied on a base of taxable income, which is gross income less certain deductions. The tax due is then calculated using a progressive rate schedule. But that's where the similarity ends. The rate schedules for corporations and people are very different as are the rules for determining taxable income. We'll have a look at the basic calculation procedures for both in the following pages.

PERSONAL TAXES

Taxes on people are called *personal* or *individual* taxes. The taxpaying unit is a *household*, usually a family of some kind. There are separate schedules for single individuals, married couples filing jointly, married people filing separately, and certain heads of households who aren't married. This last category is largely for single parents. In this book we'll focus on two personal tax schedules, those for single individuals and married couples filing joint returns.

Early in 2001 Congress passed The Economic Growth and Tax Relief Reconciliation Act of 2001. The purpose of the act was to stimulate a slowing economy by lowering personal tax rates gradually over five years. The rates for 2001 are shown in Table 2.4. Under this legislation, the rates will continue to decline until 2006, after which they will remain constant. For example, notice that the top tax rate in 2001 is 39.1%. That represents a reduction of 0.5% from the previous top rate of 39.6%, which had been in effect for many years. Under the Act that top rate declines to 35% in 2006.

TABLE 2.4

Personal Tax Schedules

Single Individuals		Married Couples Filing Jointly	
Income ($)	Rate (%)	Income ($)	Rate (%)
0–6,000	10	0–12,000	10
6,000–27,050	15	12,000–45,200	15
27,050–65,550	27.5	45,200–109,250	27.5
65,550–136,750	30.5	109,250–166,500	30.5
136,750–297,350	35.5	166,500–297,350	35.5
Over 297,350	39.1	Over 297,350	39.1

INSIGHTS

Practical Finance

The Marriage Penalty

Notice that the tax system seems to favor being married. Although the rates are the same, the lower brackets are longer for married households, so a married couple pays less tax on a given income than a single person. Think of the logic behind this as coming from the days when most families had just one income, and married wage earners had more people to support than single people. The tax system therefore gave a break to the traditional family.

The full effect of the structure, however, is more subtle. The system favors being married if only one person works. However, if both work, the effect is reversed. Today, a great many two-income couples pay more tax married than they would if they were single. This effect is called the **marriage penalty**.

To see this, calculate the tax liability for a married couple filing jointly with a taxable income of $100,000. Then calculate the tax liabilities for two single people each earning $50,000 and add them together. See how the result differs if one member of the couple makes more than half of the total income. For example, suppose one makes $80,000 and the other makes $20,000.

The 2001 tax relief act has addressed the marriage penalty. If the act goes into effect as planned, the inequity will be largely eliminated by 2009. The changes, however, aren't scheduled to begin being phased in until 2005.

Do you see any ethical or moral issues with the marriage penalty?

In addition to the rate changes we've just described, the personal tax schedules are adjusted each year to compensate for the effects of inflation. That's done by raising the break points between the brackets each year by a factor that reflects a general increase in prices throughout the economy.

We'll use the 2001 rate schedules in Table 2.4 for illustrative purposes, but you should realize that the schedules for subsequent years will be somewhat different.

Taxable Income

Items of income such as wages, profits, interest, and dividends are either *taxable* or *exempt*. The most significant exempt item is interest on **municipal bonds**. Municipals, or **munis**, are bonds issued by governmental authorities below the federal level. These include states, counties, and cities. Notice that interest on federal bonds is *not* exempt, but it is taxable. Exempt income can also be called an exclusion.

● Interest on **municipal bonds** is **exempt** from federal tax.

Personal taxable income is calculated by adding up all of a taxpayer's income, excluding exempt items, and subtracting amounts known as **deductions** and **exemptions**.

● **Taxable income** is total non-exempt income less **exemptions** and **deductions**.

DEDUCTIONS   Deductions are personal expenditures that the tax code permits people to subtract from income before calculating their tax. The most significant deductions for most people are interest on a home mortgage, certain taxes paid to state and local authorities (mainly income and real estate), and donations to recognized charities. If a household hasn't spent much money on these things, a *standard deduction* is allowed.

EXEMPTIONS   *Personal and dependency exemptions* are fixed amounts that can be deducted for each person in the household to arrive at taxable income. The exemption amount changes each year to account for inflation. In 2001 it was $2,900. Be careful not to confuse personal exemptions with exempt income; they're two different ideas.

EXAMPLE 2.1

The Smith family had the following income in 2001.

Salaries	Joe	$45,000
	Sue	42,000
Interest on savings account		2,000
Interest on IBM bonds		800
Interest on Boston bonds		1,200
Dividends from General Motors		600

During 2001 they sold an investment property for $50,000 that they had purchased three years earlier for $53,000. They also sold some AT&T stock for $14,000 for which they had paid $12,000 five years before. They paid $12,000 interest on their home mortgage and $1,800 in real estate taxes. State income tax of $3,500 was withheld from their paychecks during the year. They contributed $1,200 to their church. They have two children living at home. Assume the exemption rate is $2,900 per person. What is their taxable income and their tax liability? Further, what are their marginal and average tax rates?

Solution: First add up the Smith's ordinary income, leaving out the interest on Boston bonds, which is exempt.

Salaries	$87,000
Interest	2,800
Dividends	600
	$90,400

Next calculate the net capital gain or loss.

Loss on investment property	($3,000)
Gain on stock	2,000
Net capital loss	($1,000)

The net capital loss is less than $3,000, so it can be entirely used to offset ordinary income.

Ordinary income	$90,400
Capital loss	(1,000)
Total income	$89,400

The deductions are as follows.

Mortgage interest	$12,000
Taxes	5,300
Charity	1,200
Total deductions	$18,500

Because there are four people in the household, the exemption total is

$$\$2,900 \times 4 = \$11,600.$$

Now we can determine their taxable income.

Total income	$89,400
Less	
Deductions	(18,500)
Exemptions	(11,600)
Taxable income	$59,300

The Smith's tax liability can be found by using the married filing jointly tax table (see Table 2.4). They are in the 27.5% tax bracket, so we calculate as follows.

10% of the entire first bracket

$$\$12,000 \times .10 = \quad \$1,200$$

15% of the amount in the second bracket

$$(\$45,200 - \$12,000) \times .15 = \quad \$4,980$$

27.5% of the amount in the third bracket

$$(\$59,300 - \$45,200) \times .275 = \quad \underline{\$3,878}$$

Tax liability $10,058

The Smith's average tax rate is their total tax liability divided by their taxable income.

$$\$10,058/\$59,300 = 17.0\%$$

Their marginal rate is what they'll pay on incremental income. That's the rate in their current bracket, 27.5%.

Tax Rates and Investment Decisions

http://

Tax information and forms can be found at
● **www.irs.treas.gov**

A problem arises when an investor wants to choose between a corporate bond and a municipal bond. Both have posted interest rates, but the muni is tax exempt while the corporate issue is not. That means the investor gets to keep all of the interest on the muni, but has to pay some of the interest on the corporate bond to the government in tax.

If a muni and a corporate bond are paying the same rate and the risks are similar, the muni is clearly the better deal. However, because of their tax advantage munis usually don't pay as much interest as similar corporate or federal government bonds.

Investors have to compare the rates offered by competing bonds on an equal basis. Because the stated rate on a muni is after tax, while that of a corporate bond is pretax, one or the other must be restated to get both in the same terms. It's usually easier to restate the corporate. To do that we just multiply by one minus the investor's marginal tax rate.

EXAMPLE 2.2

Suppose the Smith family in the preceding example is offered a choice between an AT&T bond paying 11% and a Boston bond paying 9%. Which is better?

Solution: The AT&T bond pays 11%, but the Smiths only get to keep

$$11\% \times (1 - .275) = 7.98\%.$$

That's their after-tax yield on the bond, and it's less than the 9% offered by Boston. Therefore the Boston bond is the better deal.

What if the Smith's marginal tax rate was only 15%? Then their after-tax rate on the AT&T bond would be

$$11\% \times (1 - .15) = 9.35\%,$$

which is more attractive than the Boston bond's 9%.

Notice that high-bracket taxpayers tend to be more interested in tax-exempt bonds than those with lower incomes.

CORPORATE TAXES

http://

Find business tax information at

www.irs.ustreas.gov/ prod/bus_info/index.html

Corporate taxes are in principle similar to individual taxes. Total income is the business's revenue. Deductions, however, are the charges and expenditures required to run the company. These are essentially the cost and expense items on the income statement. Exemptions don't exist for corporations. The income statement line item earnings before tax (EBT) is a corporation's taxable income. Tax is calculated by taking that figure to the corporate tax table.

Remember from early in this chapter that companies have tax books and financial books that may be somewhat different (page 33). The actual tax liability comes from applying the tax schedule to EBT per the tax books. When we apply the schedule to EBT on the financial books we get a *reported* tax liability. The difference is accounted for through a deferred tax account on the balance sheet. We needn't be too concerned about that difference here, other than to be aware that it often exists. In our examples, we'll assume tax and financial books are the same.

The corporate tax schedule is shown in Table 2.5. Notice that there is something different about the corporate schedule in comparison with the personal

TABLE 2.5

Corporate Income Tax Schedule

Income ($)	Rate (%)
0–50,000	15
50,000–75,000	25
75,000–100,000	34
100,000–335,000	39
335,000–10,000,000	34
10,000,000–15,000,000	35
15,000,000–18,333,333	38
Over 18,333,333	35

Practical Finance

The Other Purpose of the Tax System

The tax system in the United States has two purposes. The first, of course, is to raise money. But the government also uses the system to incentivize what it considers desirable behavior. Sometimes these desirable ends are economic and sometimes they're social. Here are a few examples.

Lower taxes on capital gains make investment more profitable so people buy more stocks and bonds. That makes more funds available for business investment, so companies undertake more new projects. That, in turn, creates jobs and expands the economy.

S-type corporations and LLCs allow small businesses to escape double taxation while enjoying the other benefits of the corporate form. That encourages the formation of new companies, which creates jobs and expands the economy.

Companies get tax credits for employing and training certain types of unskilled, difficult-to-employ people.

Tax credits are available for money spent on restoring and preserving certain historical buildings.

schedules. There are obviously eight brackets rather than six, but there's a more significant difference in the pattern of rates. The corporate rates increase to 39% and then decrease back to 34%. Then they rise to 38% before decreasing back to 35%. This pattern seems strange as well as contrary to our notion of a progressive tax system in which higher income means a higher marginal rate.

The ideas behind the current system are fairly simple, but implementing them results in the peculiar table. There are basically three goals.

1. A progressive system with income under $10 million taxed at 34% and income over that amount taxed at 35%.

2. Substantially lower rates on incomes up to $75,000.

3. Higher-income taxpayers pay the targeted rates on their *whole* incomes.

The first two goals are easy within a traditional progressive system. It's the third goal that makes things messy.

Recall that in a traditional progressive system, a high-income taxpayer retains the *benefit* of lower tax rates on income in the bottom brackets regardless of how much total income is earned. The current system is designed to take away that benefit for wealthy corporate taxpayers so that they pay a constant rate on all of their income.

This is accomplished in two steps. First, the benefit of the 15% and 25% brackets is taken away by putting an additional 5% tax on income between $100,000 and $335,000 to make up for the amount by which the tax rate is below 34% on income up to $75,000. The additional tax is called a *surtax*. (Verify for yourself that the dollar amount of extra tax collected between $100,000 and $335,000 just makes up for the undercollection below $75,000.)

Next, the benefit of a 34% tax on income up to $10 million is taken away with a 3% surtax between $15 million and $18,333,333. Beyond that all income is taxed at a flat 35%.

EXAMPLE 2.3

Calculate the tax liability for a corporation making EBT of $280,000.

Solution: Applying the corporate tax table results in the following tax liability.

$$
\begin{array}{rcl}
\$50,000 & \times .15 = & \$\ 7,500 \\
\$25,000 & \times .25 = & 6,250 \\
\$25,000 & \times .34 = & 8,500 \\
\$180,000 & \times .39 = & \underline{70,200} \\
& & \$92,450
\end{array}
$$

EXAMPLE 2.4

Calculate the tax liability for a corporation making EBT of $500,000.

Solution: This problem is easy because between $335,000 and $10 million the overall tax rate is just 34%.

$$\$500,000 \times .34 = \$170,000$$

EXAMPLE 2.5

Calculate the tax liability for a corporation making EBT of $16 million.

Solution: We don't have to go through the calculations in the bottom brackets because we know that the system recovers those benefits to an overall 34% rate up to $10 million.

$$
\begin{array}{rcl}
\$10,000,000 & \times .34 = & \$3,400,000 \\
\$5,000,000 & \times .35 = & 1,750,000 \\
\$1,000,000 & \times .38 = & \underline{380,000} \\
& & \$5,530,000
\end{array}
$$

Notice that over $18,333,333, we just calculate at a flat 35%.

Taxes and Financing

The U.S. tax system favors debt financing of business over equity financing. The reason is that interest payments made to debt investors are tax deductible to the paying company, while dividend payments made to equity investors are not.

To illustrate the point, suppose two companies are identical except that one is financed entirely by debt[3] and one entirely by equity. Assume the payments to the debt and equity investors are the same, say $20, both firms have EBIT of $120, and the tax rate is a uniform 30% (to make the illustration simple).

● The corporate **tax system favors debt** financing.

---

3. In reality, some equity is always required. We're just imagining total debt financing for the sake of the illustration.

To see the point, we have to look beyond earnings after tax (EAT) to the net amount retained by each firm after paying its investors. That is, we have to subtract dividends from EAT to arrive at the net addition to retained earnings. The comparison follows.

Firm financed by

	DEBT	EQUITY
EBIT	$120	$120
Interest	20	—
EBT	$100	$120
Tax @ 30%	30	$36
EAT	$ 70	$ 84
Dividends	—	20
Net RE addition	$ 70	$ 64

Notice that the firm financed with debt gets to keep $6 more money, about 10% in this case. The difference is in the tax line. The debt-financed firm gets to deduct the payment to its investors before calculating taxes, while the equity financed business has to pay tax on an amount that is not reduced by the dividend payment.

Dividends Paid to Corporations

In Chapter 1 we said that the major financial disadvantage of the corporate form is the double taxation of earnings. Earnings are first taxed as corporate profits and then taxed again as personal income when passed to shareholders in the form of dividends.

● Dividends paid **to another corporation** are partially **tax exempt.**

But what happens if one corporation owns another that in turn is owned by individuals? Under those conditions we'd expect *triple taxation*. To see this, consider Figure 2.2 in which corporation B is owned by corporation A, which is owned by individuals.

It's easy to see that a dollar earned by B is taxed as income to B, as dividend income to A, and as dividend income to the shareholders. If B was owned by corporation C, its earnings would be subject to quadruple taxation.

The government intends double taxation but not triple taxation and beyond. It therefore gives partial relief by exempting most of dividends paid by one corporation to another from taxation as income to the receiving company.

The percentage exempted depends on the amount of B's stock owned by A.

Ownership	Exemption
<20%	70%
20%–80%	80%
>80%	100%

In our illustration this means that if A owns 30% of B and B pays a dividend of $100 to A, A would declare only $20 as income in preparing its taxes. The remaining $80 would be exempt.

Tax Loss Carry Back and Carry Forward

Suppose that over a four-year period a business had three good years and one with a substantial loss. If we consider each year individually, its earnings before

FIGURE 2.2

Multiple Taxation

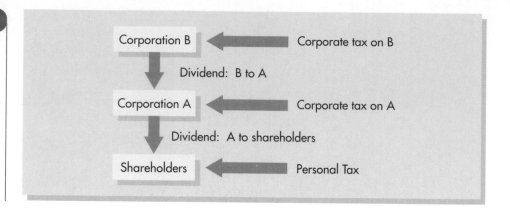

tax, tax, and earnings after tax might look as shown at the top of Figure 2.3 (we are assuming a flat 30% tax rate to make the illustration simple).

At first glance this looks reasonable. The company pays taxes when it has income and no tax when it has a loss. However, the business owner might very well claim that the IRS is putting him or her out of business if the tax system worked like this.

The entrepreneur would point to the total column and claim that over the entire four-year period, the government was trying to make the business pay $90 in tax on $50 of earnings before tax. This would not only be unfair but impossible.

Recognizing this problem, the tax system allows businesses to spread the loss in year 3 among the years before and after. In this case, $100 of the year 3 loss would be **carried back** into each of years 1 and 2, entirely offsetting income in those years. After the loss year the company would file amended tax returns for years 1 and 2 and receive refunds of the taxes paid. The remaining $50 of year 3 loss could be **carried forward** to reduce year 4 EBT. The idea is shown schematically in Figure 2.3.

Losses can be carried back for 2 years and forward for as many as 20 years.

● Business **losses** can be **carried backward** or **forward** in time to offset taxes.

FIGURE 2.3

Tax Loss Carry Back and Carry Forward

	YEAR				
	1	2	3	4	Total
EBT	$100	$100	$(250)	$100	$50
Tax	30	30	—	30	90
EAT	$70	$70	($250)	$70	($40)
	($100)	($100)		($50)	
Adjusted EBT	$ 0	$ 0	$ 0	$50	$50
Tax	0	0	0	15	15
EAT	$ 0	$ 0	$ 0	$35	$35

DISCUSSION QUESTIONS

1. Why does a financial professional working outside accounting need a knowledge of accounting principles and methods?

2. Discuss the purpose of an accounting system and financial statements in terms of the way the system represents the business.

3. Why is EBIT an important line item in the income statement? What does EBIT show us?

4. What is meant by liquidity in financial statements?

5. What are the common misstatements of balance sheet figures and why do they present a problem?

6. Do the definitions of current assets and current liabilities suggest a quick way of looking at the firm's ability to meet its financial obligations (pay its bills) over the near term? (*Hint*: Think in terms of ratios.)

7. How are capital and working capital different?

8. What is leverage and how does it work? What is the main concern about using it?

9. Define the term tax base and discuss common bases. What government units tax on each? What are these taxes commonly called?

10. What is the total effective tax rate?

11. What is taxable income for an individual? How does it differ from taxable income for a corporation?

12. What tax rate is important for investment decisions? Why?

13. Why is the tax treatment of capital gains an important financial issue?

14. Is the corporate tax schedule progressive? Why or why not?

15. What are the tax implications of financing with debt versus equity? If financing with debt is better, why doesn't everyone finance almost entirely with debt?

16. Why are dividends paid from one corporation to another partially tax exempt?

17. Explain the reasoning behind tax loss carry backs and carry forwards.

PROBLEMS

1. The Johnson Company bought a truck costing $24,000 two and a half years ago. The truck's estimated life was four years at the time of purchase. It was accounted for by using straight line depreciation with zero salvage value. The truck was sold yesterday for $19,000. What taxable gain must be reported on the sale of the truck?

2. If the Johnson Company of Problem 1 is subject to a marginal tax rate of 34%, what is the cash flow associated with the sale of the used truck?

3. Belvedere Inc. has an annual payroll of $52 million. The firm pays employees every two weeks on Friday afternoon. Last month, the books were closed on the Tuesday after payday. How much is the payroll accrual at the end of the month?

4. Gatwick Ltd. has after-tax profits (net income) of $500,000 and no debt. The owners have a $6 million equity investment in the business. If they borrow $2 million at 10% and use it to retire stock, how will the return on their investment (equity) change if net income remains the same? Assume a flat 40% tax rate and that the loan reduces equity dollar for dollar. (A business owner's return on investment or equity is ROI = ROE = Net income / Equity.)

5. Ed Fletcher is planning to start a business that requires an investment of $500,000. He has that much money, but he can also borrow virtually the whole amount from a rich relative. (This is very unusual.) Ed feels that after the business is started, it will be important to retain as much money in the company as possible to fund growth. Nevertheless, he plans to pay the investor, either himself or his relative, a $50,000 return (10% of the amount invested) each year. That's about as much as could be earned elsewhere. Considering cash retention only, should Ed borrow or invest his own money ? That is, which option will result in keeping more money in the company available to grow the business? How much more? The company's total effective tax rate will be 40%

6. The Glavits Company opened for business on Monday, June 1, with inventory of $5,000 and cash in the bank of $7,000. These were its only assets. All start-up financing was provided from the owner's personal funds, and there were no other liabilities. The firm has a line of credit at the bank that enables it to borrow up to $20,000 by writing overdraft checks on its account.

Glavits's terms of sale are net 30, but the new firm must pay its suppliers in 10 days. Employees are the company's only expense. They're paid a total of $1,000 per week each Friday afternoon for the week just ending.

On June 3, the company made a sale of $9,000 out of inventory with a cost of $3,000. On June 10 it received $2,000 of new inventory. There were no other sales or inventory receipts. The company bought a delivery truck, paying with a $6,000 check on June 30. The books were closed for the month on Tuesday, June 30.

Construct Glavits's income statement and balance sheet for June using the worksheet shown. Ignore taxes for this problem. First enter the beginning balance sheet. Next enter one number two times in each column to reflect the transaction indicated at the top of the column. Note that sometimes the numbers will be additions and sometimes they will be subtractions. Finally add across the page to get the statements for June.

Worksheet Rows	Worksheet Columns
1. BALANCE SHEET	1. Opening balance sheet
2. Assets	2. Record sales
3. Cash	3. Record cost of sale
4. Accounts receivable	4. Receive inventory
5. Inventory	5. Pay for inventory
6. Fixed assets (net)	6. Buy truck
7. Total assets	7. Pay employees—1st 4 weeks
8. (skip)	8. Pay employees—last 2 days
9. Liabilities	9. Reclassify cash overdraft as loan
10. Accounts payable	10. Record net income as income
11. Accruals	and equity
12. Debt	11. (skip)
13. Equity	12. June statements
14. Total liabilities & equity	
15. (skip)	
16. INCOME STATEMENT	
17. Sales	
18. Cost	
19. Expense	
20. Net income	

7. The Digital Systems Company was organized two years ago to take advantage of an Internet opportunity. Investors paid $12 a share for 2 million shares with a $4 par value. In the next two years the company had earnings of $2 million and $3 million, respectively. It paid dividends of $1.2 million and $1.3 million respectively in those years. At the end of the first year Digital sold another 500,000 shares of stock at $14 per share. Construct the equity section of Digital's balance sheet initially and at the end of its first and second years in business.

8. The Coolidge family has taxable income of $165,000. They live in a state in which income over $100,000 is taxed at 11%. What is their total effective (marginal) tax rate?

9. The Benjamin family had wage earnings of $65,000 in 2001. They received interest of $4,500 on corporate bonds and $1,500 on bonds issued by the state. Their dividend income was $500, and they had a $1,000 capital gain on the sale of securities.

    They paid real estate taxes of $1,450, and state income tax of $3,000, and they donated $550 to their church. They paid interest of $8,000 on their home mortgage. They have one dependent child. What is their tax liability for $2001?

10. Joan and Harry Leahy both had income in 2001. Harry made $42,500 in wages. Joan has an incorporated small business that paid her a salary of $20,000. In addition, the business had profits of $15,000, which were paid to the Leahys as dividends. They received $5,600 in interest on savings and $350 in interest on a loan made to Harry's brother, Lou. Lou also repaid $2,000 of principal on that loan during the year. The couple had interest income from two bonds, $2,200 on a 20-year IBM issue and $2,700 on a state of Michigan revenue bond.

They sold some Biotech stock for $14,000 that had been purchased five years before for $4,000. Two years ago they invested $50,000 in some rural land on the advice of a real estate agent. They sold the property in 2001 for $46,000.

The Leahys paid $12,500 in mortgage payments of which $9,000 was interest and the rest reduced principal. They paid real estate taxes of $2,750 and state income tax of $6,800 during the year. They contributed $1,500 to their church and $3,000 to the support of Joan's elderly mother. They have two young children.

a. Calculate the Leahys' taxable income.

b. What is their tax liability for 2001?

c. What is their average tax rate?

d. What is their marginal tax rate? Can there be more than one marginal rate? Explain.

11. Calculate the corporate tax on Earnings Before Tax (EBT) of

a. $37,000

b. $57,000

c. $88,500

d. $110,000

e. $5,375,000

f. $14,000,000

g. $17,350,000

h. $23,500,000

12. Microchip Inc. had the following profits and losses in the years indicated.

1999	$5,000,000
2000	$ 350,000
2001	($3,450,000)

How much federal tax will it eventually pay for 1999? The corporate rate schedule is the same for all three years.

13. The Snyder Company had the following income and expense items.

Sales	$180,870,000
Cost	$110,450,000
Expenses	$65,560,000

In addition it received both interest and dividends from the Bevins Corp, of which it owns 30%. The interest received from Bevins was $2,430,000 and the dividends were $4,700,000.

Calculate Snyder's tax liability.

Internet Problem

14. Large corporations often begin as small businesses, and both share many of the same issues. Visit the Small Business Administration at http://www.sba.gov and find information on balance sheets, income statements, and other topics discussed in this chapter. The SBA page includes links to many other useful sites, such as the Small Business Resource Guide, state business tax and license sites, and more.

The Internal Revenue Service includes information related to business tax issues, and offers tax tips, information on how to avoid costly problems, important due dates, financial guidance and resources, laws and regulations, and statistical data about small businesses. Visit their site at http://www.irs.gov/smallbiz/allbusinesses/index.htm.

Finally, visit the Census Bureau's site at http://www.census.gov/epcd/www/smallbus.html for statistics on businesses large and small.

COMPUTER PROBLEMS

15. Rachel and Harry are planning to get married. Both have successful careers and expect to earn the following this year.

	Rachel	Harry
Salary	$155,380	$146,200
Interest and dividends	$6,750	$45,325
Long-term capital gain/(loss)	$5,798	—
Total Income	$167,928	$191,525
Itemized deductions	$28,763	$15,271

a. Use the **PERSTAX** program to calculate their total tax bill as single individuals and determine how much it will cost them in taxes to get married. Assume that getting married during a year subjects the entire year's income to the married filing jointly rate schedule. Assume there are no state taxes. Review the marriage penalty on page 43 if necessary.

b. Repeat part a assuming Harry has a long-term capital loss of ($6,000) in addition to the income shown above. Compare the cost of getting married with the result of part a and explain the difference.

c. Repeat part a assuming Harry is a widower with two children.

d. Duncan and Angela are also considering getting married (neither has children), but have considerably lower incomes as follows.

	Duncan	Angela
Salary	$56,450	$37,829
Itemized deductions	$ 6,048	$ 3,224

What will it cost them to get married?

e. Evaluate and comment on the differences in the marriage penalty between the two couples. Think in terms of the percent of income paid in taxes rather than in absolute dollars.

f. What do you think about the fairness/morality of the tax system with regard to the marriage penalty? Why?

DEVELOPING SOFTWARE

16. You've been hired by the nation of Utopia to computerize its approach to calculating taxes. Utopia's progressive tax system contains only two brackets that are applicable to all households. These are as follows.

Income	Rate
Under $30,000	20%
Over $30,000	30%

The treatment of personal exemptions and itemized deductions is similar to the U.S. system, but the exemption amount is permanently fixed at $2,550 per person. There is no special consideration given to capital gains and losses.

Write a spreadsheet program to compute taxes for a typical Utopian household. Test your program with the following cases.

Income	$28,950	$96,250
# people	1	5
Deductions	$2,800	$14,457

Verify that your program works by calculating the Utopian taxes manually. (*Hint*: Use a single conditional instruction [IF statement] to identify which bracket the taxpayer is in *and* make the tax calculation.)

CHAPTER 3

Cash Flows and Financial Analysis

Chapter Outline

In Chapter 1 we made the point that the orientation of finance is toward cash flows rather than accounting results. Because of the importance of cash flow, we need to understand the concept thoroughly and be familiar with the construction of the statement of cash flows as one of a firm's financial statements. We'll develop that understanding in the first half of this chapter.

Then we'll turn our attention to financial analysis, a technique designed to get practical information about business operations out of financial statements. Before attacking either of these topics, however, we need a little background on financial information in general.

FINANCIAL INFORMATION—WHERE DOES IT COME FROM, WHO USES IT, AND WHAT ARE WE LOOKING FOR?

The term "financial information" refers to the results of business operations stated in money terms. The idea largely implies the material in financial statements but isn't entirely limited to those documents. Financial information about a company is important because people inside and outside use it as a basis for making decisions about the firm and their relationships with it.

57

Financial information is the responsibility of management. It is created by accountants within the company and reviewed by auditors, but neither accountants nor auditors guarantee its correctness.[1] This creates a conflict of interest, because managements invariably want to portray results as favorably as possible. We'll discuss this idea shortly.

Once prepared, financial information is published to a variety of audiences, who use it to make decisions about the company. Let's begin our study by looking at these users in a little more detail.

USERS OF FINANCIAL INFORMATION

Financial statements are a report on the issuing company's performance. The main user groups are investors, creditors, and management itself.

Investors and Financial Analysts

The most important function of financial statements is to convey information to outside investors. These are people or organizations that might be interested in buying the company's stock or might be asked to lend it money. Lenders are concerned with the firm's stability and cash flows. The primary focus of stockholders is more likely to be its prospects for growth.

Financial analysts interpret information about companies and make recommendations to investors.

Investors sometimes analyze financial statements themselves, but more often rely on the reports of **financial analysts** who usually work for large brokerage firms or other financial institutions. Their job is to know as much about a particular company and its industry as an outsider can and to use that knowledge to predict the firm's performance. They then make recommendations about its investment value, including whether to buy or sell its stock and whether its debt is safe. Because of their pivotal advisory role, financial analysts can be considered the main audience for investor-oriented information.

A major part of the analyst's job is a careful study of the company's recent financial statements. It's important to realize that published financial statements relate to the past, and the analyst is interested in the future. However, the past factored by current information is usually the best available indicator of the future. In this chapter we'll have a look at the basic tools used by financial analysts and sophisticated investors.

Vendors/Creditors

Vendors asked to do business with the firm on credit are another important group of statement users. Because they're advancing funds in the form of products and services, they tend to be interested in most of the same things that concern lenders. The main issue is whether the firm is likely to have cash available to pay its debts in the immediate future.

Management

The final group of statement users is the firm's own management. Financial results show successes and failures in each of the many facets of running a busi-

---

1. Auditors make certain observations and tests which provide a *reasonable level of assurance* that statements are prepared in the proper manner and that all relevant details are disclosed.

ness. Management can study those results to pinpoint relative strengths and weaknesses in operations. This process shows where to put effort to correct problems and improve performance.

SOURCES OF FINANCIAL INFORMATION

The primary source of financial information about any publicly traded company is its own **annual report.** Annual reports are required of companies that sell their stock to the general public, and typically include several years of historical financial information along with a great deal of verbiage about the firm and its business.

The financial information in an annual report must be audited by an independent accounting firm. That process doesn't guarantee complete accuracy, but it does give a fair level of assurance that the numbers are presented with reasonable objectivity and in accordance with **generally accepted accounting principles (GAAP).** However, there's a lot more latitude in the nature of the information presented in the verbiage.

In fact, there's something of a problem with annual reports. They tend to portray past performance and future prospects in a very favorable light. That is, they're biased toward reporting that the firm has done as well as could be expected in the past year and that it will do even better in the future. Reports tend to minimize or ignore mistakes and failures, exaggerate successes, and build up future opportunities in unrealistically optimistic terms.

The annual report is actually a report to stockholders prepared by the company's management. But management works for the stockholders, so they are in effect writing their own report cards. Naturally the result is biased in favor of the people running the firm.

Along these lines, most annual reports have become advertising vehicles and are prepared to be very visually appealing. They're done on glossy paper, in multicolored inks, and are filled with professional quality photographs. They frequently look more like upscale magazines than business documents.

All this isn't necessarily bad as long as readers understand the biases and don't take everything in reports as strictly true. Outright lies are rare, but the truth can be told more or less attractively, and annual reports tend to present things in a rosy glow.

Companies file a more businesslike document called the 10-K with the Securities and Exchange Commission each year. It gives more detailed information than the annual report. Most companies will send you an annual report and a 10-K for the asking.

Brokerage firms and investment advisory services provide reports on most large companies. These reports are the result of the work of their financial analysts. Brokerage firms provide the information free as a service to clients and prospective clients, while investment advisory services publish it for a fee. The best known advisory service is Value Line which provides information on approximately 1700 stocks. Advisory services provide information to paid subscribers, but it is often available free in libraries.

Value Line's June 2001 report on General Motors is shown in Figure 3.1. Study the layout of the information it contains for a few minutes. The chart at

A firm's **annual report** is the **primary source** of financial information about it.

Annual reports tend to be **biased in favor of management's performance.**

http://

Choose a company from Nasdaq's list at

http://dynamic.nasdaq. com/dynamic/ nasdaq100_activity.stm

and look at its annual report, usually found under Investor Relations on the company web sites.

Real Applications

The Devil is in the Details . . .

Annual reports are a leading source of information for investors. But since they're prepared by management, they tend to be very favorably biased. The bias takes the form of exaggerating successes and downplaying problems and threats. The 2000 annual report of Microsoft, the world's leading software company, provides a good example.

In 2000, Microsoft was under legal attack by the U.S. Justice Department for alleged violation of the Sherman Act, a law that makes certain business behavior illegal if it reduces competition and puts the violator in a monopoly position. The federal government and nineteen states sued Microsoft and demanded, among other things, that it be broken up into two companies to compensate for the alleged anticompetitive effects of its previous behavior.

During the year, the pending lawsuit was in the news constantly, and was undoubtedly a major factor in the investment community's perception of Microsoft stock. Indeed the threat it posed to the company's future probably depressed its stock price considerably. It seems reasonable to expect that a professional analysis of the firm's prospects would have included a thorough discussion of the lawsuit and an assessment of the likelihood that the firm would be damaged by it.

Yet Microsoft's annual report barely mentions the suit, even though it was still pending when the report was issued. The litigation is given only six lines in the president's discussion of results which is read carefully by most serious investors. It's mentioned in somewhat more detail in the notes to the financial statements where statements about pending litigation are required by law. But many investors don't read the notes, which are similar to "the fine print" in a contract.

Companies defend their minimal mention of such lawsuits in annual reports saying that management believes the suits are groundless, the companies will eventually win, and that investors therefore shouldn't worry about them. But even if management honestly holds that belief, aren't investors entitled to a fair and thorough disclosure of the risks arising from lawsuits, and a discussion of both management's and the other side's arguments? Perhaps, but it would be unusual to find it in an annual report.

Source: Microsoft Corporation Annual Report 2000

the top shows the stock's price performance for the last 10 years. Below that 10 to 15 years of history is shown for a variety of financial line items. Notice that some items are stated on a per-share basis.

Moving down the page, there's a short summary of the nature of the company's business followed by a verbal analysis of its current market situation and prospects for the future. At the time of this report the possibility of GM acquiring a South Korean auto manufacturer was an important issue in assessing the firm's long-term prospects. This section is the heart of the report. It tells investors what the analyst thinks is likely to happen to GM's business and by implication the price of its stock.

Notice that much of this "financial information" isn't exactly financial. It might be better described as marketing or strategic information. Keep in mind that financial results are numerical representations of what is physically going on in a business. Thus, deciding whether a firm is a good financial investment begins with a judgment about how it's doing in the market for its products.

FIGURE 3.1   Value Line's June 2001 Report on General Motors

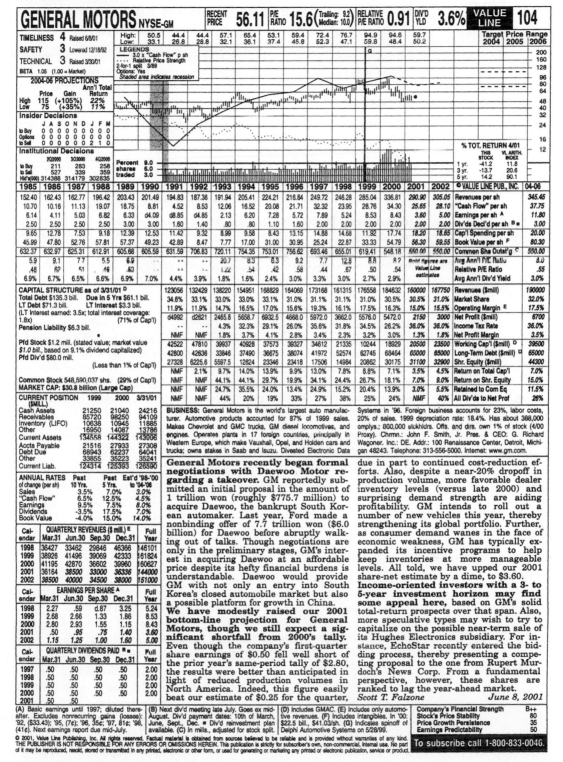

Ethics

Continuing Operations, Unusual Items, and the Ethics of Presenting Information Fairly

Financial information deals largely with the past, but investors really care only about the future. Their interest in previous financial results comes from the value those results have as predictors. But a number of things can be included in financial statements that muddy their predictive power. Here are a few issues.

Continuing Operations   Investors need to be sure the past results they consider represent a business unit that's expected to continue. For example, if a company sells off or closes a division, analysis of its prospects should be based only on past earnings from *continuing operations* excluding the unit sold. Obviously, that's because only continuing operations represent *repeatable* performance. Unfortunately separating the results of the sold unit isn't always easy, and it's possible to make what's left look better than it is.

Extraordinary Items   Some costs and expenses come along only occasionally. For example, rare events such as earthquakes and certain lawsuits may happen only once in a lifetime. Proper financial reporting separates the costs associated with those events from normally recurring expenses by displaying earnings figures before and after "unusual" or "extraordinary" items. The idea is that investors should use earnings *before* unusual items as a measure of the firm's continuing ability to make money, and ignore one-time expenses as irrelevant to future operations.

But there isn't a clear definition of what qualifies as an extraordinary expense, and some companies are stretching the definition to amazing lengths to make financial results look good. For example, Waste Management, the nation's leading trash collector, recently declared the cost of painting some of its garbage trucks one year earlier than scheduled an "unusual expense." That along with other unusual items helped the firm beat quarterly earnings expectations.* It's hard to accept that a paint job is "unusual," because it's done a little sooner than planned.

Restructuring Charges   In this context restructuring means reorganizing to face changed business conditions. It usually implies getting smaller and laying off part of the workforce. It
—continued

● THE ORIENTATION OF FINANCIAL ANALYSIS

from the CFO

Much of the information in the rest of this chapter may seem similar to material you've studied in accounting. However, our orientation is different here. In accounting we're concerned with creating financial statements. In finance we're concerned with using them to evaluate businesses and their prospects for the future. *In particular, financial analysis looks for problems, places where things aren't as they seem, or where results indicate the firm may be heading for trouble.*

For example, a statement of cash flows might indicate that a firm borrowed a lot of money last year. Accounting per se stops with the presentation of that fact along with information on the things money was spent on during the period. The financial analyst, however, must go further and ask why the borrowing occurred and what it implies for the future.

Perhaps the borrowing was to finance expansion into an exciting new venture. That might seem great, but the analyst wants to know if the firm will be

Ethics **Continued—**

also generally involves charges, which can be very large, for things like severance pay and closing of facilities.

Companies like to show income before and after restructuring charges in financial statements. The idea is that investors should consider restructuring a rare event and value the firm based on the higher income before the charge. Investors generally agree and do just that.

But in recent years some major companies, including Citicorp, Kodak, and AT&T,** have been restructuring every few years. When that happens a question arises as to whether restructuring charges are truly one-time events brought about by external forces or just cover-ups for bad management.

A Conflict of Interest Management is ultimately responsible for financial statements. But management's goal is to get investors to set as high a value on the firm's stock as possible. Executives receive personal rewards for achieving that goal. Hence there's a conflict of interest related to the presentation of things like these in financial statements. Management has an incentive to make operations appear as successful as possible and has some ability to mold the figures to do that. Accounting principles provide some control, but there's a good deal of latitude within the rules.

Ethics All of these factors lead to an ethical question. Does management have a responsibility to portray operations fairly to the market and potential investors? Or should it do everything it can to hold the stock price up for its own benefit and for that of current shareholders, including presenting certain information less than clearly?

*Aaron Elstein, "'Unusual Expenses' Raise Concerns" Wall Street Journal (August 23, 2001): C1.
Jonathan Weil, "What's the P/E Ratio? Well, Depends on What Is Meant by Earnings," Wall Street Journal (August 21, 2001): A1.

**R. Smith and S. Lipin, "Are Companies Using Restructuring Costs to Fudge the Figures?" Wall Street Journal (January 30, 1996).

● The **orientation** of the financial analyst is **critical** and **investigative**.

able to support the interest payments and whether the venture will need more borrowing later before it starts to generate a profit. On the other hand, the borrowing might be because the firm isn't collecting its receivables or is holding significant useless inventory. In that case, the analyst will want to know how the problem will be resolved and what its impact on long-run profitability will be.

Keep this orientation in mind. In finance our attitude is critical and investigative.

THE STATEMENT OF CASH FLOWS

We've made the point that income as reported in the income statement does not equal cash in the pocket of the business or its owner. Accounting income includes things like depreciation, which is one of several artificial devices designed to make the income statement a representation of the long-run condition of the enterprise. Businesses, however, are run with cold, hard cash on a day-to-day basis. Therefore another statement is needed to give users information detailing the actual movement of cash in and out of the company. That document is the statement of cash flows. It shows a reader where the firm's money came from and what it was spent on during the period covered.

TERMINOLOGY   A more formal name for the statement of cash flows is the statement of changes in financial position, but people rarely use that awkward title. It comes from the fact that the balance sheet can be called the statement of financial position, and technically the cash statement analyzes changes in the balance sheet. Common usage involves the words "cash flow" or "funds flow." Sources and uses or sources and applications of cash or funds are also ways of referring to what we will call the statement of cash flows.

Cash statements report inflows and outflows of money. Inflows are usually represented by positive numbers while outflows are negative. Negative numbers are shown in parentheses.

WHERE THE STATEMENT OF CASH FLOWS COMES FROM   The income statement and balance sheet emerge directly from closing the books. The statement of cash flows does not; it is constructed from the other two statements after they're produced.

● HOW THE STATEMENT OF CASH FLOWS WORKS—PRELIMINARY EXAMPLES

The best way to gain an understanding of the role of cash in financial statements is to appreciate how the statement of cash flows is put together from the balance sheet and income statement. The pages that follow will develop a working knowledge of the principles as well as the calculations involved.

It takes two balance sheets and an income statement to build a statement of cash flows for an accounting period. The income statement is from the period and the balance sheets are as of its beginning and end. (A beginning balance sheet is the ending balance sheet of the previous period.)

The cash statement analyzes where money has come from and gone to by doing two things. First, it takes net income for the period and adjusts it for some of the items that make it different from the everyday concept of income as cash in one's pocket. Second, it takes the two consecutive balance sheets and analyzes the *changes* in everything the company has and everything it owes to determine how those changes have affected the cash balance.

Applying these ideas can be a little difficult if we jump right into a business example. It helps to first consider personal examples involving familiar assets and liabilities. We'll begin with two such illustrations.

Buying a Car on Credit

Suppose Joe Jones has after-tax income of $50,000 and spends $40,000 on normal living expenses during a year. Also assume that at the beginning of the year he had a bank balance of $10,000 and no other assets or liabilities. Further assume that during the year he bought a new car costing $30,000, financing

$25,000 at the bank with a car loan. At the end of the year he has $15,000 in the bank.

The statement of cash flows lays out these transactions in a way that highlights where the cash comes from and goes to. The "where from" and "where to" are commonly called *sources* and *uses of cash*, respectively. The statement goes on to demonstrate that the beginning balance in the bank plus the net cash flow equals the ending balance in the bank.

The idea is illustrated conceptually as follows.

Cash income	$50,000	
Cash used on living expenses	(40,000)	
Net source of cash from income		$10,000
Source of cash from loan		$25,000
Use of cash to buy auto		($30,000)
Net inflow/(outflow) of cash		$5,000
Beginning cash balance	$10,000	
Net cash flow	5,000	
Ending cash balance	$15,000	

In this example the net source of cash from income is analogous to a business's net income adjusted for noncash items. This item is an important *source* of cash for Joe.

Joe *used* $30,000 to buy an automobile. In other words, he *increased his assets* by $30,000. In general, any time assets are increased, cash is used. Joe also *received* $25,000 from the bank when he took out the loan, which is a liability. In other words, he realized a *source* of cash of $25,000 by *increasing his liabilities*. In general any increase in liabilities results in a source or inflow of cash.

It's important to keep the car and the loan separate in your mind. In our personal lives we tend to think of going into a car dealer with a down payment and coming out with a car and loan payments all in one transaction. To understand the statement of cash flows, you have to keep the asset (the car) and the liability (the loan) separate. When he bought the car Joe didn't just spend $5,000. He spent $30,000 and borrowed $25,000 at the same time.

Adding Joe's sources (income and loan) and uses (car purchase) together we get his net cash flow. Assuming all his money is in the bank, the beginning balance plus the net cash flow has to equal the ending balance. If it doesn't, something is wrong with the record keeping or accounting.

Here's a slightly more complicated illustration.

Buying and Selling Cars

Suppose at the beginning of a year Sally Smith has an expensive car with a current market value of $20,000 and a $14,000 loan outstanding on it. At the same time her bank balance is $6,000. During the year she has after-tax income of $60,000 but spends $62,000 on living expenses. In an effort to economize, she sells her big car for $20,000 and buys a small economy model for $9,000 in cash (no loan). When she sells the old car she pays off the loan. At the end of the year her bank balance is $1,000. Sally's cash flows look something like this.

Cash income	$60,000	
Cash used on living expenses	(62,000)	
Net source of cash from income[2]		($2,000)
Source of cash from selling old car	$20,000	
Use of cash to buy new car	($9,000)	
Net source from car investments		$11,000
Use of cash to pay off old car financing		($14,000)
Net inflow/(outflow) of cash		($5,000)

Beginning cash balance	$6,000
Net cash flow	(5,000)
Ending cash balance	$1,000

In this case, Sally *reduced her assets* by selling the old car for $20,000. That sale was a *source* of cash. In general, when assets are reduced, the reduction is a source of cash. She also bought a new car, which was obviously an increase in her assets and a use of cash.

Sally paid off her car loan using cash. In doing so she *reduced a liability*. In general, a liability reduction is a use of cash.

Notice that Sally's net source of cash from income was negative simply because she spent more than she made this year. That added to the fact that she spent more than she gained on the cars and loan together means she has a net negative cash flow for the year. She accomplished that by pulling down her bank balance. If she didn't have any money in the bank, she could still have done it by borrowing. Then we would have shown an additional source due to an increase in a liability, the loan.

These examples help to illustrate the ideas involved in cash flow because we're all familiar with automobiles as assets and loans as liabilities. Basically, cash flows stem from either income or changes in assets and liabilities.

●BUSINESS CASH FLOWS

In a business, income is represented by adjusting net income from the income statement for noncash items like depreciation. Assets and liabilities are conveniently listed on balance sheets as of the beginning and end of the year, so changes in each account can be calculated easily.

However, in a business context changes in balance sheet amounts get a little confusing when assets include things like accounts receivable and liabilities include items like accounts payable and accruals. It's not as easy to see that an increase in receivables is a use of cash as it is to understand that you need cash to buy a car. A decrease in accruals is also more difficult to fathom as a use of cash than is paying off a loan.

Cash Flow Rules

In practice we don't have to worry about thinking through how cash flows in and out of every account. Four simple rules illustrated in the preceding examples can be applied to any business's financial statements. All we need to do to ana-

---

2. Because income is usually positive and a source of cash, a loss is conventionally shown as a negative source rather than as a use.

lyze cash is to keep those rules in mind. The rules are that changes in balance sheet accounts result in sources and uses of cash as follows.

$$\text{Asset increase} = \text{Use}$$

$$\text{Asset decrease} = \text{Source}$$

$$\text{Liability increase} = \text{Source}$$

$$\text{Liability decrease} = \text{Use}$$

Standard Presentation

● The **statement of cash flows** presents **operating, investing,** and **financing** activities separately.

A business's statement of cash flows is organized to show cash flows from three different kinds of activities: operating, investing, and financing.

Operating activities have to do with running the business on a day-to-day basis.

Investing activities occur when the firm buys (invests in) or sells things such as fixed assets that enable it to do business. Investing activities also include long-term purchases and sales of financial assets.[3]

Financing activities occur when the company borrows money, pays off loans, sells stock, or pays dividends. They have to do with raising money and servicing the obligations that come along with it.

Graphic Portrayals

Before tackling a numerical example, let's fix these ideas in mind by looking at two graphic representations of cash flow in a business.

Figure 3.2 shows how cash flows in and out of a company. Notice that operating activities have to do with the normal course of business and the current accounts of the balance sheet. Investing activities generally have to do with buying long-lived assets, either real or financial, and financing activities are concerned with debt and equity.

Figure 3.3 is usually called the *cash conversion cycle*, but the term *racetrack diagram* is a little more colorful and tends to fix it in mind better. Starting at the bottom of the track, a business uses cash to purchase inventory and labor to produce a product. That product is sold, resulting in a receivable. When the receivable is collected, the firm once again has cash in hand that it uses to buy more inventory and labor to produce more product and so on.

● Product is **converted** into cash, which is transformed into more product, creating the **cash conversion cycle.**

In a sense the company is running around a racetrack, converting cash to product and product to cash. You can think of the firm continually doing this equipped with some level of assets.

Given a level of assets, the firm goes around the track faster by making more sales in the period. Clearly the faster it can go around, the better off it is as long as it doesn't damage something else by going too fast. In other words, it's important to get a lot of sales per dollar of assets employed in the business. That's one of several measures of success.

However, a firm that just runs around the track putting all its money back into inventory wouldn't be doing its owners much good. A successful business has to

---

3. The term "invest" generally means buying something that is expected to return more than its cost in the future. When individuals say "invest" they usually mean buying a financial asset. However, we sometimes use the term with physical things (investing in a house) or even intangibles (investing in an education). When we talk about investment by companies we generally mean buying the equipment used in doing business such as machinery, vehicles, and real estate.

FIGURE 3.2   **Business Cash Flows**

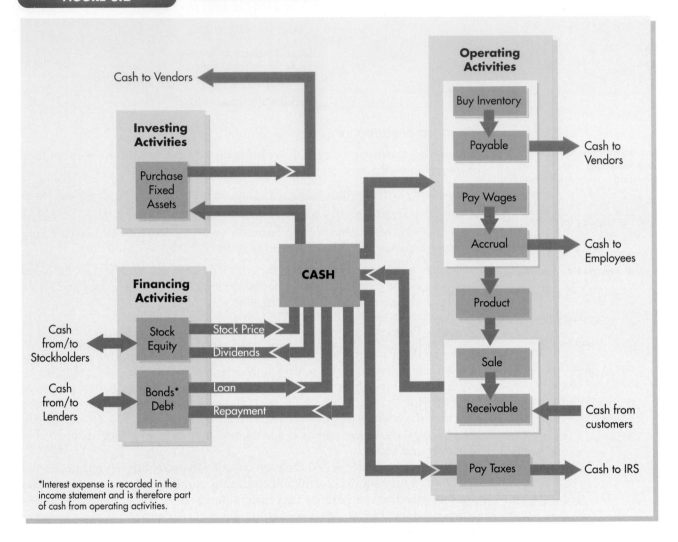

*Interest expense is recorded in the income statement and is therefore part of cash from operating activities.

pull something out each time around to buy new assets for growth and to replace old ones that wear out, to pay taxes, and for profit. Clearly, the larger the slice that can be taken out of cash flow each time around the track, the better off the firm is. This idea is simply profitability and is shown in the lower part of the figure.

Summarizing, the diagram illustrates that a business has to do two things for success: sell a lot for its level of assets and sell at a reasonable profit margin given its costs and expenses.

Notice that the two things work against each other. The business can always sell more if it charges less, but then it will have less profit. Conversely, a higher price yields more profit but lower sales. We'll come back to this idea toward the end of the chapter.

CONSTRUCTING THE STATEMENT OF CASH FLOWS

Now we can look at putting together a statement of cash flows for a business. The best way to do that is to work through a numerical example.

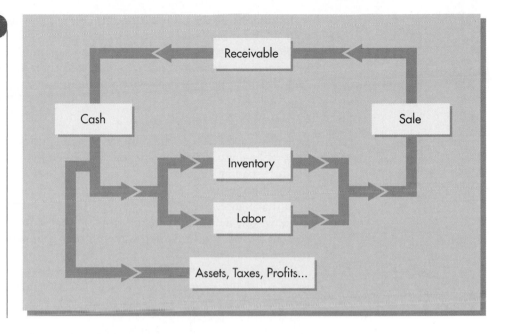

FIGURE 3.3

The Cash Conversion Cycle—The Racetrack Diagram

The Belfry Company's Cash Flows

Constructing a business cash flow statement requires balance sheets at the beginning and end of the period under consideration and an income statement for that period.

Consider the following statements for the hypothetical Belfry Company in which the balance sheets are arranged vertically.

Belfry Company
Balance Sheet
For the period ended 12/31/X2

ASSETS

	12/31/X1	12/31/X2
Cash	$1,000	$1,400
Accounts receivable	3,000	2,900
Inventory	2,000	3,200
CURRENT ASSETS	$6,000	$7,500
Fixed assets		
Gross	$4,000	$ 6,000
Accumulated deprec.	(1,000)	(1,500)
Net	$3,000	$ 4,500
TOTAL ASSETS	$9,000	$12,000

LIABILITIES

	12/31/X1	12/31/X2
Accounts payable	$1,500	$2,100
Accruals	500	400
CURRENT LIABILITIES	$2,000	$2,500
Long-terms debt	$5,000	$6,200
Equity	$2,000	$3,300
TOTAL CAPITAL	$7,000	$9,500
TOTAL LIABILITIES AND EQUITY	$9,000	$12,000

Belfry Company
Income Statement
For the period ended 12/31/X2

Sales	$10,000
COGS	6,000
Gross margin	$ 4,000
Expense	$ 1,600
Depreciation	500
EBIT	$ 1,900
Interest	400
EBT	$ 1,500
Tax	500
Net income	$ 1,000

In addition to the information on these statements, we'll assume the company sold stock for $800 during the year and paid a $500 dividend.

Notice that we've shown depreciation separately in the income statement for convenience. Most presentations don't do that. We'll develop the statement of cash flows for Belfry one activity at a time.

Operating Activities

Operating activities are the things a company does on a day-to-day basis to conduct its business. Typically they include buying inventory, producing and selling product, paying expenses and taxes, and collecting on credit sales. The focus of these activities is the production of net income, so we start the cash statement with that figure.

> ● **Operating activities** involve the **income statement** and **current** balance sheet accounts.

However, net income includes items that don't represent cash flows in the current period. Our next step is therefore to adjust those out. The result is called *operating income.*

In Belfry's case, the only adjustment necessary to calculate operating income is to add back depreciation, which was subtracted in the calculation of net income.

Net income	$1,000
Depreciation	500
Operating income	$1,500

Next we recognize that the money from operating transactions runs through the current balance sheet accounts. Therefore changes in those accounts are part of operating cash flow. We analyze the balances *other than cash* and classify the changes as sources or uses of cash according to the cash flow rules. The cash account is handled separately later.

In Belfry's case, accounts receivable decreased from $3,000 to $2,900, providing a $100 source of cash because according to the second rule an asset decrease is a source. Similarly, inventory increased from $2,000 to $3,200 for a use of $1,200 according to the first rule.

Apply the third and fourth rules to the changes in accounts payable and accruals to get the following sources and uses.

Account	Source/(Use)
Receivables	$ 100
Inventory	(1,200)
Payables	600
Accruals	(100)
	$ (600)

The sum of the current account changes and operating income is cash from operating activities. The typical presentation is illustrated for Belfry as follows.

Net income	$1,000
Depreciation	500
Net changes in current accounts	(600)
Cash from operating activities	$ 900

Investing Activities

● **Investing activities** typically include purchasing **fixed assets**.

Cash from investing activities is simple in this example. The only entry comes from an increase in Belfry's fixed assets of $2,000. This is reflected by the increase in gross fixed assets from $4,000 to $6,000, which is a use of cash according to the first rule.

Notice that we use the gross fixed assets account for this calculation rather than the net. That's because the net figure includes a reduction for accumulated depreciation, the change in which is the other side of the entry that put depreciation on the income statement. That depreciation is already included in the cash flow statement in the operating section, and we don't want to repeat it here.

Hence, cash from investing activities is

Purchase of fixed assets   ($2,000).

Financing Activities

● **Financing activities** deal with the **capital accounts, long-term debt,** and **equity.**

There are three financing activities in this example. The first is an increase in long-term debt, a source according to the third rule. The company appears to have taken out another loan. The second is a sale of stock, and the third a dividend payment. The sale of stock results in an increase in equity, a liability,[4] and is a source according to the third rule. The dividend payment is clearly a use of money. It reduces equity and is therefore a use according to the fourth rule.

Cash from financing activities is calculated as follows.

Increase in long-term debt	$1,200
Sale of stock	800
Dividend paid	(500)
Cash from financing activities	$1,500

The Equity and Cash Accounts

Notice that we haven't calculated the change in equity and classified it as a source or a use of cash. That's because the procedure breaks that change into three parts and includes them individually. Let's lay the pieces out. The change in equity is the sum of net income and the sale of new stock less the dividend paid. These are as follows for Belfry.

Net income	$1,000
Stock sale	800
Dividend	(500)
Total change in equity	$1,300

The stock sale and the dividend are included under financing activities, while the addition of net income to equity shows up under operating activities.

Also notice that we haven't done anything with the cash account. It's been omitted because the cash flow total of the three activities we've presented so far must equal the change in the cash account. That's shown as a reconciliation at the end of the statement.

---

4. Equity is a "liability" of the company to its owners. We treat it as a liability with respect to the cash flow rules.

In Belfry's case the sum of operating, investing, and financing activities is a positive $400, so we have the following reconciliation.

Beginning cash balance	$1,000
Net cash flow	400
Ending cash balance	$1,400

The entire statement of cash flows for Belfry is shown below.

To summarize, the statement of cash flows takes information from the income statement and balance sheet and displays it in a manner that highlights the movement of cash. No new information is created; what is already there is simply rearranged in a way that's more usable in the day-to-day running of the business.

Conclusions

In this case, examination of the statement of cash flows leads to some concern about the Belfry Company. The firm is quite profitable, earning 10% on sales, but still had to borrow substantially during the year. Clearly the fixed asset purchase had something to do with the additional funds required. One must ask whether that expenditure was entirely necessary. Another concern is the sudden increase in inventory. Does it mean that some of the existing inventory isn't good? If so, this could portend a big loss.

You should always keep in mind the fact that it's cash that really counts in business, not net income.

To drive that point home, let's ask another question about Belfry. Notice that during the year it had to borrow an additional $1,200 from the bank. Would a bank have been likely to extend that additional credit?

In fact, a bank might have been reluctant to advance more money to this company. Notice that the firm's capital (long-term debt plus equity) is in the neigh-

---

Belfry Company
Statement of Cash Flows
For the period ended 12/31/X2

CASH FROM OPERATING ACTIVITIES

Net income	$1,000
Depreciation	500
Net changes in current accounts	(600)
Cash from operating activities	$ 900

CASH FROM INVESTING ACTIVITIES

Purchase of fixed assets	($2,000)

CASH FROM FINANCING ACTIVITIES

Increase in long-term debt	$1,200
Sale of stock	800
Dividend paid	(500)
Cash from financing activities	$1,500

NET CASH FLOW	$ 400
Beginning cash balance	$1,000
Net cash flow	400
Ending cash balance	$1,400

● A firm that manages cash poorly can **go out of business** while making an **accounting profit**.

borhood of 70% debt. *We'll see later that such a high proportion of debt is beyond the comfort level of most lenders. The bank could have refused further advances, putting the company in a cash bind.* If that had caused Belfry to fail to make its payroll, the company could have been out of business overnight.

Yet Belfry is earning great profits in terms of net income, 10% of sales. Take the lesson to heart: A firm can go broke profitably. Small businesses do it all the time, and it happens to big companies with surprising frequency.

FREE CASH FLOWS

● Cash generated **beyond reinvestment** needs is **free cash flow**.

Free cash flow refers to whether a firm generates cash beyond its own needs. Under normal conditions, most firms generate positive cash flows from operating activities, but some of those funds have to be used to maintain a long-run competitive position. The largest such nonoperating cash requirement is typically replacing worn-out fixed assets.

Free cash flow is defined as net cash flow less such requirements. It is essentially the cash available for distribution to common stockholders. If free cash flow is negative, the firm must either borrow or raise more equity capital to be viable in the long run.

The free cash flow concept is especially important when one company acquires another. The acquiring firm needs to know whether its new business will need cash infusions after the acquisition or will generate funds that can be used elsewhere.

RATIO ANALYSIS

● **Financial ratios** are formed from sets of financial statement figures. Ratios **highlight** different aspects of **performance**.

People who make judgments about businesses by reading financial statements have developed some relatively standard methods with which they analyze information. The general technique is known as **ratio analysis**. Its use is virtually universal among financial professionals. It is therefore important that you be familiar with the basic technique and a few of the more commonly used ratios.

Ratio analysis involves taking sets of numbers out of the financial statements and forming ratios with them. The numbers are chosen so that each ratio has a particular meaning to the operation of the business.

An example will make the idea clear. There's a ratio that gives a quick indication of whether the company will have the means to pay its bills during the next year. It's called the **current ratio** and is based on the definitions of current assets and current liabilities.

Recall from Chapter 2 that the money coming into a firm from normal operations passes through current assets. Similarly, the normal outgoing money passes through current liabilities. Further, the definition of "current" is that cash will be generated or required within a year.

It's clear that to remain solvent, a company must have at least as much money coming in as it has going out. This fact suggests that comparing the sizes of current assets and current liabilities at a point in time will give an indication of whether operating cash flows will be positive or negative in the near future. The current ratio does just that. It's formed by dividing current assets by current liabilities, and must exceed 1.0 or the firm can expect to run short of cash within the next year.[5] The current ratio measures **liquidity**, which in this context refers to the company's ability to pay its bills in the short run.

---

5. The current ratio generally needs to be quite a bit greater than 1.0. If future inflows and outflows are just equal, timing problems can be expected if the outflows come first.

● For a business, **liquidity** refers to its **ability to pay its bills** in the short run.

Numerous ratios have been devised, each having a special significance like the current ratio. We'll cover several of the most commonly used ratios in the remainder of this chapter.

COMPARISONS

Ratios by themselves have some value, but not nearly as much as they have when they're compared with other similar figures. For example, a current ratio of 1.8 in a particular business might seem all right by itself, but it could cause concern if competing firms have current ratios in excess of 3.0. In such a case we would suspect that some characteristic of the business requires great liquidity, and the firm we are analyzing doesn't have it.

Ratio analysis is usually conducted in the context of one or more of three comparisons. Comparisons are made with respect to history, the competition, and budget.

HISTORY   Comparison with history means looking at a ratio next to the same figure calculated for the same organization in one or more immediately preceding accounting periods. The idea is to look for trends. If a firm's current ratio is seen to be decreasing steadily over a number of periods, the analyst would ask why.

THE COMPETITION   The performance of other companies in the same field is always a good yardstick for evaluating a firm's performance. If a particular measure is substantially off what others are doing, it's a good idea to find out why. Industry average data are often available through trade associations, government publications, banking publications, and the publications of investment analysts.

● Ratios are typically compared with similar figures from **history,** the **competition,** and **budget.**

BUDGET   Most businesses of any size develop financial plans for the future. We'll study business planning in Chapter 16. For now it's enough to understand that a plan involves a projected set of financial statements from which ratios can be developed. When financial performance is being evaluated, what the organization really did is always compared with what management said it would do in their plan (budget) for the period. Comparing planned and actual ratios highlights where management needs to put its attention in running the business.

COMMON SIZE STATEMENTS

The first step in a financial analysis is usually the calculation of a set of ratios known as **common size statements**. The common size income statement is the most frequently used. The idea can best be understood with an example.

Suppose we're interested in comparing the financial performance of two companies in the same line of business that are substantially different in size. For example, consider the income statements of Alpha and Beta.

	Alpha	Beta
Sales revenue	$2,187,460	$150,845
Cost of sales	1,203,103	72,406
Gross margin	$ 984,357	$ 78,439
Expenses	505,303	39,974
EBIT	$ 479,054	$ 38,465
Interest	131,248	15,386
EBT	$ 347,806	$ 23,079
Tax	118,254	3,462
Net income	$ 229,552	$ 19,617

It's hard to tell which company is doing a better job of controlling costs and expenses by looking at the dollar figures because Alpha is so much larger than Beta.

The comparison is made much easier by creating a *common size* statement for each company to abstract away from absolute dollars and state things in relative terms. A common size income statement is formed by stating each line as a percentage of revenue. The percentages are usually stated to the first decimal place and displayed next to the dollar figures. Let's look at the comparison of Alpha and Beta with the aid of common size statements.

	Alpha		**Beta**	
	$	%	$	%
Sales revenue	$2,187,460	100.0	$150,845	100.0
Cost of sales	1,203,103	55.0	72,406	48.0
Gross margin	$ 984,357	45.0	$ 78,439	52.0
Expenses	505,303	23.1	39,974	26.5
EBIT	$ 479,054	21.9	$ 38,465	25.5
Interest	131,248	6.0	$ 15,386	10.2
EBT	$ 347,806	15.9	$ 23,079	15.3
Tax	118,254	5.4	3,462	2.3
Net income	$ 229,552	10.5	$ 19,617	13.0

● A **common size income statement** presents each line item as a **percent of revenue.**

Each percentage figure below sales is a ratio of that line's dollars to revenue dollars. The ratio of cost of sales (or cost of goods sold) to sales revenue is generally called the *cost ratio*, while expenses as a percentage of revenue can be called the *expense ratio*. Net income as a percentage of sales has a name of its own, *return on sales*, and is one of the ratios we'll look at later.

Comparing the two columns of ratios in our example, we can immediately see significant differences in the way the two companies are operating. Alpha's cost is 55% of revenues whereas Beta's is only 48%. This is unusual because one would expect the larger company to have economies of scale in production that would make it more efficient than the smaller firm.

Several explanations are possible. Alpha might have some production problems, Beta might be particularly good at what it does, or there may be a difference in what they're making. In the last situation Alpha might be producing a simple bottom-of-the-line product that sells at a minimal markup while Beta might be making a fancy customized version of the same thing that's marked up much higher.

from the CFO

The point is that the common size analysis leads us to ask the right questions. It doesn't give us the answers, but it gets our investigation of problems started in the right direction.

Common size analysis is particularly useful in comparing a firm's performance with its own history. Unfavorable trends in cost or expense ratios from this year to last and the year before are signals to management that should never be overlooked or taken lightly.

A set of common size statements is generally the first thing an analyst prepares when starting a project.

Common size balance sheets can also be constructed that state everything as a percentage of total assets. They can be useful in determining whether a firm has relatively too much money tied up in inventory or receivables, or whether it uses more equipment than it should.

● RATIOS

In the following pages we'll present some of the more commonly used ratios of financial analysis. Each ratio is designed to illuminate some aspect of how the business is doing. In each case we'll illustrate how the ratio is calculated, discuss the rationale behind its use, and explain what it's telling the analyst.

Remember that ratios are most meaningful when used in comparisons. For that reason it's difficult to make a generalization about what a good or acceptable value is for any particular figure. For example, one of the ratios we'll be talking about measures how effectively the firm uses inventory. With respect to that ratio, a good number for a manufacturing company would be terrible for a retailer.

After we've discussed each ratio, we'll calculate its value for the Belfry Company, using the financial statements shown on page 72.

Average Values

Notice that we have a beginning and an ending balance sheet for the Belfry Company, which brings up a computational question. When a ratio calls for a balance sheet figure, should we use the beginning, the ending, or an average value?

The answer depends on what the ratio is measuring. If it pertains to a position or status at the end of the year, then ending values are appropriate. On the other hand, if the ratio measures an activity that goes on during the entire period, average balance sheet figures better reflect performance. Beginning values alone are never appropriate.

The difference between average and ending values isn't very important if the company is relatively stable and account balances aren't changing much. However, it can be significant if the firm is growing or shrinking rapidly.

As a general rule, when an income or cash flow figure appears in a ratio coupled with a balance sheet figure, an average value for the balance sheet number is appropriate. When the ratio compares two balance sheet numbers, an ending value generally is used. In our calculations for Belfry, we'll indicate which values we're using.

Categories of Ratios

Ratios can be categorized according to the kinds of issues they address. The ones we'll discuss fit into five classifications: liquidity, asset management, debt management, profitability, and market value.

● Ratios fall into five categories: **liquidity, asset management, debt management, profitability,** and **market value.**

Liquidity ratios indicate the firm's ability to pay its bills in the short run. *Asset management* ratios show how the company uses its resources to generate revenue and profit and to avoid cost. *Debt management* ratios show how effectively the firm uses other people's money and whether it's using too much borrowed money. *Profitability* ratios give us several measures by which to assess the success of the whole venture in making money. *Market value* ratios give an indication of how investors feel about the company's financial future.

● LIQUIDITY RATIOS

● **Liquidity ratios** measure the ability to meet short-term **financial obligations.**

Liquidity ratios are of particular concern to lenders and suppliers who provide products and services to the firm on credit. They want to be sure the company has the ability to pay its debts.

The Current Ratio

The current ratio is the primary measure of a company's liquidity—that is, its ability to meet its financial obligations in the near future. The calculation is

$$\text{current ratio} = \frac{\text{current assets}}{\text{current liabilities}}.$$

The reasoning behind the ratio was discussed earlier as an example. If everything coming in in the near future is a current asset today, and everything to be paid out in the near future is a current liability today, then current assets should be substantially above current liabilities to ensure solvency. That means the current ratio has to exceed 1.0. In general, a figure greater than 1.5 or 2.0 is required for comfort.

Having said that, we should point out two anomalies that occur with respect to this ratio. If you look at the balance sheets of large, sophisticated companies that are doing well, you'll often see current ratios in the neighborhood of 1.0. Does this mean these firms are in danger of insolvency?

The answer is generally no in spite of the low current ratio. The reason is that the firms are being managed very well. Holding current assets like receivables and inventory ties up money that could be used elsewhere. Hence firms try to operate with as few current assets as possible. Companies which do that well can have relatively low current ratios if they have a line of credit with a bank to cover temporary cash shortages.

from the CFO

It's also important to be aware that a high current ratio can be misleading. Inventories and receivables can be overstated, meaning some items in those accounts are valueless and will never turn into cash. If those items remain on the balance sheet, they can result in an inflated current assets figure and a falsely comforting current ratio.

We'll use ending balances for Belfry's current ratio.

$$\text{current ratio} = \frac{\$7,500}{\$2,500} = 3.0$$

The current ratio is a pure number and is generally not referred to in units of any kind.

The Quick Ratio or Acid Test

The quick ratio is conceptually similar to the current ratio.

$$\text{quick ratio} = \frac{\text{current assets} - \text{inventory}}{\text{current liabilities}}$$

The liquidity measure provided by the current ratio depends on the conversion of inventory to cash in a reasonable time. However, as we described in Chapter 2, inventory is particularly subject to valuation problems and is often overstated. Inventory also takes more time to convert to cash than other current items.

As a result of these problems, analysts look for a liquidity measure that does not depend on inventory. The quick ratio simply takes it out of current assets in the calculation. The quick ratio is also called the *acid test*, which implies a particularly tough, discerning test.

Current assets sometimes contain minor items such as prepaid expenses that never become cash; they too should be subtracted when calculating the quick ratio. Ending balances are appropriate. In Belfry's case we have

$$\text{quick ratio} = \frac{\$7,500 - \$3,200}{\$2,500} = 1.7.$$

Like the current ratio, the quick ratio isn't stated in any particular units.

● ASSET MANAGEMENT RATIOS

Asset management ratios address the fundamental efficiency with which a company is run. The issues can be long or short term and help an analyst understand the firm's basic competitiveness.

The Average Collection Period (ACP)

The **average collection period** (ACP) represents the average number of days the firm takes to collect its receivables. That is, how long does it take to get paid on credit sales? The ACP is also known as the DSO for *days sales outstanding,* or the receivables cycle. The ACP is stated in *days* and is calculated as follows.

$$ACP = \frac{accounts\ receivable}{average\ daily\ sales}$$

where average daily sales is sales/360. Multiplying the numerator and denominator by 360 gives a more convenient formulation.

$$ACP = \frac{accounts\ receivable}{sales} \times 360$$

It is common practice to use a 360-day year made up of twelve 30-day months in these calculations.[6]

Clearly, the longer a firm takes to collect its money the worse off it is. Although there are significant exceptions, most credit business is done on terms of 30 days. Frequently a discount is offered for faster payment on the order of 10 days.

from the CFO

Customers often stretch credit terms by paying a few days late, and sellers, who are anxious to keep their business, don't complain over minor delays. That means it's not unusual to see ACPs of 35 to 45 days in the normal course of business in some industries. However, if the ACP exceeds the company's terms of sale by more than 50%, there are probably serious credit problems.

Collection problems have several important implications. The most apparent is that the firm may be granting credit to customers that lack either the ability or the intent to pay. Another possibility, however, is that customers are finding something wrong with the company's product. Customer dissatisfaction frequently results in a reluctance to pay the bill.

The proper interpretation of a high ACP is very important. Although the ACP represents an average collection period, a high figure doesn't usually mean that the average customer is paying excessively slowly. It may imply that while most receivables are being collected fairly promptly, a few are very old, as much as six months or a year. These are unlikely ever to be realized in cash.

Remember from our discussion in Chapter 2 that management is sometimes reluctant to write off questionable receivables because doing so reduces profit. The result of that tendency is an overstated receivables account, which means that the firm's balance sheet is worth less than it purports to be.

Old receivables should be written off without delay or at least reserved through an addition to the allowance for doubtful accounts.

An average value of the receivables balance net of the allowance for doubtful accounts should be used in the calculation. For Belfry we have the following ACP.

$$ACP = \frac{\$2,950}{\$10,000} \times 360 = 106.2\ days$$

This is not a good result. Belfry clearly has a problem collecting money from at least some of its credit customers.

---

6. The 360-day year is common, but so is the use of a 365-day year. We'll use both conventions from time to time.

The Inventory Turnover

The inventory turnover ratio is an attempt to measure whether or not the firm has excess funds tied up in inventory. The ratio is calculated as follows.

$$\text{inventory turnover} = \frac{\text{cost of goods sold}}{\text{inventory}}$$

● **Inventory turnover** gives an indication of the **quality** of inventory as well as **how well it is managed.**

from the CFO

Holding inventory costs money. Inventory costs include interest, storage, insurance, and taxes. In addition, the more inventory a company holds, the more it has at risk of spoiling and becoming obsolete. The inventory turnover measures how many times a year the firm uses up an average stock of goods. A higher turnover is better in that it implies doing business with less tied up in inventory.

A low turnover figure can mean some old inventory is on the books that isn't being used. What is being used may be turning over adequately, but some material can just be dead weight. Such old stock should be disposed of for whatever can be gotten for it.

Operating with too little inventory can create problems too. Excessively low inventory levels cause stockouts—running out of raw material in the factory or not having the product a customer wants on hand. The result is work stoppages and lost sales. There is definitely a right amount of inventory somewhere between too much and too little. The inventory turnover ratio helps to find it.

An alternate formulation of the inventory turnover ratio involves using sales in the numerator rather than cost of goods sold. In practice the cost of goods sold formulation is preferred because cost and inventory are comparable numbers, whereas sales includes expenses and profit. Either formulation can be used if comparisons are made consistently.

Average balance sheet values are appropriate. Belfry's inventory turnover using cost of goods sold is

$$\begin{array}{c}\text{inventory turnover}\\\text{(COGS)}\end{array} = \frac{\$6,000}{\$2,600} = 2.3.$$

The alternative formulation with sales in the numerator is

$$\begin{array}{c}\text{inventory turnover}\\\text{(Sales)}\end{array} = \frac{\$10,000}{\$2,600} = 3.8.$$

Inventory turnover is a pure number, but it's usually stated in units of "turns" or "times," which are written as "×."

Fixed Asset Turnover and Total Asset Turnover

Fixed and total asset turnovers measure the relationship of the firm's assets to a year's sales.

$$\text{fixed asset turnover} = \frac{\text{sales}}{\text{fixed assets}}$$

$$\text{total asset turnover} = \frac{\text{sales}}{\text{total assets}}$$

A business can be thought of as using its assets in conjunction with the skills of its employees to generate revenue and profit. These ratios show the relationship between assets and sales. In general, a company that generates more sales with a given level of assets does better than a firm that generates fewer sales with the same assets.

The two ratios allow us to focus on either fixed or total assets. The total assets ratio tends to be more widely used. The ratio using fixed assets is appropriate in industries where significant equipment is required to do business.

These ratios are long-term measures of performance, which are of primary interest to equity investors and stock market analysts. Average balance sheet values are appropriate. Both asset values are stated net of accumulated depreciation. For the Belfry Company we have the following ratios.

$$\text{fixed asset turnover} = \frac{\$10,000}{\$3,750} = 2.7$$

$$\text{total asset turnover} = \frac{\$10,000}{\$10,500} = .95$$

The units here are generally stated as "times," sometimes with the symbol "×." For example, Belfry's fixed asset turnover might be written as 2.7× for "2.7 times."

● DEBT MANAGEMENT RATIOS

Debt management deals with how the firm uses other people's money to its own advantage. By "other people's money" we mean borrowing as well as trade credit and other liabilities. In financial analysis, we're primarily concerned that a company doesn't use so much of these funds that it assumes excessive risk. This is an important point. The problem with using other people's money is that it requires future cash outflows for interest and/or repayment. If a firm's operations don't supply enough cash for those payments, it can get in big trouble.

TERMINOLOGY   The term *debt* in ratio analysis requires a little amplification. Some authorities use the word to mean any source of money other than equity. Applied to our examples that definition means *debt* is the sum of long-term debt and current liabilities. Others prefer to restrict the idea of *debt* to interest-bearing obligations, which are generally long-term borrowings.

Theorists tend to prefer the first interpretation. They like to add current liabilities and long-term debt to arrive at a *total debt* figure for use in ratio analysis. Businesspeople, however, are more likely to limit the definition of debt to long-term, interest-bearing borrowing. Clearly this can lead to some confusion.

In this book, we'll simply be careful to say exactly what we mean. We'll call *total debt* the sum of current liabilities and long-term debt. Long-term debt will mean just that, and we'll take the word *debt* by itself to mean formal borrowing regardless of term. Where common usage is different we'll explain.

The Debt Ratio

The debt ratio uses the total debt concept and measures the relationship between total debt and equity in supporting the firm's assets. That is, it tells us how much of the firm's assets are supported by other people's money.

$$\text{debt ratio} = \frac{\text{long-term debt} + \text{current liabilities}}{\text{total assets}}$$

A high debt ratio is viewed as risky by investors, especially lenders.

The debt ratio is used to indicate the firm's riskiness at a point in time—the later the better—so ending balance sheet figures are appropriate. Debt management ratios are generally stated as percentages.

Belfry's debt ratio is

$$\text{debt ratio} = \frac{\$6,200 + \$2,500}{\$12,000} = 72.5\%.$$

Debt to Equity Ratio

The debt to equity ratio generally uses just long-term debt and is stated some-what differently than other ratios.

$$\text{debt to equity ratio} = \text{long-term debt : equity}$$

● **Fixed financial charges** like interest increase a firm's **financial risk.**

This ratio is a measure of the mix of debt and equity within the firm's total capital. It is an important measure of risk, because a high level of debt can burden the income statement with excessive interest. This makes the firm's profitability fragile in recessionary times. Interest is known as **a fixed financial charge,** and must be paid regardless of whether revenues and profits are healthy. Hence in a business downturn, large interest charges can throw a company into a loss position quickly. The riskiness associated with debt and interest is called **financial risk.**

This ratio is unusual in that it is commonly stated as a proportion rather than as a decimal or a percentage. For example, if capital of $100 includes debt of $33.33, conventional terminology would describe the debt to equity ratio as "one-third—two-thirds," or "33/67." If capital is two-thirds debt, we would say the ratio is "2 to 1 debt to equity."

For Belfry we have

$$\text{debt to equity} = \$6,200 : \$3,300.$$

This would be stated as 1.9 : 1 (1.9 to 1) because $6,200/$3,300 = 1.9. Ending balances are appropriate for the debt to equity calculation.

Times Interest Earned (TIE)

TIE gets at the idea of burdening the income statement with interest more directly. It measures the number of times interest can be paid out of earnings before interest and taxes (EBIT).

$$\text{TIE} = \frac{\text{EBIT}}{\text{interest}}$$

● A high level of **interest coverage** implies safety.

TIE is called a *coverage ratio.* For example, if EBIT is $100 and interest is $10, so TIE is 10, we would say that interest is covered 10 times. Clearly, the more times earnings cover existing interest, the safer it is to lend the firm more money.

For the Belfry Company we have

$$\text{TIE} = \frac{\$1,900}{\$400} = 4.8.$$

The appropriate unit is times.

Cash Coverage

There's an obvious problem with the TIE ratio. Interest is a cash payment, but EBIT is not exactly a source of cash. Rather, it's an income statement subtotal that may be considerably different from cash flow. In other words, more or less cash than EBIT may be available in any given year to pay interest. The problem can be partially solved by recognizing that the biggest difference between EBIT and a comparable cash figure is depreciation. It is subtracted as part of cost and expense in the calculation of EBIT.

A better approximation of coverage is available if we form another ratio with depreciation added to EBIT in the numerator. This ratio is called *cash coverage*.

$$\text{cash coverage} = \frac{\text{EBIT} + \text{depreciation}}{\text{interest}}$$

Belfry's cash coverage is

$$\text{cash coverage} = \frac{\$1,900 + \$500}{\$400} = 6.0.$$

Fixed Charge Coverage

The TIE and cash coverage ratios recognize interest as a *fixed* financing charge. The term "fixed" implies that interest must be paid regardless of business conditions, unlike dividends, which may be reduced if earnings are poor.

In recent years leasing has supplemented debt as a means of acquiring assets. Instead of borrowing to buy equipment, businesses lease the same equipment and make lease instead of interest payments.

However, if a company's leased equipment is necessary to stay in business, or if the leases are contractually noncancelable, the payments become fixed charges in the sense that they have to be paid regardless of conditions, just like interest.

We can adjust the TIE ratio to recognize this additional fixed charge. Because lease payments have been subtracted along with other costs and expenses to come to EBIT, they must be added back in the numerator to arrive at a cash figure available to pay all fixed charges. The same amounts must also be added to the denominator as fixed charges equivalent to interest. The resulting ratio is known as *fixed charge coverage*.

$$\text{fixed charge coverage} = \frac{\text{EBIT} + \text{lease payments}}{\text{interest} + \text{lease payments}}$$

Other fixed charges can be added to the numerator and denominator when appropriate.

We'll assume that the Belfry Company has $700 of lease payments within its cost and expense figures. Its fixed charge coverage is then

$$\text{fixed charge coverage} = \frac{\$1,900 + \$700}{\$400 + \$700} = 2.4.$$

Debt management ratios are important to both creditors and stockholders. Creditors want to make sure funds are available to pay interest and principal, and are therefore particularly interested in short-run coverage ratios. Stockholders are concerned about the impact of excessive debt and interest on long-term profitability.

● PROFITABILITY RATIOS

The most fundamental measure of a business's success is profit. Without profit there are no dividends, and without dividends or the expectation of them, no one will invest in stock.

Lenders don't like profitless companies either. Firms that are losing money or barely breaking even are perilously close to not being able to repay their loans.

● **Lease payments** are **fixed** financial charges similar to interest.

Profitability ratios give us relative measures of the firm's money-making success. That is, they gauge profits per dollar of sales made, assets employed, or equity invested. They're generally stated as percentages.

Return on Sales (ROS)

Return on sales is also called the *profit margin* or *net profit margin*. It is simply net income as a percentage of sales.

$$ROS = \frac{net\ income}{sales}$$

> ● **ROS** measures control of the income statement: **revenue, cost,** and **expense.**

Notice that this ratio is the bottom line of the common size income statement. It is a fundamental indication of the overall profitability of the business. It gives insight into management's ability to control the income statement items of revenue, cost, and expense.

Belfry's ROS is

$$ROS = \frac{\$1,000}{\$10,000} = 10\%\ .$$

Return on Assets (ROA)

> ● **ROA** adds the effectiveness of **asset management** to ROS.

A business uses assets and the skills of its people to earn a profit. **ROA** quantifies the success of that effort with respect to assets by stating net income as a percentage of total assets.

$$ROA = \frac{net\ income}{total\ assets}$$

ROA measures the overall ability of the firm to utilize the assets in which it has invested to earn a profit. Because income is earned over the entire year, an average assets figure is appropriate.

Belfry's ROA is

$$ROA = \frac{\$1,000}{\$10,500} = 9.5\%\ .$$

Return on Equity (ROE)

> ● **ROE** adds the effect of **borrowing** to ROA.

ROE is the most fundamental profitability ratio. It states net income as a percentage of equity.

$$ROE = \frac{net\ income}{equity}$$

ROE measures the firm's ability to earn a return on the owners' invested capital. It takes the ROA concept one step further by factoring in the effect of borrowed money. If the firm has substantial debt, ROE tends to be higher than ROA in good times and lower in bad times. If there is little or no debt, ROE and ROA are close to the same. We'll talk about the effect of borrowed money, called *leverage*, in detail in Chapter 13. An average value for equity is appropriate in the calculation. For Belfry we have

$$ROE = \frac{\$1,000}{\$2,650} = 37.7\%\ .$$

● MARKET VALUE RATIOS

The ratios we've discussed so far all pertain to the internal management of the firm. As such they are all more or less under the control of management. Another set of ratios compares certain financial statement figures to the value the stock market places on the firm. These ratios are less controllable by management because the perceptions and attitudes of the investing public are imposed on the actions of the company in arriving at market value. Management can influence those perceptions and attitudes, but it doesn't control them.

The market value of a company is reflected in the price of its stock. Multiplying the per-share price by the number of shares outstanding leads to a value for the company as a whole. However, it is common practice to think in terms of per-share values.

Price/Earnings Ratio

● The **P/E ratio** is an indication of the value the **stock market** places on a company.

This ratio compares the market price of the stock to the **earnings per share** calculated from the latest income statement. Earnings per share is simply net income divided by the number of shares of common stock outstanding. It is usually abbreviated as **EPS,** while the price/earnings ratio is referred to as the **P/E ratio.**

$$\text{P/E ratio} = \frac{\text{stock price}}{\text{EPS}}$$

The P/E ratio is very important in the stock market. Notice that it tells us how much investors are willing to pay for a dollar of the firm's earnings. For example, if a company's P/E is 10 and earnings per share are $4.50, the stock is selling for $45. Stock market people would say, "The company is selling for 10 times earnings."

Different companies carry different P/Es. Clearly, the higher the P/E the better, because a dollar of earnings translates into more shareholder wealth at higher P/Es. The most significant factor leading to a high P/E ratio is a high expected level of growth by the company.

● A firm's P/E is primarily a function of its **expected growth.**

P/Es must be used with caution. A firm that is losing money doesn't have a meaningful P/E. Further, if profits are very small but the stock has some value, the P/E can be enormous. That isn't meaningful either.

To calculate market value ratios for the Belfry Company, we need the number of shares outstanding and the price of the stock. For the sake of illustration we'll assume that there are 300 shares valued at a price of $38 per share. Earnings per share is then

$$\text{EPS} = \$1,000 \, / \, 300 = \$3.33$$

and the P/E ratio is

$$\text{P/E} = \frac{\$38}{\$3.33} = 11.4\,.$$

Market to Book Value Ratio

A company's **book value** is the total value of the equity on its balance sheet. That's equal to the value of assets less liabilities to outsiders. Notice that it may be more or less than the amount the firm could actually realize by selling everything and paying off its debts.

A healthy company is usually expected to have a market value in excess of its book value. This is sometimes known as the **going concern value** of the firm. The idea is that the combination of assets and people that creates an enterprise will generate future earnings that are worth more than the assets alone are worth today.

The market to book value ratio gets at this idea of excess value. Like P/E, it is generally thought of in per-share terms. Market value per share is just the price of the stock, and book value per share is total equity divided by the number of shares outstanding. The calculation is

$$\text{market to book value ratio} = \frac{\text{stock price}}{\text{book value per share}}.$$

The market to book value ratio is a broad indicator of what the market thinks of a particular stock. A value below 1.0 indicates grave concern about the company's future. Such a firm is said to be selling *below book.*

Speculative investors sometimes like to gamble on stocks whose market to book value ratio is below 1.0. Situations arise in which a stock's price is depressed because the market has overreacted to bad news about a fundamentally sound company. In such a case the firm's stock price sometimes rebounds quickly, and an investment at the depressed level can be very profitable. Some investors use the market to book value ratio to identify situations in which this *might* be the case.

The ending equity figure is clearly appropriate in this ratio because we're looking for a current status with respect to the market. Belfry's book value per share is its equity divided by the number of shares outstanding.

$$\text{book value per share} = \$3,300/300 = \$11$$

The market to book value ratio is then

$$\text{market to book value ratio} = \frac{\$38}{\$11} = 3.5.$$

Table 3.1 summarizes all of the foregoing ratios.

DU PONT EQUATIONS

Each of the ratios we've been talking about measures a particular aspect of running a company. However, the ratio measures aren't entirely independent, and performance on one is sometimes tied to performance on others.

Two insightful relationships between ratios are captured in the **Du Pont equations.**[7] The first is developed by writing the definition of ROA and multiplying by sales/sales (= 1, so the multiplication doesn't change the value of the expression).

$$\text{ROA} = \frac{\text{net income}}{\text{total assets}} \times \frac{\text{sales}}{\text{sales}}$$

Now reverse the order of the denominators to get

$$\text{ROA} = \frac{\text{net income}}{\text{sales}} \times \frac{\text{sales}}{\text{total assets}}.$$

Notice that we've formed two ratios, the product of which is ROA. But we've seen the new ratios before; they're return on sales and total asset turnover. Hence the Du Pont equation is

$$\text{ROA} = \text{ROS} \times \text{total asset turnover.}$$

The **Du Pont equations** express relationships between ratios that give **insights** into successful operation.

Go to SmallBizFinance for ratio analysis calculators at
www.bankrate.com/brm /news/biz/bizcalcs/ ratiocalcs.asp
to perform a ratio analysis on our hypothetical Belfry Company.

http://

---

7. So called because they were developed at the Du Pont corporation.

TABLE 3.1

Financial Ratios

Liquidity Ratios

$$\text{current ratio} = \frac{\text{current assets}}{\text{current liabilities}}$$

$$\text{quick ratio} = \frac{\text{current assets} - \text{inventory}}{\text{current liabilities}}$$

Asset Management Ratios*

$$\text{ACP} = \frac{\text{accounts receivable}}{\text{average daily sales}} = \frac{\text{accounts receivable}}{\text{sales}} \times 360$$

$$\text{inventory turnover} = \frac{\text{cost of goods sold}}{\text{inventory}}$$

$$\text{fixed asset turnover} = \frac{\text{sales}}{\text{fixed assets}}$$

$$\text{total asset turnover} = \frac{\text{sales}}{\text{total assets}}$$

Debt Management Ratios

$$\text{debt ratio} = \frac{\text{long-term debt} + \text{current liabilities}}{\text{total assets}}$$

$$\text{debt to equity ratio} = \text{long-term debt} : \text{equity}$$

$$\text{TIE} = \frac{\text{EBIT}}{\text{interest}}$$

$$\text{cash coverage} = \frac{\text{EBIT} + \text{depreciation}}{\text{interest}}$$

$$\text{fixed charge coverage} = \frac{\text{EBIT} + \text{lease payments}}{\text{interest} + \text{lease payments}}$$

Profitability Ratios

$$\text{ROS} = \frac{\text{net income}}{\text{sales}}$$

$$\text{ROA} = \frac{\text{net income}}{\text{total assets}}$$

$$\text{ROE} = \frac{\text{net income}}{\text{equity}}$$

Market Value Ratios

$$\text{P/E ratio} = \frac{\text{stock price}}{\text{EPS}}$$

$$\text{market to book value ratio} = \frac{\text{stock price}}{\text{book value per share}}$$

*Average balance sheet values may be appropriate.

The relationship is an important result. ROA is a fundamental measure of performance, indicating how well a company uses its assets to generate profits. But it is the product of two more elementary measures. The first, ROS, measures how well a firm keeps some of its sales dollars in profit. The second, total asset turnover, measures the company's ability to generate sales with the assets it has.

The Du Pont equation tells us that to run a business well, as measured by ROA, we have to manage costs and expenses well and generate a lot of sales per dollar of assets. This lesson should sound familiar. It's the same message we got from the racetrack diagram (cash conversion cycle on p. 69) earlier in this chapter.

The *extended Du Pont equation* takes the idea one step further by expressing return on equity (ROE) in terms of other ratios. We'll develop that by writing the definition of ROE and multiplying by sales/sales and by total assets/total assets.

$$\text{ROE} = \frac{\text{net income}}{\text{equity}} \times \frac{\text{sales}}{\text{sales}} \times \frac{\text{total assets}}{\text{total assets}}$$

Now rearrange the denominators to get

$$\text{ROE} = \frac{\text{net income}}{\text{sales}} \times \frac{\text{sales}}{\text{total assets}} \times \frac{\text{total assets}}{\text{equity}}$$

The last term is called the *equity multiplier*. We'll explain it in a minute, but first notice that the ROE expression is the same as the ROA expression with the last term added.

$$\text{ROE} = \text{ROS} \times \text{Total Asset Turnover} \times \text{Equity Multiplier}$$

$$\text{ROE} = \text{ROA} \times \text{Equity Multiplier}$$

The equity multiplier has to do with the idea of leverage, using borrowed money instead of your own to work for you. Hence the extended Du Pont equation says that to measure performance in terms of ROE, we add the concept of leverage to performance in terms of ROA.

To understand the equity multiplier, consider the right side of the balance sheet. It lists all of the places where the firm's money comes from: equity, debt, and liabilities. These add to total assets because both sides of the balance sheet sum to that figure. Debt and liabilities are other people's money, while equity is the firm's own money (its owners'). The equity multiplier is related to the proportion to which the firm is financed by other people's money as opposed to owner's money.

For example, suppose a firm has total assets of $100 and equity of $25. That means three quarters of its assets are financed by debt and/or liabilities ($75) and one quarter ($25) is supported by equity. The equity multiplier is ($100/$25=) 4, and the extended Du Pont equation says that the firm's ROE will be four times its ROA because of the use of other people's money.

That's very good if the business is making a profit and ROA is a positive number. For example, if ROA is 5%, ROE would be a healthy 20%. However, if times get tough, using other people's money is generally bad news. Suppose the business starts to lose money and ROA is −5%. Unfortunately, the multiplier still works the same way, and ROE will be −20%, a pretty dismal figure.

The extended Du Pont equation says something very important about running a business. The operation of the business itself is reflected in ROA. This means managing customers, people, costs, expenses, and equipment. But that result, good or bad, can be *multiplied* by borrowing. In other words, the way you *finance* a business can greatly exaggerate the results of nuts and bolts operations.

Write out the Du Pont equations for Belfry to verify the relationships.

Practical Finance

New Ideas in Financial Analysis: MVA and EVA®

In recent years the related ideas of **market value added (MVA)** and **economic value added (EVA®)** have become popular as gauges of business success. The concept behind both measures is the creation of shareholder wealth. We'll consider MVA first.

There are two ways to think about the value of a firm's equity. The *market* value of equity is just stock price times the number of shares outstanding. At the same time the equity *contributed* by shareholders is reflected in the equity accounts on the company's books (including retained earnings). If market value is greater than book value, some *additional* value has been created by the company acting as an ongoing business. This extra is MVA. It's the cumulative amount management has made for the stockholders over and above dividends since the inception of the firm.

Notice that MVA can be negative if the stock is selling below its book value. Conceptually MVA is similar to the market to book value ratio we discussed earlier. You should be able to see that a negative MVA is equivalent to a market to book ratio of less than 1.0.

The more exciting idea is EVA, economic value added. In theory it is the amount by which the firm increases or decreases MVA in the current year.

Before defining EVA precisely, it's important to notice something about traditional net income. When we calculate net income we subtract interest from revenues along with other costs and expenses. You can think of interest as the *cost* the company pays for the use of its debt capital. We do not, however, subtract a payment to stockholders for the use of equity capital.

That means financial analysis based on net income (EAT) recognizes the *cost* of debt (interest) but implicitly treats equity as a free source of capital. This presents a problem because equity capital does have a cost, basically the return demanded by stockholders on their investments. Ignoring the cost of equity makes performance seem better than it is. For example, a company with a small positive net income is profitable in an accounting sense but may be an economic failure because it doesn't provide an adequate return to stockholders on their equity investments.

A better measure of overall performance than accounting net income would be produced if we modified the income statement to subtract the cost of both debt and equity capital instead of just the interest cost of debt. This is exactly what EVA does using a concept called the **cost of capital.** We'll study the cost of capital a great deal in a later chapter. For now it's

—continued

● USING THE DU PONT EQUATIONS

Comparing the Du Pont equations between a company and an industry average can give some insights into how a firm is doing in relation to its competitors. For example, suppose we have the following data for Pillbox Inc. and its industry.

ROA = ROS × Total Asset Turnover

	ROA	ROS	Total Asset Turnover
Pillbox Inc.	12%	6%	2×
Industry	15%	5%	3×

● The Du Pont equations can be used to **isolate problems.**

If Pillbox is trying to figure out why its ROA is below average, this display focuses attention in the right direction. It says that management of the income statement items, like cost and expense, is a little better than average, but the use of assets to generate sales, as measured by total asset turnover, is very poor in comparison to the competition.

The turnover problem is probably in one or both of two areas. Perhaps the company has unnecessary or ineffective assets, such as overstated inventory or inefficient

Practical Finance

Continued—

enough to understand that it's a single, average "interest rate" that reflects the rate of return the business pays to the suppliers of its capital, both debt and equity. That rate, stated on an after-tax basis, is the "cost" of the capital funds the firm uses.

EVA is defined as follows.

$$EVA = EBIT (1 - T) - (debt + equity)(cost\ of\ capital\ \%)$$

where T is the tax rate.

The first term on the right is EBIT adjusted to an after-tax basis by multiplying by $(1 - T)$. This figure is what the firm's after-tax earnings would be if there were no charges for the use of capital, either debt or equity.

The second term on the right subtracts a charge for the use of capital. Debt + equity is total capital, so the cost of capital percentage times that sum is the dollar amount the firm pays for the use of all of its capital. This term is like the traditional interest charge in the income statement except that it's expanded to include a payment for equity. It's an after-tax figure, because the cost of capital percentage is stated after tax.

Hence, EVA is after-tax earnings less an after-tax charge for all capital. But the charge for capital is simply the minimum amount stockholders and bondholders demand for investing their money. They could make that amount by putting it in any number of alternate investments. Hence, if EVA is positive, the firm is exceeding its investors' expectations. That is, a positive EVA is an *extra,* an additional contribution to shareholders' wealth made during the year.

This is a very important idea. If EVA is zero, the firm is just earning what investors expect and demand, nothing more and nothing less. That's *adequate* performance. On the other hand, if EVA is positive, management is performing above expectations and contributing some additional value to stockholders. A negative EVA, of course, means the firm is losing ground, making a negative contribution to shareholder wealth.

EVA began to gain popularity about ten years ago and is one of the hottest ideas in financial management today. More firms seem to be using it with each passing year. Some of its better known proponents include Coca-Cola, AT&T, Briggs & Stratton, and CSX. Several attribute major gains in market value to a management focus on EVA rather than traditional net income. The EVA® and MVA concepts were developed by Stern Stewart & Co., a financial consulting firm. (http://www.eva.com)

machinery. Or maybe its promotional activities are not on target, so sales are lower than they should be. The job is now to find out what's going on and fix the problem.

● SOURCES OF COMPARATIVE INFORMATION

The best competitive information for ratio analysis is generally an industry average. These averages are available in several places.

Dun and Bradstreet (D&B) is a credit rating service. Vendors use D&B reports to make decisions about whether or not to sell to customers on credit.

D&B maintains credit files on most businesses in the United States. The files include financial information and comments on a firm's past payment history as reported by other firms that have done business with it. D&B subscribers can order reports on specific companies to help in making the credit decision.

D&B has summarized its data to provide industry average ratios for about 800 lines of business. The information is published in *Industry Norms and Key Business Ratios.*

The Risk Management Association is an association of bank lending officers. It publishes summarized ratio information on 250 industries in *Statement Studies.*

http://

Visit these sites: D&B at

www.dnb.com

and Value Line at

● **www.valueline.com**

The *U.S. Commerce Department* publishes the *Quarterly Financial Report,* which contains summarized ratio information for a large number of industries. Government reports on industry are usually organized by the Standard Industrial Classification (SIC) Code that provides a systematic segregation and cataloging of industrial activity.

Value Line and similar investment advisory services provide industry profiles as well as reports on individual companies.

LIMITATIONS AND WEAKNESSES OF RATIO ANALYSIS

Although ratio analysis is a powerful tool, it has some significant shortcomings. Analysts have to be careful not to apply the techniques blindly to any set of statements they come across. Here are a few of the more significant problems.

● Ratio analysis is **not an exact science** and requires judgment and **experienced interpretation.**

Diversified companies, large firms with consolidated operations, create what is probably the biggest analysis problem. Such companies often have divisions operating in significantly different industries. The financial information they publish *consolidates* the results of those different operations into one set of statements. Because the interpretation of ratios is highly dependent on industry norms, this mixing of results from different businesses can greatly reduce the informative value of analysis.

Financial reporting standards set by the accounting profession for diversified businesses require the disclosure of some *segment information,* but it is generally of limited scope and use.

Window dressing refers to practices at year end that make balance sheets look better than they otherwise would through improvements that don't last. Here's a simple example. Imagine a firm with a current ratio that's too low whose business is fundamentally sound so it can borrow long term. Suppose this company takes out a long-term loan a few days before the end of the year, holds the proceeds in cash over year end, and repays the loan a few days later. It thus increases year-end current assets with no impact on current liabilities, thereby improving the reported current ratio.

Accounting principles allow a great deal of latitude in reporting. That means similar companies might report the same thing differently, making their financial results artificially dissimilar. Depreciation is a good example. The choice between accelerated and straight line depreciation is up to the firm, but the difference can double reported depreciation in a given period. That in turn can make a big percentage difference in net income between two essentially identical firms.

Inflation often distorts financial statements. Real estate purchased years ago, for example, will be carried on the balance sheet at its original cost. Yet it may be worth many times that amount in today's market. During periods of rapid inflation, inventory, cost of goods sold, and depreciation can badly distort true results.

The *interpretation* of ratios isn't always clear. Recall our discussion of the current ratio and inventory turnover.

The most important thing to remember with respect to these issues is that *ratio analysis doesn't give answers; it helps you ask the right questions.*

DISCUSSION QUESTIONS

1. List the main user groups of financial information. What are the reasons for their interest?

2. Where do analysts get financial information about companies? What are their concerns about the information?

3. Financial analysts are generally optimists who believe what they're told. Right or wrong? Explain.

4. If a company's cash account increases from the beginning to the end of the year, there's more cash on hand so that must be a source of cash. Yet the cash account is an asset, and the first cash flow rule says that an asset increase is a use of cash. Explain this apparent conflict.

5. The present format for the statement of cash flows is organized according to operating activities, investing activities, and financing activities. That format has only been in use since the late 1980s. The previous format first listed all sources and then all uses of cash, giving a subtotal for each. Cash flow was then the difference between the two subtotals. What advantages or disadvantages do you see of the current format in relation to the old one? Which would you prefer if you had a choice?

6. Why don't we calculate the difference in the equity account between the beginning and end of the year and consider that difference as a source or use of cash? Why do we similarly exclude the cash account?

7. What are free cash flows? Who is likely to be most interested in them? Why?

8. Outline the thinking behind ratio analysis in brief, general terms (a few lines; don't go into each ratio individually).

9. Financial ratios don't do you much good by themselves. Explain.

10. A company has been growing rapidly for the last three years. It was profitable before the growth spurt started. Although this year's revenues are almost three times those of three years ago, the firm is now losing money. What's the first thing you would do to try to pinpoint where the problem(s) may be?

11. The term "liquidity" is used in several ways. What does it mean in the context of an asset or liability, such as those on the balance sheet? What does it mean when applied to an operating company? What does the similar term "liquidate" mean when applied to a company?

12. What is the reasoning behind using the current ratio as a measure of liquidity?

13. Why do we need the quick ratio when we have the current ratio?

14. A company's terms are net 30 and the ACP is 35 days. Is that cause for alarm? Why or why not?

15. The industry average inventory turnover ratio is 7 and your company's is 15. This could be good or bad news. Explain each possibility. How would you find out whether it is bad news?

16. Discuss the different definitions of debt in ratio analysis.

17. Why do people view having too much debt as risky? If you were interested in determining whether a company had too much debt, what measure would you use? Why? How much debt do you think would generally be considered too much?

18. It can be argued that the TIE ratio doesn't make much sense. Why? How would you change the measure to be more meaningful? (Hint: Think in terms of cash flows.)

19. Can managers affect market value ratios?

PROBLEMS

1. The Waterford Wax Company had the following current account activity last year.

	Beginning	Ending		Beginning	Ending
Cash	$ 160	$ 333	Accounts payable	$722	$2,084
Accounts receivable	1,875	3,810	Accruals	$217	456
Inventory	438	2,676			
Current assets	$2,473	$6,819	Current liabilities	$939	$2,540

a. Calculate and display the current account detail required for the Cash from Operating Activities section of the Statement of Cash Flows.

b. If you also knew that Waterford's revenues had risen by 20% last year, would you be concerned about the firm's financial health? Why? (Words only.)

2. Timberline Inc. has the following current accounts last year. ($000)

	Beginning	Ending		Beginning	Ending
Cash	$ 175	$ 238	Accounts payable	$205	$182
Accounts receivable	1,456	2,207	Accruals	$ 95	83
Inventory	943	786			
Current assets	$2,574	$3,231	Current liabilities	$300	$165

In addition, the company had sales revenues of $9,453,000 and costs and expenses (including interest and tax) of $7,580,000. Depreciation of $1,462,000 is included in the cost and expense figures.

Construct a statement showing Timberline's Cash From Operating Activities, including a detail of changes in balance sheet accounts.

3. Fred Klein started his own business recently. He began by depositing $5,000 of his own money (equity) in a business account. Once he'd done that his balance sheet was as follows.

Assets		Liabilities and Equity	
Cash	$5,000	Equity	$5,000
Total	$5,000	Total	$5,000

During the next month, his first month of business, he completed the following transactions. (All payments were made with checks out of the bank account.)

- Purchased $2,500 worth of inventory, paying $1,500 down and owing the vendor the remainder.
- Used $500 of the inventory in making product.
- Paid employees' wages on the last day of the month of $1,100.
- Sold all the product made in the first month on credit for $3,000.
- Paid rent of $1,200.

a. Construct a balance sheet for Fred's business at the end of its first month. (*Hint:* Fred's business has only current assets, current liabilities, and an equity account. Calculate the ending balance in each of the current accounts from the information given. The ending equity account balance will be the difference between the current assets and liabilities at month end.)

b. Construct Fred's income statement. (*Hint:* Fred's revenue is the credit sale. His costs/expenses consist of the inventory used in product sold plus the things other than inventory for which he wrote checks. Ignore taxes.)

c. Construct Fred's statement of Cash Flows for the month. (*Hint:* Fred's beginning balance sheet has only two accounts, cash and equity, each with a $5,000 balance. All other accounts open with zero balances.)

d. Is Fred's business profitable in an accounting sense? In a cash flow sense? (Words only.)

e. Can the business fail while making a profit? How might that happen in the next month or so? (Words only.)

4. The Blandings Home Construction Company purchased a new crane for $350,000 this year. They sold the old crane for $80,000. At the time it had a net book value of $20,000. Assume any profit on the sale of old equipment is taxed at 25%. These were the only transactions that affected Investing Activities this year. Construct the Cash Flow from Investing Activities section of the Statement of Cash Flows to concisely convey the maximum information to readers of the company's financial statements.

5. Lansing Inc., a profitable food products manufacturer, has undertaken a major expansion that will be financed by new debt and equity issues as well as earnings. During the last year the company borrowed $5 million for a term of 30 years to finance a new building to house the expanded operations. It also sold 60,000 shares of $4 par value stock at $51 per share to pay for new equipment. It also paid off short-term loans that support inventory and receivables totaling $700,000 as they came due and took out new short-term debt for the same purpose of $850,000, which was outstanding at year end. Lansing also made a scheduled payment of $500,000 on an old long-term loan with which it had acquired production equipment several years ago. The payment included interest of $425,000. Finally the firm paid dividends of $2.50 per share on 700,000 shares of outstanding common stock. Calculate and display the Cash from Financing Activities section of Lansing's Statement of Cash Flows.

6. Axtel Company has the following financial statements.

Axtel Company
Balance Sheet
For the period ended 12/31/X1
($000)

ASSETS

	12/31/X0	12/31/X1
Cash	$ 3,514	$ 2,875
Accounts receivable	6,742	5,583
Inventory	2,573	3,220
CURRENT ASSETS	$12,829	$11,678
Fixed assets		
Gross	$22,478	$24,360
Accumulated deprec.	(12,147)	(13,313)
Net	$10,331	$11,047
Total Assets	$23,160	$22,725

LIABILITIES

Accounts payable	$ 1,556	$ 1,702
Accruals	268	408
CURRENT LIABILITIES	$ 1,824	$ 2,110
Long-term debt	$ 7,112	$ 6,002
Equity	14,224	14,613
TOTAL CAPITAL	$21,336	$20,615
TOTAL LIABILITIES AND EQUITY	$23,160	$22,725

Axtel Company
Income Statement
For the period ended
12/31/X1
($000)

Sales	$36,227
COGS	19,925
Gross margin	$16,302
Expense	$10,868
EBIT	$ 5,434
Interest	713
EBT	$ 4,721
Tax	1,605
Net income	$ 3,116

In addition, Axtel *retired* stock for $1,000,000 and paid a dividend of $1,727,000. Depreciation for the year was $1,166,000. Construct a statement of cash flows for Axtel for 20X1. (*Hint:* Retiring stock means buying it back from shareholders. Assume the purchase was made at book value, and treat it like a negative sale of stock.)

7. Calculate all of the ratios discussed in the chapter for Axtel Company of Problem 6. Use ending or average balance sheet figures as appropriate. Assume Axtel had leasing costs of $7,267 in 20X1 and had 1,268,000 shares of stock outstanding valued at $28.75 per share at year end.

8. Partridge Inc. sells about $45 million a year on credit. Good credit and collections performance in the industry result in a 35-day ACP. (For convenience, calculate with ending balances only.)

   a. What is the maximum receivables balance Partridge can tolerate and still receive a good rating with respect to credit and collections?

   b. If Partridge is now collecting an average receivable in 40 days, by how much will it have to lower the receivables balance to achieve a good rating?

9. Epsom Co. manufactures furniture and sells about $40 million a year at a gross margin of 45%. (For convenience, calculate with ending balances only.)

   a. What is the maximum inventory level the firm can carry to maintain an inventory turnover (based on COGS) of 8.0?

b. If the inventory contains $1.2 million of obsolete and damaged goods that don't turn over at all, how fast would the active inventory have to turn over to achieve an overall turnover rate of 8.0?

10. The Nelson Sheetmetal Company has current assets of $2.5 million and current liabilities of $1.0 million. The firm is in need of additional inventory and has an opportunity to borrow money on a short-term note with which it can buy the needed material. However, a previous financing agreement prohibits the company from operating with a current ratio below 1.8. What is the maximum amount of inventory Nelson can obtain in this manner? (*Hint:* The note and the inventory are both current items of equal size on the balance sheet.)

11. Sweet Tooth Cookies, Inc. has the following ratios.

$$ROE = 15\%$$
$$T/A \text{ turnover} = 1.2$$
$$ROS = 10\%$$

What percentage of its assets are financed by equity?

12. The Paragon Company has sales of $2,000 with a cost ratio of 60%, current ratio of 1.5, inventory turnover ratio (based on cost) of 3.0, and average collection period (ACP) of 45 days. Complete the following current section of the firm's balance sheet assuming the ratios given are based on ending balance sheet figures.

Cash	$ _____	Accounts payable	$ _____
Accounts receivable	_____	Accruals	60
Inventory	_____		
Current assets	$ _____	Current liabilities	$ 750

13. You are given the following selected financial information for The Blatz Corporation. Assume ratios are calculated by using only year-end balances.

Income Statement		Balance Sheet	
COGS	$750	Cash	$250
Net income	$160	Net fixed assets	$850

Ratios	
ROS	10%
Current ratio	2.3
Inventory turnover	6.0×
ACP	45 days
Debt ratio	49.12%

Calculate accounts receivable, inventory, current assets, current liabilities, debt, equity, ROA, and ROE.

14. Companies often use ratios as a basis for planning. The technique is to assume the business being planned will achieve targeted levels of certain ratios and then calculate the financial statement amounts that will result in those ratios. The process always starts with a dollar assumption about revenue. Forecast the balance sheet for Lambert Co. using the following information ($000). Round all projections to the nearest thousand dollars. Assume ratios are calculated with ending balances only.

Sales	$10,000
Cash	$500
Accruals	$50
Gross margin	45%
ACP	42 days
Inventory turns	7.0×
Total asset turnover	1.25×
Current ratio	2.0
Debt : equity	1 : 3

ASSETS		LIABILITIES	
Cash	_____	Accounts payable	_____
Accounts receivable	_____	Accruals	_____
Inventory	_____	Current liabilities	_____
Current assets	_____		
		Debt	_____
Net fixed assets	_____	Equity	_____
Total assets	_____	Total liabilities & equity	_____

15. **Comprehensive Problem.** The Protek Company is a large manufacturer and distributor of electronic components. Because of some successful new products marketed to manufacturers of personal computers, the firm has recently undergone a period of explosive growth, more than doubling its revenues during the last two years. However, the growth has been accompanied by a marked decline in profitability and a precipitous drop in the company's stock price.

You are a financial consultant who has been retained to analyze the company's performance and find out what's going wrong. Your investigative plan involves conducting a series of in-depth interviews with management and doing some independent research on the industry. However, before starting, you want to focus your thinking to be sure you can ask the right questions. You'll begin by analyzing the firm's financial statements over the last three years.

The following additional information is also provided with the financial statements. Depreciation for 20X1, 20X2, and 20X3 was $200, $250, and $275 million, respectively. No stock was sold or repurchased, and, like many fast-growing companies, Protek paid no dividends. Assume the tax rate is a flat 34%, and the firm pays 10% interest on its debt.

PROTEK COMPANY
INCOME STATEMENTS

For the periods ended 12/31
($000,000)

	20X1	20X2	20X3
Sales	$1,578	$2,106	$3,265
COGS	631	906	1,502
Gross margin	$ 947	$1,200	$1,763
Expenses			
Marketing	$ 316	$ 495	$ 882
R&D	158	211	327
Administration	126	179	294
Total expenses	$ 600	$ 885	$1,503
EBIT	$ 347	$ 315	$ 260
Interest	63	95	143
EBT	$ 284	$ 220	$ 117
Tax	97	75	40
EAT	$ 187	$ 145	$ 77

BALANCE SHEETS

For the periods ended 12/31
($000,000)

	20X1	20X2	20X3
ASSETS			
Cash	$ 30	$ 40	$ 62
Accounts receivable	175	351	590
Inventory	90	151	300
Current assets	$ 295	$ 542	$ 952
Fixed assets			
Gross	$1,565	$2,373	$2,718
Accumulated depreciation	(610)	(860)	(1,135)
Net	$ 955	$1,513	$1,583
Total assets	$1,250	$2,055	$2,535
LIABILITIES			
Accounts payable	$ 56	$ 81	$ 134
Accruals	15	20	30
Current liabilities	$ 71	$ 101	$ 164
Capital			
Long-term debt	$ 630	$1,260	$1,600
Equity	549	694	771
Total liabilities & equity	$1,250	$2,055	$2,535

a. Construct common size income statements for 20X1, 20X2, and 20X3. Analyze the trend in each line. What appears to be happening? (*Hints:* Think in terms of both dollars and percentages. As the company grows, the absolute dollars of cost and expense spending go up. What does it mean if the percentage of revenue represented by the expenditure increases as well? How much of an increase in spending do you think a department could manage efficiently? Could pricing of Protek's products have any effect?)

b. Construct statements of cash flows for 20X2, and 20X3. Where is the company's money going to and coming from? Make a comment about its free cash flows during the period. Is it likely to have positive or negative free cash flows in the future?

c. Calculate the indicated ratios for all three years. Analyze trends in each ratio and compare each with the industry average. What can you infer from this information? Make specific statements about liquidity, asset management, especially receivables and inventories, debt management, and profitability. Do not simply say that ratios are higher or lower than the average or that they are going up or down. Think about what might be going on in the company and propose *reasons* why the ratios are acting as they are. For convenience, use only ending balance sheet figures to calculate your ratios. Do certain specific problems tend to affect more than one ratio? Which ones?

	Industry Average	20X1	20X2	20X3
Current ratio	4.5			
Quick ratio	3.2			
ACP	42 days			
Inventory turnover	7.5			
Fixed asset turnover	1.6			
Total asset turnover	1.2			
Debt ratio	53%			
Debt : equity	1 : 1			
TIE	4.5			
ROS	9.0%			
ROA	10.8%			
ROE	22.8%			
Equity multiplier	2.1			

d. Construct both Du Pont equations for Protek and the industry. What, if anything, do they tell us?

e. One hundred million shares of stock have been outstanding for the entire period. The price of Protek stock in 20X1, 20X2, and 20X3 was $39.27, $26.10, and $11.55, respectively. Calculate the firm's earnings per share (EPS) and its price/earnings ratio (P/E). What's happening to the P/E? To what things are investors likely to be reacting? How would a slowdown in personal computer sales affect your reasoning?

f. Would you recommend Protek stock as an investment? Why might it be a very bad investment in the near future? Why might it be a very good one?

Internet Problem

16. Learning about different companies is an important part of the financial manager's job. Go to http://www.reportgallery.com and click on the latest annual report for Merck.

    a. Go to "Executive Speeches." Then to the "Shareholder's Meeting." Find the Chairman's Report. Was it a good year for the company? Why?

    b. Check out the company's income statement. By what percent did its sales change from the prior year?

    c. What do you think contributed to this change? Read what management has to say by going to the sections in the report where management analyzes the company's financial condition.

COMPUTER PROBLEMS

17. At the close of 2002, the financial statements of Northern Manufacturing were as follows.

Northern Manufacturing

Balance Sheet
For the period ended 12/31/02
($000)

ASSETS	12/31/01	12/31/02
Cash	$ 500	$ 200
Accounts receivable	6,250	7,300
Inventory	5,180	6,470
CURRENT ASSETS	$11,930	$13,970
Fixed assets		
Gross	$ 7,500	$ 9,000
Accum depr	($2,400)	(3,100)
Net	$ 5,100	$ 5,900
TOTAL ASSETS	$17,030	$19,870
LIABILITIES		
Accounts payable	$ 1,860	$ 2,210
Accruals	850	220
CURRENT LIABILITIES	$ 2,710	$ 2,430
Long-term debt	$11,320	$12,335
Equity	3,000	5,105
TOTAL CAPITAL	$14,320	$17,440
TOTAL LIABILITIES AND EQUITY	$17,030	$19,870

Northern Manufacturing

Income Statement
For the period ended 12/31/02
($000)

Sales	$22,560
COGS	11,506
Gross mrgn	$11,054
Expense	$ 5,332
Depreciation	700
EBIT	$ 5,022
Interest	1,180
EBT	$ 3,842
Tax	1,537
Net income	$ 2,305

In addition, Northern paid dividends of $1.2 million and sold new stock valued at $1.0 million in 2002. Use the CASHFLO program to produce Northern's statement of cash flows for 2002.

18. Comparative historical financial statements for Northern Manufacturing of Problem 17 are as follows.

Northern Manufacturing

Income Statements ($000)
For the years ended

	12/31/00	12/31/01	12/31/02
Sales	$17,850	$20,510	$22,560
COGS	9,100	10,665	11,506
Gross margin	$ 8,750	$ 9,845	$11,054
Expense	$ 5,180	$ 5,702	$ 5,332
Depreciation	600	650	700
EBIT	$ 2,970	$ 3,493	$ 5,022
Interest	800	910	1,180
EBT	$ 2,170	$ 2,583	$ 3,842
Tax	868	1,033	1,537
Net income	$ 1,302	$ 1,550	$ 2,305
Dividends paid	$ 650	$ 750	$ 1,200
Stock sold	0	0	$ 1,000
Lease payments	$ 500	$ 700	$ 800

Northern Manufacturing

Balance Sheet ($000)
For the years ended

	12/31/99	12/31/00	12/31/01	12/31/02
		ASSETS		
Cash	$ 955	$ 980	$ 500	$ 200
Accounts receivable	3,103	3,570	6,250	7,300
Inventory	2,890	3,033	5,180	6,470
CURRENT ASSETS	$ 6,948	$ 7,583	$11,930	$13,970
Fixed assets				
Gross	$ 5,800	$ 6,650	$ 7,500	$ 9,000
Accum depr	(1,150)	(1,750)	(2,400)	(3,100)
Net	$ 4,650	$ 4,900	$ 5,100	$ 5,900
TOTAL ASSETS	$11,598	$12,483	$17,030	$19,870
		LIABILITIES		
Accounts payable	$ 1,860	$ 1,650	$ 1,860	$ 2,210
Accruals	385	742	850	220
CURRENT LIABILITIES	$ 2,245	$ 2,392	$ 2,710	$ 2,430
Long-term debt	$ 7,805	$ 7,891	$11,320	$12,335
Equity	1,548	2,200	3,000	5,105
TOTAL CAPITAL	$ 9,353	$10,091	$14,320	$17,400
TOTAL L & E	$11,598	$12,483	$17,030	$19,870
Number of shares		300,000	300,000	315,000
Stock price		$ 78.12	$ 70.00	$ 65.88

a. Use the ANALYS program to prepare common size statements and a set of financial ratios for each of the last three years. Notice that ANALYS calculates ratios using average balance sheet figures where appropriate.

b. Analyze the results of ANALYS for Northern Manufacturing. The firm has been quite successful in terms of revenue and profit growth so far. Do the ratios reveal any disturbing trends that might indicate future problems?

DEVELOPING SOFTWARE

19. Write a program to generate a statement of cash flows yourself. It isn't as hard as you might think.

First set up the income statement and two balance sheets on the spreadsheet just as they appear in Problem 17. Let the amounts in individual accounts such as Cash, A/R, Revenue, COGS, Interest, and Tax be input items, and let the program calculate all the totals and subtotals such as Current Assets, Total Assets, Gross Margin, and Net Income.

Next take a different area of the spreadsheet and set up the changes in the current accounts and the statement of cash flows shown on page 102.

Take all of the items shown in lowercase xxx's from the statements in the first part of your spreadsheet. Some will be single items like Net Income and depreciation, but most will be differences between beginning and ending balances like the increase or decrease in long-term debt or the change in receivables. Finally, program the spreadsheet to add up the subtotals where the uppercase XXX's appear and display the reconciliation.

The trickiest part is keeping the signs straight in your subtractions for sources and uses.

Once you have your program written, test it with the inputs to the CASHFLO program and see if you get the same results.

20. Write your own analysis program to calculate a common size income statement and the ratios introduced in this chapter. To keep the exercise reasonably simple, just provide for one year of ratios and one common size statement. Also, use year-end balance sheet figures only in the calculations.

Construct an input area in your spreadsheet in the form of an income statement and a balance sheet. Input the accounts and have the program calculate all totals and subtotals. Define your common size income statement alongside the input income statement by dividing each input line item by revenue. Define your ratios in another area drawing the numerators and denominators from the input statements.

Test your program using the 2002 statements for Northern Manufacturing from Problem 18. Compare your results with those of the ANALYS program, keeping in mind that some of the ratios will be different because ANALYS uses average balance sheet figures on some ratios.

When does the use of average balance sheet figures make a significant difference?

Northern Manufacturing

Summary of Changes to Current Accounts
For the year ended 12/31/02
($000)

ACCOUNT	SOURCE/(USE)
Receivables	$xxx
Inventory	xxx
Payables	xxx
Accruals	xxx
	$XXX

Northern Manufacturing

Statement of Cash Flows
For the year ended 12/31/02
($000)

CASH FROM OPERATING ACTIVITIES	
Net income	$x,xxx
Depreciation	xxx
Net changes in current accounts	xxx
Cash from operating activities	$XXX

CASH FROM INVESTING ACTIVITIES	
Purchase of fixed assets	($x,xxx)

CASH FROM FINANCING ACTIVITIES	
Increase (Decrease) in long-term debt	$x,xxx
Sale of stock	xxx
Dividend paid	(xxx)
Cash from financing activities	$X,XXX

NET CASH FLOW	$XXX

RECONCILIATION	
Beginning cash balance	$x,xxx
Net cash flow	XXX
Ending cash balance	$X,XXX

CHAPTER 4

The Financial System and Interest

Chapter Outline

In Chapter 1 we touched on the nature of the financial system when we described financial assets and markets. In this chapter we'll expand on those ideas. We'll have a closer look at the money flows in the economy and gain a better understanding of the manner in which investors, companies, and securities come together in stock and bond markets. Finally, we'll take an in-depth look at interest, the price of money.

THE FINANCIAL SYSTEM

An industrialized economy consists of three sectors: consumption, production, and government. The consumption sector is made up of households buying and consuming products and services that are created in the production sector. The government sector produces services that are used by both consumers and producers, and collects taxes from both.

It's important to understand that the sectors are conceptual, and that individual people are generally in at least two sectors at the same time. For example, when workers are on the job they're in the production sector, but when they go home they become part of the consumption sector.

http://

Check the Economic Statistics Briefing Room for data on production and consumption at

● www.whitehouse.gov/fsbr/ esbr.html

With respect to the issues we'll be illustrating here, the government sector acts a great deal like the production sector. It pays its employees wages and creates services that are "purchased" with tax dollars. It also issues debt securities that function much like those of corporations. Therefore, we'll lump government and production together and talk about just two sectors, production and consumption.

●CASH FLOWS BETWEEN THE SECTORS

Money flows back and forth between the production and consumption sectors every day. The wages workers receive for their roles in the production process represent income to the consumption sector. The income consumers spend on products and services in turn becomes income to the production sector. Producers spend their income on inputs used to produce more product, including wages that flow back to the consumption sector, and so on, creating a cyclical flow of money. These normal, everyday flows are illustrated in Figure 4.1.

●SAVINGS AND INVESTMENT

Two important features of the system are not included in Figure 4.1. The first involves the consumption sector. People generally don't spend their entire incomes on consumption. Most save at least a little and need a place to put savings in which a return can be earned.

The second missing feature involves the production sector. In addition to doing everyday business, companies occasionally spend large sums of money on projects such as new factories, additional equipment, and starting new enterprises.

In other words, each sector has a need that isn't pictured in Figure 4.1. Consumers need a way to save the income they don't spend, and companies need a way to obtain extra money for occasional major projects.

These needs are happily coincidental. The economic system contains a source of money in consumer savings and a use for it in funding business projects. All that's lacking is a way to connect the two. That is, we have to put companies' needs for extra money together with the availability of money saved by consumers.

FIGURE 4.1

Everyday Money Flows between Sectors

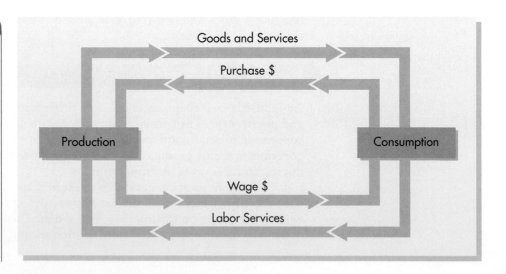

FIGURE 4.2

Flows between Sectors

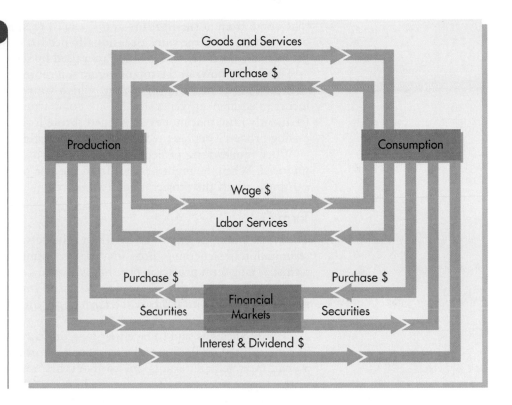

The connection is provided by *financial markets* in which buyers and sellers of financial assets meet. Companies that need money issue securities, usually stocks or bonds, which are sold to individuals. Consumers buy the securities with their savings, and companies use the proceeds to do their projects.

Consumers are said to *invest* in the securities, which are expected to generate a *return* on the money invested in their purchase. That return comes in the form of interest on bonds or dividends and price appreciation in the case of stock.

Figure 4.2 shows the financial system redrawn to include the previously omitted features. In short, financial markets provide a conduit for the transfer of savings from the consumption sector to the production sector. When the production sector uses this money it is said to be *investing* in projects, enterprises, and assets. Hence economists say that *savings equals investment* in the economy.[1]

Financial markets are extremely important to the health of an economy. Their role and function will be a major focus of our study in this book.

Raising and Spending Money in Business

Here's another way to think about the system shown in Figure 4.2. We can think of a company as spending two kinds of money. One kind is the day-to-day funds

● **Financial markets** connect production's need for money with consumption's available savings.

● Consumer **savings equals** industrial **investment**.

---

1. Notice that the term "invest" seems to have two slightly different meanings. Individuals are said to invest in financial assets, while firms invest in production facilities and equipment. What economists actually mean when they say savings equals investment is that investment by consumers in financial assets (savings) equals investment by companies in the means of production.

that come from normal profits and are used to support routine activities. The other kind is the large sums occasionally needed to support major projects and get businesses started. These funds are raised by selling financial assets.

The money flows at the top of Figure 4.2 represent the routine day-to-day activities. The second kind of money, which supports large projects and investments in equipment, generally doesn't come from operating funds. Firms more frequently raise that money as needed through financial markets. This money-raising process is represented in the bottom portion of Figure 4.2.

When money for a project is raised by borrowing, we say the project is *debt financed*. When the money comes from the sale of stock or from the company's earnings, we say the project is *equity financed*.

Term

The word "term" refers to the length of time between the present and the end or *term*ination of something. Both financial investments and physical projects have terms. A long-term project is one that will take a long time to complete. A long-term loan is one that doesn't have to be repaid for several years. The word "maturity" is also used to indicate the term of a loan. Debt *matures* on the day it is to be repaid.

Debt financing is said to be either long or short term depending on the length of time allowed until it has to be paid back. Short term generally means less than a year, intermediate term is one to five years, and long term is more than five years. People frequently leave out the intermediate-term concept and just think of long- and short-term debt as being more or less than one year.

Stocks have an indefinite term in that they have no specified repayment date. Therefore they're thought of as very long-term financing.

The projects we talked about in the last section tend to be long term, like getting businesses started or buying fixed assets. It's common practice to match the term of a project or asset with the term of the financing that pays for it. For example, funding for a project expected to take 10 years shouldn't need to be repaid in much less than 10 years. The practice is called **maturity matching.**

● **Maturity matching:** A project's duration should match the term of the financing that supports it.

● FINANCIAL MARKETS

Financial markets are classified in several ways. We'll discuss classifications with respect to term and purpose.

Capital Markets

● **Capital markets** deal in long-term debt and stock.

Money acquired for long periods is referred to as **capital,** and the financial markets that deal with it are known as **capital markets.** They trade in stocks and in debt securities having terms longer than one year.

Money Markets

● **Money markets** deal in short-term debt.

Markets in which short-term debt is traded are called **money markets.** They play an important role in setting interest rates for the rest of the economy, which we'll get into later in the chapter.

In business, most of the money that supports day-to-day operations is generated by sales. However, companies do borrow short term to cover temporary operating shortages. Most of the time, short-term corporate borrowing is done from banks, but there are financial markets that deal in short-term debt instruments[2] known as *notes*, *bills*, and *commercial paper*.

The federal government is especially active in issuing short-term debt. In the last 40 years, the government consistently spent more than it took in, creating a *federal budget deficit* in nearly every year. The accumulated sum of the annual deficits is the **national debt**. The government borrows to fund yearly deficits and to replace old debt as it matures. There is currently an annual *surplus* of tax receipts over government spending, but a large national debt remains. More than half of the national debt is short term, so there's a very active market in short-term federal debt.

● Federal borrowing supports yearly **deficit spending** and the **national debt**.

Primary and Secondary Markets

The basic purpose of financial markets is to facilitate the flow of funds from the saving public to the production sector for investment in business projects. However, most of what goes on in the largest and best known markets has little to do with that transfer.

Funds are actually transferred from individual investors to companies only when securities are issued and purchased for the first time. Immediately after that first sale, securities belong to individual investors who may or may not choose to retain them permanently. In most cases, investors hold onto securities for a while but eventually sell them to others. Security sales subsequent to the first one are *between investors* and don't involve the issuing company at all.

● The initial sale of a security is a **primary market** transaction. Subsequent sales between investors are in the **secondary market**.

The first sale of a security, in which the money proceeds go to the issuing company, is called a **primary market** transaction. Subsequent sales of the security, between investors, are called **secondary market** transactions. The vast majority of transactions in traditional financial markets like the stock market are secondary.

Corporate financial managers are concerned about secondary stock market transactions even though there's no immediate cash impact on their companies. The secondary market sets the level of a stock's price and therefore influences how much can be raised in future issues. *In addition, senior managers' compensation is usually tied to the company's stock price, and that tends to generate an intense interest in the secondary market.*

from the **CFO**

Direct and Indirect Transfers, Financial Intermediaries

Primary market transactions, which transfer money from individual investors to companies, can occur directly or indirectly through a financial intermediary. Let's consider the direct method first.

In a direct transfer, an investor simply buys the security of a company. That kind of transfer is shown in Figure 4.3a, but it's a rare occurrence as illustrated. Companies don't usually market new securities to the public by themselves. Rather, they use the services of an **investment bank,** an organization that helps market new securities.

● An **investment bank** helps companies market their securities.

The investment bank typically lines up investors interested in buying a new issue beforehand, and functions as a broker bringing buyers and sellers together. A direct transfer through such an organization is illustrated in Figure 4.3b. The transfer is direct because, even though the investment bank may take temporary possession of the securities, it actually just passes them through to the buyer.

---

2. The term **financial instrument** is another expression for a security or a document evidencing a debt.

FIGURE 4.3

Transfer of Funds from Investors to Businesses

(a)
Direct Transfer

(b)
Direct Transfer through Investment Banker

(c)
Indirect Transfer through Financial Intermediary

● A **financial intermediary** sells shares in itself and invests the funds collectively on behalf of its investors.

The indirect transfer is illustrated in Figure 4.3c. Although the diagram looks similar to 4.3b, something very different is taking place. In an indirect transfer, a **financial intermediary** collects money from many individuals, pools it, and then makes investments with it. The securities purchased are not passed through to the individual investors. Instead the financial intermediary holds onto those securities and gives the individual investors a *security of its own*. That is, it gives them some kind of claim upon itself.

A *mutual fund* is a good example. It takes money from many individual investors and uses it to buy a portfolio of stocks and bonds. (A portfolio is a collection of financial assets.) Each investor receives a number of *shares in the fund* proportionate to the size of his or her investment, but none of the individual stocks and bonds from the portfolio.

The important point is that the portfolio is owned *collectively* by individuals who have invested in the fund, but no one can identify any particular stock or bond as his or her own. An important result of this arrangement is that the fund's management controls the pooled resources of many people, which often amounts to a vast sum of money. As a result, funds have a great deal of influence in stock and bond markets.

● Financial intermediaries are **institutional investors**.

Mutual funds and similar financial intermediaries are called **institutional investors** and play a major role in today's financial markets. They own about one quarter of the stocks listed on the major exchanges but make about three quarters of the trades. That makes them very influential in setting prices and trends in the secondary market.

Here are some other kinds of financial intermediaries.

Pension funds receive the retirement contributions of workers and employers, and invest the money in stocks, bonds, and real estate. Employees own pension accounts representing their proportionate share of the fund assets.

Insurance companies collect premiums from customers and invest the money to provide a pool of assets from which to pay claims.

Banks receive deposits from individuals and make loans to companies. The bank's portfolio of financial assets is its loan portfolio, while depositors' accounts represent claims on those assets.

THE STOCK MARKET AND STOCK EXCHANGES

We briefly described the stock market in Chapter 1. In this section we'll amplify that description and develop an understanding of the market's workings.

OVERVIEW

http://

Visit the Education site at the NYSE at

www.nyse.com

Select "About the NYSE," and then click on "Education."

The stock market is a financial system or organization embedded within the larger economic system of the nation. It isn't a single place where people go to buy and sell stocks, although many people associate it with the New York Stock Exchange (NYSE).

Rather, the stock market is a network of **exchanges** and **brokers**. An exchange is actually a company that provides a physical marketplace and the administrative capability of transferring stocks from one owner to another. **Brokerage** firms, or **houses,** are also companies. They employ individuals (the brokers) who are licensed by the government to assist people in buying and selling securities. Both the exchanges and the brokers earn a living from commissions and fees charged on transactions made by people who buy and sell securities.

The government grants the exchange the basic right to make a market in securities. Brokers are *members* of stock exchanges. Each exchange has a limited number of *seats* that are purchased by brokerage firms. Owning a seat makes one a member and confers the right to do business on the exchange.

TRADING—THE ROLE OF BROKERS

To buy or sell stocks, an individual investor must have an account with a broker. The investor is said to be the broker's customer or client. When customers want to trade in stocks, they place orders with their brokers to buy or sell. It's common practice to do this by telephone. Major brokerage houses have offices located throughout the country, and people usually deal with individual brokers located in a nearby office.

Brokerage firms also have representatives at the exchange. Upon receiving orders from customers, local brokers call them to representatives known as **floor brokers** on the trading floor of the exchange.

Each stock is traded in a particular spot on the exchange floor in an auction-like process, which is supervised by an individual called a **specialist** in that stock. Specialists are responsible for conducting an orderly market in the stocks they are assigned.

● **Floor brokers** trade on the floor of the exchange.

● **Specialists** make markets in designated securities.

FIGURE 4.4

Schematic Representation of a Stock Market Transaction

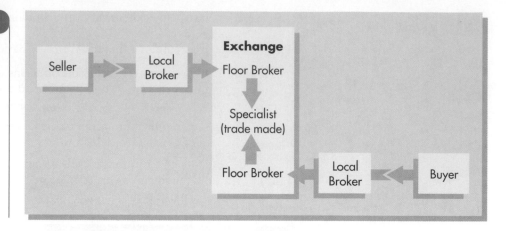

Floor brokers take the phoned-in orders to the spots where representatives of buyers and sellers meet and execute transactions. Once trades are made, confirmations are passed back to the local brokers and their clients. Actual settlement of the sale and transfer of the stock doesn't happen until a few days later. Figure 4.4 is a representation of the process.

Figure 4.5 is a photograph of the trading floor of the New York Stock Exchange. Notice that people are doing business while standing in groups at various places around the floor. Trading between floor brokers and specialists goes

FIGURE 4.5

The Trading Floor of the New York Stock Exchange

© MALANCA ETTORE AEF/GETTY IMAGES

© INDEX STOCK IMAGERY, INC.

http://

The AMEX site contains market information and other features at
www.amex.com/floor

● The sale of securities is regulated by the federal government through the **Securities and Exchange Commission (SEC)**.

● Securities law is primarily aimed at **disclosure**.

on in such groups continually while the exchange is open. Figure 4.6 shows the imposing exterior of the exchange.

● EXCHANGES

There are several stock exchanges in the United States. By far the largest is the New York Stock Exchange (NYSE) in the downtown financial district of New York City, the area collectively referred to as Wall Street. The NYSE deals in the securities of over 3,000 American and more than 400 foreign companies. Those stocks are said to be *listed* on the exchange. The NYSE handles most of the stock trading activity in the nation. The American Stock Exchange (AMEX) is located a few blocks away. The companies it lists are also relatively large but not quite as large or as old as those listed on the NYSE.

In addition to the NYSE and the AMEX there are several regional exchanges located in other major cities. They generally list companies of local interest.

Today the exchanges are linked electronically, which makes them function like one big exchange for many purposes.

The Market

All the activity we've just described and more makes up the *stock market*. Although the exchange represents a physical center for much of what goes on, the term "market" refers to the entire interconnected set of places, organizations, and processes.

Regulation

Securities markets are regulated under both state and federal laws, but the most important rules are federal. The Securities Act of 1933 required companies to disclose certain information to potential investors when promoting new securities in the primary market. The Securities Exchange Act of 1934 extended the disclosure requirements to existing stocks and set up the **Securities and Exchange Commission (SEC)** to oversee financial market activities.

The laws are primarily aimed at disclosure and the prevention of certain kinds of manipulative and deceptive behavior. Disclosure means that investors must be given full and accurate information about the companies and people behind stocks that are offered for sale. Manipulation means taking advantage of an official or privileged position to make profits on fluctuations in the prices of securities.

For example, it's illegal to make short-term profits on **insider information**, which is information available to an executive of a company but not to the general public. Suppose a drug company is about to release information about a powerful new cancer treatment that is expected to be a big money maker in the future. That information release could be expected to drive the stock's price up considerably. It would be illegal for an insider to buy stock just before the announcement and sell it just after, making a short-term profit on the price increase.

Securities law is a large and complex field. For now all we need to do is be aware that it exists and understand its basic direction.

● PRIVATE, PUBLIC, AND LISTED COMPANIES, AND THE OTC MARKET

Suppose you notice a small company in your neighborhood that seems to be doing well and decide to buy some of its stock. Could you do this as easily as you could buy shares of IBM or General Motors, with a simple call to your broker?

If a company is small, buying its stock might not be easy and you might not be able to get any at all. That's because all companies aren't traded on exchanges, and many aren't for sale to the public. Let's trace the life of a typical business enterprise to see how and when its stock becomes available for investment.

Suppose an entrepreneur starts a small unincorporated business. Because the firm isn't a corporation, it has no stock for outsiders to buy, and ownership is entirely vested in the entrepreneur. If the business is successful and the owner wants to raise money for expansion, he can incorporate in order to sell stock to others. We'll assume he does that.

Privately Held Companies

Privately held companies can't sell securities to the general public.

At this point the firm is said to be a **privately held,** or **closely held, company.** The stock of privately held companies can be sold to other people, but those sales are severely restricted by federal regulations. Generally there can't be a large number of stockholders and sales solicitations can't be made across state lines. These regulations are aimed at limiting fraudulent investment schemes in which confidence artists offer bogus securities to unwary and unsophisticated investors.

Suppose our entrepreneur raises money by selling stock to a few people he knows and continues to expand the company. We'll assume that things continue to go well and, after some time, more and bigger growth opportunities present themselves. Taking advantage of such opportunities requires a lot more funding, but the business owner has run out of friends and relatives. To sell a substantial amount of stock he has to make an offering to a large number of people.

Public Companies

A **publicly traded company** can sell securities broadly after a **prospectus** is approved by the SEC.

Offering securities for sale to the general public requires the approval of the SEC and the registration of each security offered with the commission. A firm that has received such approval is known as a *public company* or a **publicly traded company.** The process of obtaining approval and registration is known as *going public.*

Going public requires the assistance of an investment bank. The bank determines whether a market can be expected to exist for the company's stock and the likely price at which a block of stock can be sold. If the estimated price is acceptable to the firm's owners, the registration procedure begins with the preparation of a document known as a **prospectus.**

The prospectus gives detailed information about the firm's business, its financing, and the background of its principal officers. When securities are eventually offered for sale, a copy of the prospectus must be provided to potential investors. However, the prospectus must be submitted to the SEC and approved before anything can be sold.

The purpose of the prospectus is *disclosure.* That is, the document must truly and accurately inform potential investors of the nature of the business and the risks involved. If the president was recently in jail for securities fraud, for example, that fact must be disclosed. Similarly, if the company is depending on the success of some new technological process or the granting of a patent, those facts must be revealed.

The law provides severe penalties for fraud on the part of *anyone* involved in the preparation of a prospectus—not only owners and officers of the company but accountants, lawyers, and bankers who might have been hired to assist in the process.

● An unapproved prospectus is called a **red herring.**

While the SEC is reviewing a prospectus, the firm may not offer its securities for sale to the public. However, it may circulate the prospectus stamped with the word "PRELIMINARY" in red letters. Such a document is known as a **red herring**, indicating it does not yet represent an actual offering.

It's important to understand that approval of a prospectus by the SEC doesn't represent an endorsement of the security as a good investment opportunity. That is, a firm could be in an absolutely terrible business, one almost guaranteed to fail (like selling saltwater at the beach!) and still receive SEC approval because all the appropriate information was disclosed. In fact, SEC approval doesn't even guarantee that everything relevant is disclosed, because the commission doesn't have the resources to check much of the information that's submitted.

The IPO

● The market for **initial public offerings (IPOs)** is very volatile and risky.

When a prospectus is approved by the SEC, the securities described may be sold to the public. This initial sale is called an *initial public offering,* abbreviated **IPO.**

IPOs constitute a subdivision of the general stock market and are considered quite risky. The prices of newly traded companies sometimes advance very rapidly after their IPOs, but can drop dramatically as well.

Investment bankers generally line up buyers for IPOs before the securities are actually released, so the general public doesn't usually get involved right away. Institutional investors such as mutual funds are frequent buyers.

Notice that the initial public offering is a primary market transaction. Once the securities are placed with investors, further trading will involve secondary market transactions.

If our entrepreneur went through all this, he would probably have retained a majority of the firm's stock for himself. The IPO would have placed a value on the shares of the stock that were sold and thereby would have implicitly valued the shares still held by the entrepreneur. In a successful IPO that value is far in excess of book value and the entrepreneur can become a millionaire overnight, at least on paper!

The OTC Market

http://

See which companies have IPOs at

www.ipocentral.com

At this point the company is partially owned by investors, probably institutional, who purchased shares in its IPO, and partially owned by the entrepreneur and anyone who bought in before the firm went public. Now suppose any of these investors want to sell some or all of their holdings. How can that be accomplished?

Notice that we haven't as yet said anything about a stock exchange in this scenario. Also recall that stock exchanges trade only in certain stocks that are *listed* on those exchanges. In other words, our firm's securities aren't listed on an exchange, so investors can't buy or sell shares there. A vast number of companies fit this description. They're public and therefore available to be generally traded, but they're not listed on an exchange.

● Smaller public companies are traded on the **over the counter (OTC)** market.

Such unlisted securities can be bought and sold by the general public in what is known as the **over the counter (OTC) market.** This market consists of a loosely organized network of brokers who contact one another to find buyers and sellers for the securities of smaller companies. The OTC market is computerized on a nationwide system called **NASDAQ,** which stands for the National Association of Securities Dealers Automated Quotation System. Although most of the stocks traded over the counter are issued by relatively small firms, a few very large companies are traded in this market.

Real Applications

It's all in the Timing— IPOs Are a Risky Business

The first time a company sells its stock to the general public the sale is called an initial public offering, an IPO in the jargon of the financial world. IPOs represent one of the most volatile and risky segments of the investment industry. The prices of IPO stocks frequently skyrocket shortly after the shares are issued, and as frequently drop precipitously. Hence early investors in brand new stocks can make or lose a great deal of money quickly.

The reason behind the volatility is that it's hard to judge just how much the investing community will pay for a share of the new stock. If the company, its investment bankers, and the initial buyers underestimate the price investors are generally willing to pay, the stock increases in value rapidly after it's issued, and the lucky buyers do very well. However, the reverse is also possible. When the initial price is too high, the stock's price drops quickly, and early buyers suffer big losses.

It's also common for the prices of recent IPOs to increase rapidly for a relatively short time and then to come tumbling down just as rapidly. The people who really get hurt then are those who buy shortly after the initial sale when the price is near its peak.

One reason for all this volatility is that investors tend to anticipate IPOs in certain "hot" industries and from particular companies. IPOs in those fields are met with a frenzy of buying activity when they first come out. But that enthusiasm often cools rapidly.

In recent years the most prominent IPO darling has been Internet stocks. But their love affair with investors seems to have run its course and died. A prominent example tells the story.

In 1995, an IPO for Netscape, maker of one of the most popular Internet browsers, hit the market. The initial offering was priced at $28, but the stock's price soared to $72.76 in the first year of trading. This almost three-fold increase was a precursor to a spectacular run of Internet IPOs over the next five years. For a while it appeared that investors couldn't get enough of "hot" IPOs with an Internet connection.

Six years later, Marc Andreessen, the co-founder of Netscape, tried his luck in the IPO market again with shares in Loudcloud, a firm that provides services aimed at managing customers' Internet operations. Backers hoped the connection to Andreessen, who was Loudcloud's chairman, would result in enthusiastic investor acceptance of the IPO based on his experience with Netscape. In February 2001, Loudcloud attempted to sell an IPO of 20 million shares priced between $8 and $10.

But by then the market's infatuation with Internet stocks was over. Lower expectations were the norm, and the price had to be dropped to $6 to sell twenty-five million shares. Further, the post IPO price run-up never happened. During the next six months the stock traded at a high of only $7.00 and dropped as low as $1.28. According to Ben Holmes, an acknowledged expert and president of IPOpros.com, "Loudcloud was probably the last of the Internet follies . . . The door for equity financing is closing for deals like this." Interestingly, Marc Andreessen was part of the beginning, and in at the end of the spectacular IPO run for Internet stocks.

Sources: http://cgi.cnnfn.com/output/pfv/2001/03/09/deals/loudcloud/
http://pfquotes.netscape.com/finance/quotes/qoutes.tmpl?symbol=LDCL
http://www.jsonline.com/bym/news/ap/mar01/ap-loudcloudipo030501.asp

http://

Find information on small companies at

www.smallcapinvestor.com

or at

www.nasdaq.com

● Companies **list** themselves on an exchange to make trading their securities easier.

http://

Select a company from the NYSE list at

www.nyse.com/listed/listed.html

Select "Listed," then check on its stock quotes and its market data.

It's generally more expensive to trade in the smaller firms handled on the OTC market than in stocks listed on exchanges. Because few investors tend to be interested in any particular small company, brokers have to work hard to match up buyers and sellers. For that service they receive higher commissions and fees than those paid for trades in stocks listed on exchanges where there is an active market all the time.

Listing on an Exchange

Now suppose the company we've been talking about continues to grow and becomes popular among investors. It's in the company's interest to make it easy for those investors to trade in the secondary market for the firm's stock even though no money from those trades goes to the company itself. That's because a smoothly operating secondary market in the stock will make further new issues of the firm's securities easier to sell in the future.

So, if the trading volume warrants, the company can *list* its stock on an exchange. This is a relatively easy process if the exchange's requirements for size and length of time in business are met. After that the firm is a **listed company.**

● READING STOCK QUOTATIONS

Stock prices are reported every day in a variety of newspapers. The leading source of daily quotations is the *Wall Street Journal,* published by Dow Jones & Company, Inc. Quotations summarize the trading activity of the previous business day on the New York Stock Exchange, the American Stock Exchange, and the OTC market. The New York Stock Exchange listing shows "composite transactions," meaning it includes transactions in the stocks shown that may have been made on other exchanges.

The format in which stock market information is presented requires a little explanation. We'll illustrate with the listing for General Motors shown in Figure 4.7. This listing is from Wednesday, August 1, 2001, so the information reflects trading on Tuesday, July 31, 2001.

Let's look at each of the columns starting with the fourth. (The column numbers don't appear in the newspaper.) The fourth column, labeled Stock (SYM), gives the abbreviated name of the company followed by the firm's tickertape symbol in boldface type. This latter is an even shorter abbreviation used in displaying and transmitting trading information from the exchange floor.

Columns 2 and 3 show the highest and lowest prices at which the stock was traded during the past year. Notice how big the swing in value was, roughly between $77 and $48. The highest price was more than 60% above the lowest

FIGURE 4.7
Stock Market Quotation for General Motors Corporation Wednesday, August 1, 2001
Source: *The Wall Street Journal.*

Column Numbers

1	2	3	4	5	6	7	8	9	10
YTD % CHG	52 WEEKS Hi	Lo	Stock (SYM)	DIV	YLD %	PE	VOL 100s	LAST	NET CHG
+24.9	76.63	48.44	Gen Motor **GM**	2.00	3.1	33	21393	63.60	+0.70

Practical Finance

Efficient Financial Markets

In an effort to explain certain characteristics of the behavior of stock prices theorists have hypothesized that U.S. financial markets are *efficient*. In this context efficiency means information travels around the market so fast that it's virtually impossible to find a bargain.

The idea is that there's an army of analysts working in the securities industry, and that analysts, brokers, and investors are wired together electronically by phone and computer. When some new piece of information comes out that suggests a stock may be worth more or less than its current price, it's disseminated with lightning speed and investors bid the price up or down within hours if not minutes.

The implication of efficiency is that an investor can't *consistently* beat the market by studying up on stocks, because all available information is already reflected in stock prices. Beating the market means earning above-average returns by consistently finding bargains.

Don't be discouraged. Not everyone agrees that the **efficient market hypothesis** is correct. We'll have more to say about the idea in Chapter 8.

---

price in the period, and this is a well-known and relatively stable company. Column 1 shows the percentage price change the stock has undergone since the beginning of the current calendar year.

Column 5 gives the last dividend paid by the company on an annualized basis. Because dividends are usually paid quarterly, this figure is generally the latest dividend multiplied by 4. Column 6 shows the **dividend yield,** also known as the **current yield,**[3] which is simply the dividend in column 5 divided by the stock's current price, expressed as a percentage.

- The **dividend yield** gives an indication of the current income an investor can expect.

The dividend yield gives an immediate indication of how much an investor can expect to make on his or her investment without depending on price increases. It's important because it shows how much cash or current income can be expected while the stock is held.

Column 7 gives the P/E ratio we described in Chapter 3. On this date General Motors was selling for 33 times earnings. Column 8 shows the day's trading volume in lots of 100 shares. We see that 2,139,300 shares of GM stock changed hands on July 31.

- The **closing price** records the last trade of the day.

Column 9 reports the price of the day's last or final trade, also known as the **closing price.** Finally, column 10 shows the net change up or down from the previous day's last price.

Serious investors check the financial press several times a week for the progress of stocks they've purchased. Local newspapers often carry some stock market information, but the format isn't necessarily the same as that of the *Wall Street Journal*.

INTEREST

Investing in a security implies entrusting money to the organization that issued the security. The issuer uses the money and pays the investor for the use. The

---

3. "Yield" is another word for return, which is similar to interest rate. We'll discuss this in detail in later chapters.

http://

Interest rate info in a nut-shell is available at

● www.Channel3000.com/ money

● A debt's **term** or **maturity** is the time until it must be repaid.

payment is called the *return* on the investment, and is usually stated in terms of a percentage of the money invested.

The term **interest** is reserved for the return on a debt investment, meaning the investor lends money to the issuer of the security. The primary vehicle for making debt investments is the **bond.** An investor in a bond is making a loan to the issuing company even though we say he or she buys the bond. Every bond has an associated interest rate that is paid to the investor who holds it.

People often talk about *the* interest rate as though there were only one. In fact there are many rates, depending on the nature of the debt and on the characteristics of the borrowers and lenders. The various interest rates tend to move up and down more or less together. A statement like "the interest rate is moving up" is a reference to an approximate, average level rather than to anything specific.

Debt investments are loans and have **terms.** The term of a loan or a bond is the time measured from the present until the obligation must be repaid. A bond is said to *mature* at the end of its term on its *maturity date.* The word "maturity" can be synonymous with "term." That is, a bond with a 10-year term can also be said to have a **maturity** of 10 years.

It's important to notice that bonds are *non-amortized* debt. An amortized debt is one in which the principal is paid back regularly along with interest over the life of the loan. Most consumer credit, including home mortgages and car loans, is amortized. Most business and government debt is non-amortized. Borrowers issuing bonds pay interest only, usually semiannually, until the maturity date, and then must repay the entire principal at once.

● **Stocks** (equity) and **bonds** (debt) **compete** for investor's dollars. Stocks offer higher returns but have **more risk**.

● THE RELATIONSHIP BETWEEN INTEREST AND THE STOCK MARKET

Returns on stock investments and interest rates on debt are related. Investors always have a choice between investing in debt instruments like bonds or savings accounts or in equity securities like stock. (When you put money into a savings account you're lending it to the bank.) In other words, stocks (equity) and bonds (debt) compete for investors' dollars.

Debt investments are generally safer than stocks so people prefer them if the expected return on the stock and the interest on the debt are nearly equal. As a result, stocks have to offer higher returns than debt to induce people to invest in equity. As interest rates on debt move up and down over time, the return on stock investments moves up and down as well, usually remaining somewhat above the interest rate on debt.

This movement has a significant effect on the stock market because of the relationship between the return on a stock investment and the price of a share. *A higher return is associated with a lower price.* This should be clear if you think in terms of bargains. Suppose a particular stock is expected to produce a barely acceptable return over the next year. You're thinking of buying some shares, but you aren't quite sure if it's a good deal. Then imagine that the price is suddenly cut in half, while nothing else changes. That makes the stock a much better deal, a bargain. The return it now offers as a percentage of the lower invested price is much higher.

● Interest rates and security prices **move in opposite directions**.

In general, the market changes the return on a share of stock by changing its price, so if stock returns move up, prices move down, and if returns move down, prices move up. We'll understand this idea much better when we study the material in Chapter 7. For now the basic principle is what's important: *Stock prices and returns move in opposite directions.*

But remember what we just said about returns and interest rates. Changes in the overall level of stock returns are driven by changes in interest rates on debt investments. That means the general price level of the stock market is driven up and down by changes in interest rates on debt. As interest rates go up, stock prices go down, and as rates go down, prices go up.

That's a very good reason for us to be familiar with the inner workings of interest rates! Interest isn't the only thing that affects the general price level of stocks, but it's very important and more predictable than other influences.

INTEREST AND THE ECONOMY

The interest rate has a significant effect on the economy in general. High interest rates tend to stifle economic activity, whereas low rates tend to promote it. That's because both in business and in our personal lives a lot is done on credit.

● **Lower interest rates** stimulate business and economic activity.

Consider a family interested in buying a new home. If interest rates are high, their mortgage payments will be high and they may not be able to afford the house they want. Lower interest rates mean lower payments, so houses become more affordable in general and the family is more likely to buy.

When interest rates are low, people buy more houses, cars, refrigerators, and just about everything else. Because someone has to manufacture those products, more sales lead to more jobs and a healthier economy.

The same idea applies to business. Companies often use borrowed money to buy new equipment and undertake new projects. When interest rates are high, borrowing is expensive, and not many projects look good because they don't earn enough to cover their interest cost. When rates are low, more projects are viable and are undertaken. The increased activity in turn leads to a healthier economy.

All this causes the financial community to be very interested in interest rates, and gives us good reason to examine exactly what's in an interest rate and how rates are determined.

DEBT MARKETS

Interest rates are set by the forces of supply and demand in debt markets. To understand how these forces work, we need to review an analytic tool from economics, the supply and demand diagram.

Supply and Demand—A Brief Review

A demand curve is a graph relating price and quantity in the market for a product or service. It reflects the desires and abilities of buyers at a particular point in time. The graph's vertical axis represents price and its horizontal axis indicates the quantity purchased in a period. Figure 4.8 shows a demand curve labeled D.

Virtually all demand curves slope downward to the right. That simply means people will buy more of the product if the price is low and less if it's high.

A supply curve relates prices with quantities supplied by producers. The curve is upsloping, indicating that suppliers are willing to produce and sell more product at higher prices than at lower prices. The supply curve is labeled S in Figure 4.8.

Drawing both curves on the same set of axes shows that there's only one point at which both buyers and sellers are happy: the intersection of the two curves. The market tends to operate at that point, and we say it is in equilibrium there. These ideas are depicted in Figure 4.8 where the equilibrium price and quantity are represented by P* and Q*, respectively.

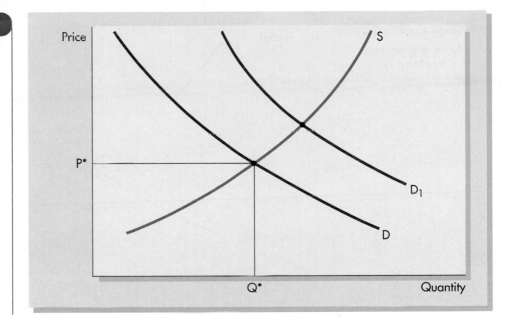

FIGURE 4.8

Supply and Demand Curves for a Product or Service

If the conditions of supply or demand change, the curves shift their positions and the market sets a new equilibrium price. Suppose, for example, buyers' preferences change so that they generally want more of the product at any price. Such a change is reflected in the diagram as a shift to the right of the demand curve to D_1. If supply doesn't change at the same time, the new equilibrium point will be higher along the supply curve, resulting in a higher P* and Q*.

Supply and Demand for Money

In the market for debt, people are borrowing and lending money rather than buying and selling a commodity. Instead of buyers we have borrowers, and instead of sellers we have lenders. It's important to understand that point. The supply curve in a debt market represents the willingness of people to lend money and the demand curve represents people's (companies') desire to borrow.

In the diagram for a debt market, the horizontal (quantity) axis is the amount borrowed in a time period. The vertical axis is the price of borrowing. *That price is interest.* You can think of borrowing as renting a lender's money for a period of time, and interest as the rent payment. It's customary to express this price of borrowing as the percentage of principal required for a one-year rental. That's simply the annual interest rate with which we're all familiar.

A supply and demand graph for a debt market is shown in Figure 4.9. The letter k is used to represent the interest rate. The debt securities in this market are called *bills, notes,* and *bonds,* depending on their term when initially issued. For convenience we'll just refer to them all as bonds.

Borrowers are companies and the government. They *sell* bonds. The downsloping demand curve indicates that they will borrow more (sell more bonds) if interest rates are low. Lenders are individuals and organizations that *buy* bonds. The upsloping supply curve indicates that they are willing to lend more (buy more bonds) when interest rates are high.

Don't be confused by the reversal of the traditional buy and sell roles in the market for debt. In the traditional supply and demand curve depicted in Figure 4.8,

● In debt markets **lenders represent supply** and **borrowers represent demand**.

● Interest is the **price** of money in a debt market.

● Borrowers **sell** bonds. Lenders **buy** bonds.

FIGURE 4.9

Supply and Demand Curves for Money (Debt)

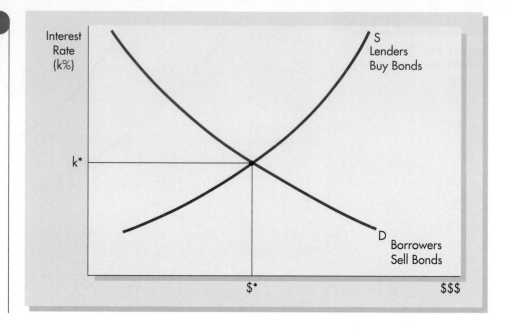

demanders do the buying and suppliers do the selling. Here demanders sell (borrow), while suppliers buy (lend). The reversal is just a result of the peculiar terminology of finance in which buying a bond means lending money.

The Determinants of Supply and Demand

When we described the supply and demand picture for a product or service we said that changes in conditions cause the curves to slide back and forth. The same is true in debt markets.

The demand for borrowed funds depends on the opportunities available to use those funds and the attitudes of people and businesses about doing things on credit. If people feel good about the economy and their futures, they'll be willing to buy houses, cars, vacations, and other things with borrowed money. Similarly, businesses will borrow for expansion and new projects if demand for their products is strong and they have confidence in the future. If these conditions aren't met, they'll borrow only what they have to.

The supply of loanable funds ultimately depends on what economists call the time preference for consumption of individuals. The time preference for consumption refers to whether a person is inclined to spend a dollar of income on current consumption or invest it to grow into something more. Most people have a definite preference for current consumption and spend most of their income as it's earned, saving only a fraction.

Remember that money saved by individuals becomes available for borrowing when people invest their savings in debt securities and savings accounts. So people's time preference for consumption dictates the level of their savings and therefore the supply of loanable funds. A decrease in the preference for current consumption, for example, leads to increased savings and an increase in the supply of debt. This is reflected in a rightward shift in the supply curve in Figure 4.9.

Changes in these conditions occur constantly throughout the economy, causing the supply and demand curves for borrowed money to slide back and forth over time. As a result, the market interest rate is moving up or down most of the time.

For most of the twentieth century movement was modest. The rates stayed at relatively low levels, about 3% to 6% until the early 1970s when the fluctuation became much more dramatic. In the early 1980s some rates exceeded 20%. In the 1990s and early 2000s, rates have again been low and stable. The ability to forecast interest rates would clearly be very valuable, but as yet no one has been able to do it with any consistency.

THE COMPONENTS OF AN INTEREST RATE

● Interest rates include **base rates** and **risk premiums**.

Any interest rate can be broken into two pieces, each of which can be further subdivided into components. Let's look at the two major pieces first.

All rates can be thought of as the sum of a base rate and a premium for risk borne by the lender. We'll represent the interest rate by the letter k, so we can write

(4.1) $$k = \text{base rate} + \text{risk premium} .$$

● COMPONENTS OF THE BASE RATE

● The base rate is **pure interest** plus **expected inflation**.

The base rate is the rate at which people lend money when there's no risk involved in the loan. It has two components, the **pure interest rate** and the expected rate of inflation over the life of the loan. The pure interest rate is also called the *earning power of money*. We'll use the symbols k_{PR} to denote that idea and INFL to represent the expected inflation rate. Then we can write

(4.2) $$\text{base rate} = k_{PR} + \text{INFL} .$$

The Pure Interest Rate

● The **pure interest rate** is the earning power of money.

The **pure interest rate** is more of an abstract concept than anything observable in the real world. It's the rate that would exist in a perfect economy in which there is no inflation, securities can always be sold quickly for their full value, and people always live up to their promises.

In another sense you can think of the pure rate as the average return that can be earned with money available for investment in business. Again the idea is unadjusted for inflation or risk. This is the sense in which we call the pure rate the basic earning power of money.

The pure rate can be thought of as compensation to lenders for the loss of the productive power of their money. It's generally taken to be between 2% and 4%.

The Inflation Adjustment

Inflation refers to a general increase in prices. We usually assume that the increase is uniform over all prices and wages although in reality some things inflate faster than others.

The key notion behind the idea of inflation is the cost of a particular bundle of goods. If the bundle costs $100 at the beginning of a year and prices inflate by 5% during the year, the same bundle will cost $105 at year end. In other words, $100 won't buy as much at the end of the year as it did in the beginning. Money will have lost some of its value.

Now imagine that you loaned someone $100 at 5% interest during a year in which the inflation rate was also 5%. Assume the loan is successfully paid off with interest so you have $105 at year end. Are you any better off than you were at the beginning of the year? The answer, of course, is no, because your year-end $105 won't buy any more than $100 bought before you made the loan. To come out ahead, you have to charge an interest rate that *exceeds* the inflation rate.

In fact, that's exactly what lenders do. Interest rates always include the anticipated inflation rate over the loan period as an add-on to the pure rate. That addition is reflected in the formulation of equation 4.2. INFL in the equation can be thought of as an inflation adjustment equal to the *average* inflation rate anticipated over the life of the loan.

● Interest rates include **estimates of average annual inflation** over loan periods.

RISK PREMIUMS

Risk in lending refers to the chance that a lender will receive less than the full value of the principal advanced plus the agreed interest in return for making a loan. In general, loans have varying degrees of risk. Some are very secure, so the chance of not being fully repaid is virtually zero. Others involve a substantial possibility that the lender will receive less than he or she bargained for.

Most lenders are willing to make loans that involve risk. However, they always demand compensation for bearing higher levels of risk. That simply means they want to be paid more for making a risky loan than for making a safe one. Because the payment lenders receive is interest, they demand more of it in the form of higher rates when making riskier loans.

● Lenders demand a **risk premium** of extra interest for making risky loans.

The difference between the interest rate charged on a given loan and the rate charged on a zero-risk loan is called the loan's **risk premium.** This idea is expressed in equation 4.1 where the base rate is implied to have zero risk.

Different Kinds of Lending Risk

We'll think of business loans as typically being made through bond issues. In that context, lenders face risks that come from several sources. The simplest to understand is default, which occurs when a borrower doesn't repay the obligation. Other risks are associated with bond prices.

When people lend by buying bonds they generally terminate their investments long before the bonds mature by selling them to other investors. This involves risk because the price at the time of sale may be different from the amount the investor paid for the bond. If the price is lower, selling will cause a loss. The situation is especially difficult if the lender has an immediate need for funds and has to get out of the investment quickly at whatever price is available.

The important point is that bond lending losses can be associated with fluctuations in the prices of bonds as well as with the failure of borrowers to repay the loans. In what follows we'll describe three sources of risk and formulate a distinct risk premium for each. The sum of these premiums will be the overall risk premium in equation 4.1. The three sources of risk are *default, liquidity,* and *maturity*.

Default Risk

● **Default risk** is the chance the lender won't pay principal or interest.

Default risk represents the chance that the borrower won't repay the entire obligation consisting of principal and interest. Losses due to default can be anywhere from the entire amount loaned to a fraction of the interest due. It's important to keep in mind that default isn't solely associated with failure to repay principal at the end of a loan's term. A borrower can default at any time by failing to pay periodic interest.

The size of the *default risk premium* demanded by lenders depends on their perception of the creditworthiness of the borrowing company. That perception is based on the firm's financial condition and its record of paying off its debts in the past. Premiums range from 0% to 6 or 8%. It's important to realize that default premiums don't increase without limit. When a company gets too risky it simply becomes unable to borrow at any interest rate.

Default most commonly occurs when business conditions deteriorate and borrowers don't have funds to service their debt. This doesn't always result in failure or a major loss. Temporarily delayed interest payments are fairly common when companies are in trouble.

Default doesn't actually have to occur for related problems to exist. Suppose a company borrows money through a bond issue and subsequently gets into financial trouble. Assume the loan principal isn't due and the firm continues to make the required interest payments, but financial analysts can tell that each payment is a close call. In other words, the company isn't in default, but its continuing ability to avoid default is in question. New investors would be very reluctant to buy the firm's bonds at full price. To sell, an individual holding such a bond would probably have to reduce its price to get out of the investment.

A time dimension also is involved in the risk of default. Suppose a large, strong company issues a one-year debt instrument. Investors considering the issue won't be concerned about default because a serious deterioration in the firm's financial condition is unlikely to occur in only one year. However, if the issue is a long-term bond, investors will be somewhat concerned because even the strongest companies can get into trouble over a long period.

This kind of thinking indicates that for strong companies, the default risk premium is very small for short-term debt but is significant for longer issues.

Liquidity Risk

Some companies' bonds are more difficult to sell than others even if there's nothing wrong with them. The debt of small firms that are not widely known can be particularly hard to market, because only investors who know the firm or its management will be interested in buying. Such bonds are said to be *illiquid*. The sellers must reduce their prices enough to interest buyers with no previous knowledge of the company. That's likely to mean taking a loss.

● **Liquidity risk** is associated with being unable to sell the bond of a little known issuer.

Liquidity risk refers to the chance of incurring that kind of loss, and the *liquidity risk premium* is extra interest demanded by lenders as compensation for bearing it.

Liquidity risk is somewhat variable with the term of the security. Very short-term obligations don't generally involve much liquidity risk, because a lender in need of funds can just wait out the period until maturity.

Maturity Risk

The primary reason for changes in bond prices is movement in the interest rate in the debt market. It is a fundamental principle of finance and economics that bond prices and interest rates move in opposite directions. We made a similar statement about stocks earlier, but the relation is more precise and predictable for bonds than for stocks.

At this point in our study we haven't developed enough knowledge to understand why this relationship between prices and interest rates occurs and exactly how it works. We'll gain a full understanding of the phenomenon when we study

Chapter 6. For now we have to accept two things. The first is what we've already said, that prices and rates move against each other. The second is that the price change associated with a given interest rate change is larger for bonds with a longer maturity (time to go until they are due to be repaid) than for bonds with a shorter maturity.

Let's be very clear about that second point. If a bond is due to mature in a short time, a change in the interest rate will have a small effect on its value. On the other hand, if the principal isn't to be repaid for many years, the same interest rate change will have a significant effect on the bond's value. The longer the maturity, the bigger the price change.

Price changes due to interest rate fluctuations are another source of risk for lenders who invest in bonds. If interest rates increase after an investor purchases a bond, its price will decline and the investor will take a loss if he or she has to get out of the investment quickly. If the bond's term is short, the loss is small and can almost be ignored. But if the security has a long maturity, the loss can be significant.

This means longer-term bonds are riskier for investors than shorter-term bonds. We call this idea **maturity risk** because it varies with the term or maturity of the bond. Investors demand a *maturity risk premium,* which ranges from virtually nothing for short-term instruments to 2% or more for longer-term issues. Slight variations on this idea are called **price risk** and **interest rate risk.**

It's important to notice that the loss we're talking about here doesn't occur if the investor holds the bond to maturity. It only happens if he or she has to sell early at a depressed price.

● **Maturity risk** arises because long-term bond prices change more with interest rate swings than short-term bond prices.

● PUTTING THE PIECES TOGETHER

We can now rewrite equation 4.1, substituting the elements we've discussed for the base rate and the risk premium.

(4.3) $$k = k_{PR} + INFL + DR + LR + MR$$

where: k_{PR} = pure interest rate

INFL = inflation adjustment (the average expected inflation rate over the life of the loan)

DR = default risk premium

LR = liquidity risk premium

MR = maturity risk premium

● The **interest rate model.**

This important equation says that an interest rate generally consists of the pure earning power of money, plus an allowance for inflation, plus an adjustment for each of three identifiable sources of risk.

We'll call equation 4.3 the *interest rate model,* meaning that it's an abstract portrayal of how interest rates work.

People often refer to k on the left side of the equation as the *nominal* or *quoted* interest rate. It's the market rate that we've been talking about all along.

Setting Interest Rates

It's important to understand that equation 4.3 represents a theoretical construct. People don't actually sit around thinking up how much each of the elements should be and then add them to come up with a rate to charge on a loan. Rates are set by the forces of supply and demand. If a particular lender doesn't feel the going rate is high enough, he or she simply doesn't invest.

The equation is an economic *model* of reality, an *explanation* of what generally has to be behind the interest rate given the needs of investors. However, like most economic models, it occasionally doesn't seem to be consistent with reality.

For example, at times a reasonable estimate of the pure rate plus the current inflation rate equals or exceeds the prevailing interest rate in some markets. That means the risk premiums in those markets must be zero or negative, which doesn't make a lot of sense.

The model is a way of thinking, a tool to aid our understanding. Occasionally things happen in the real world that aren't included in the model, and during those periods it doesn't quite work. But that's not a reason to condemn it as valueless.

FEDERAL GOVERNMENT SECURITIES, RISK-FREE AND REAL RATES

The interest rate model represented by equation 4.3 enables us to understand three special situations that are important in practical finance. We'll consider each in turn.

Federal Government Securities

Governmental bodies at all levels issue debt securities that are similar to those issued by companies. Cities, states, and the federal government issue long-term bonds, but the federal treasury also issues a great many short-term securities. Treasury bills have terms from 90 days to a year, while notes mature in 1 to 10 years.[4] The interest rate model, equation 4.3, can be applied to government debt as well as to corporate debt securities.

However, federal government debt has an important characteristic that isn't shared by anyone else's: There's no default risk associated with it. Therefore the default risk premium in equation 4.3 is zero when the model is applied to treasury securities.

It's tempting to think that the reason behind this confidence on the part of the investors is a belief that there will always be a federal government. (If there isn't, we won't be worried about money and interest rates anyway!) But the reason is more subtle. For example, as long as there's a federal government, we'd expect state governments to exist. Yet state default risks and the associated premiums are definitely not zero. Think about this for a moment before reading on. Can you figure out why the federal government can never default on a loan?

The answer lies in a power that the federal treasury keeps to itself. It can print money! No one else can. The federal government could pay off all of its debt by simply printing huge stacks of money. It doesn't do so because such an action would create a massive inflation that would terribly disrupt the economy, but the capability is always there. As a result, there's no chance of federal default.

As a practical matter, liquidity risk is also zero for federal debt. That's because there's always an active market in the federal government's obligations. The chance of being unable to sell a federal bond, note, or bill at the going price is very small. That statement definitely cannot be made for the securities of lower governmental units. In fact, a major problem with the obligations of local governments (cities, counties, etc.) is that they are often illiquid.

For info on government securities see
www.publicdebt.treas.gov/sec/sec.htm

● **Treasury (federal government) securities** are default and liquidity risk free.

---

4. The securities of the federal government are called *treasury* securities.

Maturity risk is not zero for government securities. It's the same as it is for any other borrower.

The Risk-Free Rate

The foregoing ideas give rise to the notion of a risk-free interest rate. This rate includes the pure rate and an allowance for inflation, but nothing for any of the risks we've been talking about.

● The **risk-free rate** is approximately the yield on short term treasury bills.

Noting that government debt has no default or liquidity risk, and that maturity risk is insignificantly small for short-term debt, we can surmise that short-term treasury securities are essentially risk free. In fact, people generally take the 90-day treasury bill rate to be the current **risk-free rate.**

Notice that the risk-free rate is the same as the base rate we used to introduce the idea of the components of interest (see equations 4.1 and 4.2). All interest rates are essentially the risk-free rate plus premiums for various risks.

The-risk free rate is an important idea in financial theory. It provides an alternative place for investors to put their money that's always available. In other words, if investors don't like the general opportunities available in debt markets, they can always park their money in short-term government securities until something more attractive comes along. It can also be viewed as a conceptual floor for the structure of interest rates. If investors can always get the risk-free rate without bearing risk, no investment that does have risk can offer a lower rate. When we encounter the risk-free rate, we'll denote it as k_{RF}.

The Real Rate of Interest

● **Real** interest rates have no adjustment for inflation.

In economics the term *real* refers to figures and statistics that are adjusted to remove the effects of inflation. The *real* interest rate is the rate that currently exists less the inflation adjustment. In terms of equation 4.3, INFL is zero.

The real interest rate tells investors if they're actually getting ahead. Suppose, for example, you invest some money in a long-term security at 8% interest. Several years later, you discover that the inflation rate has risen to 10%, and you're actually losing purchasing power on your investment at a rate of 2% per year.

This situation hasn't been unusual in the last 30 years. For that reason people have become reluctant to make long-term commitments at lower market rates. The solution has often been to make long-term contracts at variable interest rates that move up and down as the inflation rate and the nominal interest rate change.

There are also occasional periods in which the real interest rate is negative on most investment opportunities. That can happen because we don't really know what the rate of inflation is at a point in time until the government statistics come out several months later. If inflation rises rapidly while supply and demand forces push interest rates down, the actual interest rate can wind up below the inflation rate for some period. Obviously, when that happens the model expressed in equation 4.3 isn't working very well.

The Real Risk-Free Rate

Putting the last two concepts together results in the idea of a real risk-free rate, a term that is sometimes used in financial circles. "Real" implies the inflation adjustment is zero, and "risk free" implies that all the risk premiums are also zero.

Looking at the interest rate model, we can immediately see that the real risk-free rate is conceptually identical to the pure interest rate, k_{PR}.

EXAMPLE 4.1

You're a junior analyst in the treasury department of the Bullwork Company. The treasurer is contemplating raising money for a new plant expansion by issuing debt securities, but is unsure of the interest rates the company might have to pay. He has asked you to estimate the interest cost of issues with maturities ranging from 1 to 10 years.

You are aware that rates are actually set by supply and demand forces in the debt market, but feel the interest rate model (equation 4.3) will provide some reasonable estimates under normal conditions. The following assumptions seem to provide a reasonable starting point.

(a) The pure rate of interest is 3%.

(b) Inflation is expected to rise in the near future and then subside. Your favorite economist projects the following pattern.

Year	Inflation Rate
1	4%
2	6
3	8
4	6
5–10	5

(c) The default risk premium will be zero for one-year debt, but it will increase .2% for each additional year of term to a maximum of 1%.

(d) The liquidity premium is zero for one- and two-year debt and .5% for longer issues.

(e) The maturity risk premium is zero for a one-year term and increases by .3% for each additional year of term to a maximum of 2.5%

Prepare a table showing the projected interest rate for loans of various terms and the components of each rate.

Solution:

First we'll calculate the inflation adjustment for securities having terms from 1 to 10 years. That involves taking the average inflation rate over the entire projected term.

Year	Inflation Rate	Inflation Adjustment
1	4.0%	4.0%
2	6.0	5.0
3	8.0	6.0
4	6.0	6.0
5	5.0	5.8
6	5.0	5.7
7	5.0	5.6
8	5.0	5.5
9	5.0	5.4
10	5.0	5.4

Next we'll create a table with a column for each of the elements of the model and fill in each column according to the assumed behavior of the factor. The estimated interest rate is simply the sum of each row across the columns.

Term	k_{PR} +	INFL +	DR +	LR +	MR =	k
1	3.0	4.0	0.0	0.0	0.0	7.0%
2	3.0	5.0	0.2	0.0	0.3	8.5
3	3.0	6.0	0.4	0.5	0.6	10.5
4	3.0	6.0	0.6	0.5	0.9	11.0
5	3.0	5.8	0.8	0.5	1.2	11.3
6	3.0	5.7	1.0	0.5	1.5	11.7
7	3.0	5.6	1.0	0.5	1.8	11.9
8	3.0	5.5	1.0	0.5	2.1	12.1
9	3.0	5.4	1.0	0.5	2.4	12.3
10	3.0	5.4	1.0	0.5	2.5	12.4

Notice that the interest rate is higher for longer-term loans. That's the normal state of affairs, although sometimes the reverse is true. In this case the rising rate can be traced to the action of the risk factors. Each increases with increasing term for its own reason. The inflation factor has an unusual impact in this instance. It first rises and then falls away as the projected annual rates of inflation rise and then subside to a constant level.

YIELD CURVES—THE TERM STRUCTURE OF INTEREST RATES

As the example in the last section illustrates, interest rates generally vary with the term of the debt. The relationship is known as the *term structure of interest rates*.

A graphic portrayal of the term structure is known as a **yield curve. Yield** is simply another term for return or interest. Figure 4.10 shows two yield curves of different shapes.

Most of the time short-term rates are lower than long-term rates and the yield curve is upsloping to the right. This is called a *normal* yield curve because it is the most common. Sometimes, however, long rates are lower than short rates and the curve slopes downward. That's called an *inverted* yield curve.

A great deal of thought has gone into trying to explain the forces that drive the yield curve to take a particular shape. That is, why should long and short rates differ in either direction? Three explanations have emerged, all of which have some appeal.

The Expectations Theory

The **expectations theory** says that the curve slopes up or down on the basis of people's expectations about the general level of future interest rates. For example, suppose on a given day all interest rates are a uniform 5% regardless of term, and everyone expects them to stay there indefinitely. That means the yield curve is flat at 5%. Then imagine something happens to cause everyone to believe interest rates will increase to 10%, but only after remaining at 5% for two more years. Put yourself in the place of a lender under these conditions. You'd be willing to make a loan of up to two years at 5%, because that would be the pre-

The **yield curve** plots interest against term for otherwise similar loans. The **normal curve** slopes upward reflecting higher rates on longer loans.

Expectations theory: Today's rates rise or fall with term as future rates are expected to rise or fall.

FIGURE 4.10

Yield Curves

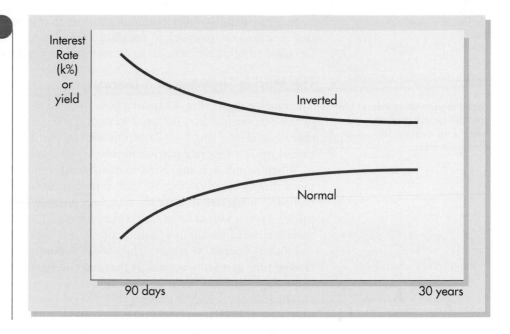

To learn more about interest rates and yield curves go to

www.smartmoney.com/ tools

vailing rate during that entire period. But would you make a three-year loan at 5%? Clearly you wouldn't, because in the third year you'd be stuck earning 5% on your money while everyone else is making 10%.

However, you might be willing to make the loan at a rate that reflects an average of two years at 5% and one year at 10%, [(5 + 5 + 10)/3 =] 6.67%. That way your overall yield would be the same as it would be if you'd made three one-year loans.

What if someone wanted to borrow for four years? You'd want a rate that averaged two 5% years and two 10% years for 7.5%. Notice that the average rate is increasing as the term of the loans increases and we get more 10% years into the calculation. That increase is the essence of an upward-sloping normal yield curve.

A variation on the expectations theory says that the shape of the curve depends on people's expectations about inflation. But because the inflation rate is a large part of the interest rate (see equation 4.3), expectations of increasing inflation are essentially equivalent to expectations of an increasing interest rate.

The Liquidity Preference Theory

● **Liquidity preference theory:** Investors prefer shorter term securities and must be induced to make longer loans.

The **liquidity preference theory** says that the yield curve should be upsloping because lenders generally prefer short-term loans. They're more liquid, making it easier to get invested cash back if you have to. As a result of that preference, there has to be an additional interest inducement to lend long term. Hence long rates will usually be higher, and the normal yield curve slopes up.

This argument involves two of the ideas we discussed in the development of the interest rate model of equation 4.3. One is the liquidity risk concept, that short-term loans are better for lenders because people can wait for maturity rather than selling their bonds. The second is the maturity risk idea, that short bonds are better for bondholders (lenders) because they are less subject to price variation due to interest rate movement. That makes them less risky and perhaps easier to sell.

In a nutshell, liquidity preference means that investors like short-term securities because they're easier to get out of in a hurry. Therefore longer-term securities have to offer higher rates to attract buyers (lenders).

The Market Segmentation Theory

● **Market segmentation theory:** Loan terms define independent segments of the debt market, which set separate rates.

The **market segmentation theory** goes back to the forces of supply and demand in the market for debt pictured in Figure 4.9. It says that the debt market isn't represented by a single set of supply and demand curves, but by many sets, each representing a separate market for money of a specific term.

When people are interested in borrowing money, they have a definite term in mind that is based on the use they intend to make of the funds. For example, a company interested in building a factory wouldn't want to fund it by borrowing for 90 days; it would be in the market for a very long-term loan. If it couldn't get that, it wouldn't want any loan at all.

Lenders operate similarly. They want to commit their funds for a definite period of time at a known yield. If they have long-term money available, they don't want short-term borrowers.

This results in a debt market that's *segmented* by term. Each segment has its own supply and demand picture with an independent set of forces pushing the curves back and forth. That means the market interest rate in each segment is independently determined, and not related to the market rate in other segments.

This independence leads to a pattern of rates that just happens. Most of the time market forces are such that short rates are lower than long rates and the yield curve takes its normal upsloping shape. However, at times independent market forces push short rates higher and the yield curve slopes down.

APPENDIX 4-A

Can There Be Interest without Money? The Desert Island

We've just concluded a discussion of the nature of interest in the context of a society that has a well-developed financial system. In what we've said, interest seems to be entirely wound up with money. But does there have to be money for interest, or a concept like interest, to exist? Would some or all of the ideas underlying interest exist if we lived in a primitive world without money? Let's explore that question with a story about being stranded on a desert island where there is no money. We'll gain some basic insights into the ideas we've been talking about that are well worth the time we'll spend.

On a Desert Island

Imagine that Rob Carusoe is a successful businessperson taking a well-deserved ocean cruise in the South Pacific. During a lifeboat drill Rob is separated from the other passengers and crew, and through no fault of his own finds himself adrift in a small rubber raft. Fortunately, he drifts ashore on an uncharted island after only a day on the raft. He's stranded!

Suppose the climate on the island is very pleasant, so Rob has little or no need for shelter or protective clothing. And after a little exploration, he finds a natural spring that provides all the water he needs.

Food, however, is something of a problem. The only edible item on the island turns out to be a certain palm root that Rob learned about from a PBS special when he was in high school and had time to watch TV. Unfortunately, it grows underground and has to be dug up. Because he was cast ashore with nothing but the clothes on his back, Rob has to dig up his food with his bare hands, which isn't very efficient.

After a few days, it becomes apparent that Rob has to spend all his time digging just to get enough to eat. In other words, one full day's labor spent in food production supplies his consumption need for just about one day. This doesn't mean that he'll starve instantly if he doesn't work all day every day, but in general he has no time for leisure and no ability to make anything extra. Life is pretty dull.

Making a Tool

One day Rob gets an idea. He could dig a lot more effectively if he had a tool, in particular a shovel. Looking around, he notices some flat rocks that might serve as a shovel blade, some bamboo stalks that would do as a handle, and some vines that might be used to fasten the two together. However, because he has no other tools with which to make the shovel, it's obvious that it's going to take a long time to fashion it by hand, say five whole days.

This presents a problem. Rob has to dig up roots every day to get enough to eat, so building a shovel means spending at least some time hungry. After due consideration, he decides it's worth the sacrifice and begins spending every second afternoon building the implement. At that rate, 20 partially starved days must elapse before he has anything to show for his efforts. This represents quite a bit of suffering, but in the end the task is complete and Rob is shovel-equipped.

Life with Tools—Savings and Investment

Rob begins to use the shovel on the twenty-first day and discovers that he can dig twice as fast with it as without it. (It's a crude shovel.) That makes his life on the island a lot better. Now he has some choices. He can work as hard as before and eat twice as much. Or he can eat as much as before by working half the time. This option gives him some leisure. Of course, any combination in between is also possible.

Let's digress for a moment and apply some economic terminology to what's been going on. Notice that the shovel is a piece of *capital equipment,* a tool or implement that makes production more effective. Further, Rob *invested* his *savings* to make it.

We normally think of savings as income that's not consumed. In this case Rob saved productive capacity by not digging food during every second afternoon. That saving represents a sacrifice in that he could have eaten more, but he elected not to. He was willing to forgo current consumption to devote resources to something else. That's what saving is.

The saved labor resource was invested in producing the shovel. Investment means spending resources on something that's expected to produce more in the future rather than on something that will be consumed and then be gone. Rob used his savings to invest in the shovel.

A New Arrival—And a Request to Borrow

Now let's return to the island and imagine that Rob has been using his shovel and enjoying a better life for some time. Then imagine that one morning a great event occurs. Another castaway washes up on the island several hundred yards down the beach. We'll call the newcomer Joe. While reasonably civil, Joe turns out to be something of a loner. He sets up some distance from Rob's camp and seems determined to remain by himself.

Rob watches Joe scratch out a hand-to-mouth existence digging roots by hand, while Joe watches Rob living much better with the aid of his shovel. This goes on for several weeks.

Finally, Joe shows up at Rob's camp with a request (and the point of our story). He wants to *borrow* Rob's shovel.

The Cost of Borrowed Shovels

Rob isn't entirely opposed to the idea but feels that if he does lend, some compensation is in order. (The compensation could be paid in food or in labor services.) The key question is, what things should Rob demand compensation for before lending?

Thinking about it, he comes up with the following ideas.

1. He has to receive the incremental productive power of the shovel in his own hands—that is, the amount of extra food he can produce with the shovel as opposed to the amount he can produce without it. If he doesn't get that, he's back where he was originally. (Notice that for borrowing to make sense for Joe, he would have to be able to produce more than Rob can with the shovel.)

2. Next, Rob worries that he might not get the shovel back. Joe might break it, lose it, disappear with it, or just refuse to return it. He feels he should get something for bearing this risk.

3. Finally, Rob is concerned that the shovel may be somewhat worn out when it's returned—not broken, but worth less than when it was lent. We'd normally use the term "depreciated" to describe this idea, but on the island we'll just say "reduced in value." Rob wants to be paid for any reduction in value his shovel suffers while being used by Joe.

The exact amount of these items isn't important. It's the concepts that count. Rob will demand rent for his shovel made up of amounts related to the three items above.

Tying Back to Interest

Now let's go back to the interest rate model expressed in equation 4.3 and conceptually relate Rob's three requirements to the five elements of the model. We'll rewrite 4.3 here for convenience.

(4.3) $$k = k_{PR} + INFL + DR + LR + MR$$

where:

k_{PR} = pure interest rate

INFL = inflation adjustment

DR = default risk premium

LR = liquidity risk premium

MR = maturity risk premium

Rob's first requirement, the incremental productive power of the shovel, is exactly the idea behind the pure interest rate. It's the amount you can earn with the resource, shovel or money, if you keep it and use it yourself.

Rob's second concern, compensation for the chance of losing the shovel altogether, is just like the idea of default risk in the model. If the borrowing company defaults severely, the lender can lose everything just as Rob can lose everything if Joe takes a hike to the other side of the island with the shovel.

Rob's third worry is that the shovel might be worn out or reduced in value upon its return. That's exactly what happens to money in inflationary times; it loses its value. Dollars returned after a year of inflation buy less than the dollars lent in the beginning of the year. So Rob's third issue is just like the inflation adjustment in the model.

The last two elements in the model are also analogous to the idea of a reduction in value. Both liquidity risk and maturity risk involve price reductions if a lender has to get out of a loan quickly by selling it to another investor. If that happens, borrowers' obligations in lenders' hands are worth less money, and a reduction in value has occurred. LR and MR are actually premiums for bearing the risk of that happening, but the analogy is still quite close.

Conclusion

The point of our story is that when we pick interest apart into its component pieces, we see that it's more basic than money. Interest really involves control over the productive power of resources as well as the ideas of capital, investment, and saving, all overlaid by the concept of risk. These ideas are more fundamental than money. Of course interest relates to money, but only because money represents control over resources in an advanced economy.

DISCUSSION QUESTIONS

1. Describe the sectors into which economists divide an industrialized economy and outline the financial flows between them.

2. What do we mean when we say businesses spend two kinds of money? Where does each kind come from? How is each used?

3. What is the primary purpose of financial markets?

4. Define the following terms: primary market, secondary market, capital market, money market.

5. Harry, a friend of yours, is taking a course in economics, and has become confused by some of the terminology because of the way people commonly use the same words. The economics professor says investment occurs when companies buy equipment and build factories. Yet Harry has always heard people talk about investing as a method of saving when they put money in the bank or purchase securities. He's confused by these dissimilar uses of the word and has asked you to explain. After asking for your help, Harry happily states that there's one thing he does understand perfectly about what the econ prof says, and that is "savings equals investment." Because investing in stocks and bonds is also saving money, it's obvious that savings equals investment! Write a brief explanation to help Harry out.

6. What's the difference between a direct and an indirect transfer of money between investors and firms?

7. Brokers and mutual funds do the same thing: invest your money for you. Is that statement true or false? Explain. What kind of financial institution is a mutual fund? What is its distinguishing feature? Describe how savings banks and insurance companies are similar to mutual funds.

8. Your friend Sally just returned from a trip to New York where she was very impressed by a visit to the stock market. Is it correct to say that she visited the stock market? What exactly did Sally visit? Is there more than one place in New York that she might have visited? Explain exactly what the stock market is and how it's related to what Sally visited.

9. Describe the process that occurs when an investor places an order with a broker to buy or sell stocks.

10. Your friend Charlie is excited about a newly issued stock. You've looked at the company's prospectus and feel it's a very risky venture. You told Charlie your opinion, and he said he wasn't worried because the stock has been approved by the SEC and therefore must be OK. Write a paragraph to help Charlie out. What is the main thrust of federal securities regulation?

11. Describe insider trading. Why is it illegal?

12. Explain the following terms: privately held company, publicly traded company, listed company, OTC market, IPO, prospectus, and red herring.

13. Define term and maturity. Is there a difference?

14. Interest is said to drive the stock market. But interest is paid on bonds and loans, while stocks pay dividends, never interest. It would seem that interest has nothing to do with the stock market. Explain this apparent contradiction.

15. Discuss the similarities and differences between supply and demand for a good (product or service) and supply and demand in a money (debt) market.

16. Briefly explain the idea of representing an interest rate as a collection of components. What is represented by the base rate? What is the risk premium for? Explain the idea of risk in lending.

17. Why is inflation important to lenders? How do they take it into consideration?

18. Explain the nature of the potential lending losses associated with each of the following: default risk, liquidity risk, maturity risk.

19. Do all loans have default, liquidity, and maturity risk more or less equally? Are some types of loans relatively free of some risks? Is the debt of a particular organization free of certain risks? If so, explain who, what, and why.

20. Explain the ideas of a risk-free rate and the real rate of interest. Are either of them approximated by anything that exists in the real world?

21. Does the so-called risk-free rate actually have some risk? (This is a tough question that isn't discussed in the chapter. Think about what makes up the risk-free rate and what among those pieces is an estimate of the future.)

22. What is a yield curve? Briefly outline three theories that purport to explain its shape. How does the yield curve influence the behavior of lenders?

23. The concept of interest is grounded in money. Without money there could be no interest. Is this statement true or false? Explain and discuss. (This question is based on Appendix 4-A.)

24. Your Aunt Sally has a large portfolio of corporate bonds of different maturities. She has asked your advice on whether to buy more or get rid of some. You anticipate an increase in interest rates in the near future. How would you advise her? Would your advice depend on the maturity of individual bonds?

PROBLEMS

1. Adams Inc. recently borrowed money for one year at 9%. The pure rate is 3%, and Adams's financial condition warrants a default risk premium of 2% and a liquidity risk premium of 1%. There is little or no maturity risk in one-year loans. What inflation rate do lenders expect next year?

2. Mountain Sports Inc. borrowed money for two years last week at 12%. The pure rate is 2%, and Mountain's financial condition warrants a default risk premium of 3% and a liquidity risk premium of 2%. The maturity risk premium for two-year loans is 1%. Inflation is expected to be 3% next year. What does the interest rate model imply the lender expects the inflation rate to be in the following year?

3. The Habender Company just issued a two-year bond at 12%. Inflation is expected to be 4% next year and 6% the year after. Habender estimates its default risk premium at about 1.5% and its maturity risk premium at about .5%. Because it's a relatively small and unknown firm, its liquidity risk premium is about 2% even on relatively short debt like this. What pure interest rate is implied by these assumptions?

4. Charles Jackson, the founder and president of the Jackson Company, is concerned about his firm's image in the financial community. The concern arose when he went to the bank for a one-year loan and was quoted a rate of 12%, which was considerably more than the firm had been paying recently. He has asked you, the treasurer, for an analysis that could shed some light on what might be causing the bank to ask for such a high rate.

Your research indicates the following. The economy is stable with a 3% inflation rate that isn't expected to change in the near future. The local banking community consistently considers the pure interest rate to be about 4%. Liquidity risk for companies of Jackson's size and reputation is generally not more than 1%, and maturity risk is virtually zero for one-year loans. In the past Jackson's reputation has warranted a low default risk premium of 2%. The firm's financial condition has been stable for some time. Two months ago Jackson had a major dispute with one of its suppliers. Charles refused to pay for a large shipment due to poor quality. The vendor did not agree and claimed that Jackson was just using the quality issue to avoid paying its bills.

5. Use the interest rate model to solve the following problem. One-year treasury securities are yielding 12% and two-year treasuries yield 14%. The maturity risk premium is zero for one-year debt and 1% for two-year debt. The real risk-free rate is 3%. What are the expected rates of inflation for the next two years? (*Hint:* Set up a separate model for each term with the yearly inflation rates as unknowns.)

6. Inflation is expected to be 5% next year and a steady 7% each year thereafter. Maturity risk premiums are zero for one-year debt but have an increasing value for longer debt. One-year government debt yields 9%, whereas two-year debt yields 11%.

  a. What is the real risk-free rate and the maturity risk premium for two-year debt?

  b. Forecast the nominal yield on one- and two-year government debt issued at the beginning of the second year.

7. The interest rate outlook for Montrose Inc., a large, financially sound company, is reflected in the following information.

  • The pure rate of interest is 4%.

  • Inflation is expected to increase in the future from its current low level of 2%. Predicted annual inflation rates follow.

Year	Inflation Rate
1	2%
2	3
3	4
4	5
5–20	6

  • The default risk premium will be .1% for one-year debt, but will increase by .1% for each additional year of term to a maximum of 1%.

  • The liquidity premium is zero for one- and two-year debt, .5% for three-, four-, and five-year terms, and 1% for longer issues.

  • The maturity risk premium is zero for a one-year term and increases by .2% for each additional year of term to a maximum of 2%.

a. Use the interest rate model to estimate market rates on the firm's debt securities of the following terms: 1 to 5 years, 10 years, and 20 years.

b. Plot a yield curve for the firm's debt.

c. Using different colors on the same graph, sketch yield curves for

    i. federal government debt and

    ii. Shaky Inc., a firm currently in financial difficulty.

d. Explain the pattern of deviation from Montrose's yield curve for each of the others.

 Internet Problem

8. Go to http://www.nyse.com for a tour of the New York Stock Exchange.

a. Go to *About the NYSE.* Click on *Education* and then *Educational Publications,* and next *You and the Investment World.* Go to Chapter 3, *How the New York Stock Exchange Operates,* and page through the text. How many seats are there on the NYSE? How much does a seat on the exchange cost? Write a paragraph or two describing the job of a specialist.

b. Go back to the home page and click on *Market Regulation* and *Surveillance.* Write a paragraph or two describing Stock Watch.

c. Get an *International View* of the Exchange. Print the listing of Non-U.S. Listed Companies.

PART TWO

Discounted Cash Flow and the Value of Securities

CHAPTER 5

Time Value of Money

Chapter Outline

The time value of money is based on the idea that a sum of money in your hand today is worth more than the same sum promised at some time in the future, even if you're absolutely certain to receive the future cash.

The idea is pretty easy to grasp if you think in terms of having a bank account and being promised an amount of money a year from now. Money in the bank earns interest, so it grows over time. The value today of the sum promised in one year is an amount that will grow into that sum if deposited in the bank now. In other words, a sum promised in a year is worth only as much as you'd have to put in the bank today to have that sum in a year.

That value obviously depends on the interest rate the bank is paying. The higher the interest rate, the faster money grows, so the less you'd have to deposit today to get a given amount next year.

Let's look at an example using a future amount of $1,000. How much would a promise of $1,000 in one year be worth today if the bank paid 5% interest? That question is equivalent to asking how much money will grow into $1,000 in one year at 5% interest. The answer is $952.38; we'll worry about how we got it a little later. The important thing to understand now is that if we deposit $952.38 for one year, we'll earn interest of 5% of that amount,

$$\$952.38 \times .05 = \$47.62 ,$$

which when added to the original deposit yields $1,000.

$$\$952.38 + \$47.62 = \$1,000.00$$

Therefore, a guaranteed promise of $1,000 in a year is worth $952.38 today *if* the interest rate is 5%.

We say that $952.38 is the **present value** of $1,000 in one year at 5%. Alternatively, we say that $1,000 is the **future value** of $952.38 after one year at 5%.

If the interest rate were 7%, the present value of $1,000.00 in one year would be $934.58, a smaller number:

$$\$934.58 \times .07 = \$65.42$$

and

$$\$934.58 + \$65.42 = \$1,000.00.$$

In other words, a higher rate of interest makes the present value of a future amount smaller. This makes sense; the bank deposit is earning faster, so you don't have to put as much in to get to the desired amount at the end of the year.

The time value of money is one of the most important principles in finance and economics today. It's based on the simple ideas we've just stated, but the applications can get quite complicated as we'll see later in this chapter.

The subject can also be called **discounted cash flow,** abbreviated as DCF. Using that terminology in our first example, we would say the $952.38 is the *discounted* value of the $1,000.

Here's another way of looking at the same thing. Suppose you have a firm, written contract promising to pay you $1,000 in one year's time, but you need as much cash as you can get today. You could take the contract, called a note, to a bank, which would **discount** it for you at whatever interest rate it charges. If the bank's interest rate was 5%, it would give you $952.38 for the note. If the rate was 7%, the bank would be willing to give you only $934.58.

● The **present value** of a sum at a future time is the amount that must be deposited at interest today to have the sum at that time.

● The **discounted** value of a sum is its present value.

OUTLINE OF APPROACH

Our study of time value will involve learning to deal with *amounts* and *annuities.* An amount problem is similar to what we've already been talking about, involving a single amount of money that grows at interest over time into a larger sum. An annuity problem deals with a stream of equal payments, each of which is placed at interest and grows over time.

We'll further divide each of these categories into two more. Within each we'll look at situations dealing with present values and those dealing with future values.

In all we'll be looking at four types of problems.

amount—present value

amount—future value

annuity—present value

annuity—future value

After we've mastered these, we'll put the techniques together and work with some relatively complicated compound problems.

MATHEMATICS   As we approach each of the four categories, we'll develop a formula suited to doing that type of problem. The algebra needed to develop the formula may look a little intimidating to readers who aren't strong in math.

Don't be alarmed. The math required to do the financial problems once you accept the formula is quite simple. Developing the formulas is background that's good to know, but you don't have to remember it to do the practical work.

TIME LINES   Students sometimes find time value problems confusing. The time line is a graphic device that helps keep things straight. Time is divided into periods and portrayed along a horizontal line. Time zero is the present, and we count periods to the right.

● A **time line** is a graphic portrayal of a time value problem.

Time 1 is the *end* of the first period, time 2 the end of the second, and so on. We can make notations above and below the time line to keep track of various pieces of the problem we're working on, such as interest rates and amounts. For example, a time line for the illustration we talked about before would look like this.

Most people don't need time lines for simple situations like this one, but the devices can help a lot in more complicated problems. We'll use them where appropriate as we go forward. We'll begin with yearly periods, but later we will introduce shorter spans.

A NOTE ABOUT THE EXAMPLES   Several of the examples in this chapter are used to teach important financial practices as well as to illustrate computational techniques. You should be sure to learn and understand the business situations described in each of these illustrations. The first one you'll encounter is in Example 5.2, which describes the equivalence of deferred payment terms and a cash discount.

AMOUNT PROBLEMS

Amount problems involve a single sum of money that can be thought of as moving back and forth through time under the influence of interest. As it moves into the future, the sum gets larger as it earns interest. Conversely, as it moves back in time, the sum gets smaller. We'll begin with future value-oriented situations.

● THE FUTURE VALUE OF AN AMOUNT

To find the future value of an amount, we need a convenient way to calculate how much a sum of money placed at interest will grow into in some period of time. Let's start with a simple situation. Suppose we invest a sum of money in the bank at interest rate k. How much will it be worth at the end of one year?

Call the sum today PV, for present value, and the amount we'll have at the end of the year FV_1, for future value in one year (k is the decimal equivalent of the interest rate—.05 for 5%).

At the end of a year we'll have the amount originally invested, PV, plus the interest on that amount, kPV. So we can write

$$FV_1 = PV + kPV .$$

Factor PV out of the right side, and we have

(5.1) $$FV_1 = PV(1 + k) .$$

Now suppose we leave FV_1 in the bank for another year, and we want to know how much we'll have at the end of that second year. We'd call that FV_2. The second year's calculation will be the same as the one we just did, but we'll use FV_1 instead of PV.

$$FV_2 = FV_1 + kFV_1$$

Factor out FV_1.

$$FV_2 = FV_1 (1 + k)$$

Now substitute for FV_1 from equation 5.1 to get

$$FV_2 = PV(1 + k)(1 + k) ,$$

(5.2) $$FV_2 = PV(1 + k)^2 .$$

Notice the similarity between equations 5.1 and 5.2. FV_1 is equal to PV times $(1 + k)$ to the *first* power, while FV_2 is PV times $(1 + k)$ to the *second* power. It's easy to see that if we performed the same calculation for a third year, FV_3 would be equal to PV times $(1 + k)$ to the *third* power, and so on for as many years into the future as we'd care to go.

We can *generalize* the relationship and write

(5.3) $$FV_n = PV(1 + k)^n$$

for any value of n. This expression gives us a very convenient way to calculate the future value of any present amount given that we know the interest rate, k, and the number of years the money is invested, n.

For example, if we deposited $438 at 6% interest for five years, how much would we have? Using equation 5.3 gives

$$FV_5 = \$438(1.06)^5$$

Raising 1.06 to the fifth power on a calculator gives 1.3382, so

$$FV_5 = \$438(1.3382)$$

$$= \$586.13.$$

The only messy part of the calculation is raising 1.06 to the fifth power. Looking at equation 5.3, we can see that calculating $(1 + k)^n$ will always be tedious, especially for larger values of n.

However, notice that the value of $(1 + k)^n$ depends only on the sizes of k and n, and that in business situations these variables take on a relatively limited number of values. Therefore, it's feasible to make up a table that contains the value of $(1 + k)^n$ for common combinations of k and n. We'll call $(1 + k)^n$ the *future*

TABLE 5.1	**The Future Value Factor for k and n $FVF_{k,n} = (1 + k)^n$**						
				k			
n	1%	2%	3%	4%	5%	6%	. . .
1	1.0100	1.0200	1.0300	1.0400	1.0500	1.0600	. . .
2	1.0201	1.0404	1.0609	1.0816	1.1025	1.1236	. . .
3	1.0303	1.0612	1.0927	1.1249	1.1576	1.1910	. . .
4	1.0406	1.0824	1.1255	1.1699	1.2155	1.2625	. . .
5	1.0510	1.1041	1.1593	1.2167	1.2763	1.3382	. . .
6	1.0615	1.1262	1.1941	1.2653	1.3401	1.4185	. . .
⋮	⋮	⋮	⋮	⋮	⋮	⋮	

● The **future value factor** for k and n is the calculated value of $(1 + k)^n$.

value factor for k and n, and write it as $FVF_{k,n}$ Table 5.1 is a partial table of values for this factor. A more extensive version is given in Appendix A-1 for use in solving problems.

We can now rewrite equation 5.3 in a more convenient form by referring to the table.

(5.4) $$FV_n = PV[FVF_{k,n}] .$$

EXAMPLE 5.1

How much will $850 be worth if deposited for three years at 5% interest?

Solution: To solve the problem, write equation 5.4 and substitute the amounts given.

$$FV_n = PV[FVF_{k,n}]$$

$$FV_3 = \$850[FVF_{5,3}]$$

Look up $FVF_{5,3}$ in the three-year row under the 5% column of Table 5.1, getting 1.1576, and substitute.

$$FV_3 = \$850[1.1576]$$

$$= \$983.96$$

Problem-Solving Techniques

● In time value problems, **three** of four variables are **given**, and **we solve for the fourth**.

Equation 5.4 is the first of four formulas that you will use to solve a variety of time value problems. Each equation contains four variables. In this case the variables are PV, FV_n, k, and n. Every problem will give you three of the variables and ask you to find the fourth.

If you're asked to find PV or FV_n, the solution is very easy. Simply look up the factor for the given k,n combination in the table, and substitute in the equation along with the given PV or FV_n. The last problem gave us PV and asked for FV_n. Here's one that gives us the future value and requires us to find the present value.

EXAMPLE 5.2

Ed Johnson sold 10 acres of land to Harriet Smith for $25,000. The terms of the agreement called for Harriet to pay $15,000 down and $5,000 a year for two years. What was the real purchase price if the interest rate available to Ed on invested money is 6%?

Solution: What Ed is getting today is $15,000 plus the present value of two $5,000 payments, each to be received at different times in the future. The problem is to compute these PVs and add them to the $15,000.

The present value of the payment due at the end of the first year is calculated by writing equation 5.4 and substituting the known elements.

$$FV_n = PV[FVF_{k,n}]$$

$$\$5,000 = PV[FVF_{6,1}]$$

Table 5.1 or Appendix A-1 gives $FVF_{6,1} = 1.0600$. Substitute and solve for PV.

$$\$5,000 = PV[1.0600]$$

$$PV = \$4,716.98$$

The second calculation is the same, but the payment is two years away, so we use $FVF_{6,2} = 1.1236$. That gives a present value of $4,449.98.

In a present value sense, the actual sale amount is the sum of these two PVs and the down payment,

$$\$15,000.00 + \$4,716.98 + \$4,449.98 = \$24,166.96.$$

That's $833.04 less than the $25,000 price quoted.

In real estate finance we would say that the *terms of sale* resulted in an effective price reduction of $833.04, even though the real estate records would indicate a transaction price of $25,000. Terms of sale state when and how the purchase price has to be paid. The seller's willingness to accept part of the price later is worth a specific amount of money. In other words, it is the equivalent of a cash discount.

The Opportunity Cost Rate

Notice that in the last problem we calculated the present values by using the interest rate available to the seller, 6%, even though nothing was actually invested at that or any other rate. We used the 6% rate because if the seller had received the full price at the time of sale, he would have been able to invest the deferred payments at that rate. Therefore, in a sense, he lost the income from that investment by giving the deferred payment terms.

● The **opportunity cost** of a resource is the benefit that would have been available from its next best use.

We say that the lost interest income is the *opportunity cost* of giving the discount. In this case, because the seller's alternative is stated as a rate of interest at which he could have invested, we call it the *opportunity cost rate*.

The opportunity cost concept is a bit slippery. For example, you could argue that Ed Johnson might not have been able to sell the property to anyone without giving the deferred terms or an equivalent discount, and therefore there wasn't really any cost to the deferred terms at all. Nevertheless, we still say that the opportunity cost rate from Johnson's viewpoint is 6%.

The opportunity cost rate frequently isn't the same to different parties in the same transaction. In Example 5.2, Ed Johnson's opportunity cost rate is 6%, because that's the rate at which he can invest. But suppose Harriet Smith has to borrow to pay for the land and that she must do so at a rate of 10%. Her opportunity cost rate is then 10%, not 6%. To her the deferred payment terms are worth a discount of $1,322.32, quite a bit more than what they implicitly cost Ed Johnson. (Verify this by calculating the effective price at 10% as we did in the example at 6%.)

In this example the deferred terms are a pretty good deal. They're worth more to the recipient than to the donor!

In general, the opportunity cost of using a resource in some way is the amount it could earn in the next best use.

FINANCIAL CALCULATORS

Financial calculators take most of the drudgery out of time value problems. They work directly with mathematical relationships like equation 5.3 rather than with tables.

There's a temptation to skip the mathematical work we've been doing here and go directly to using a calculator without mastering the algebraic approach. That's a big mistake. If you go straight to the calculator, you'll never truly understand what's behind time value or be comfortable with it. Certainly in practice we use calculators almost exclusively, but it's very important to know what's behind the numbers that flash on the display.

In the rest of this chapter we'll concentrate on the approach we've been developing that uses financial tables, but we'll also show calculator solutions in the page margins.

How to Use a Typical Financial Calculator in Time Value

Recall that there are four variables in any time value problem. Values for three are given, and the fourth is unknown. Financial calculators have a key for each variable. To use a calculator, enter the three known variables, pressing the appropriate key after each input. Then press a compute key, followed by the key for the unknown variable. The calculator responds by displaying the answer.

There are actually five time value keys, because annuities require one that isn't used in the amount problems we've looked at so far. When we solve a problem, we use four keys and zero, or ignore, the fifth. The keys selected tell the calculator which kind of problem is being done. The time value keys and their meanings are as follows.

> **http://**
>
> Some web sites have present/future value calculators, such as the one at
> ● www.ssfcu.org/tools.htm

n	—Number of time periods
I/Y	—Interest rate (other labels: %i, I/YR, I% YR)
PV	—Present value
FV	—Future value
PMT	—Payment

The last key is the periodic payment associated with an annuity. We'll talk about it later when we get to annuities. For now it should be ignored (if you clear the time value registers before starting) or set to zero.

The compute key is usually labeled either CPT or 2nd. On some calculators there isn't a compute key; the calculator just knows the last key hit is the unknown.

Before trying a problem, take a look at your calculator's instruction manual. You may have to get into a particular mode of operation and clear the time value registers before starting. Advanced calculators also have a feature regarding the interest rate that needs to be set properly. They take the interest rate input and automatically divide it by a number of compounding periods per year. The default setting is usually 12, for 12 months a year. We'll get into non-annual compounding periods later. For now, set the calculator for one (1) period per year.

Now solve Example 5.1, using your calculator. Here's how.

1. The problem runs for three years. Enter 3 and then press n.
2. The interest rate is 5%. Enter 5 and then press I/Y.
3. The present value is $850. Enter 850 and then press PV.
4. Press 2nd or CPT (if necessary) and then press FV.
5. The calculator displays 983.98 or −983.98.

Some calculators use a sign convention intended to reflect inflows as positive numbers and outflows as negatives. For example, if PV is entered as a positive, FV shows up as a negative. The idea is that PV is a deposit and FV is a withdrawal.

Notice that a calculator solution may be a little off a table solution because the table only carries four decimal places. The calculator carries 12 or more significant digits. Also notice that the interest rate is generally entered as a whole number even though the equations work with the decimal form.

In the remainder of this chapter we'll show abbreviated calculator solutions for examples in the margins. Here's an illustration showing the first $5,000 payment in Example 5.2.

Key	Input
n	1
I/Y	6
FV	5,000
PMT	0
	Answer
PV	4,716.98

● THE EXPRESSION FOR THE PRESENT VALUE OF AN AMOUNT

Notice that we are able to use equation 5.4 to solve problems asking for *either* the present value or the future value. However, the expression is set up to make the future value calculation a little easier, because FV_n is isolated on the left side.

For convenience, we can develop another equation that's oriented toward solving the present value problem. We'll begin with equation 5.3,

$$FV_n = PV(1 + k)^n.$$

Now simply solve for PV by dividing through by $(1 + k)^n$ and switching the terms to opposite sides.

(5.5) $$PV = FV_n \frac{1}{(1 + k)^n}$$

Slightly more sophisticated mathematical notation enables us to write the same thing with a negative exponent.

(5.6)
$$PV = FV_n(1 + k)^{-n}$$

The term $(1 + k)^{-n}$ can be thought of as a factor depending only on k and n that can be tabulated. We'll call that factor the **present value factor for k and n** and write it as $PVF_{k,n}$. The values of $PVF_{k,n}$ are given in Appendix A-2. We can now rewrite equation 5.6 by using this factor and reference to the table.

(5.7)
$$PV = FV_n[PVF_{k,n}]$$

We use this expression and the associated table just like we used equation 5.4. It too can be used to solve for either present or future values, but it is more conveniently formulated for present values. Do Example 5.2 on your own using equation 5.7.

The Relation between the Future and Present Value Factors

● The future and present value factors are **reciprocals**. **Either** amount equation can be used to solve any amount problem.

It's important to notice that equations 5.4 and 5.7 really express the same relationship, since they both come from equation 5.3. It's also important to realize that the present and future value factors are reciprocals of one another. That is,

(5.8)
$$FVF_{k,n} = \frac{1}{PVF_{k,n}} .$$

More on Problem-Solving Techniques

● Solving for **k or n** involves searching a table.

So far we've looked at problems that ask us to solve for FV_n or PV. When the unknown element in the equation is k or n, the approach is a little different. Notice that in both equations 5.4 and 5.7, k and n appear as subscripts on the factors referring to table values. That means we can't use traditional algebraic methods to solve for an unknown k or n.

We'll change Example 5.1 a little to illustrate what we mean. In that problem we asked how much $850 would grow into in three years at 5% interest and got an answer of $983.96.

EXAMPLE 5.3

● **Calculator Solution**

Key	Input
n	3
PV	850.00
FV	983.96
PMT	0
	Answer
I/Y	5.0

Suppose instead we were asked what interest rate would grow $850 into $983.96 in three years. In this case we have FV_3, PV, and n, but we don't have k.

Solution: We'll use equation 5.7 this time, just for variety. The general approach is to write the equation

$$PV = FV_n[PVF_{k,n}]$$

and substitute what's known,

$$\$850.00 = \$983.96[PVF_{k,3}] .$$

Notice that this equation can't be solved algebraically for k.

The approach we must take is to solve for the whole factor, $PVF_{k,3}$, and then find its value in the table. Once we've done that, we can read off the unknown value for k from the column heading. Solving for the factor gives

$$PVF_{k,3} = \$850.00/\$983.96 = .8639.$$

We have to find .8639 in Table A-2, but we don't have to search the entire table for it. We know that in this problem n = 3, so we can confine our search to the row for three years. Looking along that row we don't find .8639 exactly, but we do find .8638. That's close enough to assume that the difference is due to rounding error. Looking up to the top of the column, we read 5% as the solution to the problem.

Solutions between Columns and Rows

Most of the time, solutions for k and n don't come out exactly on numbers in the table. That is, the calculated factor is somewhere between the columns or rows. The appropriate approach when that happens depends on the accuracy needed in the solution. For some purposes it's enough to round the answer to the closest tabulated row or column. If a more accurate answer is necessary and you're using tables like the ones provided here, you have to estimate between columns and rows.

In practice, financial calculators are used to solve time value problems. They give exact results without using tables. Before financial calculators were invented, people used enormously detailed tables that filled entire volumes. For illustrative purposes in what follows we'll just round to the nearest table value of n or k.

EXAMPLE 5.4

● **Calculator Solution**

Key	Input
I/Y	14
FV	2
PV	1
PMT	0
	Answer
n	5.29

How long does it take money invested at 14% to double?

Solution: Don't be confused by the fact that we're not given a present and future value in this case. What we are given is a relation between the two. If the money is to double in value, the future value must be twice the present value. Alternatively, we could ask how long it would take $1 to double into $2. We'll use equation 5.4 in this case,

$$FV_n = PV[FVF_{k,n}].$$

Solving for the factor and substituting yields

$$FVF_{14,n} = FV_n/PV = 2.000 .$$

Next we look for 2.0000 in Appendix A-1, confining our search to the column for k = 14%. We find the table value is between five and six years.

n	14%
5	1.9254
6	2.1950

Clearly, 2.0000 is closer to 1.9254 than it is to 2.1950; therefore the nearest whole integer number of years is 5. Notice that the calculator solution gives an exact answer of 5.29 years.

ANNUITY PROBLEMS

The second major class of time value problems involves streams of payments called *annuities*. These are generally more complex than amount problems and harder to visualize, so using time lines can be important.

● ANNUITIES

An **annuity** is a stream of equal payments, made or received, separated by equal intervals of time. Hence $5 a month for a year is an annuity. A stream of monthly payments that alternates from $5 to $10 is not an annuity, nor is a stream of $5 payments that skips an occasional month. Both the amount and the time interval must be constant to have an annuity.

When payments occur at the end of the time periods, we have what's called an *ordinary annuity.* This is the usual situation. If the payments occur at the beginning of each period, we call the stream an *annuity due.* Figures 5.1 and 5.2 show time lines for both cases for a stream of four $1,000 payments.

● An **annuity** is a finite series of equal payments separated by equal time intervals.

Annuities have definite beginning and end points in time; they don't go on forever. A stream of equal payments at regular time intervals that does go on forever is called a *perpetuity.* It has to be handled by its own rules, which we'll study later in the chapter.

The Time Value of Annuities

Annuities are common in business and have important time value implications. For example, suppose a long-term contract calls for payments of $5,000 a year for 10 years. A question that arises immediately concerns the value of the agreement today. That is, if the recipient wants to discount all the payments for immediate cash, how much will they be worth in total?

A similar question asks for the future value of the entire annuity if all 10 payments are put in the bank when received and left there until the end of the contract.

Either of these questions can be answered by taking the present or future value of each payment separately and adding the results. That is a tedious process, however, involving 10 separate calculations. It's much more convenient to develop expressions that enable us to calculate the present or future value of the entire annuity at once.

We'll begin with the future value problem.

FIGURE 5.1

Ordinary Annuity

FIGURE 5.2

Annuity Due

THE FUTURE VALUE OF AN ANNUITY—DEVELOPING A FORMULA

We can develop an expression for the future value of an annuity that's similar to the formulas we studied for amounts. We'll approach the task by examining the future value of a three-year ordinary annuity, using the tools we acquired in dealing with amounts.

We'll portray the annuity along a time line and represent the yearly cash payment as a variable called *PMT,* as shown in Figure 5.3.

The Future Value Problem

● The **future value of an annuity** is the sum, at its end, of all payments and all interest if each payment is deposited when received.

Precisely stated, the assumption behind the future value of an annuity is that each amount, PMT, earns interest at some rate, k, from the time it appears on the time line until the end of the last period. The future value of the annuity is simply the sum of all the payments and all the interest. This is the same as taking the future value of each PMT treated as an amount and adding them.

For example, imagine someone gives you $100 a year for three years and that you put each payment in the bank as soon as you get it. The future value of an annuity problem is to calculate how much you have at the end of the third year. It's clearly more than $300 because of interest earned.

The Future Values of the Individual Payments

We'll develop an expression for the future value of an annuity by projecting the future value of each payment to the end of the stream individually. The approach is illustrated in Figure 5.4. We'll call the end of the third year time 3, the end of the second time 2, and so on.

First consider the third payment. It occurs at the end of the annuity, so it spends no time earning interest at all. Therefore, its value at time 3 is simply PMT.

The second payment occurs at time 2, one year before the end of the annuity, and spends one year earning interest. Its value at time 3 is PMT(1 + k). Think of this as the future value of the present amount PMT for one year at interest rate k. This comes from equation 5.1 with PMT substituted for PV.

Now consider the first payment. It occurs at the end of the first year and spends two years earning interest. Its value by the end of the annuity is PMT $(1 + k)^2$.

All this is portrayed graphically in Figure 5.4, along with the sum of the future values of the three payments, which we're calling FVA$_3$ for future value of an annuity of three periods.

The Three-Year Formula

Let's rewrite the expression for FVA$_3$ from Figure 5.4 with two changes and then examine what we have. The first change will be to explicitly recognize the exponent of 1 on (1 + k) in the middle term on the right. That is, $(1 + k) = (1 + k)^1$. It's simply common practice not to write an exponent of one even though it's there. The second change involves recognizing that anything raised to a zero

No interest

FIGURE 5.3
Time Line Portrayal of an Ordinary Annuity

0   1   2   3

PMT   PMT   PMT

FIGURE 5.4

Future Value of a Three-Year Ordinary Annuity

exponent equals one. That is, $x^0 = 1$ for any value of x. In this case we're going to multiply the first term on the right by $(1 + k)^0$. This gives

(5.9) $$FVA = PMT(1 + k)^0 + PMT(1 + k)^1 + PMT(1 + k)^2.$$

Notice the regular progression of the terms on the right side of equation 5.9. Each contains PMT multiplied by an increasing power of $(1 + k)$ starting from zero. Notice also for this three-year case that there are three terms and that the exponents start with zero and increase to two, one less than the number of years.

Generalizing the Expression

Now imagine we have a four-year annuity, and we want to develop a similar expression for it. How would that expression differ from what we've written here for the three-year case?

In a four-year model the first payment would earn interest for three years, so its future value would be $PMT(1 + k)^3$. The second payment would earn interest for two years, and the third for one year; the fourth would earn no interest at all. These latter payments would be just like the ones in the three-year case, so the only thing different in the four-year model is the addition of the new term $PMT(1 + k)^3$. That addition fits our progression perfectly. It adds one more term with the next higher exponent.

You should be able to see that this could be done for any number of additional years. Each will add one more term with the next higher exponent of $(1 + k)$. Further, the highest exponent will always be one less than the number of years. Hence we can *generalize* equation 5.9 for any number of years, n.

(5.10) $$FVA_n = PMT(1 + k)^0 + PMT(1 + k)^1 + PMT(1 + k)^2 +$$
$$\ldots + PMT(1 + k)^{n-1}$$

Equation 5.10 can be written more conveniently by using the mathematical symbol Σ, which implies summation over the values of some index.

(5.11) $$FVA_n = \sum_{i=1}^{n} PMT(1 + k)^{n-i}$$

As i ranges from 1 to n, each of the terms of equation 5.10 is formed in reverse order. For example, when $i = 1$, $n - i = n - 1$, and we get the last term. When i = 2 we get the next to last term, and so on until i = n and n − i = 0, which gives us the first term.

Because PMT appears identically in every term, we can factor it outside of the summation.

(5.12) $$FVA_n = PMT \sum_{i=1}^{n} (1 + k)^{n-i}$$

The Future Value Factor for an Annuity

Now look at the entire summation term. It depends only on the values of n and k. For example, for n = 3 years the summation is

$$(1 + k)^0 + (1 + k)^1 + (1 + k)^2,$$

which is equivalent to

$$1 + (1 + k) + (1 + k)^2.$$

In general, the summation term for n years is

$$1 + (1 + k) + (1 + k)^2 + \ldots + (1 + k)^{n-1}.$$

This expression can be calculated for pairs of values of n and k and placed in a table. The idea is identical to what we did in developing the future value factor for an amount $[FVF_{k,n} = (1 + k)^n]$, only this expression is more complex.

We'll call the summation in equation 5.12 the *future value factor for an annuity* and write it as $FVFA_{k,n}$. Values for ranges of k and n are given in Appendix A-3.

The Final Formulation

The future value factor for an annuity can replace the summation in equation 5.12 like this.

$$FVA_n = PMT \boxed{\sum_{i=1}^{n} (1 + k)^{n-i}}$$

$$= FVFA_{k,n}$$

Rewriting 5.12 using the factor, we get

(5.13) $$FVA_n = PMT[FVFA_{k,n}].$$

⬤ THE FUTURE VALUE OF AN ANNUITY—SOLVING PROBLEMS

We'll use equation 5.13 to solve future value problems where annuities are involved. Notice that there are four variables in this equation: FVA_n (the future value itself), PMT (the payment), k (the interest rate), and n (the number of periods). Problems will generally give three of them and ask for the fourth. The first step in problem solution is always writing down the equation and substituting the known elements. Once this is done, the solution procedure is very similar to that used for amount problems.

Annuity problems tend to be a bit more complex than amount problems, so it helps to draw a time line to keep the pieces straight.

EXAMPLE 5.5

The Brock Corporation owns the patent to an industrial process and receives license fees of $100,000 a year on a 10-year contract for its use. Management plans to invest each payment until the end of the contract to provide a fund for development of a new process at that time. If the invested money is expected to earn 7%, how much will Brock have after the last payment is received?

● **Calculator Solution**

Key	Input
n	10
I/Y	7
PMT	100,000
PV	0
Answer	
FV	1,381,645

Solution: The time line for this straightforward problem looks like this.[1]

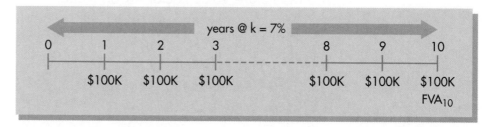

First write equation 5.13,

$$FVA_n = PMT[FVFA_{k,n}] ,$$

and substitute the given information,

$$FVA_{10} = \$100,000[FVFA_{7,10}] .$$

Next look up $FVFA_{7,10}$ in Appendix A-3, getting 13.8164. Substitute and solve for the future value.

$$FVA_{10} = \$100,000[13.8164]$$
$$= \$1,381,640 .$$

Notice that the actual money received is only $1,000,000; the rest is interest.

Calculator Solutions for Annuities

Annuity problems are similar to amount problems in that they have four variables of which three are given and one is unknown. However, the variables are somewhat different.

All amount problems involve both the present and future values of the amount. Annuity problems involve a payment (PMT) and *either* the future value *or* the present value of the annuity. Hence, in an annuity problem we use the PMT key, and we zero either PV or FV, depending on the nature of the problem.

Example 5.5 is a future value of an annuity problem, so we use the FV key, and we zero the PV key. That along with putting in a value for PMT tells the calculator what kind of a problem it's doing. Notice that although we write the future and present values of annuities as FVA and PVA, we just use the FV and PV buttons on the calculator.

---

1. A capital K is frequently used to denote thousands of dollars, replacing a comma and three zeros. M can be used to denote millions.

The Sinking Fund Problem

In Chapter 4 we learned that companies borrow money by issuing bonds for periods as long as 30 or 40 years. Bonds are non-amortizing debt, meaning borrowers make no repayment of principal during bonds' lives. Borrowers pay only interest until maturity, and then they must repay the entire principal in a lump sum. This means that on the maturity date, a bond-issuing company must either have a great deal of money on hand or must reborrow to pay off the old bonds coming due.

Lenders can become quite concerned about this practice. They may feel that a borrowing company can generally earn enough to pay annual interest, but it won't have enough cash on hand at maturity to pay off principal. If the borrower's financial position deteriorates or if financial markets become tight, it may not be able to reborrow either. This can spell bankruptcy for the bond-issuing company and a big loss for the investor/lender.

The solution to the problem can be a **sinking fund**. A sinking fund is a series of payments made into an account that's dedicated to paying off a bond's principal at maturity. Deposits are planned so that the amount in the bank on the date the bonds mature will just equal the principal due.

If lenders require a sinking fund for security, it's included as a provision in the bond agreement. The sinking fund problem is to determine the periodic deposit that must be made to ensure that the appropriate amount is available at the bond's maturity. This is a future value of an annuity problem in which the payment is unknown.

from the **CFO**

● A **sinking fund** provides cash to pay off a bond's principal at maturity.

EXAMPLE 5.6

The Greenville Company issued bonds totaling $15 million for 30 years. The bond agreement specifies that a sinking fund must be maintained after 10 years, which will retire the bonds at maturity. Although no one can accurately predict interest rates, Greenville's bank has estimated that a yield of 6% on deposited funds is realistic for long-term planning. How much should Greenville plan to deposit each year to be able to retire the bonds with the money put aside?

Solution: First recognize that the time period of the annuity is the last 20 years of the bond issue's life, because the bond agreement states that the sinking fund must be maintained only after 10 years. In other words, time zero isn't today but the beginning of the eleventh year in the bond's life.

The problem's time line looks like this.

● **Calculator Solution**

Key	Input
n	20
I/Y	6
FV	15,000,000
PV	0
	Answer
PMT	407,768.35

First write the future value of an annuity formula, equation 5.13.

$$FVA_n = PMT[FVFA_{k,n}]$$

In this case, the future value itself is known. It's the principal amount of the bond issue that will have to be repaid, $15 million. Also, k is 6% and n is 20 years, the duration of the sinking fund according to the contract. Substitute these values.

$$\$15,000,000 = PMT[FVFA_{6,20}]$$

Next look up $FVFA_{6,20}$ in Appendix A-3, getting 36.7856, and substitute.

$$\$15,000,000 = PMT[36.7856]$$

Finally, solve for PMT.

$$PMT = \$407,768.26$$

Greenville will have to deposit just under $408K per year starting in the eleventh year of the bond issue's life to ensure that the bonds will be retired on schedule without a problem.

At this point we're going to digress from time value problems themselves to study a little more detail about the workings of interest rates.

COMPOUND INTEREST AND NON-ANNUAL COMPOUNDING

Until now we've been working with annually compounded interest. Although interest rates are always quoted in annual terms, they're usually not compounded annually, and that varies the actual amount of interest paid. Before going any further, let's be sure we know exactly what the term **compound interest** means.

● **Compounding** refers to earning interest on interest.

Compound Interest

Compounding refers to the idea of earning interest on previously earned interest. Imagine putting $100 in the bank at 10%. We'd earn $10 in the first year and have a balance of $110 at year end. In the second year we'll earn $11 for a balance of $121, in the third year $12.10, and so on. The interest is larger each year because it's calculated on a balance that increases with the accumulation of all prior interest.

Under compound interest the balance in the bank grows at an exponential rate. Graphically, an amount placed at compound interest grows as shown in Figure 5.5. The increasing steepness of the curve as time progresses is characteristic of exponential growth.

Compounding Periods

Every interest rate has an associated **compounding period**. Commonly used periods are annual, semiannual, quarterly, and monthly. When none is mentioned, an annual period is implied.

The compounding period associated with an interest rate refers to the frequency with which interest is credited into the recipient's account for the purpose of calculating future interest. The shorter the period, the more frequently interest is credited and the more interest is earned *on interest*.

● Interest is usually compounded **annually, semiannually, quarterly,** or **monthly**.

An example will make the idea clear. If a bank pays 12% interest compounded annually, someone depositing $100 is credited with $12 at the end of a year, and the basis for the second year's interest calculation is $112. A time line portrayal of the year would look like this.

If the 12% is compounded semiannually, the year is divided into two halves and 6% interest is paid in each. However, the first half year's interest is credited to the depositor at midyear and earns additional interest in the second half. The additional interest is 6% of $6 or $.36. The time line portrayal looks like this.

Compounding 12% quarterly involves dividing the year into four quarters, each paying (12%/4 =) 3%. Each quarter's interest is credited at the end of the quarter. The time line looks like this.

FIGURE 5.5

The Effect of Compound Interest

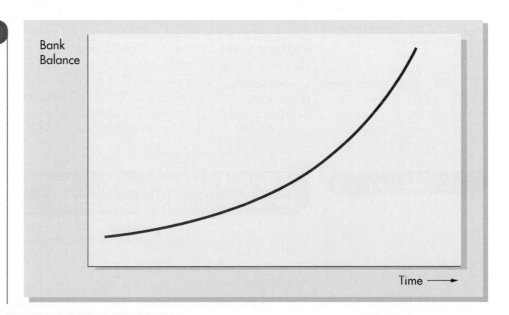

It's easy to get each successive quarter's ending balance by multiplying the previous balance by one plus the *quarterly* interest rate in decimal form. That's 1.03 in this case. This is just the (1 + k) idea we've been working with, but k is stated for a quarterly compounding period.

Compounding 12% monthly involves dividing the year into 12 monthly periods, each bearing a 1% interest rate. If $100 is initially deposited, the year-end balance will be $112.68.

It's common practice to quote an annual rate and state the compounding period immediately afterward. The quarterly case in our 12% example would be quoted as "12% compounded quarterly." Those words literally mean 3% interest paid on quarterly periods.

● Interest rates are quoted by stating the **nominal rate** followed by the **compounding period.**

The quoted rate, 12% in this case, is called the **nominal interest rate.** We'll write it as k_{nom}. The word "nominal" just means named.

It's possible to pay interest compounded on any time period; however, the periods we've mentioned are the most common in business. Daily compounding is encountered only rarely.

The theoretical limit as periods become shorter is continuous compounding in which interest is instantaneously credited as earned. Continuous compounding takes some special math that we'll discuss later.

The Effective Annual Rate

Notice in the 12% example above that the final bank balance increases with more frequent compounding. Let's summarize those calculations. For an initial deposit of $100 and a nominal rate of 12%, Table 5.2 shows the amounts in the bank at the end of one year.

These differences in a depositor's balance mean that although all four rates are quoted as 12%, different amounts of interest are actually being paid. As we've explained, the difference is due to the frequency of compounding.

It's important to quantify the effect of different compounding methods to avoid confusion in financial dealings. That is, people need to know just how much more monthly or quarterly compounding pays than annual compounding at any nominal rate. This need for clarification has led to the idea of an *effective annual rate,* referred to as EAR. It's the rate of annually compounded interest that is just equivalent to the nominal rate compounded more frequently. Stated another way, it's the annually compounded rate that gets the depositor the same account balance after one year that he or she would get under more frequent compounding.

● The **effective annual rate (EAR)** is the annually compounded rate that pays the same interest as a lower rate compounded more frequently.

Let's consider 12% compounded monthly as an example. What annually compounded interest rate will get a depositor the same interest? Table 5.2 shows that monthly compounding results in an ending balance of $112.68 on an initial deposit of $100; hence the total interest paid is $12.68.

TABLE 5.2

Year-End Balances at Various Compounding Periods for $100 Initial Deposit and k_{nom} = 12%

Compounding	Final Balance
Annual	$112.00
Semiannual	112.36
Quarterly	112.55
Monthly	112.68

The annually compounded rate that pays this much interest is calculated by dividing the interest paid by the principal invested.

$$\$12.68/\$100.00 = 12.68\%$$

Hence 12.68% compounded annually is *effectively* equal to 12% compounded monthly. What are the EARs for semiannual and quarterly compounding at 12%?

Truth in lending legislation requires that lenders disclose the EAR on loans. Watch for it the next time you see an advertisement for a bank.

In general the EAR can be calculated for any compounding period by using the following formula.

(5.14) $$\text{EAR} = \left(1 + \frac{k_{nom}}{m}\right)^m - 1$$

where m is the number of compounding periods per year (12 for monthly, 4 for quarterly, and 2 for semiannually).

The effect of more frequent compounding is greater at higher interest rates. Table 5.3 illustrates this point. At a nominal rate of 6%, the effective increase in interest due to monthly rather than annual compounding is only .17%, which represents a 2.8% increase in the rate actually paid (.17/6.00 = .028 = 2.8%). At 18%, however, the effective increase is 1.56%, which represents an 8.7% increase in what's actually paid.

The APR and the EAR

Credit card companies charge monthly interest on unpaid balances at rates in the neighborhood of 1.5%. This represents a monthly compounding of interest on the cardholder's debt. They advertise that the annual percentage rate, known as the APR, is 18%, twelve times the monthly rate.

● The **annual percentage rate (APR)** associated with credit cards is actually the nominal rate and is less than the **EAR**.

Don't confuse the APR with the EAR. The APR is actually the nominal rate. Table 5.3 shows that at a nominal rate of 18% the EAR for monthly compounding is 19.56%, somewhat more than 18%.

Compounding Periods and the Time Value Formulas

Each of the time value formulas contains an interest rate, k, and a number time of periods, n. In using the formulas, the time periods must be compounding periods, and the interest rate must be the rate for a single compounding period.

The problems we've dealt with so far have all involved annual compounding. In that case, the compounding period is a year, and the appropriate interest rate

TABLE 5.3

Changes in the Effect of Compounding at Different Rates

Nominal Rate	EAR for Monthly Compounding	Effective Increase	Increase as % of k_{nom}
6%	6.17%	.17%	2.8%
12	12.68	.68	5.7
18	19.56	1.56	8.7

is the nominal rate itself. Things are a little more complicated with non-annual compounding periods. Let's consider quarters as an example.

Suppose we have a time value problem that runs for five years and has an interest rate of 12%. If compounding is annual, k and n are simply 12 and 5, respectively. However, if compounding is quarterly, the appropriate period is one quarter and the rate for that period is (12%/4 =) 3%. Further, the time dimension of the problem needs to be stated as 20 quarters rather than five years (5 years × 4 quarters/year = 20 quarters). Hence k and n for the problem should be 3 and 20, respectively.

Whenever we run into a problem with non-annual compounding, we have to calculate the appropriate k and n for use in the formulas from the nominal rate and time given in the problem. Some simple rules make that relatively easy to do.

If a problem gives a nominal rate and states time in years, compute k and n for use in the formulas as follows.

$$\text{Semiannual:} \quad k = k_{nom}/2 \quad n = \text{years} \times 2$$
$$\text{Quarterly:} \quad k = k_{nom}/4 \quad n = \text{years} \times 4$$
$$\text{Monthly:} \quad k = k_{nom}/12 \quad n = \text{years} \times 12$$

Recall that some calculators will automatically divide the interest input by a number of compounding periods for you. That feature is convenient if you're working with the same kind of compounding all the time. But because we're switching from one to another, it's better to leave the setting at one (1) and input the interest rate for the compounding period.

Let's try two problems involving the future value of an annuity to get used to these ideas (Examples 5.7 and 5.8).

EXAMPLE 5.7

You want to buy a car costing $15,000 in $2\frac{1}{2}$ years. You plan to save the money by making equal monthly deposits in your bank account, which pays 12% compounded monthly. How much must you deposit each month?

Solution: In this situation the future value of a series of payments must accumulate to a known amount, indicating a future value of an annuity problem.

First calculate the correct k and n. Because compounding is monthly,

$$k = \frac{k_{nom}}{12} = \frac{12\%}{12} = 1\%$$

and

$$n = 2.5 \text{ years} \times 12 \text{ months/year} = 30 \text{ months}.$$

Next write the future value of an annuity expression and substitute.

$$FVA_n = PMT[FVFA_{k,n}]$$
$$\$15,000 = PMT[FVFA_{1,30}]$$

Use Appendix A-3 to find $FVFA_{1,30} = 34.7849$ and substitute.

$$\$15,000 = PMT[34.7849]$$

Finally, solve for PMT.

$$PMT = \$431.22$$

● **Calculator Solution**

Key	Input
n	30
I/Y	1
FV	15,000
PV	0
Answer	
PMT	431.22

EXAMPLE 5.8

Jeff and Susan Johnson have a daughter, Molly, just entering high school, and they've started to think about sending her to college. They expect to need about $50,000 in cash when she starts. Although the Johnsons have a good income, they live extravagantly and have little or no savings. Susan analyzed the family budget and decided they could realistically put away $750 a month or $2,250 per quarter toward Molly's schooling. They're now searching for an investment vehicle that will provide a return sufficient to grow these savings into $50,000 in four years. If quarterly compounding is assumed, how large a return (interest rate) do the Johnsons have to get to achieve their goal? Is it realistic?

Solution: Once again we recognize this as a future value of an annuity problem because of the stream of payments involved and the fact that the Johnsons are saving for a known future amount.

Because the problem runs for four years and the compounding is quarterly, n is calculated as

$$n = 4 \text{ years} \times 4 \text{ quarters/year} = 16 \text{ quarters}.$$

Equation 5.13 gives the future value of an annuity expression.

$$FVA_n = PMT[FVFA_{k,n}]$$

Substituting values from the problems, we have

$$\$50,000 = \$2,250[FVFA_{k,16}].$$

Solving for the factor yields

$$FVFA_{k,16} = 22.2222.$$

In Appendix A-3 we search for this value along the row for 16 periods and find that it lies between 4% and 4.5%. In this case it's fairly easy to estimate that the factor is about half of the way between 4% and 4.5%.

Hence the approximate solution is 4.2%; however, that's a quarterly rate. The appropriate nominal rate is

$$4.2\% \times 4 = 16.8\%.$$

This is a high rate of return to expect on invested money. Is it reasonable to expect such a rate to be sustained over four years?

There's no definite answer to that question. There have been times when that expectation would have been reasonable, but such a high rate can always be expected to involve substantial risk. Because they probably don't want to risk not being able to send Molly to college, the Johnson's should probably try to save a little more and opt for a more conservative investment.

● **Calculator Solution**

Key	Input
n	16
PMT	2,250
FV	50,000
PV	0
	Answer
I/Y	4.2

●THE PRESENT VALUE OF AN ANNUITY—DEVELOPING A FORMULA

The present value of an annuity is simply the sum of the present values of all of the annuity's payments. We could always calculate these individually, but it's much easier to develop a formula to do all the calculations in one step as we did with the future value. The method we'll use is similar to that used in developing the future value formula, but we'll proceed more quickly because we've used the approach before.

http://

Stone Street Capital will buy your winning lottery ticket by paying you its present value. See their site at

● www.stonestreet.com

We begin with a time line portrayal of a three-period annuity and write down the present value of each payment in terms of the interest rate, k. In this case we divide by powers of $(1 + k)$ instead of multiplying as in the future value case. Review equations 5.5 and 5.6 to see that this gives the present value of an amount. Figure 5.6 is the time line portrayal.

The present value is formed for the first payment by dividing the payment amount by $(1 + k)$, for the second payment by dividing by $(1 + k)^2$, and so forth. Notice that this is equivalent to multiplying by present value factors, because $1/(1 + k)$ is the present value factor for k and one period, $PVF_{k,1}$; $1/(1 + k)^2$ is the present value factor for k and two periods; and so on.

The present value of the three-period annuity is

(5.15) $$PVA = \frac{PMT}{(1 + k)} + \frac{PMT}{(1 + k)^2} + \frac{PMT}{(1 + k)^3},$$

which can also be written as

(5.15) $$PVA = PMT(1 + k)^{-1} + PMT(1 + k)^{-2} + PMT(1 + k)^{-3}$$

with negative exponents to indicate one over the powers of $(1 + k)$.

Notice how regular the expression is. Every payment produces a term involving PMT divided by $(1 + k)$ to a successively larger power beginning with one.

Examining Figure 5.6, we can easily see that adding more periods to the annuity would just add more terms to the equation. For example, a fourth payment would produce a term $PMT(1 + k)^{-4}$, and so on.

Thus we can generalize equation 5.15 for any number of periods, n, as follows.

(5.16) $$PVA = PMT(1 + k)^{-1} + PMT(1 + k)^{-2} +$$
$$\dots + PMT(1 + k)^{-n}$$

Next we can factor PMT out of the right side of equation 5.16 and use summation notation to represent the terms involving negative powers of $(1 + k)$.

(5.17) $$PVA = PMT\left[\sum_{i=1}^{n} (1 + k)^{-i}\right]$$

Once again, we notice that the expression in the brackets is a function of only k and n, and can be tabulated for likely values of those variables. This is the present value factor for an annuity and is written as $PVFA_{k,n}$.

FIGURE 5.6

Present Value of a Three-Period Ordinary Annuity

(5.18)
$$PVFA_{k,n} = \sum_{i=1}^{n} (1 + k)^{-i}$$

Values of the present value factor for an annuity are tabulated in Appendix A-4.

Finally, we can rewrite equation 5.17 by substituting from equation 5.18. The resulting expression is convenient for use in solving problems when used in conjunction with Appendix A-4.

(5.19)
$$PVA = PMT[PVFA_{k,n}]$$

● THE PRESENT VALUE OF AN ANNUITY—SOLVING PROBLEMS

Equation 5.19 for the present value of an annuity works just like equation 5.13 does for the future value of an annuity. There are four variables: PVA (the present value itself), PMT (the payment), k (the interest rate), and n (the number of periods). Problems will generally present three of them as known and ask you to find the fourth. The general approach is similar to what we've already been doing.

EXAMPLE 5.9

The Shipson Company has just sold a large machine to Baltimore Inc. on an installment contract. The contract calls for Baltimore to make payments of $5,000 every six months (semiannually) for 10 years. Shipson would like its cash now and asks its bank to discount the contract and pay it the present (discounted) value. Baltimore is a good credit risk, so the bank is willing to discount the contract at 14% compounded semiannually. How much will Shipson receive?

Solution: The contract represents an annuity with payments of $5,000. The bank is willing to buy it for its present value at a relatively high rate of interest. The higher the rate of interest, the lower the price the bank is willing to pay for the contract.

First calculate the appropriate k and n for semiannual compounding.

$$k = k_{nom}/2 = 14\%/2 = 7\%$$
$$n = 10 \text{ years} \times 2 = 20 .$$

The time line looks like this.

● **Calculator Solution**

Key	Input
n	20
I/Y	7
PMT	5,000
FV	0
Answer	
PV	52,970.07

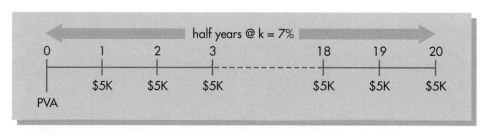

Write equation 5.19 and substitute the known information.

$$PVA = PMT[PVFA_{k,n}]$$
$$PVA = \$5,000[PVFA_{7,20}]$$

Appendix A-4 gives $PVFA_{7,20} = 10.5940$. Substituting and solving for PVA yields

$$PVA = \$52,970 .$$

Practical Finance

The Lottery: Congratulations, You're Rich— But Not as Rich as You Thought

State lottery jackpots are enormous sums of money, but they're not really as big as they're made out to be. That's because of the time value of money and the way the prizes are paid. Large lottery prizes are typically paid over 25 years, but the lottery authority states the winnings as the sum of the payments without consideration of time value. For example, a $25 million prize is really $1 million a year for 25 years, an annuity.

What the winner really has today is the present value of that annuity. If a lucky player wants her money immediately, she has to accept the discounted value of the stream of payments. Suppose the interest rate is 7%. A calculation using the present value of an annuity formula reveals that the winner's real prize is about $11.7 million. That's nothing to sneeze at, but it is a far cry from $25 million.

To make matters worse, winnings are taxable, largely in the top bracket. Let's be optimistic and assume the winner hires a good tax accountant and only winds up paying about 37% in taxes. That knocks down the immediately available, after-tax winnings to about $7.4 million, less than a third of the amount advertised.

Spreadsheet Solutions

Time value problems can be solved using spreadsheet programs like Lotus 123™ or Microsoft Excel™. The technique is similar to using a calculator. We'll explain the technique assuming that you're familiar with the basics of spreadsheet software.

Recall that there are four variables in every time value problem, but they're different depending on whether we're dealing with amounts or annuities. In amount problems we have PV, FV, k, and n, while in annuity problems we have *either* PVA *or* FVA, PMT, k, and n. Also recall that when using a calculator we use the PV and FV keys for both amounts and annuities. We can do this because the calculator is programmed to solve an annuity problem if we input a positive value for PMT and zero for either PV or FV. It solves an amount problem if we input zero for PMT. Hence there are a total of five possible variables as follows.

$$k \quad n \quad PV \quad FV \quad PMT$$

To solve a problem with a calculator we enter three numbers and zero a fourth. The calculator then gives us the unknown fifth variable.

A spreadsheet program uses similar logic. There are five spreadsheet time value functions. Each is used to calculate one of the five time value variables. Each function takes the *other* four variables as inputs. We'll use Microsoft Excel to illustrate. The five functions are as follows

To Solve For	Use Function
FV	FV(k, n, PMT, PV)
PV	PV(k, n, PMT, FV)
k	RATE(n, PMT, PV, FV)
n	NPER(k, PMT, PV, FV)
PMT	PMT(k, n, PV, FV)

To solve any time value problem, select the function for the unknown variable, put the problem values for the three known variables in the proper order within the parentheses, and input zero for the fourth variable. (Zero PMT for all amount problems, zero PV for future value of an annuity (FVA) problems, and zero FV for present value of an annuity (PVA) problems.)

There are two minor complications in the procedure. The first is simply that interest rates are entered in decimal form rather than as whole numbers, so use .07 for 7%. The second involves the signs of the cash figures. Notice that there are three cash variables—FV, PV, and PMT—one of which is always zero. Hence in every problem there are two dollar variables. These must be of opposite signs.

The easiest way to think of this issue is in terms of inflows and outflows. Imagine, for example, a simple problem in which we're depositing a sum of money in a bank today (PV) and withdrawing it with interest (FV) some years later. If we define flows into the bank as positives, then flows out must be negatives. Hence if PV is positive, FV is negative, whether the figures are inputs or outputs of the calculation. The reverse definition is also OK, as long as the variables have opposite signs.

This convention can create a bit of a problem if you forget it and input only positive figures. In some applications the program simply gives you the correct answer with a negative sign, but in others the program doesn't work at all. Hence the first thing to check when you get an error is the sign of your inputs.

Here's an example of the whole process. Suppose we want to calculate the amount we'll have in the bank after six years if we deposit $4,000 today at 7% interest. We're looking for the future value of an amount, so we choose the first function,

$$FV(k, n, PMT, PV) ,$$

and input as follows.

$$FV(.07, 6, 0, -4000) .$$

Notice that we input 0 for PMT because we're not doing an annuity problem, we input the interest rate in decimal form, and we input the PV as a negative.

Now let's change things just a little to illustrate an annuity problem. Suppose we want to know the future value of a $4,000 annual annuity for six years at 7%. We choose the future value (FV) function again and input as follows.

$$FV(.07, 6, -4000, 0)$$

Notice we're now telling the program that it's dealing with an annuity by inputting a nonzero number for PMT. And because there's no present value in a future value of an annuity calculation (see equation 5.13 on page 153), we input 0 for PV. The cell carrying this function will display the present value of our annuity.

Boot up your computer and verify that these examples yield answers of $6,002.92 and $28,613.16, respectively.

EXAMPLE 5.10

The bank in Example 5.9 discounts contracts for customers like Shipson frequently. Contracts can have payments of any constant amount for any number of periods, and the bank's interest rate changes frequently. Write a spreadsheet program for the bank that will calculate the discounted amount that should be paid on any contract like Shipson's after the interest rate, the term of the contract (in payment periods), and the amount of the payment are input into conveniently labeled cells.

Solution: In this case the bank wants to calculate the present value of an annuity, so we'll use the PV function

$$PV(k, n, PMT, FV) .$$

Since this program will only be used for one thing, we can customize the formula by zeroing FV and making the PMT variable negative.

$$PV(k, n, -PMT, 0)$$

Then the banker just has to input the appropriate interest rate, number of periods, and payment as a positive number. Here we'll input .07 for k, one-half of the annual 14% rate, 20 semiannual periods, and payments of $5,000. Notice that we do have to deal with non-annual compounding just as we did using calculators or tables.

Here is a spread sheet that does the job, along with a note detailing the operative formula. Notice that the input cells are programmed directly into the PV function along with a negative sign for the payment and a zero for the future value variable. The banker inputs the appropriate values into the green cells, and the discounted amount of the contract appears in the red cell.

	A	B	C	D	E	F	G
1							
2			DISCOUNTING A CONTRACT				
3							
4							
5		Inputs					
6							
7		Interest Rate			0.07		
8							
9		Payment Periods			20		
10							
11		Payment Amount			5000		
12							
13							
14		Discounted Value			$52,970.07		
15							
16							
17							
18		The formula in E14 is =PV(E7,E9,-E11,0)					
19							
20							0

Amortized Loans

The most common application of the present value of an annuity concept is in dealing with amortized loans. Debt is said to be amortized when the principal is paid off gradually during its life. Car loans, home mortgages, and many business loans are amortized.

● An **amortized loan's** principal is paid off regularly over its life.

An amortized loan is generally structured so that a *constant* payment is made periodically, usually monthly, over the loan's term. Each payment contains one month's interest and an amount to reduce principal. Interest is charged on the outstanding loan balance at the beginning of each month, so as the loan's principal is reduced, successive interest charges become smaller. Because the monthly payments are equal, successive payments contain larger proportions of principal repayment and smaller proportions of interest.

In applying the present value of an annuity formula to a loan, the amount borrowed is always the present value of the annuity, PVA, and the loan payment is always PMT.

EXAMPLE 5.11

Suppose you borrow $10,000 over four years at 18% compounded monthly repayable in monthly installments. How much is your loan payment?

● **Calculator Solution**

Key	Input
n	48
I/Y	1.5
PV	10,000
FV	0
Answer	
PMT	293.75

Solution: First notice that for monthly compounding k and n are

$$k = k_{nom}/12 = 18\%/12 = 1.5\%$$

$$n = 4 \text{ years} \times 12 \text{ months/year} = 48 \text{ months} .$$

Then write equation 5.19 and substitute.

$$PVA = PMT[PVFA_{k,n}]$$

$$\$10,000 = PMT[PVFA_{1.5,48}]$$

Appendix A-4 gives $PVFA_{1.5,48} = 34.0426$, and

$$PMT = \$293.75 .$$

EXAMPLE 5.12

Suppose you want to buy a car and can afford to make payments of $500 a month. The bank makes three-year car loans at 12% compounded monthly. How much can you borrow toward a new car?

● **Calculator Solution**

Key	Input
n	36
I/Y	1
PMT	500
FV	0
Answer	
PV	15,053.75

Solution: For monthly compounding,

$$k = k_{nom}/12 = 12\%/12 = 1\%$$

$$n = 3 \text{ years} \times 12 \text{ months/year} = 36 \text{ months}.$$

Write equation 5.19 and substitute.

$$PVA = PMT[PVFA_{k,n}]$$

$$PVA = \$500[PVFA_{1,36}]$$

Appendix A-4 gives $PVFA_{1,36} = 30.1075$, and

$$PVA = \$15,053.75 .$$

That is, the bank would lend you $15,053.75.

Loan Amortization Schedules

A loan amortization schedule lists every payment and shows how much of it goes to pay interest and how much reduces principal. It also shows the beginning and ending balances of unpaid principal for each period.

To construct an amortization schedule we have to know the loan amount, the payment, and the periodic interest rate. That's PVA, PMT, and k. Let's use the loan in the last example as an illustration. Table 5.4 shows the completed computation for the first two lines. Follow the explanation in the next paragraph for the first line, verify the second line, and fill in the third and fourth lines yourself.

The loan amount is $15,053.75. This is the beginning balance for the first monthly period. The payment is a constant $500.00; that amount is entered on every row in the payment column. Although the nominal interest rate in this case is 12%, the monthly interest rate is 1% because compounding is monthly. Therefore the monthly interest charge is calculated as 1% of the month's beginning loan balance.

$$\$15,053.75 \times .01 = \$150.54$$

As the payment is $500 and $150.54 goes to interest, the remaining ($500.00 − $150.54 =) $349.46 reduces principal. The ending loan balance is the beginning balance less the principal reduction, ($15,053.75 − $349.46 =) $14,704.29. This amount becomes the beginning balance for the next period, and the process is repeated.

This procedure carried out for 36 monthly periods will bring the ending balance to zero at the end of the last period. It's important to notice what happens to the composition of the payment as the loan is paid down. The interest charge declines, and the portion devoted to principal reduction increases, while the total payment remains constant.

Mortgage Loans

Loans used to buy real estate are called **mortgage loans** or just *mortgages*. A home mortgage is often the largest single financial transaction in an average person's life. A typical mortgage is an amortized loan with monthly compounding and payments that run for 30 years; that's 360 payments.

In the beginning of a mortgage's life, nearly all of the payment goes to pay interest. For example, consider that a 30-year mortgage at 12% (compounded

● **Loan amortization schedules** detail the interest and principal in each loan payment.

TABLE 5.4

A Partial Amortization Schedule

Period	Beginning Balance	Payment	Interest @ 1%	Principal Reduction	Ending Balance
1	$15,053.75	$500.00	$150.54	$349.46	$14,704.29
2	14,704.29	500.00	147.04	352.96	14,351.33
3	_____	500.00	_____	_____	_____
4	_____	500.00	_____	_____	_____
⋮	⋮	⋮	⋮	⋮	⋮

● Early mortgage payments are **almost all interest** and provide a big tax savings.

monthly) for $100,000 has a monthly payment of $1,028.61 (verify this by using equation 5.19 and Appendix A-4).[2] The first month's interest on such a loan is 1% of $100,000 or $1,000. Hence, only $28.61 is applied to principal. The first payment is 97.2% interest!

This situation reverses toward the end of the mortgage when most of the payment is principal. In other words, during the early years of a mortgage, the principal is paid down very slowly, but near the end it's amortized quickly.

This payment pattern has two important implications for homeowners. The most important is related to the fact that mortgage interest is tax deductible. Early mortgage payments provide homeowners with a big tax deduction, while later payments don't.

Consider the first payment on the loan we just used as an example. If the homeowner is in the 28% tax bracket, he or she will save $280 in taxes by making that payment because it contains deductible interest of $1,000.

Hence, the *effective* cost of the loan payment is found as follows.

Payment	$1,028.61
Tax savings	$280.00
Net	$748.61

In effect, the government shares the cost of home ownership, especially in the early years. Later on, although equity builds up faster, the tax benefit isn't nearly as great. (In this context equity means the portion of the home's value that belongs to the homeowner as opposed to being supported by a bank loan.)

The second implication of the mortgage payment pattern is that halfway through a mortgage's life, the homeowner hasn't paid off half the loan. To see that in the loan we've been talking about, let's calculate the present value of the second half of the payment stream as of the end of year 15. That will be the amount one could borrow making 180 payments of $1,028.61. Because this is what's left after 15 years, it must represent the remaining loan balance. We'll use the same expression for the present value of an annuity.

$$PVA = PMT[PVFA_{k,n}]$$
$$= \$1,028.61[PVFA_{1,180}]$$
$$= \$1,028.61[83.3217]$$
$$= \$85,705.53.$$

Thus, halfway through the life of this $100,000 mortgage, almost $86,000 is still outstanding. In other words, only about 14% of the original loan has been paid off.

Another interesting feature of a long-term amortized loan like a mortgage is the total amount of interest paid over the entire term. At 12% the homeowner pays almost twice the amount of the loan in interest even after considering the tax savings.

2. 12% would be a very high mortgage rate in today's financial market. We're using it for illustrative purposes because it gives a convenient 1% monthly rate.

Total payments ($1,028.61 × 360)	$370,299.60
Less original loan	100,000.00
Total interest	$270,299.60
Tax Savings @ 28%	75,683.89
Net interest cost	$194,615.71

Of course, this effect varies dramatically with the interest rate. Over the last 25 years, rates have varied between 7% and 16%. Recently, during the 1990s and early 2000s, they've been on the low end of that range. Verify that the net after-tax interest cost of a $100,000 mortgage loan at 8% is $118,190.59.

AMORTIZED LOANS AND TAX PLANNING   Because interest payments on business loans and home mortgages are tax deductible, we're sometimes interested in projecting the total interest and principal payments to be made during a particular future year of a loan's life. If we don't want to write out the entire amortization schedule, we can solve the problem by calculating the loan balance at the beginning and end of the year.

To illustrate, let's calculate the principal and interest payments in the third year of the $100,000 loan with which we've been working. The loan balance at the beginning of the third year will be the amount left after 24 payments have been made and there are 336 left to go. We find it by using equation 5.19.

$$PVA = PMT[PVFA_{k,n}]$$
$$= \$1,028.61[PVFA_{1,336}]$$
$$= \$1,028.61[96.4680]$$
$$= \$99,227.95$$

Similarly, 324 payments will be left after three years.

$$PVA = \$1,028.61[PFVA_{1,324}]$$
$$= \$1,028.61[96.0201]$$
$$= \$98,767.24$$

The difference between these balances, $460.71, is the amount paid into principal during the year. There are 12 payments totaling ($1,028.61 × 12 =) $12,343.32, so the interest portion is this amount less the contribution to equity.

Total payments	$12,343.32
Principal reduction	(460.71)
Deductible interest	$11,882.61

● Calculator Solution

Key	Input
n	336
I/Y	1
PMT	1,028.61
FV	0
Answer	
PV	99,227.97

● Calculator Solution

Key	Input
n	324
I/Y	1
PMT	1,028.61
FV	0
Answer	
PV	98,767.21

●THE ANNUITY DUE

So far we've dealt only with ordinary annuities in which payments occur at the ends of time periods. When payments occur at the beginnings of time periods, we have an annuity due, and our formulas need to be modified somewhat.

FIGURE 5.7

Future Value of a Three-Period Annuity Due

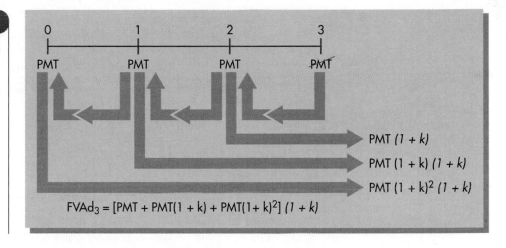

FIGURE 5.7

Future Value of a Three-Period Annuity Due

● In an **annuity due** payments occur at the **beginning** of each period.

The Future Value of an Annuity Due

First consider the future value of an annuity formula as developed in Figure 5.4. Because the end of one period is the beginning of the next, we can create the annuity due by simply shifting each payment back one period in time. This is shown schematically in Figure 5.7. There is now a payment at time 0, but none at time 3.

Because each payment is received one period earlier, it spends one period longer in the bank earning interest. Therefore each payment's future value at the end of the annuity will be whatever it was before times $(1 + k)$. The additional $(1 + k)$ is shown in italics in the diagram.

The future value of the annuity due, which we'll call $FVAd_3$, is then

$$FVAd_3 = PMT(1 + k) + PMT(1 + k)(1 + k) + PMT(1 + k)^2(1 + k) ,$$

which can be rewritten by factoring out the additional $(1 + k)$ as

(5.20) $FVAd_3 = [PMT + PMT(1 + k) + PMT(1 + k)^2](1 + k) .$

It's easy to see that no matter how many periods we choose to add, every term in an annuity due will be the same as it is in an ordinary annuity multiplied by an extra $(1 + k)$. Therefore we can generalize equation 5.20 to n periods.

(5.21) $FVAd_3 = [PMT + PMT(1 + k) +$

$$\ldots + PMT(1 + k)^{n-1}](1 + k)$$

Once we've done that, the term inside the brackets can be developed into the ordinary annuity formula just as before. The only thing changed is the addition of the $(1 + k)$ factor on the right. Hence the final formula for an annuity due is just our old formula for an ordinary annuity multiplied by $(1 + k)$.

(5.22) $FVAd_n = PMT[FVFA_{k,n}](1 + k)$

Situations in which an annuity due is appropriate can be recognized when words such as "starting now," "starting today," or "starting immediately" are used to describe a payment stream.

EXAMPLE 5.13

The Baxter Corporation started making sinking fund deposits of $50,000 per quarter today. Baxter's bank pays 8% compounded quarterly, and the payments will be made for 10 years. What will the fund be worth at the end of that time?

● Calculator Solution

Key	Input
n	40
I/Y	2
PMT	50,000
PV	0
Answer	
FV	3,020,099
	× 1.02
	3,080,501

Solution:

First calculate k and n.

$$k = 8\%/4 = 2\%$$

$$n = 10 \text{ years} \times 4 \text{ quarters/year} = 40 \text{ quarters}$$

Next write equation 5.22 and substitute known values from the problem.

$$FVAd_n = PMT[FVFA_{k,n}](1 + k)$$

$$FVAd_{40} = \$50,000[FVFA_{2,40}](1.02)$$

Get $FVFA_{2,40} = 60.4020$ from Appendix A-3 and substitute.

$$FVAd_{40} = \$50,000[60.4020](1.02)$$

$$= \$3,080,502$$

Advanced calculators let you set annuity payments at either the beginning or end of periods. If you set the beginning, the calculator takes care of the $(1 + k)$ multiplication automatically. However, if you're only doing an occasional annuity due problem, it's just as easy to multiply manually.

The Present Value of an Annuity Due

Applying very similar logic to the derivation of the present value of an annuity expression developed in Figure 5.7 yields a formula for the present value of an annuity due, which we'll call PVAd.

(5.23) $$PVAd = PMT[PVFA_{k,n}](1 + k)$$

This expression is used in the same way as equation 5.22.

As an exercise, work your way through the development of equation 5.23 by using Figure 5.7 and the approach we've just gone through in developing equation 5.22.

Recognizing Types of Annuity Problems

The most common error in working annuity problems results from confusion over whether to use the present or future value technique. Here's a little guidance on how to keep the two straight.

First, an annuity problem is always recognized by the presence of a *stream* of *equal* payments. Whether the value of the payments is known or unknown, a series of them means an annuity.

Annuity problems always involve some kind of a transaction at one end of the stream of payments or the other. If the transaction is at the end of the stream, you have a future value problem. If the transaction is in the beginning, you have a present value problem. Here's a graphic representation of this idea.

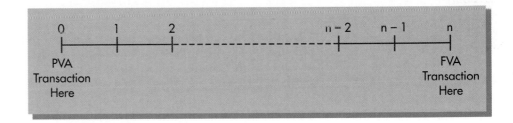

A loan is always a present value of an annuity problem. The annuity itself is the stream of loan payments. The transaction is the transfer of the amount borrowed from the lender to the borrower. That always occurs at the beginning of the payment stream.

Putting aside money to pay for something in the future (saving up) is always a future value of an annuity problem. For example, suppose we're saving up to buy a car by depositing equal sums in the bank each month. The deposits are the payments, and the car purchase is the transaction at the end of the payment stream.

PERPETUITIES

A **perpetuity** is a stream of regular payments that goes on **forever**.

A series of equal payments that occur at equal intervals and go on forever is called a **perpetuity**. You can think of a perpetuity as an infinite annuity although it's not really an annuity.

The concept of future value clearly doesn't make sense for perpetuities, because there's no end point in time to which future values can be projected. The present value of a perpetuity, however, does make sense.

The present value of a perpetuity, like that of an annuity, is the sum of the present values of all the individual payments. At first that doesn't seem to make sense either, because you'd think the sum of the present values of an infinite number of payments would be an infinite number itself.

However, the *present value* of each payment in an infinite stream is a diminishing series of numbers. Each payment's PV contribution to the sum is smaller than that of the one before because of the fact that it's farther out into the future. Mathematically, the sum of such a diminishing series of numbers turns out to be finite. Further, the computation of that finite value turns out to be rather simple.

The present value of a perpetuity of payments of amount PMT, at interest rate k, which we'll call PV_p, is just

(5.24)
$$PV_p = \frac{PMT}{k},$$

where k is the interest rate for the period on which the payment is made. For example, if the payment is made quarterly and interest is compounded quarterly, k is the interest rate for quarterly compounding, $k_{nom}/4$.

Notice that the present value of a perpetuity at a given interest rate is a sum that if deposited at that rate will just earn the amount of the payment each period without compounding.

EXAMPLE 5.14

Preferred Stock

● **Preferred stock** dividends are a perpetuity.

The Longhorn Corporation issues a security that promises to pay its holder $5 per quarter indefinitely. Money markets are such that investors can earn about 8% compounded quarterly on their money. How much can Longhorn sell this special security for?

Solution: Longhorn's security represents a perpetuity paid on a quarterly basis. The security is worth the present value of the payments promised at the going interest rate.

$$PV_P = \frac{PMT}{k} = \frac{\$5.00}{.02} = \$250$$

Securities that offer a deal like this are called *preferred stocks.* We'll study preferred stocks in some detail in Chapter 7.

EXAMPLE 5.15

Capitalization of Earnings

● A steady stream of **earnings** is **capitalized** at its present value as a perpetuity.

Ebertek is a privately held corporation that is currently being offered for sale. Big Corp. is considering buying the firm. Ebertek's revenues and earnings after tax have averaged $40 million and $2.5 million, respectively, for the last five years without much variation around those averages. Interest rates are about 10%. What is a realistic starting point for price negotiations?

Solution: If the parties agree that Ebertek's earnings stream is stable, a fair price for the company is the present value of those earnings in perpetuity. In other words, the fair price is the present value of a perpetuity of annual payments equal in size to the annual earnings. In this case the company should be worth approximately

$$PV_P = \frac{PMT}{k} = \frac{\$2,500,000}{.10} = \$25,000,000 \ .$$

This valuation process is called the *capitalization of earnings,* at the relevant interest rate, which is 10% in this case. In essence, we equate the stream of payments to an amount of capital that would earn an equivalent series of payments at the current interest rate.

In this situation, negotiations would move up or down from this starting point depending on whether future earnings prospects look better or worse than the earnings record of the recent past.

Continuous Compounding

In the section on compound interest earlier in this chapter, we discussed compounding periods of less than a year. We specifically addressed annual, semiannual, quarterly, and monthly periods.

Compounding periods can theoretically be even shorter than a day. Hours, minutes, or seconds are indeed possible. In the limit, as time periods become infinitesimally short, we have the idea of *continuous compounding* whereby interest is instantaneously credited to the recipient's account as it is earned.

The development of formulas for continuous compounding is more mathematically advanced than we want to deal with in this text. Therefore we'll just present an expression for amount problems without derivation.

(5.25) $$FV_n = PV(e^{kn})$$

where k is the nominal rate *in decimal form,* and n is the number of years in the problem.

The letter e represents a special number in advanced mathematics whose decimal value is 2.71828 . . . . All financial and engineering calculators have an e^x key for calculating exponential values of e. Notice that you can use equation 5.25 to solve for either the present or future value of an amount. Fractional values for k and/or n can be used directly in this equation.

EXAMPLE 5.16

The Twelfth National Bank of Podunk is offering continuously compounded interest on savings deposits. Such an offering is generally more of a promotional feature than anything else.

a. If you deposit $5,000 at 6½% compounded continuously and leave it in the bank for 3½ years, how much will you have?

b. What is the equivalent annual rate (EAR) of 12% compounded continuously?

Solution: To solve part a, write equation 5.25 and substitute from the problem.

$$FV_n = PV(e^{kn})$$
$$FV_{3.5} = \$5,000(e^{(.065)(3.5)})$$
$$= \$5,000(e^{.2275})$$

Use a calculator to calculate $e^{.2275} = 1.255457$, then multiply.

$$FV_{3.5} = \$6,277.29$$

For part b, calculate the interest earned on a $100 deposit at 12% compounded continuously in one year.

$$FV_n = PV(e^{kn})$$
$$FV_1 = \$100(e^{(.12)(1)})$$
$$= \$100(e^{.12})$$
$$= \$100(1.1275)$$
$$= \$112.75$$

Because the initial deposit was $100, the interest earned is $12.75, and the EAR is $12.75/$100 = 12.75%.

Compare this result to the year-end balances and resulting EAR's for other compounding periods at 12% shown in Table 5.2 on page 158 and the related discussion.

Table 5.5 summarizes all of the time value formulas we've developed.

TABLE 5.5

Time Value Formulas

Equation Number	Formula	Table
	Amounts	
5.4	$FV_n = PV[FVF_{k,n}]$	A-1
5.7	$PV = FV_n[PVF_{k,n}]$	A-2
	Ordinary Annuities	
5.13	$FVA_n = PMT[FVFA_{k,n}]$	A-3
5.19	$PVA = PMT[PVFA_{k,n}]$	A-4
	Annuities Due	
5.22	$FVAd_n = PMT[FVFA_{k,n}](1 + k)$	A-3
5.23	$PVAd = PMT[PVFA_{k,n}](1 + k)$	A-4
	Perpetuity	
5.24	$PV_p = PMT/k$	
	Continuous Compounding	
5.25	$FV_n = PV(e^{kn})$	

A NOTE ON THE SIMILARITY OF THE EQUATIONS   Either of the two amount equations can be used to solve any amount problem, because both come from equation 5.3. The four variables are the same, and the time value factors are reciprocals of one another.

The two annuity expressions appear to have the same symmetry, but they don't. The annuity equations are not interchangeable, and each is suited only to its own type of problem. Further, there isn't a reciprocal relationship between the factors. You therefore must choose the correct annuity formula before starting a problem.

● MULTIPART PROBLEMS

Real situations often demand putting two or more time value problems together to get a final solution. In such cases, a time line portrayal can be critical to keeping things straight. Here are two examples.

EXAMPLE 5.17

Exeter Inc. has $75,000 invested in securities that earn a return of 16% compounded quarterly. The company is developing a new product that it plans to launch in two years at a cost of $500,000. Exeter's cash flow is good now but may not be later, so management would like to bank money from now until the launch to be sure of having the $500,000 in hand at that time. The money currently invested in securities can be used to provide part of the launch fund. Exeter's bank has offered an account that will pay 12% compounded monthly. How much should Exeter deposit with the bank each month to have enough reserved for the product launch?

Solution: Two things are happening at once in this problem. Exeter is saving up money by making monthly deposits (an annuity), and the money invested in securities (an amount) is growing independently at interest.

To figure out how much the firm has to deposit each month, we need to know how much those deposits have to accumulate into by the end of two years. That's not given, but it can be calculated. The stream of deposits must provide an amount equal to $500,000 less whatever the securities investment will grow into.

Thus, we have two problems that must be handled sequentially. First we have an amount problem to find the future value of $75,000. Once we have that figure, we'll subtract it from $500,000 to get the contribution required from the annuity. Then we'll solve a future value of an annuity problem for the payment required to get that amount.

It's important to notice that k and n aren't the same for the two parts of the problem. For the amount problem, we have quarterly compounding over two years at 16%, so k = 4% and n = 8 quarters. In the annuity problem, we have monthly compounding of 12% for two years, so k = 1% and n = 24 months. The two-part time line follows.

● Calculator Solution

Key	Input
n	8
I/Y	4
PV	75,000
PMT	0
Answer	
FV	102,643

Find the future value of $75,000 by using equation 5.4.

$$FV_n = PV[FVF_{k,n}]$$

$$FV_8 = \$75,000[FVF_{4,8}]$$

$$= \$75,000[1.3686]$$

$$= \$102,645$$

Then the savings annuity must provide

$$\$500,000 - \$102,645 = \$397,355.$$

In other words, the future value of the annuity of the savings deposits is $397,355. Use equation 5.13 to solve for the required payment.

● Calculator Solution

Key	Input
n	24
I/Y	1
FV	397,355
PV	0
Answer	
PMT	14,731

$$FVA_n = PMT[FVFA_{k,n}]$$

$$\$397,355 = PMT[FVFA_{1,24}]$$

$$\$397,355 = PMT[26.9735]$$

$$PMT = \$14,731$$

EXAMPLE 5.18

The Smith family plans to buy a new house three years from now for $200,000. They'll take out a traditional 30-year mortgage at the time of purchase. Mortgage lenders generally base the amount they'll lend on the borrower's gross family income, allowing roughly 25% of income to be applied to the mortgage payment. The Smiths anticipate that their family income will be about $48,000 at the time they'll purchase the house. The mortgage interest rate is expected to be about 9% at that time.

   The mortgage alone won't provide enough cash to buy the house, and the family will need to have a down payment saved to make up the difference. They have a bank account that pays 6% compounded quarterly in which they've already saved $10,000. They plan to make quarterly deposits from now until the time of purchase to save the rest. How much must each deposit be?

Solution: We need three time lines to visualize this problem: one for the $10,000 already in the bank, one for the loan, and one for the savings to be made over the next three years. A time line diagram is usually necessary in problems like this one.

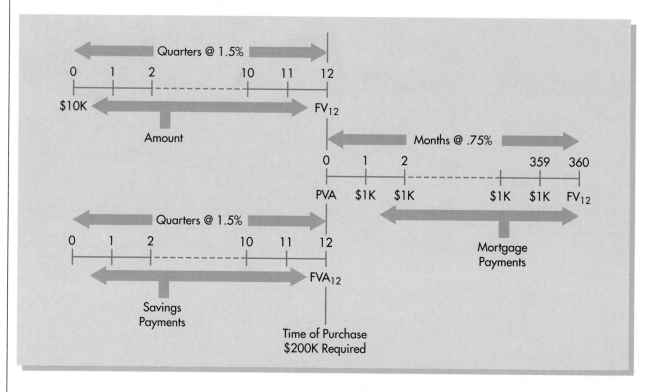

   Notice that the problem is focused around the date of purchase of the house. The amount problem and the annuity of the savings end at that time, but that's when the loan begins. That is, time 0 for the loan isn't the present but a time three years in the future. Nevertheless, we'll refer to the loan amount as the present value of the annuity of the payments.

   The problem asks us to calculate how much the Smiths need to save each quarter. To do that we have to know how much they need to save up in total. That's the future value of the annuity of their savings, FVA_{12} in the diagram. That sum is going to be $200,000 less the amount that can be borrowed, less the amount that the money already in savings will have grown into. Those amounts are PVA and FV_{12}, respectively, in the diagram.

First calculate the amount that can be borrowed by using the present value of an annuity formula (equation 5.19). A 30-year mortgage at 9% implies k = .75% and n = 360. The Smith's annual income is $48,000 or $4,000 a month. Generally about twenty-five percent of that amount, $1,000, can be used for a mortgage payment.

$$PVA = PMT[PVFA_{k,n}]$$
$$= \$1,000[PVFA_{.75,360}]$$
$$= \$1,000[124.282]$$
$$= \$124,282$$

Next calculate the future value of the $10,000 already in the bank by using equation 5.4. Six percent compounded quarterly for three years implies k = 1.5% and n = 12.

$$FV_{12} = \$10,000[FVF_{1.5,12}]$$
$$= \$10,000[1.1956]$$
$$= \$11,956$$

The savings requirement is $200,000 less these amounts; that's $63,762. This sum is the future value of the annuity of the savings deposits. We can solve for the required deposit by using the future value of an annuity formula (equation 5.13). Because this money is going into the same bank account as the previous $10,000, k and n are the same.

$$FVA_n = PMT[FVFA_{k,n}]$$
$$\$63,762 = PMT[FVFA_{1.5,12}]$$
$$\$63,762 = PMT[13.0412]$$
$$PMT = \$4,889$$

Don't be confused by the fact that the savings deposits and the $10,000 already saved are in the same account. For purposes of calculation, they can be treated as though they're in identical but separate accounts.

Our figures show that the Smiths would have to deposit almost $4,900 a quarter, which is about $1,630 a month. That's probably a bit too much to be realistic at their income level.

● **Calculator Solution**

Key	Input
n	360
I/Y	.75
PMT	1,000
FV	0
	Answer
PV	124,282

● **Calculator Solution**

Key	Input
n	12
I/Y	1.5
PV	10,000
PMT	0
	Answer
FV	11,956

● **Calculator Solution**

Key	Input
n	12
I/Y	1.5
FV	63,762
PV	0
	Answer
PMT	4,889

●UNEVEN STREAMS AND IMBEDDED ANNUITIES

Many real-world problems involve streams of payments that aren't even. When that occurs, we can't use the annuity formulas to calculate present and future values, and generally we must treat each payment as an independent amount problem. For example, consider the payment stream represented by the following time line.[3]

---

3. Although we haven't shown one here, you should recognize that one or more payments in a stream like this can be negative. A negative payment simply means that money is going the other way. For example, if a series of payments represents projected profits from a business, a negative number would just reflect a loss in some period. It would make a negative contribution to the present or future value calculation.

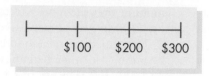

The only way to deal with this stream is to handle each payment as an individual amount. That's not too hard if we're looking for the present or future value, but it's quite difficult if we're looking for an interest rate that yields a particular present or future value.

For example, we might be asked to find the interest rate at which the PVs of the individual amounts just add up to $500.

The correct approach to that question is iterative. That means we guess at an interest rate and calculate the PV of the stream. If the calculated PV isn't $500, we make another, better guess and recalculate. As we'll see shortly, there's a way of making sure the second guess moves us closer to the solution. We'll do this problem as an illustration.

EXAMPLE 5.19

Calculate the interest rate at which the present value of the stream of payments shown above is $500.

Solution: We'll use the present value of an amount formula for each successive payment and start off by guessing at an interest rate of 12%. The present value of the entire stream is then

$$PV = FV_1[PVF_{k,1}] + FV_2[PVF_{k,2}] + FV_3[PVF_{k,3}]$$
$$= \$100[PVF_{12,1}] + \$200[PVF_{12,2}] + \$300[PVF_{12,3}]$$
$$= \$100(.8929) + \$200(.7972) + \$300(.7118)$$
$$= \$462.27 .$$

This figure is lower than the $500 we're looking for, so our guess was wrong. Because our guess discounted the figures by too much, and higher interest rates discount amounts more, we conclude that the next guess should be lower.

Using 11% gives $471.77, which is closer but still not high enough. Try a few more iterations to show that the answer is between 8% and 9%.

Imbedded Annuities

Sometimes uneven streams have regular sections, and we can use the annuity formula to reduce the number of calculations required to compute the present or future values.

Consider calculating the present value of the following uneven stream in which the third through sixth payments represent a $3 annuity of four periods.

● The **"present value"** of an imbedded annuity is moved back in time **as an amount.**

Instead of calculating the present value of each term, we can recognize the annuity and use the PVA formula for that part. However, we have to remember that the annuity formula gives the present value at the beginning of the annuity. In this case that's at time 2, not at time 0. Hence, we have to bring the "present" value of the annuity back another two periods as an amount to get its "present" value as of time 0 as indicated schematically in the diagram.

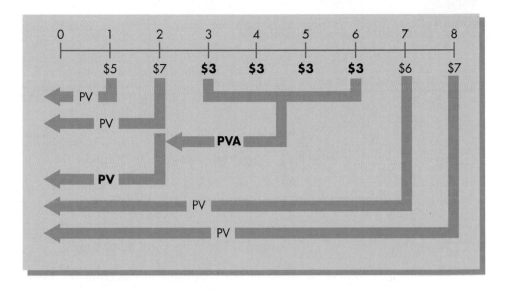

EXAMPLE 5.20

Calculate the present value of the uneven stream above at 12%.

Solution: First handle the first two and the last two payments as simple amount problems.

$$\text{Payment 1: PV} = FV_1[PVF_{12,1}] = \$5(.8929) = \$4.46$$
$$\text{Payment 2: PV} = FV_2[PVF_{12,2}] = \$7(.7972) = \$5.58$$
$$\text{Payment 7: PV} = FV_7[PVF_{12,7}] = \$6(.4523) = \$2.71$$
$$\text{Payment 8: PV} = FV_8[PVF_{12,8}] = \$7(.4039) = \$2.83$$

Next find PVA for the annuity at the beginning of period 3 (end of period 2), and bring it back two years as an amount.

$$\text{PVA} = PMT[PVFA_{12,4}] = \$3(3.0373) = \$9.11$$

and

$$\text{PV} = FV_2[PVF_{12,2}] = \text{PVA}(.7972) = \$9.11(.7972) = \$7.26$$

Now add up all the PVs to get the final answer of $22.84.

CALCULATOR SOLUTIONS FOR UNEVEN STREAMS   Financial calculators have the ability to handle uneven streams with a limited number of payments. They're generally programmed to find the present value of the stream given an interest rate or the interest rate that will yield a particular present value. Your calculator's operating manual includes instructions on how to input uneven cash flows and produce these results.

Spreadsheets have functions that do the same thing and are generally easier to use than calculators.

Evaluating uneven streams is a key element of an important financial technique known as capital budgeting which we'll study in great detail in Chapters 9, 10, and 11. We'll look into calculator and spread sheet solutions at that time.

DISCUSSION QUESTIONS

1. Why are time value concepts important in ordinary business dealings, especially those involving contracts?

2. Why are time value concepts crucial in determining what a bond or a share of stock should be worth?

3. In a retail store a discount is a price reduction. What's a discount in finance? Are the two ideas related?

4. Calculate the present value of one dollar 30 years in the future at 10% interest. What does the result tell you about very long-term contracts?

5. Write a brief verbal description of the logic behind the development of the time value formulas for annuities.

6. Deferred payment terms are equivalent to a cash discount. Discuss and explain this idea.

7. What's an opportunity cost interest rate?

8. Discuss the idea of a sinking fund. How is it related to time value?

9. The amount formulas share a closer relationship than the annuity formulas. Explain and interpret this statement.

10. Describe the underlying meaning of compounding and compounding periods. How does it relate to time value? Include the idea of an effective annual rate (EAR). What is the annual percentage rate (APR)? Is the APR related to the EAR?

11. What information is contained in a loan amortization schedule?

12. Discuss mortgage loans in terms of the time value of money and loan amortization. What important points should every homeowner know about how mortgages work?

13. Discuss the idea of capitalizing a stream of earnings in perpetuity. Where is this idea useful? Is there a financial asset that makes use of this idea?

14. When an annuity begins several time periods into the future, how do we calculate its present value today? Describe the procedure in a few words.

PROBLEMS

Amount Problems

1. The Lexington Property Development Company has a $10,000 note receivable from a customer due in three years. How much is the note worth today if the interest rate is

a. 9%?

b. 12% compounded monthly?

   c. 8% compounded quarterly?

   d. 18% compounded monthly?

   e. 7% compounded continuously?

2. What will a deposit of $4,500 left in the bank be worth under the following conditions?

   a. Left for nine years at 7% interest

   b. Left for six years at 10% compounded semiannually

   c. Left for five years at 8% compounded quarterly

   d. Left for 10 years at 12% compounded monthly

3. What interest rates are implied by the following lending arrangements?

   a. You borrow $500 and repay $555 in one year

   b. You lend $1,850 and are repaid $2,078.66 in two years

   c. You lend $750 and are repaid $1,114.46 in five years with quarterly compounding

   d. You borrow $12,500 and repay $21,364.24 in three years under monthly compounding

   (*Note:* In c and d, be sure to give your answer as the annual nominal rate.)

4. How long does it take for the following to happen?

   a. $856 grows into $1,122 at 7%

   b. $450 grows into $725.50 at 12% compounded monthly

   c. $5,000 grows into $6724.44 at 10% compounded quarterly

5. Sally Guthrie is looking for an investment vehicle that will double her money in five years.

   a. What interest rate, to the nearest whole percentage, does she have to receive?

   b. At that rate, how long will it take the money to triple?

   c. If she can't find anything that pays more than 11%, approximately how long will it take to double her investment?

   d. What kind of financial instruments do you think Sally is looking at? Are they risky? What could happen to Sally's investment?

6. Branson Inc. has sold product to the Brandywine Company, a major customer, for $20,000. As a courtesy to Brandywine, Branson has agreed to take a note due in two years for half of the amount due.

   a. What is the effective price of the transaction to Branson if the interest rate is: (1) 6%, (2) 8%, (3) 10%, (4) 12%?

   b. Under what conditions might the effective price be even less as viewed by Brandywine?

7. John Cleaver's grandfather died recently and left him a trunk that had been locked in his attic for years. At the bottom of the trunk John found a packet of 50 World War I "liberty bonds" that had never been cashed in. The bonds were purchased for $11.50 each in 1918 and pay 3% interest as long as they're held. (Government savings bonds like these accumulate and compound their interest, unlike corporate bonds which regularly pay out interest to bond holders.)

a. How much are the bonds worth in 2003?

b. How much would they have been worth if they paid interest at a rate more like that paid in recent years, say 7%?

c. Comment on the difference between the answers to parts a and b.

8. Paladin Enterprises manufactures printing presses for small-town newspapers that are often short of cash. To accommodate these customers, Paladin offers the following payment terms.

⅓ on delivery

⅓ after six months

⅓ after 18 months

The Littleton *Sentinel* is a typically cash-poor newspaper considering one of Paladin's presses.

a. What discount is implied by the terms from Paladin's point of view if it can invest excess funds at 8% compounded quarterly?

b. The *Sentinel* can borrow limited amounts of money at 12% compounded monthly. What discount do the payment terms imply to the *Sentinel*?

c. Reconcile these different views of the same thing in terms of opportunity cost.

9. Charlie owes Joe $8,000 on a note that is due in five years with accumulated interest at 6%. Joe has an investment opportunity now that he thinks will earn 18%. There's a chance, however, that it will earn as little as 4%. A bank has offered to discount the note at 14% and give Joe cash that he can invest today.

a. How much ahead will Joe be if he takes the bank's offer and the investment does turn out to yield 18%?

b. How much behind will he be if the investment turns out to yield only 4%?

Annuity Problems

10. How much will $650 per year be worth in eight years at interest rates of

a. 12%?

b. 8%?

c. 6%?

11. The Wintergreens are planning ahead for their son's education. He's eight now and will start college in 10 years. How much will they have to set aside each year to have $65,000 when he starts if the interest rate is 7%?

12. What <u>interest rate</u> would you need to get to have an annuity of $7,500 per year accumulate to $279,600 in 15 years?

13. How many years will it take for $850 per year to amount to $20,000 if the interest rate is 8%?

14. What would you pay for an annuity of $2,000 paid every six months for 12 years if you could invest your money elsewhere at 10% compounded semiannually?

15. Construct an amortization schedule for a four-year, $10,000 loan at 6% interest compounded annually.

16. A $10,000 car loan has payments of $361.52 per month for three years. What is the interest rate? Assume monthly compounding and give the answer in terms of an annual rate.

17. Joe Ferro's uncle is going to give him $250 a month for the next two years starting today. If Joe banks every payment in an account paying 6% compounded monthly, how much will he have at the end of *three* years?

18. How long will it take a payment of $500 per quarter to amortize a loan of $8,000 at 16% compounded quarterly. Approximate your answer in terms of years and months. How much less time will it take if loan payments are made at the beginning of each quarter rather than at the end?

19. What are the monthly mortgage payments on a 30-year loan for $150,000 at 12%? Construct an amortization table for the first six months of the loan.

20. Construct an amortization schedule for the last six months of the loan in Problem 19. (*Hint:* What is the unpaid balance at the end of 29½ years?)

21. How soon would the loan in Problem 19 pay off if the borrower made a single additional payment of $17,936.29 to reduce principal at the end of the fifth year?

22. What are the payments to interest and principal during the twenty-fifth year of the loan in Problem 19?

23. Amy's uncle died recently and left her some money in a trust that will pay her $500 per month for five years starting on her twenty-fifth birthday. Amy is getting married soon, and she would like to use this money as a down payment on a house now. If the trust allows her to assign its future payments to a bank, and her bank is willing to discount them at 9% compounded monthly, how much will she have toward her down payment on home ownership? Amy just turned 23.

24. The Orion Corp. is evaluating a proposal for a new project. It will cost $50,000 to get the undertaking started. The project will then generate cash inflows of $20,000 in its first year and $16,000 per year in the next five years, after which it will end. Orion uses an interest rate of 15% compounded annually for such evaluations.

  a. Calculate the "Net Present Value" (NPV) of the project by treating the initial cost as a cash outflow (a negative) in the present, and adding the present value of the subsequent cash inflows as positives. .

b. What is the implication of a positive NPV? (Words only.)

c. Suppose the inflows were somewhat lower, and the NPV turned out to be negative. What would be the implication of that result? (Words only.)

(This problem is a preview of a technique called Capital Budgeting, which we'll study in detail in Chapters 9, 10, and 11.)

Multipart Problems

25. The Tower family wants to make a home improvement that is expected to cost $60,000. They want to fund as much of the cost as possible with a home equity loan but can afford payments of only $600 per month. Their bank offers equity loans at 12% compounded monthly for a maximum term of 10 years.

a. How much cash do they need as a down payment?

b. Their bank account pays 8% compounded quarterly. If they delay starting the project for two years, how much would they have to save each quarter to make the required down payment if the loan rate and estimated cost remain the same?

26. The Stein family wants to buy a small vacation house in a year and a half. They expect it to cost $75,000 at that time. They have the following sources of money.

1. They have $10,000 currently in a bank account that pays 6% compounded monthly.

2. Uncle Murray has promised to give them $1,000 a month for 18 months starting today.

3. At the time of purchase, they'll take out a mortgage. They anticipate being able to make payments of about $300 a month on a 15-year, 12% loan.

In addition, they plan to make quarterly deposits to an investment account to cover any shortfall in the amount required. How much must those additions be if the investment account pays 8% compounded quarterly?

27. Clyde Atherton wants to buy a car when he graduates college in two years. He has the following sources of money.

1. He has $5,000 now in the bank in an account paying 8% compounded quarterly.

2. He will receive $2,000 in one year from a trust.

3. He'll take out a car loan at the time of purchase on which he'll make $500 monthly payments at 18% compounded monthly over four years.

4. Clyde's uncle is going to give him $1,500 a quarter starting today *for one year.*

In addition, Clyde will save up money in a credit union through monthly payroll deductions at his part-time job. The credit union pays 12% compounded monthly. If the car is expected to cost $40,000 (Clyde has expensive taste!), how much must he save each month?

Internet Problem

28. Let's assume you will retire at age 65. Use the retirement calculator at http://www.firstcitizens.com/ops_c_sfr.shtml to calculate how much you would need to save each month if your goal is to accumulate a $1million nest egg and you start saving at

a. age 30.

b. age 40.

c. age 50.

COMPUTER PROBLEMS

29. At any particular time, home mortgage rates are determined by market forces, and individual borrowers can't do much about them. The length of time required to pay off a mortgage loan, however, varies a great deal with the size of the monthly payment made, which is under the borrower's control.

You're a junior loan officer for a large metropolitan bank. The head of the mortgage department is concerned that customers don't fully appreciate that a relatively small increase in the size of mortgage payments can make a big difference in how long the payments have to be made. She feels homeowners may be passing up an opportunity to make their lives better in the long run by not choosing shorter-term mortgages that they can readily afford.

To explain the phenomenon to customers, she's asked you to put together a chart that displays the variation in payment size with term at typical interest rates. The starting point for the charts should be the term for a typical 30-year (360-month) loan. Use the TIMEVAL program to construct the following chart.

Mortgage Payments per $100,000 Borrowed as Term Decreases

		Mortgage Term in Years		
Rates		30	25	20	15
	6%				
	8%				
	10%				
	12%				

Write a paragraph using the chart to explain the point. What happens to the effect as interest rates rise? Why?

30. Amitron Inc. is considering an engineering project that requires an investment of $250,000 and is expected to generate the following stream of payments (income) in the future. Use the TIMEVAL program to determine if the project is a good idea in a present value sense. That is, does the present value of expected cash inflows exceed the value of the investment that has to be made today?

Year	Payment
1	$63,000
2	$69,500
3	$32,700
4	$79,750
5	$62,400
6	$38,250

a. Answer the question if the relevant interest rate for taking present values is 9%, 10%, 11%, and 12%. In the program, notice that period zero represents a cash flow made at the present time, which isn't discounted. The program will do the entire calculation for you if you input the initial investment as a negative number in this cell.

b. Use trial and error in the program to find the interest rate (to the nearest hundredth of a percent) at which Amitron would be just indifferent to the project.

This problem is a preview of an important method of evaluating projects known as *capital budgeting*. We'll study the topic in detail in Chapters 9, 10, and 11. In part a of this problem, we find the *net present value (NPV)* of the project's cash flows at various interest rates and reason intuitively that the project is a good idea if that figure is positive. In part b, we find the return inherent in the project itself, which is called the *internal rate of return (IRR)*. We'll learn how to use that in Chapter 9.

31. The Centurion Corp. is putting together a financial plan for the company covering the next three years, and it needs to forecast its interest expense and the related tax savings. The firm's most significant liability is a fully amortized mortgage loan on its real estate. The loan was made exactly ten and one half years ago for $3.2M at 11% compounded monthly for a term of 30 years. Use the AMORTIZ program to predict the interest expense associated with the real estate mortgage over the next three years. (*Hint:* Run AMORTIZ from the loan's beginning and add up the months in each of the next three years.)

DEVELOPING SOFTWARE

32. Write your own program to amortize a 10-year, $20,000 loan at 10% compounded annually. Input the loan amount, the payment, and the interest rate. Set up your spreadsheet just like Table 5.4, and write your program to duplicate the calculation procedure described.

CHAPTER 6

The Valuation and Characteristics of Bonds

Chapter Outline

Valuation is a systematic process through which we establish the price at which a security *should* sell. We can call that price the security's *intrinsic* value.

THE BASIS OF VALUE

Securities are pieces of paper, and unlike real assets they have no utility of their own. Real assets such as houses and cars have worth because they provide services like shelter and transportation. Paper assets must rely on something else to make them valuable. That something is the expectation of future income that goes along with owning securities. This is an important point. *Every* financial asset depends for its value on the future cash flows that come with it.

Since money expected in the future is worth its present (discounted) value today, *a security's value is equal to the present value of its expected future cash flows*. Further, the security should sell in financial markets for a price very close to that value.

There are often differences of opinion about what the price of a security should be. They arise because people make different assumptions about what the

● Securities are worth the **present value of the future cash income** associated with owning them.

189

security's cash flows will turn out to be and about the appropriate interest rate to use in taking present values. The most arguable cash flows are associated with stocks, because future dividends are never guaranteed and the eventual selling price of a share is always speculative.

The idea of valuation is bound closely to the concept of return on investment. Because of the precise nature of the work we're about to undertake, we need to be very exact in our understanding of what the terms "investment" and "return" mean.

INVESTING

● **Investing** means using a resource to benefit the future rather than for current satisfaction.

Investing means using a resource in a way that generates future benefits rather than in a way that results in immediate satisfaction. We say an investor *forgoes current consumption* in order to improve his or her position in the future. In everyday language that means a person buys securities or puts money in the bank rather than spending it on a new car or going out to dinner.

In finance, investing means putting money to work to earn more money, generally by entrusting it to a person or an organization that uses it and pays the owner for its use. The two most common methods of entrusting money are lending and buying an ownership interest in a business. They are called debt and equity investments, respectively. The vehicle for a debt investment is generally a bond, while for an equity investment it's a share of stock.

RETURN

Returns on One-Year Investments

Return is what an investor receives for making an investment. It can be expressed as a dollar amount or as an annual rate. For investments held for one year, the *rate of return is what the investor receives divided by what he or she invests.*

For debt that's simply the interest received divided by the amount loaned, which is the interest rate we've been calling k. Let's look at the idea a little more deeply in terms of the time value of money.

An amount PV loaned for one year at interest rate k earns interest of kPV. If the lender receives the principal plus the interest at the end of the year, these are the future cash flows that come from making the original investment of PV. Call these future cash flows FV_1 and write

$$FV_1 = PV + kPV$$
$$FV_1 = PV(1 + k) .$$

We recognize this as equation 5.1 from our study of the time value of money.

Now solve for the original investment.

$$PV = \frac{FV_1}{(1 + k)}$$

● The rate of return on a security is the interest rate that **equates the present value of its expected future cash flows with its current price**.

Again we recognize this expression from our study of time value. It's the present value of a future amount due in one year, equation 5.5, with n = 1.

In the context of valuing a security that represents a loan (usually a bond), think of PV as the *price* of the security that returns cash flows FV_1. Then the rate of return, k, can be thought of as the *interest rate that makes the present value of the future cash flows equal to the price.* This is a fundamental definition that applies to any investment held for any length of time.

The details are a bit more involved for equity (stock) investments than for debt, because the future cash flows are more complicated. Nevertheless, the basic rule is the same. We'll discuss the returns to equity investments in Chapter 7.

Returns on Longer Term Investments

When the holding period is longer and there are a number of cash flows at different times, the concept remains the same. The return is still the discount rate that makes the present value of the future cash flows equal to the price.

For example, suppose someone offers to sell you an investment that will pay $200 one year from now and $250 two years from now for $363 paid today. If you accept the offer, the return on your investment will be the interest rate at which the present value of the two payments just equals the $363 "price" of the investment today. A time line for the arrangement looks like this.

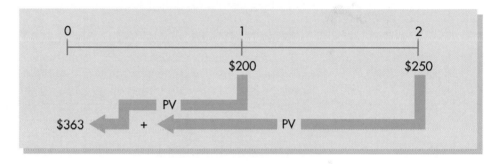

● The terms **yield, return,** and **interest** mean essentially the same thing.

As an exercise, show that the return on this hypothetical investment would be very close to 15%.

The term "yield" is synonymous with "rate of return." Its use is especially common with debt securities and traditional loans.

In the remainder of this chapter we'll look closely at the valuation of bonds and then at their institutional[1] characteristics. We'll turn our attention to stocks in Chapter 7.

BOND VALUATION

● A **bond issue** allows an organization to borrow from many lenders at one time under a single agreement.

Bonds represent a debt relationship in which the issuing company borrows and the buyer lends. A bond issue is an arrangement through which one company can borrow from many people at once. For example, suppose a large firm wants to borrow $10 million but can't find anyone willing to lend that much. Many people might be willing to lend smaller amounts, however, if the firm's credit reputation is good. If the company issues 10,000 bonds at $1,000 each, as many as 10,000 people could participate in the loan by buying one bond apiece. Bonds enable firms to raise large amounts by spreading a loan among a number of lenders.

Before we get into the valuation of bonds, we need to learn a little about terminology and practice. We've introduced some of these ideas before, but will repeat them here for convenience.

---

1. The term "institutional" refers to the rules and practices according to which things are done in an organized society.

BOND TERMINOLOGY AND PRACTICE

● A bond's **term** or **maturity** is the time from the present until the principal is to be returned.

A bond represents a loan made by the buyer to the issuer for a period known as the *term*. The bond itself is a **promissory note** that serves as legal evidence of the debt. Bonds are said to *mature* on the last day of their terms. Every bond issued has a *par* or *face value*, which is printed on the face of the document. This is the amount the issuing company intends to borrow; in effect, it's the principal of the loan.

Bonds are *non-amortized* debt. That means no repayment of principal is made during the term. Rather, the face value is repaid in a lump sum on the maturity date. Interest is paid regularly during the term, however, usually semiannually.

Any lender is said to extend *credit* to borrowers. Therefore bondholders are called *creditors* of the company issuing the bonds. The term "creditor" also applies to banks that make loans to companies and vendors that sell products without receiving immediate payment.

Newly issued bonds are called *new issues,* as one might expect, while older bonds are commonly called **seasoned issues.**

The Coupon Rate

● A bond's **par** or **face value** is the amount the issuer intends to borrow at the **coupon rate** of interest.

Most bonds pay interest at rates set at the time of issue called **coupon rates.** The coupon rate applied to the face value of a bond yields the dollar amount of interest paid, called the **coupon payment.** Coupon rates and payments are generally fixed throughout the life of a bond regardless of what happens to interest rates in financial markets.

The term "coupon" is outdated but is still in common use. Years ago, bonds were issued with a number of coupons attached that looked something like a sheet of postage stamps. When an interest payment was due, a bond owner would clip off a coupon and send it to the issuing company, which would return a check for the interest. Hence the term "coupon" became associated with bond interest.

Coupons are rarely used today. Interest payments are now mailed directly to bondholders whose names and addresses are *registered* with the issuing company or its agent. Nevertheless, the term "coupon" is still associated with bond interest.

BOND VALUATION—BASIC IDEAS

Now we have enough background to begin studying bond valuation. Keep in mind that valuation simply means determining the price a security should command in the financial market in which it is traded.

Adjusting to Interest Rate Changes

Let's put several facts from our earlier work together with what we've just learned about bonds. First recall from Chapter 4 that securities including bonds are sold in both primary and secondary markets. A primary market transaction refers to the original sale of the bond by the issuing company, and secondary market transactions are subsequent trades among investors. Second, recall from our discussion of financial markets in Chapter 4 that interest rates change all the time. Finally, we've just learned that most bonds pay interest at coupon rates that are fixed throughout their lives.

All this raises a question. How can a bond that pays a fixed rate be sold in the secondary market if interest rates have changed since it was originally issued? An example will make the idea clear.

Suppose Tom Benning, a typical investor, buys a newly issued 20-year bond directly from the Groton Company for its face value of $1,000. We'll assume that the bond pays interest at a coupon rate of 10%, which is the market rate for bonds of comparable risk at the time. From the discussion we've already had about valuation, we know that Tom has actually purchased a stream of future income. He'll receive interest payments of $100 a year (10% of $1,000) for 20 years and a payment of $1,000 returning principal along with the last interest payment.

Now imagine that a few days after Tom's purchase, interest rates rise to 12%. Also assume that coincidentally something occurs in Tom's financial situation that requires him to get out of the bond investment. That is, he needs the cash he used to buy the bond for something else, perhaps an emergency.

Tom can't go back to Groton, the issuing company, and ask for a refund. The company borrowed the funds expecting to keep them for 20 years, and it would be unwilling to give up those terms. So to get his money back, Tom has to sell the bond to another investor in a secondary market transaction.

Let's suppose Tom approaches Sandra Fuentes, a friend who he knows is in the market for an investment, and asks if she'd like to buy his Groton Company bond. She says she might be interested and asks how much he wants. Tom answers that he bought it only a few days ago for $1,000 and would like to get about that much. What would Sandra's reaction be to Tom's asking price?

Unfortunately for Tom, Sandra wouldn't be willing to pay $1,000. That's because the increase in interest rates has given her better options. New bonds now being issued offer 12%, which means they'll pay $120 a year for 20 years plus the final $1,000. Sandra, as a rational investor, would have to refuse Tom's offer.

But suppose Tom is desperate and really has to sell his bond. What is he to do? Clearly the only way he'll interest a buyer is to lower the price. In fact, he'll have to lower the price until the return to the new buyer on his or her investment is just 12%. It turns out that he'd have to lower the price to exactly $849.51. We'll see how that figure is calculated later in the chapter. For now the important thing to understand is that the price of bonds on the secondary market *drops* in response to an increase in interest rates.

What would have happened if interest rates had fallen rather than having gone up? In that case, new issues would have offered less interest than Tom's bond, and he could have sold it for *more* than $1,000. In general, bond prices *rise* in response to a *drop* in interest rates.

● Bond **prices** respond to **changes** in the market rate of **interest** by moving in a direction **opposite** to the change.

Summarizing, we see that *bond prices and interest rates move in opposite directions.* This phenomenon is a fundamental and critically important law of finance and economics. When interest rates decline, the prices of debt securities go up; when rates increase, prices go down. The price changes are just enough to keep the yields (returns) on investments in seasoned issues equal to the yields on new issues of comparable risk and maturity. In other words, *bonds adjust to changing yields by changing their prices.*

As a result of all this, bonds don't generally sell for their face values. They trade for more or less, depending on where the current interest rate is in relation to their coupon rates. The terminology associated with this phenomenon is important. Bonds selling above their face values are said to be trading at a *premium,* while those selling below face value are said to trade at a *discount*. If at a point in time the market interest rate returns to a bond's coupon rate, the bond sells for its face value at that time. At such a time, we say the bond is trading at *par value*.

● DETERMINING THE PRICE OF A BOND

We made the point earlier that the value and hence the price of any security should be equal to the present value of the expected future cash flows associated with owning that security. In the case of bonds, those future cash flows are quite predictable, because they're specified by the bond agreement.

Bondholders receive interest payments periodically and a lump sum return of principal at the bond's maturity. Yearly interest is determined by applying the coupon rate to the face value of the bond, and the principal is simply the face value itself.

Let's illustrate the pattern of these payments by setting up a time line to display the cash flows coming from a $1,000 bond with a coupon rate of 10% whose maturity date is 10 years off. Most bonds pay interest semiannually, but for illustrative purposes we'll assume this one pays annually. The time line of cash flows is illustrated in Figure 6.1.

Notice that the amount received in the tenth year is the sum of the last interest payment and the return of principal. Also notice that the interest payments are all the same and occur regularly in time.

It's important to realize that it doesn't matter whether the bond is new at time zero. The picture shown would be valid for a new 10-year bond, a 20-year bond that's currently 10 years old, or any other 10% $1,000 bond that has 10 years to go until maturity. Time zero is now, and the only thing that matters in today's valuation is *future* cash flows. Past cash flows are gone and irrelevant to today's buyer.

Having used Figure 6.1 to visualize bond cash flows in a simple numerical case, let's generalize the idea by showing a time to maturity of n periods, an interest payment represented as PMT, and a face value of FV. Recognize that each of these elements varies with different bonds. The general case is represented by the time line at the top of Figure 6.2.

In practice most bonds pay interest semiannually. That means the periods represented along the time line in Figure 6.2 are usually half years. Under those conditions, the interest payment, PMT, is calculated by applying the coupon rate to the face value and dividing by two. For example, if the bond in Figure 6.2 had 10 years to go until maturity, had a face value of $1,000, and paid 10% interest semiannually, the time line would contain 20 periods, and each PMT would be $50.

FIGURE 6.1

Cash Flow Time Line for a Bond

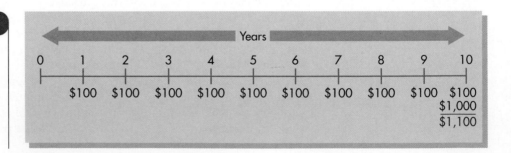

FIGURE 6.2

Bond Cash Flow and Valuation Concepts

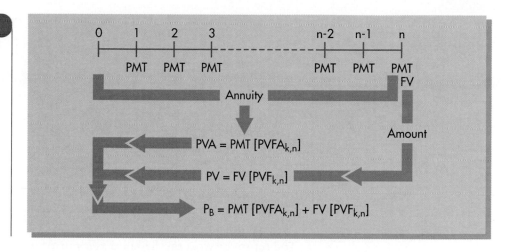

The Bond Valuation Formula

As we've been saying, a security's price should be equal to the present value of all the cash flows expected to come from owning it. In the case of a bond, the expected cash flows consist of a series of interest payments and a single payment returning principal at maturity. Hence the price of a bond, which we'll write as P_B, is the present value of the stream of interest payments plus the present value of the principal repayment.

(6.1) $P_B = PV(\text{interest payments}) + PV(\text{principal repayment})$

Because the interest payments are made regularly and are constant in amount, they can be treated as an annuity, and we can calculate their present value by using equation 5.19, the present value of an annuity formula. We'll rewrite that formula here for convenience.

(5.19) $PVA = PMT[PVFA_{k,n}]$

Applying this formula directly to the bond's interest, we can write

(6.2) $PV(\text{interest payments}) = PMT[PVFA_{k,n}]$,

where PMT is the bond's regular interest payment, n is the number of interest-paying periods remaining in the bond's life, and k is the current market interest rate for comparable bonds for the interest-paying period.

A bond's principal is always equal to its face value, so the return of principal is an expected payment of that amount n periods in the future. Its present value can be calculated by using equation 5.7, the present value of an amount formula, which we'll repeat here.

(5.7) $PV = FV_n[PVF_{k,n}]$

We'll drop the subscript on FV_n and think of FV as face value rather than future value in this application. Then we can write

(6.3) $PV(\text{principal repayment}) = FV[PVF_{k,n}]$.

Substituting equations 6.2 and 6.3 in 6.1, we get a convenient expression for calculating the price of a bond based on its future cash flows using our familiar time value techniques.

● A bond's value is the sum of the present value of the **annuity of its interest payments** plus the present value of the **return of principal**, both taken at the current **market rate** of interest.

(6.4) $$P_B = PMT[PVFA_{k,n}] + FV[PVF_{k,n}]$$

The approach is illustrated graphically in Figure 6.2. In essence, pricing a bond involves doing an annuity problem and an amount problem together, and summing the results.

Two Interest Rates and One More

It's important to notice that two interest rates are associated with pricing a bond. The first is the coupon rate, which when applied to the face value determines the size of the interest payments made to bondholders. The second is k, the current market yield on comparable bonds at the time the price is being calculated. Don't confuse the two. The rate at which the present value of cash flows is taken is k. The only thing you do with the coupon rate is calculate the interest payment.

The return or yield on the bond investment to the bond holder is k. It is the interest rate that makes the present value of all the payments represented in Figure 6.2 equal to the price of the bond. Because this return considers all payments until the bond's maturity, it's called the yield to maturity, abbreviated YTM. When people refer to a bond's yield, they generally mean the YTM.

The third yield associated with a bond is called the *current yield*. This is a summary piece of information used in financial quotations and is not associated with the pricing process. The current yield is the annual interest payment divided by the bond's current price.

Solving Bond Problems with a Financial Calculator

In Chapter 5 we noted that financial calculators have five time value keys. When doing amount or annuity problems we used four of the five keys and zeroed the fifth.

In bond problems we use all five keys. The calculator is programmed to recognize the five inputs as two problems and add the results together. In a bond problem the keys have the following meanings.

Yield-to-maturity is easily calculated using the financial calculator at

● http://financenter.com/

    n—number of periods until maturity

    I/Y—Market interest rate

    PV—price of the bond—that is, the present value of all the cash flows

    FV—Face value of the bond

    PMT—Coupon interest payment per period

The unknown is either the price of the bond (PV) or the market interest rate (IY), which is equal to the bond's yield to an investor buying at the current price. To solve a problem, we enter the four known variables first, press the compute key, and then press the key for the unknown variable.

Sophisticated calculators have a "bond mode" that allows you to input exact calendar dates for the present and the bond's maturity as well as some additional details about the payment of principal and interest. This facilitates the exact pricing of bonds sold in the middle of the month and issues with unusual provisions. Traders operating in fast-moving bond markets use such calculating options all the time. The time value keys are sufficient for our purposes, since our goal is simply to gain a broad understanding of bond operations.

EXAMPLE 6.1

The Emory Corporation issued an 8%, 25-year bond 15 years ago. At the time of issue it sold for its par (face) value of $1,000. Comparable bonds are yielding 10% today. What must Emory's bond sell for in today's market to yield 10% (YTM) to the buyer? Assume the bond pays interest semiannually. Also calculate the bond's current yield.

Solution: This is the typical bond problem. We're given a bond's face value, coupon rate, and remaining term, and are asked to find the price at which it must sell to achieve a particular return. Since the return is the market interest rate, we're being asked to find the market price of the bond. The question is equivalent to asking for the present value of the bond's expected cash flows at today's interest rate.

To solve the problem, we first write equation 6.4, the bond valuation formula.

$$P_B = PMT[PVFA_{k,n}] + FV[PFV_{k,n}]$$

Then we put the information given in the proper form for substitution into the equation.

The interest payment is found by applying the coupon rate to the face value and dividing by two, because payments are semiannual.

$$PMT = [coupon\ rate \times face\ value]/2$$

$$= (.08 \times \$1,000)/2$$

$$= \$40.00$$

Next we need n, the number of interest-paying periods from now until the end of the bond's term. This bond, like most, pays interest semiannually, so we multiply the number of years until maturity by two to get n. Notice that n represents the time from now until maturity. It doesn't matter how long the bond has been in existence previously. In this case,

$$n = 10\ years \times 2 = 20 .$$

Next we need k, the current market interest rate. Recall that when using time value formulas for non-annual compounding, we have to state n and k consistently for the compounding period. Here, n represents a number of semiannual periods, so k must be stated for semiannual compounding. That just means dividing the nominal rate by two,

$$k = 10\%/2 = 5\% .$$

Finally, the face value is given directly as $1,000, so

$$FV = \$1,000 .$$

Substitute these values into the bond equation,

$$P_B = \$40[PVFA_{5,20}] + \$1,000[PVF_{5,20}] ,$$

and use Appendix A for the factors. A-4 gives

$$PVFA_{5,20} = 12.4622 ,$$

while A-2 yields

● **Calculator Solution**

Key	Input
n	20
I/Y	5
FV	1,000
PMT	40
Answer	
PV	875.38

$$PVF_{5,20} = .3769 .$$

Substituting, we get

$$P_B = \$40[12.4622] + \$1,000[.3769]$$
$$= \$498.49 + \$376.90$$
$$= \$875.39 .$$

This is the price at which the Emory bond must sell to yield 10%. It won't be competitive with other bonds at any higher price. Notice that it's selling at a discount, a price below its face value, because the current interest rate is above the coupon rate.

The bond's current yield is calculated as follows.

$$\text{current yield} = \frac{\text{annual interest}}{\text{price}} = \frac{\$80}{\$875.39} = 9.14\%$$

Although using the bond valuation formula is easy once you get used to it, students often have trouble knowing where to put what at first. Here's a self-test example using the method we've just illustrated. It will help your understanding a great deal if you work it yourself *before* looking at the solution.

EXAMPLE 6.2

Self-Test

Carstairs Inc. issued a $1,000, 25-year bond five years ago at 11% interest. Comparable bonds yield 8% today. What should Carstairs's bond sell for now?

Solution: The variables are as follows (as usual, assume semiannual interest).

$$PMT = (.11 \times \$1,000)/2 = \$55 ,$$
$$n = 20 \times 2 = 40 ,$$
$$k = 8\%/2 = 4\%, \text{ and}$$
$$FV = \$1,000$$

Then, using equation 6.4,

$$P_B = PMT[PVFA_{k,n}] + FV[PVF_{k,n}]$$
$$= \$55[PVFA_{4,40}] + \$1,000[PVF_{4,40}]$$
$$= \$55(19.7928) + \$1,000(.2083)$$
$$= \$1,088.60 + \$208.30$$
$$= \$1,296.90$$

The current yield is

$$\text{current yield} = \$110/\$1,296.90 = 8.48\% .$$

● **Calculator Solution**

Key	Input
n	40
I/Y	4
FV	1,000
PMT	55
Answer	
PV	1,296.89

Estimating the Answer First

If we think of the bond as having been issued at a time when the market rate was equal to the coupon rate, we can make a rough estimate of the current price before starting the problem. That provides a good reasonableness check on the solution we come up with. We base the estimate on the fact that bond prices and interest rates move in opposite directions.

In Example 6.1, we knew the current price of the bond had to be *below* the face value of $1,000. That's because the market interest rate had *risen* from 8% at the time of the bond's issue to its current value of 10%. Further, the increase was fairly substantial, so we were looking for a significant drop in price, which is what we found.

It doesn't matter whether the interest rate fluctuated up and down past 8% after the bond was issued or moved directly to 10%. The only rates that count for today's price are the original coupon rate and the current rate.[2]

Before starting a bond problem, you should always decide whether the new price will represent a premium or a discount from the face value.

In general, price changes due to a given interest rate change will be larger the more time there is remaining until maturity. We'll see that more clearly in the next section.

● MATURITY RISK REVISITED

In Chapter 4 we developed an interest rate model in which rates generally consist of a base rate plus premiums for various risks borne by lenders. In particular, the model recognizes *maturity risk,* which is related to the term of the debt. We're now in a position to fully understand this important idea.

The risk arises from the fact that bond prices vary (inversely) with interest rates. When an investor buys a bond, the only way to recover the invested cash before maturity is to sell it to someone else. If interest rates rise and prices fall while the investor is holding the bond, the sale to someone else will be at a loss. (Review page 123 if necessary.)

This is exactly what happened to Tom Benning in our illustration of price adjustments to interest rate changes. The possibility of such a loss viewed at the time of purchase is the risk we're talking about.

> ● **Maturity risk** exists because the prices of **longer term** bonds **fluctuate more** in response to **interest rate changes** than the prices of shorter term bonds.

Maturity risk has two other names, *price risk* and *interest rate risk*. These terms reflect the fact that bond *prices* move up and down with changes in *interest rates*.

The expression *maturity risk* emphasizes the fact that the *degree* of risk is related to the maturity (term) of the bond. The longer the term (time until maturity), the greater the maturity (price, interest rate) risk. The reason is that the prices of longer term bonds change more in response to interest rate movements than do the prices of shorter term bonds.

---

2. Bonds aren't always issued at coupon rates equal to the current market interest rate, but it helps to understand the pricing process if we imagine that they are. In practice, coupon rates are usually targeted at or near the current market rate. However, the mechanics of printing and issuing cause a delay between the time the rate is chosen and the time the bond actually hits the market. As a result there's usually a slight difference between coupon rates and current market rates. Bonds issued above or below market rates simply sell at premiums or discounts, respectively, when offered on the primary market. Because market rates change constantly some discount or premium is almost always associated with a new issue.

TABLE 6.1	Price Changes at Different Terms Due to an Interest Rate Increase from 8% to 10%		
	Time to Maturity	Price	Drop from $1,000
	2 years	$964.54	$ 35.46
	5	922.77	77.23
	10	875.39	124.61
	20	828.36	171.64

To see that, let's look again at the bond in Example 6.1. It was issued at 8% and had 10 years to go until maturity. Interest rates rose to 10%, and the price dropped to $875.39. Let's calculate what the price would have become under varying assumptions about the remaining term to maturity without changing anything else in the problem.

Table 6.1 gives the bond's price and the price drop from $1,000 at terms of 2, 5, 10, and 20 years. You might want to verify that these figures are correct as an exercise. Each of the price changes in Table 6.1 is the result of the same increase in interest rates, from 8% to 10%. Notice how much larger the price drop becomes as the term of the bond increases. This is the essence of maturity risk. The possible loss on debt investments due to interest-rate-induced price changes increases with the term of the debt.

Realizing this fact, investors demand a premium to compensate for the additional risk they bear with longer issues. This is the *maturity risk premium*.

As Time Goes By

Let's consider the original Emory Corporation bond in Example 6.1 again. Recall that the interest rate rose from 8% to 10%, and the price fell from $1,000 to $875.39 with 10 years of term to go.

Let's imagine a very unlikely event just to enhance our understanding of the processes involved in bond pricing.

What would happen to the price of the Emory bond as time goes by *if interest rates didn't change again* for the remainder of the bond's life (a practical impossibility)? Would the price remain at $875.39, or move to something else? Test your understanding by answering the question before reading on.

In fact, the bond's price would slowly rise to $1,000 as maturity approached. If you have trouble seeing that, think of what it would be worth on the day before maturity. Someone buying at that time would be getting virtually no interest, because the last interest payment would be prorated almost entirely to the person who owned the bond during most of the last period. A buyer on the day before maturity would be buying a payment of $1,000 to be made the next day. That would be worth very nearly $1,000. This logic tells us that as we get closer to maturity, the price has to approach the bond's face value of $1,000.

We've already calculated what the price would be at two points along the way to maturity in our hypothetical example. Table 6.1 tells us that with five years to go the price will be $922.77 and when just two years remain it will be $964.54. Graphically, the progression in prices is shown in Figure 6.3.

FIGURE 6.3

Price Progression with Constant Interest Rate

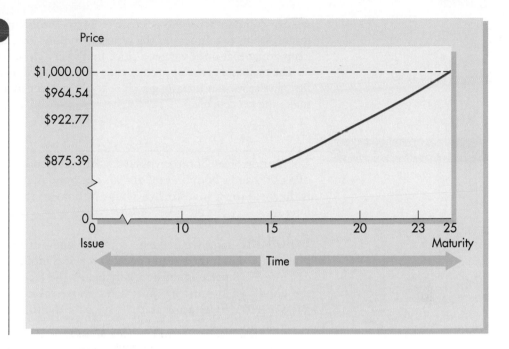

FINDING THE YIELD AT A GIVEN PRICE

Basically only two questions are asked about the dollars and cents of bonds. We've just explored the first, finding the price at which a bond achieves a specified yield. The second question is the reverse of the first. It asks for the yield on a bond investment if the security sells at a particular price. In the bond valuation formula, equation 6.4, this question asks us to find the market interest rate, k, given a value for P_B.

Let's rewrite equation 6.4 for convenient reference.

(6.4) $$P_B = PMT[PVFA_{k,n}] + FV[PVF_{k,n}]$$

Recall that finding P_B when the market yield is known simply involves doing two time value problems and adding the results together. We do a present value of an annuity problem for the interest payments and a present value of an amount problem for the return of the face value. Finding k when P_B is known is conceptually the same but much more difficult.

Recall the time value problems we studied in Chapter 5. In both amount and annuity problems we were able to solve for an unknown k quite easily. We did so by solving one of the time value formulas for a factor, and then finding the factor in the table.

Even though the bond formula utilizes present value factors and the same tables we used in Chapter 5, this approach doesn't work. It fails because equation 6.4 uses two time value factors at the same time. As we have only one equation, we can't solve for both, and therefore can't find the right column and row in each table simultaneously.

This mathematically unfortunate state of affairs means we have to resort to a rather tedious approach to solving the problem, trial and error. We begin by guessing at a solution for k. Then we value the bond at that return by using equation 6.4 and whatever other information we have. That process results in a price we can compare with the price given by the problem. If they're significantly different, we have to guess at the return again and reevaluate for another price. We keep doing that until we get a price that's very close to the one we're looking for.

The trial and error approach isn't as haphazard as it may seem. By applying a little logic, we can usually get close to the answer in a few tries. An example will make the process clear.

EXAMPLE 6.3

The Benson Steel Company issued a 30-year bond 14 years ago with a face value of $1,000 and a coupon rate of 8%. The bond is currently selling for $718. What is the yield to an investor who buys it today at that price? (Assume semiannual interest.)

Solution: First we make an educated guess at the answer on the basis of our knowledge that interest rates and bond prices move in opposite directions. In this case the $718 price is substantially below the face value of $1,000, so we know the bond's yield must be quite a bit above the coupon rate. Let's make a first guess at 10%. Evaluating at 10%, we have the following variables.

$$PMT = (.08 \times \$1,000)/2 = \$40$$

$$n = 16 \times 2 = 32$$

$$k = 10\%/2 = 5\%$$

$$FV = \$1,000$$

Then, using Equation 6.4, we have

$$P_B = PMT[PVFA_{k,n}] + FV[PVF_{k,n}]$$

$$= \$40[PVFA_{5,32}] + \$1,000[PVF_{5,32}]$$

$$= \$40(15.8027) + \$1,000(.2099)$$

$$= \$632.11 + \$209.90$$

$$= \$842.01 .$$

Clearly 10% isn't the solution, because we're looking for the rate that yields a price of $718. Our choice has brought the price down from $1,000, but not far enough. That means we have to bring the rate up quite a bit more. For illustrative purposes, let's jump all the way to 14% (we probably wouldn't go that far if we weren't trying to make a point). The only input that changes from our last try is k, which is now

$$k = 14\%/2 = 7\% .$$

Substitute into equation 6.4 and verify that the calculation leads to

$$P_B = \$620.56 .$$

This figure is substantially *below* the target of $718, so we've pushed our interest rate too high. Now we know the answer has to be between 10% and 14%. Let's try a figure right in the middle. Evaluate the bond at 12% to verify that the resulting price is

$$P_B = \$718.36 .$$

● **Calculator Solution**

Key	Input
n	32
PV	718.00
FV	1,000
PMT	40
	Answer
I/Y	6 × 2 = 12.0

This is just a shade higher than the actual selling price, so the true yield is just below 12%. For most purposes, declaring 12% the solution would be close enough.

Financial calculators are programmed to solve bond programs, including finding yields. The internal workings of such calculators do exactly what we've just done, find the solution by trial and error.

CALL PROVISIONS

Circumstances sometimes arise in which bond issuers want to pay off their indebtedness early. This commonly occurs when interest rates drop a great deal after bonds are issued.

For example, suppose a company issues a 30-year bond with a 15% coupon rate when interest rates are at about that level. Some years later, suppose rates drop to 7%. The firm will be stuck paying above-market rates on the bond's principal until maturity unless it can somehow get out of the loan arrangement with the bondholders.

Companies that issue bonds anticipate this sort of thing, and like to include call provisions in bond agreements to protect themselves. A call provision is a clause that gives the issuing organization the right to pay off the bond prior to maturity. In our illustration, the company would like to borrow money at the new lower interest rate of 7%, and use it to retire the old bond that pays 15%. The process is called *refunding* the debt.

> ● **Call provisions** allow bond issuers to **retire** bonds **before maturity** by paying a premium (penalty) to bondholders.

Investors who buy bonds don't like call provisions because they feel the clauses give firms the opportunity to renege on interest rate obligations. In the example we've just described, the bondholders were getting a 15% return on funds in a market that currently offered only 7%. If the bond is paid off early, they'll lose that 15% and will have to reinvest at 7%.

These conflicting interests are reconciled with a two- or three-part compromise. First, call provisions are generally written to include a *call premium* that must be paid to bondholders if the feature is exercised. This means that if the company chooses to pay a bond off early, it must pay lenders (bondholders) some extra money as compensation for their loss of the original deal. The premium is usually stated in terms of extra interest at the coupon rate, and diminishes as the bond's maturity approaches.

Second, issuers usually agree that the bond won't be called for a certain number of years at the beginning of its life. This initial time is the period of *call protection*. Finally, to attract buyers, a bond with a call provision may require a somewhat higher interest rate than similar bonds without call provisions.

Call provisions are also sometimes exercised to free companies of restrictions imposed by certain agreements associated with bond contracts called *indentures*. We'll discuss indentures later in the chapter.

Figure 6.4 portrays a declining call premium starting at one year's interest on a 10%, $1,000 bond with a term of 10 years and a call-protected period of five years.

The call premium is also known as a *call penalty*. This apparent conflict is easily explained by point of view. The payment is a premium to the investor who receives it but a penalty to the company that pays it. Call provisions are also called *call features*.

INSIGHTS

Practical Finance

Can a Bond Be a Bond without Paying Interest?

The answer to that mysterious question is yes; they're called **zero coupon bonds**.

To understand the idea think about a bond issued at a very low coupon rate—say, half the market rate. It would sell at a deep discount because the interest payments would be less than investors could get elsewhere. But offsetting the low interest payments, investors would receive the bond's face value at maturity, which would be more than they paid for it. In other words, investors who chose the bond would be trading some current income for a capital gain later on. But that capital gain would be unusual in that it wouldn't come from changing market values. It would actually be interest earned on the debt all along but not paid until maturity.

If we take this idea to the extreme making the coupon interest smaller and smaller until it's gone, we've got a zero coupon bond. Essentially it's just a promise to pay a face amount in the future that sells for the present value of that amount today.

The "zero" has some interesting tax implications. You'd think the investor would pay no tax until maturity because no money is received until then. But that isn't the case. The IRS *imputes* interest during the bond's life and demands tax on the phantom income.

We're all familiar with zeros under another name, U.S. savings bonds. They operate in exactly the same way. We buy a bond for the present value of its face at maturity. They're a popular gift because a $100 bond only costs about $60. There is one big difference, however. The government gives buyers of its own "zeros" a break by not taxing the interest until maturity.

● A **zero coupon bond** pays no interest during its life, but imputed interest is still taxable.

The Effect of a Call Provision on Price

A special situation arises when a bond with a call provision is in its protected period, but appears certain to be called as soon as that period is over. In such a case the traditional bond valuation procedure doesn't work because it includes cash flows projected to occur after the protected period. These cash flows aren't likely to be forthcoming because the bond will probably be paid off exactly at the end of the protected period. In such cases, bondholders will actually receive normal interest payments up until call, at which time they'll receive the bond's face value plus the call premium. The situation is illustrated graphically in Figure 6.5.

Examine the diagram carefully. It shows the entire life of a bond that was originally intended to pay interest for 10 semiannual periods. This would normally be a five-year bond. The first three years are call protected in this example. We're

FIGURE 6.4

The Call-Protected Period and a Declining Call Premium

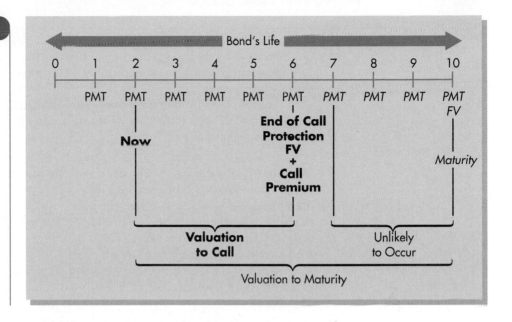

FIGURE 6.5

Valuation of a Bond Subject to Call

assuming the first year has past, so the present is indicated by **"Now"** at the end of period 2.

We assume the interest rate has dropped substantially, so the bond is very likely to be called at the end of the third year, period 6. Cash flows planned after that time probably won't happen. These are shown in italics.

We'd normally value this bond by taking the present value of all the payments from **Now** until maturity, including the return of the face value at maturity. This would mean that in the bond valuation formula we would use n = 8 and substitute the face value for FV.

What's actually going to happen, however, is a shorter series of interest payments ending with the sixth, and a final payment equal to FV *plus* the call premium.

Valuing the Sure To Be Called Bond

We can value this bond with the same formula we've used up until now by making two simple modifications to our inputs. All we have to do to realistically represent what is likely to happen is let n equal the time to call instead of the time to maturity, and add the call premium to the face value when we portray the final payment. The sum of the face value and the call premium is known as the *call price*.

We can express these ideas in a modification of the bond formula as follows.

(6.5) $$P_B(\text{call}) = \text{PMT}[\text{PVFA}_{k,m}] + \text{CP}[\text{PVF}_{k,m}] \,,$$

where

$$m = \text{number of periods to call}$$

$$\text{CP} = \text{call price} = \text{face value} + \text{call premium}$$

PMT and k are computationally the same as in the problem without a call. However, k is known as the yield to call, abbreviated YTC, because it's used in taking the present value of cash flows only until the call is likely to occur.

EXAMPLE 6.4

The Northern Timber Co. issued a $1,000, 25-year bond five years ago. The bond has a call provision that allows it to be retired any time after the first 10 years with the payment of an additional year's interest at the coupon rate. Interest rates were especially high when the bond was issued, and its coupon rate is 18%. Interest rates on bonds of comparable risk are now 8%. What is the bond worth today? What would it be worth if it didn't have the call feature? Assume interest payments are semiannual.

Solution: This problem asks us to evaluate the price of the bond, first assuming the call feature will be exercised (which is very likely) and then in the normal way. The basic assumption is that the bond must *yield* the current rate of interest in either case. That is, even if the bond is going to be called, the price will adjust to bring the yield to the market rate of 8%. A graphic depiction of the problem follows (the interest payments are omitted).

Notice that the time line shows semiannual periods rather than years. The call premium is 18% of $1,000 or $180, so the call price is ($1,000 + $180 =) $1,180.

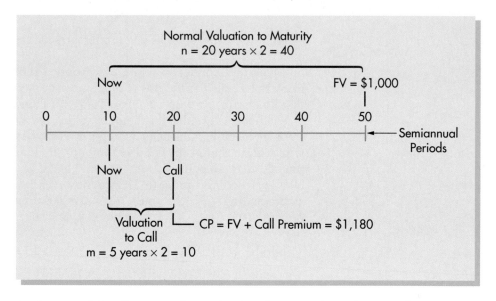

At the top of the diagram, above the time line, we show the period over which the bond would normally be evaluated and the face value to be returned of $1,000. At the bottom we show the relevant period for a likely call and a call price of $1,180.

First we'll evaluate to maturity using equation 6.4.

$$P_B = PMT[PVFA_{k,n}] + FV[PVF_{k,n}] .$$

The variables follow.

$$PMT = (.18 \times \$1,000)/2 = \$90$$

$$n = 20 \times 2 = 40$$

$$k = 8\%/2 = 4\%$$

$$FV = \$1,000$$

● **Calculator Solution**

Key	Input
n	40
I/Y	4
FV	1,000
PMT	90
	Answer
PV	1,989.64

Substituting, we have

$$P_B = \$90[PVFA_{4,40}] + \$1,000[PVF_{4,40}]$$
$$= \$90[19.7928] + \$1,000[.2083]$$
$$= \$1,781.35 + \$208.30$$
$$= \$1989.65.$$

Notice how much the price has risen, almost doubling the original $1,000. That's because the drop in the interest rate was very substantial *and* the bond has a long time to go until maturity. This price represents the present value of Northern Timber's (the bond issuer) cash flow commitment if the bond isn't called.

Next we'll evaluate to call using equation 6.5.

$$P_B(call) = PMT[PVFA_{k,m}] + CP[PVF_{k,m}].$$

The variables follow.

$$PMT = (.18 \times \$1,000)/2 = \$90$$
$$m = 5 \times 2 = 10$$
$$k = 8\%/2 = 4\%$$
$$CP = \$1,000 + .18(\$1,000) = \$1,180$$

Substituting,

$$P_B(call) = \$90[PVFA_{4,10}] + \$1,180[PVF_{4,10}]$$
$$= \$90[8.1109] + \$1,180[.6756]$$
$$= \$729.98 + \$797.21$$
$$= \$1,527.19.$$

● **Calculator Solution**

Key	Input
n	10
I/Y	4
FV	1,180
PMT	90
	Answer
PV	1,527.15

Notice that the price is substantially above $1,000 but is much less than the price without a call. From the point of view of a bond buyer, the only relevant price is $1,527.19, because the likelihood of call is very high. This price represents the value of Northern Timber's cash flow commitment if the bond is called. Notice how much Northern will save if it calls the bond.

The Refunding Decision

Whenever the current interest rate is substantially below a bond's coupon rate and the issue has a call feature, the issuing company has to decide whether or not to exercise the call. The company has to compare the interest savings from calling the bond with the cost of making the call and issuing a new bond to raise the money required to pay the old one off.

The difference in bond prices in the last example shows the interest savings associated with a call and includes a major cost item, the call premium. However, the figure does not include administrative expenses or the cost of issuing a new bond.

The costs incurred in issuing new bonds are known as *flotation costs* and can be rather substantial. They're primarily brokerage fees paid to investment bankers, but they also include administrative expenses and the costs of printing and engraving.

As a result of these costs, interest rates have to drop a lot before it's advisable for a company to refund by calling in one bond issue and floating another.

Dangerous Bonds with Surprising Calls

from the **CFO**

Bonds can occasionally have obscure call features buried in their contract terms that can cause unwary investors real grief. These generally take the form of a clause that says if some particular event occurs the bond will be called at face value.

The most common of these clauses involve *sinking fund* provisions. Recall that in Chapter 5 we described a sinking fund as a way lenders guarantee that borrowers will have enough money put aside to pay off a bond's principal when it comes due. (Review pages 155–156 if necessary.) There we said that borrowing firms can make deposits in a separate account whose future value will be the amount of the bond's principal.

Another way to provide for an orderly payoff of principal is to require that the individual bonds of an issue be called in and paid off over a series of years rather than all at once. For example, suppose a company borrowed a million dollars for 25 years by issuing 1,000 25-year bonds, each with a face value of $1,000. Repayment could be made a lot more secure if, instead of paying off all the bonds at the maturity date, the company called and retired a few each year during the last five years of the issue's life.

Sinking fund provisions often require companies to do just that, call in and retire a fixed percentage of the issue each year toward the end of the term. Since this procedure is for the benefit of the bondholders (to increase their security), the agreements don't generally include a call premium. The bonds called are usually determined by a *lottery,* so no one knows which bonds will be called early and which will continue to maturity.

Now, suppose a particular bond that's subject to sinking fund provisions like these happens to be selling at a premium because of interest rate changes. An unlucky investor might buy a $1,000 face value bond for, say, $1,100, and in short order receive a call at $1,000 that results in an immediate loss of $100! This does happen, even though bond investments are supposed to be relatively safe.

Here's another example. Government agencies issue bonds that are backed by mortgages on residential real estate. If the mortgages underlying the bonds are held to maturity, the bonds pay interest until maturity. But if the mortgages are paid off early, the funds are used to retire the bonds at face value. Because no one knows how fast people will pay off their home mortgages, you can never be sure the mortgage-backed bonds won't be called early.

Needless to say, it's wise to check the details of bond agreements before investing.

● RISKY ISSUES

Sometimes bonds sell for prices far below those indicated by the valuation techniques we've described so far in this chapter. For example, suppose we applied equation 6.4 to a particular $1,000 face value bond and came up with a value of $950. However, suppose we checked the financial pages of a newspaper and found the bond to be trading at $500.

from the **CFO**

This would usually mean the company that issued the bond is in financial trouble, and there is some question about its ability to honor the obligations of the bond agreement. In other words, analysts feel it might default on the payment of interest and/or principal. Obviously such a risk will cause investors to lower their estimates of what any security is worth.

Financial purists argue that in such a situation equation 6.4 still gives the right answer if we properly select the interest rate k. The argument is that the increased risk should be reflected in a higher expected return to the investor. Using a higher k results in a lower calculated price. In other words, the bond has slipped into a lower quality class, which should be reflected by the requirement of a higher yield to compensate for the chance that the investor may lose everything if things go poorly for the company.

However you look at it, a major deterioration in a bond-issuing company's financial performance will substantially depress the price of its securities, including bonds.

INSTITUTIONAL CHARACTERISTICS OF BONDS

In the remainder of this chapter we'll describe some of the more important features of bonds and bond agreements that aren't directly related to pricing. Keep the fundamental definition of a bond in mind as we go forward. A bond is a device that enables an organization (generally a corporation or a government unit) to borrow from a large number of people at the same time under one agreement.

REGISTRATION, TRANSFER AGENTS, AND OWNERS OF RECORD

Bonds are classified as either **bearer bonds** or **registered bonds**. Bearer bonds belong to whoever possesses them, a convention that makes them dangerously subject to loss and theft. Bearer bonds have coupons attached for the payment of interest as described earlier.

The owners of registered bonds are recorded with a **transfer agent**. This is an organization, usually a bank, that keeps track of the owners of stocks and bonds for issuing companies. When one investor sells a security to another, the agent *transfers* ownership in its records as of the date of the sale. On any given date, there is a particular *owner of record* on the transfer agent's books for every bond (and share of stock) outstanding. Interest payments are sent directly to the owners of record of registered bonds as of the date the interest is paid.

A record of owners of **registered securities** is kept by a **transfer agent**. Payments are sent to **owners of record** as of the dates the payments are made.

KINDS OF BONDS

Several distinguishing features divide bonds into different categories. We'll briefly discuss a few of the more important distinctions.

Secured Bonds and Mortgage Bonds

Secured bonds are backed by the value of specific assets owned by the issuing company. If the firm defaults, the secured bondholders can take possession of the assets and sell them to recover their claims on the company. The essence of the secured arrangement is that the assets tied to specific debt aren't available to other creditors until that debt is satisfied. When the securing assets are real estate, the bond is called a **mortgage bond**.

Debentures

Debentures are unsecured bonds. They rely on the general creditworthiness of the issuing company rather than the value of specific assets. Debentures are clearly more risky than the secured debt of the same company. Therefore, they must usually be issued to yield higher returns to investors.

http://

Current bond investment articles can be found in MONEY magazine at

www.money.com

in Kiplinger's Personal Finance magazine at

www.kiplinger.com

in Business Week at

www.businessweek.com

and in Smart Money at

www.smartmoney.com

Subordinated Debentures and Senior Debt

The term "subordinated" means lower in rank or priority. In terms of debt, it means having lower priority than other debt for repayment in the event the issuing company fails. Debentures can be subordinated to specific issues or to all other debentures in general. The debt having priority over a *subordinated debenture* is known as s*enior debt*.

Conceptually, subordination arises with the senior debt. For example, suppose a lender is considering making a loan but fears the borrower will take on more debt from other lenders in the future. Then if the borrower failed, whatever assets were available to satisfy unpaid loans would have to be shared among a large number of creditors. Some security is afforded to the first lender by writing a clause into the loan agreement requiring the subordination of all future debt.

● **Subordinated debt** is **lower in priority** for payment of principal and interest than **senior debt.**

Because subordinated debt is riskier than senior or unsubordinated debt, it generally requires a higher yield than those issues.

Convertible Bonds

Convertible bonds can be converted into a specified number of shares of stock at the option of the owner. Bondholders generally *exercise the conversion privilege* if the stock's price rises enough to make the converted shares of stock worth more than the bond.

● **Convertible bonds** can be exchanged for specified amounts of stock.

Recall that an important distinction between stocks and bonds is that stocks have a potential for significant price appreciation if the issuing company does very well, but bonds do not. Convertible features are designed to share a limited amount of that appreciation potential with bondholders. Hence, they're sweeteners that make bonds more attractive.

For example, a $1,000 bond might be convertible into 50 shares of stock, implying a conversion price of $20 per share. The bond is issued when the price of the stock is substantially below $20. Then suppose the stock's price rises to $25. The bondholder converts, effectively paying $20 for shares with a market value of $25, making a gain of

$$\$5 \times 50 \text{ shares} = \$250 \,.$$

Of course, if the stock's price never exceeds $20, the conversion feature is never exercised and turns out to have no value.

Convertibles can generally be issued at somewhat lower interest rates than regular bonds. Such a rate reduction reflects the value placed on the conversion potential by the market. Further, companies can occasionally borrow using convertibles when traditional debt would be impossible to market because of risk.

Junk Bonds

Junk bonds are issued by companies that are not in particularly sound financial condition or are considered risky for some other reason. They generally pay interest rates that are as much as 5% higher than the rates paid by the strongest companies. Hence they're also called *high-yield* securities.

● **Junk bonds** are issued by risky companies and pay high interest rates.

Before the mid-1970s it was virtually impossible for risky firms, especially new, small companies, to borrow by issuing unsecured bonds. Investors were simply unwilling to accept the risks associated with such firms at any promised rate of return. At that time, however, a concept of pooling risky bonds arose and seemed to make high-risk, high-yield issues viable in the sense of being reasonably safe investments. For a few years the volume of junk bonds exploded, growing until it represented 10% to 20% of the total domestic bond market.

In the late 1980s and early 1990s, the safety perceived in the pooling technique evaporated when the economy went into a sustained recession. As a result, the junk bond vehicle lost most of its popularity. We'll discuss junk bonds again in Chapter 17.

● BOND RATINGS—ASSESSING DEFAULT RISK

Recall that in Chapter 4 we discussed several risks associated with bonds, including the risk of default (pages 122–123). In practice, investors and the financial community go to great lengths to assess and control exposure to default risk in bonds.

● **Bond ratings** gauge the probability that issuers will fail to meet their obligations.

Bonds are assigned quality ratings that reflect the probability of their going into default. Higher ratings mean lower default probabilities. The bond ratings are developed by *rating agencies* that make a business of staying on top of the things that make bonds and the underlying firms more or less risky. The best known rating agencies are Moody's Corporation (known as Moody's) and Standard & Poor's Corporation (generally called S&P).

The agencies rate bonds by examining the financial and market condition of the issuing companies and the contractual provisions supporting individual bonds. It's important to realize that the analysis has these two parts. A bond's strength is fundamentally dependent on that of the issuing corporation, but some things can make one bond safer than another issued by the same company. For example, a mortgage bond backed by real estate will always be stronger than an unsecured debenture issued by the same company. Similarly, senior debt is always superior to subordinated debt.

The process of rating a bond begins with a financial (ratio) analysis of the issuing firm using the kinds of tools we developed in Chapter 3. To that the agencies add any knowledge they have about the company, its markets, and its other dealings. For example, suppose a firm has good financial results and a prosperous market outlook but is threatened by a major lawsuit. If the lawsuit is very serious, it can lower the rating of the firm's bonds.

Bond ratings are not precise in the sense of being the result of a mathematical formula. Although they do rely heavily on standard numerical (ratio) analyses, they also include qualitative judgments made by the rating agencies.

Rating Symbols and Grades

Moody's and S&P use similar scales to describe the bonds they rate. It's important to be generally familiar with the meaning of the terms. Table 6.2 summarizes the symbols used by the two firms and their meanings. The distinction between bonds above and below the Baa/BBB is especially significant. Bonds at or above that level are said to be **investment grade**, whereas those below are considered substandard. The latter can be called *junk bonds*.

Why Ratings Are Important

Throughout our study, we've stressed the fact that risk and return are related, and that investors *require* higher returns on riskier investments. Ratings are the primary measure of the default risk associated with bonds. Therefore they're an important determinant of the interest rates investors demand on the bonds of different companies.

TABLE 6.2	**Moody's and S&P Bond Ratings**		
	Moody's	S&P	Implication
	Aaa	AAA	Highest quality,
	Aa	AA	extremely safe
	A	A	Good quality,
	Baa	BBB	"investment grade"
	Ba	BB	Poor quality,
	B	B	risky
	Caa	CCC	Low quality,
	Ca	CC	very risky
		C	
	C	D	

http://

Bonds Online Internet provides information about investing in bonds at **www.bonds-online.com**.

In effect, the rating associated with a firm's bonds determines the rate at which the firm can borrow. A lower rating implies the company has to pay higher interest rates. That generally means it's more difficult for the company to do business and earn a profit, because it's burdened with a higher cost of debt financing. To be precise about what we've just said, the idea is laid out in Figure 6.6.

All bond yields (interest rates) move up and down over time, but there's always a *differential* between the rates required on high and low quality issues. The lower curve associated with high-quality bonds means that the issuing companies can borrow at lower rates (more cheaply) than those associated with risky, low-quality bonds. The safest, highest quality bond is a federal treasury bond, which has no default risk (Chapter 4, page 125). Its yield plotted on a graph like Figure 6.6 would be lower than that of any other bond.

A bond's rating affects the size of the differential between the rate it must pay to borrow and the rate demanded of high quality issues. It does not affect the overall up and down motion of the rate structure. Clearly, the differential reflects

FIGURE 6.6	
The Yield Differential between High- and Low-Quality Bonds	

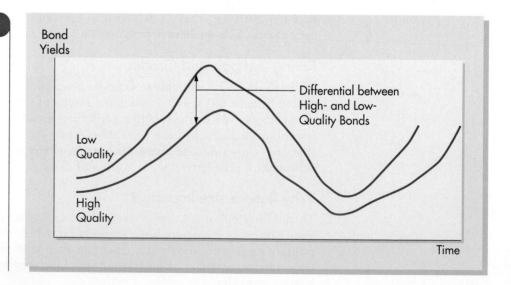

Real
Applications

Even the Safest Companies Can Default on Bonds—The Perils of Utility Deregulation in California

Public utilities like water and power companies have traditionally issued some of the safest securities available. That's because until recently they were all "regulated monopolies." This means customers have to buy their water and electricity from the utilities, but prices are set by government commissions that ensure customers get a fair deal.

This generally makes investment in utility stocks and bonds safe but unexciting. Under normal conditions, regulated utilities just about can't lose money, but they can't make much either. As a result, returns on their securities are stable and relatively risk free. Utility bonds have always been particularly safe havens for investors concerned about risk, and traditionally received high grades from bond rating agencies.

However, in recent years there's been a general movement by state governments to deregulate utilities, that is, to take away their monopoly status and eliminate price controls. The rationale is that the pressure of competition will result in greater efficiency and lower prices for consumers. California moved toward an unregulated approach to the electric power business with laws passed in 1996.

Electric power is provided in a two-step process. Suppliers generate electricity and sell it wholesale to electric utilities, who sell it to homes and businesses at retail prices. Traditionally both wholesale and retail transactions were regulated. In California, legislation was designed to phase in deregulation by introducing market pricing of the utilities' purchase of power from power suppliers first, and then to later introduce market pricing to the end consumer. It was believed this two-step procedure would prevent consumers from experiencing a big jolt at the start of deregulation.

Unfortunately, the convergence of unregulated wholesale prices and regulated retail prices had an unexpected outcome that put some of California's huge electric utilities in great peril. They were forced to buy their power in a market in which suppliers could raise prices at will, but they had to sell it in regulated markets in which they couldn't raise prices to match their costs.

From May of 2000 until May of 2001, companies like Southern California Edison ran up massive bills as prices to purchase wholesale electricity surged to unforeseen highs. With customer prices controlled, Southern California Edison was unable to pass on its higher cost and accumulated losses of $3.3 billion. That loss caused the company to default on many of its bond obligations in January of 2001. Seeing the trouble coming, Moody's downgraded the bonds' rating from A1 to A2 in November of 2000. Then, after the default, the debt's rating was further lowered to "junk" status of Caa2.

The downgrading of Southern California Edison's debt wasn't surprising since there was serious talk about the company going into bankruptcy. In October of 2001, the state stepped in and entered into an agreement with the company to help it pay off its debt. That was great news for the bondholders who had invested in these securities before the series of downgrades and for those who took a chance and invested later when the company was in default.

Whether Southern California Edison will regain its investment grade status in the near future is still uncertain. Although the current debt crisis has been handled, the fact that Southern California Edison still cannot pass on the wholesale cost of energy to consumers will continue to make investors cautious.

Sources: Jacob Fine, "California's Silver Lining", *The Bond Buyer* (January 31, 2001): 1; Christopher O'Leary, "Wall Street Pans for gold in the Detritus of California's Big Utilities", *The Investment Dealers' Digest* (January 15, 2001): 3–4; Mark Golden, *Dow Jones Newswires* (October 5, 2001).

the risk of default perceived to exist with lower quality bonds. This is the default risk premium we discussed in Chapter 4.

THE DIFFERENTIAL OVER TIME Notice that the quality differential tends to be larger when interest rates are generally high than when they're low. This is an important fact and makes logical sense. High rates tend to be associated with recessions and tough economic times. It's during those periods that marginal companies are prone to fail. In other words, the risk of default associated with weak companies is greater in bad times than in good times. Because it expresses the level of risk, the differential tends to be larger in recessionary periods.

> ● The **differential** between the yields on high- and low-quality bonds is an indicator of the health of the economy.

In fact, this phenomenon is strong enough to be considered an *economic indicator*. That means a high differential is taken as a signal that harder times are on the way.

THE SIGNIFICANCE OF THE INVESTMENT GRADE RATING Most bonds are purchased by institutional investors rather than by individuals. These investors include mutual funds, banks, insurance companies, and pension funds. Many such institutions are required by law to make only relatively safe, conservative investments. Therefore they can deal only in investment grade bonds. This requirement severely limits the market for the debt of companies whose bonds aren't considered investment grade.

● BOND INDENTURES—CONTROLLING DEFAULT RISK

In Chapter 1 we discussed a conflict of interest between creditors and stockholders (page 18). Virtually all business operations involve some risk. However, higher levels of risk are usually associated with higher rewards. The conflict of interest arises because the rewards of successful risk taking accrue largely to stockholders, while the penalties for failure can be shared between stockholders and creditors.

Indeed, bondholders can be hurt even if failure doesn't occur. If a company is perceived to become more risky, the return investors require on its debt increases immediately, which in turn drives down the market price of its bonds. When that happens, bondholders suffer an immediate loss.

Investors contemplating lending to a company by buying its bonds look at the current level of risk associated with the business. If they're comfortable with that level, they purchase bonds, but remain concerned that future operations could become more risky. That might happen if the firm takes on riskier projects, encounters financial problems, or is managed unwisely.

> ● **Bond indentures** attempt to prevent firms from becoming riskier after the bonds are purchased.

To ensure that bond-issuing companies maintain an even level of risk, lenders usually insist that bond agreements contain restrictions on the borrower's activities until the bonds are paid off. The contractual document containing such *restrictive covenants* is called the bond **indenture**.

Typical indenture provisions preclude entering certain high-risk businesses and limit borrowing more money from other sources. Indentures may also require that certain financial ratios be held above minimum levels. For example, an indenture might require that times interest earned (TIE) be maintained above a particular figure, say seven.

Every bond issue has a *trustee* whose job is to administer and enforce the terms of the indenture on behalf of the bondholders. Trustees are usually banks.

Ethics **Ethical Debt Management**

Suppose a firm borrows through a bond issue with a relatively weak indenture that doesn't say anything about additional future debt. Then suppose it wants to borrow more later on, but the new lender is concerned about safety, and insists that its debt be made *senior* to existing debt. If the firm agrees it will damage the investors who hold the old bonds.

It's fairly obvious that the original bondholders will suffer if the firm fails, because they'll stand behind the new creditors in being paid out of any assets that survive the failure. But they may be hurt even if the firm does well. That's because the old bond's rating is likely to be lowered because of its new subordinate status. That means the market will perceive the issue as having more risk, and is likely to lower its price immediately. Hence old bondholders will take a loss if they sell.

Is it ethical for a firm to do that without in some way compensating the old bondholders? What if management argues that the firm desperately needs the new money and will be in big trouble without it. What would you do if you were CFO?

Sinking Funds

● **Sinking funds** provide money for the repayment of bond principal

Recall that bonds are non-amortized debt, meaning that the borrowed principal is not repaid until maturity. This creates a risk for bondholders in that borrowing firms may not have the funds to make large principal repayments.

Considerable safety is provided by a *sinking fund* that spreads the repayment of principal over time. We've already discussed two sinking fund arrangements. The first calls for periodic deposits such that the amount available at maturity is equal to the principal to be repaid. We illustrated that approach as a future value of an amount problem in Example 5.6 on page 155. A second arrangement involves randomly calling in some bonds for retirement prior to maturity. We discussed that approach starting on page 208 of this chapter.

Still another approach is to issue serial bonds, splitting the total amount borrowed into several separate issues with different maturities, usually about a year apart.

DISCUSSION QUESTIONS

1. What is valuation, and why are we interested in the results?

2. Contrast real assets and financial (paper) assets. What is the basis for the value of each?

3. How can two knowledgeable people come to different conclusions about the value of the same security? Can this happen if they have access to the same information?

4. Describe the nature of a bond. Include at least the following ideas.

term/maturity	face value
debt versus equity	"buying" a bond
non-amortized	one borrower/many lenders
risk	conflict with stockholders

5. What is a call provision? Why do companies put them in bonds? Define call-protected period and call premium/penalty.

6. Two interest rates are associated with pricing a bond. Name and describe each. How are they used? Describe a third rate not used in pricing.

7. If bonds pay fixed interest rates, how can they be sold year after year on the secondary market? Include the idea of how yields adjust to changing market interest rates.

8. Why do bonds have indentures?

9. Describe bond pricing as two time value of money problems.

10. What is the relationship between bond prices and interest rates? Verbally describe how this relationship comes about. How can we use this relationship to estimate the value of a bond?

11. What is interest rate or price risk? Why is it sometimes called maturity risk? Explain fully.

12. What causes maturity risk? In other words, *why* do long-term bonds respond differently to interest rate changes than short-term bonds? (*Hint:* Think about how the present value formulas work.)

13. Using words only, describe the process of finding a bond's yield at a given selling price.

14. Under what conditions is a bond almost certain to be called at a particular date in the future? How does this condition affect its price?

15. You're an analyst in the finance department of Flyover Corp., a new firm in a profitable but risky high-tech business. Several growth opportunities have come along recently, but the company doesn't have enough capital to undertake them. Stock prices are down, so it doesn't make sense to try to raise new capital through the sale of equity. The company's bank won't lend it any more money than it already has, and investment bankers have said that debentures are out of the question. The treasurer has asked you to do some research and suggest a few ways in which bonds might be made attractive enough to allow Flyover to borrow. Write a brief memo summarizing your ideas.

16. The Everglo Corp., a manufacturer of cosmetics, is financed with a 50–50 mix of debt and equity. The debt is in the form of debentures that have a relatively weak indenture. Susan Moremoney, the firm's president and principal stockholder, has proposed doubling the firm's debt by issuing new bonds secured by the company's existing assets, and using the money raised to attack the lucrative but very risky European market. You're Everglo's treasurer, and have been directed by Ms. Moremoney to implement the new financing plan. Is there an ethical problem with the president's proposal? Why? Who is likely to gain at whose expense? (*Hint:* How are the ratings of the existing debentures likely to change?) What would you do if you really found yourself in a position like this?

17. You're the CFO of Nildorf Inc., a maker of luxury consumer goods that, because of its product, is especially sensitive to economic ups and downs (people cut back drastically on luxury items during recessionary times). In an executive staff meeting this morning, Charlie Suave, the president, proposed a major expansion. You felt the expansion would be feasible if the immediate future looked good, but were concerned that spreading resources too thin in a recessionary period could wreck the company. When you expressed your concern, Charlie said he wasn't worried about the economy because the spread between AAA and B bonds is relatively small, and that's a good sign. You observed, however, that rates seem to have bottomed out recently and are rising along with the differential between strong and weak companies. After some general discussion, the proposal was tabled pending further research. Later in the day, Ed Sliderule, the chief engineer, came into your office and asked, "What in the world were you guys talking about this morning?" Prepare a brief written explanation for Ed.

18. How and why do sinking funds enhance the safety of lenders?

PROBLEMS

Assume all bonds pay interest semiannually.

1. The Altoona Company issued a 25-year bond five years ago with a face value of $1,000. The bond pays interest semiannually at a 10% annual rate.

   a. What is the bond's price today if the interest rate on comparable new issues is 12%?

   b. What is the price today if the interest rate is 8%?

   c. Explain the results of parts a and b in terms of opportunities available to investors.

   d. What is the price today if the interest rate is 10%?

   e. Comment on the answer to part d.

2. Calculate the market price of a $1,000 face value bond under the following conditions.

	Coupon Rate	Time Until Maturity	Current Market Rate
a.	12%	15 years	10%
b.	7	5	12
c.	9	25	6
d.	14	30	9
e.	5	6	8

3. The Sampson Company issued a $1,000 bond 5 years ago with an initial term of 25 years and a coupon rate of 6%. Today's interest rate is 10%.

   a. What is the bond's current price if interest is paid semiannually as it is on most bonds?

   b. What is the price if the bond's interest is paid annually? Comment on the difference between a and b.

   c. What would the price be if interest was paid semiannually and the bond was issued at a face value of $1,500?

4. The Mariposa Co. has two bonds outstanding. One was issued 25 years ago at a coupon rate of 9%. The other was issued five years ago at a coupon rate of 9%. Both bonds were originally issued with terms of 30 years and face values of $1,000. The going interest rate is 14% today.

a. What are the prices of the two bonds at this time?

b. Discuss the result of part a in terms of risk in investing in bonds.

5. Longly Trucking is issuing a 20-year bond with a $2,000 face value tomorrow. The issue is to pay an 8% coupon rate, because that was the interest rate while it was being planned. However, rates increased suddenly and are expected to be 9% when the bond is marketed. What will Longly receive for each bond tomorrow?

6. John Wilson is a conservative investor who has asked your advice about two bonds he is considering. One is a seasoned issue of the Capri Fashion Company that was first sold 22 years ago at a face value of $1,000, with a 25-year term, paying 6%. The other is a new 30-year issue of the Gantry Elevator Company that is coming out now at a face value of $1,000. Interest rates are now 6%, so both bonds will pay the same coupon rate.

a. What is each bond worth today? (No calculations should be necessary.)

b. If interest rates were to rise to 12% today, estimate without making any calculations what each bond would be worth. Review page 199 on estimating if necessary.

c. Calculate the prices in part b to check your estimating ability. If interest rates are expected to rise, which bond is the better investment?

d. If interest rates are expected to fall, which bond is better? Are long-term rates likely to fall much lower than 6%? Why or why not? (*Hint:* Think about the interest rate model of Chapter 4 and its components.)

7. Smithson Co.'s Class A bonds have 10 years to go until maturity. They have a $1,000 face value and carry coupon rates of 8%. Approximately what do the bonds yield at the following prices?

a. $770

b. $1,150

c. $1,000

Problems 8 through 10 refer to the bonds of the Apollo Corporation, all of which have a call feature. The call feature allows Apollo to pay off bonds anytime after the first 15 years, but requires that bondholders be compensated with an extra year's interest at the coupon rate if such a payoff is exercised.

8. Apollo's Alpha bond was issued 10 years ago for 30 years with a face value of $1,000. Interest rates were very high at the time, and the bond's coupon rate is 20%. The interest rate is now 10%.

a. At what price should an Alpha bond sell?

b. At what price would it sell without the call feature?

9. Apollo's Alpha-1 bond was issued at a time when interest rates were even higher. It has a coupon rate of 22%, a $1,000 face value, an initial term of 30 years, and is now 13 years old. Calculate its price if interest rates are now 12%, compare it with the price that would exist if there were no call feature, and comment on the difference.

10. Apollo's Beta bond has just reached the end of its period of call protection, has 10 years to go until maturity, and has a face value of $1,000. Its coupon rate is 16% and the interest rate is currently 10%. Should Apollo refund this issue if refunding costs a total of 8% of the value of the debt refunded plus the call penalty?

11. Pacheco Inc. issued convertible bonds 10 years ago. Each bond had an initial term of 30 years, had a face value of $1,000, paid a coupon rate of 11%, and was convertible into 20 shares of Pacheco stock, which was selling for $30 per share at the time. Since then the price of Pacheco shares has risen to $65, and the interest rate has dropped to 8%. What are the bonds worth today? Comment on the function of the bond valuation procedure for convertibles.

Internet Problem

12. Moody's Investors Services at http://www.moodys.com/ provides information to help investors select bonds more prudently. Click on RATING Actions and choose two issues that have recently undergone a change in bond rating. Write a short report in each issue explaining how the rating was changed and why.

COMPUTER PROBLEMS

13. You are a securities salesperson. Many of your clients are elderly people who want very secure investments. They remember the days when interest rates were very stable (before the 1970s) and bond prices hardly fluctuated at all regardless of their terms. You've had a hard time convincing some of them that bonds, especially those with longer terms, can be risky during times when interest rates move rapidly.

Use the BONDVAL program to make up a chart to help illustrate your point during discussions with your clients.

The Value of a $1,000 Par, 12% Coupon Bond as a Function of Term as Interest Rates Change

		Bond Term in Years			
		1	5	10	25
Market Rates	6%				
	8%				
	10%				
	12%				

Write out a brief paragraph outlining your warning about bond price volatility to an elderly customer. Refer to your chart.

14. Use BONDVAL to find the YTM of the following $1,000 par value bonds.

	1	2	3
Market Price	$752.57	$1,067.92	$915.05
Coupon Rate	6.5%	7.24%	12.5%
Term	15.5 yrs	8.5 yrs	2.5 yrs

CHAPTER 7

The Valuation and Characteristics of Stock

Chapter Outline

In this chapter we'll be concerned with determining the value of equity securities, including common and preferred stock. We'll find the process is much less precise than the procedures we studied for bonds because of the nature of equity cash flows.

COMMON STOCK

Corporations are owned by the holders of their common stock. Stockholders choose directors, who in turn appoint managers to run the company. In theory this means that stockholders have a voice in running the company through the board of directors.

However, most large companies are *widely held,* meaning that stock ownership is spread among a large number of people with no individuals or groups controlling more than a few percent. Under those conditions, stockholders have little power to influence corporate decisions, and stock ownership is simply an investment.

● Most **equity** investors aren't interested in a role as **owners**.

In other words, we don't tend to think of having any role as *owners* when we buy stock. We're just interested in the future cash flows that come from owning shares. In that sense, *equity* (stock) investments are just like *debt* (bond) investments; the only thing we're interested in is money.

● THE RETURN ON AN INVESTMENT IN COMMON STOCK

In a stock investment, income comes in two forms. Investors receive dividends and realize a gain or loss on the difference between the price they pay for stock and the price at which they eventually sell it. This last part is called a *capital gain* or *loss*.

It pays to be precise about this idea and write it as an equation. Suppose we buy a share of stock, hold it for one year, and then sell it. Call the price we pay today P_0 and the price at the end of one year P_1. If we receive a dividend during the year, call that D_1. Then our income is the dividend, D_1, plus the difference in prices, $(P_1 - P_0)$, and our investment is the original price, P_0. The return, k, can be written as

(7.1)
$$k = \frac{D_1 + (P_1 - P_0)}{P_0}.$$

Notice that the return on a stock investment can be a negative number if the stock's price decreases while the investor holds it. In the equation, this means $P_1 < P_0$.

Next we'll solve equation 7.1 for P_0, the stock's price today. To do that multiply through by P_0,

$$kP_0 = D_1 + (P_1 - P_0),$$

add it to each side, and factor it out on the left.

$$P_0 + kP_0 = D_1 + P_1$$
$$(1 + k)P_0 = D_1 + P_1$$

Finally, divide through by $(1 + k)$ to get

(7.2)
$$P_0 = \frac{D_1 + P_1}{(1 + k)}.$$

● The **future cash flow** associated with stock ownership consists of **dividends** and the eventual **selling price** of the shares.

Notice that D_1 and P_1 are the future cash flows that come from buying the stock today at price P_0. Further notice that division by $(1 + k)$ is equivalent to multiplying by the present value factor for interest rate k and one year.

Therefore, equation 7.2 says that *the return on our stock investment is the interest rate that equates the present value of the investment's expected future cash flows to the amount invested today, the price P_0.*

This result is fundamental. The return on any stock investment is the rate that makes the present value of future cash flows equal to the price paid for the investment today. This principle also holds for investments held for more than one year.

Dividend and Capital Gain Yields

The return on a stock investment can be broken into two parts related to the two sources of income associated with stock ownership. Rewrite equation 7.1 as two fractions.

(7.3)
$$k = \frac{D_1}{P_0} + \frac{(P_1 - P_0)}{P_0}$$

● The **return** on a stock investment comes from **dividends** and **capital gains**.

The first part, D_1/P_0, is known as the **dividend yield,** and the second part, $(P_1 - P_0)/P_0$, is called the **capital gains yield.**

● THE NATURE OF CASH FLOWS FROM COMMON STOCK OWNERSHIP

As we've said, an investor who buys stock can expect two forms of future cash flow: a stream of dividends and the proceeds of the eventual sale of the shares.

Figure 7.1 is a time line reflecting these ideas for an investment made today and held for n years. In our work with stock valuation, we'll use annual time periods[1] and indicate payments in a particular year by subscripting the symbol for the payment with the number of the year.

For example, D_1 and D_2 will mean the dividends paid in the first and second years, respectively, and P_n will mean the price of the stock at the end of the nth year. We'll indicate the present with a zero subscript, so P_0 means the price today and D_0 means today's dividend or the most recent one paid.

We'll assume an investor buying today pays P_0, but does not receive D_0, which went to the last owner.

Comparison of Cash Flows from Stocks and Bonds

Notice that the cash flow pattern for stocks appears similar to the one associated with bonds. In both cases a series of regular payments is followed by a single larger payment that can be thought of as the return of the original investment. That is, dividends seem analogous to interest payments, while the final sale of stock appears to be like the return of a bond's principal.

In fact, however, the similarity is rather superficial because of the differing natures of the cash flows in the two cases. It's worthwhile to explore those differences rather carefully. We'll begin by comparing interest and dividends.

A bond's interest payments are guaranteed by the borrower, and are therefore fairly certain to be received. Companies have to be very close to failure before they default on bond interest. Dividends, on the other hand, carry no such guarantee. This is an important point. There's no agreement associated with common stock that makes any representation about the payment of dividends. Investors depend on them for value, but nothing is committed, promised, or guaranteed by

FIGURE 7.1		
Cash Flow Time Line for Stock Valuation		

---

1. Dividends are generally paid quarterly, but for valuation purposes things are simplified by working in annual terms.

the company. Indeed, a firm with a long history of paying dividends can stop at any time, especially if business turns bad.

Next, recall that the interest payments associated with a bond are constant in amount. That makes it easy to develop a formula to value bonds, because interest can be represented as an annuity. Dividends, on the other hand, are rarely constant. In fact, people generally expect dividends to increase over time as the company grows.

Things are equally imprecise with respect to the final payments received by stockholders versus bondholders. With a bond, the payment is the contractually promised loan principal equal to the bond's face value. A stockholder, on the other hand, has to sell his or her shares at the prevailing market price to realize a final payment. This price can be higher or lower than the price originally paid.

Let's emphasize that last point even further. There's no provision in a common stock investment for the repurchase of shares or for any return of the investor's capital by the company. That means the money for the final payment comes from another investor rather than from the issuing company as it does with a bond.[2]

In summary, the cash flows associated with stock ownership are dividends and the proceeds of the eventual sale of the shares. Both are distinctly imprecise and difficult to forecast.

THE BASIS OF VALUE

● The **basis for stock value** is the **present value** of expected **cash inflows** even though dividends and stock prices are difficult to forecast.

In spite of the imprecision of forecasted dividends and prices, the value of stock depends on the present value of those future cash flows. In terms of the portrayal in Figure 7.1, the stock's value is the sum of the present value of the n dividend payments and the present value of the selling price in the nth period. Keep in mind that the successive dividends generally have different values, so we have to distinguish between them by carrying the subscripts in D_1, D_2, through D_n.

Valuing a stock involves making some *assumptions* about what its future dividends and its eventual selling price will be. Once this has been done we take the present value of the *assumed* (projected) cash flows at an appropriate interest rate to estimate the share's current price. Contrast this with bond valuation. There we had no need to make any assumptions about the future cash flows because they were spelled out by the bond contract.

We can write a generalized stock valuation formula from these ideas by treating the dividends and the selling price as a series of independent amounts to be received at various times in the future.

Equation 5.7 on page 148 gave us an expression for the present value of an amount to be received n periods in the future at interest rate k. We'll repeat that expression here for convenience.

(5.7) $$PV = FV_n[PVF_{k,n}]$$

Now think of each dividend and the eventual selling price shown in Figure 7.1 as an FV_n, where n is the number of periods into the future until that particular amount is received. The present value of the first dividend can be written as $D_1[PVF_{k,1}]$. The second is $D_2[PVF_{k,2}]$, and so on through the nth dividend and the price in the nth period.

2. If a bond isn't held until maturity, it too must be sold to another investor, but the bondholder always has the option of holding until maturity and receiving the face value.

P_0, the value of the stock today, is the sum of all these amounts, and can be written as follows.

(7.4) $P_0 = D_1[PVF_{k,1}] + D_2[PVF_{k,2}] + \ldots + D_n[PVF_{k,n}] + P_n[PVF_{k,n}]$

EXAMPLE 7.1

Joe Simmons is interested in the stock of Teltex Corp. He feels it is going to have two very good years because of a government contract, but may not do well after that. Joe thinks the stock will pay a dividend of $2 next year and $3.50 the year after. By then he believes it will be selling for $75 a share, at which price he'll sell anything he buys now. People who have invested in stocks like Teltex are currently earning returns of 12%. What is the most Joe should be willing to pay for a share of Teltex?

Solution: Joe shouldn't pay any more than the present value of the cash flows he expects. Those are $2 at the end of one year and $3.50 plus $75 at the end of two years. Writing equation 7.4 for two years, we have

$$P_0 = D_1[PVF_{k,1}] + D_2[PVF_{k,2}] + P_2[PVF_{k,2}]$$
$$= \$2.00[PVF_{12,1}] + \$3.50[PVF_{12,2}] + \$75.00[PVF_{12,2}]$$
$$= \$2.00[.8929] + \$3.50[.7972] + \$75.00[.7972]$$
$$= \$64.37 \, .$$

If the market price of Teltex is below about $64, Joe should buy; if not, he shouldn't invest.

A stock's **intrinsic value** is based on **assumptions** about future cash flows made from **fundamental analyses** of the firm and its industry.

http://

Stock quotes and other financial data can be found at

www.wsrn.com

The Intrinsic (Calculated) Value and Market Price

Example 7.1 illustrates a basic principle of securities analysis. Joe's research led him to forecast the future dividends and price given in the example. According to his analysis, the present value of those cash flows is fundamentally what the stock is worth. We call that the stock's **intrinsic value** (according to Joe).

However, if other investors don't agree with Joe's dividend and price estimates, their ideas of Teltex's intrinsic value will differ from his. The firm's market price is generally thought to be a consensus of the intrinsic values calculated by everyone watching the stock. If Joe's value is higher than the consensus, and if he's right, he'll be getting a bargain if he buys.

The process of developing intrinsic values and comparing them with market prices is known as *fundamental analysis*. We'll come back to the idea later in the chapter.

GROWTH MODELS OF COMMON STOCK VALUATION

Equation 7.4 is a convenient way to look at stock valuation when we have a relatively short planning horizon and some reason to make specific assumptions about future prices and dividends. Generally, however, we can't forecast the future in that much detail. We're more likely to look at a company and simply forecast a *growth rate* of earnings and dividends into the future starting from wherever they are now.

● Stock valuation models are based on **predicted growth rates,** because forecasting exact future prices and dividends is very difficult.

For example, suppose a company has grown at an average rate of 5% per year over the last three or four years, and we expect its condition to improve slightly in the short run. The future being as uncertain as it is, it's difficult to make the detailed forecast of dividends and future prices needed to use equation 7.4. However, most of us would be comfortable in saying that the company and its dividends are likely to grow at 6% into the indefinite future.

Because that's the best we can often do in predicting the future, we'll find it useful to develop expressions that value stocks on the basis of only their present positions and assumptions about growth rates.

●DEVELOPING GROWTH-BASED MODELS

Notice that equation 7.4 treats the stock's dividends and eventual selling price as separate amounts in the present valuing process. Each is multiplied by the present value factor for the appropriate interest rate and time, which is represented in the equation as $PVF_{k,i}$, where i takes values from 1 to n.

In Chapter 5 we developed the formulation of any $PVF_{k,i}$, which we'll repeat here for convenience.

(5.5)
$$PVF_{k,i} = \frac{1}{(1 + k)^i}$$

Clearly, multiplying by $PVF_{k,i}$ is equivalent to dividing by $(1 + k)^i$. Review equation 5.5 on page 147 if this isn't familiar.

In what follows, we'll find it convenient to represent present values of amounts by dividing by $(1 + k)^i$ instead of multiplying by the factor of $PVF_{k,i}$. Rewriting equation 7.4 to reflect this change in notation, we have

● A stock's **value today** is the sum of the **present values** of the **dividends** received while the investor holds it and the **price** for which it is eventually sold.

(7.5)
$$P_0 = \frac{D_1}{(1 + k)} + \frac{D_2}{(1 + k)^2} + \cdots + \frac{D_n}{(1 + k)^n} + \frac{P_n}{(1 + k)^n} .$$

An Infinite Stream of Dividends

Notice again that our stock valuation formula, now represented by equation 7.5, involves a stream of dividends followed by a final selling price. This portrayal fits well with our concept of stock ownership: buy, hold for a while, and then sell. However, it's not convenient to work with in terms of valuation.

Think about P_n, the price at the end of the holding period. At that time, the nth period, it will represent the current price just as P_0 represents the current price today. Therefore its value then will involve a stream of dividends that starts in period n + 1 and a selling price at some point farther into the future, say period m. In other words, the person who buys the stock in period n will hold it until period m and then sell it. That person's valuation model will look like this.

$$P_n = \frac{D_{n+1}}{(1 + k)} + \cdots + \frac{D_m}{(1 + k)^{m-n}} + \frac{P_m}{(1 + k)^{m-n}}$$

Conceptually we can replace P_n in equation 7.5 with this expression, and wind up with a revised expression containing a longer stream of dividends and a final price farther away in time.

We can conceptually do the same thing again at period m. That is, we can think about the next sale, and replace P_m with another series of dividends followed by a price in the still more distant future. We can do that as many times as we like and push the eventual selling price as far into the future as we like. Indeed, we can conceptually push the final P infinitely far into the future!

However, the present value of any amount that is infinitely far away in time is clearly zero, so equation 7.5 becomes the present value of an infinitely long stream of dividends and nothing else.

In short, we've replaced the final selling price with the rest of the dividends forever. This more useful valuation expression is written as follows by using summation notation.

(7.6)
$$P_0 = \sum_{i=1}^{\infty} \frac{D_i}{(1 + k)^i}$$

A MARKET-BASED ARGUMENT   If shifting from equation 7.5 to 7.6 seems strange, here's another way to convince yourself that it makes sense.

Imagine that we're pricing a primary market transaction, one in which the firm is initially offering its stock to the investing public. Think of the investment community *as a whole* setting the stock's price. In other words, ignore the fact that individual investors will subsequently trade the stock back and forth among themselves, and think of them as one unified body setting a price for the stock when it's issued. In fact, that's exactly what the market process does.

This price, set by the market acting collectively, must be based on the present value of future cash flows moving from the company to the investing community. But there's only one kind of payment that moves from the company to investors, and that's dividends. So the only basis for valuation by the community as a whole is the entire future stream of dividends; there's nothing else available. This leads directly to equation 7.6.

Working with Growth Rates

Growth rates work just like interest rates. If we're told that something whose value is $100 today will grow at 6% next year, the amount of the growth is

$$\$100 \times .06 = \$6$$

and the new size of the variable is

$$\$100 \times 1.06 = \$106 .$$

We usually represent growth rates with the letter g, which takes the decimal value of the percentage rate. For example, a 6% growth rate implies g = .06.

Growth rates are usually used to predict future values of variables whose values are known today. For example, if today's dividend is D_0 and we want to forecast year 1's dividend, D_1, assuming growth rate g, we can write

$$D_1 = D_0 + gD_0$$
$$= D_0(1 + g) .$$

Year 2's dividend is just year 1's multiplied by $(1 + g)$ again.

$$D_2 = D_1(1 + g)$$

Noticing the expression for D_1 just above, we can substitute and write

$$D_2 = D_0(1 + g)^2 .$$

● Conceptually, it's possible to **replace** the final selling **price** with an **infinite series of dividends.**

D_3 is this expression multiplied by $(1 + g)$ again, and so on for as many subsequent D's as we need. In general the ith dividend is

(7.7) $D_i = D_0(1 + g)^i$.

When successive values of a growing dividend are needed, we just multiply by $(1 + g)$ repeatedly.

EXAMPLE 7.2

Apex Corp. paid a dividend of $3.50 this year. What are its next three dividends if it is expected to grow at 7%?

Solution: In this case $D_0 = \$3.50$ and $g = .07$, so $(1 + g) = 1.07$. Then

$$D_1 = D_0(1 + g) = \$3.50(1.07) = \$3.75,$$
$$D_2 = D_1(1 + g) = \$3.75(1.07) = \$4.01, \text{ and}$$
$$D_3 = D_2(1 + g) = \$4.01(1.07) = \$4.29.$$

●THE CONSTANT GROWTH MODEL

Equation 7.6 says that the value of a stock is the present value of an infinite stream of dividends but makes no statement about what those dividends are. In other words, the $D_1, D_2, \ldots, D_n$ can have any values, randomly chosen or a regular progression of numbers.

When we know D_0, the last dividend paid, and we assume dividends will grow at some constant rate in the future, equation 7.7 gives us a convenient way to forecast any particular dividend.

We can put these two ideas together by substituting equation 7.7 into 7.6 and rewriting as follows.

(7.8) $P_0 = \sum_{i=1}^{\infty} \dfrac{D_0(1 + g)^i}{(1 + k)^i}$

This expression is the basis of the constant growth model. It represents the sum of an infinite series of fractions as follows.

$$P_0 = \frac{D_0(1 + g)}{(1 + k)} + \frac{D_0(1 + g)^2}{(1 + k)^2} + \frac{D_0(1 + g)^3}{(1 + k)^3} + \ldots \infty$$

Notice that the numerators represent a series of dividends, each of which is larger than the last because of multiplication by the factor $(1 + g)$. The denominators reflect the present value factors for successive years into the future. These too get successively larger because of multiplication by $(1 + k)$.

Because D_0 appears in each term of the series, it can be factored out.

(7.9) $P_0 = D_0\left[\dfrac{(1 + g)}{(1 + k)} + \dfrac{(1 + g)^2}{(1 + k)^2} + \dfrac{(1 + g)^3}{(1 + k)^3} + \ldots \infty \right]$

Now, *if k is larger than g,* the fractions in the brackets get smaller as the exponents get larger. Both the numerators and denominators become larger numbers as the exponents grow, but if k is bigger than g, the denominators get large faster. Any fraction whose denominator is much larger than its numerator is a very small number. In this case the successive fractions approach zero as the exponents get big.

As a result, the entire expression in brackets is a *finite* number when k is larger than g. This leads to a finite value for P_0 even though we're summing an infinite stream of numbers to get it.

● In stock valuation, **normal growth** occurs when **k > g**.

When k is larger than g, we say we're forecasting *normal growth*. When g is greater than k, we say we have *super normal growth*. Super normal growth can occur in business, but lasts for limited periods. We'll consider it in detail later. For now we'll concentrate on normal growth situations.

Constant Normal Growth—The Gordon Model

Equations 7.8 and 7.9 look pretty intimidating, but can be reduced to something simple with a little mathematics that we needn't worry about here. We'll just accept the result.

The simplified form of equation 7.8 is

● The **Gordon model** is a simple expression for forecasting the **price** of a stock that's expected to **grow at a constant, normal rate.**

(7.10)
$$P_0 = \frac{D_0(1 + g)}{k - g} = \frac{D_1}{k - g}.$$

This expression is known as the *constant growth model,* because it assumes that the stock's dividends are going to grow at the constant rate, g, into the indefinite future. It is also called the **Gordon model** after Myron J. Gordon, a scholar who was behind its development and popularization.

Notice that the equation makes sense only if growth is normal—that is, if k > g. Otherwise the denominator is negative (or zero), leading to a negative (or undefined) price which isn't meaningful.

Also notice that the numerator can be expressed either as $D_0(1 + g)$ or as D_1. Keep in mind that D_0 is the most recent dividend paid to the stock's former owner. D_1 is the next dividend. It is the first one that will be received by someone who buys the stock today. Think of D_1 as the *first dividend into the period of normal growth*. That image will help your understanding later in the chapter.

The constant growth model is easy to use. Here's a straightforward example.

EXAMPLE 7.3

Atlas Motors is expected to grow at a constant rate of 6% a year into the indefinite future. It recently paid a dividend of $2.25 a share. The rate of return on stocks similar to Atlas is about 11%. What should a share of Atlas Motors sell for today?

Solution: Write equation 7.10 and substitute D_0 = $2.25, k = .11, and g = .06.

$$P_0 = \frac{D_0(1 + g)}{k - g} = \frac{\$2.25(1.06)}{.11 - .06} = \$47.70$$

This price includes the value of all dividends to be paid after time zero but does not include D_0, which has already been paid to the stock's current owner.

The Zero Growth Rate Case—A Constant Dividend

It is of interest to value a stock that's expected to pay a constant, never-changing dividend. In that case we don't need a subscript on the variable representing the dividends because they're all the same. We'll call each dividend D.

This case can be represented by equation 7.10 if we let g equal zero; then $D_0 = D_1 = D$ and 7.10 becomes

(7.11) $$P_0 = \frac{D}{k}$$

● A **zero growth** stock is a **perpetuity** to the investor.

You should recognize equation 7.11 as the expression for the present value of a perpetuity from our work in Chapter 5. (See pages 173–174.) A perpetuity is an unchanging payment made regularly for an indefinite period of time. That's exactly what we're describing in the constant dividend model.

EXAMPLE 7.4

Lexington Corp. is in a stagnant market, and analysts foresee a long period of zero growth for the firm. It's been paying a yearly dividend of $5 for some time, which is expected to continue indefinitely. The yield on the stock of similar firms is 8%. What should Lexington's stock sell for?

Solution: Write equation 7.11 and substitute.

$$P_0 = \frac{D}{k} = \frac{\$5}{.08} = \$62.50$$

People don't usually assume that common stock will pay the same dividend forever. It's more usual to assume some positive growth rate. There is, however, a security known as *preferred stock* that does pay the same dividend year after year with no expectation of increase or decrease. We'll study it later in the chapter.

THE EXPECTED RETURN

The Gordon model can be recast to focus on the return on the stock investment implied by the constant growth assumption. This is easily done by solving equation 7.10 for k. In this formulation, k represents an **expected return,** and is often written as k_e.

● The **expected return** reflects investors' **knowledge** of a company. It is input to the Gordon model through the growth rate assumption.

(7.12) $$k_e = \frac{D_1}{P_0} + g$$

The concept of expected return will be important in the next chapter. In this case, it says that if an investor's knowledge and predictions about a company's stock are rolled up into a forecast growth rate, the return implied by the forecast is given by equation 7.12.

If we take $D_1 = D_0(1 + g)$ and assume that D_0 and P_0 are actual values of the latest dividend and the current price, the equation gives an estimate of the return to be had by investing in the stock at price P_0.

It's worthwhile to compare equation 7.12 with 7.1, which we'll repeat here for convenience.

(7.1)
$$k = \frac{D_1}{P_0} + \frac{(P_1 - P_0)}{P_0}$$

Recall that the two terms on the right side of equation 7.1 are the dividend yield and the capital gains yield. Compare equation 7.12 with 7.1 and notice that they're identical in all but the second term on the right. This implies that those terms have the same meaning in both equations. In other words, the capital gains yield in the Gordon model is nothing but the growth rate. That makes intuitive sense because the whole company, including dividends and stock prices, is assumed to be growing at rate g.

●TWO-STAGE GROWTH

Situations sometimes arise in which a firm's future growth isn't expected to be constant. Specifically, we often know something about the near-term future that can be expected to have a *temporary* effect on the firm's prospects. For example, the release of a new product might create a period of rapidly expanding demand after which further growth slows to normal.

The usual *two-stage* forecast involves a rapid, *super normal* growth rate for one, two, or even three years and a *normal* rate thereafter. Recall that super normal means a rate in excess of k, the return on the stock. Our task is to use the tools we've developed thus far to value a stock that's expected to behave in this way.

First let's look at a time line picture of such an investment opportunity. The top of Figure 7.2 shows a general case in which the firm grows at rate g_1, the super normal rate, for two years and then grows indefinitely at rate g_2, the slower normal rate.

We can value this stock by using the constant growth model, but we have to apply it carefully. The model gives us a value for a share of stock *at the beginning of an infinite period of constant, normal growth.*

In Figure 7.2 we have constant, normal growth, but it doesn't start at time zero. It starts at the end of the second year. Therefore we have to apply the Gordon model at that point in time.

● The **two-stage growth model** allows us to value a stock that's expected to grow at an unusual rate for a **limited time.**

When we do that, the result is a price for the stock at the end of the second year, or equivalently at the beginning of the third. We'll call that price P_2. It includes the value of all dividends to be paid subsequent to year 2, but not the dividend of year 2 itself, D_2. In other words, it takes into account D_3, D_4, D_5, and so on.

FIGURE 7.2	
Two-Stage Growth Model	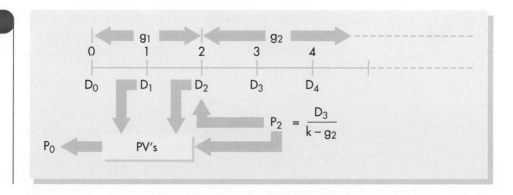

Using the Gordon model at the end of the second year requires a modification of the notation we used before. Look back at equation 7.10. Notice that the numerator in that expression is D_1, which is *the first dividend into the period of normal growth*. In the model we're working with now, that's D_3, because the growth rate changes at the end of year 2.

In addition, the denominator of equation 7.10 contains the normal growth rate g. In this case we have two growth rates but the normal one that continues indefinitely is g_2, so that's the one we must use. The correct way to formulate the constant growth model in this application is

$$P_2 = \frac{D_3}{k - g_2}.$$

This expression is portrayed in Figure 7.2 along with its position along the time line.

A person buying this stock today gets three things in the future: D_1, D_2, and P_2. The two dividends are clearly cash flows forecast at the ends of years 1 and 2. P_2, on the other hand, is an actual cash flow only if the purchaser sells the stock at the end of the second year. Nevertheless, we'll treat P_2 just as though it was a cash flow expected two years in the future.

The value of a security today is the present value of future cash that comes from owning it, so the value of the stock represented in Figure 7.2 is the sum of the present values of D_1, D_2, and P_2. This is indicated schematically in the diagram.

EXAMPLE 7.5

Zylon Corporation's stock is selling for $48 a share according to *The Wall Street Journal*. We've heard a rumor that the firm will make an exciting new product announcement next week. By studying the industry, we've concluded that this new product will support an overall company growth rate of 20% for about two years. After that, we feel growth will slow rapidly and level off at about 6%. The firm currently pays an annual dividend of $2.00, which can be expected to grow with the company. The rate of return on stocks like Zylon is approximately 10%. Is Zylon a good buy at $48?

Solution: To determine whether Zylon is a good buy, we'll estimate what it *should* be worth on the basis of the present value of future cash flows, and compare that result with the listed price. If our valuation is higher, we might conclude that the stock is a bargain and buy it.

Drawing a diagram similar to Figure 7.2 generally helps in problems like this. The following time line shows the growth rates and dividends.

The dividend paid recently, D_0, is given as $2.00. The first future dividend is forecast by growing $2.00 at the first year's growth rate. That's accomplished by multiplying by one plus the growth rate in that year.

$$D_1 = D_0(1 + g_1) = \$2.00(1.20) = \$2.40$$

To get the second year's dividend we multiply by $(1 + g_1)$ again.

$$D_2 = D_1(1 + g_1) = \$2.40(1.20) = \$2.88$$

We do *nearly* the same thing for D_3. The firm is now growing at rate g_2, which is 6% in this example.

$$D_3 = D_2(1 + g_2) = \$2.88(1.06) = \$3.05$$

Next we use the Gordon model *at the point in time where the growth rate changes and constant growth begins.* That's year 2 in this case, so

$$P_2 = \frac{D_3}{k - g_2} = \frac{\$3.05}{.10 - .06} = \$76.25 \ .$$

This result is also indicated in the diagram.

All that remains in calculating a price is to take the present value of each of the elements to which a buyer at time zero is entitled and add them up; these are D_1, D_2, and P_2.

$$P_0 = D_1[PVF_{k,1}] + D_2[PVF_{k,2}] + P_2[PVF_{k,2}]$$

$$P_0 = \$2.40[PVF_{10,1}] + \$2.88[PVF_{10,2}] + \$76.25[PVF_{10,2}]$$

$$P_0 = \$2.40[.9091] + \$2.88[.8264] + \$76.25[.8264]$$

$$P_0 = \$67.57$$

Now we compare $67.57 with the listed price of $48.00. Clearly our valuation is larger. If our assumptions are correct, the stock should be worth almost $20 more than its current market price. If we're right, the price will rise substantially in a relatively short time, so we would be wise to buy.

● PRACTICAL LIMITATIONS OF PRICING MODELS

from the CFO

It's important to remember that the growth rate models we've been studying are abstractions of reality. They're simplified representations of the real world that at best can give us only approximations of what's likely to occur in the future. We have to be careful not to view them as being accurate to the penny even though our calculations result in figures like the $67.57 in the last example.

It's especially important to understand that our results can never be any more accurate than the inputs that go into the model. In this case those inputs are the projected growth rates and the interest rate.

Growth rate estimates <u>are guesses</u> that can be off by quite a bit. For example, in the case we've just illustrated the predicted 20% growth rate could actually turn out to be anything from 15% to 25%. Rates at either end of this range will make a big difference in the figure we finally get for P_0.

The exact interest rate isn't always known either. The rates of return that people require to invest in stocks vary according to the risk they perceive in any particular company. Different investors have different perceptions, so our 10% rate might easily be 9% or 11%.

Another big source of inaccuracy comes from the denominator of the Gordon model. Notice that it's the difference between two of our inputs, the interest rate and a growth rate. If those numbers are estimated to be close together, their difference is small and the calculated price blows up because a small denominator makes the value of a fraction large.

Look at the calculation of P_2 in Example 7.5. The denominator of the fraction, $k - g_2$, is $(.10 - .06 =) .04$. But suppose our estimates of k and g_2 were a little off, and k should have been 9% and g_2 more like 7%. Then the denominator would have been $(.09 - .07 =) .02$ and P_2 would have been $154.08. [The numerator would also change to $(\$2.88 \times 1.07 =) \$3.08$.] This would have made P_0 $131.89 rather than $67.57. That's a 95% difference in the estimated value of the stock coming from input errors that are relatively much smaller (10% for k and 17% for g_2)!

The point is that when it comes to estimating stock prices, finance is not engineering! Our numbers just aren't all that accurate. Keep that in mind when using the results the way we did in the last example. The estimated value of the stock turned out to be $67.57, which looked very good in comparison with the $48 market price. But suppose the stock had been selling for $62 instead of the example's $48. Could we have concluded that it was still a bargain, although not as big a one? In other words, could we expect to make $5.57 on the purchase of a share?

The answer to that question is probably no. The difference of about $5 out of $67 isn't large enough to overcome the margin for error inherent in the estimating process. At a market price of $48 we'd be pretty sure we had something, but at $62 we really can't say much at all. Basically, the result would be saying the stock is worth in the neighborhood of $65 or $70. Any finer estimates than that are meaningless.

- **Stock** valuation models give **approximate** results because the inputs are approximations of reality. **Bond** valuation is **precise** because the inputs are exact.

Comparison with Bond Valuation

The comments about inaccuracy in the last section refer only to stock valuation; bonds are a completely different story. The bond pricing model gives a precise valuation for the security, because the future cash flows are contractually guaranteed in amount and time. Unless a borrowing company defaults on its obligation, which is rare among higher grade issues, we can predict the exact pattern of future interest and principal payments. Having that, we can determine the price exactly for any yield. Yields in turn are established quite accurately by market forces influenced by the stability of the issuing company and the term of the debt.

Stocks That Don't Pay Dividends

Some companies pay no dividends even when their profits are high. Further, many openly state their intention never to pay dividends. Nevertheless, the stocks of such firms can have substantial value.

The growth models we've been working with base stock values solely on the present value of a dividend stream. How can such a model be valid if there are stocks with value that pay no dividends?

- Stocks that **don't pay dividends** have value, because there's a general expectation that **some day they will.**

The answer to this puzzling question lies in understanding when and why firms pay no dividends to stockholders. Firms that don't pay dividends even

Practical Finance

Reconciling Valuation Theory and Practice

People who work with stock investing day in and day out aren't likely to think of valuation in terms of present value models. Brokers and frequent investors are more likely to work with earnings per share and price/earnings ratios to predict short-term price movements. The EPS model is expressed by the following relation.

(a)
$$P_0 = EPS \times P/E$$

where P_0 is the stock's price, EPS is earnings per share, and P/E is the price/earnings ratio.

According to this view, to the extent that companies have different P/E ratios, the market values their earnings differently. For example, if two firms each earn $1 per share, and their P/Es are 10 and 20, their stocks will sell for $10 and $20 regardless of the fact that their earnings are the same. In other words the market puts a different value on a dollar of earnings depending on who makes it.

This doesn't seem consistent with the valuation models we've been studying, which say price is based on the present value of *dollar* earnings *only*.

Things get more confusing if you look at the relationship expressed in equation (a) closely. Mathematically, it's just an identity because P/E is just price over EPS. Hence it reduces to

$$P_0 = EPS \times \frac{P_0}{EPS}$$

or

$$P_0 = P_0$$

which doesn't have much value for anything.

But in fact there's more to it than that. The stock market tends to fix short-run P/E ratios within ranges by industry. And within industries better performers get higher P/Es than poor performers. In other words certain favored industries and certain favored companies are rewarded with higher than normal P/Es. That is, in the short run the P/E ratio is relatively stable, so price changes depend mainly on changes in recent earnings, EPS.

That still doesn't seem to reconcile well with the models that value stocks according to the present value of *future* cash flows until you realize two things. First, recent earnings are predictors of future earnings, so a higher EPS today means more earnings and dividends in the future. Second, countless studies have shown that the primary determinant of who gets what P/E is expected growth. The higher a company's expected growth, the higher its P/E.

That means equation (a) works like a crude Gordon model in which higher growth rates and higher current earnings both imply a higher current stock price. In other words the seat-of-the-pants approach used by rough and tumble practitioners is very consistent with sophisticated valuation theory. That should give us all a sense of calm and well-being.

when their earnings are good are usually in an early period of their development and growing rapidly. Growth requires cash, and managements feel it's futile to pay out dividends only to turn around and borrow or issue more stock to raise money to support that growth. Stockholders agree because they hope to own a piece of a much larger company if growth continues.

However, most people understand that rapid growth doesn't go on forever. When growth in the industry and firm slows down, even the most vocal non-dividend payers eventually begin paying. In other words, stocks that don't pay dividends today are expected to pay large dividends at some time in the future. It's those distant dividends that impart value.

If a company truly never paid a dividend, there would be no way for the investing community as a whole to *ever* get a return on its investment. And that doesn't make much sense.

There is an alternate, somewhat comical, explanation known as the *greater fool theory of investing*. It goes like this. People buy non-dividend-paying stocks for price appreciation—that is, with the intention of selling to other investors at higher prices than those at which they bought. But only a fool would buy an investment with no payback, so a buyer is depending on finding a *greater fool* later to buy at a higher price.

There's no doubt that investors sometimes behave as though they were operating under the greater fool theory, but in general we prefer the explanation involving the eventual payment of dividends.

http://

Current stock market information and data can be found at

● www.businessweek.com/investor/index.html

SOME INSTITUTIONAL CHARACTERISTICS OF COMMON STOCK

Common stock represents an investment in equity (ownership) that theoretically implies control of the company. That is, it's logical to assume that an ownership interest means a stockholder has some influence on the way the company is run.

As a practical matter, however, influence depends on how much stock is held by any one person or group. Because most management issues are decided by a majority vote, stockholders owning minority interests have little power when someone else has a clear majority or when no one owns a substantial percentage of the firm. To understand how all of this works, we have to look at how companies are run.

● CORPORATE ORGANIZATION AND CONTROL

Corporations are controlled by **boards of directors** whose members are elected by stockholders. The board appoints the firm's senior management, which in turn appoints middle and lower management and runs the company on a day-to-day basis. Major strategic decisions are considered by the board, and a few really big issues, like mergers, must be voted on by the stockholders.

Corporate boards are generally made up of the company's top managers and a number of *outside directors*. Board members may be major stockholders, but they don't have to be.

● Top **management** effectively controls widely held companies, because no stockholder group has enough power to remove them.

Companies are said to be widely held when stock ownership is distributed among a large number of people and no single party has a significantly large share. When that happens it is very difficult to make a change in the board, because it's hard to organize voting stockholders against the incumbent members. In such situations, members of top management on the board have effective control of the company with little accountability to stockholders.

The outside directors are supposed to be a restraint on this autonomy of management, but generally don't do much along those lines.[3] Of course, when a substantial percentage of stock is under the control of a single group, that group has effective control of the company because it can elect board members. In widely held companies, 15% to 25% is generally enough for effective control if no one else has more than a few percent.

---

3. There have been a few notable exceptions in recent years in which CEOs have been removed by groups led by outside directors.

The Role of the Equity Investor

As we said early in the chapter, most of the investors who buy stock in sizable companies don't look for a role in running the company. They're simply interested in the cash flows that come from stock ownership.

Preemptive Rights

Preemptive rights allow stockholders to maintain their proportionate ownership of corporations. When new shares are issued, common stockholders have the right to purchase a portion of the new issue equal to the percentage of the outstanding shares they already own. If preemptive rights exist, current stockholders must be offered this option before the new shares can be sold to anyone else.

Preemptive rights are common, but there's generally no law requiring them. Hence if stockholders have preemptive rights, it's because they were written into the company's rules of operation (called its charter, articles, or bylaws) by the people who originally formed the corporation.

VOTING RIGHTS AND ISSUES

Most common stock comes with voting rights. That means each share gets an equal vote in the election of directors and on major issues. Voting issues are usually limited to changes in the company's charter, which broadly defines what it does, and questions about mergers.

Stockholders vote on directors and other items at an *annual stockholders' meeting* that corporations are required by law to hold. Most shareholders don't attend, however, and vote by **proxy** if at all. Proxies give the authority to vote shares to a designated party. Generally, the current board members solicit shareholders by mail for their proxies. If the firm's performance has been reasonably good, the proxies are given and the board is reelected.

A **proxy fight** occurs if parties with conflicting interests solicit proxies at the same time. This usually happens when a stockholder group is unhappy with management and tries to take over the board. We'll talk about proxy fights more in Chapter 17.

> Each share of **common** stock has one vote in the election of directors, which is usually cast by **proxy.**

Majority and Cumulative Voting

Suppose a company's stock is held by two groups of stockholders with differing interests. Also assume one group has a clear majority of the shares outstanding. Traditional *majority voting* gives the larger group control of the company to the virtual exclusion of the minority group. This is because each director is chosen in a separate election, so the majority group can win every seat.

Cumulative voting is a way to get some minority representation on the board. Under the cumulative method, each share of stock gets one vote for every seat being elected. Minority stockholders can then cast all their votes for one seat or split them up among several elections. This means the minority interest can concentrate its votes on one or two seats and be sure to win, thereby getting some representation on the board.

> **Cumulative voting** gives minority interests a chance at some representation on the board.

Shares with Different Voting Rights

It's possible to issue more than one class of stock with different rights associated with each class. Along these lines, a practice that affects control involves issuing a class of stock with limited voting rights or with no votes at all. If such an issue

Real
Applications

Corporate Control in Large Companies: The Revolt of Institutional Shareholders

Do stockholders really control the companies they own through the election boards of directors? In smaller companies the answer is definitely yes. Owners typically elect themselves or close associates to the board, and control their businesses more or less directly. But in large, "widely held" corporations the answer to this question has traditionally been no. When stock ownership is so dispersed that no one owns more that a small fraction of the enterprise, it's been virtually impossible for dissatisfied shareholders to influence management. They simply can't get enough votes together to influence the board, which can alter corporate policy or change top management.

This condition has led to a rather serious problem. Top executives of major corporations act essentially without accountability. That means they're unlikely to lose their positions of wealth and power for making poor or self serving decisions. They're paid fantastically well, and often pursue business strategies that seem more related to their own empire building interests than to the benefit of stockholders.

But a modern investing phenomenon is beginning to change that condition. Institutional investors are organizations that invest the pooled contributions of many individuals, and therefore control vast amounts of money.* Because of their size, institutions often acquire substantial blocks of stock in major companies. When that happens, they can exert considerable influence on corporate boards of directors. In extreme cases they can engineer the removal of chief executives with whom they're dissatisfied.

The trend started in 1992 when institutional investors instigated the ouster of Robert Stempel, the CEO of General Motors. Since then similar groups have initiated changes in several top managements that ordinarily wouldn't have happened unless the firm in question was taken over by another company. The CEOs of IBM, Archer-Daniels, and AT&T all departed under shareholder pressure during the middle of the 1990's. And top executives at Compaq, NatWest, and Rite Aid made early departures in 1999.

Prior to these shareholder revolts, dissatisfied investors would just sell their holdings if they felt management wasn't acting in their best interests. Now the institutions have found

receives the same dividends as traditional voting stock, it may be attractive to the typical investor who has no interest in control anyway.

Nonvoting stock was fairly common in the early part of this century, but has been unusual since the 1930s. At that time there was a general resistance to it from the government, the stock exchanges, and investors. The idea has reemerged recently, however, in association with mergers and acquisitions.

● STOCKHOLDERS' CLAIMS ON INCOME AND ASSETS

Stockholders have a **residual claim** on both income and assets. That means they are the last in line among all the claimants on the firm's resources.

With respect to income, stockholders own what's left after all operating costs and expenses are paid, after bondholders receive their interest and any principal due, and after preferred stockholders get their dividends. That doesn't sound like a very good deal, but it often is.

that controlling as few as one or two seats on the board lets them assert some control over management decisions. In 1999, unhappy institutional shareholders influenced the boards of at least thirty major corporations.

This increased pressure from unhappy investors has led to more contentious relationships between CEOs and their boards. Indeed it's been observed that CEOs are managing the information boards receive and are demanding more generous severance packages in their contracts because they know they can be removed.

CEOs aren't the only target of large institutional investors who want more performance out of their stock. In 1999, the General Motors board of directors faced a challenge related to getting the most out of GM's 68% interest in Hughes Electronics, the provider of DirecTV and the largest satellite television provider in the United States. Slow growth in the auto industry had led institutional investors to believe the value of Hughes Electronics was not fully reflected in the price of GM shares because of poor performance by other GM divisions. In response to investors' concerns, GM put its stake in Hughes up for sale in 2000 .

Dissatisfied institutional shareholders have become outspoken activists in the last ten years. Whether they're interested in changing top management or just influencing business decisions, these organizations are no longer willing to sit around and wait for managements to "maximize shareholder wealth." Instead they're becoming proactive participants in the decisions made by corporate America.

* We're using the term *institutional* in two slightly different ways on these pages. An institutional investor is a financial organization that owns stock in corporations. Mutual funds, banks and insurance companies can be institutional investors. The institutional characteristics of stock in the heading to this section refers to the rules and rights associated with stock ownership.

Sources: "Thank You and Goodbye," *The Economist* (October 30, 1999): 67–68. Andrew Bary, "Strong Signals," *Barron's* (December 6, 1999):19–20. John Lippman and Gregory L. White, "GM Agrees to Sell Hughes to EchoStar," *The Wall Street Journal* (October 29, 2001): A3.

● Common stockholders are **last in line** to receive income or assets, and so bear **more risk** than other investors. But their **residual** interest is large when the firm does well.

When business is bad, stockholders are in the worst position of all, because the company's money is more likely to run out before they're paid than before other claimants are paid. That's why stock is considered the riskiest investment.

When business is good, however, the residual after everyone else is paid can be enormous, and it all belongs to the stockholders. Essentially, the "upside" potential in stock ownership is limitless.

The residual income belonging to stockholders is essentially earnings (EAT). It is either paid out to them in dividends or retained and reinvested in the business. Both options are clearly beneficial to stockholders. Dividends are immediate money in their pockets, while retained earnings contribute to growth that makes the stock more valuable.

With respect to assets, the residual position means that if the corporation fails and is liquidated, stockholders don't get anything until everyone else is paid. That often means they don't get anything at all.

PREFERRED STOCK

Preferred stock is a security that has some of the characteristics of common stock and some of those of bonds. It's often referred to as a *hybrid* of the two—that is, a cross between common stock and bonds.

Preferred stock pays a constant dividend forever. When a share is initially issued, two things are specified: the initial selling price (in the primary market) and the dividend. The ratio between the two reflects the current return on investments of similar risk, the market interest rate.

For example, if the interest rate is 10% and a company wants to issue preferred shares at $100 each, it would offer a dividend of $10. This would be referred to as a $10 preferred issue rather than a 10% preferred issue.

You can think of the 10% rate as being similar to the coupon rate on a bond. The preferred's initial selling price (issue price) is conceptually similar to a bond's face value. Preferred stock is generally issued at prices of $25, $50, and $100.

It's important to notice that preferred stock carries no provision for the return of capital to the investor.

VALUATION OF PREFERRED STOCK

An investor who purchases a share of preferred stock receives a constant dividend forever. Because all securities are worth the present value of their future cash flows, a share of preferred is worth the present value of that infinitely long stream of dividend payments.

In Chapter 5 we said that a constant stream of payments stretching into the indefinite future is a *perpetuity*. We also learned a simple formula to calculate a perpetuity's present value, which we'll repeat here for convenience.

(5.24)
$$PV_p = \frac{PMT}{k}$$

> ● **Preferred stock** pays a constant dividend and is valued as a **perpetuity**.

We'll use this basic equation for preferred stock, but will change the variable names to more appropriately reflect the application. The perpetuity's payment (PMT) is the preferred dividend, which we'll call D_p. The present value of the perpetuity (PV_p) must equal the security's price, which we'll call P_p. The interest rate will remain k. Then the expression for the price of a preferred share is

(7.13)
$$P_p = \frac{D_p}{k}.$$

Notice that the valuation of a preferred share is conceptually identical to that of a zero growth common share discussed earlier in this chapter.

Like bonds, preferred stock is issued to yield approximately the current rate of interest. When interest rates change, preferred shares have to offer competitive yields to new secondary market buyers. This is accomplished through price changes.

Prices of preferred stocks, like those of bonds, move inversely with interest rates. However, calculating new preferred prices is much easier than calculating bond prices. We simply insert the new interest rate into equation 7.13 and solve for P_p.

EXAMPLE 7.6

Roman Industries's $6 preferred originally sold for $50. Interest rates on similar issues are now 9%. What should Roman's preferred sell for today?

Solution: Just substitute the new market interest rate into equation 7.13 for today's price.

$$P_p = \frac{D_p}{k} = \frac{\$6.00}{.09} = \$66.67$$

Notice that the original yield on the issue was ($6/$50 =) 12%. Because the interest rate dropped from 12% to 9%, we know the price has to be above its original value of $50. This gives a reasonableness check on our answer.

CHARACTERISTICS OF PREFERRED STOCK

As a security, preferred stock has some unique characteristics relative to traditional debt and equity. We'll summarize a few issues.

The Cumulative Feature

● Common dividends can't be paid unless the dividends on **cumulative preferred** are current.

Nearly all preferred stock comes with a **cumulative feature** designed to enhance its safety for investors. The cumulative feature generally states that if preferred dividends are passed (not paid) in any year or series of years, no common dividends can be paid until the preferred dividends in arrears are caught up.

For example, if a firm gets into financial trouble and doesn't pay dividends on a $5 preferred for three years, no common dividends can be paid until each preferred shareholder has received the cumulative total of $15 per share.

Comparing Preferred Stock with Common Stock and Bonds

Some of the features of preferred stock are like those of bonds, while some are more like those of common stock. Some are in between. Let's consider a few specifics.

PAYMENTS TO INVESTORS The fact that preferred dividends are constant and don't increase even if the company grows makes them similar to the constant interest payments of a bond. They're unlike the dividends on common stock, which are usually expected to grow with the firm.

● The features of **preferred stock** allow it to be characterized as a **cross between common stock and bonds.**

MATURITY AND RETURN OF PRINCIPAL A bond has a maturity date on which the principal is returned. Preferred stock has no maturity, and never returns principal. In that respect it's like common stock, which never returns principal either.

ASSURANCE OF PAYMENT Interest must be paid or bondholders can force a company into bankruptcy. Common stock dividends can be passed indefinitely. Preferred dividends can be passed, but are subject to a cumulative feature. In this respect it is somewhere between bonds and common stock.

PRIORITY IN BANKRUPTCY   In the event of bankruptcy, bondholders have a claim on the company's assets to the extent of the unpaid principal of the bonds. Common stockholders are entitled only to what's left after all other claimants have been paid. Preferred stockholders are again in between. They have a claim in the amount of the original selling price of the stock, but it is subordinate to the claims of all bondholders. That is, it comes before the interests of common stockholders but after those of bondholders.

VOTING RIGHTS   Common stockholders have voting rights, while preferred stockholders do not. In that respect preferred stock is like bonds.

TAX DEDUCTIBILITY OF PAYMENTS TO INVESTORS   Interest is tax deductible to the paying company, whereas dividends, common or preferred, are not. In this respect, preferred stock is very much equity.

Preferred stock is legally equity, but from what we've just said it's clearly more like debt in many ways. For that reason, it's generally treated separately in financial analysis.

The Order of Risk

The features we've been talking about create an ordering of risk associated with the three securities. Bonds are the safest, common stock is the most risky, and preferred is in the middle. The compensation for the risk in common stock is that the return—through dividend increases and price appreciation—can be very high if the company does exceptionally well. That possibility doesn't exist with either of the other two.

The name "preferred" stock comes from the idea that of the two types of equity, you'd rather have preferred stock if the firm does poorly or fails.

Taxes and Preferred Stock Investors

The U.S. tax code treats preferred dividends just like common dividends in that they're not tax deductible to the company paying them. That makes preferred stock a relatively expensive source of financing.

Like common dividends, preferred dividends received by another corporation are 70% or more exempt from taxation. (See Chapter 2, page 49.) This partial tax exemption coupled with preferred stock's relatively low risk makes it especially attractive to some institutional investors. Hence, those investors bid up preferred prices until they're not attractive to individual investors who don't have the tax exemption. The result is that not many *people* invest in preferred stock.

SECURITIES ANALYSIS

● **Securities analysis** is the art and science of selecting investments.

Valuation is part of a broader process aimed at selecting investments known as **securities analysis**. The term is applied to both stocks and bonds, but most of the activity relates to selecting stocks. There are two basic approaches to analysis; we'll briefly describe each.

Fundamental Analysis

Fundamental analysis involves doing research to discover everything possible about a firm, its business, and its industry. Once analysts become expert in a

● **Fundamental analysis** looks at a company and its business to forecast value.

company's field, they forecast its sales and expenses over the coming years. From that they project earnings and then a stream of dividends based on the firm's stated or implied dividend policy. The forecast dividend stream is used as input to the valuation models we've been discussing.

In short, fundamental analysis involves learning the fundamentals of a business and applying that knowledge to forecasting its future cash flows. Value follows directly.

Technical Analysis

● **Technical analysis** bases value on the pattern of past prices and volumes.

Technical analysts take a different approach. Technicians believe market forces dictate prices and, more importantly, price movements. They also believe movement patterns tend to repeat themselves over time. By studying past price changes, technicians believe they can recognize patterns that precede major up or down movements in the prices of individual stocks.

Technicians prepare elaborate charts displaying the prices and volumes[4] of virtually all stocks traded. These are examined in an effort to discern patterns that precede major moves. Because of this technique, technical analysts are also called **chartists.**

Technicians feel one doesn't have to know *why* a firm's stock has value in terms of underlying cash flows. Rather, they believe it's enough to accept that it does have value, and rely on predictable market phenomena to make investment decisions.

Fundamentalists versus Technicians

http://

Microsoft Money Central at
● http://moneycentral.msn.com/home.asp
offers access to a wealth of stock data.

The two schools of thought are rather vocally opposed to one another, although many people use ideas from both camps. Scholars are almost universally fundamentalists. Nevertheless, the technical school of thought has a significant following.

A number of statistical studies have been done in attempts to prove or disprove the validity of technical analysis once and for all. To date no one has definitely proven anything to the satisfaction of the other side.

The Efficient Market Hypothesis (EMH)

● The **efficient market hypothesis** says information moves so rapidly in financial markets that price changes occur immmediately, so it's impossible to **consistently** beat the market to bargains.

The *efficient market hypothesis* (EMH) pertains to information flows within financial markets in the United States. It says that financial markets are efficient in that new information is disseminated with lightning speed.

The theory asserts that information moves so fast around the thousands of analysts, brokers, and investors who make up the stock market that prices adjust to new information virtually immediately. In other words, when some new knowledge about a stock becomes available, it is analyzed and disseminated so fast that the market price adjusts to reflect the information in a matter of hours or less.

For example, suppose a pharmaceutical company announced that it had discovered a cure for cancer. That would certainly raise the price of the firm's stock. The EMH says that the price rise will happen immediately, because analysts will be on the phone right away telling client investors the news, and they'll bid the price up as fast as they can.

---

4. Volume refers to the number of shares traded in a period. A price change at a low volume of trading isn't generally as significant as the same change accompanied by a higher volume.

The implication is that at any time, all available information is already reflected in stock prices, and studying historical patterns of price movement can't consistently do an investor any good. Hence the EMH is a direct refutation of the validity of technical analysis.

However, the EMH implies that we won't find many bargains by using fundamental analysis and the valuation models either. That's because an army of professionals is doing fundamental analysis all the time, and they will have already discovered and disseminated anything an individual can figure out.

The validity of the EMH is subject to dispute. It will probably never be proven to be either right or wrong. At this point in your study, you should just be aware of its existence and have a basic grasp of what it says.

DISCUSSION QUESTIONS

1. Discuss the nature of stock as an investment. Do most stockholders play large roles in the management of the firms in which they invest? Why or why not?

2. Compare and contrast the nature of cash flows stemming from an investment in stock with those coming from bonds.

3. Verbally rationalize the validity of a stock valuation model that doesn't contain a selling price as a source of cash flow to the investor. Give two independent arguments.

4. Why are growth rate models practical and convenient ways to look at stock valuation?

5. What is meant by normal growth? Contrast normal and super normal growth. How long can each last? Why?

6. Describe the approach to valuing a stock that is expected to grow at more than one rate in the future. Can there be more than two rates? What two things have to be true of the last rate?

7. Discuss the accuracy of stock valuation, and compare it with that of bond valuation.

8. Do stocks that don't pay dividends have value? Why?

9. Your cousin Charlie came into a large inheritance last year and invested the entire amount in the common stock of IBD Inc., a large computer company. Subsequently he's been very interested in the company and watches it closely. Recently the newspaper carried a story about major strategic changes at IBD, including massive layoffs and business realignments. Charlie was devastated. He doesn't understand how the firm could have made such changes without the knowledge or approval of its stockholders. Write a brief letter to Charlie explaining how things really work.

10. Preferred stock is said to be a hybrid of common stock and bonds. Explain fully. Describe the cash flows associated with preferred and their valuation.

11. Discuss the relative riskiness of investment in bonds, common stock, and preferred stock.

12. Compare fundamental analysis and technical analysis. Which makes more sense to you?

13. What does the efficient market hypothesis say? What is its implication for stock analysis?

PROBLEMS

1. The stock of Sedly Inc. is expected to pay the following dividends.

	Year			
	1	2	3	4
Dividend	$2.25	$3.50	$1.75	$2.00

At the end of the fourth year its value is expected to be $37.50. What should Sedly sell for today if the return on stocks of similar risk is 12%?

2. Fred Tibbits has made a detailed study of the denim clothing industry. He's particularly interested in a company called Denhart Fashions that makes stylish denim apparel for children and teenagers. Fred has done a forecast of Denhart's earnings and looked at its dividend payment record. He's come to the conclusion that the firm will pay a dividend of $5.00 for the next two years followed by a year at $6.50. Fred's investment plan is to buy Denhart now, hold it for three years, and then sell. He thinks the price will be about $75 when he sells. What is the most Fred should be willing to pay for a share of Denhart if he can earn 10% on investments of similar risk?

3. The Spinnaker Company has paid an annual dividend of $2 per share for some time. Recently, however, the board of directors voted to grow the dividend by 6% from now on. What is the most you would be willing to pay for a share of Spinnaker if you expect a 10% return on your stock investments?

4. The Pancake Corporation recently paid a $3 dividend and is expected to grow at 5% forever. Investors generally require an expected return of at least 9% before they'll buy stocks similar to Pancake.

a. What is Pancake's intrinsic value?

b. Is it a bargain if it's selling at $76 a share?

5. Tyler Inc's most recent annual dividend was $3.55 a share. The firm has been growing at a consistent 4% rate for several years, but analysts generally believe better times are ahead and future growth will be in the neighborhood of 5%. The stock is currently selling for $75. Stocks similar to Tyler earn returns ranging from 8% to 10%.

a. Calculate values for a share of Tyler at interest rates of 8%, 9%, and 10%.

b. Do you think Tyler is a good investment for the long run—that is, for someone planning to hold onto it for 10 or more years?

c. Do you think it's a good investment for the short term? That is, should you buy it with the expectation of selling in a relatively short period, say a year or less?

d. Repeat the calculations in part a assuming that instead of rising, Tyler's growth rate (1) remains at 4% or (2) declines to 3%.

e. Comment on the range of prices that you've calculated in parts a and d.

6. The Anderson Pipe Co. just paid an annual dividend of $3.75 and is expected to grow at 8% for the foreseeable future. Harley Bevins generally demands a return of 9% when he invests in companies similar to Anderson.

a. What is the most Harley should be willing to pay for a share of Anderson?

b. Is your answer reasonable? What's going on here? What should Harley do with this result?

7. The Miller Milk Company has just come up with a new lactose-free dessert product for people who can't eat or drink ordinary dairy products. Management expects the new product to fuel sales growth at 30% for about two years. After that competitors will copy the idea and produce similar products, and growth will return to about 3%, which is normal for the dairy industry in the area. Miller recently paid an annual dividend of $2.60, which will grow with the company. The return on stocks like the Miller company is typically around 10%. What is the most you would pay for a share of Miller?

Problems 8 through 10 refer to Softek Inc., a leader in the computer software field. Softek has two potentially big-selling products under development. Alpha, the first new product, seems very likely to catch on and is expected to drive the firm's growth rate to 25% for the next two years. However, software products have short lives, and growth can be expected to return to a more normal rate of 6% after that period if something new isn't launched immediately

Beta, the second product, is a logical follow-on, but management isn't as confident about its success as it is about Alpha's. Softek's most recent yearly dividend was $4.00, and firms in the industry typically return 14% on stockholder investments.

8. You are an investment analyst for a brokerage firm and have been asked to develop a recommendation about Softek for the firm's clients. You've studied the fundamentals of the industry and the firm, and are now ready to determine what the stock should sell for based on the present value of future cash flows.

a. Calculate a value for Softek's stock assuming product Alpha is successful but Beta isn't. In other words, assume two years of growth at 25% followed by 6% growth lasting indefinitely.

b. Calculate a price assuming Beta is also successful and holds Softek's growth rate at 25% for two additional years.

9. Calculate a price for Softek assuming Alpha is successful and Beta is successful but doesn't do quite as well as Alpha. Assume Softek grows at 25% for two years and then at 18% for two more. After that it continues to grow at 6%. (*Hint*: Don't be confused by the fact that there are now three growth periods. Just calculate successive dividends, multiplying by one plus the growth rate in effect until you get the first dividend into the period of normal growth. Then apply the Gordon model. A time line is a must for this problem.)

10. How would you advise clients about Softek stock as an investment under the following conditions? Give reasons for your advice. (No calculations.)

a. Softek is currently selling at a price very near that calculated in part a of Problem 8.

b. It is selling near the price calculated in Problem 9.

c. It is selling at a price slightly above that calculated in part b of Problem 8.

11. Blackstone Corporation's $7 preferred was issued five years ago. The risk-appropriate interest rate for the issue is currently 11%. What is this preferred selling for today?

12. Fox Woodworking Inc. issued preferred shares at a face value of $50 to yield 9% 10 years ago. The shares are currently selling at $60. What return are they earning for investors who buy them today?

Internet Problem

13. The Sara Lee Corporation provides an excellent 10-year summary of financial data at http://www.saralee.com. Use the constant growth model to estimate the value of Sara Lee. You can get the most recent dividend and the dividend growth rate (use the 10-year rate) from the web site. Use a 14% required rate of return. How does the value from the model compare to Sara Lee's current market price?

COMPUTER PROBLEMS

14. The Rollins Metal Company is engaged in a long-term planning process and is trying to choose among several strategic options that imply different future growth rates for the company. Management feels that the main benefit of higher growth is that it enhances the firm's current stock price. However, high growth strategies have a cost in that they generally involve considerable risk. Higher risk means that investors demand higher returns, which tends to depress current stock price.

Management is having a hard time evaluating this cost–benefit trade-off because growth and risk are conceptual abstractions. In other words, it's hard to visualize how growth and risk interact with each other as well as with other things to produce stock prices. Management can, however, intuitively associate each strategy option with a growth rate and a required rate of return implied by risk.

You are a financial consultant who's been hired to help make some sense out of the situation. You feel your best approach is to develop a systematic relationship between return, growth, and stock price that you can show to management visually.

Use the STCKVAL program to develop the following chart assuming the strategic options result in different constant growth rates that start immediately. The firm's last dividend was $2.35 per share.

The Price of Rollins Stock as a Function of Growth Rate and the Return Required by Investors

		Growth Rates (g)			
		6%	8%	10%	12%
Required Returns (k)	7%		—	—	—
	9%			—	—
	11%				—
	13%				

Can you make any general comments about the risk return trade-off based on your chart?

15. Suppose the strategic options available to the Rollins company in Problem 14 result in *temporarily* enhanced growth. Each option can be associated with a super normal growth rate that lasts for some period after which growth returns to the firm's normal 5%. Further suppose the duration of the super normal growth is a variable which can also be affected by strategic policy. Use the STCKVAL program for two-stage growth to develop the following chart assuming a required return of 10%.

The Price of Rollins Stock as a Function of Temporary Growth Rate and Duration at a Required Return Rate of 10%

		Super Normal Growth Rates (g_1)			
		12%	14%	16%	18%
Duration of g_1 in Years (n)	2				
	4				
	6				
	8				

Can you use your chart to make any general comments about the risk return trade-off under this assumption about the nature of the strategic options?

DEVELOPING SOFTWARE

16. Program your own two-stage growth model for two years of super normal growth (g_1) followed by normal growth (g_2) lasting forever. Treat both growth rates, the last dividend (D_0), and the required rate of return (k) as inputs. Here's how to do it. (Refer to Figure 7.2 and Example 7.5 on pages 231–233. You'll be programming exactly that procedure.)

1. Lay out four cells horizontally in your spreadsheet (to represent a time line starting with time zero).
2. Put D_0 in the first cell.
3. Form the next two cells by multiplying the one before by $(1 + g_1)$.
4. Form the fourth cell by multiplying the third by $(1 + g_2)$.
5. Calculate P_2 in another cell using the Gordon model with the fourth cell in the numerator and $(k - g_2)$ in the denominator.
6. Form P_0 as the sum of the present values of the middle two cells in the time line and the present value of the cell carrying P_2.

17. Program a model for three years of super normal growth.

CHAPTER 8

Risk and Return

Chapter Outline

This chapter explores the relationship between risk and return inherent in investing in securities, especially stocks. In what follows we'll define risk and return precisely, investigate the nature of their relationship, and find that there are ways to limit exposure to investment risk.

The body of thought we'll be working with is known as *portfolio theory*. The ideas behind the theory were motivated by observations of the returns on various investments over many years. We'll begin by reviewing those observations.

WHY STUDY RISK AND RETURN?

As we've said before, there are fundamentally two ways to invest: debt and equity. Debt involves lending by buying bonds or putting money into savings accounts. Equity means buying stock.

Scholars looked at these two investment vehicles over a long period of time, about 75 years, and noticed that on the average the returns to equity investments were much higher than the returns to debt investments. Equity returns averaged an annual rate of over 11%, while debt returns averaged only 4 or 5%. During the same period, inflation also averaged about 3%, so people who invested in debt didn't get ahead by very much at all.[1]

● The **return on equity (stock)** investments has historically been **much higher** than the **return on debt** investments.

---

1. *Stocks, Bonds, Bills, and Inflation,*® Valuation Edition, 2001 Yearbook, Ibbotson Associates.

But the average returns weren't the whole story. Although equity returns were much higher in terms of the long-run average, they were subject to huge swings during shorter periods. In a given one- or two-year period, for example, the annual return on stock investments might have been as high as 30% or as low as −30%. The high side of this range is great news, but the low side would be a disaster to most investors.

○ **Equity** is historically much **riskier** than debt.

The short-term variability of equity returns was a very important observation, because few people invest for 75 years. Most everyone has a much shorter time horizon of 2, 10, or perhaps 20 years, but never 75. The variability means that if you invest in stock today with a goal of putting a child through college in 5 years, there's a good chance that you'll lose money instead of making it. That's a frightening possibility to most people.

As a result of these observations, people began to wonder if there wasn't some way to invest in equities (stocks) that would take advantage of their high average rate of return but minimize their risk at the same time.

Thinking about that question resulted in the development of some techniques that enable investors to control and manage the risk to which they subject themselves while searching for high returns. These techniques involve investing in combinations of stocks called *portfolios.*

○ **Portfolios** are collections of financial assets held by investors.

In the rest of this chapter we'll gain a better understanding of the concept of risk and see how it fits into the portfolio idea. Keep in mind throughout that the reason we do this is to *capture the high average returns of equity investing while limiting the associated risk as much as possible.*

○THE GENERAL RELATIONSHIP BETWEEN RISK AND RETURN

People usually use the word "risk" when referring to the probability that something bad will happen. For example, we often talk about the risk of having an accident or of losing a job.

In financial dealings risk tends to be thought of as the probability of losing some or all of the money we put into a deal. For example, we talked about the risk of default on a loan in Chapter 4, meaning the probability that the loan wouldn't be paid back and the lender would lose his or her investment. Similarly, an investment in a share of stock results in a loss if the price drops before an investor sells. The probability of that happening is what most people think of as risk in stock investments.

In general, investment opportunities that offer higher returns also entail higher risks. Let's consider a hypothetical example to illustrate this central idea.

Suppose you could invest in a stock that will do one of two things. It will either return 15% on your investment or become valueless, resulting in a total loss of your money. Imagine for the sake of illustration that there's no middle ground; you either make 15% or lose everything. Suppose the chance of total loss is 1% and the chance of a 15% return is 99%. The *risk* associated with investing in this stock can be thought of as a 1% chance of total loss.

Let's further assume that all stocks behave in this peculiar way and offer only two possible outcomes, some positive return or a total loss. However, the level of positive return and the probability of total loss can be different for each stock.

It's important to visualize this hypothetical world. Every stock has a positive level of return that's quite likely to occur. *Investors more or less expect to receive that return,* yet they realize that every stock investment also carries some risk, the probability that they'll lose their entire investment instead.

● Stocks with **higher likely returns** generally also have **higher risks of loss**.

Now, suppose you're not happy with the 15% return offered by the stock we started with, so you look around for an issue that offers a higher rate. *As a general rule, you'd find that stocks offering higher likely returns also come with higher probabilities of total loss.* For example, an issue offering a 20% return might entail a 3% chance of total loss, while something offering a 25% return might have a 10% chance of loss, and so on.

This relationship is the financial expression of a simple fact of business life. Higher profit business opportunities are generally untried ventures that have a good chance of doing poorly or failing altogether. As a result, higher likely return goes hand in hand with higher risk.

Of course, in the real world there aren't just two possible outcomes associated with each investment opportunity. The actual return on a stock investment can be more or less than the most likely value by any amount. The illustration's total loss is in fact a worst case situation. The real definition of risk therefore has to be more complex than the one in the illustration. Nevertheless, the general rule remains the same: Higher financial rewards (returns) come with higher risks.

Unfortunately, it isn't easy to understand how the real risk/return relationship works—that is, to predict just how much risk is associated with a given level of return. Understanding the real risk/return relationship involves two things. First we have to define risk in a measurable way, and then we have to relate that measurement to return according to some formula that can be written down.

It's important to realize that the true definition of risk isn't simple and easily measurable the way it was in the illustration. There we had only one bad outcome, total loss, so risk was just the probability of that outcome. In reality there are any number of outcomes that are less favorable than we'd like, and each has a probability of happening. Some outcomes are very bad, like losing everything, while others are just mildly unpleasant, like earning a return that's a little less than we expected. Somehow we have to define risk to include all of these possibilities.

Portfolio Theory—Modern Thinking about Risk and Return

Recent thinking in theoretical finance, known as **portfolio theory,** grapples with this issue. The theory defines investment risk in a way that can be measured, and then relates the measurable risk in any investment to the level of return that can be expected from that investment in a predictable way.

Portfolio theory has had a major impact on the practical activities of the real world. The theory has important implications for how the securities industry functions every day, and its terminology is in use by practitioners all the time. Because of the central role played by this piece of thinking, it's important that students of finance develop a working familiarity with its principles and terminology. We'll develop that knowledge in this chapter.

● THE RETURN ON AN INVESTMENT

We developed the idea of a return on an investment rather carefully in the last two chapters. Recall that investments could be made in securities that represent either debt or equity, and that the return was the discount (interest) rate that equated the present value of the future cash flows coming from an investment to its current price.

In simpler terms you can think about the return associated with an investment as a rate of interest that the present valuing process makes a lot like the interest

Two Internet sources of up-
to-date rates of return are
BanxQuote at
www.banx.com/
and Bank Rate Monitor at
www.bankrate.com/

rate on a bank account. In effect, the rate of return ties all of an investment's future cash flows into a neat bundle, which can then be compared with the return on other investments.

One-Year Investments

In what follows we'll use the idea of returns on investments held for just one year to illustrate points, so it's a good idea to keep those definitions in mind in formula form. We developed the expressions in Chapters 6 and 7, but will repeat them here for convenience.

A debt investment is a loan, and the return is just the loan's interest rate. This is simply the ratio of the interest paid to the loan principal.

(8.1)
$$k = \frac{\text{interest paid}}{\text{loan amount}}$$

This formulation leads to the convenient idea that a return is what the investor receives divided by what he or she invests. A stock investment involves the receipt of dividends and a capital gain (loss). If a stock investment is held for one year, the return can be written as

(8.2)
$$k = \frac{D_1 + (P_1 - P_0)}{P_0}.$$

Here P_0 is the price today, while P_1 and D_1 are respectively the price and dividend at the end of the year. This is equation 7.1, which we developed on page 222.

Returns, Expected and Required

Whenever people make an investment, we'll assume they have some expectation of what the rate of return will be. In the case of a bank account, that's simply the interest rate quoted by the bank. In the case of a stock investment, the return we expect depends on the dividends we think the company is going to pay and what we think the future price of the stock will be. This anticipated return is simply called the **expected return**. It's based on whatever information the investor has available about the nature of the security at the time he or she buys it. In other words, the expected return is based on equation 8.2 with *projected* values inserted for P_1 and D_1.

It's important to realize that *no rational person makes any investment without some expectation of return.* People understand that in stock investments the actual return probably won't turn out to be exactly what they expected when they made the investment, because future prices and dividends are uncertain. Nevertheless, they have some expectation of what the return is most likely to be.

At the same time, investors have a notion about what return they must receive in order to make particular investments. We call this concept the **required return** on the stock.

The required return is related to the perceived risk of the investment. People have different ideas about the safety of investments in different stocks. If there's a good chance that a company will get into trouble, causing a low return or a loss on an investment in its stock, people will require a higher expected return to make the investment.

A person might say, "I won't put money into IBM stock unless the expected return is at least 9%." That percentage is the person's *required return* for an in-

The **expected return** on a stock is the return investors feel is most likely to occur based on currently available information.

The **required return** on a stock is the minimum rate at which investors will purchase or hold a stock based on their perceptions of its risk.

● Significant investment in a stock occurs only if the **expected return exceeds the required return** for a substantial number of investors.

vestment in IBM. Each individual will have a different required return for every stock offered. Exactly how people form required returns is a central subject of this chapter. The important point is that *substantial investment will take place in a particular stock only if the generally expected return exceeds most people's required return for that stock*. In other words, people won't buy an issue unless they think it will return at least as much as they require.

● RISK—A PRELIMINARY DEFINITION

We talked about risk earlier, and alluded to the fact that its definition in finance is somewhat complicated. The definition we'll eventually work with is a little different from the way we normally use the word. We'll need to develop the idea slowly, so we'll begin with a simple definition that we'll modify and add to as we progress. The simple definition is consistent with our everyday notion of risk as the chance that something bad will happen to us.

● A preliminary definition of investment **risk** is the **probability that return will be less than expected.**

For now, **risk** *for an investor is the chance (probability) that the return on an investment will turn out to be less than he or she expected when the investment was made.* Notice that this definition includes more than just losing money. If someone makes an investment expecting a return of 10%, risk includes the probability that the return will turn out to be 9%, even though that's a positive return. Let's look at this definition of risk in the context of two different kinds of investment.

First consider investing in a bank account. What's the chance that a depositor will receive less interest than the bank promised when the account was opened? Today that chance is very small, because most bank accounts are insured by the federal government. Even if the bank goes out of business, depositors get their money, so we're virtually guaranteed the promised return. A bank account has virtually zero risk because there's little or no chance that the investor won't get the expected return.

Now consider an investment in stock. Looking at equation 8.2, we can see that the return is determined by the future price of the stock and its future dividend. Because there are no guarantees about what those future amounts will be, the return on a stock investment may turn out to be different from what was expected at the time the stock was purchased. It may be more than what was anticipated or it may be less. Risk is just the probability that it's anything less.

Feelings about Risk

Most people have negative feelings about bearing risk in their investment activities. For example, if investors are offered a choice between a bank account that pays 8% and a stock investment with an expected return of 8%, almost everyone would choose the bank account because it has less risk. People prefer lower risk if the expected return is the same. We call this characteristic **risk aversion,** meaning that most of us don't like bearing risk.

● **Risk averse** investors prefer lower risk when expected returns are equal.

At the same time, most people see a trade-off between risk and return. If offered a choice between the 8% bank account and a stock whose expected return is 10%, some will still choose the bank account, but many will now choose the stock.

It's important to understand that risk aversion doesn't mean that risk is to be avoided at all costs. It is simply a negative that can be offset with more anticipated money—in other words, with a higher expected return.

We're now armed with sufficient background material to attempt an excursion into portfolio theory.

PORTFOLIO THEORY

Portfolio theory is a statistical model of the investment world. We'll develop the ideas using some statistical terms and concepts, but will avoid most of the advanced mathematics. We'll begin with a brief review of a few statistical concepts.

REVIEW OF THE CONCEPT OF A RANDOM VARIABLE

A **random variable** is the outcome of a chance process and has a probability distribution.

In statistics, a random variable is the outcome of a chance process. Such variables can be either *discrete* or *continuous*. Discrete variables can take only specific values whereas continuous variables can take any value within a specified range.

Suppose you toss a coin four times, count the number of heads, and call the result X. Then X, the number of heads, is a random variable that can take any of five values: zero, one, two, three, or four. For any series of four tosses, there's a probability of getting each value of X [written P(X)] as follows.[2]

X	P(X)
0	.0625
1	.2500
2	.3750
3	.2500
4	0.0625
	1.0000

Such a representation of all the possible outcomes along with the probability of each is called the *probability distribution for the random variable X*. Notice that the probabilities of all the possible outcomes have to sum to 1.0. The probability distribution can be shown in tabular form like this or graphically, as in Figure 8.1.

---

2. The probabilities can be calculated by enumerating all of the 16 possible head–tail sequences in four coin tosses and counting the number of heads in each. Each sequence has an equal one-sixteenth probability (.0625) of happening. The probability of any number of heads is one-sixteenth times the number of sequences containing that number of heads.

The number of heads in a series of coin tosses is a *discrete* random variable because it can take on only a limited number of discrete values, each of which has a distinct probability. In our example, the only outcomes possible are 0, 1, 2, 3, and 4. There can't be more than four heads or fewer than zero, nor can there be a fractional number of heads.

The Mean or Expected Value

● The **mean** or **expected value** of a distribution is the most likely outcome for the random variable.

The value that the random variable is most likely to take is an important statistical concept. In symmetrical probability distributions with only one peak like the one in Figure 8.1, it's at the center of the distribution under its highest point. We call this most likely outcome the *mean* or the *expected value* of the distribution, and write it by placing a bar over the variable. In the coin toss illustration, the mean is written as

$$\overline{X} = 2 .$$

Thinking of the mean as the value of the random variable at the highest point of the distribution makes intuitive sense, but the statistical definition is more precise. The mean is actually the weighted average of all possible outcomes where each outcome is weighted by its probability. This is written as

$$\overline{X} = \sum_{i=1}^{n} X_i P(X_i).$$

where X_i is the value of each outcome and $P(X_i)$ is its probability. The summation sign means that we add this figure for each of the n possible outcomes.

Calculating the mean for discrete distributions is relatively easy. For the coin toss illustration, we just list each possible outcome along with its probability, multiply, and sum.

X	P(X)	X * P(X)
0	.0625	0
1	.2500	.25
2	.3750	.75
3	.2500	.75
4	0.0625	0.25
	1.0000	$\overline{X}$ = 2.00

The mean is simply the mathematical expression of the everyday idea of an average. That is, if we repeat the *series* of coin tosses a number of times, the average outcome will be 2. Notice that the process of multiplying something related to an outcome (in this case the outcome itself) by the probability of the outcome and summing gives an average value. We'll use the technique again shortly.

The Variance and Standard Deviation

A second important characteristic of a random variable is its variability. The idea gets at how far a typical observation of the variable is likely to deviate from the mean. Here's an example.

Suppose we define a random variable by estimating the heights of randomly selected buildings in a city. Allow 12 feet per story. The results might range from 12 feet for one-story structures to more than 1,000 feet for skyscrapers. Suppose the average height turned out to be 30 stories or 360 feet. It's easy to see that a typical building would have a height that's very different from that average. Some office buildings would be hundreds of feet higher, while all private homes would be hundreds shorter.

Now, suppose we did the same thing for telephone poles, measuring to the nearest foot, and got an average height of 30 feet. Unlike buildings, we'd find that telephone poles don't vary much around 30 feet. Some might be 31 feet and some 29, but not very many of them would be far out of that range.

The point is that there's a great deal of difference in *variability around the mean* in different distributions. Telephone pole heights are closely clustered around their average, while building heights are widely dispersed around theirs.

In statistics, this notion of how far a typical observation is likely to be from the mean is described by the *standard deviation* of the distribution, usually written as the Greek letter sigma, σ. You can think of the standard deviation as the average (standard) distance (deviation) between an outcome and the mean. For example, in our building illustration the "average" (typical) building might be 20 stories different in height than the mean height of all buildings. As we'll explain shortly, that interpretation isn't quite right because of the way standard deviations are calculated, but it's a good way to visualize the concept.

● The **standard deviation** gives an indication of how far from the mean a typical observation is likely to fall.

The standard deviation idea intuitively begins as an average distance from the mean. One would think that could be calculated in the same way as the mean itself. That is, by taking the distance of each possible outcome from the mean, multiplying it by the probability of the outcome, and summing over all outcomes. Mathematically that would look like this:

$$\sum_{i=1}^{n} (X_i - \overline{X}) \, P(X_i)$$

The problem with this formulation is that the deviations [the $(X_i - \overline{X})$'s] are of different signs depending on the side of the mean on which each outcome (X_i) is located. Hence they cancel each other when summed. Statisticians avoid the problem by squaring the deviations before multiplying by the probabilities and summing. This leads to a statistic called the *variance* written as

$$\text{Var } X = \sigma_x^2 = \sum_{i=1}^{n} [(X_i - \overline{X})^2] P(X_i).$$

In words, the variance is the average *squared* deviation from the mean. The *standard deviation* is the square root of the variance.

Intuitively, taking the square root of the variance reverses the effect of the earlier squaring to get rid of the sign differences. Unfortunately, it doesn't quite work. The square root of the sum of squares isn't equal to the sum of the original amounts. Hence the standard deviation isn't an average distance from the mean, but it's *conceptually* close. This is why we use the term *standard* deviation instead of average deviation. In any event, standard deviation and variance are the traditional measures of variability in probability distributions and are used extensively in financial theory.

For a discrete distribution like our coin toss, we calculate the variance and then the standard deviation by (1) measuring each possible outcome's distance from the mean, (2) squaring it, (3) multiplying by the probability of the outcome, (4) summing the result over all possible outcomes for the variance, and then (5) taking the square root for the standard deviation. Of course, the mean has to be calculated first.

X_i	$(X_i - \bar{X})$	$(X_i - \bar{X})^2$	$P(X_i)$	$(X_i - \bar{X})^2 * P(X_i)$
0	−2	4	.0625	0.25
1	−1	1	.2500	0.25
2	0	0	.3750	0.00
3	1	1	.2500	0.25
4	2	4	.0625	0.25

$$\text{Var } X = \sigma_X^2 = 1.00$$
$$\text{Std Dev} = \sqrt{\text{Var } X} = \sigma_X = 1.00$$

This example is unusual in that the variance is exactly 1, so the standard deviation turns out to be the same number.

Keep in mind that the terms "variance" and "standard deviation" are both used to characterize variability around the mean.

The Coefficient of Variation

The *coefficient of variation,* CV, is a *relative* measure of variation. It is the ratio of the standard deviation of a distribution to its mean.

$$CV = \frac{\sigma_X}{\bar{X}}$$

It is essentially standard variability as a fraction of the average value of the variable. In our coin toss example, the mean outcome is two heads in a series of four tosses. The standard deviation is one head, meaning a typical series will vary by one from the mean of two. The coefficient of variation is then (½ =) .5, meaning the typical variation is one half the size of the mean.

Continuous Random Variables

Other random variables are continuous, meaning they can take any numerical value within some range. For example, if we choose people at random and measure their height, that measurement could be considered a random variable called H. A graphic representation of the probability distribution of H is shown in Figure 8.2. In this graph, probability is represented by the area under the curve and above the horizontal axis. That entire area is taken to be 1.0.

FIGURE 8.2

Probability Distribution for a Continuous Random Variable

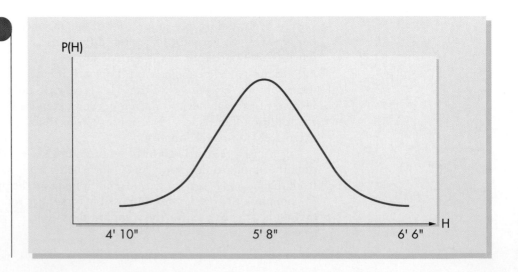

When the random variable is continuous, we talk about the probability of an actual outcome being *within a range* of values rather than turning out to be an exact amount. For example, it isn't meaningful to state the probability of finding a person whose height is *exactly* 5'2", because the chance of doing that is virtually zero. However, it is meaningful to state a probability of finding a person whose height is between 5'1⅞" and 5'2⅛". In the distribution, that probability is represented by the area under the curve directly above and between those values on the horizontal axis.

Calculating the mean and variance of a continuous distribution is mathematically more complex than in the discrete case, but the idea is the same. The mean is the average of all possible outcomes, each weighted by its probability. When the distribution is symmetrical and has only one peak, the mean is found under that peak.

⬤ THE RETURN ON A STOCK INVESTMENT AS A RANDOM VARIABLE

⬤ In financial theory, the **return on a stock investment** is considered a **random variable**.

In portfolio theory, the return on an investment in stock is considered a random variable. This makes sense because return is influenced by a significant number of uncertainties. Consider equation 8.2. In that expression, the value of the return depends on the future market price of the stock, P_1, and a future dividend, D_1. Both of these amounts are influenced by the multitude of events that make up the business environment in which the company that issued the stock operates. The price is further affected by all the forces that influence financial markets. In other words, there's an element of uncertainty or randomness in both the future price and the future dividend. It follows that there's an uncertainty or randomness to the value of k, and we can consider it a random variable.

Return is a continuous random variable whose values are generally expressed as percentages. Equation 8.2 calculates the decimal form of those percentages (e.g., .10 for 10%). In straightforward stock investments, the lowest return possible is –100%, a total loss of invested money, but there's technically no limit to the amount of positive return that's possible.

Like any random variable, the return on a stock investment has an associated probability distribution. Figure 8.3 is a graphic depiction of a probability distribution for the return on a stock we'll call X. We'll call the return on X k_X. The values the return can take appear along the horizontal axis, and the probabilities of those values appear on the vertical axis. The shape of the distribution depicts the likelihood of all possible actual values of k_X according to areas under the curve.

The total area under the curve is 1.0, and the proportionate area under any section represents the probability that an actual return will fall along the horizontal axis in that area. For example, the shaded area in the diagram represents the probability that in any particular year the actual return on an investment in stock X will turn out to be between 8.0% and 8.5%. If that area is .1 or 10% of the total area under the curve, the probability of the actual return being between 8.0% and 8.5% in any year would be 10%.

⬤ The mean of the distribution of returns is the stock's **expected return**.

The mean or expected value (the most likely outcome) is usually found under the highest point of the curve. It's indicated as $\overline{k}_X$ in the diagram.

The mean is the statistical representation of the average investor's expected return that we talked about earlier. This is an important point. Portfolio theory assumes that all of the knowledge the investment community has about the future performance of a stock is reflected in the probability distribution of returns perceived by the investors. In particular, the mean of that perceived distribution is the expected return investors plan on receiving when they buy.

FIGURE 8.3

The Probability Distribution of the Return on an Investment in Stock X

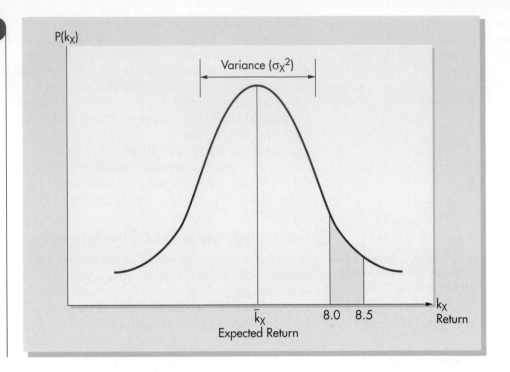

The variance and standard deviation of the distribution show how likely it is that an actual return will be some distance away from the expected value. A distribution with a large variance is more likely to produce actual outcomes that are substantially away from the expected value than one with a small variance.

Figure 8.3 shows the variance conceptually as the width of the distribution. We'll use σ_x^2 to indicate that we're talking about the distribution of returns for stock X. Similarly, σ_x will be the standard deviation for stock X. A large variance implies a wide distribution with gently sloping sides and a low peak. A narrow distribution with steeply sloping sides and a high peak has a small variance and standard deviation. Figure 8.4 shows distributions with large and small variances.

Notice that the large variance distribution has more area under the curve farther away from the mean than the small variance distribution. This pattern means that more actual observations of the return are likely to be far away from the mean when the distribution's variance is large. Stated another way, returns will tend to be more different, or more variable, from year to year when the variance is large. When the variance is small, actual returns in successive years are more likely to cluster closely around the mean or expected value.

RISK REDEFINED AS VARIABILITY

● In financial theory **risk** is defined as **variability** in return.

The meaning of risk in portfolio theory differs from the definition we gave earlier. Before we said that risk is the probability that return will be less than expected. In portfolio theory, risk is variability. That is, a stock whose return is likely to be significantly different from one year to the next is risky, while one whose returns are likely to cluster tightly is less risky. Stated another way, a risky stock has a high probability of producing a return that's substantially away from the mean of the distribution of returns, while a low-risk stock is

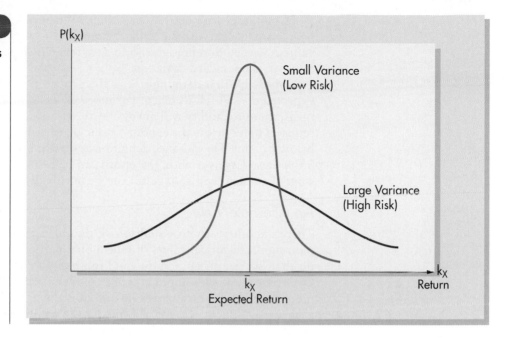

FIGURE 8.4

Probability Distributions with Large and Small Variances

unlikely to produce a return that differs from the expected return by very much.

But this is exactly the idea of variance and standard deviation that we've been talking about, so in portfolio theory, a stock investment's risk is defined as the standard deviation of the probability distribution of its return. A large standard deviation implies high risk and a small one means low risk. In practical terms, high risk implies *variability* in return, meaning that returns in successive years are likely to be considerably different from one another.

Figure 8.4 can be interpreted as showing a risky stock and a low-risk stock with the same expected return. The difference is in the variances, which can be visually observed as the widths of the distributions.

This definition is somewhat inconsistent with the earlier version in which we said risk was the probability that return would be *less than* what was expected. One would think that a more appropriate definition in statistical terms would equate risk with only the left side of the probability distribution, because in that area return is less than expected. Defining risk as the entire standard deviation includes the probability that the return turns out to be more than expected, and we're certainly not concerned if that happens.

Indeed, a left-side-only definition would make more intuitive sense. However, it would be very difficult to work with mathematically. Theorists solved the problem by noticing that return distributions are usually relatively symmetrical. This means that a large left side always implies a large right side as well. Why not therefore define risk for mathematical convenience as total variability, understanding that we're really only concerned with the probability of lower than expected returns (those on the left)? Indeed this is what was done. The resulting technical definition of risk is a little strange in that it includes good news as well as bad news, but that doesn't bother us if we keep the reason in mind.

So we actually have two definitions of risk that are both correct. In practical terms, risk is the probability that return will be less than expected. In financial theory, risk is the variability of the probability distribution of returns.

Terminology isn't entirely consistent. When talking conceptually about risk people are likely to use the terms "variance" or "variability." But when a precise value is needed to represent risk in a mathematical equation, it's more common to use σ, the standard deviation.

Notice also that defining risk as the probability that return will be less than expected doesn't tell us much. For more or less symmetrical distributions of returns, that probability will always be about 50%. But for some investments the return is never below the expected value by very much, while for others it can be below by a lot. The variance definition gets right at this distinction. If the distribution has a large variance, the return can be below the expected value by a substantial amount, and an investor can be hurt badly.

An Alternate View

There's another way to visualize risk that many students find helpful. Imagine plotting the historical values of return on a particular stock over time. When we do that, we get an up and down graph like one of those shown in Figure 8.5. Over time the stock's return is seen to oscillate around its average value, $\overline{k}_X$. The more the stock's return moves up and down over time, the more risky we say it is as an investment. That is, the greater the amplitude of the swings, the riskier the stock. This view is simply a graphic result of the variance of the distribution. In the diagram, stock A is relatively high risk and stock B is relatively low risk. We will use this representation again shortly.

● RISK AVERSION

● **Risk aversion** means investors prefer lower risk when **expected returns are equal.**

Now we're in a position to define **risk aversion** more precisely. The axiom simply states that people prefer investments with less risk to those with more risk if the expected returns are equal. Figure 8.6a illustrates the idea with probability

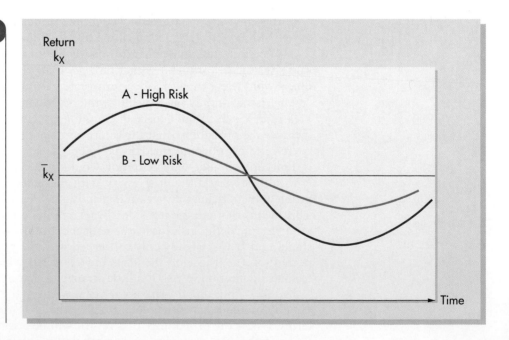

FIGURE 8.5

Investment Risk Viewed as Variability of Return Over Time

FIGURE 8.6

Risk Aversion

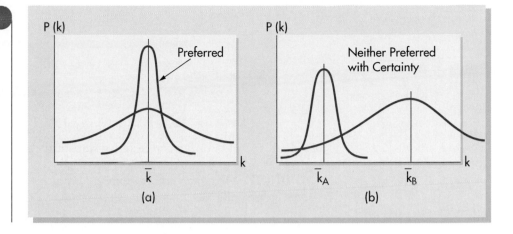

distributions. The narrower distribution has less risk and will be preferred to the wider, riskier distribution.

It's important to understand that this preference is assumed to hold universally only in cases where the expected returns are exactly equal. When the choice is as illustrated in Figure 8.6b, the principle of risk aversion tells us nothing. There, investment A is preferred on the basis of risk, while investment B is preferred on the basis of expected return. Which will be chosen depends on the individual investor's tolerance for risk.

EXAMPLE 8.1

Evaluating Stand-Alone Risk

The notions of risk we've just developed are associated with owning shares of a single stock by itself. That can be characterized as *stand-alone risk,* because the stock's variability stands alone independent of anything happening in the owner's portfolio.

Harold MacGregor is considering buying stocks for the first time and is looking for a single company in which he'll make a substantial investment. He's narrowed his search to two firms, Evanston Water Inc. and Astro Tech Corp. Evanston is a public utility supplying water to the county, and Astro is a relatively new high-tech company in the computer field.

Public utilities are classic examples of low-risk stocks because they're *regulated monopolies.* That means the government gives them the exclusive right to sell their products in an area but also controls pricing so they can't take advantage of the public by charging excessively. The *utility commission* usually sets prices aimed at achieving a reasonable return for the company's stockholders.

On the other hand, young high-tech firms are classic examples of high-risk companies. That's because new technical ideas can be enormously profitable, complete failures, or anything in between.

Harold has studied the history and prospects of both firms and their industries, and with the help of his broker has made a discrete estimate of the probability distribution of returns for each stock as follows.

Evanston Water		Astro Tech	
k_E	$P(k_E)$	k_A	$P(k_A)$
6%	.05	−100%	.15
8	.15	0	.20
10	.60	15	.30
12	.15	30	.20
14	.05	130	.15

Evaluate Harold's options in terms of statistical concepts of risk and return.

Solution: First calculate the expected return for each stock. That's the mean of each distribution.

Evanston Water			Astro Tech		
k_E	$P(k_E)$	$k_E * P(k_E)$	k_A	$P(k_A)$	$k_A * P(k_A)$
6%	.05	.3%	−100%	.15	−15.0%
8	.15	1.2	0	.20	0.0
10	.60	6.0	15	.30	4.5
12	.15	1.8	30	.20	6.0
14	.05	.7	130	.15	19.5
		$\bar{k}_E = \overline{10.0\%}$			$\bar{k}_A = \overline{15.0\%}$

Next calculate the variance and standard deviation of the return on each stock.

Evanston Water

k_E	$k_E - \bar{k}_E$	$(k_E - \bar{k}_E)^2$	$P(k_E)$	$(k_E - \bar{k}_E)^2 * P(k_E)$
6%	−4%	16	.05	0.8
8	−2	4	.15	0.6
10	0	0	.60	0.0
12	2	4	.15	0.6
14	4	16	.05	0.8

Variance $\sigma_E^2 = 2.8$

Standard Deviation: $\sigma_E = 1.7\%$

Astro Tech

k_A	$k_A - \bar{k}_A$	$(k_A - \bar{k}_A)^2$	$P(k_A)$	$(k_A - \bar{k}_A)^2 * P(k_A)$
−100%	−115%	13,225	.15	1,984
0	−15	225	.20	45
15	0	0	.30	0
30	15	225	.20	45
130	115	13,225	.15	1,984

Variance: $\sigma_A^2 = 4,058$

Standard Deviation: $\sigma_A = 63.7\%$

Finally, calculate the coefficient of variation for each stock's return.

$$CV_E = \frac{\sigma_E}{\bar{k}_E} = \frac{1.7}{10.0} = .17 \qquad CV_A = \frac{\sigma_A}{\bar{k}_A} = \frac{63.7\%}{15\%} = 4.25$$

Discussion: If Harold considers only the expected returns on his investment options, he'll certainly choose Astro. It's most likely return is half again as high as

Evanston's. But a glance at the distributions reveals that's not the whole story. With Evanston, Harold's investment is relatively safe, because the worst he can do is a return of 6% rather than the expected 10%

Investing in Astro is a completely different story. While Harold's most likely return there is 15%, a substantial chance (15%) exists that he'll lose everything. There's also a 20% chance he'll earn a zero return. Possibilities like these give people concerns about investing in this kind of stock.

It's also important to appreciate the high side of the two distributions. With Evanston, Harold isn't likely to do much better than the expected return, because the highest yield available is only 14%. The utility commission's pricing regulations guarantee that. But with Astro there's a chance of more than doubling invested money in a relatively short time. That's reflected in the 15% chance of a 130% return. That tends to offset the depressing loss possibilities in the minds of some investors.

It should be clear that on a stand-alone basis, Astro is a relatively risky stock, while Evanston is relatively safe. Astro's risk and Evanston's lack of it come from the *variation* in the distributions of their returns, which we just observed by examining the distributions in detail. But the idea is also available in summarized form from the standard deviations and coefficients of variation.

First notice that Astro's standard deviation is 63.7%. That means a "typical" return has a good chance of being about 64% above or below the expected return of 15%. That's an enormous range for return, from −49% to 79%. On the other hand, Evanston's standard deviation is only 1.7%, meaning a typical return will probably be less than two percentage points off the expected return.

It's tempting to compare the two companies by saying Astro's risk is (63.7/1.7=) 37 times that of Evanston. But that's not quite fair because Astro has a higher expected return. It makes more sense to compare the coefficients of variation, which state the standard deviations in units of their respective means. Evanston's CV is .17 while Astro's is 4.25, so it's more reasonable to say that Astro is (4.25/.17=) 25 times as risky as Evanston.

A picture is even more telling. Continuous approximations of the two distributions are plotted as follows.

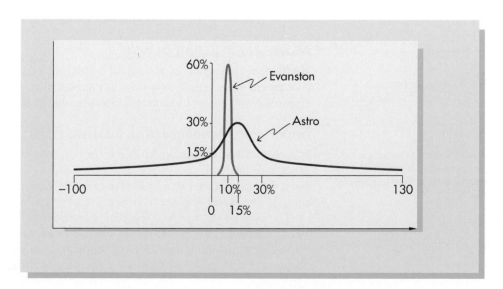

So, after having said all that, which stock should Harold choose?

Although our analysis has laid out the solution clearly, no one but Harold can answer that question. That's because his choice depends on his degree of *risk aversion*. Evanston is the better choice with respect to risk, but Astro is better with respect to expected return. Which dominates is a personal choice that only the investor can make.

DECOMPOSING RISK—SYSTEMATIC (MARKET) AND UNSYSTEMATIC (BUSINESS-SPECIFIC) RISK

● The **returns** on securities tend to **move** up and down **together.**

A fundamental truth of the investment world is that the returns offered on various securities tend to move up and down together. They don't move exactly together, or even proportionately, but for the most part stocks tend to go up and down at the same times.

Events and Conditions Causing Movement in Returns

Returns on stock investments move up and down in response to various events and conditions that affect the environment. Some things influence all stocks, while others affect only specific companies. News of politics, inflation, interest rates, war, and economic events tend to move most stocks in the same direction at the same time. A labor dispute in a particular industry, on the other hand, tends to affect only the stocks of firms in that industry.

Although certain events affect the returns of all stocks, some returns tend to respond more than others to particular things. Suppose news of an impending recession hits the market. The return on most stocks can be expected to decline, but not by the same amount. The return on a public utility like a water company isn't likely to change much. That's because people's demand for water doesn't change much in hard times, and the utility is a regulated monopoly whose profitability is more or less guaranteed by the government. On the other hand, the return on the stock of a luxury goods manufacturer may drop sharply, because recession signals a drying up of demand for the company's product.

In short, there's a general but disproportionate movement together upon which is superimposed a fair amount of individual movement.

Movement in Return as Risk

Remember that one way to look at a stock's risk is to consider the up and down movement of its return over time as equivalent to that risk (Figure 8.5). Think of that total movement as the total risk inherent in the stock.

Separating Movement/Risk into Two Parts

● A stock's risk can be separated into **systematic or market** risk and **unsystematic or business-specific** risk.

It's conceptually possible to separate the total up and down movement of a stock's return into two parts. The first part is the movement that occurs along with that of all other stocks in response to events affecting them all. That movement is known as *systematic risk*. It systematically affects everyone.

The second part is whatever movement is left over after the first part has been removed. This movement is a result of events that are specific to particular companies and industries. Strikes, good or bad weather, good or bad management, and demand conditions are examples of things that affect specific companies. This remaining movement is called *unsystematic risk*. It affects specific companies.

Systematic and unsystematic risk can also be called **market risk** and **business-specific risk**, respectively.

PORTFOLIOS

Most equity investors hold stock in a number of companies rather than putting all of their funds in one firm's securities. We refer to an investor's total stock holding as his or her *portfolio*.

Risk and Return for a Portfolio

● Portfolios have **their own** risks and returns.

Each stock in a portfolio has its own expected return and its own risk. These are the mean and standard deviation of the probability distribution of the stock's return. As might be expected, the total portfolio also has its own risk and return.

The return (actual or expected) on a portfolio is simply the average of the returns of the stocks in it, where the average is weighted by the proportionate dollars invested in each stock. For example, suppose we have the following three-stock portfolio.

Stock	$ Invested	Return
A	$ 6,000	5%
B	$ 9,000	9
C	$15,000	11
	$30,000	

The return on the portfolio, expected or actual, is

$$k_p = w_A k_A + w_B k_B + w_C k_C,$$

where k_p is the portfolio's return and the w's are the fractions of its total value invested in each asset. The weighted average calculation is as follows.

$$k_p = \frac{\$6K}{\$30K}(5\%) + \frac{\$9K}{\$30K}(9\%) + \frac{\$15K}{\$30K}(11\%)$$

$$= (.2)(.05) + (.3)(.09) + (.5)(.11)$$

$$= 9.2\%$$

The risk of a portfolio is the variance or standard deviation of the probability distribution of the portfolio's return. That depends on the variances (risks) of the returns on the stocks in the portfolio, but not in a simple way. We'll understand more about this relationship of portfolio risk to stock risk as we move on.

The Goal of the Investor/Portfolio Owner

As we said earlier, the goal of investors is to capture the high average returns of equities while avoiding as much of their risk as possible. *That's generally done by constructing diversified portfolios to minimize portfolio risk for a given return.*

Investment theory is based on the premise that portfolio owners care only about the financial performance of their whole portfolios and not about the stand-alone characteristics of the individual stocks in the portfolios.

● Investors are concerned with how stocks **impact portfolio performance** and not with their stand-alone characteristics.

In other words, an investor evaluates the risk and return characteristics of a new stock only in terms of how that stock will affect the performance of his or her portfolio and not on the stand-alone merits of the stock. How a stock's characteristics can be different in and out of a portfolio will become clear shortly.

● DIVERSIFICATION—HOW PORTFOLIO RISK IS AFFECTED WHEN STOCKS ARE ADDED

Our basic goal in investing, to capture a high portfolio return while avoiding as much risk as possible, is accomplished through diversification. **Diversification** means adding different, or diverse, stocks to a portfolio. It's the investor's most basic tool for managing risk. Properly employed, diversification can reduce but not eliminate risk (variation in return) in a portfolio. To achieve the goal, however, we have to be careful about how we go about diversifying. We'll need to address unsystematic (business-specific) risk and systematic (market) risk separately.

Business-Specific Risk and Diversification

If we diversify by forming a portfolio of the stocks of a fairly large number of different companies, we can imagine business-specific risk as a series of essentially random events that push the returns on individual stocks up or down. The stimuli that affect individual companies are separate events that occur across the country. Some are good and some are bad.

● **Business-specific risk** is essentially random and can be **diversified away**.

Because events causing business-specific risk are random from the investor's point of view, their effects simply cancel when added together over a substantial number of stocks. Therefore we say that business-specific risk can be "diversified away" in a portfolio of any size. In other words, the good events offset the bad ones, and if there are enough events the net result tends to be about zero.

However, a word of caution is in order. For this idea to work, the stocks in the portfolio have to be from companies in fundamentally different industries. For example, if all the companies in a portfolio were agricultural, the effect of a drought wouldn't be random. It would hit all of the stocks. Therefore the business-specific risk wouldn't be diversified away.

This is an easy but powerful concept. For investors who hold numerous stocks, business-specific risk simply doesn't exist at the aggregate level because it's "washed out" statistically. Individual stocks still have it, but portfolios do not, and the portfolio is all the investor cares about.

Systematic (Market) Risk and Diversification

Reducing market risk in a portfolio calls for more complicated thinking than does handling business-specific risk. It should be intuitively clear that if the returns of all stocks move up and down more or less together, we're unlikely to be able to eliminate all of the movement in a portfolio's return by adding more stocks. In fact, systematic or market risk in a portfolio can be reduced but never entirely eliminated through diversification. However, even the reduction of market risk requires careful attention to the risk characteristics of the stocks added to the portfolio.

THE PORTFOLIO   To appreciate the issue, imagine we have a portfolio of stocks that has an expected return $\overline{k}_p$. In what follows, we'll assume for simplicity that all the stocks have the same expected return. It's all right to make this unrealistic assumption for illustrative purposes, because the points we're getting at involve the interplay of risk among stocks and not of returns.

Our portfolio will have its own risk or variation in return, which is determined by the stocks in it. We'll assume the portfolio has been put together to mirror exactly the makeup of the overall stock market. That is, if the prices of the stocks in the overall market are such that General Motors makes up 2% of the market's value, we'll spend 2% of our money on General Motors stock, and so on through all the stocks listed on the market. If the portfolio is constituted in this way, its return will move up and down just as the market's return does. In other words, the portfolio's risk will just equal the market's risk. The behavior of the portfolio's return over time is illustrated in Figure 8.7 by the heavy line labeled P.

THE IMPACT ON PORTFOLIO RISK OF ADDING NEW STOCKS   We now want to consider the impact on the portfolio's risk of adding a little of *either* of two new stocks to it. We'll call these stocks A and B. The special behavior of the return on each is shown in Figure 8.7. Notice that we're not talking about adding both stocks A and B at the same time. Rather the idea is to assess the impact on the risk of the resulting portfolio of adding a little of A *or* a little of B to the original portfolio.

First consider stock A. What happens to the risk of the portfolio if we add a few shares of A? Notice that A's return achieves its highs and lows at exactly the same times as does the portfolio's, and that its peaks and troughs are higher and lower, respectively, than the portfolio's. It should be clear that the inclusion of a little A will tend to heighten the portfolio's peak returns and depress its lowest returns. In other words, it will make the swings in the portfolio's return larger. That means it will add risk to the portfolio.

In statistical terms, A's return is said to be perfectly positively correlated with the portfolio's return. That means the two returns move up and down at exactly the same times. Such stocks will generally add risk to a diversified portfolio.

FIGURE 8.7

Risk in and out of a Portfolio

Now consider the pattern of returns on stock B over time. Its peaks occur with the portfolio's valleys, and its valleys coincide with the portfolio's peaks. The return on stock B is always moving up or down in a direction opposite the movement of the return on the portfolio.

What will happen to the pattern of returns of the portfolio if we add a few shares of B? Clearly, the peaks will be lower and the valleys will be higher—that is, the swings won't be as wide. According to our definitions, that means the risk will be lowered by adding some B. In statistical terms, B's return is said to be perfectly negatively correlated with the portfolio's return. Such stocks will always lower the portfolio's risk.

In short, A adds risk to a portfolio while B reduces the portfolio's risk.

THE RISK OF THE NEW ADDITIONS BY THEMSELVES AND IN PORTFOLIOS

Now consider the relative riskiness of stocks A and B without reference to a portfolio. That is, how risky is each one standing alone? Figure 8.7 shows that A's and B's returns have about the same level of variation. That is, their peaks and troughs are about the same height. Therefore their stand-alone risks as individual stocks are about the same.

● Stocks with **equal stand-alone risk** can have **opposite risk impacts on a portfolio** because of the timing of the variations in their returns.

However, in a portfolio sense, A is risky and B is safe in that A adds and B subtracts risk. This is a central and critically important concept. *Although A and B are equally risky on a stand-alone basis, they have completely opposite risk impacts on a portfolio.*

The portfolio definition of a stock's risk is related to the timing of the variability of the stock's return rather than to the magnitude of the variation. It has to do with the way the new stock's return changes when the portfolio's return changes. Or, if the portfolio is constituted like the market as we've assumed, it has to do with the way the stock's return changes with the return on the market.

However, the degree to which a stock's return moves with the market is what we've called market risk. Hence we can say that *a stock's risk in a portfolio sense is its market risk.*

CHOOSING STOCKS TO DIVERSIFY FOR MARKET RISK

How do we diversify to reduce market risk in a portfolio? Figure 8.7 might imply that it's easy: Just add stocks like B until the movement of the portfolio is virtually dampened out. Unfortunately, stocks like B that move counter cyclically with the market are few and far between.

The classic example of such a stock is shares in a gold mine. When returns on most stocks are down, people flee from paper investments and put money in tangible assets, notably gold. That drives the price of gold up. A higher price for gold means a gold mine becomes more profitable, which elevates the return on its stock. Hence when the return on most stocks is down, the return on gold mine stocks tends to be up. The reverse happens when stock returns are generally high.

Although people do diversify with gold mine stocks to stabilize portfolios, there aren't enough of them to do the job thoroughly. There simply aren't many stocks around that are negatively correlated with the market.

● Market risk in a portfolio can be reduced but not eliminated by diversifying with stocks that are **not perfectly positively correlated** with the portfolio.

However, a great number of stocks are available whose returns behave in a manner somewhere between those of A and B in the diagram. In terms of the behavior of return, that kind of stock can be thought of as a combination of A and B. Such a stock is illustrated by line C in Figure 8.7. Stocks like C are said to be *not* perfectly positively correlated with the portfolio.

Adding some C to the portfolio will generally reduce its risk somewhat. If we think of C as a hybrid or cross between A and B, its addition is a way to get a little B into the portfolio indirectly. An intuitive way to put it is to say that C contains a little of the "personality" of B.

In summary, market risk generally can be reduced but not eliminated by diversifying with stocks like C that are not perfectly positively correlated with the portfolio.

The Importance of Market Risk

Let's return to stocks A and B in Figure 8.7 for a moment. The illustration is constructed to point out two different concepts of risk. Considered individually the stocks are equally risky, yet in a portfolio one is risky and the other is not. Which interpretation is appropriate and when?

The relative risk attributes of the two stocks are entirely changed if we assume investors focus on portfolios rather than on individual stocks. Modern portfolio theory is based on that assumption. *What matters is how stocks affect portfolios rather than how they behave when considered alone. And how they affect portfolios depends only on market risk.*

● **Caution:** The concepts of risk associated with portfolio theory **may not be appropriate for individual investors.**

This is a fundamental result of portfolio theory. According to the theory, what matters in the investment world is market risk alone. *It is also a dangerous* result. Business-specific risk is truly diversified away only in the context of large portfolios. For the small investor with a limited portfolio, that effect simply doesn't occur. An individual business reversal can devastate an investment program if the stock represents a significant portion of a small portfolio. Hence while the thinking behind portfolio theory may be appropriate for running a mutual fund, it should not be applied blindly to managing one's personal assets.

● MEASURING MARKET RISK—THE CONCEPT OF BETA

Because market risk is of such central importance to investing, it's appropriate to look for a way to measure it for individual stocks.

● A stock's **beta** measures its **market risk.**

A statistic known as a stock's **beta** coefficient has been developed that is commonly considered to be the measure of a stock's market risk. Essentially, beta captures the variation in a stock's return which *accompanies* variation in the return on the market.

Developing Beta

● A stock's **characteristic line** reflects the average relationship between its return and the market's. **Beta is the slope of the characteristic line.**

A stock's beta coefficient is developed by plotting the historical relationship between the return on the stock and the return on the market.[3] Figure 8.8 shows such a plot. Each point represents a past time period for which we plot the stock's return, k_X, on the vertical axis and the market's return, k_M, on the horizontal axis. Doing this for a number of past periods results in a "scatter diagram" of historical observations. A regression line fitted to these data points is known as the *characteristic line* for the stock.

The characteristic line represents the average relationship between the stock's return and the market's return. Its slope is particularly rich in information. The slope tells us *on the average* how much of a change in k_X has come about with a

3. The return on the market is estimated by calculating the return on a market index such as the Standard & Poor's 500.

INSIGHTS

Practical Finance

Is It Investing or Gambling?

Investing is putting money at risk in the hope of earning more money—a return. But isn't that also a definition of gambling? Certainly it is, so what's the difference between investing and gambling, and why do we have such different moral and ethical attitudes about them?

Investing has economic value to the society that gambling doesn't. But, aside from that, from an individual's perspective it's fair to ask about the distinction between playing the stock market and taking a trip to Las Vegas.

Viewing both processes in terms of the probability distributions of their returns provides some insight. Investing tends to be characterized by probability distributions with positive expected values (means) and relatively small probabilities of very large gains or losses. Gambling on the other hand generally has a zero or negative expected value and offers a good chance of losing everything placed at risk. The attraction of gambling is that there's also a visible chance of winning many times the amount risked along with its entertainment value. Think of playing roulette in a Las Vegas casino. It's no secret that the odds are stacked slightly in favor of the house, and that many visitors leave town with empty pockets. But there are also a few well-publicized examples of people who hit the jackpot. Graphically the distributions might look something like this.

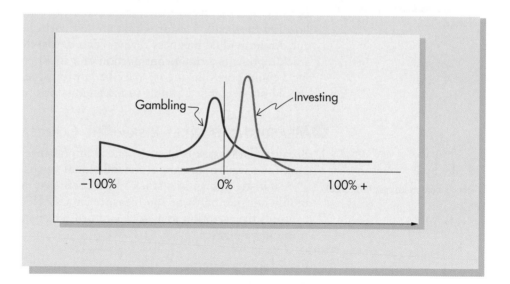

This view leads to another logical question. Are there activities that people normally call investing that are more like gambling? The answer is a resounding yes. Buying the stock of a high-risk new venture might be an example. There are also some financial markets that are risky to the point of bordering on gambling (e.g., commodities and futures markets, which are beyond the scope of this book).

In fact, the whole idea of portfolio theory is to move the investor's exposure toward the investment profile we've just described and away from the gambling profile.

The important thing to take away from this discussion is that something isn't "investing" just because it happens through the financial industry. Brokers like to characterize all their offerings as investing because it has a nobler image. But, in fact, some financial "investments" are really more like gambles.

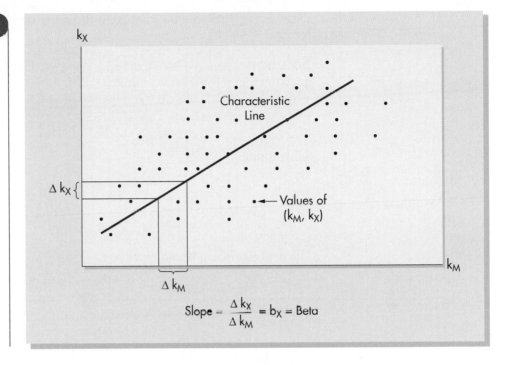

FIGURE 8.8

The Determination of Beta

Slope = $\dfrac{\Delta k_X}{\Delta k_M}$ = b_X = Beta

given change in k_M. This is exactly what we're looking for in terms of measuring market risk. The slope is an indication of how much variation in the return on the stock goes along with variation in the return on the market.

To see this, notice that as we move along the characteristic line, a change in k_M, Δk_M, comes with a change in k_X, Δk_X. The relationship between these changes is reflected in the slope of the line.

(8.3)
$$\text{slope} = \frac{\text{rise}}{\text{run}} = \frac{\Delta k_X}{\Delta k_M} = b_X = \text{beta}$$

Market risk is defined as the degree to which the return on the stock moves with the return on the market. That idea is summarized perfectly by the slope of the characteristic line. The slope can therefore be *defined* as the measure of market risk for the stock. This measure is called the beta coefficient, or simply *beta*, for the stock.

Projecting Returns with Beta

Knowing a stock's beta enables us to estimate changes in its return given changes in the market's return.

EXAMPLE 8.2

Conroy Corp. has a beta of 1.8 and is currently earning its owners a return of 14%. The stock market in general is reacting negatively to a new crisis in the Middle East that threatens world oil supplies. Experts estimate that the return on an average stock will drop from 12% to 8% because of investor concerns over the economic impact of a potential oil shortage as well as the threat of a limited war. Estimate the change in the return on Conroy shares and its new return.

Solution: Beta represents the past average change in Conroy's return relative to changes in the market's return.

$$b_{Conroy} = \frac{\Delta k_{Conroy}}{\Delta k_M}$$

Substituting,

$$1.8 = \frac{\Delta k_{Conroy}}{4\%}$$

$$\Delta k_{Conroy} = 7.2\%$$

The new return can be estimated as

$$k_{Conroy} = 14\% - 7.2\% = 6.8\% \,.$$

Understanding Beta

It's important to understand that beta represents an average relationship based on past history. To appreciate this, consider the movement from one data point to the next in Figure 8.8.

The change between any two successive values of k_X represents movement caused by the combination of market risk forces and business-specific risk forces. In other words, such a change is part of the stock's total risk. By regressing k_X versus k_M, we're making the assumption that movement along the line representing an average relationship between the variables reflects only market-related changes. In this view, movement from one data point to the next has two components, movement to and from the line and movement along the line. Movement to and from the line represents business-specific risk, whereas movement along the line represents market risk.

Forecasting with beta, as in the last example, uses only the average relationship between the returns, which is assumed to be market related. It says nothing about business-specific risk factors.

EXAMPLE 8.3

Suppose Conroy Corp. in Example 8.2 is a defense contractor that makes sophisticated antimissile systems. Would the estimate of return done in that example be valid? What if Conroy were in the orange juice business?

Solution: It's unlikely that the estimate would be much good if Conroy were a defense contractor. The threat of a limited war could be expected to have a positive impact on the company because of its defense-related line of business. In other words, such a threat is likely to have a major business-specific risk impact on the firm's return that would act in a direction opposite the market-related decline.

If Conroy made orange juice, we wouldn't expect a business-specific risk change due to the Middle East crisis, so the market-related estimate would be more realistic.

● Betas are developed from **historical data** and **may not be accurate** if a **fundamental change** in the business environment occurs.

BETA OVER TIME   Any firm's beta is derived from observation of the behavior of its return in the past relative to the return on the market. Use of the statistic implicitly assumes that the relationship between the two returns is going to remain constant over time. In other words, using beta assumes the stock's return will behave in the same way in the future that it did in the past relative to the market's return. This assumption is usually reasonable, but at times it may not be.

INSIGHTS

Real Applications

Just How Risky Is AT&T—Really? A Problem with Betas

Calculating beta is a pretty simple procedure. It's just a straightforward linear regression of a stock's return versus the market's. Unfortunately, in some cases several problems can make calculated betas unreliable. One of the biggest involves the evolution of the company whose risk is being assessed. If the firm has changed significantly during the period from which the historical return data comes, beta may be virtually meaningless. That's because the company as it stands today isn't the same business that generated the returns used in the regression analysis. AT&T provides an excellent example.

Before 1983, AT&T was "the" phone company in the United States. It supplied all long distance service and local service in most metropolitan areas, and operated Bell Laboratories, which handled communications technology and manufacturing. But AT&T was sued by the Justice Department for violation of Antitrust laws that prohibit monopolies. As a result, the firm agreed to break into eight separate companies. Long distance service and Bell Labs continued to operate under the AT&T name, while local service was divided among seven regional firms collectively referred to as "Baby Bells."

AT&T continued to provide long distance service and technology through the late 1980s and early 90s, but acquired NCR, a major computer manufacturer, in 1991. It operated these three businesses for five years until 1996, when it again split, this time along the lines of those businesses. The AT&T name stayed with long distance operations, while technology and computers were split off as Lucent Technologies and NCR, respectively.

In 2001, AT&T split into four pieces: AT&T Business, AT&T Wireless, AT&T Broadband, and AT&T Consumer. These represent several new lines AT&T developed after the 1996 split, including cable television, Internet service, cell phone service, and local phone service. Complicating matters even further was the fact that the telephone communications business was being deregulated during this period. Before 1983 phone companies were regulated monopolies. Today the industry is essentially a competitive free-for-all. That's significant because the risk characteristics of companies in regulated and competitive industries are vastly different.

So how meaningful is AT&T's beta today? Probably not very meaningful, because the company hasn't been a consistently defined enterprise over any period from which data on returns can be collected.

Sources: Margaret Johnston, "Searching for Value, AT&T Splits Four Ways," *Infoworld* (October 30, 2000): 10. "AT&T's Three-Way Split," *The Economist* (September 23, 1995): 51.

EXAMPLE 8.4

Let's consider the Conroy Corp. of the last two examples once more. Think of the early 1990s when the Cold War was ending and military budgets were being reduced dramatically. Would a projection using beta have been valid at that time?

Solution: This situation makes the future of Conroy's beta somewhat uncertain. The data from which the firm's characteristic line was developed would have been from earlier periods during the Cold War when military spending and lucrative defense contracts were considered a way of life that was likely to continue forever. The new climate of reduced defense budgets looked much more tentative and risky for high-technology defense production. Therefore the future beta is likely to have been different from the past value at that time.

Volatility

Beta measures volatility in relation to market changes. In other words, it tells us whether the stock's return moves around more or less than the return of an average stock.

A beta of 1.0 means the stock's return moves on average just as much as the market's return. Beta > 1.0 implies the stock moves more than the market. Beta < 1.0 means the stock tends to move with the market but less. Beta < 0 means the stock tends to move against the market, that is, in the opposite direction. Such stocks are rare. Stock B of Figure 8.7 is a negative beta stock. Gold mines are the primary real-world example of such stocks.

● Small investors should remember that **beta doesn't measure total risk.**

The idea of beta immediately suggests an investment strategy. When the market is moving up, hold high-beta stocks because they move up more. When the market is moving down, switch to low-beta stocks because they move down less!

Beta for a Portfolio

Because beta measures market risk, the degree to which a stock moves with the market, it makes sense to think about market risk and beta for an entire portfolio. In fact, the concept is rather simple. Beta for a portfolio of stocks is just the weighted average of the betas of the individual stocks where the weights are the dollar amounts invested in each stock.

For example, suppose a two-stock portfolio is made up like this.

Stock	Beta	Current Dollar Value	Portion of Value
A	.7	800	.8
B	1.1	200	.2
		1,000	1.0

Then the portfolio's beta, written b_p, is calculated as follows.

$$b_p = .8b_A + .2b_B = .8(.7) + .2(1.1) = .78$$

A NOTE ON DECIMAL ACCURACY   Notice that the portfolio beta we just calculated is expressed to two decimal places. You'll sometimes see betas calculated to three decimal places. However, if you think about the nature of beta and the way it's derived for individual stocks, it's apparent that such accuracy is meaningless. Rounding off to one decimal place is generally sufficient.

● USING BETA—THE CAPITAL ASSET PRICING MODEL (CAPM)

The things we've been discussing in this chapter are inputs to a sophisticated mathematical model of the financial world called the **capital asset pricing model**, abbreviated as CAPM. The terminology can be a little confusing. A "capital asset" is a share of stock, and "pricing model" implies an attempt to explain how stock prices are set in the market.

The CAPM has been around for some time. It was developed during the 1950s and 1960s by economists Harry Markowitz and William F. Sharpe, who shared the 1990 Nobel Prize in economics for their work.

The CAPM's Approach

The model's approach to determining how prices are set is to explain how the required rate of return on a stock comes about. Recall that the required rate of return is the return that just holds investors in the stock. It's the amount an individual has to expect to get in order to be willing to put his or her money in a particular issue. It's related to the riskiness of the issue as perceived by the investor. (Review pages 253–254 if necessary.) People won't invest unless the expected return is at least equal to their required return.

Price Depends on Return

● The **CAPM** attempts to explain **stock prices** by explaining how investors' **required returns** are determined.

In general, once a return is specified, price follows. For example, consider equation 8.2, our definition of the return on a stock investment (page 253). If we solve that equation for the current price, P_0, we get

$$P_0 = \frac{D_1 + P_1}{(1 + k)}.$$

If we make assumptions about the future price and dividend, P_1 and D_1, the current price of the stock, P_0, depends on knowing the rate of return, k.

Another approach involves the Gordon model, equation 7.10 from Chapter 7, on stock valuation. We'll repeat that expression here for convenience.

(7.10) $$P_0 = \frac{D_0(1 + g)}{k - g}$$

Notice that if the last dividend, D_0, is known and an assumption is made about the growth rate, g, the current price depends on knowing k, the return. We'll use this relationship in some problems shortly.

All this says that if we understand how required returns are set, we'll understand a great deal about how prices are established.

Rates of Return, the Risk-Free Rate, and Risk Premiums

At this time, we have to make a few points about rates of return in general. First, interest is the rate of return on debt and is conceptually identical to the rate of return on an equity investment. Therefore we can mix the two ideas as we like. Specifically, we can have both interest rates and rates of return on stock investments within the same equation.

Next we need to recall the concept of a risk-free rate of return from Chapter 4. (Review page 126 if necessary.) A risk-free investment is one in which there is no possibility of receiving less than the expected return. Federally insured bank accounts are essentially risk free, as are investments in short-term treasury debt. The current rate of interest paid on three-month treasury bills is generally taken to be the prevailing risk-free rate, written as k_{RF}.

The rate of return on any other investment involves some allowance for bearing risk added to the risk-free rate. The allowance is known as the *risk premium* for the investment. If we call some investment Y, we can write the return on Y as

$$k_Y = k_{RF} + k_{RPY}$$

where k_{RPY} is the risk premium on investment Y. Solving for the risk premium, we have

$$k_{RPY} = k_Y - k_{RF} .$$

● The **CAPM** purports to explain how the **risk premiums** in required rates of return are formed.

That is, Y's risk premium is the difference between the return on Y and the risk-free rate.

The required rate of return on an investment in a stock is then the risk-free rate plus some *premium* for bearing the risk associated with that stock. The mystery is to try to explain just what that risk premium depends on. This is what the capital asset pricing model purports to do.

Putting the Pieces Together

Each of the concepts we've talked about so far, including return as a random variable, risk defined as variance, risk aversion, all the portfolio ideas, and beta, are necessary assumptions undergirding the CAPM.

All of these ideas can be stated in mathematical terms. When they are, some advanced math can be used to derive a single, simple equation that defines the required return on a stock in terms of its risk. That equation, called the **security market line, SML,** is the heart of the CAPM.

The beauty of the model and probably the reason for its wide acceptance is the simplicity of this result.

The Security Market Line (SML)

The security market line proposes that required rates of return are determined by the following equation.

● The **SML** is the heart of the **CAPM.**   **(8.4)**

$$k_X = k_{RF} + \overbrace{(k_M - k_{RF})b_X}^{\text{Stock X's Risk Premium}}$$

Market Risk Premium

where: k_X is the required return on stock X

k_{RF} is the risk-free rate

k_M is the return on the market

b_X is stock X's beta coefficient

First notice that the right side of the equation is in two parts: the risk-free rate and a risk premium for stock X. This is consistent with the ideas we expressed earlier about rates of return in general.

Next we'll consider the risk premium in detail. It's made up of two parts, the expression in parentheses and beta. Beta, of course, is our measure of market risk for stock X. The expression in parentheses is the difference between the return on the market and the risk-free rate.

THE MARKET RISK PREMIUM   In the section before last we said that the difference between the return on an investment and the risk-free rate is the risk premium for that investment. Therefore the term in parentheses in equation 8.4 is the risk premium for an investment in the market as a whole. That can be interpreted as an investment in an "average" stock or in a portfolio constituted to mirror the market.

● The **market risk premium,** $(k_M - k_{RF})$, is a reflection of the investment community's level of **risk aversion.**

The market risk premium reflects the average tolerance for risk of all investors at a point in time. In other words, it's indicative of the degree of *risk aversion* felt by the investing community.

THE RISK PREMIUM FOR STOCK X   The risk premium for stock X is just the market, or "average," risk premium multiplied by stock X's own beta, the measure of its market risk.

What the SML is saying is simple and yet profound. It alleges that a stock's risk premium is determined *only* by the market risk premium factored by the stock's beta.

Notice that the only thing in the equation that relates specifically to company X is b_X, the measure of X's *market* risk! So if management wants to influence stock price, an important way to try to do so is by changing the volatility of the firm's return and thereby its beta.

● The **CAPM** asserts that the only **company-specific** thing affecting required return is **market risk.**

The important implication of the SML is that *only market risk counts*. Business-specific risk doesn't enter the equation; market risk does through beta. Put another way, investors are rewarded with extra return only for bearing market risk, not for bearing business-specific risk. This makes sense because we've assumed that business-specific risk is diversified away for portfolio investors.

The SML holds for any company. That's why we've used the generic "X" to represent the company's name. The model says that any firm's required rate of return, as generally perceived by most investors, can be found by just putting that company's beta into equation 8.4.

The SML as a Portrayal of the Securities Market

The SML can be thought of as representing the entire securities market, most notably the stock market. To show this we'll plot the line in *risk return space*. That simply means the graph will have return on the vertical axis and risk along the horizontal axis. The variable representing risk will be beta. The SML is portrayed graphically in Figure 8.9, where it's seen as a straight line.

Recall the standard formulation for plotting a straight line from algebra.

(8.5) $$y = mx + b$$

Here y is traditionally the vertical axis variable and x is the horizontal axis variable. When the equation of a straight line is in this form, m is the slope of the line and b is its y intercept.

FIGURE 8.9

The Security Market Line

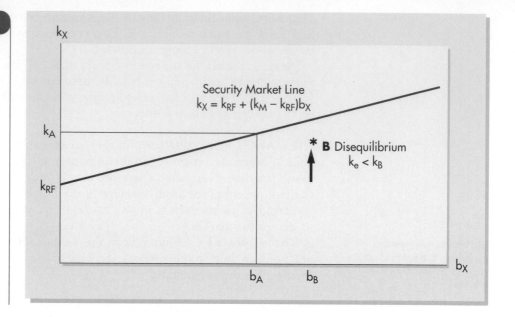

In our graph of the SML, the variable on the vertical axis is k_X and the variable on the horizontal axis is b_X. We can write equation 8.4 in the same form as equation 8.5 and compare the two.

$$k_X = \underbrace{(k_M - k_{RF})}\ \underbrace{b_X} + \underbrace{k_{RF}}$$

$$y = \qquad m \qquad x \ + \ b$$

● The **slope of the SML** plotted in **risk-return space** reflects the general level of risk aversion.

The comparison shows that the slope of the SML is the market risk premium $(k_M - k_{RF})$. Thus the slope of the SML is a reflection of the risk tolerance or level of risk aversion felt by investors in general. If investors become more risk averse, the spread between k_M and k_{RF} will increase because people will demand a larger premium for bearing any level of risk. When that happens, the SML will get steeper. Conversely, if people become less concerned about risk, the market risk premium will shrink and the SML will become flatter.

It's important to understand that attitudes about risk do change over time, and that the changes are indeed reflected in real differences between k_M and k_{RF}.

Next consider the intercept of the SML with the vertical axis. This is the y-intercept in the traditional equation. The value of k_X at the intercept point is clearly k_{RF}. This makes sense because risk, represented by beta, is zero at the left side of the graph. The intercept point is simply saying that an investor always has the option of putting his or her money into government securities earning k_{RF} with no risk.

● The **vertical intercept** of the SML represents investment in short-term government securities.

The SML portrays the market in terms of risk and return in that any stock can be thought of as occupying a point along the line determined by its level of risk. For instance, stock A is shown on the diagram. If we enter the graph at A's beta, b_A, we can find A's required return by moving up to the line and then over to the vertical axis at k_A.

The SML as a Line of Market Equilibrium

A system is said to be in *equilibrium* if it tends to remain in a constant state over time. The equilibrium condition is said to be *stable* if when the system is displaced, forces are created that tend to push it back into the equilibrium position.

The SML represents an equilibrium situation if for every stock along the line, the expected rate of return is equal to the required rate of return. In that case investors holding stocks are happy because their expected and required rates of return are at least equal. There is no excess of either buyers or sellers, and in theory the market remains where it is.

Now suppose conditions change in such a way that the expected return on some stock becomes less than its required return. This situation is represented by point B in the diagram where the expected return, shown as k_e, is less than the required return for stock B, which is on the SML above b_B.

In this case, people who own the stock will be inclined to sell because the anticipated return no longer meets their needs. That is, it is below their required return, which is on the SML. However, potential buyers will not be interested in purchasing the stock because the expected return is also lower than their required returns. In other words, we have would-be sellers but no interested buyers. When that happens in the market for anything, there's only one solution if trading is to take place—sellers must lower their asking prices. In other words, the market price falls.

● The SML represents a condition of **stable equilibrium.**

Now examine equation 8.2 once again (page 253). Notice that the current market price is represented as P_0. If P_0 falls while the other variables in the equation remain unchanged, the value of k on the left side of the equation *increases*. That means the expected return becomes higher as new investors have to spend less for the same future cash flows.

In Figure 8.9, this means market forces drive the expected return back up toward the equilibrium line of the SML. Hence the stock market equilibrium is stable, because when some external occurrence displaces a return away from the equilibrium line, forces are created to push it back.

In reality the market is never quietly in equilibrium, because things are always happening that move stock prices and returns around. The important point of the theory is that market forces are constantly being created that tend to push things back *toward* an equilibrium position with respect to risk and return.

Valuation Using Risk-Return Concepts

We can use the ideas of the capital asset pricing model in another approach to stock valuation. The method assumes that the marginal investor buys and sells the stock at the return determined by the SML, and that those sales determine market price.

● The SML and the Gordon model provide a two-step **approach to valuation.**

Given that assumption, we can calculate the price in two steps. First we use the SML to calculate a required rate of return. Then we use that return in the Gordon model to arrive at a price.

EXAMPLE 8.5

The Kelvin Company paid an annual dividend of $1.50 recently, and is expected to grow at 7% into the indefinite future. Short-term treasury bills are currently yielding 6%, and an average stock yields its owner 10%. Kelvin stock is relatively volatile. Its return tends to move in response to political and economic changes about twice as much as does the return on the average stock. What should Kelvin sell for today?

Solution: First write the SML for Kelvin from equation 8.4.

$$k_{Kelvin} = k_{RF} + (k_M - k_{RF})b_{Kelvin}$$

Next notice that the inputs to the SML have been specified in the problem description without being named. The return on short-term treasury bills reflects the current risk-free rate, k_{RF}, and the return on the "average stock" is equivalent to the return on the market, k_M. Finally, recognize that we've been given beta in rather cryptic terms. Political and economic changes are things that tend to affect all stocks and the response to them relates to market risk. Therefore, saying Kelvin's return responds twice as much as the average to those things implies that Kelvin's beta is 2.0.

Substituting for Kelvin's required return we have

$$k_{Kelvin} = 6 + (10 - 6)2.0 = 14\% \ .$$

Next write the Gordon model and substitute using k_{Kelvin} for k in the denominator.

$$P_0 = \frac{D_0(1 + g)}{k - g}$$

$$= \frac{\$1.50(1.07)}{.14 - .07}$$

$$= \$22.93$$

The Impact of Management Decisions on Stock Prices

The fact that management decisions can affect both beta and likely future growth rates makes the SML approach to valuation relevant for policy decisions.

EXAMPLE 8.6

The Kelvin Company described in the last example has an exciting new opportunity. The firm has identified a new field into which it can expand using technology it already possesses. The venture promises to increase the firm's growth rate to 9% from the current 7%. However, the project is new and unproven, so there's a chance it will fail and cause a considerable loss. As a result, there's some concern that the stock market won't react favorably to the additional risk. Management estimates that undertaking the venture will raise the firm's beta to 2.3 from its current level of 2.0. Should Kelvin undertake the new project?

Solution: A strategic decision such as this should be based on the primary objective of the firm's management, maximizing shareholder wealth. That's equivalent to maximizing the price of the company's stock.

An increased growth rate will have a positive effect on stock price. Convince yourself of this by examining how the growth rate, g, influences the value of P_0 in the Gordon model in the last example. A bigger g makes the numerator larger and the denominator smaller, both of which contribute to an increase in P_0. (Remember that g must remain less than k.)

On the other hand, examining the SML of equation 8.4, we see that a larger beta results in a larger risk premium and therefore a larger required rate of return. That in turn goes into the denominator of the Gordon model as k, and a larger k in the Gordon denominator results in a smaller price.

Hence, taking on the new project involves two things that tend to move the stock's price in opposite directions. Faster growth will increase stock price, while higher risk will decrease it. The question is which effect will dominate. We can find out by calculating an estimated price assuming the project is undertaken.

First recalculate the required rate of return.

$$k_{Kelvin} = 6 + (10 - 6)2.3 = 15.2\%$$

Then recalculate the price using the Gordon model with the new return and the new estimated growth rate.

$$P_0 = \frac{D_0(1 + g)}{k - g} = \frac{\$1.50(1.09)}{.152 - .09} = \$26.37$$

The resulting price of $26.37 is higher than the $22.93 price before the project, indicating that the positive effect of the increased growth rate outweighs the negative effect of increased risk. Therefore the venture looks like a good idea.

In actual practice it would be difficult to make accurate estimates of the effect of a project like this on a firm's growth rate and beta. Such estimates would be subjective guesses at best. The impact on beta would be particularly vague. Nevertheless an exercise like this would give management a valuable insight into the potential effects of their actions on stock price.

Adjustments to Changing Market Conditions

As the securities market changes over time, the equilibrium of the SML accommodates to the altered conditions by shifting its position. We'll consider two such movements.

● The SML shifts **parallel** to itself in response to changes in the **risk-free rate.**

THE RESPONSE TO A CHANGE IN THE RISK-FREE RATE   When the risk-free rate changes, all other things held equal, the SML simply shifts up or down parallel to itself. The new equilibrium position is determined by the new rate at the vertical axis intercept. The idea is illustrated in Figure 8.10 for an increase in the risk-free rate from k_{RF} to $k_{RF'}$.

The shift illustrated in Figure 8.10 contains a subtlety. The parallel shift of the SML implies that its slope remains the same. Recall that the slope of the SML is the market risk premium ($k_M - k_{RF}$), which reflects the general degree of investors' risk aversion.

If the slope of the SML doesn't change when k_{RF} changes, k_M must also increase or decrease by the amount of the change in k_{RF}. This makes sense because the market rate, like any other rate, consists of the risk-free rate plus a risk premium.

THE RESPONSE TO A CHANGE IN RISK AVERSION   A change in the general sensitivity of investors to risk will be reflected in a change in the market risk premium, represented as ($k_M - k_{RF}$) and as the *slope* of the SML in the diagram. We'll assume that k_M changes with no accompanying change in k_{RF}.

FIGURE 8.10

A Shift in the Security Market Line to Accommodate an Increase in the Risk-Free Rate

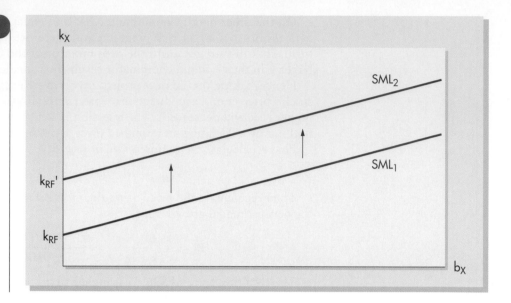

FIGURE 8.11

A Rotation of the Security Market Line to Accommodate a Change in Risk Aversion

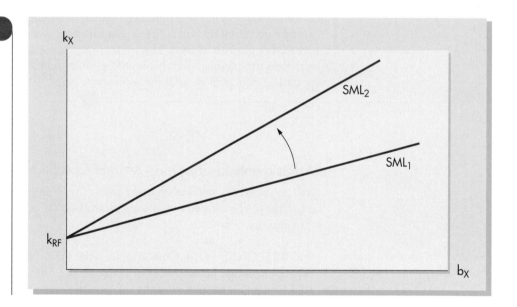

● Changes in **attitudes toward risk** are reflected by **rotations of the SML** around its vertical intercept.

A change in slope alone is reflected by a rotation of the SML around the constant vertical intercept point at k_{RF}. The idea is illustrated in Figure 8.11.

In the illustration SML_1 rotates to SML_2 in response to an *increase* in risk aversion. In other words, the average investor demands a higher risk premium on any investment to compensate for his or her increased aversion to risk. The higher premium is reflected in a steeper slope for the resulting SML.

EXAMPLE 8.7

The Sidel Company has a beta of 1.25. The risk-free rate is currently 6%, and the market is returning 10%. According to the SML, Sidel's required rate of return is

$$k_S = k_{RF} + (k_M - k_{RF})b_S = 6 + (10 - 6)1.25 = 11.0 \ .$$

a. Calculate Sidel's new required rate of return if the risk-free rate increases to 8% and investors' risk aversion remains unchanged.

b. Calculate the new required rate if the return on the market increases to 11% with the risk-free rate remaining at the original 6%.

Solution:

a. If the risk-free rate changes with no change in risk aversion, the market return has to change with it, so the difference between the two remains constant. Substituting into the SML, we have

$$k_S = k_{RF} + (k_M - k_{RF})b_S = 8 + (12 - 8)1.25 = 13.0\% \ .$$

In this case, interest rates in general will rise by the increase in the risk-free rate.

b. If the market return changes by itself, simply substitute the new value into the SML as follows.

$$k_S = k_{RF} + (k_M - k_{RF})b_S = 6 + (11 - 6)1.25 = 12.25\%$$

Here the increase in the market return reflects a higher risk premium, meaning people are more concerned about bearing risk. As a result, the rate on all risky investments will rise.

In both cases, the price of Sidel stock will fall.

THE VALIDITY AND ACCEPTANCE OF THE CAPM AND ITS SML

The capital asset pricing model is like the other models we've discussed in that it is an abstraction of reality. It's a simplification of the complex securities world, designed to help in making predictions about what stock prices and returns will do. Such predictions can then be used to make various investment decisions.

The main reason for CAPM's popularity is probably its simplicity. The model's operative equation, the SML, is short and easy to understand. This is unusual among mathematical and statistical models, which are typically very difficult.

In addition, CAPM provides something that's very relevant in finance, a tangible statement of the relationship between risk and return. Everyone intuitively feels there's a relation between the two, and that higher risk goes along with higher return. But until CAPM came along, no one had a usable handle on the idea. In other words, there wasn't anything that said *this* much risk is appropriate for *that* much return, and therefore I'll invest, but otherwise I won't.

Unfortunately, because models that simplify the real world have to leave a lot out, they don't always work. CAPM is no exception to that general rule. Scholars are deeply divided on its validity and usefulness. Many question whether there is any real predictive value in the SML at all, while others feel the equation is sound but that people tend to apply it incorrectly. Staunch proponents maintain that the model is entirely valid and works under most conditions.

The most important attack on the CAPM has come from the work of two well-known scholars, Eugene Fama of the University of Chicago and Kenneth

● The CAPM is **not universally accepted,** and a continuing debate exists as to its relevance and usefulness.

http://

Visit the MATLAB Computing Environment for Economic and Financial Engineering at

● www.mathworks.com/products/matlab

Practical Finance

Beta in Practice

The concept of beta as a measurement of risk is probably the most widely used piece of stock market theory today. Investment advisory services publish betas for all heavily traded stocks, and people in the securities industry talk about beta all the time.

However, it's quite likely that many of the people who use the term aren't aware of exactly what it means. Beta measures risk, and risk means volatility of return, both up and down. Most people are aware of that much. But beta measures market-related volatility, not total volatility. That's what the average person forgets.

Beta means market risk only, and that's the relevant measure only if you're dealing with a large, well-diversified portfolio. If you're a moderate or small investor, beta tells only part of the story, and you can get hurt pretty badly by the part it doesn't tell.

French of Yale. They found no historical relationship between the returns on stocks and their betas.[4] The CAPM, of course, assumes that a relationship does exist as expressed by the SML. If Fama and French are right, the CAPM isn't worth much. Other researchers, however, have challenged their work on both empirical and theoretical grounds. A lively controversy continues in the scholarly literature that is as yet inconclusive.

It's unlikely that the leading scholars in this area will come to an agreement any time soon. CAPM and beta, the associated measure of risk, are part of the framework of theoretical finance and will probably remain so for the foreseeable future.

For our purposes, you should understand the ideas and assumptions leading up to the SML and appreciate what the equation is saying in terms of the relation between risk and return. We'll assume that it's a pretty good representation of reality most of the time.

It is important, however, to keep one important limitation in mind. The model's risk as measured by beta is market risk only, and not a stock's total risk. As we said earlier, that limits the concept substantially.

DISCUSSION QUESTIONS

1. What is the fundamental motivation behind portfolio theory? That is, what are people trying to achieve by investing in portfolios of stocks rather than in a few individual stocks or in debt? What observations prompted this view?

2. What is the general (in words) relationship between risk and return?

3. Define and discuss (words only, no equations) the concepts of expected return and required return.

4. Give a verbal definition of risk that's consistent with the way we use the word in everyday life. Discuss the weaknesses of that definition for financial theory.

---

4. Eugene Fama and Kenneth French, "The Cross-Section of Expected Stock Returns," *Journal of Finance,* 47, No. 2 (June 1992): 427–65.

5. Define risk aversion in words without reference to probability distributions. If people are risk averse, why are lotteries so popular? Why are trips to Las Vegas popular? (*Hint:* Think in terms of the size of the amount risked and entertainment value.)

6. The following definition applies to both investing and gambling: Putting money at risk in the hope of earning more money. In spite of this similarity, society has very different moral views of the two activities.

a. Develop an argument reconciling the differences and similarities between the two concepts. That is, why do people generally feel good about investing and bad about gambling? (*Hint:* Think of where the money goes and what part of of a person's income is used.)

b. Discuss the difference between investing and gambling by referring to the probability distributions shown on page 272. Identify the representations of a total loss, a big win, and likely outcomes.

7. Why does it make sense to think of the return on a stock investment as a random variable? Does it make sense to think of the return on a bond investment that way? How about an investment in a savings account?

8. In everyday language, risk means the probability of something bad happening. Risk in finance, however, is defined as the standard deviation of the probability distribution of returns.

a. Why do these definitions seem contradictory?

b. Reconcile the two ideas.

9. Analyze the shape of the probability distribution for a high-risk stock versus that of a low-risk stock. (*Hint:* Think in terms of where the area under the curve lies.)

10. Describe risk in finance as up and down movement of return. Does this idea make sense in terms of the variance definition?

11. Define and discuss the idea of separating risk into two parts. Describe each part carefully.

12. Describe the goal of a portfolio owner in terms of risk and return. How does he or she evaluate the risk characteristics of stocks being considered for addition to the portfolio?

13. Discuss lowering portfolio risk through diversification. Consider

a. Unsystematic (business-specific) risk.

b. Systematic (market) risk.

14. Describe the concept of beta. Include what it measures and how it's developed.

15. You've just begun work at the brokerage firm of Dewey, Cheatam, and Howe as a stock analyst. This morning you read an article in the paper that said a large-scale reduction in defense spending is imminent. Fred Fastbuck, a broker at the firm, has several clients who are elderly retirees. You recently learned that he's actively putting those clients into several defense industry stocks he describes as low risk. Fred has told you that he feels the stocks are low risk because they have betas of 1.0 or less. How would you advise Fred? Consider the real meaning of beta and its constancy over time.

16. Describe the SML in words. What is it saying about how investors form required rates of return? Thoroughly evaluate the implications of the SML's message.

17. How does the SML determine the price of a security?

18. How is risk aversion reflected in the SML?

19. The CAPM purports to explain how management decisions about risk can influence the well-being of stockholders. Describe in words the mechanism through which this works.

20. Is the CAPM a true and accurate representation of the securities world?

PROBLEMS

1. The Duncan Company's stock is currently selling for $15. People generally expect its price to rise to $18 by the end of next year. They also expect that it will pay a dividend of $.50 per share during the year.

a. What is the expected return on an investment in Duncan's stock?

b. Recalculate the expected return if next year's price is forecast to be only $17 and the dividend $.25.

c. Calculate the actual return on Duncan if at the end of the year the price turns out to be $13 and the dividend actually paid was just $.10.

2. The Rapscallion Company's stock is selling for $43.75. Dave Jones has done some research on the firm and its industry, and he thinks it will pay dividends of $5 next year and $7 the following year. After those two years Dave thinks its market price will peak at $50. His strategy is to buy now, hold for the two years, and then sell at the peak price. If Dave is confident about his financial projections but requires a return of 25% before investing in stocks like Rapscallion, should he invest in this opportunity? (*Hint:* The return on a multiyear investment is the discount (interest) rate that makes the present value of the future cash flows equal to the price. See page 191 at the beginning of Chapter 6.)

3. Conestoga Ltd. has the following estimated probability distribution of returns.

Return	Probability
4%	.20
12%	.50
14%	.30

Calculate Conestoga's expected return, the variance and standard deviation of its expected return, and the return's coefficient of variation.

4. The probability distribution of the return on an investment in Omega Inc.'s common stock follows.

Return	Probability
5%	.05
8	.25
10	.40
12	.25
15	.05

Graph the probability distribution. Calculate the expected return, the standard deviation of the return, and the coefficient of variation. (Notice that to make the calculations manageable, we've made the unrealistic assumption that the probability distribution of returns is discrete.)

5. Calculate the expected return on an investment in Delta Inc.'s stock if the probability distribution of returns is as follows.

Return	Probability
−5%	.10
5	.25
10	.30
15	.25
25	.10

Plot the distribution on the axes with Omega Inc. in Problem 4. Looking at the graph, which company has the lower risk/variance? If offered the choice between making an investment in Delta and in Omega Inc. of Problem 4, which would most investors choose? Why?

6. The Manning Company's stock is currently selling for $23. It has the following prospects for next year.

Next Year's		
Stock Price	Dividend	Probability
$25	$1.00	.25
30	1.50	.50
35	2.00	.25

Calculate Manning's expected return for a one-year holding period.

7. Imagine making choices in the following situation to test your degree of risk aversion. Someone offers you the choice between the following game and a sure thing.

The game: A coin is tossed. If it turns up heads, you get a million dollars. If tails, you get nothing.
The sure thing: You're given $500,000.

a. What is the expected value of each option?

b. Which option would you choose?

c. Viewing the options as probability distributions, which has the larger variance? What is the variance of the sure thing? (No calculations.)

d. Suppose the game is changed to offer a payoff of $1.2 million for a head but still offers nothing for a tail. The sure thing remains $500,000. What is the expected value of each option now? Which option would you choose now?

e. Most people will have chosen the sure thing in part d. Assuming you did too, how much would the game's payoff have to increase before you would choose it over the sure thing?

f. Relate this exercise to Figure 8.6 on page 263.

8. A portfolio consists of the following four stocks.

Stock	Current Market Value	Expected Return
A	$180,000	8%
B	145,000	10
C	452,000	12
D	223,000	5
	$1,000,000	

What is the expected return of the portfolio?

9. Charming Co. manufactures decorating products. Treasury bills currently yield 5.4% and the market is returning 8.1%.

a. Calculate Charming Co.'s beta from its characteristic line as depicted below.

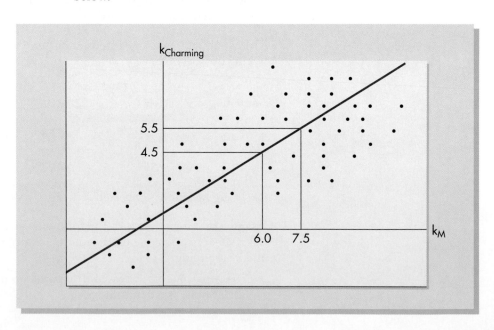

b. What expected return would an average investor require to buy shares of Charming?

c. Would the answer to part b be a "fair" return? Why?

10. A four-stock portfolio is made up as follows.

Stock	Current Value	Beta
A	$4,500	.8
B	2,900	.6
C	6,800	1.3
D	1,200	1.8

Calculate the portfolio's beta.

11. The CFO of Ramekin Pottery Inc. is concerned about holding up the price of the company's stock. He's asked you to do an analysis starting with an estimate of the return investors are likely to require before they will invest in the firm. The overall stock market is currently returning 16%, 90 day treasury bills yield 6%, and the return on Ramekin's stock typically responds to changes in the political and economic environment only about 60% as vigorously as does that of the average stock.

a. Prepare an estimate of the firm's required return using the CAPM.

b. Is a higher or lower required return good for the company? Why?

c. Suppose the CFO asks you what management can do to improve the required return. How will you respond?

d. What will you tell him if he wants it done in within the next three months?

12. You are a junior treasury analyst at the Palantine Corporation. The treasurer believes the CAPM gives a good estimate of the company's return to equity investors at any time, and has asked you to prepare an estimate of that return by using the SML. Treasury bills currently yield 6%, but may go up or down by 1%. The S&P 500 shows a return of 10% but may vary from that figure up to 12%. Palantine's beta is .8. Construct a table showing all possible values of $k_{Palantine}$ for 1% increments of k_{RF} and k_M (nine entries). For this problem treat k_M and k_{RF} separately. That is, do not assume an increase in k_M when k_{RF} changes.

13. Seattle Software Inc. recently paid an annual dividend of $1.95 per share and is expected to grow at a 15% rate indefinitely. Short-term federal government securities are paying 4%, while an average stock is earning its owner 11%. Seattle is a very volatile stock, responding to the economic climate two and a half times as violently as an average stock. This is, however, typical of the software industry.

a. How much should a share of Seattle be worth?

b. Do you see any problems with this estimate? Change one assumption to something more reasonable and compare the results.

14. The Aldridge Co. is expected to grow at 6% into the indefinite future. Its latest annual dividend was $2.50. Treasury bills currently earn 7% and the S&P 500 yields 11%.

a. What price should Aldridge shares command in the market if its beta is 1.3?

b. Evaluate the sensitivity of Aldridge's price to changes in expected growth and risk by recalculating the price while varying the growth rate between 5% and 7% (increments of 1%) and varying beta between 1.2 and 1.4 (increments of .1).

15. Lipson Ltd. expects a constant growth rate of 5% in the future. Treasury bills yield 8% and the market is returning 13% on an average issue. Lipson's last annual dividend was $1.35. The company's beta has historically been .9. The introduction of a new line of business would increase the expected growth rate to 7% while increasing its risk substantially. Management estimates the firm's beta would increase to 1.2 if the new line were undertaken. Should Lipson undertake the new line of business?

16. The Picante Corp.'s beta is .7. Treasury bills yield 5% and an average stock yields 10%.

a. Write and sketch the SML and locate Picante on it. Calculate Picante's required rate of return and show it on the graph.

b. Assume the yield on treasury bills suddenly increases to 7% with no other changes in the financial environment. Write and sketch the new SML, calculate Picante's new required rate, and show it on the new line.

c. Now assume that besides the change in part b, investors' risk aversion increases so that the market risk premium is 7%. Write and sketch the resulting SML, calculate Picante's required return, and show it on the last line.

 Internet Problem

17. Visit the Vanguard web site at **http://majestic.vanguard.com/EPA/DA**. Click on "An Investing Primer" and select "What is a Realistic Rate of Return?" in the Lesson Directory. What is the range of possible returns when the holding period is only 1 year? How does the range of possible returns change when the holding period is extended to 10 years and to 20 years? What does this data suggest with respect to how risky investing in the stock market really is? What strategy can an investor use to reduce the risk of investing in common stocks?

COMPUTER PROBLEMS

 18. Problem 14 in Chapter 7 concerned the Rollins Metal Company, which is engaged in long-term planning. The firm is trying to choose among several strategic options that imply different future growth rates and risk levels. Reread that problem on page 247 now.

The CAPM gives some additional insight into the relation between risk and required return. We can now define risk as beta, and evaluate its effect on stock price by constructing a chart similar to the one called for in Problem 14 of Chapter 7, replacing k on the left side with beta (b).

Rollins's beta calculated from historical data is .8. However the risky strategies being considered could influence that figure significantly. Management feels beta could rise to as much as 2.0 under certain strategic options. Treasury bills currently yield 3%, while the S&P index is showing a return of 8%. Recall that Rollins's last dividend was $2.35.

a. Use the CAPMVAL program to construct the following chart.

The Price of Rollins Stock as a Function of Growth Rate and Beta

		Growth Rates (g)			
		6%	8%	10%	12%
	.8				
Beta (b)	1.2				
	1.6				
	2.0				

b. The effect of beta on required return and price is influenced by the general level of risk aversion, which in the CAPM is represented by $(k_M - k_{RF})$, and the market risk premium (which is also the slope of the SML). In part a of this problem the market risk premium is $(8\% - 3\% =)$ 5%. Economists, however, predict a recession that could sharply increase risk aversion. Reconstruct the chart above assuming the market risk premium increases to 7% (k_M rises to 10% with no change in k_{RF}).

c. Do your charts give any new insights into the risk-return-growth relationship? (i.e., how does the reward for bearing more risk in terms of stock price change in recessionary times?) Write the implied required return on your charts next to the values of beta. Then compare the charts with the one from Problem 14 of Chapter 7.

d. Does the inclusion of beta and the CAPM really make management's planning job any less intuitive? In other words, is it any easier to associate a strategy's risk level with a beta than directly with a required return?

DEVELOPING SOFTWARE

19. Write a spreadsheet program to calculate the expected return and beta for a portfolio of 10 stocks given the expected returns and betas of the stocks in the portfolio and their dollar values.

The calculation involves taking a weighted average of the individual stocks' expected returns and betas where the weights are based on the dollar values invested in each stock.

Set up your spreadsheet like this:

	Stock	Value	Weight	Beta	Factor	k_e	Factor
1.	ABC	$ 5,530	.0645	.93	.0600	8.0%	.5160
2.	EFG	$ 2,745	.0320	1.25	.0400	12.2%	.3904
⋮	⋮	⋮	⋮	⋮	⋮	⋮	⋮
10.	XYZ	$ 9,046	.1055	1.12	.1182	11.5%	1.2133
		$85,715	1.0000		XXX		XXX

Sum columns for: Portfolio beta
                  Portfolio k_e

The computational procedure is as follows.

1. Input the names of the stocks, their dollar values, their betas, and their k_e's.

2. Sum the value column.

3. Calculate the weight column by dividing each row's value cell by the cell carrying the sum of the values.

4. Calculate the beta and k_e factors by multiplying the individual beta and k_e cells by the cells in the weight column on the same row.

5. Sum the two factor columns for the results indicated.

Is your program general in that it will handle a portfolio of *up to* 10 stocks, or will it only work for exactly 10? If it is general, what do you have to be careful about with respect to inputs?

Extra: Assume you have $1M to invest in stocks. Look up several stocks' betas in Value Line and estimate k_e for each. Look up the current price of each stock in *The Wall Street Journal*, and form a hypothetical portfolio by allocating your money among the stocks. Find your portfolio's expected return and beta using your program.

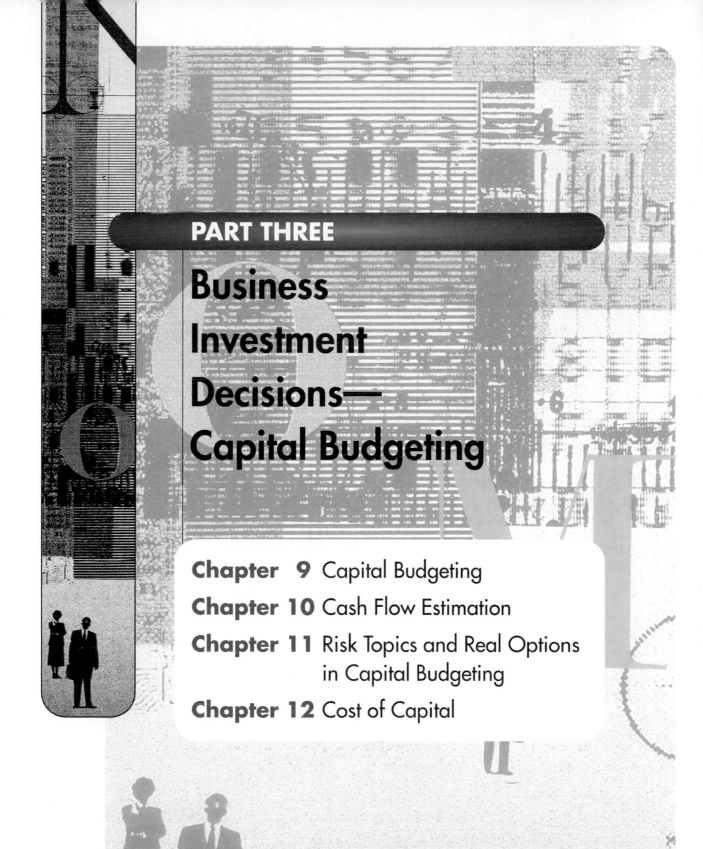

PART THREE

Business Investment Decisions— Capital Budgeting

CHAPTER 9

Capital Budgeting

Chapter Outline

Characteristics of Business Projects
    Project Types and Risk
    Stand-Alone and Mutually Exclusive Projects
    Project Cash Flows
    The Cost of Capital
Capital Budgeting Techniques
    Payback Period
    Net Present Value (NPV)
    Internal Rate of Return (IRR)

Comparing IRR and NPV
NPV and IRR Solutions Using Financial
    Calculators and Spreadsheets
Projects with a Single Outflow and
    Regular Inflows
Profitability Index (PI)
Comparing Projects with Unequal Lives
Capital Rationing

The money companies spend in the normal course of business can be divided into two categories. Funds are expended on an everyday basis to buy inventory, pay expenses, and compensate employees. These expenditures can be thought of as short term in that they support daily activity.

In addition to such short-term expenditures, firms spend large sums on special projects from time to time. For example, machines normally wear out and need to be replaced every few years. The replacement expenditures tend to be relatively large, but they are infrequent. New business ventures provide a second example because they generally require initial spending to get started. Start-up amounts are usually large, but the opportunities don't come along often. Spending on things like these is long term because the projects involved tend to last for long periods. As a general rule, money spent on long-term projects is called *capital*.

The field known as **capital budgeting** *involves planning and justifying how capital dollars are spent on long-term projects.* It provides methods through which projects are evaluated to decide whether they make sense for a particular business at a point in time. It also provides a basis for choosing between projects when more than one is under consideration at the same time.

> ● **Capital budgeting** involves planning and **justifying large expenditures** on long-term projects.

CHARACTERISTICS OF BUSINESS PROJECTS

● PROJECT TYPES AND RISK

Projects fit into three general categories: replacement, expansion, and new venture. We've already used the first and the last of these as examples in the opening section. Expansion simply involves doing something the firm already does on a larger scale. It usually requires investing money in additional resources and equipment similar to those already on hand.

⦿ Capital projects have **increasing risk** according to whether they are **replacements, expansions,** or **new ventures.**

A risk is associated with investing money in any project. For now we'll define that risk simply as the chance of making less on the project than management expects when the decision to go ahead is made.

Broadly speaking, risk varies with project type, increasing as we move from replacement to expansion to new venture. A replacement is the safest endeavor because we're doing something that's already being done. Expansion projects are riskier because they're based on a forecast increase in demand for the company's product that may not materialize. Finally, the riskiest project is a new venture, something the company hasn't done before. No one ever knows whether they'll be successful at something they haven't tried.

⦿ STAND-ALONE AND MUTUALLY EXCLUSIVE PROJECTS

Projects can be evaluated in either of two contexts. The first involves a proposal without a competing alternative. For example, suppose an old machine is wearing out and there's only one replacement product on the market. The choice is simply whether to buy the new machine (the project) or to do nothing.

This single-project situation is known as a **stand-alone project.** We need to decide on a project's viability by itself, standing alone. Is it a good deal for the company or not? Another way to think of it is to say that no other project is currently competing for the resources required to do this one.

⦿ A **stand-alone project** has no competing alternatives.

The second situation involves choosing between projects. It occurs either when there's more than one way to do something, or two different things are proposed but there's only enough money to do one of them. As an example of the first circumstance, assume the worn-out machine can be replaced by either of two new ones. Suppose the first option is relatively cheap to buy but is expensive to operate and produces low-quality output. The second costs more initially but runs less expensively and produces better product. Which should the firm choose? Notice that it must choose one or the other, because only one replacement is required. In this context, the alternatives are said to be **mutually exclusive,** since choosing either excludes the other.

Sometimes projects can be mutually exclusive even if they're totally different physically. That occurs when a firm has only enough resources to do one project at a time. For example, suppose an electronics firm has new venture opportunities in computer technology and radio transmission, but it has only enough money to undertake one new idea. The projects are mutually exclusive because doing one precludes doing the other, even though from business and technical viewpoints they're entirely separate. Further, the limiting resource doesn't have to be money. It might be trained personnel, plant capacity, or management's time.

⦿ PROJECT CASH FLOWS

⦿ The first and usually most difficult step in capital budgeting is **reducing projects to a series of cash flows.**

The first step in the capital budgeting process requires that any project under consideration be represented as a series of cash flows that is incremental to the business.

This requirement is easiest to picture in the context of a new venture. Imagine that such a new business will take an initial investment of $50,000, will lose $10,000 in the first year, and is expected to generate $15,000 in cash each year for the next five years before being shut down. For capital budgeting purposes, the project can be summarized as just that series of yearly cash outflows and inflows. If we call the cash flow in the ith year C_i, and let C_0 be the initial investment at the beginning of year 1, we can represent the project as follows, where the numbers in parentheses are negative and represent outflows.

C_0	($50,000)
C_1	(10,000)
C_2	15,000
C_3	15,000
C_4	15,000
C_5	15,000
C_6	15,000

● Business projects involve **early cash outflows** and later inflows. The **initial outlay** is required to get started.

It's important to notice the pattern of cash flows shown here. Projects nearly always involve an initial outflow of funds followed by inflows at later dates. C_0 is virtually always negative because it represents the *initial outlay* necessary to get a project started. The remaining figures tend to be positive, although they may include some negatives as in the example.

It's conceptually easy to identify incremental cash flows for a new venture. The representation can be more difficult to see when we're talking about a replacement project. Then incremental cash flows are things like savings on fuel and maintenance or improved profitability due to higher quality product. That kind of incremental cash flow can be hard to quantify.

In fact, the most difficult and inaccurate part of capital budgeting is estimating project cash flows. For the time being we'll proceed by assuming the estimates are given for the projects we'll be talking about. In the next chapter, we'll return to the issue and consider cash flow estimation in more detail, along with some questions about accuracy and risk.

● THE COST OF CAPITAL

Capital budgeting theory is based on the time value of money and the idea of return on investment. A central concept in the theory is the idea of a firm's *cost of capital*. This is the rate of return the firm pays to its long-term investors for the use of their money.

The purpose of the concept is intuitively obvious: An investment makes sense only if it earns more than the cost of funds put into it.

● A firm's **cost of capital** is the **average rate it pays its investors** for the use of their money.

For example, suppose you want to start a business in which you expect to earn a return of 15% on invested money. Further suppose you have no money of your own, but you can borrow from a relative who demands 18% interest. Does it make sense to start the business? Of course not; you'd be losing money from the outset because you'd have to pay more for your funds than you could earn using them. It would make sense to begin the business only if you could borrow the start-up money at *less than* 15%. In this illustration, the cost of capital is the rate at which you can borrow to undertake the venture.

In general, firms have two sources of capital—equity and debt—and pay different rates of return to the investors who supply each. In practice, the cost of capital is a single rate that reflects the average of the rates for those two sources.

Here's a simple example. Suppose the total dollar amount of a firm's capital is 75% equity and 25% debt. Assume the stockholders (equity) are receiving a

10% return, while the creditors (debt) are getting 8% interest. The cost of capital is the *weighted average* of the two returns, where the weights are the proportionate amounts of money invested in each of the two kinds of capital. The calculation follows.

	Portion		Return	
Equity	.75	×	10%	= 7.5%
Debt	.25	×	8%	= 2.0%
Weighted average cost of capital				= 9.5%

In other words, the cost of capital is a blending of the rates the company provides to its investors. The idea seems simple enough, but can get very complicated in practice.[1] It's an important concept, and we'll devote an entire chapter to it later in the book. For now we'll assume that every firm knows what its cost of capital is, and measures opportunities against it.

CAPITAL BUDGETING TECHNIQUES

In what follows, we'll look at four capital budgeting techniques. Each consists of a series of calculations and a set of decision rules. Using any technique involves calculating a number that the technique associates with a project and then applying the decision rules to that number. Each technique has slightly different decision rules for stand-alone and mutually exclusive situations.

● PAYBACK PERIOD

The simplest capital budgeting technique is the payback period. In it we calculate the amount of time it takes for a project's planned cash flows to "pay back" the initial outlay. In other words, we measure the time it takes for the project to break even. This time period is the parameter used for making comparisons. Payback is most meaningful when there's just one cash outflow at the beginning of the project. The technique is most easily understood through a numerical illustration.

In the following table, an initial outlay of $200,000 precedes four inflows of $60,000. The payback period is easily visualized by displaying the cumulative cash flow below the yearly cash flows.

			Year		
	0	1	2	3	4
Cash flow (C_i)	($200,000)	$60,000	$60,000	$60,000	$60,000
Cumulative cash flow	($200,000)	($140,000)	($80,000)	($20,000)	$40,000

Payback period = 3.33 years

● The **payback period** is the time it takes to recover early cash outflows. **Shorter** paybacks are preferred.

Notice that the cumulative cash flow is negative by $20,000 after three years and positive by $40,000 after four years. If cash is assumed to flow evenly throughout the year, breakeven occurs after 3.33 years—that is, after three years and four months. This length of time is the **payback period** for the project.

---

1. We've oversimplified for the sake of this preliminary illustration. As we'll see in Chapter 12, the cost of debt must take into account the tax deductibility of interest.

Payback Decision Rules

STAND-ALONE PROJECTS   Decision rules in the payback technique are based on the idea that it's better to recover invested money sooner rather than later. Companies that use the technique generally have stated policies for the maximum time allowable for capital recovery. The stand-alone decision rule is simply that an acceptable project's payback period must be less than that policy maximum. We can state that rule conveniently as follows.

$$payback\ period < policy\ maximum \longrightarrow accept$$

$$payback\ period > policy\ maximum \longrightarrow reject$$

MUTUALLY EXCLUSIVE PROJECTS   By the same reasoning, we generally prefer a project that pays back sooner to one that pays back later. Therefore the mutually exclusive decision rule for payback is simply *shorter is better*. If P/B_A and P/B_B represent the payback periods for projects A and B, respectively, we can write the decision rule like this.

$$P/B_A < P/B_B \longrightarrow choose\ project\ A\ over\ project\ B$$

Weaknesses of the Payback Method

Payback is a generally unsophisticated approach to capital budgeting that is criticized for two major shortcomings. First, it ignores the time value of money. Thus future dollars are weighted equally with current dollars in the calculations. This is clearly a distortion of values. Second, it ignores cash flows after the payback period. This deficiency can lead to the wrong answer even in simple cases.

EXAMPLE 9.1

Use the payback period technique to choose between mutually exclusive projects A and B.

	Project A	Project B
C_0	($1,200)	($1,200)
C_1	400	400
C_2	400	400
C_3	400	350
C_4	200	800
C_5	200	800

Solution: Project A's payback period is clearly three years, because its initial $1,200 investment is entirely recovered in that time. Project B is identical to A for the first two years and only slightly different in the third year, when the cash inflow is just $50 lower. However, that slightly lower payment in year 3 means that B's payback isn't complete until sometime in the fourth year. In other words, the payback period is a little longer for project B than for project A. The payback decision rule therefore chooses A over B. But B is clearly the better project because of what goes on after year 3 when B receives much larger cash inflows. The differences in years 4 and 5 overwhelm the minor difference in year 3 but are ignored by the method.

Why Use the Payback Method?

It's reasonable to ask why anyone uses the payback method given these weaknesses. The answer is that the method is quick and easy to apply, and it serves as a rough screening device.

If a project flunks payback, it's likely to be dismissed without further consideration. If it passes, one of the more sophisticated methods will be applied in further analysis.

The Present Value Payback Method

A variation on the method attempts to correct one of its deficiencies, the fact that it ignores time value. In this approach the payback calculation is made after taking the present value of all the cash flows at an appropriate discount rate.

This approach makes logical sense but still leaves the second deficiency unaddressed while losing the method's "quick and dirty" simplicity. As a result, it's rarely used.

● NET PRESENT VALUE (NPV)

A fundamental principle of finance and economics is that the *present value* of future cash flows is what counts when making decisions based on value. The **net present value** technique applies this idea to the analysis of projects.

> A project's **NPV** is the sum of the present values of its cash inflows and outflows at the **cost of capital.**

In the net present value technique, we calculate the present value of each of a project's cash flows and add them together. The result is the net present value of the *project,* usually referred to as the *NPV.* The word "net" implies an offsetting of pluses against minuses which reflects the fact that some flows are positive (inflows) and others are negative (outflows). Decisions about which projects to undertake are then based on project NPVs.

The present value calculations are made using the firm's *cost of capital* as an interest rate. This is an important point; the appropriate discount rate for most NPV calculations is the firm's cost of capital as described earlier in this chapter.

We can represent a project's NPV with the following equation.

$$(9.1) \quad NPV = C_0 + \frac{C_1}{(1+k)} + \frac{C_2}{(1+k)^2} + \cdots + \frac{C_n}{(1+k)^n}$$

where C_i represents the project's cash flow in the ith year and C_0 reflects the initial outlay. Notice that we're representing the present value calculation as division by powers of $(1+k)$.[2] Also notice that C_0 isn't divided by anything. That's because the initial cash flow is assumed to occur immediately, in the present.

It's important to think about the signs of the C's in equation 9.1, remembering that negatives are cash outflows and positives are inflows. As we said earlier, the negatives tend to occur first, followed by the positives. Equation 9.1 says that the NPV is the difference between the present values of all the positives and all the negatives. If the present value of the inflows (positives) is greater, NPV is a positive number. NPV is negative if the present value of the outflows is larger.

NPV and Shareholder Wealth

An insightful way to look at capital spending projects involves their impact on shareholder wealth. A project's net present value is the net effect that its undertaking

http://

Go to the Business Owner's Toolkit for more on how to complete a cost–benefit analysis using financial analysis tools. Click on *Managing Your Business Finances, Major Purchases and Products* to learn how to tell if a project makes sense over the long haul. Visit

● www.toolkit.cch.com

2. Review equations 5.5 through 5.7 on pages 147–148 if it isn't clear to you that this is equivalent to multiplying by the present value factors $PVF_{k,1}$, $PVF_{k,2}$, and so on.

is expected to have on the value of the firm. If a positive-NPV project is taken on and successfully completed, the economic value of the firm should be increased by exactly the amount of the project's NPV. Conversely, a negative-NPV project will decrease the value of the firm by the amount of the negative NPV.

Therefore a capital spending program that maximizes the NPV of projects undertaken will contribute to maximizing shareholder wealth, the ideal goal of management. This direct link to shareholder wealth maximization makes NPV the most theoretically correct capital budgeting technique.

So far we've been discussing NPVs for projects to be undertaken in the future. It's important to realize that cash flows may not actually turn out as expected. So a project that has a high *planned* NPV may turn out to have a very different impact on shareholder wealth after it's completed. Nevertheless, before the fact, the planned NPV is our best estimate of the future outcome. We'll talk a lot more about the differences between planned and actual numbers in the next chapter.

Decision Rules

● A **positive NPV** implies an acceptable project on a **stand-alone** basis.

STAND-ALONE PROJECTS Clearly, a project in which the present value of planned cash inflows exceeds the present value of outflows is desirable. Conversely, one in which the outflows are larger is undesirable. These situations correspond to projects with positive and negative NPVs, respectively. This logic leads to the *stand-alone decision rule.*

$$\text{NPV} > 0 \longrightarrow \text{accept}$$

$$\text{NPV} < 0 \longrightarrow \text{reject}$$

EXAMPLE 9.2

Project Alpha has the following cash flows.

C_0	C_1	C_2	C_3
($5,000)	$1,000	$2,000	$3,000

If the firm considering Alpha has a cost of capital of 12%, should the project be undertaken?

Solution: Project Alpha's NPV is found by summing the present value of each of the cash flows at the firm's cost of capital. We'll calculate the present values by multiplying each cash flow by the present value factor for 12% and one, two, or three years, respectively. This is equivalent to dividing by powers of $(1 + k)$ as shown in equation 9.1. (See equations 5.5, 5.6, and 5.7 on pages 147–148.) Remember that C_0 isn't factored because it's a present cash flow.

Year	Cash Flow	PV Factor	PV of Cash Flow
0	($5,000)	1.0000	($5,000.00)
1	1,000	.8929	892.90
2	2,000	.7972	1,594.40
3	3,000	.7118	2,135.40
			NPV = ($ 377.30)

Project Alpha's NPV is negative at the firm's cost of capital, so it should not be undertaken.

It's important to notice that even though a project's total inflows exceed its outflows, it can still have a negative NPV. The reason is that the inflows are generally farther in the future, so the present valuing process diminishes their value more than it does that of the outflows. In the example, the undiscounted value of the inflows adds to $6,000, while the single outflow is only $5,000. Nevertheless, on a present value basis, the inflows are less than the outflows.

● In a **mutually exclusive** context, projects with **larger NPVs** are preferred.

MUTUALLY EXCLUSIVE PROJECTS   The more the present value of cash inflows exceeds outflows, the larger is a project's NPV and the more it can be expected to contribute to shareholder wealth. In other words, *a bigger NPV is better than a smaller NPV.* This leads to the *mutually exclusive decision rule.*

$$\text{NPV}_A > \text{NPV}_B \longrightarrow \text{choose project A over B}$$

where NPV_A and NPV_B are the net present values of projects A and B, respectively.

The idea is straightforward on its face: Choose the project with the largest NPV. However, several questions come up in actual practice. The following example provides another drill on calculating NPVs and applying the decision rules; at the same time it raises some issues related to the practical application of the method.

EXAMPLE 9.3

The Xavier Motor Company makes outdoor power equipment including lawn mowers and garden tractors and is considering two diversification ventures. The first involves manufacturing a larger, more powerful tractor than the firm has made up until now. Market research indicates a substantial demand for more powerful equipment, and some competitors are already moving in that direction. The second opportunity involves building snowblowers. The manufacturing and engineering technology required for making snowblowers is essentially the same as that for building garden equipment, but Xavier has never made snowblowers before.

Management wants to make a decision based on only five years of projected cash flows, because it feels the future beyond that time is too vague to form a basis for current decisions. In other words, if a project isn't expected to earn enough to justify itself in five years, management considers it too risky.

Working with representatives from the marketing, engineering, and manufacturing departments, a financial analyst has put together a set of projected incremental cash flows for each project. Xavier's cost of capital is 9%.

Xavier Motor Company Project Estimates ($000)

Year	Tractor	Snowblower
0	($3,000)	($3,500)
1	(250)	(700)
2	500	800
3	1,000	1,200
4	1,500	2,000
5	1,500	2,000

A financial analysis of the project situation should provide answers to the following questions.

   a. If these projects were being considered on a stand-alone basis, would either or both be acceptable?

   b. If Xavier can raise no more than $5 million for new projects, which of these projects should be chosen?

   c. If Xavier's management was willing to consider two more years of projected cash flow, and the contributions continued at the level of the last two years, which project would be chosen?

   d. Are any risk considerations relevant beyond the numbers in this situation?

Solution: We begin by calculating the NPV for each project. We'll show these calculations in tabular form, multiplying the yearly cash flows by the present value factor for 9% and the appropriate year ($PVF_{9,i}$), rather than dividing by powers of $(1 + k)$.

Xavier Motor Company NPV Project Analysis ($000)

		Cash Flows		PV of Cash Flows	
Year	Factor	Tractor	Snowblower	Tractor	Snowblower
0	1.0000	($3,000)	($3,500)	($3,000)	($3,500)
1	.9174	(250)	(700)	(229)	(642)
2	.8417	500	800	421	673
3	.7722	1,000	1,200	772	927
4	.7084	1,500	2,000	1,063	1,417
5	.6499	1,500	2,000	975	1,300
				NPV = $2	$ 175

We can answer the first two questions immediately from the foregoing calculations.

   a. Both projects have a positive NPV and are therefore acceptable on a stand-alone basis. However, neither is positive by very much in relation to the size of the investments involved. The tractor project is especially marginal. This result is bound to raise some questions about the advisability of the projects. For now we'll just note that the projects are acceptable in accordance with the NPV method and return to the issue of accuracy later.

   b. The projects are mutually exclusive, because their initial outlays total $6.5 million and the company only has $5.0 million available for capital projects. In the mutually exclusive situation, the snowblower appears to have the edge, but not by much.

   c. The distant future is always hard to pin down. It's easy to forecast great sales and profitability six or more years in the future. Exuberant sales and marketing people do it all the time. The question is, how much of those forecasts should a reasonably prudent financial manager accept when making decisions about the commitment of substantial amounts of money? Let's calculate the impact of another two years on the NPV analysis.

Xavier Motor Company NPV Project Analysis ($000)

Year	Factor	Cash Flows Tractor	Cash Flows Snowblower	PV of Cash Flows Tractor	PV of Cash Flows Snowblower
6	.5963	$1,500	$2,000	$ 894	$1,193
7	.5470	1,500	2,000	821	1,094
			Addition to NPVs	1,715	2,287
			Previous NPVs	2	175
			New NPVs	$1,717	$2,462

Notice how the entire complexion of the problem has changed. Both projects now clearly appear favorable on a stand-alone basis. That is, the NPVs are substantially positive relative to the size of the early investments. Further, the snowblower now seems to be an obvious choice with a substantial NPV advantage.

d. *This question raises another big issue: Are the forecasts for the two projects equally reliable? There's a strong argument that they are not. Snowblowers are a new business for Xavier whereas the tractor is an extension of something they're already doing. The implication is that the snowblower project may be much riskier than the tractor project. If that's the case, is a simple comparison of the NPVs valid?*

● Capital budgeting techniques are easy to apply, but **interpreting** the results requires considerable judgment.

For now you should concentrate on being sure you understand the mechanics of the NPV method—that is, how to calculate NPVs and how to apply the decision rules. However, keep the concerns brought up by this problem in mind. We'll return to them in the next two chapters.

●INTERNAL RATE OF RETURN (IRR)

Instead of comparing present value dollar amounts, the **internal rate of return (IRR)** technique focuses on rates of return. The IRR concept can be defined in two ways. In fundamental terms a project's IRR is just the return it earns on invested funds. However, the concept can also be defined in terms of the NPV equation, 9.1. We'll have a close look at both approaches.

The Project as an Investment

In the IRR method we view a project as an investment of the company's money, which in principle is similar to the purchase of a financial asset. In this view, the cash outlay at the beginning of a project is like an investor paying cash to purchase a stock or a bond. Subsequent cash inflows from the project are similar to interest or dividend payments received by the investor.

The analogy is easy to visualize when a project has only one cash outflow occurring at its beginning, time zero. Consider the project in Example 9.2; we'll repeat those cash flows here for convenience.

C_0	C_1	C_2	C_3
($5,000)	$1,000	$2,000	$3,000

● A project's **IRR** is the return it generates on the **investment** of its cash outflows.

Notice that the project calls for one outflow, or payment, of cash followed by three inflows. The initial $5,000 outlay can be thought of as the "price" of receiving the subsequent inflows. In other words, accepting the project financially amounts to putting up the initial $5,000 in return for which the investing company receives the later inflows.

Recall that in Chapters 6 and 7 we defined the return on an investment as the interest rate at which the discounted value of the future cash flows just equals the price of the investment. The same idea applies here. The IRR is the interest rate at which the present value of the three inflows just equals the $5,000 outflow (price).

In this view, the IRR is analogous to the yield on a bond. Recall that purchasing a bond entitles the owner to a series of interest payments and a repayment of principal. These are cash inflows for which the investor pays the bond's price. The interest rate that equates the present value of the investor's inflows to the price of the bond (outflow) is the bond's yield. Similarly, the rate that equates the present value of a project's inflows to the initial outlay is the IRR.

The idea is a little harder to see when there's more than one outflow—for example, if there are two negative cash flows before the inflows start. In such a case, the IRR is the interest rate that equates the present value of all inflows with the present value of all outflows. That is, by definition, the IRR is just the return on the investment of the outflows.

Defining IRR through the NPV Equation

We can gain additional insight by relating the IRR concept to the NPV method. The two approaches are closely related in that both NPV and IRR can be defined by essentially the same equation.

● The **IRR** is the interest rate that **makes a project's NPV zero.**

In the last section we defined a project's NPV with equation 9.1. Referring to that expression, IRR is simply the value of the interest rate, k, at which NPV equals zero. This occurs when the present value of all the inflows is just equal to the present value of all the outflows, and they offset one another. This means IRR is the solution to the NPV equation with the interest rate treated as the unknown and NPV set to zero. This is the same as saying that *the IRR is the interest rate at which a project's NPV equals zero.*

Rewriting 9.1 with NPV = 0 and using IRR in place of k yields the expression that defines IRR.

$$(9.2) \quad 0 = C_0 + \frac{C_1}{(1 + IRR)} + \frac{C_2}{(1 + IRR)^2} + \cdots + \frac{C_n}{(1 + IRR)^n}$$

When the C_i are given for a particular project, equation 9.2 is one equation in one unknown, IRR. The solution is *the* IRR for the project. Every project of practical interest has an IRR just as every project has an NPV.

Decision Rules

IRR decision rules follow directly from thinking in terms of a return on an investment.

STAND-ALONE PROJECTS   In the stand-alone case, we're asking whether investment in a project is a good use of the company's money. The answer depends on the rate the firm pays to use that money. We described that rate as the company's *cost of capital* earlier in this chapter.

● A project is acceptable on a stand-alone basis if its **IRR exceeds the cost of capital.**

Recalling the illustration given there, we can generalize by saying that no one should invest in anything unless the return on the investment is expected to exceed the rate paid for the use of the money invested.

Because a project's IRR is the return on funds invested in the project, and the cost of capital reflects the average rate the company pays for the use of long-term money, the stand-alone decision rule follows from this generalization: *Invest in a project only if its IRR exceeds the firm's cost of capital.* Or,

$$IRR > k \longrightarrow accept$$

$$IRR < k \longrightarrow reject$$

where k is the firm's cost of capital.

● In a **mutually exclusive** context, projects with **larger IRRs** are **preferred.**

MUTUALLY EXCLUSIVE PROJECTS   The decision rule for mutually exclusive projects also follows from the definition of IRR as a return on an investment. We prefer investments with higher rates of return to those with lower rates. Hence, *a bigger IRR is better.* Or, if IRR_A and IRR_B relate to projects A and B, respectively,

$$IRR_A > IRR_B \longrightarrow \text{choose project A over project B .}[3]$$

Calculating IRRs

Examination of equation 9.2 shows that calculating internal rates of return for a general series of cash flows isn't easy. A project's IRR is the solution to that equation when a fixed set of numbers has been substituted for the C_i. Notice that the equation is a polynomial of order n in the variable IRR. Further, it's a very messy polynomial, because the powers of the unknown appear in the denominators of the fractions on the right. In general, such an equation can't be solved algebraically for values of n greater than two.

We get around this difficulty by using an iterative, numerical approach to solving the equation. In fact, we actually use equation 9.1 from which 9.2 is derived to find a solution to the latter.

Equation 9.1 defines a project's NPV and enables us to calculate that figure for any interest rate, k, given a set of cash flows (the C_i). To find a project's IRR, we simply try different values for k in equation 9.1 until we find one at which the NPV is zero. That value of k is the IRR, and at that value equation 9.1 *becomes identical* to 9.2.

● **Finding IRRs** usually requires an **iterative**, trial-and-error technique.

To solve a problem, we guess at the project's IRR and calculate an NPV by using the guess as the interest rate in equation 9.1. If the NPV doesn't come out to be zero, the first guess was incorrect, and we guess again. However, the result of the first calculation contains information that indicates the direction in which the second guess should be made. An illustrative example will make the procedure clear.

EXAMPLE 9.4

Find the IRR for the series of cash flows in Example 9.2.

C_0	C_1	C_2	C_3
($5,000)	$1,000	$2,000	$3,000

3. We'll see shortly (pages 311–312) that the IRR decision rule can occasionally lead to the wrong choice in mutually exclusive situations.

If the firm's cost of capital is 8%, is the project a good idea? What if the cost of capital is 10%?

Solution:

We'll start by guessing that the IRR is 12% and calculating the project's NPV at that rate. As it happens, we've already done that calculation in Example 9.2. Review that calculation on page 302 now and see that the resulting NPV is ($377.30).

Clearly, the project's NPV at 12% is not zero, so we have to make another guess. Look at the preceding pattern of the cash flows. The positive numbers are in the future, displayed on the right. These positives are affected by the discounting process when we take present values. In effect, they're shrunk by their respective present value factors before being combined with the negative $5,000 to form the NPV. *Notice that a larger interest rate shrinks the positive numbers more than a smaller rate, but it doesn't affect the initial outlay at all, because it isn't discounted.*

Our first guess of 12% shrunk the positive numbers too much, so that they became less than the negative outlay of $5,000 by $377.30. We'd like our next guess to shrink the positive cash flows less, so we'll choose a *smaller* interest rate.

We can summarize this thinking by saying that the magnitude of a project's NPV moves inversely with the interest rate used in its calculation. This relationship is portrayed graphically in Figure 9.1.

● A project's **NPV profile** is a graph of its NPV versus the cost of capital. It **crosses** the horizontal **axis** at the **IRR.**

The graph depicted is known as an *NPV profile.* Every project with a defined set of cash flows (the C_i) has an NPV profile that appears as a line on the graph. The lines will generally be downsloping to the right and cross the horizontal axis at some point. The IRR is the point at which the project's NPV is zero. That occurs where the NPV profile crosses the k axis as shown in the graph.

It's important to realize that the NPV profiles of capital budgeting projects slope downward to the right, because the pattern of cash flows generally involves outflows first (negative numbers) and inflows later (positive numbers). A higher discount rate therefore affects the positives more than the negatives, and has the net effect of shrinking the NPV. The analysis of unusual patterns is left as an exercise.

Finding a project's IRR is equivalent to locating the crossover point of the NPV profile and the horizontal axis by testing points on either side. In the current problem, our first guess has taken us to the right of the crossover. Our next guess must be a lower interest rate to move the NPV up and get closer to the IRR.

We'll keep track of our calculations by setting up a two-column table to portray each interest rate choice and the NPV calculated to go along with it. Use the calculation method shown in Example 9.2 to verify that the entries shown below are correct. NPVs are shown rounded to the nearest whole dollar.

Interest Rate Guess	Calculated NPV
12%	($377)
10	(184)
9	(83)
8	22
7	130

The calculated NPV changes sign between 9% and 8%, which means the IRR is between those interest rates.

If the firm's cost of capital is 8%, the project is marginally favorable. If the cost is 10%, it's clearly unfavorable.

Notice that this technique is similar to the iterative approach we used to find the yield on a bond given its price in Chapter 6 (pages 201–202).

Some financial calculators are programmed to find the IRR for a general set of cash flows. Internally such machines are going through the iterative process we've just illustrated.

Technical Problems with IRR

Two technical problems are associated with the IRR method. They *rarely* present practical difficulties, but anyone using the technique should be aware of them.

MULTIPLE SOLUTIONS   The IRR for a project is defined as the solution to equation 9.2 with the project's cash flows substituted for the C_i and IRR treated as the unknown. The expression comes from the NPV equation operating at the point where NPV equals zero.

A problem arises because equation 9.2 is an nth-order equation in the variable IRR. That means it can have as many as n solutions. How do we know which one is correct? At first glance, this seems like a fatal problem for the IRR method, but in reality it isn't.

Solutions to the equation can be either positive, negative, or what mathematicians call imaginary.[4] Negative and imaginary solutions aren't practically meaningful, so we needn't be concerned about them. We worry only when there's more than one positive solution.

> ● Unusual projects can have **more than one IRR,** but they rarely present practical difficulties.

FIGURE 9.1

NPV Profile

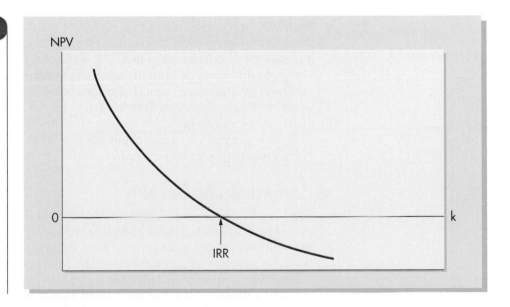

---

4. Imaginary numbers are functions of the square root of minus one. They are the subject of an entire branch of advanced mathematics.

It turns out that the number of positive solutions to equation 9.2 depends on the pattern of the project's cash flows. There can be no more positive solutions than there are *sign reversals* in the cash flow stream. A sign reversal occurs when the C_i change from negative to positive or from positive to negative.

The normal pattern of project cash flows involves only one sign change. There's almost always a negative initial outlay, C_0, followed by a series of periods with positive cash flows. C_0 is sometimes followed immediately by a few negative flows before the inflows start, but even then there's only one sign change from negative to positive. That means there's only one positive solution for IRR, which is the correct one.

In the occasional project with one or two negative cash flow years interspersed among the positives, there can be more than one IRR solution. However, in practical problems there's generally only one solution within a reasonable range of values for an interest rate, say, between 0% and 50%. That's the one we're looking for. When other positive solutions exist, they tend to be figures like 300% or 400%. Because we solve for the IRR by using an iterative approach starting with a reasonable guess, we rarely find such answers.

As a practical matter, the multiple-solution issue can be all but ignored.

THE REINVESTMENT ASSUMPTION   Examine equation 9.2 once again. Suppose we have a typical case with a negative C_0 followed by a long series of cash inflows. The IRR method makes an implicit assumption about what happens to those cash inflows after they're received. It assumes that inflows are *reinvested* at the IRR until the end of the project's life.

The reinvestment assumption presents a problem in the case of especially profitable ventures. Suppose a project has an IRR of 50%. The company is unlikely to find other opportunities with returns that high in which to reinvest the funds thrown off by the project. Therefore, the reinvestment assumption is unlikely to be satisfied. But that casts a doubt on the reality of the 50% solution. In other words, the return rate is very high, but it may not truly be 50%.

Contrast IRR with the NPV method in such a situation. A project with a very high IRR would also have a high NPV, but the reinvestment assumption in that method requires only that cash flows be reinvested at the cost of capital. That's because the discount rate in the NPV technique is just k, the cost of capital, as shown in equation 9.1. Such investments are virtually always available.

The reinvestment problem is also somewhat academic—that is, not a practical concern. When returns on projects are in the 50% neighborhood, people don't worry about *exactly* how high they are. In other words, if a project computes to a 50% IRR, people don't argue about whether it's 50% or only 40%. In either case, if the projected cash flows are correct, they indicate a very good opportunity.

● COMPARING IRR AND NPV

The internal rate of return and the net present value methods are the two major approaches to evaluating capital budgeting projects. It's logical to ask whether they always give the same solutions to problems. Surprisingly, the answer to that question is no. Let's explore why with the aid of the NPV profile that we introduced earlier.

The NPV profile *for a project* is a graphic representation of the relationship between a project's NPV and the interest rate at which it's calculated. It is simply the graph of equation 9.1 for a particular set of cash flows (the C_i).

Look back at the NPV profile in Figure 9.1. The related discussion demonstrated that the line of the profile slopes downward to the right for projects that involve early cash outflows and later cash inflows. Because that is invariably the case for business projects, all profiles of interest to us slope downward to the right. However, their shapes aren't identical, and they cross the horizontal axis at different points. In addition, the profiles of different projects *may* cross one another, as illustrated in Figure 9.2. We can use the NPV profiles depicted there to show how the NPV and IRR methods can give conflicting directions when we are choosing among mutually exclusive projects.

Notice in Figure 9.2 that project A's profile crosses the k axis to the right of project B's. That means $IRR_A > IRR_B$. Therefore the IRR method chooses project A over project B. Does the NPV method also choose project A? It depends on the cost of capital. We'll demonstrate by graphically evaluating the two projects against each other using the NPV method at different values of k.

To determine graphically any project's NPV at a particular cost of capital, we find k on the horizontal axis and move vertically to the project's NPV profile. From there we move left to the vertical axis and read the value of NPV.

First choose cost of capital k_1 and locate NPV_A and NPV_B, the NPVs for projects A and B, respectively. These are shown toward the bottom of the vertical axis in the diagram. Notice that NPV_A is above (is larger than) NPV_B, indicating that the NPV method chooses project A just as the IRR method does.

Now do the same thing for cost of capital k_2, which is to the left of the point at which the two profiles cross. The resulting NPVs are shown toward the top of the vertical axis. Notice that the result is reversed. This time the NPV method chooses project B over A, a result opposite that of the IRR method.

Examination of the diagram provides some insight into when this phenomenon may occur. To give conflicting results, the NPV profiles have to cross in the first quadrant of the graph at interest rates that are of practical interest. That doesn't happen often. Even when it does, we can generally expect the two methods to agree when the cost of capital isn't too far below the project IRRs.

● The NPV and IRR methods can occasionally give **conflicting results** in mutually exclusive decisions.

FIGURE 9.2

Projects for Which IRR and NPV Can Give Different Solutions

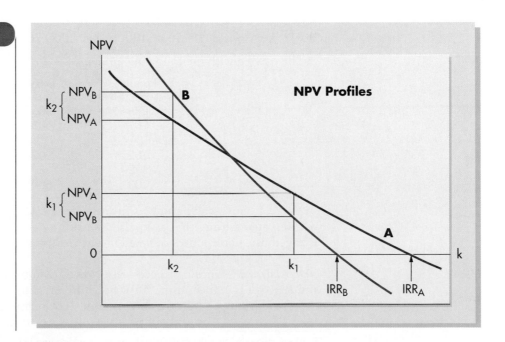

The Preferred Method in Case of Conflict

As a practical matter, conflicts between the IRR and NPV methods are rare. When they do occur, *the NPV method is preferred,* because its *reinvestment assumption* is more easily satisfied.

●NPV AND IRR SOLUTIONS USING FINANCIAL CALCULATORS AND SPREADSHEETS

Modern financial calculators and spreadsheet software take most of the drudgery out of calculating NPVs and IRRs. The machines are especially convenient when we need to find an IRR because they allow us to avoid the tedious iterative process described earlier.[5] We'll outline how to solve problems using a Texas Instruments BAII PLUS™ calculator and Microsoft's Excel™ spreadsheet. Inputting to the calculator can be a little tricky, so you'll probably have to refer to its user's manual as well.

Calculators

A calculator will find a project's NPV or IRR quickly once the associated cash flows are entered. To enter cash flows on the BAII PLUS, begin by pressing the CF button to enter the cash flow mode, and then clear the working memory by pressing 2nd and then CLR Work.

The calculator is programmed to prompt the user for the cash flows one at a time, starting with the initial outlay that it calls CFo (we've called this figure C_0). Type in the value, make it negative (an outflow) by hitting the $+/-$ key, and then press ENTER. (After entering a number, press the $\downarrow$ key to move to the prompt for the next input item.)

The machine then prompts for up to 24 *different* cash flows, referred to as C01, C02, . . . ,C24. However, after each of these cash flows is entered, the machine prompts for a "frequency" displayed as F01, F02, . . . ,F24. The frequency allows you to repeat the last cash flow entered up to 9,999 times before moving on to the next *different* cash flow. If you don't enter a frequency, the machine assumes 1. For example, the series

$$-500 \quad 100 \quad 200 \quad 200 \quad 200 \quad 800$$

can be entered with the following inputs.

Prompt	Entry
CFo	−500
C01	100
F01	
C02	200
F02	3
C03	800

You can move back and forth through the cash flow and frequency figures you've entered using the $\uparrow\downarrow$ keys. Cash flows can also be inserted, deleted, or changed using procedures outlined in the user's manual.

NPV AND IRR   Once a project's cash flows are in the machine, calculating NPV and IRR is easy. To find the NPV begin by pressing the NPV button. The machine will prompt for I, the interest rate at which you want to do the present

---

5. It's worth noting that the machines are programmed to find IRRs using a similar iterative process.

value calculation (this is generally the cost of capital we've called k). Type the interest rate as a whole number (e.g., 12 for 12%) and press ENTER. Now press ↓ and then CPT (for compute). The project's NPV will appear on the screen. To get IRR, just press IRR and then CPT.

As an exercise, use your calculator to compute NPVs and IRRs for the project cash flows in Examples 9-2 and 9-3.

Spreadsheets

Spread solutions for NPV and IRR are very easy to do. We simply arrange the project's cash flows in a series of consecutive cells along a row or column and use the spreadsheet software's NPV and IRR functions. Here's an example using Microsoft Excel™ and the cash flows from Example 9-2.

	A	B	C	D	E
1	Project Cash Flows:				
2		–$5,000	$1,000	$2,000	$3,000
3					
4	Cost of Capital: k =		0.12		
5					
6	NPV =	($377.41)			
7					
8	IRR =	8.2%			

The formula in cell B6 is

$$= B2 + NPV(C4, C2{:}E2) \, .$$

Let's first focus on the NPV function. Its first argument is an interest rate—the cost of capital in this case—which we've put in cell C4. The other argument is the range of cells containing the project's *future* cash flows, C2 to E2. Notice that the NPV function calculates the present value of the *future* cash flows only. That means we have to add the initial outlay separately, which we do by including B2 in the formula.

The IRR function, on the other hand, takes the whole series of cash flows including the initial outlay. The formula in cell B8 is simply

$$= IRR(B2{:}E2) \, .$$

● PROJECTS WITH A SINGLE OUTFLOW AND REGULAR INFLOWS

Many projects are characterized by a single initial cash outflow followed by a finite number of equal inflows coming at regular time intervals. As an illustration, take the project in our last example and shift $1,000 from the third year to the first.

C_0	C_1	C_2	C_3
($5,000)	$2,000	$2,000	$2,000

● **Annuity formulas** can be used to calculate NPV and IRR when projects have **single outlays and regular inflows**.

This pattern is much easier to work with because the inflows can be treated as an annuity. In such cases we can rewrite the equations, defining NPV and IRR by using the present value of an annuity formula.[6]

---

6. We're using the present value of an annuity from Chapter 5, page 163; but replacing PMT with C just to be more consistent with our present notation, which represents cash flows as C's.

Equation 9.1 defining NPV becomes

(9.3) $NPV = C_0 + C[PVFA_{k,n}]$

where C is the constant annual inflow, k is the cost of capital, n is the project's life in years, and C_0 is the initial outlay. Remember that C_0 is a negative number. The second term on the right is the present value of the annuity formed by the project's positive cash flows over a period of n years at interest rate k.

Similarly, equation 9.2 defining IRR becomes

(9.4) $0 = C_0 + C[PVFA_{IRR,n}]$.

Equation 9.4 is especially convenient, because it lets us avoid the iterative procedure otherwise necessary to find IRRs.

EXAMPLE 9.5

Find the NPV and IRR for the project used as an illustration immediately above. Assume the cost of capital is 12%.

Solution: To calculate NPV, write equation 9.3 and substitute from the cash flow pattern.

$$NPV = C_0 + C[PVFA_{k,n}]$$
$$NPV = -\$5,000 + \$2,000[PVFA_{12,3}] .$$

Find the present value factor for an annuity in Appendix A-4 and substitute

$$NPV = -\$5,000 + \$2,000(2.4018)$$
$$NPV = -\$196.40 .$$

To calculate the IRR, write equation 9.4 and substitute

$$0 = C_0 + C[PVFA_{IRR,n}]$$
$$0 = -\$5,000 + \$2,000[PVFA_{IRR,3}] .$$

Solve for the factor.

$$PVFA_{IRR,3} = \$5,000 / \$2,000$$
$$= 2.5000$$

Now search for 2.5000 in Appendix A-4 along the row for three periods. The solution is between 9% and 10%.

Compare these results for NPV and IRR with those we calculated in Examples 9.2 and 9.4. Did shifting the $1,000 forward by two years make a big difference?

● PROFITABILITY INDEX (PI)

IRR and NPV are the most widely used capital budgeting techniques. Payback is used frequently but generally as a preliminary screening device before one of the other methods. Although new approaches are proposed from time to time, none has caught on in a big way. One approach, however, is used enough to make it worth mentioning briefly. The **profitability index (PI)** is essentially a variation on the NPV method. We'll define it by referring to equation 9.1.

The PI compares the present value of a project's *future* cash flows with the initial outlay required to get the project started, making the comparison in the form of a ratio.

Recall that the initial outlay is C_0. Hence PI is defined as the sum of all the terms to the right of C_0 in equation 9.1 divided by C_0.

● The **profitability index (PI)** is the ratio of the present value of inflows to the initial outlay. Projects are **acceptable if PI > 1**. **Larger PIs** are preferred.

$$(9.5) \qquad PI = \frac{\dfrac{C_1}{(1+k)} + \dfrac{C_2}{(1+k)^2} + \cdots + \dfrac{C_n}{(1+k)^n}}{C_0}$$

The PI is also known as the benefit/cost ratio, reflecting the idea that the positive cash flows expected in the future are benefits, while the initial outlay is a cost.

The concept is poorly defined if some of the early C's after C_0 are negative. In such a case it isn't clear whether those should be considered costs and added to the denominator or negative benefits and subtracted from the numerator. The idea works best when the initial outlay, C_0, is the only negative cash flow, which is a fairly common situation. (We should really write $-C_0$, but generally don't.)

Essentially, the PI is the ratio

$$\frac{\text{present value of inflows}}{\text{present value of outflows}}.$$

NPV, by way of contrast, is the *difference* between the present value of inflows and the present value of outflows.

When the present value of inflows exceeds the present value of outflows, the PI will be greater than one. This condition is equivalent to a positive NPV. Further, a larger PI is preferable to a smaller PI, because it implies more inflows relative to outflows in a present value sense. This is equivalent to preferring a larger to a smaller NPV.

Decision Rules

All this leads to the decision rules for the profitability index.

STAND-ALONE PROJECTS

$$PI > 1.0 \longrightarrow \text{accept}$$
$$PI < 1.0 \longrightarrow \text{reject}$$

MUTUALLY EXCLUSIVE PROJECTS

$$PI_A > PI_B \text{ choose project A over project B}$$

where PI_A and PI_B are the profitability indices for projects A and B, respectively.

COMPARISON WITH NPV   The comparison with NPV decision rules is not exact. In the stand-alone case, a PI > 1.0 always coincides with NPV > 0. However, the two methods may compute the relative desirability of projects differently and may not make the same choices among options.

INSIGHTS

Practical Finance

Which Methods Do Businesses Prefer?

Big Companies

Virtually all large companies do capital budgeting using sophisticated, time value–based methods. However, although NPV is theoretically the best technique, companies use IRR more frequently. That's probably because people are more comfortable with rates than with sums of present valued dollars. We're all familiar with interest rates on savings accounts from childhood. We learn about returns on stock investments early in our adult lives, and businesspeople talk about returns on sales, assets, and equities all the time.

NPV on the other hand is a little abstract. Most people don't learn about it until college, and you can't hold the present value of a dollar in your hand. Executives understand NPV, but the concept is a little alien. As a result most gravitate toward IRR. This preference isn't likely to change much in the foreseeable future.

Small Companies

Things are very different in small businesses. A study done some years ago indicated that more than 80% of small businesses commit capital on the basis of the payback method or don't do any formal analysis at all.*

There are probably two reasons for that finding. First, it's likely that most small firm managers simply haven't been educated in finance and don't know how to apply the more sophisticated techniques. Second, the small firm focus is just about always on very short-term cash flow. In the very short run, payback does a creditable job, so entrepreneurs may feel they don't need anything else.

*Runyon, L. R. "Capital Budgeting Decision Making in Small Firms," *Journal of Business Research* 11 (September 1983): 389–97.

EXAMPLE 9.6

Compute the profitability index for a project with the following cash flows if the cost of capital is 9%. Is the project acceptable on a stand-alone basis?

C_0	C_1	C_2	C_3
($4,500)	$1,500	$2,000	$1,600

Solution: The present value of future cash flows is computed as follows:

Year (i)	C_i	$PVF_{9,i}$	PV
1	$1,500	.9174	$1,376
2	2,000	.8417	1,683
3	1,600	.7722	1,236
			$4,295

Then, from equation 9.5, the PI is

$$PI = \frac{\$4,295}{\$4,500} = .95 .$$

Because the profitability index is less than one, the project is not acceptable.

COMPARING PROJECTS WITH UNEQUAL LIVES

● Projects with substantially **unequal lives** aren't directly comparable.

Mutually exclusive decisions are sometimes complicated by the fact that the competing projects don't extend over the same period of time. When the disparity is significant, it can make a direct comparison of the projects meaningless.

For example, suppose a manufacturing company is replacing a production machine and must choose between two new models that have different lives. Assume both new machines save $750 per year in cost, but the longer-lived model is expected to last six years, whereas the other will be good for only three years. Of course, the more durable replacement will be more expensive. Assume the costs are $2,600 and $1,500, respectively. The comparison is shown in Figure 9.3 for an assumed 8% cost of capital.

Notice that the shorter project has a better IRR, but the longer has a superior NPV. This conflict is due to the disparity in the project's lives.

The problem arises mainly with the NPV method. To visualize the difficulty, think of a replacement machine as having an annual benefit to the firm during its entire life. In broad terms, that just means it will produce income every year in excess of its cost on a present value basis.

The problem here is that the NPV method adds up six years of benefits for one project and only three years for the other. Therefore, the longer-lived machine just about always winds up with a higher NPV.

Putting it another way, the fact that one machine has a six-year life forces us to look at a six-year time horizon for analysis, and the shorter-lived project is implicitly assumed to have nothing going on in the second three years.

The Replacement Chain Method

To solve the dilemma we have to realize that if the company buys the cheaper machine, it will have to buy another replacement at the end of the first three years.

The correct way to compare the two projects in Figure 9.3 is to explicitly include a replacement for the short-lived machine at the end of its life. In essence,

---

FIGURE 9.3

Comparing Projects with Different Lives

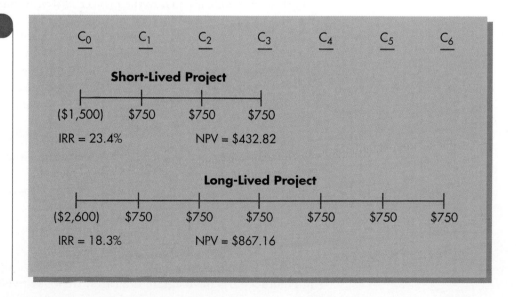

FIGURE 9.4

A Three-Year Project Chained into Six Years

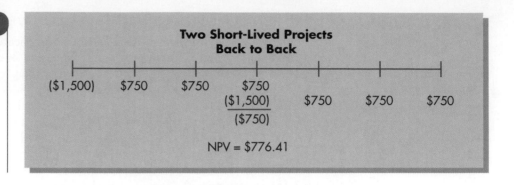

**Two Short-Lived Projects
Back to Back**

($1,500) $750 $750 $750 $750 $750 $750
                                   ($1,500)
                                   ─────────
                                   ($750)

NPV = $776.41

● The **replacement chain method** extends projects until a common time horizon is reached.

we *chain* two of the short projects together to cover the same time span as the longer project. The idea is portrayed graphically in Figure 9.4. The time line pictured there should replace the short line in Figure 9.3.

In this example, the long-lived project still has a higher NPV, so it would be chosen. However, the NPV comparison is more reasonable now that the second three-year period is considered in the short-lived case.

In theory, any pair of projects with different lives can be compared using the *replacement chain method* by chaining both until a common time period is reached. For example, a 3- and a 4-year project could be compared by chaining both to 12 years.

The approach has a significant drawback in that a large number of replacements may be necessary to get equal time horizons for the competing projects. For example, if one option lasts 5 years and the other 8, we'd have to look at 40 years of replacements to make the comparison, and that isn't realistic.

The Equivalent Annual Annuity (EAA) Method

Turning each project into an *equivalent annual annuity* (EAA) is the easiest way to solve the time disparity problem. To understand the method, think in terms of chaining projects the way we did in the last section. However, replace each project link in the chain by its NPV. Then replace that with an annuity of the same length whose NPV is equal to the project's NPV. A numerical example will make the idea clear.

● The **equivalent annual annuity** method replaces each project with an equivalent perpetuity.

The shorter-lived project we've been working with has a life of three years and an NPV of $432.82 (Figure 9.3). The equivalent three-year annuity is found by substituting that amount into the present value of an annuity formula along with three years and the appropriate interest rate as follows.

$$PVA = PMT[PVFA_{k,n}]$$

$$\$432.82 = PMT[PVFA_{8,3}]$$

Now find the factor in Appendix A-4, substitute, and solve for the annuity payment, which is the EAA.

$$\$432.82 = PMT(2.5771)$$

$$PMT = \$167.95$$

$$= EAA$$

The idea is illustrated in Figure 9.5 for the three-year project shown chained in Figure 9.4. As the diagram indicates, we make two conceptual steps. First we

FIGURE 9.5

Replacing a Project with Its NPV and EAA

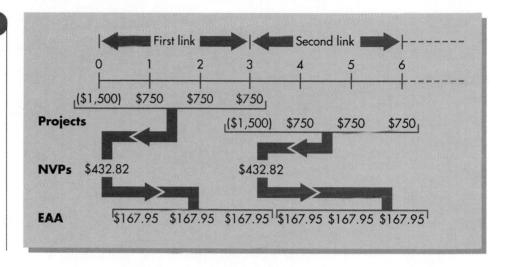

replace the project with its NPV. Then we replace that with an annuity of the same length which has the same NPV. In this way we replace the project with an equivalent stream of equal benefits.

Because we can chain the project forward through time as long as we like, we can represent it by an indefinitely long stream of payments equal to the EAA. It's important to realize that this is true even though the EAA calculation is based on the number of years in the life of the original project.

Further, we can calculate an EAA for *any* project regardless of its life. And because all EAAs are infinite annuities, we can choose among projects by comparing their annuity payments.

The longer-lived project in our illustration has an NPV of $867.16 and a life of six years. Its EAA is calculated as follows.

$$PVA = PMT[PVFA_{k,n}]$$

$$\$867.16 = PMT[PVFA_{8,6}]$$

$$\$867.16 = PMT(4.6229)$$

$$PMT = \$187.58$$

$$= EAA$$

This is larger than the shorter project's EAA of $167.95, so we again come to the conclusion that the longer project is better.

Notice that we can also compare EAAs on the basis of their present values by using the present value of a perpetuity formula. This simply amounts to dividing the EAA by the decimal value of the relevant interest rate. Because the cost of capital is the same for both projects, this will result in the same choice.

● CAPITAL RATIONING

A firm's *capital budget* is the total amount of money to be spent on capital projects in a period of time, usually a year. How large should that amount of money be?

In theory, the answer to that question is easy. Every project with a positive NPV is expected to increase shareholder wealth and should be undertaken. Therefore, the optimal capital budget would be large enough to undertake all

FIGURE 9.6

Capital Rationing

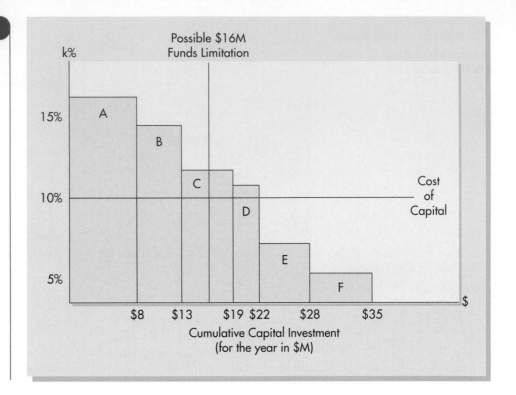

available projects with positive NPVs or equivalently with IRRs that exceed the cost of capital.

The idea is illustrated conceptually in Figure 9.6, a plot of interest rates against capital spending. Each lettered block represents a proposed project. A block's height represents the project's IRR, and the width is the amount of capital required to do the project. In most cases that's the initial outlay, C_0. Notice that the projects are arranged in decreasing order of IRR, and that the firm's cost of capital is shown as a horizontal line. The projects shown represent either stand-alone opportunities or the best choice among mutually exclusive options.

This portrayal makes it easy to see which projects have IRRs that exceed the cost of capital and therefore should be done. In this case, if there is no funds limitation, the firm will maximize shareholder wealth by undertaking projects A, B, C, and D while foregoing projects E and F.

In practice, however, there is rarely enough money available to do all proposed projects that appear to have positive NPVs. Some capital constraint is likely to be imposed like the one shown in the diagram at $16M. When such a constraint is imposed, we have **capital rationing** in that available capital dollars have to be rationed among projects.

Capital rationing creates a problem because projects are generally not divisible. In this case we can't do part of project C, so we can't do it at all. That leaves some unused money within the budget between the end of project B and the constraint. The rationing problem is to choose the best set of projects that fit into the capital constraint. By "best" we mean the set that maximizes NPV. In the illustration the choice appears to be easy because D, the next best project, just fits into the space available. In some cases, however, the choice isn't so obvious. It's

● **Capital rationing** involves selecting projects subject to a funding limitation.

possible that the selection of projects that maximizes NPV could omit one of the higher-rated projects in favor of one or more lower-rated projects that fit better within the constraint.

Finding the best possible solution to a capital rationing problem involves using techniques from a field of mathematics known as constrained maximization. The subject is quite complex and beyond the scope of this book, but you should be aware of its existence.

Using sophisticated mathematics to find a precise solution to capital rationing problems implies attributing a great deal of accuracy to the NPV and IRR estimates of the projects being considered. In the next chapter we'll learn that such accuracy frequently isn't possible.

from the **CFO**

In practice, financial managers ration capital intuitively, choosing among projects for a variety of reasons, not all of which may be strictly financial. In that way they make choices that are usually close to the best, but not exactly optimal.

DISCUSSION QUESTIONS

1. You are a financial analyst for the Ajax Company, which uses about $1M of inventory per month. The purchasing manager has come to you for help with a buying decision. He can get a big discount on $15M of inventory by buying it all at once. However, there is some risk of obsolescence when buying that far in advance. He understands that large purchases are frequently analyzed by means of capital budgeting techniques, and he asks for your help in deciding whether to buy the specially priced inventory. How would you advise him? Is capital budgeting appropriate?

2. Risk in capital projects is the probability that a project will earn less than expected. Make up and describe one hypothetical project in each of the replacement, expansion, and new venture categories. List a few ways that each might go wrong and cause the cash flows to be less favorable than expected. Can you think of situations in which projects could result in losses? Could the losses exceed the initial investment (C_0)?

3. Charlie Brown is thinking about starting Wing-It Airlines to fly a commuter route in and out of a major city. Four planes are on the market that will do the job, but each has different flight, load, and operating characteristics. Charlie is unsure of the demand for his service, and feels that it may depend to some extent on the type of plane chosen. Whether the business is feasible may depend on which airplane is used in conjunction with the demand estimate assumed. Are capital budgeting techniques appropriate for analysis of this problem? If so, is the issue a stand-alone or mutually exclusive decision?

4. Define mutual exclusivity and describe ways in which projects can be mutually exclusive.

5. Capital budgeting is based on the idea of identifying incremental cash flows, so overheads aren't generally included. Does this practice create a problem for a firm which, over a long period of time, takes on a large number of projects that are just barely acceptable under capital budgeting rules?

6. Relate the idea of cost of capital to the opportunity cost concept (pages 145–146). Is the cost of capital the opportunity cost of project money?

7. The payback technique is criticized for not using discounted cash flows. Under what conditions will this matter most? That is, under what patterns of cash flow will payback and NPV or IRR be likely to give different answers?

8. Explain the rationale behind the NPV method in your own words. Why is a higher NPV conceptually better than a lower one?

9. Projects A and B have approximately the same NPV. Their initial outlays are similar in size. Project A has early positive cash flows, and little or nothing is expected to come in later on. Project B has much larger positive cash flows than B, but they're farther in the future. Can you make any general statement about which project might be better?

10. Suppose the present value of cash ins and outs is very close to balanced for a project to build a new $50M factory, so that the NPV is +$25,000. The same company is thinking about buying a new trailer truck for $150,000. The NPV of projected cash flows associated with the truck is also about $25,000. Does this mean that the two projects are comparable? Is one more desirable than the other? If the cash flows have similar risks, are the projects equally risky? (*Hint:* Think in terms of the size of the investment placed at risk in relation to the financial rewards expected.)

11. Think about the cash flows associated with putting $100,000 in the bank for five years, assuming you draw out the interest each year and then close the account. Now think about a set of hypothetical cash flows associated with putting the same money in a business, operating for five years, and then selling out. Write an explanation of why the IRR on the business project is like the bank's interest rate. How are the investments different?

12. What is it about the cash flows associated with business projects that makes the NPV profile slope downward to the right? Would the NPV profile of any randomly selected set of positive and negative flows necessarily slope one way or the other? Why?

13. The following set of cash flows changes sign twice and has two IRR solutions. Identify the sign changes. Demonstrate mathematically that 25% and 400% are both solutions to the IRR equation.

C_0	C_1	C_2
($320)	$2,000	($2,000)

On the basis of this example, why would you expect multiple solutions to be an unusual problem in practice?

14. Under what conditions will the IRR and NPV methods give conflicting results for mutually exclusive decisions? Will they ever give conflicting results for stand-alone decisions? Why?

15. Why is the profitability index more appropriately described as a variation on the NPV technique than as a variation on the IRR technique?

16. Show that the profitability index (PI), the initial outlay (C_0), and the net present value (NPV) of a project are related by the following equation.

$$NPV = C_0(1 - PI)$$

(*Hint:* State both the NPV and the PI in terms of C_0 and the sum of all other cash flows.)

17. The Budwell & Son Oil Company is looking at two drilling proposals. One project lasts for three years, costs $20 million to start, pays back quickly, and has an NPV of $15 million. The other project also costs about $20 million to start, but has an expected life of seven years, takes much longer to pay back, and has an NPV of $17 million. Mr. Budwell, the company's founder, favors the shorter project because of the quick investment recovery. His son Billy, however, has taken finance in college and insists that the only way to judge projects is on NPV. He therefore favors the longer project. They've engaged you as their financial advisor to settle the issue. How would you advise them?

18. Webley Corp. has a capital budget limited to $20 million. Five relatively high IRR projects are available that have initial investments totaling $15 million. They are all roughly the same size. A sixth project has an IRR only slightly lower than those of the first five but requires an $8 million investment. Several other smaller projects are available with IRRs quite a bit lower than the sixth. The president has stated that it's too bad the firm has to pass up the sixth project, but it just doesn't fit into the budget. How would you advise him?

PROBLEMS

1. A project has the following cash flows.

C_0	C_1	C_2	C_3
($700)	$200	$500	$244

a. What is the project's payback period?
b. Calculate the project's NPV at 12%.
c. Calculate the project's PI at 12%.

2. Calculate an IRR for the project in Problem 1 using an iterative technique. (*Hint:* Start by guessing 15%.)

3. Clancy Inc. is considering a project with the following cash flows.

C_0	C_1	C_2	C_3
($7,800)	$2,300	$3,500	$4,153

a. Clancy has a policy of rejecting all projects that don't pay back within three years outright and analyzing those that do more carefully with time value based methods. Does this project warrant further consideration?

b. Should Clancy accept the project based on its NPV if the company's cost of capital is 8%?

c. What conclusion will the firm reach based on PI?

4. Should the project being considered in Problem 3 be accepted or rejected based on IRR? (*Hint:* Start by guessing 11% for IRR.)

5. Hamstring Inc. is considering a project with the following cash flows.

C_0	C_1	C_2	C_3	C_4
($25,000)	$10,000	$12,000	$5,000	$8,000

The company is reluctant to consider projects with paybacks of more than three years. If projects pass the payback screen, they are considered further by means of the NPV and IRR methods. The firm's cost of capital is 9%.

a. What is the project's payback period? Should the project be considered further?

b. What is the project's NPV? Does NPV indicate acceptance on a stand-alone basis?

c. Calculate the project's IRR by using an iterative approach. Start by using the cost of capital and the NPV calculation from part a. Does IRR indicate acceptance on a stand-alone basis?

d. What is the project's PI? Does PI indicate acceptance on a stand-alone basis?

6. Project Alpha requires an initial outlay of $35,000 and results in a single cash inflow of $56,367.50 after five years.

a. If the cost of capital is 8%, what are Alpha's NPV and PI? Is the project acceptable under each of these techniques?

b. What is project Alpha's IRR? Is it acceptable under IRR?

c. What are Alpha's NPV and PI if the cost of capital is 12%? Is the project acceptable under that condition?

d. What is Alpha's payback period? Does payback make much sense for a project like Alpha? Why or why not?

7. The Sampson Company is considering a project that requires an initial outlay of $75,000 and produces cash inflows of $20,806 each year for five years. Sampson's cost of capital is 10%.

a. Calculate the project's payback period by making a single division rather than accumulating cash inflows. Why is this possible in this case?

b. Calculate the project's IRR, recognizing the fact that the cash inflows are an annuity. Is the project acceptable? Did your calculation in this part result in any number(s) that were also calculated in part a? What is it about this problem that creates this similarity? Will this always happen in such cases?

c. What is the project's NPV? Is the project acceptable according to NPV rules?

8. Calculate the IRR, NPV, and PI for projects with the following cash flows. Do each NPV and PI calculation at costs of capital of 8% and 12%. Calculate IRRs to the nearest whole percent.

a. An initial outlay of $5,000 and inflows of $1,050 for seven years.

b. An initial outlay of $43,500 and inflows of $14,100 for four years.

c. An investment of $78,000 followed by 12 years of income of $11,500.

d. An outlay of $36,423 followed by receipts of $8,900 for six years.

9. Island Airlines Inc. needs to replace a short-haul commuter plane on one of its busier routes. Two aircraft are on the market that satisfy the general requirements of the route. One is more expensive than the other but has better fuel efficiency and load-bearing characteristics, which result in better long-term profitability. The useful life of both planes is expected to be about seven years, after which time both are assumed to have no value. Cash flow projections for the two aircraft follow.

	Low Cost	High Cost
Initial cost	$775,000	$950,000
Cash inflows, years 1 through 7	$154,000	$176,275

a. Calculate the payback period for each plane and select the best choice.

b. Calculate the IRR for each plane and select the best option. Use the fact that all the inflows can be represented by an annuity.

c. Compare the results of parts a and b. Both should select the same option, but does one method result in a clearer choice than the other based on the relative sizes of the two payback periods versus the relative sizes of the two IRRs?

d. Calculate the NPV and PI of each project assuming a cost of capital of 6%. Use annuity methods. Which plane is selected by NPV? By PI?

e. Calculate the NPV and PI of each project, assuming the following costs of capital: 2%, 4%, 6%, 8%, and 10%. Use annuity methods. Is the same plane selected by NPV and PI at every level of cost of capital? Investigate the relative attractiveness of the two planes under each method.

f. Use the results of parts b and e to sketch the NPV profiles of the two proposed planes on the same set of axes. Show the IRRs on the graph. Would NPV and IRR ever give conflicting results? Why?

10. Calculate the NPV for the following projects.

a. An outflow of $7,000 followed by inflows of $3,000, $2,500, and $3,500 at one-year intervals at a cost of capital of 7%.

b. An initial outlay of $35,400 followed by inflows of $6,500 for three years and then a single inflow in the fourth year of $18,000 at a cost of capital of 9%. (Recognize the first three inflows as an annuity in your calculations.)

c. An initial outlay of $27,500 followed by an inflow of $3,000 followed by five years of inflows of $5,500 at a cost of capital of 10%. (Recognize the last five inflows as an annuity, but notice that it requires a treatment different from the annuity in part b.)

11. Calculate the IRR for the following projects.

a. An initial outflow of $15,220 followed by inflows of $5,000, $6,000, and $6,500.

b. An initial outflow of $47,104 followed by inflows of $16,000, $17,000, and $18,000.

12. Calculate the NPV at 9% and the IRR for the following projects.

a. An initial outlay of $69,724 and an inflow of $15,000 followed by four consecutive inflows of $17,000.

b. An initial outlay of $25,424 followed by two zero cash years and then four years of inflows at $10,500.

c. An outlay of $10,672 followed by another outlay of $5,000 followed by five inflows of $5,000.

13. Calculate the NPV at 12% and the IRR for the following projects. Find IRRs to the nearest whole percent.

a. An initial outflow of $5,000 followed by three inflows of $2,000.

b. An initial outflow of $5,000 followed by inflows of $1,000, $2,000, and $3,000.

c. An initial outflow of $5,000 followed by inflows of $3,000, $2,000, and $1,000.

d. Notice that in parts a, b, and c, a total of $6,000 is received over three years. Compare the NPVs and IRRs to see the impact of shifting $1,000 between years.

14. Grand Banks Mining Inc. plans a project to strip-mine a wilderness area. Setting up operations and initial digging will cost $5 million. The first year's operations are expected to be slow and to net a positive cash flow of only $500,000. Then there will be four years of $2 million cash flows after which the ore will run out. Closing the mine and restoring the environment in the sixth year will cost $1 million.

a. Calculate the project's NPV at a cost of capital of 12%.

b. Calculate the project's IRR to the nearest whole percent.

15. Bagel Pantry Inc. is considering two mutually exclusive projects with widely differing lives. The company's cost of capital is 12%. The project cash flows are summarized as follows.

	Project A	Project B
C_0	($25,000)	($23,000)
C_1	14,742	6,641
C_2	14,742	6,641
C_3	14,742	6,641
C_4		6,641
C_5		6,641
C_6		6,641
C_7		6,641
C_8		6,641
C_9		6,641

a. Compare the projects by using payback.

b. Compare the projects by using NPV.

c. Compare the projects by using IRR.

d. Compare the projects by using the replacement chain approach.

e. Compare the projects by using the EAA method.

f. Choose a project and justify your choice.

Internet Problem

16. For a comprehensive application of the capital budgeting process go to the University of Florida–Institute of Food and Agricultural Science web site at http://edis.ifas.ufl.edu/. Search the EDIS database using the key word "capital budgeting." Write a one-page summary of the process described in the article entitled *Capital Budgeting for a New Dairy Facility*. Describe each of the investment tools discussed. Describe the methods suggested by the author for dealing with risk.

COMPUTER PROBLEMS DEVELOPING SOFTWARE

17. Write a spreadsheet program to calculate the NPV of a project with an irregular pattern of cash flows for up to 10 periods without using the spreadsheet software's NPV function. Essentially, the task is to program equation 9.1 with n = 10.

First input the interest rate (k) in a single cell.

Next set up three horizontal rows of 11 cells (including C_0). The top row will receive the cash flows as inputs.

Program the present value factor for each period into the second row of cells using the interest rate you input earlier as follows.

Period	0	1	2	...	...	10
Factor	1	$\dfrac{1}{1 + k}$	$\dfrac{1}{(1 + k)^2}$	...	...	$\dfrac{1}{(1 + k)^{10}}$

Note that we're calling the interest rate k, but it will appear as a cell name in your program.

Next form the third row by multiplying the top two cells in each column together. This makes the third row the present value of each cash flow.

Finally, sum the values along the third row in another cell to form the project's NPV.

Notice that your program will handle a project of less than 10 periods if you simply input zero (or leave blank) the cash flow cells from n + 1 to 10.

Also notice that you can easily extend your program to any reasonable number of periods by extending the horizontal rows and the programming logic. Test your program on the data in Example 9.3 on pages 303–304 to make sure it works correctly.

18. The Tallahassee Motor Company is thinking of automating one of its production facilities. The equipment required will cost a total of $10.0 million and is expected to last 10 years. The company's cost of capital is 9%. The project's benefits include labor savings and a quality improvement that will lower warranty costs. Savings are estimated as follows.

Year	Cost Savings ($000)
1	$ 574
2	864
3	1,246
4	2,748
5	3,367
6	2,437
7	2,276
8	1,839
9	1,264
10	623

a. Use the program developed in Problem 17 to find the project's NPV. Is the project acceptable?

b. Use the program to develop the data for an NPV profile. Evaluate the NPV for interest rates (costs of capital) from 6 to 14%.

c. Use the program to iteratively find the project's IRR to one hundredth of a percent.

CHAPTER 10

Cash Flow Estimation

Chapter Outline

Early in the last chapter we said that any project to be analyzed by capital budgeting techniques must be represented as a series of estimated cash flows. We portrayed the flows for a typical project as C_0, C_1, . . . , C_n, and assumed that they were readily available. In this chapter we'll consider exactly how such cash flow estimates are developed. In the next chapter we'll look into some modern developments in capital budgeting that deal with incorporating risk into the analysis.

CASH FLOW ESTIMATION

We'll begin by placing cash flow estimation within the overall capital budgeting process and making some important observations about people's perceptions.

● CAPITAL BUDGETING PROCESSES

Capital budgeting consists of two distinct processes. The first is estimation of the cash flows associated with projects. The second is evaluation of the estimates using techniques like NPV and IRR. There is a tendency to take the forecast cash flows for granted and to overlook the difficulties involved in their estimation. Further, once a set of projections is made, people tend to treat it as a concrete fact not subject to error.

The same tendency leads to associating the capital budgeting concept solely with the evaluation techniques, especially NPV and IRR, and becoming caught up in an incorrect perception of the accuracy and precision of the whole process. Indeed, the techniques we studied in the last chapter seem like "financial engineering" in their direct and unambiguous approach to the task of choosing among projects. Problem solutions come out to what seems like hair-splitting accuracy, and it's easy to get a feeling of comfort and security in the correctness of the method.

However, this secure feeling of great accuracy is misplaced. The results of an NPV or IRR analysis are only as accurate as the cash flow estimates used as inputs. And those estimates are forecasts of the *future,* which are always difficult to make and subject to considerable error.

● **Estimating** project **cash flows** is the **most difficult** and error-prone part of capital budgeting.

In practice, forecasting accurate project cash flows is the more difficult and arbitrary of the two capital budgeting processes. In a sense it's the more important, because it's where error and bias can creep into the analysis. Applying NPV and/or IRR is a straightforward task that isn't likely to result in error or misinterpretation. The calculation may be complicated, but it's easy in the sense that we don't have to make any judgments about what we're doing. Making cash flow estimates, on the other hand, requires the exercise of a good deal of judgment about what to include, what to leave out, and how heavily to weight things in relation to one another. As a result, a particular set of estimated flows may be very good or very bad depending on the nature of the project and who's doing the estimating.

This is an important point that's often overlooked. Anyone can make the right capital budgeting decisions with NPV and IRR *given* a set of cash flows. It's developing the right set of cash flows that's tough.

In this chapter we'll take a close look at what goes into estimating cash flows. We'll be especially concerned with the practical matter of ambiguities and uncertainties in the process.

PROJECT CASH FLOWS—AN OVERVIEW AND SOME SPECIFICS

First we'll sketch a broad approach to the estimating process, then we'll consider a few issues that require special treatment, and finally we'll look into some detailed examples.

● THE GENERAL APPROACH TO CASH FLOW ESTIMATION

Cash flow estimation can be a messy calculation, but it's conceptually quite simple. We just think through all the events a project is expected to bring about, and write down the financial implications of each event in the future time period in which we expect it to occur. Then we add up everything in each time period.

● Cash estimates are done on **spreadsheets** by enumerating the issues that impact cash and forecasting each over time.

We generally use a spreadsheet format for our estimations. The sheet's columns are time periods starting with the present and extending into the future over the project's life. The rows are financial items that will either generate or require cash.

For example, a sales forecast leads to an estimate of cash inflows from customers, while an expense projection leads to a pattern of outflows to employees and vendors. When everything is enumerated, we add up each column to arrive at a forecast of each future period.

It will help your perspective if you look ahead at Table 10.1 on page 339 to get an idea of what the finished product looks like.

Forecasts for new ventures tend to be the most complex, so we'll consider them before talking briefly about expansion and replacement projects. For those projects we generally just leave out some of the issues considered for new ventures. It helps to organize our thinking if we consider things in several separate categories. A general outline for estimating new venture cash flows follows.

PRE–START-UP, THE INITIAL OUTLAY   Enumerate everything that has to be spent before the project is truly started. Include expenses and assets that have to be purchased. Also include the tax impact of expense items. The sum of these things is C_0, the *initial outlay*.

THE SALES FORECAST, UNITS AND REVENUES   The incremental business expected from the project is laid out in spreadsheet form (on paper or in a computer) over future time periods. It's best to forecast in terms of units and then multiply by projected prices to arrive at sales dollars.

COST OF SALES AND EXPENSES   Plan for costs directly related to the new sales forecast as well as expenses necessary for indirect support of the increased activity level. To do that, assume relationships between sales and cost and between sales and expense based on the nature of the business being analyzed.

ASSETS   New assets to be acquired with cash are planned over the project's life whenever they're expected to be acquired. Most are needed during the initial, pre–start-up period. It's important not to neglect working capital, which requires cash like any other asset.

DEPRECIATION   When planning for physical assets, it's important to forecast depreciation even though it's a noncash expense because it affects taxes.

TAXES AND EARNINGS   Summarizing the tax deductible items in each period lets us calculate the project's impact on taxes and earnings. Calculate incremental taxes and treat them like any other cash flow item.

SUMMARIZE AND COMBINE   Adjust earnings for depreciation and combine it with the balance sheet items to arrive at a cash flow estimate in each forecast period.

Expansion projects tend to require the same elements as new ventures, but generally require less new equipment and facilities.

Replacement projects are generally expected to save costs without generating new revenue, so the estimating process tends to be somewhat less elaborate. The expected dollar savings are planned over future periods along with the assets required to realize those savings. Depreciation and tax calculations are necessary in most cases.

We'll look at some examples after the next section.

●A FEW SPECIFIC ISSUES

It helps to keep a few specific items in mind when making cash flow estimates. We'll consider several before moving on to examples.

The Typical Pattern

Nearly all projects require an *initial outlay* of funds before getting started. Subsequently, flows tend to be positive (inflows) with some notable exceptions. The typical pattern is characterized by early outflows followed by later inflows.

A replacement project is generally fairly simple in this respect. The initial outlay is the cost of the new equipment less any salvage value available for the old.

Future cash flows are the savings or benefits of using the new, more efficient machinery. They start immediately and are generally relatively stable.

Other kinds of projects can have several negative cash flow periods. New ventures, for example, typically lose money for the first few years after an initial outlay, so there are several negative periods at the outset. More complex projects can require infusions of cash at different times, so it's possible to have negative flows at any time. For example, a cleanup requirement at the end can make the last flow of a project negative.

● Most cash **outflows** occur **early;** inflows happen **later.**

Project Cash Flows Are Incremental

● Only **incremental** cash flows count.

The most fundamental concept about project cash flows is that they are *incremental* to the company's normal business. Incremental means *in addition to,* and at least conceptually *separate from.* In other words, we must answer the following question: What cash flows will occur if we undertake this project that wouldn't occur if we left it undone and continued business as before?

Sunk Costs

● **Sunk costs** have already been spent and are ignored.

Some expenditures associated with a project should not be included in capital budgeting cash flows. **Sunk costs** are monies that have already been spent at the time of the analysis. The fact that sunk money is gone cannot be changed by decisions about the project.

For example, suppose a company spends money to study a new area of business and later conducts an analysis to decide whether to enter the field. The cost of the study should *not* be included in the project's cash flow stream for capital budgeting analysis, because at the time of the analysis the money has already been spent.

The analysis of a decision must include only *future* costs that are dependent on the decision. The study money is gone and won't be recovered whether the new field is entered, so it's irrelevant to the decision.

Opportunity Cost

● The **opportunity cost** of a resource is its value in its best alternative use and is included in capital budgeting analyses.

Resources aren't free even though they sometimes seem to be. Suppose a firm has an idle production facility and is evaluating a project that requires a similar resource. The idle factory will be used if the project is undertaken, and won't require a cash outlay. Does that mean the facility is a zero cost item in the project's capital budgeting analysis?

It's tempting to say yes, especially if there are no other plans for the building. However, that's not the right way to look at the problem. The appropriate cost of any resource is whatever has to be *given up* to use it. In other words, its value in the next best use.

In this example, suppose the firm has no other production use for the idle factory, but can sell it for $1 million (the next most lucrative use). In such a case we'd say $1 million is the *opportunity cost* of the factory and use that amount as a cash outflow in the analysis. In effect, the company is foregoing a $1 million cash inflow by using the facility in the project. The factory would be free only if it had no market value and no other use by the company.

Impacts on Other Parts of the Company

Projects sometimes have impacts on other parts of the company that have to be considered. Suppose a company sells a family model product and is considering introducing a luxury model. Some customers who buy the family model will probably switch to the luxury line. The result will be a loss of income in the family line that should be reflected as a negative cash flow in the analysis of the new proposal.

Overhead Levels

Basic overheads are usually considered fixed and left out of project analysis. There are times, however, when overhead changes have to be considered.

For example, suppose a company has a central personnel department that is considered overhead by operating departments. Most capital budgeting projects involve the addition of only a few new people, so the workload of the personnel department isn't increased significantly by the larger staff. But suppose a particular project calls for so many new employees that an additional personnel administrator is required for their support. In such a case the increased cost *in the personnel department* must be reflected as a cost of the project. In other words, the project has an *incremental overhead effect* that should be reflected in its projected cash flows.

Taxes

- All capital budgeting cash flows are stated **after tax.**

Capital projects are generally expected to improve profitability, but more profit usually means more taxes. It's important to calculate incremental cash flows net of any additional taxes caused by the project.

To do that we have to calculate the incremental impact of the project on earnings before tax, then calculate the extra tax and include it as a cash outflow. In other words, we deal with *after-tax cash flows* in capital budgeting.

Cash versus Accounting Results

It's important to keep the distinction between earnings and cash flows in mind when doing project projections. Capital budgeting deals only with cash flows, so in theory we hardly need mention accounting net income at all. However, business managers invariably want to know the *net income impact* of projects as well as the results of the capital budgeting analysis. It's therefore important to keep both available although separate.

Working Capital

- Projects generally require new **working capital,** which requires cash.

Projects that involve increased sales normally also require increases in receivables and inventories (partially offset by payables). In other words, higher revenue demands more working capital, which builds up during the project's early years along with revenue. It's important to recognize that increases in working capital have to be funded with cash outflows just like the acquisition of any other asset, and that these flows have to be included in the project's forecast.

Ignore Financing Costs

- **Ignore interest expense** when estimating incremental cash flows.

When project cash flows are projected, we do *not* include the interest expense of carrying a cumulative outflow over time. This is the most significant difference between cash flow estimation and the financial forecasting associated with business planning (Chapter 16). Cash flow estimation is concerned with the value of projects irrespective of how they're financed, so we look only at operating cash flows.

This is not to say that the capital budgeting concept ignores interest expenses or the time value of money. The time cost of money is explicitly accounted for in the evaluation process when the NPV and/or IRR techniques are applied. Because it's taken into account there, we don't need to consider it when estimating cash flows.

Old Equipment

Some projects, especially replacements, involve getting rid of old capital equipment. Such material generally can be sold on a secondhand market, providing a cash inflow that to some extent offsets the expense of the new equipment.

It's important to consider this source of funds in cash flow estimation. It's also important to recognize that the income from the sale of old equipment may be reduced by taxes on the accounting profit recognized with the sale.

ESTIMATING NEW VENTURE CASH FLOWS

New venture projects tend to be larger and more elaborate than expansions or replacements. However, incremental cash flows can be easier to isolate with new ventures, because the whole project is easily seen as distinct and separate from the rest of the company.

EXAMPLE 10.1

The Wilmont Bicycle Company manufactures a line of traditional multispeed road bicycles. Management is considering a new business proposal to produce a line of off-road mountain bikes. The proposal has been studied carefully and the following information is forecast.

Cost of new production equipment and machinery including
  freight and setup $200,000

Expense of hiring and training new employees...$125,000

Pre–start-up advertising and other miscellaneous expenses....................................$20,000

Additional selling and administrative expense
  per year after start-up..$120,000

Unit sales forecast

  Year 1 200

  Year 2 600

  Year 3 1,200

  Year 4 and beyond................................1,500

Unit price $600

Unit cost to manufacture (60% of revenue)..$360

Last year, anticipating an interest in off-road bicycles, the company bought the rights to a new gearshift design for $50,000.

Wilmont's production facilities are currently being utilized to capacity, so a new shop has to be acquired for incremental production. The company owns a lot near the present facility on which a new building can be constructed for $60,000. The land was purchased 10 years ago for $30,700, and now has an estimated market value of $150,000.

If Wilmont produces off-road bicycles, it expects to lose some of its current sales to the new product. Three percent of the new unit forecast is expected to come out of sales that would have been made in the old line. Prices and direct costs are about the same in the old line as in the new.

Wilmont's general overhead includes personnel, finance, and executive functions, and runs about 5% of revenue. Small one-time increments in business don't affect overhead spending, but a major continuing increase in volume would require additional support. Management estimates that additional spending in overhead areas will amount to about 2% of the new project's revenues.

New revenues are expected to be collected in 30 days. Incremental inventories are estimated at $12,000 at start-up and for the first year. After that an inventory turnover of 12 times based on cost of sales is expected. Incremental payables are estimated to be 25% of inventories.

Wilmont's current business is profitable, so losses in the new line will result in tax credits. The company's marginal tax rate is 34%.

Solution: The Initial Outlay.
First we'll consider cash flows required before start-up, which comprise the initial outlay, C_0. We'll work in thousands of dollars and carry one decimal place. That amounts to forecasting to the nearest $100, which provides more than enough detail for estimating purposes.

Expenses of an operating nature can be expected to be tax deductible against other income in the period before start-up. These include the cost of hiring, training, advertising, and other miscellaneous items.

Hiring and training	$125.0
Advertising and miscellaneous	$ 20.0
Deductible expense	$145.0
Tax credit @ 34%	$ 49.3
Net after tax expenses	$ 95.7

Next add the cash needed for physical assets necessary to get started.

Equipment	$200.0
New construction	60.0
Initial inventory	$ 12.0
Assets subtotal	$272.0

Add the operating items and the physical assets to get the total, actual pre–start-up outlay.

Net after-tax expenses	$ 95.7
Assets subtotal	$272.0
Actual pre–start-up outlay	$367.7

Next we have to recognize the opportunity cost of the land. The property has a market value of $150,000, but if it's sold for that amount, a capital gains tax will be due on the increase in value over its original cost. Corporations don't get favorable capital gains rates, so the tax rate will be 34%.

Sales price	$150.0
Cost	$ 30.7
Capital gain	$119.3
Tax @ 34%	$40.6
Cash foregone (price 2 tax)	$109.4

Summarizing, we obtain a figure for C_0.

Actual pre–start-up cash outlay	$367.7
Opportunity cost of land	$109.4
C_0 (initial outlay for analysis)	$477.1

Cash Flows After Start-up. Incremental sales forecasts often begin small, grow for a few years, and then level off. Other forecast elements commonly do the same thing, change for a few years and then remain constant. When that happens, we have to forecast out in time only until the numbers stop changing from year to year. Subsequent years are then repetitive.

In this case sales are forecast to grow for four years before leveling off. However, a change in depreciation after the fifth year affects taxes. Hence the annual cash flow estimate changes each year until the sixth year and then remains constant. We'll therefore estimate only the first six years, understanding that for a longer forecast we just need to repeat the last year as many times as we like. The calculations are laid out in Table 10.1 and discussed in the following paragraphs. **Follow Table 10.1 as you continue to read this example.**

The revenue forecast at the top of the table is developed by laying out the unit sales projection and multiplying by the projected price of $600. It's important to forecast both physical units and future prices rather than just total revenue. Maintaining unit-price detail makes it easier to alter the forecast to reflect different assumptions as well as check the reasonability of the entire estimate.

● It's generally best to forecast revenue with **unit and price** detail.

Production cost can be built up from components or forecast as a percentage of revenue consistent with previous experience in the same or similar businesses. In this case Wilmont is experienced in making bicycles, and feels that a *cost ratio* of 60% will be appropriate for the new line. Applying this ratio to the revenue figures yields the projected cost line. Gross margin follows by subtracting cost from revenue.

Next we calculate items that affect pretax income, beginning with selling, general and administrative (SG&A) expense estimated at $120,000 per year.

Deductible depreciation is in two separate pieces because equipment and buildings are depreciated over different lives. Equipment can be written off over 5 years for tax purposes, while the building has to be amortized over 39 years. We'll assume straight-line depreciation for both and ignore partial-year conventions for convenience. Then the annual depreciation is as follows.

Equipment ($200,000/5)	$40,000
Building ($60,000/39)	$ 1,538
Depreciation, first five years	$41,538
Thereafter	$ 1,538

The next line represents the expected increase in general overhead calculated at 2% of incremental revenues. Following that is an allowance for the lost business expected in the old product line. It was estimated that 3% of the unit forecast would come from the old line. Assuming the cost and price relationships are about the same in the old line as in the new, we can estimate the profit impact of this loss as 3% of the new gross margin forecast.

Add these items and subtract from gross margin for the impact on earnings before tax (EBT). The tax calculation is just 34% of EBT, which leads to the impact of the project on earnings after tax (EAT). Although this figure isn't relevant for capital budgeting purposes, it's invariably important to operating managers and should therefore be calculated and displayed as part of the analysis. The cash impact of these operating items is calculated by adding back depreciation, the only noncash charge in this example.

Finally, we calculate the cash required to build the working capital necessary to support the project. This means estimating the year-end balances for accounts receivable, inventories, and accounts payable.

We're assuming that receivables are collected in 30 days, meaning there's one month of uncollected revenue in accounts receivable (A/R) all the time. The average level during each year is therefore one-twelfth of that year's revenue. Having the average figure in two successive years, we can average them to get the year-end figure for the first of the years. The calculations for the first two years are shown here. Year 1's average monthly revenue is $10,000; in year 2 that figure builds to $30,000. On the way between the two levels, assuming the growth is smooth, it passes through $20,000 at year end.

Year	Revenue	Average A/R	Year-End A/R
1	$120,000	$10,000	$20,000
2	360,000	30,000	45,000
3	720,000	60,000	

Inventory is estimated as one month's cost of goods sold, so take the annual cost figure divided by 12 except in the first year where a $12,000 level has been assumed. Finally, payables are 25% of inventory.

Summarize these items and calculate the year-to-year *change* in working capital, which reflects the cash required to fund it over the project's life. In the first year the change in working capital is $17,000 rather than $29,000, because an initial inventory of $12,000 is assumed to have been acquired before start-up.

The after-tax cash flow estimates for years 1 through 6 are calculated by adding the working capital requirements to the operating subtotal several lines above. These figures along with the initial outlay calculated earlier represent the cash flows for the off-road bike project.

C_0	C_1	C_2	C_3	C_4	C_5	C_6
($477.1)	($52.9)	($7.1)	$73.8	$139.3	$153.5	$139.9

Notice that the cash forecasts for subsequent years will be repetitions of the sixth year if sales remain at a steady 1,500 units. Therefore, in this case, we can extend the forecast by just adding more inflows of $139,900.

It's important to notice two things that are *not* in the calculations above. First, there is no provision for the $50,000 already spent for the new gearshift design. That money is gone whether the mountain bike project is accepted or not and is therefore irrelevant. Only *future* flows that depend on the decision to go ahead should be considered in the project's analysis. Past or *sunk* costs that can't be changed or recovered aren't considered even though they're related to the project.

Second, there's no allowance for interest on accumulated cash flows as a cost or income of the project. The cost of funds is explicitly included in capital budgeting when the NPV and IRR techniques are applied. Therefore it doesn't need to be considered in the estimation of project cash flows.

TERMINAL VALUES

● Cash flows forecast to continue forever are compressed into finite **terminal values** using perpetuity formulas.

It's possible to assume the incremental cash flows associated with a project go on forever. The assumption is especially common with respect to new ventures that are expected to continue as businesses indefinitely. For example, in the Wilmont Bicycle Company problem we've just completed, it's not unreasonable to assume that the year 6 cash flow of approximately $140,000 continues into the indefinite future.

There's a convenient way to reflect this assumption in the cash flow stream that Wilmont will use in capital budgeting. The repetitive cash flow starting in period 7 is a perpetuity whose "present" value at the beginning of period 7 (end of period 6) is C_7/k, where k is the cost of capital (see perpetuities on pages 173–174). This amount, known as the project's *terminal value,* is added to the *period* 6 cash flow to reflect the continuation of the project. If Wilmont's cost of capital is 10%, the project's terminal value would be

$$\frac{\$140,000}{.10} = \$1,400,000.$$

It's also possible to assume a perpetual cash flow that grows at some rate, g. In that case the terminal value is calculated by dividing the first ongoing cash flow by $k - g$ instead of k. Suppose Wilmont forecasts a 3% growth in the mountain bike project's cash flows starting with $140,000 in period 7. The project's terminal value would then be

$$\frac{\$140,000}{.10 - .03} = \$2,000,000.$$

Notice how large the terminal value cash flow is relative to the project's earlier flows. Indeed the terminal value assumption overwhelms everything else in the projection. Also notice that the magnitude of the terminal value is very sensitive to the growth rate assumed.

from the **CFO**

This is a big problem with respect to the accuracy of capital budgeting analyses. An optimistic long-run forecast can make a project look good on an NPV or IRR basis even if the short-run projections are poor. Since the terminal period doesn't start for some time, it's hard to disprove the assumptions behind it. Hence people who propose projects tend to portray them as growing rapidly into the indefinite future. It's generally up to the finance department to keep such projections reasonable and conservative.

There's a strong argument that infinite projections shouldn't be used at all because of the uncertainty of the distant future. This position maintains that if a project can't be justified in a reasonably long time—say, 10 years—it shouldn't be undertaken.

ACCURACY AND ESTIMATES

Now that we've had a look at the estimating process we need to revisit the important point about precision that we discussed briefly at the beginning of the chapter.

The NPV and IRR techniques give the impression of great accuracy, since NPVs and IRRs are easily calculated to several decimal places. Such precision isn't real, however. Although IRR and NPV calculations are very exact, they're based on the cash flows input to the capital budgeting model. Those flows are *estimates* of the future and, like all estimates, are subject to error and bias.

TABLE 10.1

Cash Flow Estimation

Wilmont Bicycle Company
Estimated Cash Flows
Mountain Bike Project ($000s)

	Year					
	1	2	3	4	5	6+
Revenue and Gross Margin						
Units	200	600	1,200	1,500	1,500	1,500
Revenue	$120.0	$360.0	$720.0	$900.0	$900.0	$900.0
Cost	72.0	216.0	432.0	540.0	540.0	540.0
Gross margin	$ 48.0	$144.0	$288.0	$360.0	$360.0	$360.0
Tax Deductible Expenses						
SG&A expense	$120.0	$120.0	$120.0	$120.0	$120.0	$120.0
Depreciation	41.5	41.5	41.5	41.5	41.5	1.5
General overhead	2.4	7.2	14.4	18.0	18.0	18.0
Loss old line	1.4	4.3	8.6	10.8	10.8	10.8
Total	$165.3	$173.0	$184.5	$190.3	$190.3	$150.3
Profit Impact and Tax						
EBT impact	($117.3)	($ 29.0)	$103.5	$169.7	$169.7	$209.7
Tax	(39.9)	(9.9)	35.2	57.7	57.7	71.3
EAT impact	($ 77.4)	($ 19.1)	$ 68.3	$112.0	$112.0	$138.4
Add depreciation	41.5	41.5	41.5	41.5	41.5	1.5
Subtotal	($ 35.9)	$ 22.4	$109.8	$153.5	$153.5	$139.9
Working Capital						
Accounts receivable	$ 20.0	$ 45.0	$ 67.5	$ 75.5	$ 75.5	$ 75.5
Inventory	12.0	18.0	36.0	45.0	45.0	45.0
Payables	(3.0)	(4.5)	(9.0)	(11.3)	(11.3)	(11.3)
Working capital	$ 29.0	$ 58.5	$ 94.5	$108.7	$108.7	$108.7
Change in working capital	($ 17.0)	($ 29.5)	($ 36.0)	($ 14.2)	—	—
Net Cash Flow						
Net cash flow	($ 52.9)	($ 7.1)	$ 73.8	$139.3	$153.5	$139.9

● Capital budgeting results are **no more accurate** than the **projections of the future** used as inputs.

In Example 10.1, Wilmont's cash flow estimates were built on the unit sales forecast. But for a new product, that forecast could easily be off by 20%. Such variability implies that it usually doesn't pay to expend a great deal of effort to make other elements of the estimate precise. For example, an estimator might spend a lot of time determining whether the appropriate cost ratio for the mountain bike project is 60% or 61%. That would be a waste of time given the inaccuracy of the underlying sales forecast. Notice that we worked in tenths of thousands of dollars in Table 10.1, and could easily have rounded to thousands without loss of substance.

from the CFO

Estimating inaccuracies come from any number of sources, but unintentional biases are probably the biggest problem in capital budgeting. Projects are usually proposed by people who have an interest in their approval, and it's generally those same individuals who provide the technical input for the estimated cash flows used in capital budgeting. This creates an inherent conflict of interest.

For example, suppose a company's manufacturing department has proposed buying a new, state-of-the-art production machine to replace an old machine that's beginning to wear out. If the new machine is purchased, product quality will be consistently higher, and there will be fewer equipment breakdowns that cause production stoppages. Such problems create the most stress in manufacturing managers' lives and significantly affect their performance ratings. Therefore manufacturing managers are likely to perceive the new machine as a way to make their lives easier and better.

It is true that the manufacturing department will be charged with the cost of the new machine, but if that cost is included in the department's budget, it won't create an overrun that requires explaining. All things considered, manufacturing executives are likely to perceive the machine in an entirely positive light.

Representing the new machine as a series of cash flows requires putting a dollar value on the improved quality of output and on the machine's higher reliability. The implication is that the increased quality will result in higher customer satisfaction and fewer complaints. The better reliability will presumably result in less lost time on the production floor.

Making financial estimates of effects like these is a very subjective affair. We can generally say that the new machine will have a positive effect, but exactly how large it will be is hard to pin down. The results are difficult to identify even after the project is implemented. The effects of happier customers and fewer breakdowns rarely show up clearly on a financial statement. If they happen at all, they're just rolled into the normal financial results of operations.

As a result of all this, estimating the financial impact of such a project often turns out to be little more than educated guesswork that can never be proven right or wrong. But the people making the guesses are probably going to be members of the manufacturing team who proposed the project in the first place and feel that it's a terrific idea. Therefore their tendency will be to overestimate the benefits and underestimate the costs. We'll consider some of these issues in an example shortly.

● Projects are generally proposed by people who want to **see them approved** leading to **favorable biases.**

●MACRS—A NOTE ON DEPRECIATION

The U.S. government lets companies use *accelerated depreciation* when computing income for tax purposes. Under an accelerated method depreciation is shifted forward in an asset's life, so more is taken in the early years and less later on with no change in the total. This means taxable income and taxes due are lower in the early years and higher later on. In essence the scheme *defers* taxes.

This is an advantage because of the time value of money. To understand that, think of taking a dollar of deferred tax and putting it in the bank until it has to be paid several years later, and keeping the interest earned in the meantime.

Accelerated depreciation creates a problem, however, because companies don't like to show lower profits in the short run even if they'll be made up later on. As a result companies generally don't use accelerated depreciation to calculate the earnings shown to stockholders and the public. It's important to understand that it's perfectly legitimate to use two sets of accounting rules like this, one for *tax* purposes and one for *financial* purposes.

Recall that depreciation is a noncash expense item. It represents a fictitious allocation of cost over time intended to make financial results match physical activity. It doesn't represent actual spending. Also recall that in capital budgeting we're interested in cash flow, not accounting results. Hence the only reason we include depreciation in capital budgeting calculations is because of its effect on taxes, which are real cash flow items.

Therefore if a firm uses accelerated depreciation for tax purposes, it should use that depreciation in capital budgeting calculations. We haven't shown this detail in our examples to keep things simple for illustrative purposes, but you should be aware of how this feature of the tax system works.

Modified Accelerated Cost Recovery System

Many accelerated methods are available to spread depreciation over an asset's life. The tax code, however, dictates exactly how it's to be done. The method is called the **Modified Accelerated Cost Recovery System,** generally abbreviated **MACRS.** First the system classifies assets into different categories and specifies a depreciation life for each. Then it provides a table showing the percentage of the asset's cost that can be taken in depreciation during each year of life. The classification rules are fairly extensive as are the tables, so we'll just show a representative sample consisting of three-, five-, and seven-year assets as follows.

Class	Representative Equipment
3-year	Research equipment
5-year	Automobiles and computers
7-year	Furniture and equipment

	Depreciation as a Percent of Cost Property Class		
Year in Life	3-year	5-year	7-year
1	33.3%	20.0%	14.3%
2	44.4	32.0	24.5
3	14.8	19.2	17.5
4	7.5	11.5	12.5
5		11.5	8.9
6		5.8	8.9
7			8.9
8			4.5

Notice that there's depreciation in an extra year in each column, and the first entry in each column is smaller than the second. Both oddities are due to the *half year convention,* which assumes assets are placed in service in the middle of the year in which they're acquired. Hence the first entry in each column represents a half year of service and leaves another half year to be recognized at the end of the class life period.

MACRS applies only to equipment. Buildings (real estate) are depreciated straight line over 27.5 years if they're residential and over 39 years otherwise. (31.5 for some older properties.) Land isn't depreciated.

ESTIMATING CASH FLOWS FOR REPLACEMENT PROJECTS

Replacement projects generally have fewer elements to consider than new ventures, but identifying what is incremental can be trickier. It can be especially hard to specify what will happen if you don't do the project. For example, suppose a production machine is getting old and needs to be replaced. Do we compare the performance of the new machine with the current performance of the old one, or assume that the old one will continue to deteriorate? If the latter, how much additional cost will the deterioration bring about? Tax effects are also complicated in replacement projects.

EXAMPLE 10.2

Harrington Metals Inc. purchased a large stamping machine five years ago for $80,000. To keep the example simple we'll assume that the tax laws at the time permitted straight-line depreciation over eight years and that machinery purchased today can be depreciated straight line over five years. The machine has not performed well, and management is considering replacing it with a new one that will cost $150,000. If the new machine is purchased, it is estimated that the old one can be sold for $45,000. The quoted costs include all freight, installation, and setup.

The old machine requires three operators, each of whom earns $25,000 a year including all benefits and payroll costs. The new machine is more efficiently designed and will require only two operators, each earning the same amount.

The old machine has the following history of high maintenance cost and significant downtime.

	Year				
	1	2	3	4	5
Hours down	40	60	100	130	128
Maintenance expense ($000)	In warranty	$10	$35	$42	$45

Downtime on the machine is a major inconvenience, but it doesn't usually stop production unless it lasts for an extended period. This is because the company maintains an emergency inventory of stamped pieces and has been able to temporarily reroute production without much notice. Manufacturing managers estimate that every hour of downtime costs the company $500, but have no hard data backing up that figure.

The makers of the replacement machine have said that Harrington will spend about $15,000 a year maintaining their product and that an average of only 30 hours of downtime a year should be expected. However, they're not willing to guarantee those estimates after the one-year warranty runs out.

The new machine is expected to produce higher quality output than the old one. The result is expected to be better customer satisfaction and possibly more sales in the future. Management would like to include some benefit for this effect in the analysis, but is unsure of how to quantify it.

Estimate the incremental cash flows over the next five years associated with buying the new machine. Assume Harrington's marginal tax rate is 34%, and that the company is currently profitable so that changes in taxable income result in tax changes at 34% whether positive or negative. Assume any gain on the sale of the old machine is also taxed at 34%, since corporations don't receive favorable tax treatment on capital gains.

Solution: There are two kinds of cash flow items in this problem: those that can be estimated fairly objectively and those that require some degree of subjective guesswork. Let's consider the objective items first.

The initial outlay is a relatively straightforward matter. The new machine will cost $150,000 less whatever proceeds come from the sale of the old one. The old machine has a market value of $45,000, but sale at that price will result in a taxable gain. The unit was originally purchased for $80,000 and is being depreciated straight line over eight years at $10,000 per year. It's now five years old, so the remaining book value is $30,000. The after-tax proceeds are calculated as follows ($000).

Sale price	$45.0	$45.0
Book value	$30.0	
Gain on sale	$15.0	
Tax @ 34%	$5.1	(5.1)
Net cash proceeds of sale		$39.9

The project's initial outlay is as follows.

Cost of new machine	$150.0
Less proceeds from sale of old machine	$ 39.9
Initial outlay	$110.1

Now we'll consider incremental cash flows during the five-year planning period. The straightforward items are the tax implications of a new depreciation pattern and the labor savings due to requiring one less operator.

Purchasing the new machine will alter the depreciation tax shield as follows ($000).

	Year				
	1	*2*	*3*	*4*	*5*
New depreciation	$30.0	$30.0	$30.0	$30.0	$30.0
Old depreciation	$10.0	$10.0	$10.0		
Net increase in depreciation	$20.0	$20.0	$20.0	$30.0	$30.0
Cash tax savings @ 34%	$6.8	$6.8	$6.8	$10.2	$10.2

The labor savings are just the cost of one employee.

	Year				
	1	*2*	*3*	*4*	*5*
Labor savings	$25.0	$25.0	$25.0	$25.0	$25.0

Now we have to deal with the subjective items in the estimate. Three effects have to be considered. These are the differences between the new machine and the old in maintenance expense, downtime, and product quality. Each clearly has a value, but it's hard to say how much.

It is at this stage of the analysis that the role of the financial analyst is most crucial. The people putting together the proposal to buy the new machine are likely to be very optimistic about the subjective benefits. It's the job of the finance department to be the voice of reason in the decision-making process, and to make sure that only realistic estimates of subjective benefits are included.

Let's consider the issues in this example one at a time. The most concrete is the maintenance cost. We have to forecast the *difference* in the cost of maintenance on the new machine if we buy it and maintenance on the old one if it is kept. Looking at the record, we can see that the old machine's cost increased steadily for several years, but has recently leveled off at about $45,000. The

● **Subjective benefits** based on opinions are hard to quantify and lead to biases when estimated by people who want project approval.

from the CFO

● The **financial analyst** should ensure that only **reasonable estimates** of unprovable benefits are used.

question is whether to assume it will stay there or resume its increase as the machine gets older. The new machine offers a one-year warranty and promises a cost of $15,000 a year thereafter. However, that figure is not guaranteed. The issue is whether to believe the $15,000 or assume a higher number. We'll lay out a set of maintenance cost figures that reflects maintenance on the old machine continuing at $45,000 and the new machine performing as promised.

	Year				
	1	2	3	4	5
Old machine	$45.0	$45.0	$45.0	$45.0	$45.0
New machine	In warranty	$15.0	$15.0	$15.0	$15.0
Savings	$45.0	$30.0	$30.0	$30.0	$30.0

The difference between the two maintenance estimates represents the cash savings due to replacing the machine. Notice that it's possible to manipulate the analysis by varying the assumptions about either or both estimates. If we want to make the project look good, we can assume the old machine's costs will get worse and the new one's will hold at $15,000. If we assume the new machine will cost more while the old one holds at $45,000, the project looks worse.

The point is that there's a great deal of latitude in the forecast, and reasonable estimates of the maintenance cost savings can vary by quite a bit. For purposes of the example, we'll use the one shown here.

Next let's look at the downtime estimate. Here two variables are considered: how much downtime will actually be saved by the new machine and how much each hour is worth. The questions involved in estimating the hours saved are similar to those in dealing with the maintenance cost. The old machine has been having about 130 hours of downtime a year, while the new one promises 30 for a saving of 100 hours. However, good arguments can be made for raising or lowering that figure by quite a bit. The compounding question, however, is how much an hour of saved downtime is worth. It clearly should have some value, but it's difficult to say how much. This is a very common problem. We know there's a cost or benefit to something, but we're not able to estimate its value with any precision.

from the **CFO**

Manufacturing management's subjective estimate of $500 is likely to be on the high side because of the biases we discussed earlier. *A conservative approach, on the other hand, might be to refuse to include anything in the analysis for the saved downtime because its value can't be documented. Anything in between is also possible.*

In situations like this, most people favor a middle of the road approach. That implies giving some value to the saved downtime, but choosing a value substantially lower than that recommended by manufacturing. In this case, $200 per hour is probably reasonable. Combining that figure with the saved time estimate of 100 hours yields an estimated cash flow savings of $20,000 per year.

Next we'll examine the most subjective claim in favor of the new machine, increased quality of output. Once again, this issue is very common when people are trying to justify a project. The issue isn't whether the output actually will be of higher quality. That should be ascertainable as a matter of fact by testing the output of a demo machine against the output of the old one. The question is whether an increase in the quality of certain component parts will significantly increase customer satisfaction, and whether that will translate into more future sales.

Several scenarios are possible. If customers or service technicians have been actively complaining about the parts from the old machine, it's easier to argue that higher quality will have a future sales impact than if the old parts weren't a problem. But even then, the impact is likely to be very difficult to estimate. As a general rule, when the connection between a project and the claimed cash flow impact is this tenuous, financial people tend to want to leave it out of the analysis. That's what we'll do in this case.

Now we can summarize the cash flows in the years after installation of the new machine.

	Year				
	1	2	3	4	5
Labor savings	$25.0	$25.0	$25.0	$25.0	$25.0
Maintenance savings	45.0	30.0	30.0	30.0	30.0
Downtime savings	20.0	20.0	20.0	20.0	20.0
Total	$90.0	$75.0	$75.0	$75.0	$75.0
Tax	30.6	25.5	25.5	25.5	25.5
Net after tax	$59.4	$49.5	$49.5	$49.5	$49.5
Tax savings on depreciation	6.8	6.8	6.8	10.2	10.2
Cash flow	$66.2	$56.3	$56.3	$59.7	$59.7

Combining these with the initial outlay yields the project's estimated cash flow stream.

C_0	C_1	C_2	C_3	C_4	C_5
($110.1)	$66.2	$56.3	$56.3	$59.7	$59.7

Ethics **Ethics in Cash Flow Estimation**

We've just seen that strong departmental interests can attach to capital budgeting decisions, and that wide ranges of inputs can be accepted in making those decisions. It's also true that people stretch the truth to get what they want. What are the ethical issues of knowingly providing biased information to a decision-making process to get an outcome that's favorable to your own department?

In answering, recall that in ethical situations one group often has power over another (page 17). Is information power? Who benefits and who gets hurt if the company buys the new machine in Example 10.2 based on manufacturing's claims if those claims are exaggerated beyond truth?

Here's another interesting situation. Imagine that an executive puts together a proposal for a new venture. It's common for the person proposing something like that to get to run the start-up. Then, if it's successful he or she moves up the management ladder rapidly and makes a lot of money. Do you see a motivation for the executive to overstate the project's benefits and understate its negatives? Is the executive's gamble one sided in that he or she has a lot to gain and little to lose? Who loses if the project is undertaken and fails?

DISCUSSION QUESTIONS

1. You are a new financial analyst at Belvedere Corp., a large manufacturing firm that is currently looking into diversification opportunities. The vice president of marketing is particularly interested in a venture that is only marginally connected with what the firm does now. Other managers have suggested enterprises in more closely related fields. The proponents of the various ideas have all provided you with business forecasts from which you have developed financial projections, including project cash flows. You have also calculated each project's IRR with the following results.

Project	IRR	Comments
A	19.67%	Marketing's project, an almost totally new field
B	19.25%	Proposed by manufacturing, also a very different field
C	18.05%	Proposed by engineering, a familiar field

You are now in a meeting with senior managers that was called to discuss the options. You have just presented your analysis, ending your talk with the preceding information.

After your presentation the vice president of marketing stands, congratulates you on a fine job, and states that the figures clearly show that project A is the best option. He also says that your financial analysis shows that project A has the full backing of the finance department. All eyes, including the CFO's, turn to you. How do you respond?

2. Most top executives are graded primarily on their results in terms of net income rather than net cash flow. Why, then, is capital budgeting done with incremental cash flows rather than with incremental net income?

3. The typical cash flow pattern for business projects involves cash outflows first, then inflows. However, it's possible to imagine a project in which the pattern is reversed. For example, we might receive inflows now in return for guaranteeing to make payments later. Would the payback, NPV, and IRR methods work for such a project? What would the NPV profile look like? Could the NPV and IRR methods give conflicting results?

4. Creighton Inc. is preparing a bid to sell a large telephone communications system to a major business customer. It is characteristic of the telephone business that the vendor selling a system gets substantial follow-on business in later years by making changes and alterations to that system. The marketing department wants to take an *incremental* approach to the bid, basically treating it as a capital budgeting project. They propose selling the system at or below its direct cost in labor and materials (the incremental cost) to ensure getting the follow-on business. They've projected the value of that business by treating future sales less direct costs as cash inflows

They maintain that the initial outlay is the direct cost to install the system, which is almost immediately paid back by the price. Future cash flows are then the net inflows from the follow-on sales. These calculations have led to an enormous NPV and IRR for the sale viewed as a project.

Both support and criticize this approach. (*Hint*: What would happen if Creighton did most of its business this way?)

5. Webley Motors, a manufacturer of small gas engines, has been working on a new design for several years. It's now considering going into the market with the new product, and has projected future sales and cash flows. The marketing and finance departments are putting together a joint presentation for the board of directors that they hope will gain approval for the new venture. Part of the presentation is a capital budgeting analysis of the project that includes only estimated future costs and revenues. Dan Eyeshade, the head of investor relations, insists that calculations shown to the board include the money spent on research in the past several years. He says that to ignore or omit those costs would be deceiving the board about the true cost of the project, which would be both unethical and legally dangerous. Comment on Dan's position. If you disagree, prepare an argument that will convince him to change his mind, and suggest an alternative presentation that will satisfy you both.

6. The Capricorn Company is launching a new venture in a field related to but separate from its present business. Management is proposing that financing for the new enterprise be supplied by a local bank, which it has approached for a loan. Capricorn's finance department has done a capital budgeting analysis of the venture, projecting reasonable cash flows and calculating an NPV and an IRR that both look very favorable.

The bank's loan officer, however, isn't satisfied with the analysis. She insists on seeing a financial projection that calculates interest on cumulative cash flows, incorporates that interest as a cost of the project, and shows the buildup and decline of the debt necessary to accomplish the proposal. She essentially wants a business plan complete with projected financial statements.

Reconcile the bank officer's position with capital budgeting theory.

7. Wilson Petroleum is a local distributor of home heating oil. The firm also installs and services furnaces and heating systems in homes and small commercial buildings. The customer service department maintains sales and service records on current customers, who number about 400. Detailed customer records are kept manually in file cabinets, and a small computer system holds all customer names and addresses for mailing and billing purposes. One full-time clerk maintains all the records and handles all billing and customer inquiries. Customers occasionally complain if delivery or service is late, but only one or two mild complaints are received each month. Delays are primarily a result of problems in the field rather than problems in assigning calls in the service department.

A consultant has proposed a new computer system that will completely automate the customer service function. It will provide on-line billing and immediate access to all customer records. The cost of the proposed system is $50,000 initially plus about $7,000 a year for maintenance and support. It will still take a person to run it. The consultant says the new system will provide faster service and superior insight into the needs of the customer base, which will result in better customer relations and more sales in the long run.

Discuss the pros and cons of the consultant's proposal. What further justification should management demand before buying? Could the consultant have made the proposal for reasons that aren't in Wilson's best interest? Could the consultant be well meaning yet biased? Explain.

PROBLEMS

1. A project that is expected to last six years will generate a profit and cash flow contribution before taxes and depreciation of $23,000 per year. It requires the initial purchase of equipment costing $60,000, which will be depreciated over four years. The relevant tax rate is 25%. Calculate the project's cash flows. Round all figures within your computations to the nearest thousand dollars.

2. Flextech Inc. is considering a project that will require new equipment costing $150,000. It will replace old equipment with a book value of $35,000 that can be sold on the secondhand market for $75,000. The company's marginal tax rate is 35%. Calculate the project's initial outlay.

3. Tomatoes Inc. is planning a project that involves machinery purchases of $100,000. The new equipment will be depreciated over five years straight line. It will replace old machinery that will be sold for an estimated $36,000 and has a book value of $22,000. The project will also require hiring and training ten new people at a cost of about $12,000 each. All of this must happen before the project is actually started. The firm's marginal tax rate is 40%. Calculate, C_0, the project's initial cash outlay.

4. A four-year project has cash flows before taxes and depreciation of $12,000 per year. The project requires the purchase of a $50,000 asset that will be depreciated over five years straight line. At the end of the fourth year the asset will be sold for $18,000. The firm's marginal tax rate is 35%. Calculate the cash flows associated with the project.

5. Harry and Flo Simone are planning to start a restaurant. Stoves, refrigerators, other kitchen equipment, and furniture are expected to cost $50,000, all of which will be depreciated straight line over five years. Construction and other costs of getting started will be $30,000. The Simones expect the following revenue stream. ($000)

Year	1	2	3	4	5	6	7
Sales	$60	$90	$140	$160	$180	$200	$200

Food costs are expected to be 35% of revenues, while other variable expenses are forecast at 25% of revenues. Fixed overhead will be $40,000 per year. All operating expenses will be paid in cash, revenues will be collected immediately, and inventory is negligible, so working capital need not be considered. Assume the combined state and federal tax rate is 25%. Do not assume a tax credit in loss years, and ignore tax loss carry forwards. (Taxes are simply zero when EBT is a loss.) Develop a cash flow forecast for the Simones' restaurant.

6. The Leventhal Baking Company is thinking of expanding its operations into a new line of pastries. The firm expects to sell $350,000 of the new product in the first year and $500,000 each year thereafter. Direct costs including labor and materials will be 60% of sales. Indirect incremental costs are estimated at $40,000 a year. The project will require several new ovens that will cost a total of $500,000 and be depreciated straight line over five years. The current plant is underutilized, so space is available that cannot be otherwise sold or rented. The firm's marginal tax rate is 35% and its cost of capital is 12%. Assume revenue is collected immediately and inventory is bought and paid for every day, so no additional working capital is required.

a. Prepare a statement showing the incremental cash flows for this project over an eight-year period.

b. Calculate the payback period, NPV, and PI.

c. Recommend either acceptance or rejection.

d. If the space to be used could otherwise be rented out for $30,000 a year, how would you put that fact into the calculation? Would the project be acceptable in that case?

7. The Catseye Marble Co. is thinking of replacing a manual production process with a machine. The manual process requires three relatively unskilled workers and a supervisor. Each worker makes $17,500 a year and the supervisor earns $24,500. The new machine can be run with only one skilled operator who will earn $41,000. Payroll taxes and fringe benefits are an additional third of all wages and salaries.

The machine costs $150,000 and has a tax depreciation life of five years. Catseye elects straight-line depreciation for tax purposes. A service contract covers all maintenance for $5,000 a year. The machine is expected to last six years, at which time it will have no salvage value. The machine's output will be virtually indistinguishable from that of the manual process in both quality and quantity. There are no other operating differences between the manual and the machine processes. Catseye's marginal tax rate is 35%, and its cost of capital is 10%.

a. Calculate the incremental cash flows associated with the project to acquire the machine.

b. Calculate the project's payback and NPV. Would you accept or reject the project?

c. Suppose there is no alternative but to lay off the displaced employees, and the cost of severance is about three months' wages. How would you factor this information into the analysis? Does it change the project's acceptability?

d. How would you characterize this project's risk?

8. Blackstone Inc. manufactures western boots and saddles. The company is considering replacing an outmoded leather processing machine with a new, more efficient model. The old machine was purchased for $48,000 six years ago and was expected to have an eight-year life. It has been depreciated on a straight-line basis (ignore partial year conventions). The used machine has an estimated market value of $15,323. The new machine will cost $60,000 and will be depreciated straight line over five years. All depreciation assumes zero salvage.

The new machine is expected to last eight years (its economic life), and then will have to be replaced. Assume it has no actual salvage value at that time.

Assume Blackstone's marginal tax rate is 35%.

Operating cost savings are summarized as follows.

	Old	**New**
Annual maintenance cost	$2,000 increasing $200 in each future year	None for two years, $1,500 thereafter
Cost of fixing production defects	$3,000	$1,000
Operators	2 @ $20,000	1.5 @ $24,000

The shop foreman feels the new machine will produce a higher quality output and thus affect customer satisfaction and repeat sales. He thinks that benefit should be worth at least $5,000 a year, but doesn't have a way to document the figure.

a. Calculate the relatively certain incremental cash flows associated with the new machine over its projected economic life of eight years and the NPV at a cost of capital of 12% based on those cash flows. (Round to whole $.)

b. Suppose the foreman's $5,000 quality improvement estimate were to be included. How big an impact would it have in relation to the other numbers? Comment.

9. The Ebitts Field Corp. manufactures baseball gloves. Charlie Botz, the company's top salesman, has recommended expanding into the baseball bat business. He has put together a project proposal including the following information in support of his idea.

■ New production equipment will cost $75,000 and will be depreciated straight line over five years.

■ Overheads and expenses associated with the project are estimated at $20,000 per year during the first two years and $40,000 per year thereafter.

■ There is enough unused space in the factory for the bat project. The space has no alternative use or value.

■ Setting up production and establishing distribution channels before getting started will cost $300,000 (tax deductible).

■ Aluminum and wood bats will be produced and sold to sporting goods retailers. Wholesale prices and incremental costs per unit (direct labor and materials) are as follows.

	Aluminum	**Wood**
Price	$18	$12
Cost	11	9
Gross margin	$ 7	$ 3

■ Charlie provides the following unit sales forecast (000).

	Year					
	1	2	3	4	5	6
Aluminum	6	9	15	18	20	22
Wood	8	12	14	20	22	24

The sixth year sales level is expected to hold indefinitely.

- Receivables will be collected in 30 days, inventories will be the cost of one month's production, and payables are expected to be half of inventories. Assume no additional cash in the bank or accruals are necessary. (Use ¹⁄₁₂ of the current year's revenue and cost for receivables and inventories.)
- Ebitts Field's marginal tax rate is 35% and its cost of capital is 12%.

a. Develop a six-year cash flow estimate for Charlie's proposal. Work to the nearest $1,000.

b. Calculate the payback period for the project.

c. Calculate the project's NPV assuming a six-year life. Is the project acceptable?

d. Is the cost of capital an appropriate discount rate for the project considering its likely risk relative to that of the rest of the business? Why?

e. What is the project's NPV if the planning horizon is extended to eight years? (Add the incremental PV from two more years at year 6's cash flow.)

f. What is the NPV if management is willing to look at an indefinitely long time horizon? (*Hint:* Think of the cash flows in year 6 and beyond as a perpetuity.)

g. Comment on the results of parts e and f.

10. Segwick Corp. manufactures men's shoes, which it sells through its own chain of retail stores. The firm is considering adding a line of women's shoes. Management considers the project a new venture because there are substantial differences in marketing and manufacturing processes between men's and women's footwear.

The project will involve setting up a manufacturing facility as well as expanding or modifying the retail stores to carry two products. The stores are leased, so modification will involve leasing larger spaces, installing new leasehold improvements, and writing off some old leasehold improvements.[1]

The expected costs are summarized as follows.

Asset Items

New manufacturing equipment, depreciated over five years (straight line)	$ 750,000
Acquisition of a facility for design and manufacturing	
Land (no deprec)	$ 480,000
Building (Note: use 31.5 yrs deprec)	$ 630,000
	$1,110,000
Leased retail space	
Net new lease expense, per year	$40,000
New leasehold improvements depreciated over the next five years (straight line)	200,000
Write off of old improvements	90,000
Depreciation reduction due to written off improvements per year for three more years	30,000

---

1. Leasehold improvements are assets added to leased premises by the tenant. They are generally depreciated over the remaining life of the lease.

Expense Items

Cost of hiring and training new people.............................	$150,000
Initial advertising and promotion...	200,000
Yearly advertising and promotion.......................................	50,000
Yearly sales salaries	900,000
Additional corporate overhead ($000/yr)	$20, $42, $60,
	$80, $80, $80

Revenue and Cost

The unit sales forecast is as follows in thousands.

Year	Units	Average Price
1	30	$65
2	40	68
3	50	70
4 and on	60	75

Direct cost excluding depreciation is 40% of sales

Working Capital

Sales are to retail customers who pay with checks or credit cards. It takes about 10 days to clear both of these and actually receive cash.

Inventories are estimated to be approximately the direct cost of two months' sales.

Payables are estimated as one quarter of inventories.

Estimate the current accounts based on the current year's sales and cost levels.

Assume incremental cash is required equal to 2% of revenues.

Accruals are insignificant.

Other Items

Management expects a few of the company's current male customers to be lost because they won't want to shop in a store that doesn't exclusively sell men's shoes. The gross margin impact of these lost sales is estimated to be $60,000 per year.

The company has already purchased designs for certain styles of ladies' shoes for $60,000.

Segwick's cost of capital is 10%. Its marginal tax rate is 35%.

a. Develop a six-year forecast of after-tax cash flows for Segwick.

b. Calculate the project's payback period, NPV, IRR, and PI, and make a recommendation about acceptance.

> [**Preview:** In Chapter 11 we'll learn that a project's risk *should* be a factor in capital budgeting decisions, and that risker projects *should* be less acceptable. One approach to adjusting for risk is using a discount rate that's higher than the cost of captial in evaluating risky projects, which makes them less likely to be accepted. But selecting the *risk adjusted rate* is difficult. An approach available when the project is a new business is using the required rate of return offered by the Captial Asset Pricing Model (the SML, page 278) for a company already in that business.]

c. Assume you are told that the men's shoe industry is very stable, being served by the same manufacturers year after year. However, firms enter and leave the ladies' shoe business regularly.

1. Would this knowledge make you more or less comfortable with the analysis you've done of this project? Why?

2. How and why does the information affect the appropriateness of using the cost of capital in the analysis?

3. Suppose you know of a company that makes only ladies' shoes and its beta is 2.0. If treasury bills are paying 6% and an average stock investment earns 10%, what rate might be more appropriate than the cost of capital for the analysis of this problem?

 Internet Problem

11. Do a cash flow sensitivity analysis on some problems of your choice at the end of the chapter. (You can download the spreadsheet template for Microsoft Excel on this web page.) The spreadsheet template can be customized to meet your needs. For additional information, click on the link for some cash flow what ifs.

http://www.toolkit.cch.com/tools/cfsens_m.asp

COMPUTER PROBLEMS

 12. The Paxton Homes Co. is a successful builder of moderate to high-priced houses. The firm is currently considering an expansion into light commercial construction in which it would build shopping centers and small office buildings. Management considers the idea a new venture because of the major differences between commercial and residential construction.

Getting into the new line of business will require an investment of $12.5M in equipment and $3M in expenses. The equipment will be depreciated over five years. Part of the start-up money will come from the sale of some old trucks and cranes. These have a total market value of $1.8M and an NBV of $600K. Selling the equipment will result in a depreciation reduction of $200K per year for three years.

Revenue from the commercial line is expected to be $6M in the first year and to grow by $2M in each succeeding year until it reaches $20M. After that, growth is uncertain and may be anywhere from 0% to 6% per year. Costs and expenses, including incremental overhead, will be 110% of revenues in the first year, 85% in the next two years, and 70% thereafter. Economies of scale in materials purchasing are expected to save the residential business about $250K per year but not until the fourth year. Net working capital requirements are estimated at 10% of revenue. The combined federal and state tax rate on the incremental business will be 40%. Losses can be offset against other profits and can therefore be viewed as earning a tax credit at the same rate. Paxton's cost of capital is 12%.

You are a financial analyst assigned to evaluate the commercial construction proposal. Use the CAPBUD program to analyze the project and prepare a presentation in which you will make a recommendation either favoring or opposing its undertaking. Here are some ideas for approaches to your presentation.

a. Establish a base case using the information given. Forecast into the future until the numbers stop changing (eight years). Assume a terminal value based on a continuation of the eighth year's cash flows with no further growth. Is the project acceptable based on NPV and IRR given these assumptions?

b. Test the sensitivity of the base case analysis to the terminal value assumption by varying the growth rate to 3% and 6%.

   1) Comment on the difference the terminal growth rate assumption makes.

   2) Construction is a cyclical industry in that it is very subject to the ups and downs of the economy. In good times growth is enormous, but in bad times the industry and the firms in it shrink rapidly. Given that fact, how do you feel about the terminal value assumption?

   3) Evaluate the project's NPV and IRR assuming a 10-year planning horizon—that is, assuming zero cash flows after the tenth year. Does this approach make more or less sense to you than the terminal value assumptions used in part a?

c. Test the sensitivity of the analysis to changes in revenue growth. For example, suppose revenue grows by only $1M per year instead of two until the eighth year. Is the project a good idea then? What if cost/expense is a higher percentage of revenue than anticipated?

CHAPTER 11

Risk Topics and Real Options in Capital Budgeting

Chapter Outline

RISK IN CAPITAL BUDGETING—GENERAL CONSIDERATIONS

http://

See how the U.S. Department of Agriculture assesses the costs and benefits of USDA policies at

• www.usda.gov/agency/oce/oracba/

In our discussions in the last chapter, we emphasized the idea that cash flow estimates are subject to a good deal of error. Different people will make different estimates of the same thing, and actual flows are apt to vary substantially from anybody's estimates. A more concise way to put the same thing is just to say that cash flow estimates are *risky*.

In recent years the subject of risk has been given great attention in financial theory, especially in the area of portfolio theory (Chapter 8). In this section we'll take a look at some attempts that have been made to incorporate risk into capital budgeting, including one approach that applies portfolio theory methods to capital budgeting problems.

CASH FLOWS AS RANDOM VARIABLES

In everyday usage the term "risk" is associated with the probability that something bad will happen. In financial theory, however, we associate risk with random variables

FIGURE 11.1

The Probability Distribution of a Future Cash Flow as a Random Variable

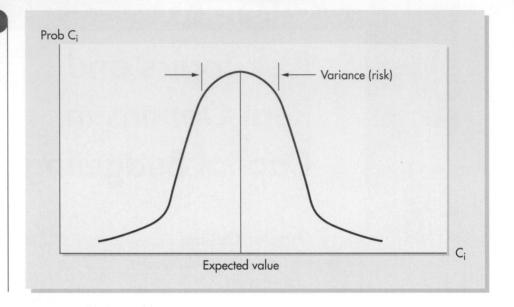

and their probability distributions. Risk is the chance that a random variable will take a value significantly different from the one we expect, regardless of whether the deviation is favorable or unfavorable. In terms of a probability distribution, the value we expect is the mean (expected value), and the chance that an observation will be significantly different from the mean is related to the variance.

Recall that in portfolio theory (Chapter 8) the return on an investment is viewed as a random variable with an associated probability distribution, and risk is defined as the variance or standard deviation of that distribution. The risk inherent in estimated cash flows can be defined in a similar way. Each future cash flow can be thought of as a separate random variable with its own probability distribution. In each case, the risk associated with the flow is related to the variance of the distribution. The idea is illustrated in Figure 11.1.

● In capital budgeting the **estimate** of each future period's **cash flow** is a **random variable.**

When cash flows are viewed like this, the NPVs and IRRs of projects are also random variables with their own probability distributions. That's because they're calculated as functions of the various cash flows, which are random variables themselves. The idea is conceptually illustrated in Figure 11.2.

● The **NPV** and **IRR** of any project are **random variables** with expected values and variances that reflect **risk.**

This view makes explicit the idea that estimated cash flows as well as the resulting NPVs and IRRs have most likely (expected, mean) values, but will probably turn out to be somewhat different from those values. The amount by which the actual value is likely to differ from the expected value is related to the distribution's variance or standard deviation, which can be visualized intuitively as the width of the bell-shaped curve.

● THE IMPORTANCE OF RISK IN CAPITAL BUDGETING

Up until now we've thought of each cash flow as a *point estimate.* That's a single number rather than a range of possibilities with a probability distribution attached. When we do that, we're computing NPVs and IRRs that are also point estimates, and ignoring the possibility that the true NPV or IRR could turn out to be higher or lower. That means there's a good chance we'll be making *wrong decisions* by using NPVs and IRRs that come from risky cash flow estimates.

FIGURE 11.2   **Risk in Estimated Cash Flows**

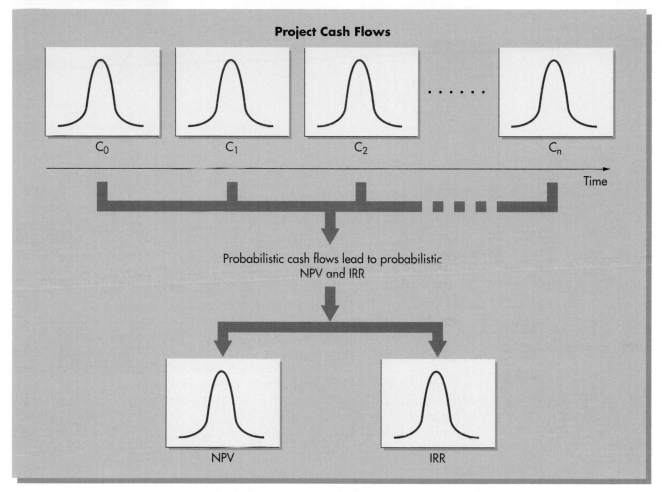

For example, suppose we're making a capital investment decision between two projects with NPVs that look like those shown in Figure 11.3. Notice that NPV_B has a higher expected value than NPV_A, but is also more risky. The capital budgeting techniques we considered in the last chapter will invariably choose project B over project A, because it has a higher expected NPV and the methods ignore project risk. But there's a good chance that project B's NPV (and IRR) will actually turn out to be less than project A's, perhaps by quite a bit. If that happens we will have made the wrong decision at a potential cost of millions.

Risk Aversion

The principle of risk aversion applies to capital budgeting just as it does to investing in portfolio theory. All other things equal, we prefer less risky capital projects to those with more risk.

To make the point plainer, imagine that projects A and B have exactly the same expected NPV. The NPV technique would be indifferent between them, yet any rational manager would prefer the one with the lower risk.

FIGURE 11.3

Project NPVs Reflecting Risky Cash Flows

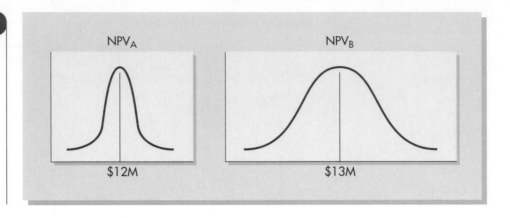

Changing the Nature of the Company

Another dimension to the risk issue goes beyond individual projects and relates to the fundamental nature of the firm as an investment. Companies are characterized by investors largely in terms of risk. That was the point of our study of portfolio theory in Chapter 8. When people buy stocks and bonds, expected returns matter, but risk matters just as much.

In capital budgeting we think of projects as incremental to the normal business of the firm. We view them as sort of *stuck onto* the larger body of what goes on every day. Yet every project affects the totality of the company, just as every stock added to a portfolio changes the nature of that portfolio. In the long run, a company is no more than a collection of all the projects it has undertaken that are still going on. In a very real sense, *a company is a portfolio of projects.*

Hence if a firm takes on new projects without regard for risk, it's in danger of changing its fundamental nature as perceived by investors. A firm that starts to adopt riskier projects than it has in the past will slowly become a riskier company. The higher risk will be reflected in a more volatile movement of the firm's return, which in turn will result in a higher beta. And that higher beta can generally be expected to have a negative impact on the price of the company's stock.

We can conclude that some consideration of risk *should* be included in project analysis. If it isn't, the full impact of projects simply isn't understood at the time they're chosen and implemented.

● **Ignoring risk** in capital budgeting can lead to **incorrect decisions** and **change the risk character** of the firm.

INCORPORATING RISK INTO CAPITAL BUDGETING— NUMERICAL AND COMPUTER METHODS

Once the idea that risk *should* be incorporated in the capital budgeting process is accepted, the question of *how* to do it has to be addressed. Considering the capital budgeting techniques we studied in the last chapter, it's not at all obvious how we ought to go about factoring in risk-related ideas.

Quite a bit of thought has been given to the subject and several approaches have been developed. We'll look at some numerical methods and then examine a more theoretical approach.

● SCENARIO/SENSITIVITY ANALYSIS

The fundamental idea behind risk in capital budgeting is that cash flows aren't likely to turn out exactly as estimated. Therefore actual NPVs and IRRs are likely to be different from those based on estimated cash flows. The management question is just *how much* an NPV or an IRR will change given some deviation in cash flows. A good idea of the relationship between the two changes can be gotten by using a procedure called scenario analysis.

In the following discussion we'll refer only to NPV, understanding that the comments apply also to IRR or to any capital budgeting technique.

Suppose a project is represented by a number of estimated future cash flows, each of which can actually take a range of values around the estimate. Also suppose we have an idea of what the best, worst, and most likely values of each cash flow are. Graphically the idea involves a picture like this for *each* cash flow.

The most likely value of each cash flow is the estimate we've been working with up until now, sometimes called a *point estimate.*

If we calculate the project's NPV by using the most likely value of each cash flow, we generally get the most likely NPV for the project. If we do the calculation with the worst possible value of each C_i, we'll get the worst possible NPV. Similarly, we'll get the best NPV if we use all the best cash flows. Notice that we can calculate an NPV with *any* combination of cash flows. That is, we could pick a worst case for C_1, a best case for C_2, something in between for C_3, and so on. All we have to do to calculate an NPV is to choose one value for each cash flow.

Every time we choose a value for each of the project's cash flows, we define what is called a *scenario,* one of the many possible outcomes of the project. When we calculate the NPV of several scenarios we're performing a **scenario analysis.**

This procedure results in a range of values for NPV along with a good estimate of the most likely value. But it doesn't give a very good notion of the probability of various values within the range. We can choose as many scenarios as we like, however, by selecting any number of different sets of outcomes for the cash flows. Evaluating a number of scenarios gives a subjective feel for the variability of the NPV to changes in our assumptions about what the cash flows will turn out to be.

EXAMPLE 11.1

Project A has an initial outflow of $1,400 and three variable cash inflows defined as follows.

	C_1	C_2	C_3
Worst case	$450	$400	$700
Most likely	550	450	800
Best case	650	500	900

Analyze project A's NPV.

Solution: The worst possible NPV will result if the three lowest cash flows all occur. Assume the cost of capital is 9%. Then the worst NPV is

$$NPV = -\$1,400 + \$450[PVF_{9,1}] + \$400[PVF_{9,2}] + \$700[PVF_{9,3}]$$

$$= -\$1,400 + \$450[.9174] + \$400[.8417] + \$700[.7722]$$

$$= -\$109.95 \ .$$

Similar calculations lead to a best case scenario with an NPV of $312.14, and an NPV of $101.10 for the scenario involving the most likely cash flow for every C_i, which is the project's traditional NPV.

Now suppose management feels pretty good about the estimates in the first two years, but is uncomfortable with the high cash flow numbers forecast for year 3. They essentially want to know what will happen to the traditional NPV if year 3 turns out badly.

To answer that question, we form a scenario including the most likely flows from years 1 and 2 and the worst case from year 3. Verify that the NPV from that scenario is $23.88. Notice that management's concern is well founded, as a worst case in the third year alone yields a marginally positive NPV.

● **Scenario/sensitivity** analysis selects worst, middle, and best outcomes for each cash flow and computes **NPV for a variety** of combinations.

Another name for essentially the same process is **sensitivity analysis**. That is, we investigate the *sensitivity* of the traditionally calculated NPV to changes in the C_i. In the last part of the last example we saw that a change of $100 in the year 3 cash flow led to a change of ($101.10 − $23.88 =) $77.22 in the project's NPV. In other words, the NPV changed by about 77% of the change in year 3 cash flow. The mathematically astute will recognize that in this simple example 77% is just the present value factor for 9% and three years.

● COMPUTER (MONTE CARLO) SIMULATION

The power of the computer can help to incorporate risk into capital budgeting through a technique called *Monte Carlo* simulation. The term "Monte Carlo" implies that the approach involves the use of numbers drawn randomly from probability distributions.

Figure 11.2 intuitively suggests the approach. Reexamine that illustration on page 357. Notice that each cash flow is itself a random variable with a probability distribution, and that they combine to create the probability distributions of the project's NPV (and IRR).

Monte Carlo simulation involves making assumptions that specify the shapes of the probability distributions for *each* future cash flow in a capital budgeting project. These assumed distributions are put into a computer model so that random observations[1] can be drawn from each.[2]

---

1. In this context, the term "observation" refers to a number drawn from a probability distribution or to the result of calculations made from such numbers.
2. In more detailed models, a probability distribution can be assumed for *each* of the elements that *goes into* the periodic cash flow estimates. For example, if period cash flows are the difference between revenue and cost, one might specify distributions for both, and calculate cash flow as the difference between an observation on revenue and one on cost.

Once all the probability distributions are specified, the computer simulates the project by drawing one observation from the distribution of each cash flow. Having those, it calculates the project's NPV and records the resulting value. Then it draws a new set of random observations for each of the cash flows, discards the old set, and calculates and records another value for NPV. Notice that the second NPV will probably be different from the first because it is based on a different set of randomly drawn cash flows.

The computer goes through this process many times, generating a thousand or more values (observations) for NPV. The calculated values are sorted into ranges and displayed as histograms reflecting the number of observations in each range. Figure 11.4 is a sample of the resulting display, where the numbers along the horizontal axis represent the centers of ranges of values for the calculated NPVs. For example, the value of 600 over the NPV value of $100 means that 600 simulation calculations resulted in NPVs between $50 and $150.

If the height of each column is restated as a percentage of the total number of observations, the histogram becomes a good approximation of the probability distribution of the project's NPV *given the assumptions made about the distributions of the individual cash flows.*

● **Simulation** models cash flows as random variables and **repeatedly calculates NPV,** building its distribution.

Armed with this risk-related information, managers can make better choices among projects. For example, look back at Figure 11.3 on page 358. Simulation would give us approximations of the shapes of the distributions shown, as well as the most likely values of NPV. In the case illustrated, decision makers might well choose project A over project B in spite of B's NPV advantage because of A's lower risk.

Drawbacks

Using the simulation approach has a few drawbacks. An obvious problem is that the probability distributions of the cash flows have to be estimated subjectively. This can be difficult. However, it's always easier to estimate a distribution for a

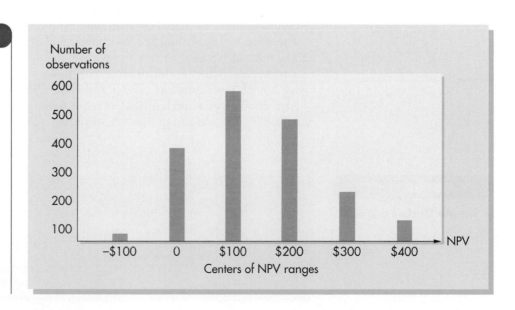

FIGURE 11.4

Results of Monte Carlo Simulation for NPV

simple element of a problem, like a single cash flow, than for a more complex element, like the final NPV or IRR.

A related issue is that the distributions of the individual cash flows generally aren't independent. Project cash flows tend to be positively *correlated* so that if early flows are low, later flows are also likely to be low. Unfortunately, it's hard to estimate the extent of that correlation.

Another problem is the interpretation of the simulated probability distributions. There aren't any decision rules for choosing among projects with respect to risk. Just how much risk is too much or how much variance is needed to overcome a certain NPV advantage isn't written down anywhere. Such judgments are subjective, and depend on the wisdom and experience of the decision makers.

In spite of these problems, simulation can be a relatively practical approach to incorporating risk into capital budgeting analyses.

●DECISION TREE ANALYSIS

● A **decision tree** is a graphic representation of a business project in which events have multiple outcomes each of which is assigned a probability.

We made the point earlier (page 359) that scenario analysis gives us a feel for the possible variation in NPV (and IRR) in a capital budgeting project, but doesn't tell us much about the probability distribution of the NPV outcome. Decision tree analysis lets us approximate the NPV distribution if we can estimate the probability of certain events within the project. A decision tree is essentially an expanded time line that "branches" into alternate paths wherever an event can turn out in more than one way.

For example, suppose a capital budgeting project involves some engineering work with an uncertain outcome that won't be completed until operations have been underway for a year. If the engineering turns out well, subsequent cash flows will be higher than if it doesn't. The situation is captured in the decision tree diagram shown in Figure 11.5.

The project starts with initial outlay, C_0 followed by cash flow C_1, but after that there are two possibilities depending on the success of the engineering work. Each of the two possible outcomes is represented by a *branch* of the decision tree. The place at which the branches separate is called a *node,* and is commonly shown as a small numbered circle to help keep track of complex projects.

The estimated probability that a branch will occur is indicated (P_1, P_2) just after the node at which it starts. In this case, the upper branch represents an engineering success, which results in high cash flows indicated by C_{2-Hi}, C_{3-Hi}. . . . The lower branch represents less success and lower cash flows C_{2-Lo}, C_{3-Lo}. . . .

Any number of branches can emanate from a node, but their probabilities must sum to 1.0, indicating that one of the branches must be taken.

FIGURE 11.5

A Simple Decision Tree

A *path* through the tree starts on the left at C_0 and progresses through node 1 along one branch or the other. There are obviously just two possible paths in Figure 11.5. An overall NPV outcome is associated with each path. In this case, the more favorable outcome is along the upper path and has cash flows C_0, C_1, $C_{2\text{-Hi}}$, $C_{3\text{-Hi}} \cdots$, while the less favorable lower path has cash flows C_0, C_1, $C_{2\text{-Lo}}$, $C_{3\text{-Lo}} \cdots$

● A **probability distribution** of a project's **NPV** can be developed using **decision tree** analysis.

Evaluating a project involves calculating NPVs along all possible paths and associating each with a probability. From that a probability distribution for NPV can be developed. The technique is best understood through an example. (We're working with NPV, but everything we say is equally applicable to IRR. Read the following example carefully; we will build on it throughout the rest of this section and the next.)

EXAMPLE 11.2

The Wing Foot Shoe Company is considering a three-year project to market a running shoe based on new technology. Success depends on how well consumers accept the new idea and demand the product. Demand can vary from great to terrible, but for planning purposes management has collapsed that variation into just two possibilities: good and poor. A market study indicates a 60% probability that demand will be good and a 40% chance that it will be poor.

It will cost $5M to bring the new shoe to market. Cash flow estimates indicate inflows of $3M per year for three years *at full manufacturing capacity* if demand is good, but just $1.5M per year if it's poor. Wing Foot's cost of capital is 10%. Analyze the project and develop a rough probability distribution for NPV.

Solution: First draw a decision tree diagram for the project ($000).

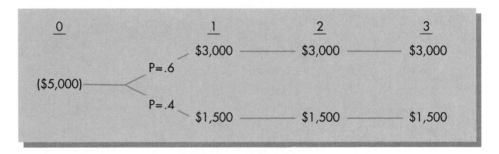

Next calculate the NPV along each path, using equation 9.3 (page 314), which we'll repeat here for convenience ($000).

(9.3) $$NPV = C_0 + C[PVFA_{k,n}]$$

Good consumer demand:

$$NPV = -\$5,000 + \$3,000[PVFA_{10,3}]$$

$$NPV = -\$5,000 + \$3,000(2.4869)$$

$$NPV = -\$5,000 + \$7,461$$

$$NPV = \$2,461$$

Poor consumer demand:

$$NPV = -\$5,000 + \$1,500(2.4869)$$
$$NPV = -\$5,000 + \$3,730$$
$$NPV = -\$1,270$$

Notice that we now have the elements of a probability distribution for the project's NPV. We know there's a 60% chance of an NPV of $2,461,000 along the upper path and a 40% chance of an NPV of $-$1,270,000$ along the lower path.

The expected NPV (the mean or expected value of the probability distribution of values for NPV) is calculated by multiplying every possible NPV by its probability and summing the results ($000). (See the review of statistics at the beginning of Chapter 8 if necessary, especially the calculation on page 256.)

Demand	NPV	Probability	Product
Good	$2,641	.60	$1,585
Poor	($1,270)	.40	(508)
		Expected NPV =	$1,077

Summarizing, we can say that the project's most likely NPV outcome is approximately $1.1M, and that there's a good chance (60%) of making about $2.6M, *but* there's also a substantial chance (40%) of losing about $1.3M.

Notice that Wing Foot's management gets a much better idea of the new running shoe project's risk from this analysis than it would from a projection of a single value of $1.1M for NPV. The decision tree result explicitly calls out the fact that a big loss is quite possible. That information is important because a loss of that size could ruin a small company. It could also damage the reputation of whoever is recommending the project.

The analysis also shows that if things turn out well, the reward for bearing the risk will probably be about half the size of the initial investment. That's also an important observation, because people are less likely to take substantial risks for modest returns than for outcomes that multiply their investment many times over.

The end result of the analysis in this case might well be a rejection of the project on the basis of risk even though the expected NPV is positive.

More Complex Decision Trees and Conditional Probabilities

Most processes represented by decision trees involve more than one uncertain event that can be characterized by probabilities. Each such event is represented by a node from which two or more new branches emerge, and the tree widens quickly toward the right. A typical tree is illustrated in Figure 11.6.

Notice that there are additional nodes along the branches that emanate from node 1, each splitting the original branch into two or three more. In this diagram there are five paths from left to right through the tree. Each starts at C_0 and ends along one of the branches on the far right. Each path has an NPV calculated using all of the cash flows along that path.

FIGURE 11.6

A More Complex Decision Tree

● The **probabilities emerging** from any decision tree **node** must **sum to 1.0.**

The probability of a path is the product of all of the branch probabilities along it. These are known as *conditional* probabilities, meaning that the probabilities coming out of node 2 are conditional on the upper branch out of node 1 happening.[3] Keep in mind that the probabilities out of each node must sum to 1.0. For example, $P_1 + P_2 = 1.0$ and $P_3 + P_4 + P_5 = 1.0$.

EXAMPLE 11.3

The Wing Foot Shoe Company of Example 11.2 has refined its market study and has some additional information about potential customer acceptance of the new product. Management now feels that there are two possibilities along the upper branch. Consumer response can be good, or it may be excellent. The study indicates that *if* demand is good during the first year, there's a 30% chance it will grow and be excellent in the second and third years. Of course, this also means there's a 70% chance demand in years 2 and 3 won't change.

If consumer response to the product turns out to be excellent, an additional investment of $1M in a factory expansion will allow the firm to make and sell enough product to generate cash inflows of $5M rather than $3M in both years 2 and 3. Hence the net cash inflows for the project will be ($5M − $1M =) $4M in year 2 and $5M in year 3. (The expansion is necessary to achieve the better financial results because Example 11.2 stated that the factory was at capacity along the upper path.) A decision tree for the project with this additional possibility is as follows.

3. The probability of a path is also called the *joint* probability of the individual branches along it.

The probabilities coming out of node 2 are conditional probabilities, meaning that they exist only along the good demand path. In other words, they are *conditional upon* good demand happening out of node 1, which itself has a probability of .6. The probability of arriving at the end of any path through the decision tree is calculated by multiplying all of the probabilities along the path. Hence the probability of the upper path is (.6 × .3 =) .18, the middle path is (.6 × .7 =) .42, and the lower path is just .40 as it was before. It's important to notice that these probabilities sum to 1.0, indicating that all possible outcomes are achieved by routes through the tree.

The NPV along each path is calculated in the traditional manner using all of the cash flows along the path. The middle and lower paths have the same cash flows as the paths in Example 11.2, so we've already calculated those NPVs. The NPV for the new upper path is just a series of three amount calculations added to the initial outlay ($000).

$$NPV = -\$5,000 + \$3,000[PVF_{10,1}] + \$4,000[PVF_{10,2}] + \$5,000[PVF_{10,3}]$$

$$= -\$5,000 + \$3,000(.9091) + \$4,000(.8264) + \$5,000(.7513)$$

$$= -\$5,000 + \$2,727 + \$3,306 + \$3,757$$

$$= \$4,790$$

Then the probability distribution for the project and the calculation of the expected return are as follows.

Acceptance	NPV	Probability	Product
Excellent	$4,790	.18	$ 862
Good	$2,641	.42	1,109
Poor	($1,270)	.40	(508)
		Expected NPV =	$1,463

The distribution is shown graphically here.

● Probabilities out of later nodes are **conditional** upon the outcome of earlier nodes along the same path.

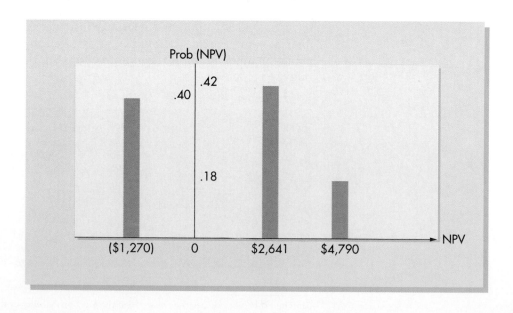

Once again it's important to notice how much more information is available through decision tree analysis than would be from a single point estimate of NPV. In this case the additional information tells us there's a fairly good chance (18%) of doing very well on the project. But there's still a substantial chance (40%) of losing money. As in Example 11.2 that outcome could be ruinous, and a prudent management might avoid it even though the expected value of the NPV is somewhat more positive than before.

REAL OPTIONS

An option is the ability or right to take a certain course of action, which in business situations generally leads to a financially favorable result.

● A **real option** is a course of action that **can be made available,** usually at a cost, which **improves financial results** under certain conditions.

Here's an example. Suppose a business sells sports apparel in a shopping mall, and specializes in jackets and sweatshirts bearing the insignia of professional football teams. Also suppose the business depends on bank credit to support routine operations, meaning it generally needs to have a loan outstanding just to keep going.[4] Assume its typical loan is $1M. Now suppose the local pro football team has a chance at the Super Bowl this year. If they make it, the demand for football jackets will double, and the business will need $2M in bank credit. But if the extra credit isn't available, the additional sales will be lost.

The situation puts the business owner in a dilemma. He doesn't want to borrow the extra $1M and pay interest on it all year, because he isn't sure the additional sales will materialize. But he also knows that if he goes to the bank for an incremental loan at the last minute, he may not get it, because the bank may be short of funds at that time.

The solution may be an arrangement with the bank in which it makes a *commitment* to lend the extra money in return for a *commitment fee,* which is usually about $\frac{1}{4}$% per year of the committed but unborrowed amount. If the business does borrow the money, the bank just charges its normal interest rate while the loan is outstanding. If it doesn't, it just pays the commitment fee, ($1M × .0025 =) $2,500 in this case.

The arrangement gives the business owner the ability to take advantage of the potential increase in demand for football apparel in that he has the *option* of borrowing the extra money to support the increased sales. We call that ability a **real option**. The word *real* means the option exists in a real, physical business sense. It's inserted to distinguish real options from financial options.[5]

---

4. That in itself doesn't mean the business is weak or in danger of failing. We'll learn about this kind of financing in Chapter 15 when we study working capital.

5. The most common financial option is the right to purchase stock at a fixed price for a specified period. That right is known as a *call option* and is for sale at an *option price.* If the stock's market price rises above the fixed price during the period, the option holder buys the stock and immediately sells it for a profit. If the market price doesn't exceed the fixed price during the period, the option expires, and the investor loses what she paid for it. Stock options are beyond the scope of this book and are covered in detail in investments texts. At this point you should simply be aware of what they are to avoid confusion with real options.

Notice that the real option has a value to the business owner. It's worth at least as much as the commitment fee he pays the bank, and it may be worth a lot more depending on the probability of the local team getting into the Super Bowl and the profit he'd make on the additional sales if that happened.

●REAL OPTIONS IN CAPITAL BUDGETING

● The **value** of a **real option** can be **estimated** as the **increase in project NPV** that its inclusion brings about.

Real options frequently occur in capital budgeting projects. Their impact is best seen when the project is analyzed using a probabilistic approach such as decision tree analysis. A real option's presence generally increases the expected NPV of a project. That increase is often a good estimate of the option's value.

EXAMPLE 11.4

Consider the Wing Foot Shoe Company's situation after the possibility of excellent demand is introduced as described in Example 11.3?

a. Is a real option present?

b. Suppose space at Wing Foot's plant is scarce, and room for an expansion is available only at $.5M cost at the project's outset. This is in addition to the $1M cost of the expansion; i.e., the project's initial outlay will increase by $.5M if the expansion option is included. If demand isn't excellent, that money will be wasted. Should the expansion space be purchased under the conditions presented in Example 11.3?

Solution:

a. Notice that in Example 11.2, Wing's factory is at full capacity at a sales level consistent with good consumer acceptance of the new product. This is shown along the top branch of the decision tree. If capacity expansion isn't possible, there's nothing management can do to take advantage of higher than expected demand. The situation differs in Example 11.3 because the firm has the option of investing an additional $1M in an expansion if larger demand is experienced. Then the project could generate more sales and increased cash flows that might more than offset the cost of the new capacity.

The opportunity to respond to the realization that consumer acceptance is excellent by expanding the plant is a real option. In other words, management has the *option* of expanding capacity at an incremental cost to meet higher than expected demand.

b. Having the extra space from the beginning of the running shoe project gives management the real option to expand. Without it they don't have that choice. Hence in order to decide whether it's wise to purchase extra space, we have to place a value on the real option of expanding capacity. We'll then compare that with the cost of maintaining the option which is $.5M

It's relatively easy to make a first approximation of the value of the real option in this case. It's just the difference in the *expected values* of the project's NPV calculated with and without the option. That makes sense because expected NPV is the basic measure of the project's value to the firm.

We calculated the expected NPV without the option in Example 11.2 and with it in Example 11.3. The option was the only difference in those situations. From those examples we have the following.

Expected NPV with option	$1,463
Expected NPV without option	$1,077
Real option value	$ 386[6]

Since the value of the real option is less than its $.5M cost, it seems that management shouldn't buy the space for the potential expansion ahead of time. However, we'll see shortly that there may be another reason to consider keeping the expansion option alive.

The Abandonment Option

Look at the decision tree in Example 11.3 (pages 365–366) once again. Notice that the lower path representing poor demand has a negative NPV of ($1,270), indicating the project will be a money-losing failure if customers are reluctant to buy the new design. Once management realizes demand is poor, say after the first year, does it make sense to continue producing the running shoes in years 2 and 3, earning inflows of just $1,500? It does if there are no alternate uses for the resources involved in making the shoes, since a positive cash contribution of $1,500 per year is better than nothing.

> The ability to **abandon** a project that is performing poorly is a common **real option** that is often inexpensive.

But suppose the facilities and equipment used to make the new shoe can be redeployed into something else. Under those conditions it may make sense to abandon the project altogether.

EXAMPLE 11.5

Wing Foot has other lines of shoes in which most of the equipment purchased for the running shoe project could be used if the new idea was abandoned. Management estimates that at the end of the first year the equipment's value in those other uses will be $4.5M. How does this information impact the analysis of the running shoe project?

Solution: If the project is abandoned and the equipment is redeployed at the end of the first year, cash flows along the bottom path of the decision tree in Example 11.3 (page 365) would be ($1,500 + $4,500 =) $6,000 in the first year and zero in years 2 and 3. The NPV along the bottom path would then be as follows.

$$\text{NPV} = -\$5,000 + \$6,000[\text{PVF}_{10,1}]$$
$$= -\$5,000 + \$6,000(.9091)$$
$$= -\$5,000 + \$5,455$$
$$= \$455$$

---

6. It's important not to confuse the value of the option in a statistical, expected value sense and with what it's worth if the expansion actually happens. Look at the calculation of the expected value of the project's NPV in Example 11.3. If demand is excellent and the expansion happens, NPV is $4,790. If demand is just good, NPV is $2,641. The difference between those figures is $2,149. That's the amount the expansion capability contributes *if* demand actually turns out to be excellent.

However, at the beginning of the project, when we're doing capital budgeting, we don't know whether that will happen. At that time we just know there's an 18% chance of excellent demand. Recognizing this, the expected value calculation adds 18% of $2,149 to the project's expected NPV, which, within rounding error, is $386. ($2,149 × .18 = $386.82)

Recalculate the project's expected NPV, assuming the bottom path is replaced by abandonment. To do that repeat the calculation in Example 11.3 replacing the NPV of ($1,270) along the bottom path with $455.

Acceptance	NPV	Probability	Product
Excellent	$4,790	.18	$ 862
Good	$2,641	.42	1,109
Poor	$ 455	.40	182
		Expected NPV =	$2,153

Notice that the expected NPV has increased from $1,463 to $2,153.

It's very important to appreciate two things about the calculations we've just done. First, abandonment is a course of action available to management that improves the project's expected NPV. Therefore if abandonment is possible, it's a real option.

Second, the existence of the abandonment option lowers the project's risk substantially. We can see that by looking at the diagram in Example 11.3 that graphically displays the probability distribution of the project's NPV (page 369). Notice that the project as originally presented has a 40% probability of a negative NPV of ($1,270). This is essentially a loss of that amount. We commented earlier that such a loss could ruin a small firm and might be a reason to avoid the project altogether.

But if the abandonment option exists as we've described it, that outcome is pushed to the right and becomes a 40% probability of a small gain of $455. That makes the project taken as a whole a lot less risky. Indeed, it's unlikely that a firm would need to avoid the project because of the risk of ruin if this abandonment option exists.

VALUING REAL OPTIONS

> The **value** of a real option is **at least** the **increase in NPV** it brings about.

In Example 11.4 we calculated the value of a real option as the increase it created in the NPV of the project in which it is embedded. That's a good starting point for valuation, but it doesn't capture the whole story because of the risk reduction we've just described.

In fact, real options are generally worth more than their expected NPV impact because of the effect they have on risk. Recall that individuals and managers are *risk averse,* meaning they prefer less risky undertakings when expected returns or NPVs are equal. That preference generally means people are willing to pay something for risk reduction over and above what they'll pay for an increase in expected NPV. Hence the value of a real option is often *more than* the amount by which it increases NPV. Unfortunately it's difficult to say just how much more, because neither a precise measure of risk nor a relationship between risk and value exists in the capital budgeting context. In other words, we know the value of real options may be enhanced by their effect on risk, but we can't say by how much.

> A real option may be **worth more** than the increase it causes in NPV, because it also **reduces project risk.**

An Approach through Rates of Return

One possible approach to valuing real options involves *risk-adjusted rates* of return. We'll discuss the idea in detail in the next section. For now it's enough to understand that lower risk should be associated with a lower rate of return in our NPV calculations. Hence if a real option lowers a project's risk, it may be appropriate to recalculate its NPV using a lower interest rate than the firm's cost of capital. Since lower interest rates produce higher present values, this procedure makes the recalculated NPV larger, thereby assigning a higher value to the real option. The difficult question is choosing the right risk-adjusted rate.

The Risk Effect Is Tricky

Consider the expansion option of Example 11.4 (page 368) in which we indicated that the expected benefit of the option may not be worth its cost. (Recall that the expected NPV increase was $386,000 while the cost of preserving the option was $500,000.) We arrived at that tentative conclusion without considering the option's effect on risk. We just said that the risk reduction properties of real options lend them extra value. If that's the case isn't it possible that the option to expand is worth more than $386,000?

Pause for a moment and answer that question before reading on. (*Hint:* Compare the effect of the abandonment option and the expansion option on the probability distribution of NPV for the project.)

Although real options often reduce risk, the risk effect of the expansion option probably doesn't help to enhance its value. We can see that by comparing its effect with that of the abandonment option carefully. The risk-reducing effect of the abandonment option is significant because it eliminates the risk of a substantial loss. The expansion option, on the other hand, makes a larger profit available if things go really well, but doesn't change the fact that there's a 40% chance of a large loss which might ruin the firm. Since that large, high probability loss is the key risk issue, there's little or no risk-reducing value in the expansion option.

All of this says that the value of real options has to be considered carefully on a case-by-case basis. A good deal of advanced theoretical work is currently being done in the area.

● DESIGNING REAL OPTIONS INTO PROJECTS

It makes sense to design projects so that they contain beneficial real options whenever possible. We've already seen two examples in which thinking about real options at the beginning of a project might make a big difference later on.

The **abandonment option** discussed in Example 11.5 increased expected NPV and lowered risk at the same time. Hence the example illustrates that it's a good idea to design the ability to quit into projects. Unfortunately that isn't always easy. Contractual obligations, for example, can make abandonment tough. In our illustration, suppose Wing Foot guaranteed retailers the new shoes for three years, signed a lease for factory space, and entered long-term purchasing contracts with suppliers. Then stopping after one year would require breaking the contracts, which could be difficult and costly. Prudent managers should always try to avoid entanglements that make exit hard.

Expansion options like the one illustrated in Example 11.4 are very common. When the ability to expand costs extra money early in the project's life, a careful financial analysis is necessary, as we've indicated. However, the option frequently requires little or no early commitment and should be planned in whenever possible.

Investment timing options also come up frequently. Here's an example. Suppose a company is looking at a project to build a new factory, and has identified an unusually good site, but it can't make a final decision for six months.

Real Applications

Volatile Energy Prices and Real Options Thinking Can Lead to Big Profits on Inefficient Facilities

Real options thinking has become especially popular in industries that require big investments in capital equipment. Classic examples are air transportation, which requires giant jet planes with enormous price tags, and the electric power industry, in which providers build costly power plants. Prior to 2001 Enron Corp was a large energy company whose base business involved building and running electric power plants as well as natural gas pipelines.* The firm's application of real options thinking to power plants in the late 1990s provides a fascinating example of the scope of the technique.

Real options reasoning was used to justify building three electric power plants in Mississippi and Tennessee that were inefficient by design. They're so inefficient that the electricity they produce will cost 50% to 70% more than the industry standard. The plants cost a lot less to build than state of the art facilities, but that's not the reason they were put in place.

Deregulation in the electric utility industry has led to amazingly volatile wholesale prices for electric power in recent years. (See the Real Applications box in Chapter 6, page 213.) Indeed the price of power has been known to vary from a normal level of about $40 per megawatt hour to an unbelievable $7,000. That volatility coupled with real options thinking makes the inefficient plants not only feasible, but a great idea.

The plants aren't intended to operate all the time. They are to be fired up only when energy rates spike to levels that are so high that production costs don't matter. For example, if a megawatt hour of electricity is selling for $1,000, it doesn't matter much whether it costs $20 or $30 to produce.

The inefficient power plants give their owner the *option* to generate and sell more electricity when rates peak. At other times they're simply left idle. The cost of building the plants is the cost of having that option. This is a classic real options situation. If the probability of peak prices is fairly high, the expected value of the extra profits the plants will bring in exceeds the cost of building those plants, and having them increases the expected NPV of power generating operations.

It turns out that these plants may only have to operate a week or two each year to more than pay for themselves. The plants represent a *flexibility option*, because they give their owner the flexibility to respond to high electricity prices with expanded output.

Although the reasoning behind real options has been around for more than twenty years, it's just starting to catch on in a big way today. It's especially popular in capital intensive industries. Enthusiastic supporters of the technique include large, well-known firms like Hewlett-Packard, and France's Airbus Industrie.

* Electric power and gas pipelines were only a small part of Enron's business by the early 2000s. By that time it had largely focused on the risky business of trading contracts for the future delivery of natural gas, electric power, and other commodities. The firm became financially overextended in those areas and filed for bankruptcy protection in late 2001. That failure was essentially unrelated to its power plant operations.

Sources: "Exploiting Uncertainty," *Business Week* (June 7, 1999). Daniel Kadlec, "Power Failure: As Enron crashes, angry workers and shareholders ask, Where were the firm's directors? The regulators? The stock analysts?" *Time* (December 10, 2001): 68.

Management doesn't want to buy the property now, because there's a chance they won't build the factory. But they don't want to lose out to another buyer because if they do decide to build later on, they'd then have to start looking for a site all over again.

The solution can be a *land option contract* in which the landowner grants the company the right to buy the site at any time in the next six months at a fixed price in return for a nonrefundable fee called the *option price*.

The option is a purchase contract between a buyer and a seller that's suspended at the discretion of the buyer for a limited time. If the buyer doesn't *exercise* the option by the end of that time, it just expires. The land option lets the firm delay its investment in the land until it's sure about other relevant issues and problems.

Flexibility options let companies respond more easily to changes in business conditions. For example, suppose a firm buys the same part from two suppliers for $1 per unit. If it gives all of its business to one supplier, the price would be $.90 per unit. But if that single supplier fails, the firm's business will suffer while it's unable to get the part. Hence the flexibility of having both suppliers available may be worth the extra $.10 per unit.

INCORPORATING RISK INTO CAPITAL BUDGETING—THE THEORETICAL APPROACH AND RISK-ADJUSTED RATES OF RETURN

The theoretical approach to incorporating risk into capital budgeting focuses on rates of return. Recall that an *interest rate* plays a central role in both the NPV and IRR methods. Up until now we've taken that key rate to be the firm's cost of capital. Let's briefly review how it is used in both techniques.

> The **cost of capital** plays a **key role** in both NPV and IRR.

In the NPV method, we calculate the present value of cash flows by using the cost of capital as the discount rate. A higher discount rate produces a lower NPV, which reduces the chances of project acceptance. In the IRR method, the decision rule involves comparing a project's return on invested funds with the cost of capital. A higher cost of capital means a higher IRR is required for acceptance, which also lowers the chance of the project being qualified.

In summary, the acceptance or rejection of projects depends on this key interest rate in both methods, with higher rates implying less likely acceptance. In what follows we'll investigate the implications of doing the calculations with an interest rate other than the cost of capital.

Riskier Projects Should Be Less Acceptable

The idea behind incorporating risk into capital budgeting is to make particularly risky projects less acceptable than others with similar *expected* cash flows. Notice that this is exactly what happens under capital budgeting rules if projects are evaluated using higher interest rates. A higher discount rate lowers the calculated NPV for any given set of cash flows, while a higher threshold rate means calculated IRRs have to be larger to qualify projects.

> Using a higher, **risk-adjusted rate** for **risky** projects **lowers their chance of acceptance.**

Therefore, a logical way to incorporate risk into capital budgeting is to devise an approach that uses the NPV and IRR methods, but analyzes riskier projects by using higher interest rates in place of the cost of capital. Logically, the higher the risk, the higher the interest rate that should be used. This approach will automatically create a bias against accepting higher risk projects. Higher rates used to compensate for riskiness in financial analysis are called **risk-adjusted rates.**

The Starting Point for Risk-Adjusted Rates

Earlier in this section we said that in the long run a company can be viewed as a collection of projects, and that adopting a large number of relatively risky endeavors can change its fundamental nature to that of a more risky enterprise.

It makes sense to take the current status of a firm as the starting point for risk measurement and to let the cost of capital be the interest rate representing that point. Then it's logical to analyze projects that are consistent with the current riskiness of the company using the cost of capital and to use higher rates for riskier projects.

Relating Interest Rates to Risk

These ideas are consistent with the interest rate fundamentals we studied in Chapter 4. Recall that every interest rate is made up of two parts: a base rate and a premium for risk. The idea was expressed as an equation that we'll repeat here for convenience.

(4.1) $$k = \text{base rate} + \text{risk premium}$$

● Projects with **risk** consistent with **current** operations should be evaluated using the **cost of capital**.

This equation says that investors demand a higher risk premium and consequently a higher interest rate if they are to bear increased risk of losing money. In capital budgeting, the company is investing in the project being analyzed, and the interest rate used in the analysis is analogous to the rate of return demanded by an investor from a security.

If the project's risk is about the same as the company's overall risk, using the firm's cost of capital is appropriate. If the project's risk is higher, a rate with a higher risk premium is needed.

Choosing the Risk-Adjusted Rate for Various Projects

The ideas we've described in this section make logical sense, but run into practical problems when they're implemented. The stumbling block is the arbitrariness of choosing the appropriate risk-adjusted rate for a particular project.

Projects are generally presented with point estimates of future cash flows. Assessing the riskiness or variability of those cash flows is usually a subjective affair, so there's little on which to base the choice of a risk-adjusted rate. However, some logical thinking can help.

Recall that projects fit into three categories of generally increasing risk: replacement, expansion, and new venture. Replacements are usually a continuation of what was being done before, but with new equipment. Because the function is already part of the business, its risk will be consistent with that of the present business. Therefore the cost of capital is nearly always the appropriate discount rate for analyzing replacement projects.

Expansion projects involve doing more of the same thing in some business area. They're more risky than the current level, but usually not very much more. In such cases a rule of thumb of adding one to three percentage points to the cost of capital is usually appropriate.[7]

New venture projects are the big problem. They usually involve a great deal more risk than current operations, but it's hard to quantify exactly how much. So choosing a risk-adjusted rate is difficult and arbitrary. However, *sometimes* we can get help from portfolio theory.

---

7. If the expansion is very large, a bigger adjustment may be necessary.

● ESTIMATING RISK-ADJUSTED RATES USING CAPM

Portfolio theory and the capital asset pricing model (Chapter 8) deal with assigning risk to investments. Under certain circumstances, the techniques developed there can be applied to risk-adjusted rates for capital budgeting.

The Project as a Diversification

● A new venture **diversifies** the company and its shareholders.

When a company undertakes a new venture, the project can be viewed as a diversification similar to adding a new stock to a portfolio. We can look at this idea in two ways.

The first involves seeing the firm as a collection of projects. A new venture simply adds another enterprise to the company's project portfolio, which then becomes more diversified. In the second view, the project diversifies the investment portfolios of the firm's shareholders into the new line of business.

This second idea is important and profound; let's explore it more deeply. Suppose a firm is in the food processing business. Stockholders have chosen to invest in the company because they're comfortable with the risks and rewards of that business. Now suppose the firm takes on a venture in electronics. To the extent of the new project, stockholders are now subject to the risks and rewards of the electronics business. They could have accomplished the same thing by selling off some of their food processing company stock and buying stock in an electronics firm. In essence the company has done that for them, probably without their permission.

Diversifiable and Nondiversifiable Risk for Projects

In Chapter 8 we separated investment risk into systematic and unsystematic components. Unsystematic risk is specific to individual firms or industries and can be diversified away by having a wide variety of stocks in a portfolio. Systematic risk, on the other hand, is related to movement with the entire market and can't be entirely eliminated through diversification.

Projects viewed as investments have two levels of diversifiable risk because they're effectively in two portfolios at the same time. Some risk is diversified away within the firm's portfolio of projects, and some is diversified away by the stockholders' investment portfolios.

These ideas lead to an additional, intermediate concept of risk, the undiversified risk added to a company by the addition of a project. The idea is illustrated in Figure 11.7.

Notice that the risk left over after the two kinds of diversifiable risk are removed is systematic risk. This is the same concept of systematic risk used in portfolio theory, but here it's associated with a project rather than a company.

Estimating the Risk-Adjusted Rate through Beta

The capital asset pricing model that we studied in Chapter 8 gives us an approach to measuring *systematic risk* for *companies* by using the security market line (SML). The SML (equation 8.4) defines the firm's required rate of return in terms of a base rate and a risk premium. We'll repeat it here for convenience.

(8.4) $$k_X = k_{RF} + (k_M - k_{RF})b_X ,$$

where k_X is the required rate of return for company X, k_{RF} is the risk-free rate, k_M is the return on the market, and b_X is company X's beta.

FIGURE 11.7

Components of Project Risk

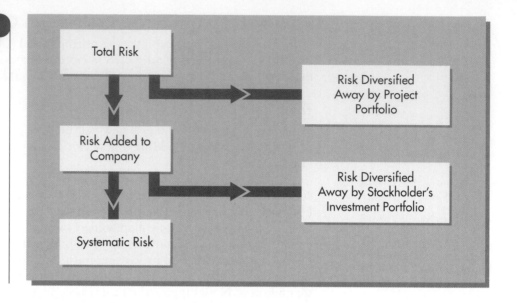

The term

$$(k_M - k_{RF})b_X$$

is the risk premium for company X's stock, which is a function of b_X, the company's beta. Beta in turn measures systematic risk, the bottom block in Figure 11.7. In other words, the SML gives us a risk-adjusted interest rate related to a particular kind of risk for the stock of a company, and we find that same kind of risk in the analysis of projects.

● Under certain conditions the **SML** can be used to determine a **risk-adjusted rate** for a **new venture** project.

If a capital budgeting project is viewed as a business in a particular field, it may make sense to use a beta common to that field in the SML to estimate a risk-adjusted rate for analysis of the project.

Recall, for example, the food processing company that takes on a venture in electronics. It might be appropriate to use a beta typical of electronics companies in the SML to arrive at a risk-adjusted rate to analyze the project. This line of thinking is especially appropriate when an independent, publicly traded company can be found that is in the same business as the venture and whose beta is known. The approach is known as the **pure play** method of establishing a risk-adjusted rate. The pure play company has to be solely in the business of the venture; otherwise its beta won't be truly appropriate.

EXAMPLE 11.6

Orion Inc. is a successful manufacturer of citizens band (CB) radios. Management is considering producing a sophisticated tactical radio for sale to the Army, but is concerned because the military market is known to be quite risky.

The military radio market is dominated by Milrad Inc., which holds a 60% market share. Antex Radio Corp. is another established competitor with a 20% share. Both Milrad and Antex make only military radios. Milrad's beta is 1.4 and Antex's is 2.0. Orion's beta is 1.1. The return on an average publicly traded stock (k_M) is about 10%. The yield on short-term treasury bills (k_{RF}) is currently 5%. Orion's cost of capital is 8%.

The military radio project is expected to require an initial outlay of $10 million. Subsequent cash inflows are expected to be $3 million per year over a five-year contract.

On the basis of a five-year evaluation, should Orion undertake the project?

Solution: The military business is clearly riskier than the CB business judging by the relative betas of Orion and its potential rivals. Therefore a CAPM-based risk-adjusted rate is appropriate for the analysis. Milrad and Antex are both pure play companies, but the fact that Milrad is the market leader probably reduces its risk. If Orion enters the field it will be in a position similar to Antex's, so a risk-adjusted rate based on that firm's beta is most appropriate.

First we calculate the risk-adjusted rate using the SML and Antex's beta.

$$k = k_{RF} + (k_M - k_{RF})b_{Antex}$$
$$= 5\% + (10\% - 5\%)2.0$$
$$= 15.0\%$$

Notice that this rate is considerably higher than Orion's cost of capital (8%).

Next calculate the proposed project's NPV using the risk-adjusted rate.

$$NPV = C_0 + C[PVFA_{k,n}]$$
$$= -\$10.0M + \$3M[PVFA_{15,5}]$$
$$= -\$10.0M + \$3M(3.3522)$$
$$= \$.1M$$

Notice that the risk-adjusted NPV is barely positive, indicating that the project is marginal.

If Orion's 8% cost of capital had been used in the analysis, the result would have been as follows.

$$NPV = -\$10.0M + \$3M[PVFA_{8,5}]$$
$$= -\$10.0M + \$3M(3.9927)$$
$$= -\$10.0M + \$12.0M$$
$$= \$2.0M$$

Compare these two results. The capital budgeting rule unadjusted for risk would clearly have accepted the project, but consideration of risk has shown it to be a very marginal undertaking. This can be a crucial managerial insight! However, in the next section we'll see that there are more questions lurking about.

PROBLEMS WITH THE THEORETICAL APPROACH—FINDING THE RIGHT BETA AND CONCERNS ABOUT THE APPROPRIATE RISK DEFINITION

Using the CAPM to estimate risk-adjusted rates as illustrated in the last section appears straightforward and unambiguous. However, it would be rather unusual for the technique to fit into the real world as neatly as it did in the example. Generally, the biggest problem is finding a pure play company from which to get an appropriate beta. For example, if Milrad and Antex were divisions of larger companies, their separate betas wouldn't be available, and the betas of their parent companies would be influenced by the operations of divisions in other fields. As a result, we're usually reduced to estimating betas based on those of firms in similar rather than exactly the same businesses. This reduces the credibility of the technique by quite a bit.

However, there's another, more basic problem. Look back at Figure 11.7. Notice that three levels of risk are attached to projects, and that the CAPM technique uses the last level, systematic risk. But systematic risk is a concept that's really only relevant in the context of a well-diversified portfolio of financial assets. It excludes all unsystematic risks that may be associated with the project itself or with the company. In the context of a firm making day-to-day business decisions, disregarding unsystematic risk may not be appropriate.

For example, suppose the military radio project in Example 11.6 fails because Orion's management doesn't know how to deal with the government.[8] That risk isn't included in systematic risk because it's related specifically to Orion. But shouldn't Orion be concerned about risks like that when considering the project? Most people would agree that it should.

This reasoning suggests that total risk as pictured in Figure 11.7 is the more appropriate measure for capital budgeting. But CAPM doesn't give us an estimate of that. All we can say is that total risk is higher than systematic risk.

Let's look at Example 11.6 again in that light. The military radio project is marginal at a risk-adjusted rate reflecting only systematic risk. If a broader definition of risk is appropriate, the risk-adjusted rate should be even higher, which would lower NPV and make the project undesirable.

Projects in Divisions—The Accounting Beta Method

Sometimes a large company has divisions in different businesses, each of which has substantially different risk characteristics. In such cases, the cost of capital for the entire firm can't be associated with any particular division, so some kind of a proxy rate has to be found for capital budgeting within divisions.

The pure play method just described might be used if pure play companies can be found in the right businesses, but that's often not possible. If an appropriate surrogate can't be found, and a division has separate accounting records, an approximate approach can be used. The approximation involves developing a beta for the division from its accounting records rather than from stock market performance. This is accomplished by regressing historical values of the division's return on equity against the return on a major stock market index like the S&P 500. The slope of the regression line is then the division's approximate beta and the SML can be used to estimate a risk-adjusted rate. This approach is called the *accounting beta method*.

A Final Comment on Risk in Capital Budgeting

Adjusting capital budgeting procedures to recognize risk makes a great deal of sense. However, the methods available to implement the concept are less than precise. As a result, risk-adjusted capital budgeting remains more in the province of the theorist than of the financial manager.

To put it another way, virtually everyone uses capital budgeting techniques, but only a few overtly try to incorporate risk. Business managers do recognize

from the CFO

---

8. This is a very real problem. Government and commercial markets are entirely different worlds.

risk, but they do it through judgments overlaid on the results of analysis when decisions are finally made.

Nevertheless, it's important that students understand the risk issue, because it's a very real part of decision making. Recognizing risk is a major step toward bringing theory in line with the real world. Even though we can't precisely put the idea that cash flows are subject to probability distributions into our analysis, we'll make better decisions for having thought about it.

DISCUSSION QUESTIONS

1. In 1983 the Bell telephone system was broken up, resulting in the creation of seven regional telephone companies. The "Baby Bells," as they were called, were freed from many of the regulatory constraints under which the Bell system had operated, and at the same time had a great deal of money. The managements of these young giants were determined to make them more than the staid old-line telephone companies they'd been in the past. They were quite vocal in declaring their intentions to undertake ventures in any number of new fields, despite the fact that virtually all of their experience was in the regulated environment of the old telephone system. Many stockholders were alarmed and concerned by these statements. Comment on what their concerns may have been.

2. A random variable is defined as the outcome of one or more chance processes. Imagine that you're forecasting the cash flows associated with a new business venture. List some of the things that come together to produce cash flows in future periods. Describe how they might be considered to be outcomes of chance processes and therefore random variables. Cash flow forecasts for a project are used in equations 9.1 and 9.2 to calculate the project's NPV and IRR. That makes NPV and IRR random variables as well. Is their variability likely to be greater or less than the variability of the individual cash flows making them up?

3. One of the problems of using simulations to incorporate risk in capital budgeting is related to the idea that the probability distributions of successive cash flows usually are not independent. If the first period's cash flow is at the high end of its range—for example, flows in subsequent periods are more likely to be high than low. Why do you think this is generally the case? Describe an approach through which the computer might adjust for this phenomenon to portray risk better.

4. Ed Draycutt is the engineering manager of Airway Technologies, a firm that makes computer systems for air traffic control installations at airports. He has proposed a new device the success of which depends on two separate events. First the Federal Aviation Administration (FAA) must adopt a recent proposal for a new procedural approach to handling in-flight calls from planes experiencing emergencies. Everyone thinks the probability of the FAA accepting the new method is at least 98%, but it will take a year to happen. If the new approach is adopted, radio makers will have to respond within another year with one of two possible changes in their technology. These can simply be called A and B. The A response is far more likely, also having a probability of about 98%. Ed's device works with the A system and is a stroke of engineering genius. If the A system becomes the industry standard and Airway has Ed's product, it will make a fortune before anyone else can market a similar device. On the other hand if the A system isn't adopted, Airway will lose whatever it's put into the new device's development.

Developing Ed's device will cost about $20 million, which is a very substantial investment for a small company like Airway. In fact, a loss of $20 million would put the firm in danger of failing.

Ed just presented his idea to the executive committee as a capital budgeting project with a $20 million investment and a huge NPV and IRR reflecting the adoption of the A system. Everyone on the committee is very excited. You're the CFO and are a lot less excited. You asked Ed how he reflected the admittedly remote possibility that the A system would never be put in place. Ed, obviously proud of his business sophistication, said he'd taken care of that with a statistical calculation. He said adoption of the A system required the occurrence of two events, each of which has a 98% probability. The probability of both happening is (.98 × .98 = .96) 96%. He therefore reduced all of his cash inflow estimates by 4%. He maintains this correctly accounts for risk in the project.

Does Ed have the right expected NPV? What's wrong with his analysis? Suggest an approach that will give a more insightful result. Why might the firm consider passing on the proposal in spite of the tremendous NPV and IRR Ed has calculated?

5. Might Ed's case in question 4 be helped by a real option? If so, what kind? How would it help?

6. Why is it desirable to construct capital budgeting rules so that higher-risk projects become less acceptable than lower-risk projects?

7. Rationalize the appropriateness of using the cost of capital to analyze normally risky projects and higher rates for those with more risk.

8. Charlie Henderson, a senior manager in the Bartok Company, is known for taking risks. He recently proposed that the company expand its operations into a new and untried field. He put together a set of cash flow projections and calculated an IRR of 25% for the project. The firm's cost of capital is about 10%. Charlie maintains that the favorability of the calculated IRR relative to the cost of capital makes the project an easy choice for acceptance, and urges management to move forward immediately.

Several knowledgeable people have looked at the proposal and feel Charlie's projections represent an optimistic scenario that has about one chance in three of happening. They think the project also has about one chance in three of failing miserably. An important consideration is that the project is large enough to bankrupt the company if it fails really badly.

Charlie doesn't want to talk about these issues, claiming the others are being "negative" and that he has a history of success with risky ventures like this. When challenged, he falls back on the 25% IRR versus the 10% cost of capital as justification for his idea.

The company president has asked you for your comments on the situation. Specifically address the issue of the 25% IRR versus the 10% cost of capital. Should this project be evaluated using different standards? How does the possibility of bankruptcy as a result of the project affect the analysis? Are capital budgeting rules still appropriate? How should Charlie's successful record be factored into the president's thinking?

9. In evaluating the situation presented in the last problem, you've found a pure play company in the proposed industry whose beta is 2.5. The rate of return on short-term treasury bills is currently 8% and a typical stock investment returns 14%. Explain how this information might affect the acceptability of Charlie's proposal. What practical concerns would you overlay on top of the theory you've just described? Do they make the project more or less acceptable? Does the fact that Bartok has never done this kind of business before matter? How would you adjust for that inexperience? Is the risk of bankruptcy still important? What would you advise doing about that? All things considered, would you advise the president to take on the project or not?

10. Evaluate the conceptual merits of applying CAPM theory to the problem of determining risk-adjusted interest rates for capital budgeting purposes. Form your own opinion based on your study of CAPM (Chapter 8) and the knowledge you're now developing of capital budgeting. The issue is concisely summarized by Figure 11.7. Is the special concept of risk developed in portfolio theory applicable here? Don't be intimidated into thinking that because the idea is presented in textbooks, it's necessarily correct. Many scholars and practitioners feel this application stretches theory too far. On the other hand, others feel it has a great deal of merit. What do you think and why?

PROBLEMS

1. The Glendale Corp. is considering a real estate development project that will cost $5M to undertake and is expected to produce annual inflows between $1M and $4M for two years. Management feels that if the project turns out really well the inflows will be $3M in the first year and $4M in the second. If things go very poorly, on the other hand, inflows of $1M followed by $2.5M are more likely. Develop a range of NPVs for the project if Glendale's cost of capital is 12%.

2. If Glendale's management in the last problem attaches a probability of .7 to the better outcome, what is the project's most likely (expected) NPV?

3. The Blazingame Corporation is considering a three-year project that has an initial cash outflow (C_0) of $175,000 and three cash inflows that are defined by the following independent probability distributions shown. All dollar figures are in thousands. Blazingame's cost of capital is 10%.

C_1	C_2	C_3	Probability
$50	$40	$75	.25
60	80	80	.50
70	120	85	.25

a. Estimate the project's most likely NPV by using a point estimate of each cash flow. What is its probability?

b. What are the best and worst possible NPVs? What are their probabilities?

c. Choose a few outcomes at random, calculate their NPVs and the associated probabilities, and sketch the probability distribution of the project's NPV.

   [*Hint:* The project has 27 possible cash flow patterns ($3 \times 3 \times 3$), each of which is obtained by selecting one cash flow from each column and combining with the initial outflow. The probability of any pattern is the product of the probabilities of its three uncertain cash flows. For example, a particular pattern might be as follows.

	C_0	C_1	C_2	C_3
C_i	($175)	$50	$120	$80
Probability	1.0	.25	.25	.50

The probability of this pattern would be

$$.25 \times .25 \times .50 = .03125 .]$$

4. Work Station Inc. manufactures office furniture. The firm is interested in "ergonomic" products that are designed to be easier on the bodies of office workers who suffer from ailments such as back and neck pain due to sitting for long periods. Unfortunately customer acceptance of ergonomic furniture tends to be unpredictable, so a wide range of market response is possible. Management has made the following two-year probabilistic estimate of the cash flows associated with the project arranged in decision tree format ($000).

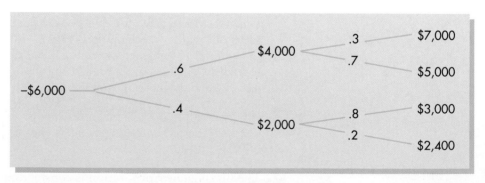

Work Station is a relatively small company, and would be seriously damaged by any project that lost more than $1.5 million. The firm's cost of capital is 14%.

a. Develop a probability distribution for NPV based on the forecast. In other words, calculate the project's NPV along each path of the decision tree and the associated probability.

b. Calculate the project's expected NPV.

c. Analyze your results, and make a recommendation about the project's advisability considering both expected NPV and risk.

5. Resolve the last problem assuming Work Station Inc. has an abandonment option at the end of the first year under which it will recover $5 million of the initial investment in year 2. What is the value of the ability to abandon the project? How does your overall recommendation change?

6. Spitfire Aviation Inc. manufactures small, private aircraft. Management is evaluating a proposal to introduce a new high-performance plane. High-performance aviation is an expensive sport undertaken largely by people who are both young and wealthy. Spitfire sees its target market as affluent professionals under 35 who have made a lot of money in the stock market in recent years.

Stock prices have been rising rapidly for some time, so investment profits have been very handsome, but lately there are serious concerns about a market downturn. If the market remains strong, Spitfire estimates it will sell 50 of the new planes a year for five years, each of which will result in a net cash flow contribution of $200,000. If the market turns down, however, only about 20 units a year will be sold. Economists think there's about a 40% chance the market will turn down in the near future.

There are also some concerns about the design of the new plane. Not everyone is convinced it will perform as well as the engineering department thinks. Indeed, the engineers have sometimes been too optimistic about their projects in the past. If performance is below the engineering estimate, word of mouth communication among fliers will erode the product's reputation, and unit sales *after the first year* will be 50% of the preceding forecasts. Management thinks there's a 30% chance the plane won't perform as well as the engineers think it will. The cost to bring the plane through design and into production is estimated at $15M. Spitfire's cost of capital is 12%.

a. Draw and fully label the decision tree diagram for the project

b. Calculate the NPV and probability along each path.

c. Calculate the project's expected NPV.

d. Sketch a probability distribution for NPV.

e. Describe the risk situation in words compared to a point estimate of NPV.

7. If Spitfire elects to do the project, what is an abandonment option at the end of year 1 worth if Spitfire can recover $8M of the initial investment into other uses at that time? If the recovery is $13M?

8. The New England Brewing Company produces a super premium beer using a recipe that's been in the owner's family since colonial times. Surprisingly, the firm doesn't own its own brewing facilities, but rents time on the equipment of large brewers who have excess capacity. Other small brewers have been doing the same thing lately, so capacity has become difficult to find, and must be contracted for several years in advance.

New England's sales have been increasing steadily, and marketing consultants think there's a possibility that demand will really take off soon. Last year's sales generated net cash flows after all costs and taxes of $5M. The consultants predict that sales will probably be at a level that will produce net cash flows of $6M per year for the next three years, but they also see a 20% probability that sales could be high enough to generate net cash inflows of $8M per year.

Meeting such an increase in demand presents a problem because of the advance contracting requirements for brewing capacity. Unless New England arranges for extra facilities now, there's a 70% chance that it won't be available if the increased demand materializes. An option arrangement is available with one of the large brewers under which it will hold capacity for New England until the last minute for an immediate, nonrefundable payment of $1M. New England's cost of capital is 9%.

a. Draw a decision tree reflecting New England's cash flows for the next three years without the option, and calculate the expected NPV of operating cash flows. (Note that there's no need to include an initial outlay because we're dealing with ongoing operations.)

b. Redraw the decision tree to include the capacity option as a real option in your calculations. What is its value? Should it be purchased?

c. Does the real option reduce New England's risk in any way?

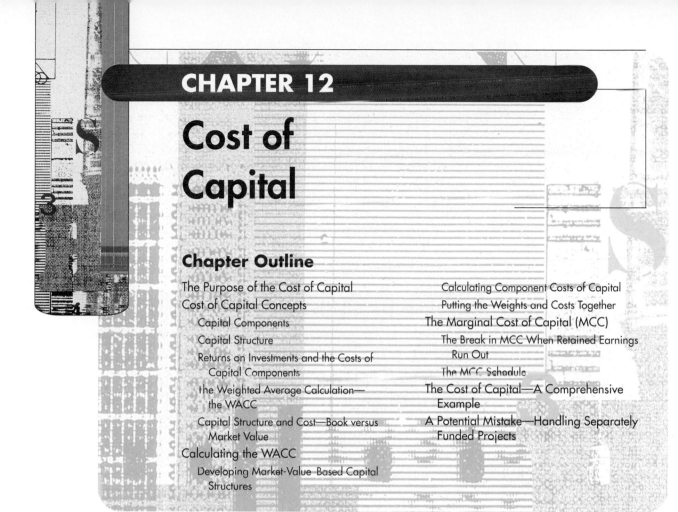

CHAPTER 12

Cost of Capital

Chapter Outline

We introduced the cost of capital briefly in Chapter 9, because we needed some appreciation of the concept to grasp the rationale behind capital budgeting. In this chapter we'll explore the idea in more detail and learn how to calculate a firm's cost of capital.

THE PURPOSE OF THE COST OF CAPITAL

A company's cost of capital is the average rate it pays for the use of its capital funds. That rate provides a benchmark against which to measure investment opportunities in the context of capital budgeting.

● The **cost of capital** is the **average rate paid** for the **use of capital funds.** It is used **primarily** in **capital budgeting.**

The idea is very straightforward. No one should invest in any project that will return less than the cost of invested funds. Because a firm's cost of capital is the best estimate of the cost of any money it invests, it should never take on a project that doesn't return at least that rate.

This is equivalent to saying that to be accepted, a project must either have an IRR that exceeds the cost of capital or an NPV that is positive when computed at that rate. These ideas were developed in Chapter 9 where we used the symbol k to represent the cost of capital. Review pages 298–299 if necessary.

It's quite important to the effective management of a company that its cost of capital be estimated accurately. Otherwise the firm is likely to make incorrect investment decisions that can jeopardize its profitability and long-run survival.

The cost of capital concept is similar to an idea we've already studied: an individual investor's required return for a particular stock. In Chapter 8 (page 253), we said that an investor wouldn't buy a stock unless its expected return was higher than his or her required return for that company. Further, we said that people base required returns on risk.

A company's cost of capital can be thought of as its required return for all capital budgeting projects that have risk levels approximately equal to its own. A project's expected return is its IRR. Hence the firm won't invest in a project unless its IRR (expected return) exceeds the firm's cost of capital (required return).

COST OF CAPITAL CONCEPTS

Capital refers to money acquired for use over long periods of time. The funds are generally used for getting businesses started, acquiring long-lived assets, and otherwise doing the kinds of projects we studied in Chapters 9 through 11 under the topic of capital budgeting. On a firm's financial statements, capital appears on the lower right side of the balance sheet.

CAPITAL COMPONENTS

● The **components** of a firm's capital are **debt, common equity,** and **preferred stock.**

Capital can be divided into **components** according to the way the money was raised. The two basic classifications are debt and common equity. Debt is borrowed money raised through loans or the sale of bonds. Common equity indicates an ownership interest, and comes from the sale of common stock or from retaining earnings.

A third kind of capital comes from the sale of preferred stock. Preferred can be thought of as a cross between debt and equity, because it has some of the characteristics of each. Legally it's a kind of equity, but for many financial purposes it behaves more like debt. Because of this hybrid nature, preferred is sometimes combined with one of the other components for purposes of analysis.

However, preferred stock offers investors a return which is generally different from that of either debt or common equity. Therefore, in the context of the cost of capital, it's handled separately as a third component.

In the rest of this chapter we'll refer to common equity simply as equity and preferred equity as preferred stock or just preferred.

CAPITAL STRUCTURE

● **Capital structure** is the **mix** of the three **capital components.**

The mix of capital components in use by a company at a point in time is known as its **capital structure.** We generally describe capital structure in percentage terms referring to the relative sizes of the components. For example, a firm that has the following capital components can be described as 30% debt, 10% preferred stock, and 60% equity.

Debt	$ 30,000,000	30%
Preferred stock	10,000,000	10
Equity	60,000,000	60
Total capital	$100,000,000	100%

INSIGHTS

INSIGHTS

Practical Finance

The Cost of Capital—Intuitively

Suppose an entrepreneur plans to open a business that will earn 12% on invested money. If he has no money of his own, but can borrow at 15%, does it make sense to start the business?

Clearly it doesn't. The enterprise is certain to lose money, because it will pay more for funds than it will earn using them. The business makes sense only if the entrepreneur can borrow at a rate below 12%.

This is the idea behind the cost of capital. We shouldn't pay more for a resource than it earns. In this simple case the cost of capital is just the rate at which borrowed funds are available. In reality firms have more than one kind of capital and each has a different cost. *The* cost of capital is a single rate that represents an average of those costs.

The Target Capital Structure

A great deal of importance is sometimes placed on operating with the "right" capital structure. However, the determination of what's right is the subject of some debate. We'll address this issue in Chapter 13. In the meantime, we'll assume that the management of a firm may have a particular mix of capital components that it considers more desirable than any other. We'll call that mix the firm's **target capital structure,** and assume that management strives to maintain it as money is raised.

Where a target capital structure has been designated, we'll see that it can be used in place of the actual capital structure for certain calculations.

● A firm's **target capital structure** is a mix of components that management **considers optimal** and strives to maintain.

Raising Money in the Proportions of the Capital Structure

As a practical matter, an exact capital structure can't be maintained continuously, because money tends to be acquired in finite amounts by issuing securities of one kind or another, one at a time.

For example, suppose a firm had the capital structure illustrated just above and that mix was also its target. Further suppose the company needed to raise an additional $1 million. To do that it would generally issue and sell $1 million of either debt, preferred stock, or common stock. Trying to sell some of each security in the proportion of 30–10–60 wouldn't be practical.

Issuing one security for the additional money would throw the proportions in the capital structure off target. Then the next time it raised capital, the company could try to move back toward the target mix.

● Cost of capital **calculations** assume that capital is **raised in the exact proportions** of some capital structure.

In spite of this practical difficulty, cost of capital calculations are generally based on the assumption that money is raised in the exact proportions of some capital structure. In this case we would assume the firm raised its $1 million by selling $300,000 in new bonds and $100,000 in new preferred stock, along with $600,000 of equity. The equity would come from a combination of retained earnings and the sale of new common stock. The assumption isn't very realistic, but the distortion it produces is generally small.

● RETURNS ON INVESTMENTS AND THE COSTS OF CAPITAL COMPONENTS

Investors provide capital to companies by purchasing their securities. The investors' returns are paid out by the companies, so those returns are costs to the firms in which the investments are made. This is a fundamental point. The return

● The **return earned** by investors on the security underlying a capital component is its **unadjusted cost.**

received by an investor on a particular type of security (debt, preferred, or equity) and the cost to the company of the funds raised through that security are opposite sides of the same coin.

For a particular company, investments in the securities underlying the three capital components tend to offer returns of different magnitudes, because each type of security has different risk characteristics. Thus each capital component has a distinct cost that's related to the return earned by the investors who provide that component. And because the returns are different, so are the costs.

● Because component securities have **different risks,** they offer **different returns** and have **different costs. Equity** is **highest, debt** is **lowest,** and preferred is between.

Generally the return on an equity investment is higher than the return on debt or preferred because the risk is higher. Hence the firm's cost of equity capital is higher than its cost of debt or preferred stock. The return/cost of debt tends to be the lowest of the three, because debt is the least risky investment. The cost of preferred is usually between the cost of debt and that of equity.

Although the cost paid out by the company is the investor's return, there are some adjustments that keep the *effective* cost and return from being exactly the same. Hence we say that cost and return are related rather than equal. We'll describe the adjustments later.

For now the important point is that there are separate component costs of capital for debt, preferred stock, and equity. And each component cost is related to the return earned by investors owning the security underlying that component.

● THE WEIGHTED AVERAGE CALCULATION—THE WACC

Calculating the cost of capital is conceptually quite simple. Firms raise capital from several sources, each of which has its own cost. A firm's overall cost of capital is just the average of the costs of its separate sources weighted by the proportion of each source used. The separate sources are the capital components we've been talking about, and the proportions are the percentages of each component in the firm's capital structure.

● The **WACC** is a **weighted average** of component costs where the weights reflect the amount of each component used.

The procedure has led to the term *weighted average cost of capital*, abbreviated **WACC.** The expression has exactly the same meaning as the simpler "cost of capital" we've been using until now. It's customary to use the expression WACC in discussions of the subject, because it avoids confusion with the cost of capital for an individual component.

Computing the WACC—An Example

To compute a WACC, we need two things: the mix of the capital components in use and the cost of each component. We'll get into how we arrive at each shortly, but first let's preview what we'll do once we have them. An example is the easiest way to understand the procedure.

EXAMPLE 12.1

Calculate the WACC for the Zodiac Company given the following information about its capital structure.

Capital Component	Value	Cost
Debt	$ 60,000	9%
Preferred stock	50,000	11
Common stock	90,000	14
	$200,000	

Solution: First we compute the capital structure weights on the basis of the dollar values given. This involves adding up the dollar amounts and stating each as a percentage of the total. That calculation results in the first two numerical columns below. The weight of the debt component, for example, is

$$\frac{\$60,000}{\$200,000} = .30 = 30\%.$$

Notice that the weights have to add up to 1.00 or 100%, and that they are the decimal equivalents of the percentages in the firm's capital structure.

Next multiply the cost of each component by its weight and sum the results as shown. The result is the WACC.

Capital Component	Value	Weight		Cost		
Debt	$60,000	.30	×	9%	=	2.70%
Preferred stock	50,000	.25	×	11	=	2.75
Common stock	90,000	.45	×	14	=	6.30
	$200,000	1.00		WACC	=	11.75%

● CAPITAL STRUCTURE AND COST—BOOK VERSUS MARKET VALUE

A major source of confusion about the WACC stems from the fact that both capital structure and component costs can be viewed in terms of either the book or market value of the underlying capital. We'll talk about structure first and then about component costs.

Capital Structure—Book versus Market

The book values of a firm's capital accounts reflect the prices at which the securities that raised its capital were originally sold, and are embodied in the capital section of its balance sheet. Market values reflect the current market prices of those same securities. The firm's capital structure can be based on either. We'll illustrate the difference with a case in which there's only debt and equity capital (no preferred stock).

Assume the Diplomat Corporation, a new firm, raises $100,000 in equity by selling 10,000 shares of common stock at $10 each. It also borrows $100,000 by selling 100 bonds at a par value of $1,000. Immediately after those transactions, Diplomat has the capital structure shown in Table 12.1, which reflects both book and market values.

Now imagine that Diplomat's stock price increases to $12, while interest rates climb and drive the price of its bonds down to $850. These market adjustments do not change the capital entries on the company's books. Therefore, the book-value–based structure remains as shown in Table 12.1.

However, the market-value–based structure does change significantly. The result is shown in Table 12.2.

Capital structures based on book and market values are generally different because the market values of securities change all the time, and those changes are not reflected on company books. Our question is which basis for structure is appropriate for calculating the WACC?

● The **value of capital** can be stated based on the **book or market prices** of the underlying securities.

TABLE 12.1	**The Diplomat Corporation's Initial Capital Structure—Book and Market Equal**			
Equity	10,000 shares ×	$10 = $100,000		50.0%
Debt	100 bonds × $1,000 =	100,000		50.0
		Total	$200,000	100.0%

TABLE 12.2	**The Diplomat Corporation's Market-Value-Based Capital Structure**			
Equity	10,000 shares ×	$12 = $120,000		58.5%
Debt	100 bonds ×	$850 =	85,000	41.5
		Total	$205,000	100.0%

Component Returns/Costs—Book versus Market

Investors' returns and the related component costs of capital can also be thought of in either book or market terms. We'll illustrate with a bond.

Suppose a firm sells a 10% coupon rate bond at its face value. Initially an investor buying the bond earns a 10% return, and the company pays the same 10% interest on the borrowed money. Suppose the market interest rate later falls to 8%.

After the market rate change, two returns can be associated with the bond. The original investor is still receiving 10% on his or her investment, and the company is still paying 10% on the original amount borrowed. However, a new investor buying the bond will have to pay a higher price and will therefore earn a return of only 8%. Hence either an 8% market rate or a 10% book rate can be associated with the debt.

Once again, our question is which should be reflected in the component cost of debt in the WACC calculation?

The Appropriate Perspective for the WACC Calculation

Which view—book or market—is more appropriate for calculating the WACC? To answer that question we have to understand exactly what the use of each implies in the context of capital budgeting.

Book values relate to capital the company already has. It was raised in the past to support past projects. Using those values to calculate the WACC results in a figure that reflects the composite cost of existing capital that's already committed.

Market values relate to the current state of capital markets. Using market values to calculate the WACC gives a figure that reflects an average of what capital would cost if it were raised today.

We use the WACC in techniques like IRR and NPV to evaluate newly proposed projects. Old capital isn't available to fund these undertakings because it's already been spent. Hence firms generally have to fund projects with new capital they have yet to raise. It therefore makes sense to evaluate those new projects against the likely cost of the new capital that will support them.

○ **Book values** reflect the cost of capital **already spent. Market values** estimate the cost of capital to be raised in the **near future.**

● **Market values** are appropriate because new projects are generally funded with **newly raised money.**

That means it's appropriate that the WACC reflect current market conditions, because those conditions are the best estimate of what capital will cost during the coming period. Hence we should use market values throughout the WACC calculation.

The Customary Approach

The customary approach is to assume that in the future, the firm will either maintain its present capital structure based on market prices or will strive to achieve some target structure also based on market prices. Either of these structures is combined with market-based component costs of capital to develop the WACC.

People are generally less concerned with the precision of the capital structure in the calculation than with the accuracy of the component costs of capital. In practice, it turns out that calculating the present structure at market prices is somewhat tedious. Further, the market-based structure is constantly changing. A reasonable target structure is often used for simplicity as much as for any other reason. The error implied is generally very small.

CALCULATING THE WACC

Calculating a real WACC involves three distinct steps. First we develop a market-value–based capital structure. Then we *adjust* the market returns on the securities underlying the capital components to reflect the company's true component costs of capital. Finally, we put these together to calculate a WACC.

● DEVELOPING MARKET-VALUE–BASED CAPITAL STRUCTURES

Developing a capital structure involves stating the dollar amounts of the capital components in use by the firm, adding them up, and then restating each as a percentage of the total. A book value structure is easy to calculate because the book values of debt, preferred stock, and equity are readily available on the balance sheet. Developing a market-value–based structure is more difficult. It requires that we compute the current market value of all the securities underlying each category of balance sheet capital, and then develop a structure from those values. The best way to understand the procedure is through an example.

EXAMPLE 12.2

The Wachusett Corporation has the following capital situation.

Debt: Two thousand bonds were issued five years ago at a coupon rate of 12%. They had 30-year terms and $1,000 face values. They are now selling to yield 10%.

Preferred stock: Four thousand shares of preferred are outstanding, each of which pays an annual dividend of $7.50. They originally sold to yield 15% of their $50 face value. They're now selling to yield 13%.

Equity: Wachusett has 200,000 shares of common stock outstanding, currently selling at $15 per share.

Develop Wachusett's market-value–based capital structure.

Solution: The market value of each capital component is the market price of the underlying security multiplied by the number of those securities outstanding.

We can use the valuation concepts from Chapters 6 and 7 to arrive at prices for the bonds and preferred stock. The price of the common stock is given.

Debt: The price of Wachusett's bonds is calculated by using the bond formula developed in Chapter 6, equation 6.4. In this case, k = 5%, n = 50, PMT = $60, and F = $1,000. (See pages 196–198.)

● A **market-value**–based capital structure uses the **current** prices of the firm's outstanding securities.

$$P_b = PMT[PVFA_{k,n}] + FV[PVF_{k,n}]$$
$$= \$60[PVFA_{5,50}] + \$1,000[PVF_{5,50}]$$
$$= \$60(18.2559) + \$1,000(.0872)$$
$$= \$1,182.55$$

Because there are 2,000 bonds outstanding, the market value of the debt is

$$\$1,182.55 \times 2,000 = \$2,365,100 .$$

Preferred stock: The preferred shares pay a $7.50 dividend and currently yield 13%. Each preferred share is valued as follows (see Chapter 7, equation 7.13, pages 240–241).

$$P_P = \frac{D_P}{k} = \frac{\$7.50}{.13} = \$57.69$$

Because there are 4,000 preferred shares outstanding, their total market value is

$$\$57.69 \times 4,000 = \$230,760 .$$

Common equity: The market value of Wachusett's common stock is just the market price times the number of shares outstanding.

$$\$15.00 \times 200,000 = \$3,000,000$$

Market-value–based weights: Next we summarize and compute the capital component weights based on market values.

Debt	$2,365,100	42.3%
Preferred	230,760	4.1
Equity	3,000,000	53.6
	$5,595,860	100.0%

http://

Go to the *Business Owner's Toolkit* at

www.toolkit.cch.com.

To learn more about how to select the appropriate discount rate, click on *Managing Your Business Finances, Major Purchases and Projects*

● CALCULATING COMPONENT COSTS OF CAPITAL

In this section we'll look into procedures for calculating the component costs of capital for debt, preferred stock, and equity. In each case, we'll start by considering the market return currently received by *new* investors on the securities underlying the component. Then we'll make certain adjustments to those returns that are necessary to reflect practical reality. We'll describe the adjustments before getting into the individual component costs.

Adjustments—The Effect of Financial Markets and Taxes

Although the returns received by investors and the costs paid out by companies are the same money, the amounts *effectively* paid and received can be different

● The returns paid to new investors are **adjusted** to arrive at **effective** costs to the company.

because of taxes and certain transaction costs associated with doing business in financial markets.

TAXES   The tax effect applies only to debt, and stems from the fact that interest payments are tax deductible to the paying firm. That effectively makes debt cheaper than it would be if it weren't deductible.

For example, if the firm's marginal tax rate is 40%,[1] the payment of $1 in interest reduces taxable income by $1, and the firm pays $.40 less tax even though the investor gets the full dollar of interest. By way of contrast, a dollar paid as a dividend is not deductible and results in no tax savings.

The dollar cost of paying an amount of interest, I, is

$$I(1 - T)$$

● The **tax deductibility of interest** makes debt an even **cheaper** source of capital than it is due to low risk.

where T is the tax rate. The same rule applies when interest is expressed as a rate of return. If the firm pays interest at a rate k_d, the effective after-tax cost of paying that rate is

$$k_d(1 - T) .$$

For example, if the interest rate is 10% and the tax rate is 40%, the cost of debt adjusted for taxes would be

$$k_d(1 - T) = 10\%(1 - .4) = 6\% .$$

Recall that the return paid to investors on debt is the lowest of the three capital components because debt is the least risky investment. The tax effect reduces the cost of debt even further in relation to the cost of the other components, making it a real bargain.

● **Flotation costs** lower the amount received when a security is issued, **increasing the cost** of the capital raised.

FLOTATION COSTS   **Flotation costs** are administrative fees and expenses incurred in the process of issuing and selling (floating) securities. You can think of flotation cost as a commission paid to firms in the investment banking industry for services performed in raising capital.

If flotation costs are f percent of the proceeds of a security issue that raises an amount P paid by investors, the amount received by the issuing company is

$$P - fP = P(1 - f),$$

where f is in decimal form in the equation. Clearly, flotation costs lower the amount of money a firm receives when it sells securities. They have the effect of making the cost of the issue higher than the return received by investors. In general we can write

$$\begin{matrix} \text{component} \\ \text{cost of} \\ \text{capital} \end{matrix} = \frac{\text{investor's return}}{(1 - f)} = \frac{k}{(1 - f)}.$$

In words, the component cost of capital is higher than the investor's return by the ratio of $1/(1 - f)$.[2]

---

1. The marginal federal income tax rate for most firms is 35%. However, most companies are also subject to state income taxes, so 40% is a reasonable approximation of an average total rate.
2. This relationship is strictly true only when the investment is expected to generate an infinite stream of cash flows. If the stream is finite, as in a bond investment, it is an approximation.

For example, if the return on a particular security is 10% and flotation costs are 20%, the component cost of capital is

$$\text{component cost of capital} = \frac{k}{(1-f)} = \frac{10\%}{(1-.20)} = 12.5\%$$

The Cost of Debt

To calculate the component cost of debt based on market returns, we take the return received by investors currently purchasing the firm's bonds and adjust it for the effects of taxes. Most debt isn't sold initially to the general public, but is *privately placed* with large investors. Therefore flotation costs are minimal, and we needn't adjust for them.

The market return on business debt is generally well known for the firm's own securities or for issues of similar risk. We'll call that return k_d. Then the cost of debt is

● The **cost of debt** is the investor's return adjusted for the **tax deductibility of interest** payments.

(12.1) $$\text{cost of debt} = k_d(1-T),$$

where $(1-T)$ adjusts for the fact that interest is tax deductible to the paying firm.

EXAMPLE 12.3

Blackstone Inc. has 12% coupon rate bonds outstanding that yield 8% to investors buying them now. Blackstone's marginal tax rate including federal and state taxes is 37%. What is Blackstone's cost of debt?

Solution: First notice that k_d is the current market yield of 8%, not the coupon rate. To calculate the cost of debt we simply write equation 12.1 and substitute from the information given.

$$\begin{aligned}\text{cost of debt} &= k_d(1-T) \\ &= .08(1-.37) \\ &= 5.04\%\end{aligned}$$

The Cost of Preferred Stock

Preferred stock provides an investor with a constant dividend as long as the share remains outstanding. Recall from our work in Chapters 5 and 7 that such an arrangement is known as a *perpetuity*.

The price of a preferred share is the present value of the perpetuity of the dividend stream, and is given by the expression

(12.2) $$P_p = \frac{D_p}{k_p},$$

where P_p is the current price of a share, D_p is the preferred dividend, and k_p is the return on the investment in preferred stock. (See Chapter 5, pages 173–174, and Chapter 7, page 240.)

Solving equation 12.2 for the investor's return yields

(12.3)
$$k_p = \frac{D_p}{P_p}.$$

Preferred dividends are not tax deductible to the issuing firm, so no tax adjustment needs to be made. However, flotation costs must be incorporated by multiplying equation 12.3 by $1/(1 - f)$. Rewriting, we have

● The **cost of preferred stock** is the investor's return adjusted for **flotation costs**.

(12.4)
$$\text{cost of preferred stock} = \frac{D_p}{(1 - f)P_p} = \frac{k_p}{(1 - f)}.$$

EXAMPLE 12.4

The preferred stock of the Francis Corporation was issued several years ago with each share paying 6% of a $100 par value. Flotation costs on new preferred are expected to average 11% of the funds raised.

a. What is Francis's cost of preferred capital if the interest rate on similar preferred stock is 9% today?

b. Calculate Francis's cost of preferred if the stock is selling at $75 per share today.

Solution: Notice that parts a and b of this problem pose the same question with slightly different given information. In part a we have the market return directly, and in part b we have the information needed to calculate it.

a. Write equation 12.4 using only the last term on the right, and adjust the market return for flotation costs directly.

$$\text{cost of preferred stock} = \frac{k_p}{(1 - f)} = \frac{9\%}{1 - .11} = 10.1\%$$

b. In this case, instead of having the yield, we're told that the stock is currently selling for $75. We also know it pays an annual dividend of 6% of $100 or $6. Write equation 12.3 using the middle term and substitute.

$$\text{cost of preferred stock} = \frac{D_p}{(1 - f)P_p} = \frac{\$6}{(1 - .11)\$75} = 9.0\%$$

The Cost of Common Equity

● The **cost of equity** is imprecise because of the **uncertainty** of future cash flows.

The market return available on an equity investment isn't as easy to come up with as the market return on debt or preferred stock. Those securities give an investor known streams of future payments in return for the prices paid, so calculating the return is easy. A stock investment, on the other hand, depends for its return on *estimates* of future dividends and prices, which are much less certain than interest payments and preferred dividends.

As a result of this uncertainty, the market return on an equity investment has to be estimated. To do that we can use some of the ideas we've developed in earlier chapters. We'll look at three approaches involving the CAPM, the Gordon model, and risk premiums.

● New equity comes from **two sources,** stock sales and retained earnings, which have **different costs.**

Another complication arises from the fact that equity comes from two sources, retained earnings and the sale of new stock. These have to be treated separately because they turn out to have different costs. We'll look at each in turn, beginning with retained earnings.

The Cost of Retained Earnings

It's tempting to think of retained earnings as free to the company, because they come from its own internal operations. However, all earnings belong to the firm's stockholders whether they're paid out as dividends or retained. To the extent that management retains earnings, they reinvest shareholders' money in the company for them.

In other words, retained earnings represents money stockholders could have spent if it had been paid out in dividends. Therefore, those stockholders deserve a return on the funds just as though the money had been paid out and reinvested through the purchase of new shares. By this logic, the market return on new shares is the appropriate starting point for estimating the cost of retained earnings.

● The cost of **retained earnings** is equal to the **unadjusted** return earned by new buyers of the firm's stock.

NO ADJUSTMENTS BETWEEN RETURN AND COST FOR RE   It's important to notice that retained earnings are the only *internally generated* capital source. They aren't raised through financial markets, so they don't incur flotation costs. They're also not tax deductible. Hence no adjustments are necessary to convert return to cost.

THE CAPM APPROACH—THE REQUIRED RATE OF RETURN   We studied the capital asset pricing model (CAPM) in Chapter 8. The model is a theory purporting to explain how investors set required rates of return for particular stocks. Recall that the required rate is the return that just induces investors to purchase a stock, and is generally assumed to be a function of the stock's risk. The expected rate of return, on the other hand, is the return investors expect in the future given the knowledge currently available about a particular stock.

Under normal market conditions stock prices are more or less *in equilibrium,* meaning that expected and required rates of return are about equal. Hence, the market return on a particular stock can be approximated by estimating either the required return or the expected return. The CAPM allows us to estimate the required return; we'll look at estimating with the expected return in the next section.

The CAPM's expression for the required rate of return is the security market line (SML). It was presented in Chapter 8 as equation 8.4. We'll relabel the expression and repeat it here for convenience.

(12.5)
$$k_X = k_{RF} - (k_M - k_{RF})b_X$$

where: k_X is the required return on stock X

k_{RF} is the risk-free rate, usually taken to be the current return on three-month treasury bills

k_M is the return on the market or on an "average" stock, usually estimated through a market index like the S&P 500

b_X is stock X's beta coefficient, the measure of company X's market risk

Equation 12.5 provides a direct estimate of the current market return available to investors on the equity of company X. It is therefore also a direct estimate of the cost of equity acquired through retained earnings, because no tax or market adjustments are necessary.

EXAMPLE 12.5

The return on the Strand Corporation's stock is relatively volatile as reflected by the company's beta of 1.8. The return on the S&P 500 is currently 12% and is expected to remain at that level. Treasury bills are yielding 6.5%. Estimate Strand's cost of retained earnings.

Solution: Write equation 12.5 and substitute directly, using the return on the S&P 500 as k_M and the treasury bill yield as k_{RF}.

$$\text{cost of RE} = k_X = k_{RF} + (k_M - k_{RF})b_X$$
$$= 6.5\% + (12\% - 6.5\%)1.8$$
$$= 16.4\%$$

THE DIVIDEND GROWTH APPROACH—THE EXPECTED RATE OF RETURN   In Chapter 7 we developed an expression for pricing a stock that is expected to grow at a constant rate into the indefinite future. The model is alternatively called the *dividend growth model* or the *Gordon model* after the scholar who developed it. The expression was presented as equation 7.10. We'll relabel and repeat it here with one minor change in notation. We'll replace k in the denominator with k_e to emphasize the idea that the rate is the expected return on an investment in the stock.

(12.6)
$$P_0 = \frac{D_0(1 + g)}{k_e - g}$$

where: P_0 is the current price of the stock
D_0 is the most recent annual dividend paid by the company
k_e is the expected return on an investment in the stock
g is the anticipated, constant growth rate of the company and its dividend stream

Solving equation 12.6 for k_e gives a direct estimate of the cost of equity capital obtained through retained earnings. The result is equation 12.7.[3]

(12.7)
$$\text{cost of RE} = k_e = \frac{D_0(1 + g)}{P_0} + g$$

3. Recall that in the Gordon model the *next* dividend is $D_1 = D_0(1 + g)$. Hence equations 12.6 and 12.7 can also be written with D_1 in the numerators of the fractions.

EXAMPLE 12.6

Periwinkle Inc. paid a dividend of $1.65 last year and its stock is currently selling for $33.60 a share. The company is expected to grow at 7.5% indefinitely. Estimate the firm's cost of retained earnings.

Solution: Write equation 12.7 and substitute for Periwinkle's expected return and the cost of RE.

$$\text{cost of RE} = k_e = \frac{D_0(1 + g)}{P_0} + g$$

$$= \frac{\$1.65(1.075)}{\$33.60} + .075$$

$$= .053 + .075 = 12.8\%$$

● The **cost of retained earnings** can be estimated using the **CAPM**, the **dividend growth (Gordon) model**, or a **risk premium**.

THE RISK PREMIUM APPROACH   Since beginning our study of interest in Chapter 4, we've recognized that any return can be thought of as the sum of a base rate and premiums for bearing risk.

Investment risk and the associated risk premiums vary among companies, but they also vary between the kinds of securities offered by a single company. Debt is the safest investment, while equity has considerably more risk.

The relationship between the risk of debt and the risk of equity is relatively constant among companies. In other words, the *increment* in risk between debt and equity is about the same for high-risk and low-risk firms. That increment tends to command an additional risk premium of between 3% and 5%.

As a result, it's feasible to estimate the return on a firm's equity by adding three to five percentage points to the market return on its debt, which is generally easy to get. We can formalize the relationship as

(12.8) $k_e = k_d + rp_e,$

where k_d and k_e are the respective market returns on debt and equity, and rp_e is the additional risk premium on equity. The cost of retained earnings is then equal to this estimate of k_e.

EXAMPLE 12.7

The Carter Company's long-term bonds are currently yielding 12%. Estimate Carter's cost of retained earnings.

Solution: Simply write equation 12.8 and substitute, using 4% for the incremental risk premium.

$$\text{cost of RE} = k_e = k_d + rp_e$$

$$= 12\% + 4\%$$

$$= 16\%$$

The Cost of New Common Stock

So far, we've been talking about equity capital from retained earnings. Firms often need to raise more equity capital than is available from earnings, and do so by selling new common stock.

Equity from new stock is just like equity from retained earnings, with the exception that raising it involves incurring flotation costs. Therefore, the expressions we've used so far to estimate the cost of equity have to be adjusted to reflect those costs. This is easiest to do in equation 12.7, the dividend growth model, because the price of the stock appears explicitly in that expression. The adjustment simply involves substituting $(1 - f)P_0$ for P_0, where f represents the fraction of the price going to flotation cost. The result is as follows.

● The cost of **new common stock** includes an adjustment for **flotation** costs.

(12.9) $$\text{cost of new equity} = k_e = \frac{D_0(1 + g)}{(1 - f)P_0} + g$$

EXAMPLE 12.8

Suppose Periwinkle Inc. of Example 12.6 had to raise capital beyond that available from retained earnings. What would be its cost of equity from new stock if flotation costs were 12% of money raised?

Solution: Write equation 12.9 and substitute from Example 12.6, including a 12% flotation cost.

$$\begin{aligned}
\text{cost of} \atop \text{new equity} &= k_e = \frac{D_0(1 + g)}{(1 - f)P_0} + g \\
&= \frac{\$1.65(1.075)}{(.88)\$33.60} + .075 \\
&= .06 + .075 = 13.5\%
\end{aligned}$$

● PUTTING THE WEIGHTS AND COSTS TOGETHER

Once we've calculated a market-value–based capital structure and a series of component costs based on market returns, the weighted average calculation for the WACC is a simple matter. The procedure is identical to the one we illustrated in Example 12.1 using the appropriate weights and costs. We'll forego presenting the same computation here.

A comprehensive example presented after the next section includes the weighted average calculation in its proper sequence.

THE MARGINAL COST OF CAPITAL (MCC)

A firm's WACC is not independent of the amount of capital raised. In fact, it tends to increase abruptly from time to time as funding requirements are increased. Changes in the WACC are reflected in the **marginal cost of capital**

(MCC) **schedule,** a graph showing how the WACC changes as a firm raises more capital during a planning period, usually a year. Glance ahead to Figure 12.1 on page 402 to see the idea expressed graphically.

The WACC/MCC terminology is a little confusing. The MCC schedule is a graph showing the values the WACC goes through as larger amounts of money are raised. We could just as easily call it a graph of the WACC. The term "marginal cost of capital" (MCC) itself means the cost of the next dollar of capital to be raised.

Notice that the WACC starts out at one level and jumps to a higher level as the total amount of capital raised passes a certain point. If still more capital were to be raised, the MCC would have more step-function jumps like the one shown. The first jump or break is of particular interest.

● The **MCC** is a graph of the **WACC** showing **abrupt increases** as larger amounts of capital are raised in a planning period.

●THE BREAK IN MCC WHEN RETAINED EARNINGS RUN OUT

The first increase in the MCC usually occurs when the firm runs out of retained earnings and starts raising external equity by selling stock. The WACC increases at that point because the cost of equity increases. We can see this phenomenon clearly by comparing two of the examples in the last section.

Examples 12.6 and 12.8 both involve the cost of equity for Periwinkle Inc. In the first example we calculated the cost of retained earnings, and in the second we dealt with the cost of equity from new stock. Notice that the 13.5% cost of new equity is higher than the 12.8% cost of retained earnings. The difference is due to the flotation costs associated with selling the new shares.

● The MCC **breaks** when **retained earnings are exhausted,** and the cost of equity increases due to **flotation** costs.

We generally assume firms use all the money available from retained earnings before selling new stock. So the cost of equity capital increases abruptly as the firm moves into externally raised money. But if the cost of equity increases at some point, the WACC must also increase at the same point because equity is an element in the weighted average calculation. A numerical illustration will make these ideas clear.

We'll assume the information shown in Table 12.3 about the Brighton Company, and develop its MCC schedule. We'll calculate the WACC, first using the cost of retained earnings and then using the cost of new equity. These are the WACCs before and after the retained earnings breakpoint. The two computations are shown in Table 12.4. Notice that the only difference between them is the cost of equity.

TABLE 12.3	**The Brighton Company's Capital Structure, Component Costs, and Requirements**

	Capital Structure	Component Cost
Debt	40%	8%
Equity	60%	From RE 10% From new stock 12%
Expected retained earnings		$3M
Total capital requirement		$10M

| TABLE 12.4 | The Brighton Company's WACC Calculations |

	Capital Structure Weights		Capital Component Cost		
With equity from RE					
Debt	.4	×	8%	=	3.2%
Equity	.6	×	10%	=	6.0%
				WACC	= 9.2%
With equity from new stock					
Debt	.4	×	8%	=	3.2%
Equity	.6	×	12%	=	7.2%
				WACC	= 10.4%

Table 12.4 shows that Brighton's WACC will increase by 1.2% as the firm uses up retained earnings and moves into new equity.

Locating the Break

The next question involves locating the break in terms of total funding. In other words, how much capital will have been raised when the WACC increases?

This turns out to be a simple matter. Recall that we assumed capital will be raised in the proportions of some capital structure. In this case the structure is 60% equity, so every dollar raised will be 60% equity. We also expect to have $3 million of retained earnings to use up before turning to new stock. Hence our question is equivalent to asking for the total funding level when 60% of that total is $3 million, or $3 million is 60% of what number?

The calculation answering that question is division by .6. Brighton will have raised a total of

$$\$3 \text{ million}/.60 = \$5 \text{ million}$$

when it runs out of retained earnings. Therefore the WACC *breaks* at $5 million.

This is an important calculation. The first breakpoint of the WACC is always found by dividing the amount of retained earnings available by the fractional proportion of equity in the capital structure.

●THE MCC SCHEDULE

Brighton's results are shown graphically in Figure 12.1. The graph shows the WACC at various funding levels. As we said earlier, the overall portrayal is referred to as the marginal cost of capital (MCC) schedule. Notice how the schedule makes a definitive break at the point where retained earnings are exhausted. Also notice that the break occurs at the level of total capital that has been raised when retained earnings run out ($5 million), not at the level of available retained earnings, $3 million in this case.

Other Breaks in the MCC Schedule

For most companies, the WACC is reasonably constant, aside from the break into external equity, as long as moderate levels of capital are raised. However,

FIGURE 12.1

The Brighton Company's Marginal Cost of Capital (MCC) Schedule

low-cost funds cannot be raised at or near the initial WACC without limit. The internal workings of capital markets tend to put restrictions on the amount of new money available to companies in any time period.

For example, suppose Brighton attempted to raise $20 million instead of $10 million. Perceiving such a large capital program as risky, investors would be likely to demand higher returns for further investments in both debt and equity. That means Brighton would have to pay higher interest rates to borrow more and accept a lower price to sell additional stock. Effectively, the MCC would have more upward steps to the right on the graph between $10M and $20M.[4]

Combining the MCC and the IOS

> The **investment opportunity schedule (IOS)** is a plot of the IRRs of available projects arranged in descending order.

A firm's available capital budgeting projects can be sorted into descending order of IRR and displayed on the same set of axes as the MCC. The idea is shown in Figure 12.2 for the Brighton Company. Each block represents a project. The heights and widths of the blocks are, respectively, the projects' IRRs and the amounts of capital they require. The pattern traced by the upper rightward boundary of the projects is known as the **investment opportunity schedule (IOS)**. The horizontal segments of the IOS are the IRRs of the respective projects.

> The **MCC and IOS plotted together** show which projects should be undertaken.

This portrayal makes clear which projects should be undertaken and which should not. Brighton should accept projects as long as the IOS (IRR) is above the MCC. Figure 12.2 shows that projects A, B, and C should be undertaken, but projects D and E should not. Notice that the first break in the MCC makes projects D and E unacceptable. If the WACC continued at 9.2% indefinitely, both of these projects would have IRRs equal to or above the cost of capital. Because the MCC breaks as new equity has to come from the sale of stock, they don't.

Interpreting the MCC

The portrayal in Figure 12.2 seems to imply that Brighton should evaluate the first $5 million of capital projects with a WACC of 9.2% and projects using the next $5 million with a WACC of 10.4%. However, this approach is cumber-

---

4. Occasionally the cost of debt or preferred increases *before* the shift from retained earnings to outside equity. Then that point isn't the *first* break in the MCC as we've described.

FIGURE 12.2

Marginal Cost of Capital (MCC) Schedule and Investment Opportunity Schedule (IOS)

some in that it requires keeping track of more than one WACC. The same effect is achieved by taking a marginal approach and defining the WACC as the rate at which the IOS and the MCC intersect, 10.4% in the illustration.

This is an important point. A firm's WACC for a planning period (usually a year) is determined by the availability of financial resources *and* the pattern of investment opportunities projected during that period.

● The firm's **WACC** for the planning period is at the **intersection** of the **MCC** and the **IOS**.

THE COST OF CAPITAL—A COMPREHENSIVE EXAMPLE

In this section we'll work through a comprehensive example of the calculations necessary to develop a firm's WACC and the MCC curve. We'll also comment on practice as we go along.

EXAMPLE 12.9

Baxter Metalworks Inc. has the following elements of capital.

Debt: Baxter issued $1,000, 30-year bonds 10 years ago at a coupon rate of 9%. Five thousand bonds were sold at par. Similar bonds are now selling to yield 12%.

Preferred stock: Twenty thousand shares of 10% preferred stock were sold five years ago at their $100 par value. Similar securities now yield 13%.

Equity: The company was originally financed with the sale of 1 million shares of common stock at $10 a share. Accumulated retained earnings are currently $3 million. The stock is now selling at $12.50.

Target capital structure: We won't get into the reasoning behind the idea that one mix of capital components might be better than another until Chapter 13. For now, assume that Baxter has chosen the following target capital structure.

Debt	20%
Preferred stock	10%
Equity	70%

This means management attempts to keep the market values of the capital components reasonably close to these proportions over time as money is raised.

Other information:

- Baxter's marginal income tax rate including federal and state rates is 40%.
- Flotation costs average 10% in the sale of common and preferred stock.
- Short-term treasury bills currently yield 7%.
- An average stock currently yields a return of 13.5%.
- Baxter's beta is 1.4.
- The firm is expected to grow at 6.5% indefinitely.
- The annual dividend paid last year was $1.10 per share.
- Next year's business plan includes earnings of $2 million, of which $1.4 million will be retained.

Calculate Baxter's capital component weights and its WACC before and after the retained earnings break. Sketch the firm's MCC.

Solution: We'll solve this problem and illustrate some important points along the way with the following steps.

1. Book values and weights (for reference only).
2. Market values and weights.
3. Compare target, book, and market weights, and comment on practice.
4. Capital component costs.
5. Computation of WACCs.
6. Sketch MCC.

1. Book Values and Weights of Baxter's Capital Components
First we'll recreate the capital section of Baxter's balance sheet.

Debt (5,000 bonds @ $1,000)..		$5,000,000
Preferred stock (20,000 shares @ $100)....................................		2,000,000
Equity		
Common stock (1 million shares @ $10) $10,000,000		
Retained earnings......................................	3,000,000	13,000,000
Total capital		$20,000,000

Now calculate the book weights by stating debt, preferred equity, and common equity as percentages of total capital. This calculation is made for reference only, because we don't use book values to calculate WACC.

Debt	$ 5,000,000	25%
Preferred	2,000,000	10
Equity	13,000,000	65
	$20,000,000	100%

2. Market Values and Weights

To calculate capital component weights based on market values, we have to find the current market value of the securities underlying each component.

Debt: The market value of Baxter's debt is based on the current price of its outstanding bonds. That price is different from face value, because the market interest rate is no longer equal to the bond's coupon rate. The calculation is made by using the bond formula developed in Chapter 6, equation 6.4. In this case k = 6%, n = 40, PMT = $45, and F = $1,000. Review pages 196–198 if this procedure is unfamiliar to you.

$$P_b = PMT[PVFA_{k,n}] + FV[PVF_{k,n}]$$

$$= \$45[PVFA_{6,40}] + \$1,000[PVF_{6,40}]$$

$$= \$45(15.0463) + \$1,000(.0972)$$

$$= \$774.28$$

Because 5,000 bonds are outstanding, the market value of the debt is

$$\$774.28 \times 5,000 = \$3,871,400 .$$

Preferred stock: The preferred shares were issued to yield 10% at a $100 par value. Therefore the preferred dividend is $10. The market yield is now 13%, so each preferred share is valued as follows (see Chapter 7, equation 7.13, page 240).

$$P_p = \frac{D_p}{k} = \frac{\$10}{.13} = \$76.92$$

For the 20,000 preferred shares outstanding, their total market value is

$$\$76.92 \times 20,000 = \$1,538,400 .$$

Common equity: The market value of Baxter's common stock is easy to calculate. The shares are selling at $12.50 and there are 1 million outstanding, so their value is

$$\$12.50 \times 1,000,000 = \$12,500,000 .$$

Market-value–based weights: Next we summarize and compute the capital component weights based on market values.

Debt	$3,871,400	21.6%
Preferred	1,538,400	8.6
Equity	12,500,000	69.8
	$17,909,800	100.0%

As you can see, calculating market value weights is somewhat tedious. This is especially true if a number of different classifications of stocks and bonds are all outstanding at the same time.

3. Book, Market, and Target Capital Structures

At this point it's appropriate to stop and compare the alternative capital structures we've talked about. These are the target structure and structures based on book and market values. The results are summarized as follows.

	Book	Market	Target
Debt	25%	21.6%	20%
Preferred Stock	10	8.6	10
Common Equity	65	69.8	70
	100%	100.0%	100%

Notice that in this example, the weights aren't very different from one another. Of course, that's not always the case, but it does happen quite a bit. It's especially true that the market-value–based weights and the target structure are quite similar.

In the rest of this example we'll use the market value weights, noticing that they're very close to the target structure.

4. Capital Component Costs

Next we'll calculate the cost of each capital component using the rules developed earlier.

Debt: The cost of debt is given by equation 12.1. It's equal to the return being received by debt investors adjusted for taxes.

$$\text{cost of debt} = k_d(1 - T)$$
$$= .12(1 - .40)$$
$$= 7.2\%$$

Preferred stock: Equation 12.4 gives us the cost of preferred either through consideration of the preferred dividend relative to its market price or by directly adjusting the market yield for flotation costs. Because we're given a market yield of 13% in this case, we'll do the latter.

$$\text{cost of preferred stock} = \frac{k_p}{(1 - f)} = \frac{13\%}{1 - .10} = 14.4\%$$

Equity: We'll deal with the cost of equity in two steps. First we'll estimate the cost of retained earnings, and then the cost of new stock.

Retained earnings: We'll approach the cost of retained earnings in the three ways we've considered, then reconcile the results.

CAPM: Equation 12.5 gives the return required on Baxter's stock by a typical investor in terms of the risk-free rate, the market return, and Baxter's beta.

$$\text{cost of RE} = k_B = k_{RF} + (k_M - k_{RF})b_B$$
$$= 7.0\% + (13.5\% - 7.0\%)1.4$$
$$= 16.1\%$$

Dividend growth: Equation 12.7 gives the expected return on Baxter's stock given its current price, recent dividend history, and anticipated growth rate.

$$\text{cost of RE} = k_e = \frac{D_0(1 + g)}{P_0} + g$$
$$= \frac{\$1.10(1.065)}{\$12.50} + .065$$

$$= .094 + .065$$

$$= 15.9\%$$

Risk premium: The risk premium approach adds a premium of 3% to 5% to the return on a firm's debt to allow for the extra risk involved in an equity investment. Using equation 12.8 and a middle value of 4% for the additional premium, we have

$$\text{cost of RE} = k_e = k_d + rp_e$$

$$= 12\% + 4\%$$

$$= 16\% \ .$$

● Some **judgment** is required in **reconciling** the results of the different approaches to the **cost of equity.**

Reconciliation: In this case the three approaches give similar results, which are summarized as follows.

CAPM	16.1%
Dividend growth	15.9%
Risk premium	16%

Hence using 16.0% for the cost of retained earnings seems reasonable.

New stock: The return on equity raised through the sale of new stock is estimated by using the dividend growth model adjusted for flotation costs. Equation 12.9 yields

$$\text{cost of RE} = k_e = \frac{D_0(1 + g)}{(1 - f)P_0} + g$$

$$= \frac{\$1.10(1.065)}{(.90)\$12.50} + .065$$

$$= .104 + .065$$

$$= 16.9\% \ .$$

Notice that the cost of new stock is .9% higher than the cost of retained earnings.

A note on accuracy: As we've said before, it's important to realize that return/cost calculations with respect to equity are not as accurate as our tenth of a percent figures seem to imply. An estimate that's good to about a half percent is generally the best we can hope for.

5. Computing the WACC

Deriving the WACC is now a straightforward weighted average calculation. We'll use weights based on market values. The calculation has to be done twice because of the two different costs of equity, for retained earnings and new stock. The results will be the WACCs before and after the retained earnings breakpoint.

The computation is laid out in the table on page 408. The entries in the weight column are the decimal equivalents of the percentages of each component in the capital structure based on market values. Treat the pre-break and after-break pairs of columns separately. Multiply the cost of each component by the number in the weight column to get the factor column. Then add the factors for the WACC. We use results rounded to the nearest tenth of a percent in applications.

Capital Component	Weight	Pre-Break		After-Break	
		Cost	Factor	Cost	Factor
Debt	.216	7.2%	1.56	7.2%	1.56
Preferred Stock	.086	14.4	1.24	14.4	1.24
Equity	.698	16.0	11.17	16.9	11.80
			WACC = 13.97%		WACC = 14.60%
		Use rounded values:	14.0%		14.6%

6. The MCC

The MCC schedule shows the WACC before and after the retained earnings breakpoint. To plot it we have to know how much capital will have been raised when the break occurs.

Baxter expects to generate $1.4 million in retained earnings next year, and every dollar raised is assumed to be 69.8% equity—either retained earnings or new stock. To locate the breakpoint we have to answer the following question: $1.4 million is 69.8% of what total capital amount? To get the answer, simply divide $1.4 million by .698, the fractional component of equity in the capital structure.

The calculation is

$$\$1,400,000/.698 = \$2,005,731 \,.$$

For practical purposes we'll round this result and assume the retained earnings breakpoint is $2 million. The plot of Baxter's MCC can then be drawn as follows.

At some point to the right the MCC would step upward again as Baxter approaches the limits of its money-raising capability, and the various capital components become more expensive. However, we can't predict exactly where those steps will be the way we can forecast the breakpoint due to running out of retained earnings.

A POTENTIAL MISTAKE—HANDLING SEPARATELY FUNDED PROJECTS

Sometimes a project is proposed that is to be funded entirely by a single source of capital. This situation can create some confusion about the application of the WACC in practice.

INSIGHTS

Practical Finance

Revisiting EVA

Recall that at the end of our study of ratio analysis in Chapter 3 (pages 88–89) we introduced two new performance measurement concepts, market value added (MVA) and economic value added (EVA). We're now in a better position to appreciate EVA.

EVA is important because of a shortcoming in the concept of net income, the traditional measure of financial performance. Net income begins with revenue and subtracts costs and expenses *including interest* to arrive at the so-called "bottom line." Hence the traditional income statement charges operations with the cost of debt, but *ignores the cost of equity and preferred stock*. That means net income implicitly treats equity and preferred as free resources which, of course, they aren't. EVA corrects that problem by charging for the use of all capital instead of just debt. The charge is calculated by multiplying total capital by the *cost of capital* as developed in this chapter. The EVA calculation is expressed as follows where equity includes preferred stock.

$$\text{EVA} = \text{EBIT} (1 - T) - (\text{debt} + \text{equity}) (\text{cost of capital } \%)$$

EBIT $(1 - T)$ is operating income *after tax*, which is then reduced by the charge for all capital used.

EVA is a very important concept in management today. It's worth your while to review the broad implications of the idea now that you have a better understanding of the cost of capital.

● **All projects** should be evaluated against the **WACC including** those with **dedicated funding.**

For example, a firm might float a bond issue and use the proceeds entirely to fund just one project. It's logical to ask whether the cost of capital used to evaluate the project should be the cost of the bond issue and not the firm's WACC. Because debt tends to be the cheapest form of capital, such an approach would make the project more likely to be accepted.

Although it seems that a close matching of a source of funds with its use would be appropriate whenever possible, it's a mistake in capital budgeting which has to be conducted within the context of the firm's overall capital-raising capability. Firms cannot continue to raise low-cost debt indefinitely without from time to time raising higher cost equity. In other words, firms have a limited debt capacity that can be used up until a further infusion of equity is made.

Let's consider an illustration in which the firm is borrowing exclusively to fund a project to see what can happen if we base the accept/reject decision on the cost of debt alone. For simplicity we'll assume the firm has no preferred stock. Imagine that its cost of debt and cost of equity are 8% and 12%, respectively, and that the capital structure is half debt and half equity so the WACC is 10%. Suppose the project proposed has an IRR of 9%, is evaluated against the 8% cost of debt, and is therefore accepted. Notice that it would have been rejected if evaluated against the WACC of 10%.

Now suppose that sometime later another project comes along with an IRR of 11%, and the firm tries to borrow to fund it. However, lenders say the company's debt capacity is exhausted and refuse to advance funds.

Suppose equity money is available to fund the project, but its cost is 12%. Using the same rationale of measuring a project against the cost of the specific capital component funding it, the firm evaluates the second project against the 12% cost of equity and rejects it.

Notice what has happened. The company has accepted a project with an IRR of 9% and rejected one with an IRR of 11%. This obvious error is a result of trying to match funding sources and uses within the constraint of one firm's capital-raising capability. Had the firm evaluated both projects at the WACC of 10%, the correct accept/reject decisions would have been made. The implication is clearly that *all* projects (which are risk consistent with the firm's operations) should be evaluated at the WACC.

DISCUSSION QUESTIONS

Visit Ibbotson Associates at www.ibbotson.com/ to see how they estimate the cost of capital.

1. You're the newly hired CFO of a small construction company. The privately held firm is capitalized with $2 million in owner's equity and $3 million in variable rate bank loans. The construction business is quite risky, so returns of 20% to 25% are normally demanded on equity investments. The bank is currently charging 14% on the firm's loans, but interest rates are expected to rise in the near future. Your boss, the owner, started his career as a carpenter and has an excellent grasp of day-to-day operations. However, he knows little about finance. Business has been good lately, and several expansion projects are under consideration. A cash flow projection has been made for each. You're satisfied that these estimates are reasonable.

The owner has called you in and confessed to being confused about the projects. He instinctively feels that some are financially marginal and may not be beneficial to the company, but he doesn't know how to demonstrate this or how to choose among the projects that are financially viable.

Assuming the owner understands the concept of return on investment, write a brief memo explaining the ideas of IRR and cost of capital and how they can solve his problem. Don't get into the detailed mechanics of the calculations, but do use the figures given above to make a rough estimate of the company's cost of capital and use the result in your memo.

2. Compare the cost of capital concept with the idea of the required return on a stock investment made by an individual. Relate both ideas to the risk of the investment. How would a very risky investment/project be handled in the capital budgeting/cost of capital context?

3. Define the idea of capital structure and capital components. Why is capital structure important to the cost of capital concept? In many capital structure discussions, preferred stock is lumped in with either debt or common equity. With respect to the cost of capital, however, it's treated separately. Why?

4. You are a new financial analyst working for a company that's more than 100 years old. The CFO has asked you and a young member of the accounting staff to work together in reviewing the firm's capital structure for the purpose of recalculating its cost of capital. As you both leave the CFO's office, your accounting colleague says this job is really going to be easy because he already has the information. In preparing the latest annual report, he worked on the capital section of the balance sheet and has the values of debt, preferred stock, and equity at his fingertips. He says the two of you can summarize these into a report in five minutes and then go out for a beer. How do you react and why? Is the fact that the firm is quite old relevant? Why?

5. You're the CFO of a small company that is considering a new venture. The president and several other members of management are very excited about the idea for reasons related to engineering and marketing rather than profitability. You've analyzed the proposal by using capital budgeting techniques and found that it fails both IRR and NPV tests with a cost of capital based on market returns. The problem is that interest rates have risen steeply in the last year, so the cost of capital seems unusually high.

You've presented your results to the management team, who are very disappointed. In fact, they'd like to find a way to discredit your analysis so they can justify going ahead with the project. You've explained your analysis and everything seems well understood except for one point. The group insists that the use of returns currently available to investors as a basis for the cost of capital components doesn't make sense. The vice president of marketing put his objection as follows. "Two years ago we borrowed $1 million at 10%. We haven't paid it back, and we're still making interest payments of $100,000 every year. Clearly, our cost of debt is 10% and not the 14% you want to use. If you'd use our 'real' cost of debt, as well as of equity and preferred stock, the project would easily qualify financially." How do you respond?

(The appropriate response is relatively short. It's worth noting that this kind of thing happens all the time in corporations. Marketing and engineering people often get carried away with "neat" projects that don't make sense financially. The CFO has to watch the bottom line and it's not unusual to be seen as a wet blanket who wants to spoil the others' fun!)

from the CFO

6. The investor's return and the company's cost are opposite sides of the same coin—almost, but not quite. Explain.

7. There's an issue of historical versus market value with respect to both the cost of capital components and the amounts of those components used in developing weights. We're willing to accept an approximation for the weights, but not for the cost/returns. Why?

8. A number of investment projects are under consideration at your company. You've calculated the cost of capital based on market values and rates, and analyzed the projects by using IRR and NPV. Several projects are marginally acceptable. While watching the news last night, you learned that most economists predict a rise in interest rates over the next year. Should you modify your analysis in light of this information? Why?

9. Establishing the cost of equity is the most arbitrary and difficult part of developing a firm's cost of capital. Outline the reasons behind this problem and the approaches available to make the best of it.

10. The engineering department at Digitech Inc. wants to buy a new state-of-the-art computer. The proposed machine is faster than the one now being used, but whether the extra speed is worth the expense is questionable given the nature of the firm's applications. The chief engineer (who has an

MBA and a reasonable understanding of financial principles) has put together an enormously detailed capital budgeting proposal for the acquisition of the new machine, which concludes that it's a great deal. You're a financial analyst for the firm and have been assigned to review the engineering proposal. Your review has highlighted two problems. First, the cost savings projected as a result of using the new machine seem rather optimistic. Second, the analysis uses an unrealistically low cost of capital.

With respect to the second point, the engineering proposal contains the following exhibit documenting the development of the cost of capital used.

> Digitech's capital structure is 60% debt and 40% equity
>
> The computer manufacturer is offering financing at 8% as a sales incentive
>
> Cost of capital = 8% × .6 = 4.8%
>
> After tax = 4.8% × (1 − T) = 4.8% × .6 = 2.9%

You've checked the market and found that Digitech's bonds are currently selling to yield 14%, and the stock is returning about 20%.

How would you proceed? That is, explain the chief engineer's error(s) and indicate the correct calculations.

11. Retained earnings are generated by the firm's internal operations and are immediately reinvested to earn more money for the company and its shareholders. Therefore such funds have zero cost to the company. Is this statement true or false? Explain.

12. Define the marginal cost of capital (MCC) and explain in words why it predictably undergoes a step-function increase (breaks) as more capital is raised during a budget period.

13. After the break in the MCC caused by using up retained earnings, the schedule can be expected to remain flat indefinitely. Is that statement right or wrong? If wrong, explain what can be expected to happen to the MCC and why.

14. Why is it appropriate to define the WACC as the highest step on the MCC under the IOS? Is anything lost by using this definition?

15. Whitefish Inc. operates a fleet of 15 fishing boats in the North Atlantic Ocean. Fishing has been good in the last few years as has the market for product, so the firm can sell all the fish it can catch. Charlie Bass, the vice president for operations, has worked up a capital budgeting proposal for the acquisition of new boats. Each boat is viewed as an individual project identical to the others, and shows an IRR of 22%. The firm's cost of capital has been correctly calculated at 14% before the retained earnings break and 15% after that point. Charlie argues that the capital budgeting figures show that the firm should acquire as many new boats as it possibly can, financing them with whatever means it finds available. You are Whitefish's CFO. Support or criticize Charlie's position. How should the appropriate number of new boats be determined? Does acquiring a large number of new boats present any problems or risks that aren't immediately apparent from the financial figures?

PROBLEMS

1. Blazingame Inc.'s capital components have the following market values.

Debt	$35,180,000
Preferred stock	$17,500,000
Common equity	$48,350,000

Calculate the firm's capital structure and show the weights that would be used for a weighted average cost of capital (WACC) computation.

2. The Aztec Corporation has the following capital components and costs. Calculate Aztec's WACC.

Component	Value	Cost
Debt	$23,625	12.0%
Preferred stock	4,350	13.5
Common equity	52,275	19.2

3. A relatively young firm has capital components valued at book and market and market component costs as follows. No new securities have been issued since the firm was originally capitalized.

Component	Value Market	Value Book	Cost
Debt	$42,830	$40,000	8.5%
Preferred stock	10,650	10,000	10.6
Common equity	65,740	32,000	25.3

a. Calculate the firm's capital structures and WACCs based on both book and market values, and compare the two.

b. What appears to have happened to interest rates since the company was started?

c. Does the firm seem to be successful? Why?

d. What should be the implication of using a WACC based on book as opposed to market values? In other words, what kind of mistakes might management make by using the book values?

4. Five years ago Hemingway Inc. issued 6,000 thirty-year bonds with par values of $1,000 at a coupon rate of 8%. The bonds are now selling to yield 5%. The company also has 15,000 shares of preferred stock outstanding that pay a dividend of $6.50 per share. These are currently selling to yield 10%. Its common stock is selling at $21, and 200,000 shares are outstanding. Calculate Hemingway's market-value–based capital structure.

5. The Wall Company has 142,500 shares of common stock outstanding that are currently selling at $28.63. It has 4,530 bonds outstanding that won't mature for 20 years. They were issued at a par value of $1,000 paying a coupon rate of 6%. Comparable bonds now yield 9%. Wall's $100 par value preferred stock was issued at 8% and is now yielding 11%; 7,500 shares are outstanding. Develop Wall's market-value–based capital structure.

6. The market price of Albertson Ltd's common stock is $5.50 and 100,000 shares are outstanding. The firm's books show common equity accounts totaling $400,000. There are 5,000 preferred shares outstanding that originally sold for their par value of $50, pay an annual dividend of $3, and are currently selling to yield an 8% return. Also, 200 bonds are outstanding that were issued five years ago at their $1,000 face values for 30-year terms, pay a coupon rate of 7%, and are currently selling to yield 10%. Develop Albertson's capital structure based on both book and market values.

7. The Dentite Corporation's bonds are currently selling to yield new buyers a 12% return on their investment. Dentite's marginal tax rate including both federal and state taxes is 38%. What is the firm's cost of debt?

8. Harris Inc.'s preferred stock was issued five years ago to yield 9%. Investors buying those shares on the secondary market today are getting a 14% return. Harris generally pays flotation costs of 12% on new securities issues. What is Harris's cost of preferred financing?

9. New buyers of Simmonds Inc. stock expect a return of about 22%. The firm pays flotation costs of 9% when it issues new securities. What is Simmonds' cost of equity

a. from retained earnings?

b. from new stock?

10. Kleig Inc.'s bonds are selling to yield 9%. The firm plans to sell new bonds **to the general public** and will therefore incur flotation costs of 6%. The company's marginal tax rate is 42%.

a. What is Kleig's cost of debt with respect to the new bonds? (*Hint*: Adjust the cost of debt formula to include flotation costs.)

b. Suppose Kleig also borrows directly from a bank at 12%.

1. What is its cost of debt with respect to such bank loans? (*Hint*: Would bank loans be subject to flotation costs?)

2. If total borrowing is 60% through bonds and 40% from the bank, what is Kleig's overall cost of debt? (*Hint*: Think weighted average.)

11. A few years ago, Hendersen Corp. issued preferred stock paying 8% of its par value of $50. The issue is currently selling for $38. Preferred stock flotation costs are 15% of the proceeds of the sale. What is Hendersen's cost of preferred stock?

12. The Pepperpot Company's stock is selling for $52. Its last dividend was $4.50, and the firm is expected to grow at 7% indefinitely. Flotation costs associated with the sale of common stock are 10% of the proceeds raised. Estimate Pepperpot's cost of equity from retained earnings and from the sale of new stock.

13. The Longlife Insurance Company has a beta of .8. The average stock currently returns 15% and short-term treasury bills are offering 6%. Estimate Longlife's cost of retained earnings.

14. The Longlife Insurance Company of Problem 13 has several bonds outstanding that are currently selling to yield 9%. What does this imply about the cost of the firm's equity?

15. The Longenes Company uses a target capital structure when calculating the cost of capital. The target structure and current component costs based on market conditions follow.

Component	Mix	Cost*
Debt	25%	8%
Preferred stock	10	12
Common equity	65	20

*The costs of debt and preferred stock are already adjusted for taxes and/or flotation costs. The cost of equity is unadjusted.

The firm expects to earn $20 million next year and plans to invest $18 million in new capital projects. It generally pays dividends equal to 60% of earnings. Flotation costs are 10% for common and preferred stock.

a. What is Longenes's initial WACC?

b. Where is the retained earnings breakpoint in the MCC? (Round to the nearest $.1M.)

c. What is the new WACC after the break? (Adjust the entire cost of equity for flotation costs.)

d. Longenes can borrow up to $4 million at a net cost of 8% as shown. After that the net cost of debt rises to 12%. What is the new WACC after the increase in the cost of debt?

e. Where is the second break in the MCC? That is, how much total capital has been raised when the second increase in WACC occurs?

f. Sketch Longenes's MCC.

16. (Integrative Problem) Taunton Construction Inc.'s capital situation is described as follows.

Debt: The firm issued 10,000 25-year bonds 10 years ago at their par value of $1,000. The bonds carry a coupon rate of 14% and are now selling to yield 10%.

Preferred stock: Thirty thousand shares of preferred stock were sold six years ago at a par value of $50. The shares pay a dividend of $6 per year. Similar preferred issues are now yielding 9%.

Equity: Taunton was initially financed by selling 2 million shares of common stock at $12. Accumulated retained earnings are now $5 million. The stock is currently selling at $13.25.

Taunton's *target capital structure* is as follows.

Debt	30.0%
Preferred stock	5.0
Common equity	65.0
	100.0%

Other information:

- Taunton's marginal tax rate (state and federal) is 40%.
- Flotation costs average 12% for common and preferred stock.
- Short-term treasury bills currently yield 7.5%.
- The market is returning 12.5%.
- Taunton's beta is 1.2.
- The firm is expected to grow at 6% indefinitely.
- The last annual dividend paid was $1.00 per share.
- Taunton expects to earn $5 million next year.
- The firm can borrow an additional $2 million at rates similar to the market return on its old debt. Beyond that, lenders are expected to demand returns in the neighborhood of 14%.
- Taunton has the following capital budgeting projects under consideration in the coming year. These represent its investment opportunity schedule (IOS).

Project	IRR	Capital Required	Cumulative Capital Required
A	15.0%	$3M	$3M
B	14.0	2M	5M
C	13.0	2M	7M
D	12.0	2M	9M
E	11.0	2M	11M

a. Calculate the firm's capital structure based on book and market values, and compare with the target capital structure. Is the target structure a reasonable approximation of the market-value–based structure? Is the book structure very far off?

b. Calculate the cost of debt based on the market return on the company's existing bonds.

c. Calculate the cost of preferred stock based on the market return on the company's existing preferred stock.

d. Calculate the cost of retained earnings using three approaches: CAPM, dividend growth, and risk premium. Reconcile the results into a single estimate.

e. Estimate the cost of equity raised through the sale of new stock using the dividend growth approach.

f. Calculate the WACC by using equity from retained earnings based on your component cost estimates and the target capital structure.

g. Where is the first breakpoint in the MCC (the point where retained earnings run out)? Calculate to the nearest $.1M.

h. Calculate the WACC after the first breakpoint.

i. Where is the second breakpoint in the MCC (the point at which the cost of debt increases)? Why does this second break exist? Calculate to the nearest $.1M.

j. Calculate the WACC after the second break.

k. Plot Taunton's MCC.

l. Plot Taunton's IOS on the same axes as the MCC. Which projects should be accepted and which should be rejected? Do any of those rejected have IRRs above the initial WACC? If so, explain in words why they're being rejected.

m. What is *the* WACC for the planning period?

n. Suppose project E is self-funding in that it comes with a source of its own debt financing. A loan is offered through an equipment manufacturer at 9%. The cost of the loan is

$$9\% \times (1 - T) = 5.4\% .$$

Should project E be accepted under such conditions?

 Internet Problem

17. Visit Ibbotson's Cost of Capital Center Web site at http://www.ibbotson.com/ research/papers/cost.asp to review a recent research paper. Click on *Cost of Capital Research Papers*. Select one of the articles listed and prepare a one-page summary highlighting the most important points.

PART FOUR

Long-Term Financing Issues

CHAPTER 13

Capital Structure and Leverage

Chapter Outline

We introduced the idea of capital structure in Chapter 12 as a necessary underpinning to the cost of capital concept. In this chapter we'll discover there's a great deal more to capital structure than calculating the WACC. In fact, its management is one of the most important things financial executives do.

Used properly, capital structure management can be an effective approach to improving financial performance. It can turn good results into better ones, and can even raise the price of a company's stock.

However, the technique has to be used with caution because its benefits come at a price. The cost of improving performance with capital structure can be increased risk. And risk, as we've already learned, is a serious problem. In this chapter, we'll learn all about the benefits and the costs of managing results through capital structure.

BACKGROUND

In Chapter 12, we said capital structure describes the mix of debt, preferred stock, and equity a firm employs. In this chapter we'll simplify that definition by assuming preferred stock is essentially a form of debt.[1] Hence from here on when we refer to capital structure, we'll mean the mix of just two components, debt and equity, within capital.

> **Financial leverage** refers to debt in the capital structure. It **multiplies** the **effectiveness** of equity but adds risk.

"Leverage" is a general term that refers to an ability to multiply the effect of some effort. The term comes from physics where a lever is used to multiply force. *Financial leverage* refers to using borrowed money to multiply the effectiveness of the equity invested in a business enterprise.

The borrowed money with which financial leverage is concerned is the debt in a company's capital structure. Hence the terms "financial leverage" and "capital structure" are somewhat synonymous. To be leveraged means to have debt. To be unleveraged means to operate with only equity capital.

The idea is quantified by the percentage of debt within total capital (debt + equity). Thus, 10% financial leverage implies a capital structure that's 10% debt and 90% equity.

THE CENTRAL ISSUE

The study of capital structure revolves around a central question: Can the use of debt (leverage) increase the value of a firm's equity? Stated slightly differently: Can it increase stock price?

We need to be sure we understand exactly what this question means. To illustrate, think about a firm with $1 million in equity capital and no debt. Then suppose it borrows $.25 million, buys up a quarter of its own stock, and retires the shares. In effect it's traded a quarter of its equity for debt. The procedure is called a **capital restructuring**.

> **Capital restructuring** involves changing leverage by **shifting the mix** of debt and equity.

Intuitively, the process shouldn't affect the price of the shares still outstanding. Three quarters of the original shares now represent three quarters of the former equity, so nothing should have changed on a per-share basis.

But in fact, adding financial leverage in the manner we've just described often increases the price of the remaining shares and the value of the firm. However, the effect isn't consistent, and there are circumstances under which adding leverage decreases stock price and a firm's value.

In other words, there's a relationship between capital structure and stock price, but it's neither precise nor totally understood. Study in the field attempts to explain the nature of the relationship better and predict when additional financial leverage will increase or decrease price and value.

> Under certain conditions, **changing leverage** increases stock price. An **optimal capital structure** maximizes stock price.

In particular, we want to discover whether there's an *optimal capital structure* that maximizes stock price, all other things held constant.

After covering a little more background, we'll look at an example to see just how leverage works.

---

1. This assumption is based on the fact that preferred stock dividends are fixed in amount, and in that respect are more like interest payments than like common stock dividends.

You can think of debt and preferred stock as offering investors returns that are more or less constant regardless of how the company is doing financially. Equity, on the other hand, offers a retrun that tends to vary with the business's performance.

● RISK IN THE CONTEXT OF LEVERAGE

In earlier chapters we learned that risk and return are related and have a great deal to do with determining stock prices. Here again, we'll find that risk plays an important role in setting values. In fact, leverage influences stock price because it alters the risk/return relationship in an equity investment. We'll understand that better as we go along.

Measures of Performance

We'll often refer to EBIT, ROE, and EPS in this chapter, so it's worthwhile to review their meaning.

● **Operating income (EBIT) is unaffected by financial leverage.**

EBIT, earnings before interest and taxes, is also called operating income. It's the lowest line on the income statement that's independent of financing. In other words, because EBIT is above interest expense, it is unaffected by whether the firm is leveraged or not.

ROE and EPS are return on equity and earnings per share, respectively. They're defined as follows

$$\text{ROE} = \frac{\text{EAT}}{\text{equity}} \quad \text{and} \quad \text{EPS} = \frac{\text{EAT}}{\text{number of shares}},$$

where EAT is earnings after tax, the bottom line of the income statement (also called net income).

● **Investors regard EPS as an important indicator of future profitability.**

ROE and EPS are *overall* measures of business performance in that they include both the results of operations and the effects of financing. Both measures are important to investors when they consider buying a company's stock, but EPS is especially significant. It is usually taken as an indication of the future earning power of the firm and is therefore a major determinant of the stock's market price.

EBIT, ROE, and EPS were treated in Chapters 2 and 3, on pages 26 and 83–84. It's not a bad idea to review those pages now.

Redefining Risk for Leverage-Related Issues

● **Leverage-related risk is variation in ROE and EPS.**

We're used to thinking of risk in finance as *variation* in the return on an investment. In this chapter we'll narrow our focus and think of risk as variation in financial performance measured by ROE and EPS.[2] This notation is separable into two pieces, business risk and financial risk.

● **Business risk is the variation in EBIT.**

BUSINESS RISK   Business risk is variation in a firm's operating performance measured by EBIT. It arises from variations in revenues, costs, and expenses. Hence **business risk** is defined as variation in EBIT itself.[3]

FINANCIAL RISK   In an unleveraged firm (one with no debt), the variation in ROE and EPS is identical to the variation in EBIT. In a leveraged firm, the varia-

---

2. Variation in ROE and EPS is a part of the broader definition of risk we used in Chapter 8. It includes much but not all of what we called *unsystematic* or *business-specific* risk there.

3. Be careful not to confuse the business risk we're talking about here with the broader concept of business-specific risk from Chapter 8. Business-specific risk includes variation in EBIT as well as other things tied to a specific company or industry. For example, concern over the possibility of federal regulation of an industry could depress stock prices even though financial results are unchanged. Federal regulation or the threat of it would then be an element of business-specific risk.

tion in ROE and EPS is always *greater than* the variation in EBIT. Further, the more leverage the firm uses, the larger is the incremental variation.

● **Financial risk** is the **additional** variation in ROE and EPS brought about by **financial leverage.**

This leads to the definition of *financial risk* as the *additional* variation in ROE and EPS that arises as a result of using financial leverage (debt). The idea is illustrated in Figure 13.1. The left column shows that business operations produce EBIT, to which we add financing to produce ROE and EPS. In other words, EBIT measures operations, but ROE and EPS measure *overall* performance, which is a combination of operations and financing.

The second and third columns show the sources of variation in the measures and how that variation is defined as risk. It's important to notice that business risk flows down into ROE and EPS by itself. Financial risk is *added* only if there is debt financing.

● LEVERAGE AND RISK—TWO KINDS OF EACH

From what we said in the last section it's clear that financial leverage is associated with, and indeed causes, financial risk. We've also defined business risk as the variation in EBIT. It turns out there's another type of leverage, which has an influence on business risk that's similar to the influence financial leverage has on financial risk. This concept is called *operating leverage.*

Operating leverage is related to a company's **cost structure** rather than to its capital structure. Cost structure describes the relative amounts of *fixed* and *variable* cost in productive and administrative processes.

When the term "leverage" is used by itself, it generally refers to financial leverage, which is the more important concept. We'll discuss operating leverage, and relate it to financial leverage later in this chapter.

FIGURE 13.1

Business and Financial Risk

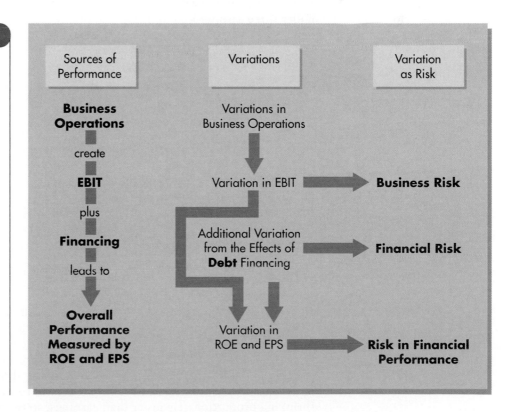

● OUR APPROACH TO LEVERAGE

In the remainder of this chapter we'll take an in-depth look at leverage. We'll begin by examining how financial leverage works in practical, real-world terms. Then we'll have an equally pragmatic look at operating leverage. After examining both, we'll make a comparison between them and look at how they interact.

Then we'll spend some time studying capital structure theory. We'll do that without much mathematics, but when we're done we'll have a good grasp of the approach taken by sophisticated scholars. We'll also see that the theoretical results are essentially the same as those we arrived at intuitively, but for somewhat different reasons.

FINANCIAL LEVERAGE

Now that we've developed the appropriate background, we can begin an investigation into just why leverage does what it does. We'll begin with an intuitive explanation.

● THE EFFECT OF FINANCIAL LEVERAGE

The underlying reason that leverage may increase stock prices is that under certain conditions it improves financial performance measured in terms of ROE and EPS. However, it sometimes makes performance worse and always increases risk. Hence it's not immediately clear when leverage will be a benefit and when it won't.

To understand how leverage works, we'll examine the financial results of a rising young company, the Arizona Balloon Corporation, ABC for short, which sells hot air balloon rides in the Arizona desert. We'll look at how ABC performs under three assumptions about its use of leverage. We'll examine a case with no debt, one with 50% debt, and a highly leveraged situation with 80% debt.

Each scenario is represented by a column in Table 13.1. The capital structures are shown at the top of each column along with the number of shares of stock outstanding. Moving from left to right, the share numbers are calculated by assuming borrowed money is used to retire stock that can be bought at its book value of $10 per share.

The issue we want to explore is what happens to financial performance as we vary leverage while holding the level of operating income (EBIT) constant. In other words, given some level of EBIT, are we better off with more or less leverage?

To answer that question we'll assume EBIT of $200,000, as displayed toward the middle of each column. The next four lines complete the income statement. Interest is 10% of debt and taxes are figured at a 40% rate.

Return on equity (ROE) and earnings per share (EPS) are displayed next. These are the performance measures in which we're most interested.

The Good News about Financial Leverage

The important thing to observe in the table is the progression of ROE and EPS as we move to the right. As leverage increases, both measures go up dramatically.

Notice why this happens in terms of computations. ROE and EPS are calculated by dividing EAT by equity and the number of shares, respectively.

As debt is added, EAT declines because of increasing interest charges. However, equity and the number of shares outstanding shrink as debt replaces equity in the capital structure and shares are retired. In this case, equity and shares are shrinking proportionately faster than earnings, so the ratios increase.

| TABLE 13.1 | **Effect of Increasing Financial Leverage When the Return on Capital Employed Exceeds the Cost of Debt** |

Leverage Analysis
Arizona Balloon Corporation
($000)

	Leverage Scenarios		
	1	*2*	*3*
	0% Debt	*50% Debt*	*80% Debt*
Capital			
Debt	$ —	$ 500	$ 800
Equity	1,000	500	200
Total	$1,000	$1,000	$1,000
Shares @ $10	100,000	50,000	20,000
Revenue	$1,000	$1,000	$1,000
Cost/expense	800	800	800
EBIT	$ 200	$ 200	$ 200
Interest (10%)	—	50	80
EBT	$ 200	$ 150	$ 120
Tax (40%)	80	60	48
EAT	$ 120	$ 90	$ 72
ROE	12%	18%	36%
EPS	$ 1.20	$ 1.80	$ 3.60

● When **profitability** is good, **EPS** and **ROE** increase as leverage increases.

This is the good news about leverage. If basic profitability is good, a dollar-for-dollar replacement of equity with debt improves financial performance as measured by ROE and EPS.[4] Then if investors react positively to the increases they may bid up the price of ABC's stock.

The Return on Capital Versus the Cost of Debt

The benefit of leverage illustrated in Table 13.1 makes sense because ABC's operating income (EBIT) represents an after-tax return on capital that exceeds its cost of debt. In other words, the company makes more with borrowed money than it pays for the privilege of borrowing.

The after-tax return on capital can be measured by a ratio called the return on capital employed (ROCE). The ROCE looks at the profitability of operations without regard to how the firm is financed, but does so after tax. This amounts to calculating what the after-tax earnings on EBIT would be if there were no deductible interest, and then dividing by total capital.

● The **ROCE** measures the profitability of **operations** before financing charges on a basis **comparable to ROE**.

The resulting number is comparable to the return on assets, the return on equity, or the after-tax cost of debt. The computation is given by equation 13.1.

(13.1)
$$\text{ROCE} = \frac{\text{EBIT } (1 - T)}{\text{debt + equity}}$$

---

4. A moderating effect that's not included in the illustration is that interest rates generally go up at high levels of debt. That means the interest cost might really be somewhat higher in the third column than the amount shown. However, the effect is unlikely to reverse the trend of increasing ROE and EPS shown.

Calculating equation 13.1 for any of the columns in Table 13.1 yields 12%. This says that ABC is able to earn 12% after tax on any capital it uses.

If you're a little confused by the ROCE concept, just concentrate on the first column. In that case, because there's no debt and no interest, the ROCE is simply the ROE, which is 12%.

Now notice that ABC's after-tax cost of debt is

$$k_d(1 - T) = 10\%(1 - .4) = 6\%,$$

where k_d is the interest rate the company pays and T is the tax rate. This is only half of what the business earns on its capital, so it makes sense to use someone else's (borrowed) money.

Whenever a firm can earn an ROCE that exceeds its after-tax borrowing rate, it *seems* to make sense to use as much borrowed money as possible. In this case, every dollar borrowed frees up a dollar of equity and earns ABC's owners the 6% difference.

We'll learn shortly that other things affect the advisability of borrowing, but it's a basic truth that recorded financial results improve as equity is traded evenly for debt if the ROCE exceeds the after-tax cost of debt.

● When the **ROCE exceeds** the after-tax **cost of debt,** more leverage **improves ROE and EPS.**

The Other Side of the Coin—The Bad News about Leverage

Unfortunately, leverage works in two directions. When a company is earning an ROCE that's *less* than the after-tax cost of debt, leverage makes results worse! To see that, we'll reconstruct Table 13.1 assuming bad weather causes a downturn in ABC's balloon business. The result is displayed in Table 13.2.

TABLE 13.2

Effect of Increasing Financial Leverage When the Cost of Debt Exceeds the Return on Capital Employed

Leverage Analysis
Arizona Balloon Corporation
($000)

	Leverage Scenarios		
	1	*2*	*3*
	0% Debt	*50% Debt*	*80% Debt*
Capital			
Debt	$ —	$ 500	$ 800
Equity	1,000	500	200
Total	$1,000	$1,000	$1,000
Shares @ $10	100,000	50,000	20,000
Revenue	$ 800	$ 800	$ 800
Cost/expense	720	720	720
EBIT	$ 80	$ 80	$ 80
Interest (10%)	—	50	80
EBT	$ 80	$ 30	—
Tax (40%)	32	12	—
EAT	$ 48	$ 18	—
ROE	4.8%	1.8%	0%
EPS	$ .48	$ .18	$ 0.00

Assume revenues and earnings fall off to the point where the ROCE is just 4.8% (see the ROE in the first column of Table 13.2). That's less than the 6% cost of debt.

Now look at the progression from column to column as the firm moves from equity into debt. ROE and EPS *decrease* with increasing leverage. That's because the firm is earning less on capital (4.8%) than it's paying for the use of borrowed funds (6%).

● When **ROCE is less than** the after-tax **cost of debt,** more leverage makes **ROE and EPS worse.**

This is another basic truth about leverage. Results are worse when ROCE is less than the after-tax cost of debt. This can cause investors to bid the price of the firm's stock down. Clearly it doesn't make much sense to increase leverage intentionally in this situation, and financial managers don't do it unless something else makes borrowing unavoidable.

Managing through Leverage

The foregoing suggests that under certain conditions management may be able to manipulate financial results and stock price by changing the firm's capital structure. This is indeed true, but it has to be done with some caution.

It takes time to change capital structure, whereas operating results can turn around overnight. That means a firm can expand leverage during good times and then be caught by an unexpected downturn. When that happens, there may be a precipitous drop in ROE and EPS as well as in stock price.

The following example illustrates the management of EPS.

EXAMPLE 13.1

Selected financial information for the Albany Corporation follows.

Albany Corporation at $10M Debt
($000 except per-share amounts)

EBIT	$23,700	Debt	$ 10,000
Interest (@ 12%)	1,200	Equity	90,000
EBT	$22,500	Capital	$100,000
Tax (@ 40%)	9,000	Number of shares = 9,000,000	
EAT	$13,500		

stock price = $10 per share

$$ROE = \frac{EAT}{equity} = \frac{\$13,500}{\$90,000} = 15\%$$

$$EPS = \frac{EAT}{number\ of\ shares} = \frac{\$13,500}{9,000,000} = \$1.50$$

Notice that Albany's total capital is $100 million. It pays 12% interest on debt of $10 million and its combined state and federal tax rate is 40%. The company's stock is selling at its book value of $10 per share. The treasurer feels debt can be traded for equity without immediately affecting the price of the stock or the rate at which the firm can borrow.

Management believes it is in the best interest of the company and its stockholders to move the firm's EPS from its current level up to $2.00 per share. However, no opportunities are available to increase operating profit (EBIT) above the current level of $23.7 million.

Will borrowing more money and retiring stock raise Albany's EPS, and if so, what capital structure will achieve an EPS of $2.00?

Solution: EPS will increase if the ROCE exceeds the after-tax cost of debt. Calculate ROCE by writing equation 13.1 and substituting from the problem.

$$ROCE = \frac{EBIT(1 - T)}{debt + equity}$$

$$= \frac{\$23.7M(1 - .4)}{\$100.0M} = \frac{\$14.2M}{\$100.0M}$$

$$= 14.2\%$$

The after-tax cost of debt is the interest rate paid times one minus the tax rate.

$$k_d(1 - T) = 12\%(1 - .4) = 7.2\% < 14.2\%$$

Hence trading equity for debt will improve EPS.

The second part of the question asks us to find the capital structure that results in an EPS of $2.00. Conceptually the easiest way to do that is trial and error. Simply choose a series of debt levels and recompute the financial results until a value is found that yields EPS = $2.00.

Let's begin with an arbitrary $20 million increase in debt to $30 million. Because Albany's stock is selling for its book value of $10, every $10 borrowed will retire one share of stock and reduce equity by the same $10. Hence the new equity will be $70 million. The revised interest expense is ($30M × .12 =) $3.6 million. From there the calculations are straightforward.

Albany Corporation at $30M Debt
($000 except per-share amounts)

EBIT	$23,700	Debt	$ 30,000
Interest (@ 12%)	3,600	Equity	70,000
EBT	$20,100	Capital	$100,000
Tax (@ 40%)	8,040	Number of shares = 7,000,000	
EAT	$12,060		

$$ROE = \frac{EAT}{equity} = \frac{\$12,060}{\$70,000} = 17.2\%$$

$$EPS = \frac{EAT}{number\ of\ shares} = \frac{\$12,060}{7,000,000\ shares} = \$1.72$$

The resulting EPS of $1.72 is less than the $2.00 target. This implies that more than $30 million in debt will be required. As an exercise, show that $45 million is very close to the right level.

● FINANCIAL LEVERAGE AND FINANCIAL RISK

Tables 13.1 and 13.2 show that financial leverage is a two-edged sword. It multiplies good results into great results, but it also multiplies bad results into terrible results. This means when business conditions change, performance measured by ROE or EPS makes wider swings for more leveraged organizations than for those with relatively less debt. The *incremental* variation in results is what we've called *financial risk*.

TABLE 13.3

Financial Leverage and Risk

| | ROE | |
	Column 1 No Debt	Column 3 80% Debt
Good times (Table 13.1)	12.0%	36.0%
Bad times (Table 13.2)	4.8%	0.0%
Difference	7.2%	36.0%
Incremental difference in ROE due to financial leverage	= 36.0% − 7.2% = 28.8%	
Change in ROE due to business risk	= 7.2%	
Change in ROE due to financial risk	= 28.8%	
Total variation in ROE	= 36.0%	

We can illustrate the idea with Arizona Balloon Corporation using Tables 13.1 and 13.2. The first table represents relatively good times, while the second reflects harder times and lower earnings. Within each table there's a no-leverage situation in the first column and a high-leverage case in the third column.

To see the effect of financial leverage on risk, we'll compare the changes in ROE in the first and third columns, respectively, between the two tables. The analysis is shown in Table 13.3.

Because there's no financial leverage in column 1 of the two tables, the difference in those ROEs represents the variability of the basic business's results. In other words, that change is due to *business risk*.[5]

The difference in the column 3 ROEs represents the *sum* of the variabilities arising from operations and from financing. The incremental variability, the difference between the two differences, is a result of *financial risk*.

In ABC's case, business risk accounts for a swing of 7.2% in ROE. The financial risk associated with 80% leverage, however, accounts for a swing of (36.0% − 7.2% =) 28.8% in ROE. In other words, financial risk is (28.8%/ 7.2% =) four times as large as business risk. The result makes sense, because 80% debt represents a high degree of leverage.

To check your understanding, show that the financial risk associated with 50% debt (column 2) is 1.25 times the level of business risk.

A good way to think of these ideas is to say that leverage magnifies changes in operating income (EBIT) into larger changes in ROE and EPS. Further, the more leverage there is, the larger is the magnification.

● **Financial risk** is the **increased variability** in financial results that comes from **additional leverage.**

● PUTTING THE IDEAS TOGETHER—THE EFFECT ON STOCK PRICE

Our study of the Arizona Balloon Corporation has demonstrated two important effects of leverage.

---

5. We generally measure business risk at EBIT, but when there's no financial leverage the result is the same at ROE. To see this, notice that *in column 1* the ratio of EBIT in Table 13.1 to EBIT in Table 13.2 is the same as the ratio of ROE in Table 13.1 to ROE in Table 13.2.

● Leverage **enhances performance** while it **adds risk,** pushing stock prices in **opposite directions.**

1. During periods of reasonably good performance, leverage enhances results in terms of ROE and EPS.

2. Leverage adds variability to financial performance when operating results change. This means performance is riskier with more leverage.

Both phenomena become more pronounced as the level of leverage increases.

These effects drive stock prices in opposite directions. The first, enhanced performance under *likely* conditions, effectively makes the expected return on a stock investment higher. That makes the stock more desirable to investors, which causes them to bid up its price.

In ABC's case, for example, suppose everyone expects prosperity consistent with Table 13.1 next year, believing the chances of a recession are very remote. Then ABC's expected EPS with no leverage is $1.20 from the first column. That expectation can be increased to $1.80 by moving to the leverage position in column 2. If no one is too worried about poor economic conditions, the higher expected performance is just accepted at its face value.

The second effect makes a stock investment riskier, and we know from the principle of risk aversion (Chapter 8, pages 254 and 262) that investors don't like that. Hence the second effect tends to drive investors away, lowering the price.

The key question is which effect dominates and when?

Real Investor Behavior and the Optimal Capital Structure

● When **leverage is low,** a little **more** has a **positive effect** on investors, but at **high** debt levels **concerns about risk dominate,** and the **effect of more is negative.**

It turns out that at low to moderate levels of debt, investors value the positive effects of leverage a great deal and virtually ignore concerns about increased risk. This is especially true if the economic outlook is good. Hence increases in leverage tend to raise stock prices when leverage is low or moderate.

As leverage increases, however, concerns about risk and poor performance begin to overwhelm the benefits of enhanced return in people's minds. Thus, at higher levels, further increases in leverage have a negative effect on stock price.

In other words, as leverage increases from nothing to very high levels (all other things held constant), stock price increases, reaches a maximum, and then decreases. The idea is shown graphically in Figure 13.2. The maximum point on the graph is conceptually important. It corresponds to the *optimal capital structure*. By definition this is the capital structure (percent debt, level of leverage) that maximizes stock price.

● As leverage increases its effect goes from **positive to negative,** which results in an **optimum capital structure.**

Finding the Optimum—A Practical Problem

No one doubts that the response pattern of stock price to leverage is generally as pictured in Figure 13.2 or that there is indeed some optimal level of debt that produces a maximum price. The problem is that no one has a way to determine exactly where the maximum is for a particular company at a particular time.

The appropriate level of leverage tends to vary with the nature of a company's business as well as with the economic climate. A firm whose basic business is relatively volatile would be expected to use less leverage than a company in a stable business. That's because a high level of business risk compounded by a high level of leverage produces an extremely risky company.

With respect to economic climate, investors are more sensitive to risk when the outlook is poor than when it's good. The optimal level of leverage therefore should be lower in bad times because investors are repelled by increasing risk sooner.

FIGURE 13.2

The Effect of Leverage on Stock Price

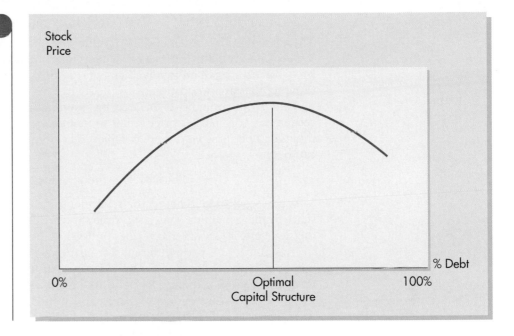

Unfortunately, these ideas aren't particularly quantifiable, so we aren't able to locate the optimum along the horizontal axis of Figure 13.2 with any accuracy.

That doesn't mean capital structure thinking is useless. However, it is more of a general guide than a precise set of instructions for managing a company. The accepted wisdom is more or less as follows.

from the CFO

1. *A firm with good profit prospects and little or no debt is probably missing an opportunity by not using borrowed money if interest rates are reasonable.*

2. *For most businesses, the optimal capital structure is somewhere between 30% and 50% debt.*

3. *Debt levels above 60% create excessive risk and should be avoided.*

● As a practical matter the optimum capital structure **cannot be precisely located.**

Keep in mind that these are rough guidelines with lots of exceptions, and not hard rules.

The Target Capital Structure

We referred to a *target capital structure* during our discussion of the cost of capital in Chapter 12. We said the target structure is one that management prefers over any other and attempts to maintain as it raises money. We're now in a position to better appreciate that idea.

● A firm's **target capital structure** is management's estimate of the optimal capital structure.

The target capital structure is just an approximation of the optimal capital structure. It is management's best guess at a level of leverage that maximizes the firm's stock price.

You may recall that in Chapter 12 we weren't concerned about stating target and actual capital structures with a great deal of precision. The reason should be apparent now. We can't find the optimal structure with a high degree of accuracy, so it doesn't make much sense to get too detailed about a guess at it.

The Effect of Leverage When Stocks Aren't Trading at Book Value

There's an important detail that shouldn't be missed in what we've been doing. We've presented illustrations of changes in leverage in which equity is replaced by debt. They have all involved changes in the number of shares of stock outstanding that are proportionate to the changes in equity.

That proportionality is ensured by assuming the stock can be purchased for retirement at a market price equal to its book value. When that isn't the case, things can be somewhat more complex. The relationship between ROE and EPS can be shown to be

$$\text{EPS} = \text{ROE} \times (\text{book value per share}).$$

When stock is purchased for retirement at book value, the book value per share of the remaining shares stays the same. And the transaction has essentially the same effect on EPS that it does on ROE. However, when stock is purchased for retirement at a price different from its book value, the book value of the remaining shares changes. Therefore a transaction can have different effects on ROE and EPS. Our results generally hold for ROE, but may not for EPS.

This phenomenon adds to the general imprecision of the ideas with which we've been working. The important point is the general direction in which leverage drives stock price, not the exact amount of the effect.

● THE DEGREE OF FINANCIAL LEVERAGE (DFL)—A MEASUREMENT

Financial leverage magnifies changes in EBIT into larger changes in ROE and EPS. It is of interest to know just how large that magnification is at any particular level of leverage.

For example, suppose a firm anticipates a 20% drop in EBIT. If the company has no debt, ROE and EPS will also drop by 20%. But what drop should be expected if the firm's capital is 30% or 40% debt? Clearly the question is important if management is interested in the effect changes in ROE and EPS may have on investors.

It's possible to answer the question by using a concept called the *degree of financial leverage,* abbreviated *DFL.* The DFL lets us quantify the effectiveness of leverage by relating *relative* changes in EPS and EBIT at any level of leverage.[6]

The idea is expressed as follows

(13.2)
$$\text{DFL} = \frac{\%\Delta\text{EPS}}{\%\Delta\text{EBIT}},$$

where %ΔEPS and %ΔEBIT mean the relative changes in EPS and EBIT, respectively.

---

6. A relative change is a percentage change. For example, a 5% change in the number 20 is a change of 1 unit, because 1 is 5% of 20. An increase to 21 is a positive 5% change. A decrease to 19 is a negative 5% change.

In general, a relative change in a number is the change divided by the number itself, expressed as a percentage. If we represent the change in the number N by ΔN, the relative change in N is expressed as

$$\%\Delta\text{N} = \frac{\Delta\text{N}}{\text{N}} \times 100.$$

If N is 20 and ΔN is 1, we have

$$\%\Delta\text{N} = \frac{1}{20} \times 100 = 5\%.$$

The best way to visualize the meaning of the DFL is to rewrite equation 13.2 by multiplying through by %ΔEBIT.

(13.2a) %ΔEPS = DFL × %ΔEBIT

● The **DFL** relates relative **changes in EBIT** to relative **changes in EPS.**

This expression says that relative changes in EBIT are multiplied by the DFL to arrive at relative changes in EPS. For example, if a firm's DFL is 1.5 and EBIT changes by 20%, EPS will change by (1.5 × 20% =) 30%.

If financial statements are available, the DFL can be calculated by assuming a small change in EBIT, working through to the resulting change in EPS, and substituting the relative changes into equation 13.2. However, that approach is rather tedious. An easier method is available by using the following formula.

(13.3)
$$DFL = \frac{EBIT}{EBIT - I}$$

where I is interest.

The derivation of equation 13.3 is a little involved, so we'll just accept the result.

EXAMPLE 13.2

Selected income statement and capital information for the Moberly Moped Manufacturing Company follow ($000).

		Capital	
Revenue	$5,580	Debt	$1,000
Cost/expense	4,200	Equity	7,000
EBIT	$1,380	Total	$8,000

Currently 700,000 shares of common stock are outstanding. The firm pays 15% interest on its debt and anticipates that it can borrow as much as it reasonably needs at that rate. The income tax rate is 40%.

Moberly is interested in boosting the price of its stock. To do that management is considering restructuring capital to 50% debt in the hope that the increased EPS will have a positive effect on price. However, the economic outlook is shaky, and the company's CFO thinks there's a good chance that a deterioration in business conditions will reduce EBIT next year. At the moment Moberly's stock sells for its book value of $10 per share.

Estimate the effect of the proposed restructuring on EPS. Then use the degree of financial leverage to assess the increase in risk that will come along with it.

Solution: First we'll calculate the proposed capital structure and display it alongside the current structure. Because equity can be traded at its book value, the restructuring is a straightforward exchange of equity for debt with a proportionate reduction in the number of shares outstanding.

	Current	Proposed
Capital		
Debt	$1,000	$4,000
Equity	7,000	4,000
Total	$8,000	$8,000
Shares outstanding	700,000	400,000

Next calculate projected EAT and EPS at the current level of business for both capital structures.

	Current	Proposed
EBIT	$1,380	$1,380
Interest (15% of debt)	150	600
EBT	$1,230	$780
Tax (@ 40%)	492	312
EAT	$738	$468
EPS	$1.054	$1.170

It's easy to see that if business conditions remain unchanged, the proposed structure will yield a higher EPS.

Next use equation 13.3 to calculate the DFL under each structure.

$$DFL_{cur} = \frac{EBIT}{EBIT - 1} = \frac{\$1,380}{\$1,380 - \$150} = 1.12$$

$$DFL_{prop} = \frac{EBIT}{EBIT - 1} = \frac{\$1,380}{\$1,380 - \$600} = 1.77$$

Now we can see why the CFO is concerned. EPS will be much more volatile under the proposed structure than it is currently. To illustrate, suppose business deteriorates and EBIT declines by 30%; that's not unusual. We can use equation 13.2a to see what will happen under both the current and proposed structures.

Under the current structure EPS will decline by a percentage calculated as follows.

$$\%\Delta EPS_{cur} = DFL_{cur} \times \%\Delta EBIT$$
$$= 1.12 \times 30\% = 33.6\%$$

But under the proposed structure the percentage decline will be

$$\%\Delta EPS_{prop} = DFL_{prop} \times \%\Delta EBIT$$
$$= 1.77 \times 30\% = 53.1\%$$

Now apply these percentage declines to the projected EPSs to see what they'll become under both structures if the business deterioration does occur.

$$\text{Current:} \quad \$1.054(1 - .336) = \$.70$$

$$\text{Proposed:} \quad \$1.170(1 - .531) = \$.55$$

The implication is that if the proposed capital structure is adopted *and* a substantial downturn occurs, the resulting EPS will be lower than the EPS under the old structure. Clearly, adopting the proposal adds substantial risk.

The impact of the proposed restructuring on stock prices is arguable. We can't say with certainty whether or not the positive effect of the EPS increase will overcome the negative effect of increased risk. It all depends on the current perceptions of investors.

The uncertainty can be expressed in terms of the graph in Figure 13.2. The question revolves around just where Moberly currently is on the graph and whether the restructuring will carry it past the peak. We can't say for sure. However, using the DFL to analyze the risk increase gives management a much better feel for the trade-offs involved than it would get if only the EPS impact were considered.

It's unfortunate that the DFL concept isn't used a great deal in practice. In the Moberly problem, many analysts would have stopped after calculating the two EPSs under good conditions. They'd have understood that risk was increased, but wouldn't have tried to quantify the increase for the benefit of the decision maker. We're certain our current readers will rectify that situation in a few years.

EBIT–EPS ANALYSIS

We've learned that financial leverage can enhance results at normal levels of operating profit, but makes those results more volatile at the same time. If that knowledge is to do any good, managers need to be able to use it to make intelligent choices about the amount of leverage their companies should employ given a set of expectations about future business.

This means managers need a way of quantifying and analyzing the trade-off between results and risk implied by moving from one level of leverage to another. EBIT–EPS analysis provides a graphic portrayal of the trade-off that makes the choice relatively straightforward.

To illustrate, let's go back to the Arizona Balloon Corporation and assume management expects the relatively good year reflected in Table 13.1 (page 425). To keep the illustration simple, we'll assume the choice is between the leverage scenarios of columns 1 and 2 only, although any other combination of debt and equity could be analyzed.

The EBIT–EPS technique involves graphing EPS as a function of EBIT for each leverage level as shown in Figure 13.3. We'll begin with the all equity case in column 1. The table gives us an EPS of $1.20 at an EBIT of $200,000. That's a point on the EBIT–EPS graph for zero leverage. EPS is a linear function of EBIT, so we need only one other point to draw the graph. We'll choose EBIT of $400,000 and calculate EPS.

FIGURE 13.3

EBIT–EPS Analysis for Arizona Balloon Corporation from Table 13.1, Columns 1 and 2

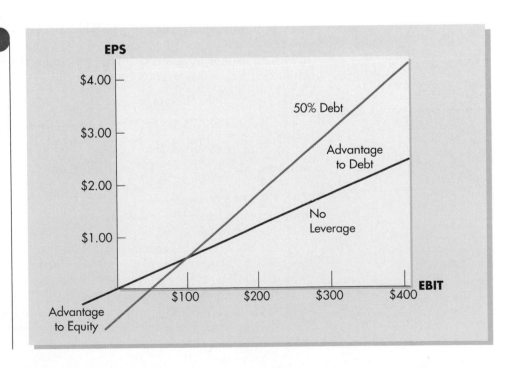

EBIT	$400,000
Interest (10%)	—
EBT	$400,000
Tax (40%)	160,000
EAT	$240,000
Number of shares	100,000
EPS	$2.40

These points determine the line labeled "No Leverage" in Figure 13.3.

For the 50% debt scenario, column 2 of Table 13.1 shows an EPS of $1.80 at an EBIT of $200,000. A calculation like the one we've just done (using $50,000 in interest and 500,000 shares of stock) gives a second point at which EPS is $4.20 when EBIT is $400,000. These points determine the line labeled "50% Debt" in the diagram.

The two lines represent EPS at various levels of operating profit under their respective assumptions about leverage. Notice that they cross one another, making different choices of leverage superior on either side of the intersection. We prefer the higher EPS of the upper line anywhere other than at the intersection, where we're indifferent between the two choices.

It's important to be able to find the indifference point. In general the formula of an EPS–EBIT line is the financial computation of EPS from EBIT stated in algebraic form.

$$EPS = \frac{(EBIT - I)(1 - T)}{\text{number of shares}}$$

$$\text{where:} \quad I = \text{interest}$$

$$T = \text{tax rate}$$

Compare the equation to the steps in the partial income statement above. In the numerator $(EBIT - I)$ is earnings before tax (EBT), which is adjusted to earnings after tax by multiplying by $(1 - T)$. That divided by the number of shares outstanding is EPS.

We can find the indifference point by equating the EPS for the no-leverage line with that for the 50% leverage line.

No Leverage		**50% Debt**
$\dfrac{(EBIT - \$0)(1 - .4)}{100,000}$	$=$	$\dfrac{(EBIT - \$50,000)(1 - .4)}{50,000}$

Solving yields

$$EBIT_{indif} = \$100,000.$$

In other words, the lines cross, and our preference for leverage changes when EBIT passes through $100,000.

Notice how useful the diagram is. It tells management that if EBIT is expected to stay above $100,000, the firm is better off with the higher leverage option. It also gives an indication of how much better off the firm will be for any level of EBIT.

The risk that comes with leverage is reflected by what happens to EPS in the 50% debt case if operating profits fall below $100,000. In that range, ABC will be on the upper line without leverage, but on the lower line with 50% debt.

● **EBIT–EPS analysis** portrays the results of **leverage** and helps to decide **how much** to use.

The analysis doesn't make the leverage decision for ABC's management. But combined with an idea of the likely variability of EBIT, it gives them all they need to make an informed choice. If EBIT is unlikely to fall much below $100,000, higher leverage is appropriate. On the other hand, if big swings are common, little or no leverage may be the wiser decision.

OPERATING LEVERAGE

We mentioned operating leverage briefly in the beginning of the chapter. The concept deals with cost rather than capital, but the functions and effects are similar to those of financial leverage. Operating leverage also has the ability to *combine* with financial leverage to produce alarmingly volatile results. For this reason we need to be familiar with the workings of operating leverage even though it's not exactly a capital structure issue. We'll begin our study with some background.

TERMINOLOGY AND DEFINITIONS

The term "operations" refers to a firm's business activities exclusive of long-term financing. In terms of the income statement, those activities involve the items from sales down to operating income (EBIT).

Risk in Operations—Business Risk

A firm's EBIT varies over time for a variety of reasons including ups and downs in sales, changes in cost conditions, and the effectiveness of management. Recall that we've already defined variation in EBIT as *business risk* (page 422).

> **Variation in EBIT** is defined as **business risk**.

It's important to realize that every business has some variation in its operating results, but some have more than others. The amount depends to a great extent on the nature of the business. Some industries have stable conditions of demand and cost, while in others things go up and down like roller coasters. Generally, most of the variation in EBIT comes about as a result of changes in the level of sales.

Fixed and Variable Costs and Cost Structure

A business's costs can be separated into two categories, *fixed* and *variable*. A fixed cost doesn't change when the level of sales changes, but a variable cost does.

Fixed costs are things like rent, depreciation, utilities, and management salaries. Variable costs include direct labor, direct materials, and other items that go up and down with volume, like sales commissions. Costs that don't fit neatly into either category can usually be separated into fixed and variable components for purposes of analysis. Ultimately, all costs and expenses can be segregated, at least roughly, into fixed and variable categories. Fixed cost is also called *overhead*.

> **Cost structure** is the mix of **fixed and variable** costs in a firm's operations.

A firm's *cost structure* is the mix of fixed and variable costs used in its operating processes. The idea is analogous to the concept of capital structure describing the mix of debt and equity within capital.

Operating Leverage Defined

Given the similar concepts of cost structure and capital structure, operating leverage is defined with respect to cost just as financial leverage is defined with respect to capital. *Operating leverage* refers to the amount of *fixed* cost in the cost structure. Thus, if a firm's costs are largely fixed, it has a great deal of operating leverage.

A good way to get a feel for cost structure and operating leverage is to imagine a factory that can be run in one of two ways, either with (1) a lot of people and a few machines or with (2) a lot of machines and a few people. We tend to describe the first organization as labor intensive or utilizing manual processes and the second as capital intensive or automated.

People represent variable cost because they can be let go when sales and production decline. Machines, on the other hand, represent fixed cost because they can't be laid off during a downturn. Hence the automated plant (2) has more operating leverage than the labor intensive plant (1).

- ● **Operating leverage** increases as the proportion of **fixed cost** increases.

●BREAKEVEN ANALYSIS

Breakeven analysis is widely used to determine the level of activity a firm must achieve to stay in business in the long run. The technique explicitly lays out the effect of sales volume on a firm's use of fixed and variable costs. In doing that it provides an excellent insight into the nature and effect of operating leverage. We'll develop the breakeven model and then use it to illustrate operating leverage.

Overview of Breakeven

The term "breakeven" means zero profit or loss, generally measured at EBIT (operating income). At breakeven, income (revenue) exactly equals outgo (costs and expenses) and the firm just survives. Breakeven analysis is a way of looking at operations to determine the volume, in either units or dollars, a company must sell to achieve this zero-profit, zero-loss situation.

In what follows we'll use the term "cost" broadly to include items generally referred to as expense. Both costs and expenses can be fixed or variable.

http://

For more on breakeven analysis go to

● www.dinkytown.net/java/
BreakEven.html.

- ● **Breakeven analysis** shows the mix of **fixed and variable** cost and the volume required for **zero profit/loss.**

●BREAKEVEN DIAGRAMS

Fixed and variable costs are represented graphically in the first two panels of Figure 13.4. Cost is plotted along the vertical axis and unit sales (Q for quantity) along the horizontal axis. Fixed cost is constant as sales increase, while variable cost increases proportionately with sales.

FIGURE 13.4

Fixed, Variable, and Total Cost

The two diagrams are generally combined by plotting variable cost on top of fixed cost. The result is shown in the third panel where the diagonal line represents total cost, the sum of fixed and variable costs.

The *breakeven diagram* is depicted in Figure 13.5. It's formed by overlaying a line representing revenue on the total cost diagram. At any level of sales, revenue is just PQ, price times quantity.

> Breakeven is at the **intersection** of revenue and total cost.

Breakeven is the level of sales at which revenue equals cost. On the diagram it's the point where the total cost line and the revenue line intersect. The breakeven volume is directly below that point on the horizontal axis, indicated by $Q_{B/E}$ on the diagram.

At any sales volume, the firm's profit or loss is the difference between revenue and total cost. This can be measured by the difference in the heights of those lines above the axis. The shaded area between the two lines to the right of their intersection represents profitable operations and the shaded area to the left represents losses.

The Contribution Margin

> Every sale makes a **contribution** of the difference between price and variable cost.

Every time a unit is sold, one unit's worth of variable cost is incurred. The amount by which price exceeds that unit variable cost is called the **contribution** made by the sale. Expressed as an equation,

(13.4)
$$C_t = P - V,$$

where: C_t is the contribution,
P is price, and
V is variable cost per unit.

The term implies a *contribution* to profit and fixed cost. Notice that the unit contribution is the same anywhere on the breakeven diagram—that is, at any level of sales.

Contribution can be expressed as a percentage of revenue by dividing by the price, P. It's then called the *contribution margin*, which we'll write as C_M. Dividing equation 13.4 by P, we have

(13.5)
$$C_M = \frac{P - V}{P}.$$

EXAMPLE 13.3

Suppose a company can make a unit of product for $7 in variable labor and materials, and sell it for $10. What are the contribution and contribution margin?

Solution: The contribution comes directly from equation 13.4.

$$C_t = P - V$$
$$= \$10 - \$7$$
$$= \$3$$

The contribution margin comes from equation 13.5.

$$C_M = \frac{P - V}{P} = \frac{\$3}{\$10} = .3 = 30\%$$

Calculating the Breakeven Sales Level

EBIT is revenue minus cost, which can be expressed in terms of price and quantity as

(13.6) $$EBIT = PQ - VQ - F_C$$

where: P = price per unit,
         V = variable cost per unit,
         Q = quantity sold, and
         F_C = total fixed cost.

Notice in this equation that P and V are multiplied by Q to represent revenue (PQ) and total variable cost (VQ), but fixed cost is represented by a single variable, F_C. EBIT is revenue minus both cost components, variable and fixed.

Breakeven occurs where revenue (PQ) equals total cost (VQ + F_C); hence EBIT = 0. To find that point, rewrite equation 13.6 with EBIT = 0.

$$0 = PQ - VQ - F_C$$

Then factor out Q, rearrange terms, and solve for the breakeven value of Q, which we've called $Q_{B/E}$.

$$Q(P - V) - F_C = 0$$

(13.7) $$Q_{B/E} = \frac{F_C}{P - V}$$

● **Breakeven** volume is **fixed cost divided by contribution**.

Notice that the breakeven volume is found by dividing fixed cost by (P − V), which is the contribution per unit sold. In words, the breakeven calculation tells how many units have to be sold to *contribute* enough money to cover (pay for) fixed costs.

The breakeven point stated in terms of dollar sales rather than units is equation 13.7 multiplied by price, P. If we call $S_{B/E}$ the breakeven dollar sales level, we have

(13.8) $$S_{B/E} = \frac{P(F_C)}{P - V}.$$

Dividing the numerator and denominator of equation 13.8 by P and substituting from equation 13.5 gives a useful expression.

(13.9)
$$S_{B/E} = \frac{F_C}{(P - V)/P} = \frac{F_C}{C_M}$$

Equation 13.9 says that the breakeven sales level is just fixed cost, F_C, divided by the *contribution margin*, C_M (stated in decimal form).

EXAMPLE 13.4

What is the breakeven sales level in units and dollars for the company in Example 13.3 if the firm has fixed costs of $1,800 per month?

Solution: For the breakeven point in units, write equation 13.7 and substitute.

$$Q_{B/E} = \frac{F_C}{P - V} = \frac{\$1,800}{\$3} = 600 \text{ units}$$

As each unit sells for $10, the breakeven sales level in dollar terms, from equation 13.8, is just

$$\$10 \times 600 = \$6,000.$$

Alternatively, the last result is available from equation 13.9 by dividing fixed cost by the contribution margin expressed in decimal form.

$$S_{B/E} = \frac{F_C}{(P - V)/P} = \frac{F_C}{C_M} = \frac{\$1,800}{.3} = \$6,000$$

This calculation essentially tells us how many dollars that each contribute 30 cents it takes to make $1,800.

Notice that breakeven volumes in either units or dollars are stated per period of time. In Example 13.4 the period is a month because fixed costs were given on a monthly basis.

● THE EFFECT OF OPERATING LEVERAGE

Breakeven analysis gives us an excellent approach to understanding exactly how operating leverage works. We'll begin by examining the breakeven diagrams for two firms that use different amounts of operating leverage. This is equivalent to saying that they differ with respect to their cost structures, one having relatively more fixed cost than the other. The diagrams are shown in Figure 13.6.

For convenience we'll assume both firms have the same breakeven volume shown at sales level A in the diagrams. Recall that the diagrams reflect profit or loss in terms of EBIT in the shaded areas on either side of the breakeven points. As output expands, profit grows as we move further to the right of breakeven. On the other hand, if volume falls below the breakeven level, losses grow as we move further to the left.

● As volume moves away from breakeven, profit or loss **increases faster** with more **operating leverage.**

The Risk Effect

Notice the relative speed with which profit or loss grows as we move away from volume level A in the two diagrams. The high operating leverage firm on the

FIGURE 13.6 **Breakeven Diagrams at High and Low Operating Leverage**

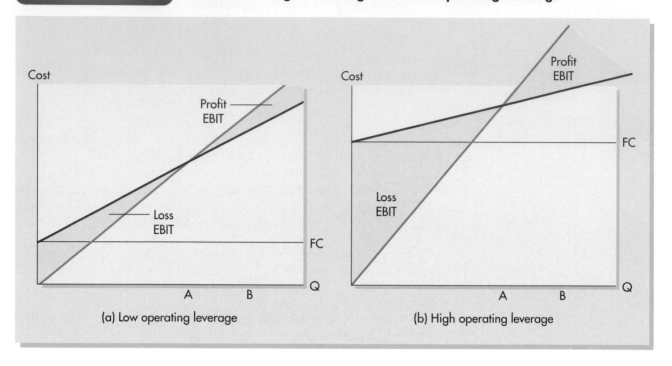

(a) Low operating leverage

(b) High operating leverage

right expands profits much faster than the low leverage firm on the left. However, it also expands losses much faster if output falls below the breakeven at A.

This is the essence of operating leverage. Any movement away from point A produces some change in EBIT in the low leverage company. The same movement away from A will produce a *larger* change in EBIT in the higher leverage firm. In other words, the increased leverage *magnifies* the change in EBIT that results from a given change in sales volume.

Thus, operating leverage can be said to increase the variation in EBIT as a result of variations in sales. Because variation in EBIT is defined as business risk, it follows that *increased operating leverage increases business risk.*

● **Variation in EBIT** (business risk) is **larger** with **more operating leverage.**

The effect can be appreciated from the geometry of the diagrams. The high leverage firm has a smaller variable cost, which makes its total cost line flatter than that of the low leverage firm. That means it diverges from the revenue line faster.

Stated another way, the high leverage firm gets a larger contribution from each sale, so it accumulates profits or losses faster as it moves away from the breakeven. Of course, this is true for movement between any two sales levels along the horizontal axis. The trade-off is that the high leverage firm has more fixed cost to cover before it makes a profit than the low leverage firm.

The Effect on Expected EBIT

More operating leverage implies higher operating profit at any output above the breakeven. To see this consider point B in both diagrams of Figure 13.6. The geometry of the diagrams shows that at the same distance above the breakeven output, the higher fixed cost firm will always make more EBIT.

In general, the higher the fixed cost, the higher profit is at a given point above breakeven. Imagine the F_C line sliding upward in the diagram of Figure 13.6b with the breakeven point staying the same. That would flatten the total cost line and widen the profit triangle.

Hence if a firm is relatively sure of its output level, it's better off to trade variable costs for fixed. In other words, increasing operating leverage multiplies operating income (EBIT) at likely output levels.

What we've said assumes a higher fixed cost is accompanied by a proportionately lower variable cost so the breakeven point stays more or less the same. If that doesn't happen, higher fixed cost doesn't necessarily mean anything.

EXAMPLE 13.5

Suppose the low leverage firm in Figure 13.6a has fixed costs of $1,000 per period, sells its product for $10, and has variable costs of $8 per unit. Further suppose that the high leverage firm in Figure 13.6b has fixed cost of $1,500 and also sells product for $10 a unit.

The diagram shows the breakeven volumes for the two firms to be the same. What variable cost per unit must the high leverage firm have if it is to achieve the same breakeven point as the low leverage firm? State the trade-off at the breakeven point. Which structure is preferred if there's a choice?

Solution: Compute the breakeven volume for the low leverage firm (a) by writing equation 13.7.

$$Q_{B/E-a} = \frac{F_C}{P - V} = \frac{\$1,000}{\$10 - \$8} = 500 \text{ units}$$

This will also be $Q_{B/E-b}$, the breakeven volume for the high leverage firm.

Now write equation 13.7 for the high leverage firm, showing the variable cost per unit as an unknown, V_b. Then substitute the given price and fixed cost and the calculated breakeven volume.

$$Q_{B/E-b} = \frac{F_C}{P - V_b}$$

$$500 \text{ units} = \frac{\$1,500}{\$10 - V_b}$$

Solving for V_b yields

$$V_b = \$7.$$

And

$$C_t = \$10 - \$7 = \$3.$$

Summarizing, we have the following.

	Low Leverage	High Leverage
Contribution	$2	$3
Fixed cost	$1,000	$1,500

Thus, at the breakeven, a $1 differential in contributions makes up for a $500 difference in fixed cost.

For an expected level of sales somewhat above the breakeven, the preferable structure depends on volatility. If expectations are for relatively stable business, the high fixed cost model gives better operating results. However, if sales are likely to bounce around a lot, especially below the breakeven point, the low fixed cost structure might be better in the long run.

THE DEGREE OF OPERATING LEVERAGE (DOL)—A MEASUREMENT

Operating leverage amplifies changes in sales volume into larger changes in EBIT. It can be quantified and measured with an idea called the *degree of operating leverage,* abbreviated *DOL.* The concept is similar to the DFL we discussed earlier.

The DOL is the ratio of the relative change in EBIT to a relative change in sales. We can write this as

● The **DOL** relates relative **changes in volume (Q)** to relative **changes in EBIT.**

(13.10)
$$\text{DOL} = \frac{\%\Delta\text{EBIT}}{\%\Delta\text{Q}}.$$

We'll forego the derivation here, but it can be shown that the DOL can be expressed as follows.

(13.11)
$$\text{DOL} = \frac{Q(P - V)}{Q(P - V) - F_C}$$

where the variables have the meanings we've been using.

EXAMPLE 13.6

The Albergetti Corp. sells its products at an average price of $10. Variable costs are $7 per unit and fixed costs are $600 per month. Evaluate the degree of operating leverage when sales are 5% and then 50% above the breakeven level.

Solution: First compute the breakeven volume by using equation 13.7.

$$Q_{B/E} = \frac{F_C}{P - V} = \frac{\$600}{\$10 - \$7} = 200 \text{ units}$$

Breakeven plus 5% and 50% implies sales of 210 and 300 units, respectively. Use equation 13.11 to calculate the DOL at 210 units per month and at 300 units. At 210 units we have

$$\text{DOL}_{Q=210} = \frac{Q(P - V)}{Q(P - V) - F_C}$$
$$= \frac{210(\$10 - \$7)}{210(\$10 - \$7) - \$600}$$
$$= 21.$$

At 300 units, we have

$$\text{DOL}_{Q=300} = \frac{300(\$10 - \$7)}{300(\$10 - \$7) - \$600}$$
$$= 3.$$

Notice that the DOL *decreases* as the output level increases above the breakeven.

As a brief exercise, show that the DOL is infinite (not defined) in equation 13.11 at the breakeven point.

COMPARING OPERATING AND FINANCIAL LEVERAGE

Operating leverage connects sales with EBIT in much the same way that financial leverage connects EBIT with ROE and EPS.

● Financial and operating leverage are similar in that **both** can enhance results while increasing variation.

Recall that financial leverage can improve performance in ROE and EPS, and that it amplifies changes in EBIT into larger relative changes in those ratios. Similarly, operating leverage can enhance EBIT at a given sales level, and expands variations in sales into larger relative variations in EBIT. The idea is illustrated in Figure 13.7.

Another similarity has to do with the nature of operating and financial costs. Financial leverage involves substituting debt for equity in the firm's capital structure, while operating leverage involves substituting fixed cost for variable cost in its cost structure.

Notice, however, that debt is a *fixed* cost method of financing in that it pays a fixed amount of interest to investors regardless of how well the company does. Equity, on the other hand, is a *variable* cost form of financing, because the dividends paid to stockholders can be varied or eliminated if the firm isn't doing well. Hence both forms of leverage involve substituting fixed cash outflows for variable cash outflows.

Finally, there's a similarity but not an exact match between the two kinds of leverage with respect to the two kinds of risk we've defined. Financial risk is the additional variation in ROE and EPS caused by financial leverage, while business risk is variation in EBIT that's enhanced by operating leverage. Both kinds of leverage make their respective risks larger as the levels of leverage increase. However, financial leverage is the sole cause of financial risk, while some business risk

FIGURE 13.7

The Similar Functions of Operating and Financial Leverage

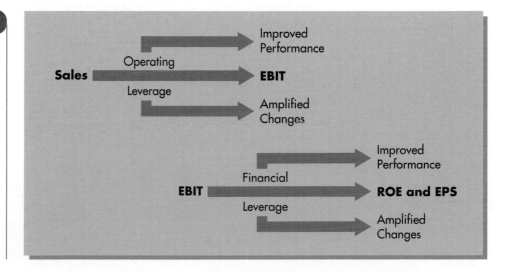

FIGURE 13.8

Risk and Cost Relationships between Operating and Financial Leverage

would exist even if there were no operating leverage. These last ideas are summarized in Figure 13.8.

Two final points of comparison are worth noting. First, virtually all productive processes involve the use of some equipment that generates fixed cost. Therefore all firms have some operating leverage. On the other hand, many firms use no debt and therefore have no financial leverage.

Second, financial leverage is more controllable than operating leverage. Technology dictates the minimum and maximum amounts of machinery needed to make most products, so management's choice of an operating leverage level is relatively limited. On the other hand, management can generally choose the amount of debt a firm uses within very broad limits.

THE COMPOUNDING EFFECT OF OPERATING AND FINANCIAL LEVERAGE

● The effects of **financial and operating** leverage **compound** one another.

An important result of the existence of two kinds of leverage is that they compound one another. Changes in sales are amplified by operating leverage into larger relative changes in EBIT, which in turn are amplified into still larger relative changes in ROE and EPS by financial leverage. The net effect is quite large because the combined effect of the two kinds of leverage is *multiplicative* rather than additive.

This means that fairly modest changes in the level of sales can lead to dramatic swings in ROE and EPS in companies that use both operating and financial leverage. The idea is illustrated in Figure 13.9.

FIGURE 13.9

The Compounding Effect of Operating and Financial Leverage

● The **DTL** reflects the combined effect of both kinds of leverage.

The compound effect of operating and financial leverage can be measured by a concept called the *degree of total leverage,* abbreviated *DTL.* The DTL is simply the product of DOL and DFL.

(13.12) $$\text{DTL} = \text{DOL} \times \text{DFL}$$

EXAMPLE 13.7

The Allegheny Company is considering replacing a manual production process with a machine. The money to buy the machine will be borrowed. The replacement of people with a machine will alter the firm's cost structure in favor of fixed cost, while the loan will move the capital structure in the direction of more debt. The firm's leverage positions at expected output levels with and without the project are summarized as follows.

	DOL	DFL
Current	2.0	1.5
Proposed	3.5	2.5

The economic outlook is uncertain and some managers fear a decline in sales of as much as 10% in the coming year. Evaluate the effect of the proposed project on risk in financial performance.

Solution: Currently, the degree of total leverage is

$$\text{DTL} = \text{DOL} \times \text{DFL}$$
$$= 2(1.5)$$
$$= 3.$$

This means that a 10% decline in sales could result in a 30% decline in EPS. Stated another way, the relative volatility of EPS is three times that of sales.

Under the proposed conditions, the DTL would be much larger.

$$\text{DTL} = \text{DOL} \times \text{DFL}$$
$$= 3.5(2.5)$$
$$= 8.75$$

Here, EPS is almost nine times as volatile as sales, and a 10% drop in volume could produce as much as an 88% decrease in EPS. In other words, EPS could be virtually wiped out. That's likely to affect stock prices a great deal more than a 30% decline.

The conclusion is that the proposal has a great deal more inherent risk than one might think at first glance.[7]

---

7. The degree of leverage concepts are both a little tricky. The volatility implied by both ratios increases with the addition of debt or fixed cost, but it's even more sensitive to the proximity of breakeven points.

Examine equation 13.3 for the DFL and equation 13.11 for the DOL. Notice that both denominators are zero at breakeven points. In the case of the DOL, the denominator is EBIT, which is zero at the breakeven we've been talking about in this section. For the DFL, the denominator is EBT, which is zero when interest equals operating income.

In the neighborhood of those points, the denominators are very small so the fractions are very large. Hence we get large *relative* changes in EPS or EBIT, but those changes may not be very large in absolute terms because we're operating at EPS or EBIT levels near zero.

CAPITAL STRUCTURE THEORY

During the last 50 years, financial scholars have devoted a great deal of thinking to capital structure. They've essentially been addressing the same question we posed at the beginning of this chapter: Does capital structure affect stock price and the market value of the firm, and if so, is there an optimal structure that maximizes either or both?

The scholarly approach is more mathematical than the work we've been doing, but the results are essentially the same. Structure does affect price and value, and there is an optimum, but there's no way to find it with any precision.

Capital structure theory is one of the more important elements of modern financial thought, and has yielded some valuable insights into real-world problems. Hence it's important that professionals be familiar with the theoretical approach and understand the nature of the results. Fortunately, we can do that without mastering a great deal of mathematics.

● BACKGROUND—THE VALUE OF THE FIRM

Theory approaches capital structure by focusing on the market value of the firm and its cost of capital. The assumption is that if market value can be increased by manipulating capital structure, an increase in stock price must follow.

We'll need to become familiar with the terminology and principles used before getting into the theory itself.

Notation

First let's define the notation (symbols) we'll be using. The market value of the firm is the total market value of all of its debt and equity securities represented as follows.

V_d = market value of the firm's debt

V_e = market value of the firm's stock (equity)

V_f = market value of the firm in total

Hence

(13.13) $V_f = V_d + V_e.$

Investors' returns on the firm's securities will be

k_d = return on an investment in debt (bonds) and

k_e = return on an investment in equity (stock).

● Theory begins by assuming a world **without taxes or transaction costs,** so investors' returns are exactly component capital costs.

In our study of the cost of capital (Chapter 12), we said that the firm's costs of debt and equity were the investors' returns adjusted for flotation costs and taxes. Theory operates in an abstract world. It assumes away flotation costs and begins by assuming there are no taxes. Therefore the costs of debt and equity are exactly k_d and k_e, respectively. The cost of capital is then a weighted average of these, which we'll write as

k_a = average cost of capital.

Value Is Based on Cash Flow Which Comes from Income

The value of any security is the present value of the cash flows that come from owning it, and all cash flows paid to investors come from earnings. Hence earnings ultimately determine value.

Practical Finance

Leverage and Business Strategy

Business strategy involves understanding the factors that define industrial competition. An important issue in strategy is predicting how companies will react to troubled times or competitive challenges. Leverage plays a big part in those predictions.

The more heavily a firm is leveraged, either financially or operationally, the more quickly it loses money when volume decreases. The effect is compounded when both forms of leverage are present. This means leveraged companies react aggressively when something threatens their volume. They cut prices, increase advertising, and offer special promotions at the drop of a hat to keep volume up. That tends to make the industries in which they operate chaotic and less attractive for everyone. Japanese firms provide a great example of the phenomenon. They're known for their competitiveness, some of which can be traced to exceptional leverage.

Business credit is relatively easy in Japan, and companies tend to carry two or three times the debt of American firms. In other words, they're highly leveraged financially. Firms are also focused on low unit cost, which they achieve with large automated plants. That implies high fixed cost and commensurately high operating leverage.

Beyond these factors, Japanese culture acts to increase leverage. Employment is a lifetime proposition there, and firms just don't lay off employees when business decreases. Hence labor, the traditional variable cost, is essentially fixed. That increases operating leverage still further.

Taken together, these things imply an extraordinarily high degree of total leverage in Japanese companies. Strategically, they seem to behave accordingly.

We'll focus on operating income (EBIT), which is by definition the earnings stream available to either debt or equity investors. To avoid some notational confusion later, we'll refer to operating income as OI rather than EBIT in this section.

Assume OI is completely divided between interest and dividend payments, so we can write

(13.14) $$OI = I + D$$

where: I = total annual interest payment to bondholders and

D = total annual dividend payment to stockholders.

Debt is assumed to be perpetual. Whenever principal is paid off, a new amount of equal size is immediately borrowed; hence I is constant year after year. Because no income is retained, the company doesn't grow, and OI remains constant as well. Then equation 13.14 implies that dividend payments are also constant. In other words, each stream of annual payments, I and D, is a *perpetuity*.

The values of the firm's debt and equity are then the present values of these perpetuities, and we can write

● Dividend and interest payments are both **perpetuities,** and the firm's market value is the sum of their present values.

(13.15) $$V_d = \frac{I}{k_d}$$

and

(13.16) $$V_e = \frac{D}{k_e}$$

where k_d and k_e are the costs of debt and equity. Using equation 13.13, we can also write

(13.17)
$$V_f = \frac{I}{k_d} + \frac{D}{k_e}.$$

The nature of the weighted average return is such that the following expression is essentially equivalent to equation 13.17.

(13.18)
$$V_f = \frac{OI}{k_a}$$

In words, these equations say that the value of the firm is determined by the costs of its debt and equity, and that we can look at them together through the average cost of capital, k_a. Keep in mind that lower rates mean higher values.

● **Returns drive value** in an inverse relationship.

This is an important way of looking at things. It means we can think of returns as driving value. For example, if something causes investors to require a higher return on an investment in a company's stock, equation 13.16 says that will drive the value of the firm's equity down. If the return on debt remains the same, the cost of capital, k_a, will also rise and overall value will drop.

Graphic Portrayals

The foregoing means we can look at value by tracking the behavior of the three returns, k_d, k_e, and k_a, as capital structure changes. We're particularly concerned with the behavior of k_a, the average cost of capital, because of its relation to overall value.

Earlier we talked about stock price and value increasing to a maximum as leverage increases. Equation 13.18 tells us that this is equivalent to k_a decreasing to a minimum. The idea is illustrated in Figure 13.10, where value and stock price, V_f and P_s, achieve a maximum, while k_a reaches a minimum at the same capital structure.

In what follows, we'll find it useful to include k_e and k_d in the bottom graph of portrayals like Figure 13.10 to analyze how changes in the two component costs of capital influence the average cost.

● THE EARLY THEORY BY MODIGLIANI AND MILLER

The theoretical ball got rolling in 1958 when two well-known scholars named Franco Modigliani and Merton Miller published a paper on the effect of capital structure on value.[8] Modigliani and Miller are cited often, and it's become common to refer to them as MM.

Restrictive Assumptions in the Original Model

MM's work was a sophisticated mathematical model of the financial world. It included a number of restrictions on the behavior of firms and individuals that made it less than realistic. Nevertheless, it provided important insights into the effects of capital structure on value. Later work relaxed some of the restrictions and led to the state of the theory as it is today.

---

8. See Franco Modigliani and Merton H. Miller, "The Cost of Capital, Corporation Finance, and the Theory of Investment," *American Economic Review*, 48 (June 1958): 261–297.

FIGURE 13.10

Variation in Value and Average Return with Capital Structure

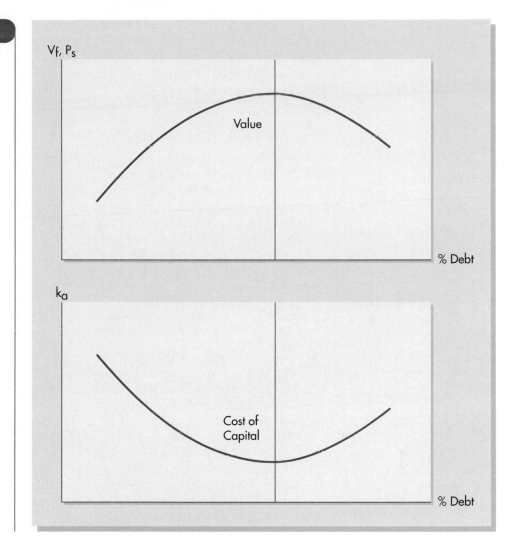

For our purposes the most important restrictions were the following.

1. There are no income taxes.

2. Securities trade in perfectly efficient capital markets in which there are no transaction costs.

3. Investors and companies can borrow as much as they want at the same rate. That is,

   a. Rates don't go up as one borrows more money, and

   b. The rate is the same for investors and companies.

The second assumption contains an important subtlety. Among other things, it says that there are no costs associated with bankruptcy. This idea sounds like a contradiction to many students and needs to be explained.

● MM initially assumed there were **no costs to bankruptcy.**

A bankrupt company goes through two processes. First it loses value because of deteriorating business conditions; then it goes into bankruptcy proceedings, which involve either a restructuring of debt or a liquidation of assets.

The assumption of zero bankruptcy cost implies that no legal or administrative fees are incurred in restructuring or liquidating, and if liquidation is required assets are sold for a value close to what they were worth to the company.

In other words, bankruptcy costs are fees and losses on the sale of used assets. The term does not refer to the loss in value that put the business into a bankruptcy situation in the first place.

The Assumptions and Reality

Clearly, the assumptions of the original MM model were unrealistic. First and most obvious, there are income taxes.

Second, the legal and administrative expenses of bankruptcy are quite large, and assets sold under duress usually bring only a fraction of their original value. In fact, these costs often eat up most of what's left in a bankrupt company.

Third, individuals usually pay higher interest rates than firms, and anyone's rates generally go up as more money is borrowed.

In spite of these problems, the MM model made an insightful contribution to thinking on the subject of capital structure and provided a starting point for a great deal more effort.

The Result

● Under MM's initial set of restrictions, **value** is **independent** of capital structure.

MM showed that under the restrictive assumptions we've discussed and several others, the firm's total value is unaffected by capital structure. The result is called the **independence hypothesis,** because it shows value to be independent of structure. It can be described in terms of a firm's cost of debt and equity and its average cost of capital. The ideas are illustrated in Figure 13.11.

The top graph is straightforward. The firm's value is constant with increasing leverage as we move from left to right on the graph. Stock price can also be shown to be unchanging. The bottom graph requires more explanation.

Notice that along the vertical axis, at zero debt, we have only equity capital, so $k_e = k_a$. Also notice that k_d is lower than k_e, reflecting the fact that an investment in debt is somewhat safer than an investment in the same company's equity. The assumption that the firm can borrow at a constant rate is reflected by displaying k_d as a horizontal line for all percentages of debt.

Now consider what happens as the firm replaces equity with debt and moves to the right in the graph. Because the debt is lower in cost, you'd expect the average cost of capital, k_a, to fall as more debt is added to the financing mix. It doesn't, however, because k_e rises as the debt load increases, compensating in the average for the lower cost debt.

● As **cheaper debt** is added, the **cost of equity increases** because of increased risk such that the weighted average **cost of capital remains constant.**

Some increase in k_e will always come about when debt is added, because additional debt increases the financial risk on equity holders. As risk increases, equity holders demand higher rates of return. But a constant k_a and the associated constant value implies that k_e increases *exactly* enough to offset the benefit of the increasing amount of lower cost debt being used.

MM's Result Supports the Operating Income View

MM's result wasn't exactly new. Many people already held what can be called an operating income view that's largely the same.

This position maintains that because the firm's value is the present value of its expected operating income stream, a rational market will implicitly hold the total value of that stream constant no matter how the capital is divided between debt and equity. In a sense, this view says that you can't make something out of noth-

FIGURE 13.11

**The Independence
Hypothesis**

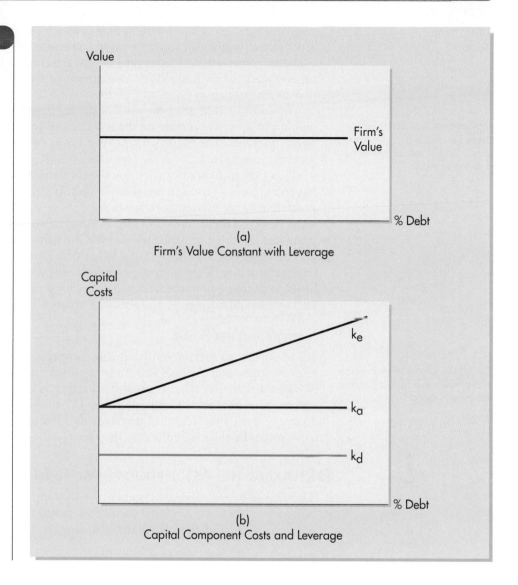

(a)
Firm's Value Constant with Leverage

(b)
Capital Component Costs and Leverage

ing. The firm's investment value is whatever it is on the basis of income, and that's that. You can't magically create more value by fooling around with the mix.

However, until MM came along, no one had a very good explanation of how this would happen in the marketplace. That is, no one could satisfactorily explain a *process* that would hold investment value constant as leverage is added or subtracted.

The Arbitrage Concept

MM proposed that a process of *arbitrage*[9] driven by equity investors seeking to *maximize their returns* would hold the value of a firm constant through changes in leverage. The argument is quite complex, but essentially says that if the value

---

9. Arbitrage means making a profit by buying and selling the same thing at the same time in two different markets. For example, suppose you noticed that a stock was selling for $45 in New York and $50 in Boston. You could make a profit by placing a buy order in New York and a sell order in Boston at the same time, and delivering the share in Boston that you bought in New York.

of a firm were to go up due to adding leverage, shareholders could get a better return by selling its shares, borrowing some money on their own, and investing in a similar but unleveraged company (the arbitrage is between the leveraged and unleveraged companies). MM's assumption of uniform interest rates comes into play as investors borrow money on their own.

● MM propose that **arbitrage** between leveraged and unleveraged firms will hold **value constant** as debt increases.

The selloff would drive the price of the leveraged firm down, while the buying would put upward pressure on the price of the unleveraged firm, driving the two values together. The entire process then holds the value of any firm constant as leverage is increased.

(Don't try to figure out why this should work from what we've said here. We haven't gone into enough detail to do that. It's enough that you get a rough appreciation of the conceptual approach.)

MM were said to have provided *behavioral support* for the operating income argument. In other words, they showed how the behavior of investors in financial markets might hold the total value of a firm constant through changes in capital structure. Keep in mind, however, that to do this they had to assume the absence of taxes, no transaction costs for investing (like commissions), and that everyone could borrow as much as they wanted at the same rate.

Interpreting the Result

● The MM result implies that leverage affects value because of **market imperfections.**

It's important to understand what this early result implies about the real world. It doesn't say that a firm's value and its stock price are unaffected by leverage. We know that isn't true. What it does imply is that the *reason* leverage affects value stems from *market imperfections,* like taxes and transaction costs, and not from the basic interaction of investors and companies. That's an important insight into why things are the way they are.

● RELAXING THE ASSUMPTIONS—MORE INSIGHTS

Things really got interesting when the assumptions that excluded taxes and bankruptcy costs were relaxed. Before we get into the effect of those changes we need to understand an important point about the workings of the tax system.

Financing and the U.S. Tax System

The tax system favors debt over equity financing because interest payments are deductible to the paying company but dividends are not. We'll illustrate with the two companies depicted in Table 13.4. Assume they're identical except that one is financed entirely with equity and the other is 50% debt financed. Also assume both pay out all after-tax earnings in dividends, the interest rate is 10%, and the tax rate is 40%.

Both companies pay all available earnings to the investors who furnish capital. In the case of the equity-financed company, that means all EAT goes to stockholders. However, the other firm pays interest to bondholders and EAT to stockholders.

● The tax system **favors debt financing** because **interest is tax deductible,** while dividends are not.

The important point is shown at the bottom of the table. *Total* payments to investors are *higher* for the leveraged company. The difference comes from the fact that the leveraged firm can deduct interest from taxable income and therefore *pays less tax*.

Including Corporate Taxes in the MM Theory

In the presence of taxes, operating income (OI) has to be split between investors and the government. Because value is ultimately based on income received by in-

TABLE 13.4	**The Tax System Favors Debt Financing**		

	All Equity	50% Debt 50% Equity
EBIT	$100	$100
Interest (10% of debt)		50
EBT	$100	$ 50
Tax (40% of EBT)	40	20
Net income (EAT)	$ 60	$ 30
Dividend	60	30
Net retained	$ 0	$ 0
Capital		
Debt	$ 0	$ 500
Equity	1,000	500
Total capital	$1,000	$1,000
Payments to Investors		
Interest	$ 0	$ 50
Dividends	60	30
Total	$ 60	$ 80

vestors, this lowers the firm's value from what it would be if there were no taxes. However, the amount of the value reduction depends on the firm's use of leverage, because that affects how much tax the government collects.

Let's focus on how much the government gets. The amount depends on the tax rate and the distribution of funds between debt and equity investors.

In the absence of debt, all of OI is taxable. If the tax rate is T, the government gets

(a)
$$T(OI) .$$

However, interest is tax deductible, so if there's debt and an amount of interest, I, the government gets only

(b)
$$T(OI - I) = T(OI) - TI .$$

The difference in what the government gets with and without debt is the difference between a and b, which is TI. Thus, when a firm uses debt financing, the government's take is reduced by TI every year.

Stated conversely, debt results in a yearly perpetuity of TI dollars to be divided among investors that wouldn't be available if debt weren't used. The amount TI is called the *tax shield* associated with debt financing.

The impact of the tax shield on value is simply the present value of the perpetuity TI capitalized at discount rate k_d.

⬤ In the MM model with taxes **interest** provides a **tax shield** that reduces government's share of the firm's earnings.

(13.19)
$$\text{PV of tax shield} = \frac{TI}{k_d}$$

This can be written more conveniently by recognizing that interest is just debt times the interest rate.

(13.20)
$$I = Bk_d$$

where B = debt.

Substituting into equation 13.19 yields

(13.21) $$\text{PV of tax shield} = \frac{\text{TI}}{k_d} = \frac{\text{TBk}_d}{k_d} = \text{TB}.$$

● **Value is increased** by the **PV** of the **tax shield.** The **benefit of debt** is the **tax rate** times the **debt** amount.

TB is also referred to as the *benefit of debt*. In words, equation 13.21 says that *having debt in the capital structure increases a firm's value by the magnitude of that debt times the tax rate.*

For example, suppose an all-equity firm that has a tax rate of 40% and a market value of $2 million restructures by trading $1 million in stock for the same amount in bonds. The implication of the theory with taxes is that the firm's market value will increase by

$$.4 \times \$1\text{M} = \$400,000$$

to $2.4 million.

● The benefit of debt accrues **entirely to stockholders** because bond returns are fixed.

Further, the *increment in value will all accrue to the stockholders* because the value of the bonds is fixed by the terms of the bond contract and current interest rates.

This is a very significant conclusion. It says that a firm can increase its value and the wealth of shareholders at a constant rate by trading equity for debt until it is financed virtually 100% with debt (we say virtually because there has to be some equity). The result is represented in Figure 13.12.

● In the MM model with taxes **value increases** steadily as **leverage is added.**

The top graph shows the market value of the firm increasing from its all-equity value as the addition of debt increases the present value of the tax shield along with leverage. The lower graph shows the behavior of the component and weighted average costs of capital. Notice that with the inclusion of taxes the cost of debt is $k_d(1 - T)$ rather than just k_d.

In this representation, the average cost of capital falls with the inclusion of more low-cost debt. The cost of equity increases at the same time, but not fast enough to overcome the effect of the low-cost debt.

Including Bankruptcy Costs in the MM Theory

● **Bankruptcy costs** eventually make investors **raise required rates,** which **lowers value.**

The probability of business failure increases as a firm takes on more debt. As explained earlier, bankruptcy costs are *additional* losses that accrue primarily to stockholders when companies fail. As leverage increases past some point, investors become conscious enough of bankruptcy costs to begin raising their required rates of return. In other words, investors begin to worry that *they* will incur losses due to bankruptcy cost if the firm fails. This happens first to equity investors and later to bondholders. As investor required rates go up, so do the firm's capital costs.

The effect is shown in Figure 13.13b. As we move to the right, critical points are passed after which k_e and then k_d begin to climb. It's important to notice that the average cost of capital, k_a, does not begin to increase as soon as k_e starts upward. That's because it is still being driven downward by the mix change coming from the replacement of high-cost equity with low-cost debt. The minimum value of k_a is reached only after k_e has gone up quite a bit, perhaps reinforced by an increase in k_d.

● The **MM model** with taxes and bankruptcy costs concludes that an **optimal capital structure exists.**

Now consider the top diagram that shows the firm's value. According to equations 13.15 through 13.18, increasing required returns have a depressing effect on value as we continue to the right after one or both of the returns begin to rise. However, the growing tax shield continues to add value at the same time.

At first the rate effect isn't strong enough to overcome the tax effect and the net result of more leverage is still an increase in value. Before long, however, the

FIGURE 13.12

MM Theory with Taxes

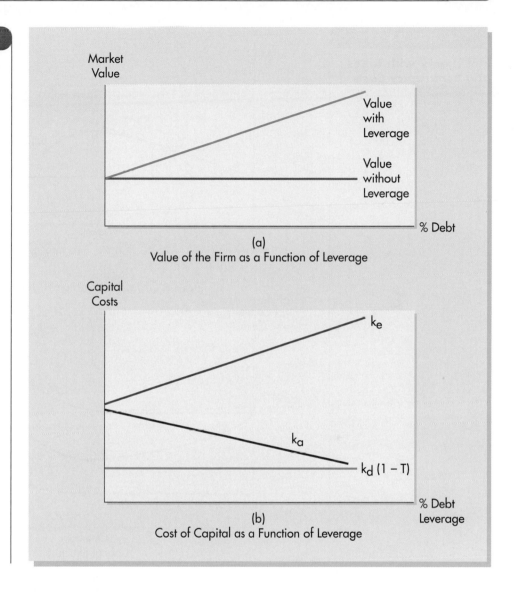

growing specter of failure overwhelms the tax effect, and value begins to decline with additional leverage. The peak in value coincides with the minimum in k_a.

Summarizing the Results

In short, the MM model with taxes and bankruptcy costs says that additional leverage increases the value of a firm when total leverage is relatively low. However, a maximum is eventually reached, after which further increases reduce value. Unfortunately, the theory does not provide a method for finding the maximum.

Notice that this result is essentially the same as the one we developed by using an intuitive approach early in the chapter. A little leverage helps, a lot hurts, and it's hard to find the perfect amount.

However, the reasons for the conclusion are different. The MM model attributes the benefit of leverage solely to taxes, while the intuitive approach relies on

FIGURE 13.13

MM Theory with Taxes and Bankruptcy Costs

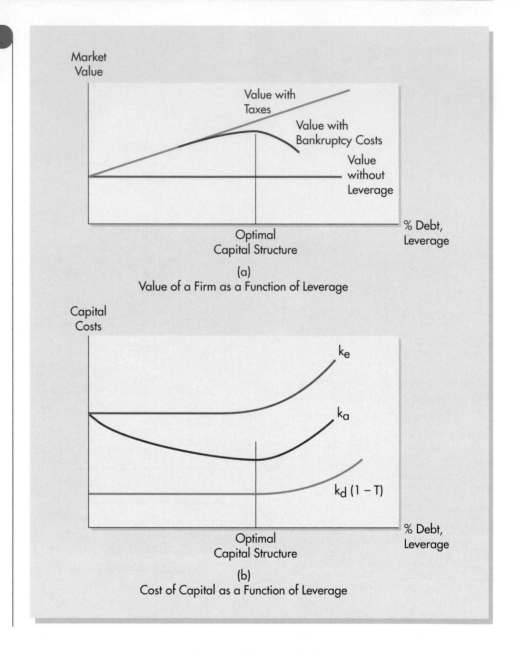

(a)
Value of a Firm as a Function of Leverage

(b)
Cost of Capital as a Function of Leverage

the impact of improved performance on investors' attitudes and perceptions. Both attribute leverage's negative effects to risk.

● AN INSIGHT INTO MERGERS AND ACQUISITIONS

Corporate mergers happen in a number of ways that we'll study in some detail in Chapter 17. For now we just need to understand that in many mergers one company simply buys the stock of another company called the *target*.

To obtain control quickly, the buying company has to purchase most of the shares of the target over a short period of time. That means it can't just buy them in the stock market at the going price, because at any particular time most stockholders aren't interested in selling at that price.

To overcome this difficulty, the acquiring firm offers to buy the target's stock at a *premium* over its current market price. The offer is made to all of the target's stockholders at once and may be extended directly or through the firm's management.

This process means that a corporate buyer usually pays a great deal more for a target company than the pre-merger market value of its stock. Paying twice that value isn't unheard of.

This raises an interesting question. How can any sane acquiring company rationalize paying as much as 50% or 100% over market value for a target company? Are the financial high rollers who do such deals crazy, or do they know something others don't?

One rationale for high acquisition premiums involves capital structure theory and the method of financing the purchase. Target companies are frequently thought to be undervalued because they aren't using much debt. In other words, their capital structures are near the left sides of the graphs in Figure 13.13. The implication is that a restructuring which adds debt might substantially increase their value.

Acquiring firms often raise the money to purchase a target's stock by borrowing. The resulting merged business ends up with a new owner and a great deal more debt than it had before. This seems like a sucker deal for the new owner. *But* if the increase in market value due to adding debt (and moving to the right in Figure 13.13) is greater than the total premium paid for the stock, everyone can come out a winner, the buyers as well as the old owners.

● **Borrowing** to pay a **premium** in an **acquisition** may be theoretically **justified** if value is increasing with leverage.

In other words, the increase in leverage brought about by a merger can *theoretically* produce a value increment that is available to be divided between the new and old owners. If the increment is big enough, and the new owners negotiate wisely enough, they can get rich! On the other hand, if they misjudge the effect of the leverage increase, they can go broke.

The argument certainly has validity, but it tends to be somewhat overblown. Indeed, many acquisitions involve premiums that seem far beyond anything that could be achieved through a leverage-based value increment.

DISCUSSION QUESTIONS

1. The user of leverage might be thought of as taking advantage of the provider. Between stockholders and bondholders, who is the user and who is the provider? Give a word explanation or illustration that might support this view. What does the used party get in return?

2. The central issue underlying the study of leverage is whether or not it influences stock price and whether there's an optimal structure. But the whole idea seems kind of fuzzy and uncertain. Why are people so interested? (*Hint:* Think of management's goals and of the world of mergers.)

3. Relate business and financial risk as defined in this chapter to the risks described in Chapter 8.

4. Why are ROE and EPS such important measures of performance to investors?

5. Both business risk and financial risk would exist with or without either type of leverage. Leverage just makes them more significant. Are those statements true or false? Explain.

6. Briefly explain the pros and cons of financial leverage. In other words, what are its benefits, and what are the costs that come along with those benefits?

7. The Armageddon Corp. is in big trouble. Sales are down and profits are off. On top of that, the firm's credit rating has been reduced, so it's facing very high interest rates on anything it borrows in the future. Current long-term borrowing represents 60% of capital but at fixed interest rates, so it won't be affected.

   The firm's major stockholder, the Apocalypse Group, has scheduled a conference with management to discuss the company's problems. Everyone is very nervous about this conference, and the executive team is meeting to decide what to tell Apocalypse.

   Charlie Gladhand, the director of marketing, came into the meeting wearing a wide grin. He explained that he'd read an article about leverage that contained the solution to the company's problem. The article told of several successful firms that had, to the delight of their owners, become more successful by borrowing money. Charlie suggests that Armageddon dazzle the Apocalypse Group by borrowing heavily in the next few days before the conference.

   Critique Charlie's idea.

8. You're interested in investing in the Peters Company, which has shown a remarkable increase in EPS during the last three years. Investigating, you find that the company's debt to equity ratio has increased dramatically over the same period and is now four to one. How does this information affect your feelings about Peters as an investment?

9. Explain in words the ROCE test for the advisability of adding leverage. That is, what is the test really telling us? When will it indicate a company is doing the wrong thing?

10. The risk added by financing is small and insignificant in relation to the inherent risk in most businesses. Is that statement true or false? Discuss.

11. Describe generally how leverage affects stock prices. What forces are at work, driven by what effects?

12. You're the CFO of Axelrod Trucking, a privately held firm whose owner, Joe Axelrod, is interested in selling the company and retiring. He therefore wants to pump up its value by any means possible. Joe read an article about leverage in a business magazine the other day, and has sent you a memo directing that you restructure the firm's capital to the "optimum" in order to maximize the company's value. Prepare a brief response to Joe's memo.

13. The Revere Company currently has good earnings and a capital structure that's 20% debt. Its EPS is in the upper quarter of firms in its industry. Top management's compensation is in large part based on the year-end price of the company's stock. It's now October and the president, Harry Upscale, is looking for ways to pump that price before December 31. Harry invests in stocks himself and pays a great deal of attention to EPS when buying and selling. He also understands that leverage can magnify EPS. However, he knows little more than that about finance. Harry has strongly suggested to the treasurer that Revere restructure its capital to 65% debt to enhance EPS and increase stock price.

You're an analyst in the firm's treasury department. The treasurer has asked you to prepare an analysis of Harry's proposal to help him talk the boss out of the idea. You've calculated the company's current DFL at 2.2, and projected that it would be 5.8 at the proposed leverage level. Draft a memo from the treasurer to Harry tactfully explaining why his idea may not work and might actually have a result opposite to what he wants to achieve.

14. Explain the difference between a fixed and a variable cost. How do these concepts change as the time horizon lengthens? In other words, are the same things fixed over a 5-year planning period that are fixed in a typical 1-year period? What about a 10-year period? What's the relevant period when we're talking about operating leverage?

15. Why do labor-intensive processes involve less operating leverage than automated processes? What fixed costs are associated with automation? Why can't those costs be eliminated by just selling the machinery?

16. Explain the idea of breakeven analysis in a brief paragraph.

17. Describe the concept of the breakeven point in words by using the concept of contribution and fixed costs. (Short answer.)

18. Summarize the effect of operating leverage on EBIT.

19. The Appleridge Company is a large manufacturer of capital goods. (The demand for capital goods typically swings up and down a great deal between good and bad economic times.) Business has been good lately and is expected to remain so in the foreseeable future. The firm is currently relatively labor intensive in its processes. The chief engineer, Mike Quickwrench, has suggested a major project to modernize and automate the plant. At the output level planned for next year, the project will reduce total cost by 10%. Mike has presented the idea to the management team in a totally positive light. The other executives are caught up in Mike's enthusiasm and are ready to proceed. You're Appleridge's CFO, and feel that all sides of an issue should be discussed before it is approved. What concerns do you have? How would you present them in a way that keeps you from appearing to be overly negative?

20. The Braithwaite Tool Co. is considering a major modernization and automation of its plant using borrowed funds. Fully discuss a serious financial negative that could result from the project.

21. Explain the idea of bankruptcy costs. Why are they important to investors? When do investors start to worry about them?

22. Briefly describe the result of MM's original restrictive model. Why was it important in spite of its serious restrictions?

23. Briefly summarize the operating income argument that was supported by the original MM result.

24. Outline the arbitrage process proposed by MM that supports the operating income argument. What is the arbitrage between?

25. Explain in words how the tax system favors debt financing.

26. In a short paragraph, describe the result of adding taxes to the MM model.

27. In another short paragraph, describe the effect of adding bankruptcy costs to the MM model with taxes.

28. Compare the implications of the MM model with taxes and bankruptcy costs to the things we discovered by studying the Arizona Balloon Corporation.

29. The Wycombe Company is doing well and is interested in diversifying, so it's been looking around for an acquisition target. The Albe Company has been found with the help of an investment banker. Albe is quite profitable and is about half the size of Wycombe. This size relationship is reflected in their market values. Both firms are financed entirely by equity. The investment banker has advised that it will be necessary to pay a premium of about 30% over market price to acquire Albe. Wycombe's president is having a hard time with this news and has asked you for advice. Construct and explain an approach to the acquisition that might make the premium easier to rationalize. Would it affect your argument if neither Albe nor Wycombe were particularly profitable? If so, how?

PROBLEMS

1. The Connecticut Computer Company has the following selected financial results.

	10% Debt	40% Debt	75% Debt
Debt	$ 10,000		
Equity	90,000		
Total Capital	$100,000		
Shares @ $5	18,000		
EBIT	$ 18,000		
Interest (15%)	1,500		
EBT	$ 22,500		
Tax (40%)	9,000		
EAT	$ 13,500		
ROE			
EPS			

The company is considering a capital restructuring to increase leverage from its present level of 10% of capital.

a. Calculate Connecticut's ROE and EPS under its current capital structure.

b. Restate the financial statement line items shown, the number of shares outstanding, ROE, and EPS if Connecticut borrows money and uses it to retire stock until its capital structure is 40% debt assuming EBIT remains unchanged and the stock continues to sell at its book value. (Develop the second column of the chart shown.)

c. Recalculate the same figures assuming Connecticut continues to restructure until its capital structure is 75% debt. (Develop the third column of the chart.)

d. How is increasing leverage affecting financial performance? What overall effect might the changes have on the market price of Connecticut's stock? Why? (Words only. *Hint:* Consider the move from 10% to 40% and that from 40% to 75% separately.)

2. Reconsider the Connecticut Computer Company of Problem 1 assuming the firm has experienced some difficulties and its EBIT has fallen to $8,000.

a. Reconstruct the three-column chart developed in Problem 1 assuming Connecticut's EBIT remains at $8,000.

b. Interpret the result in terms of stock price and the advisability of restructuring capital under these conditions.

c. Could these results have been predicted more easily? Use the ROCE concept to come to the same conclusion.

3. Assume Connecticut Computer Company of the last two problems is earning an EBIT of $15,000. Once again, calculate the chart showing the implication of adding more leverage. Verbally rationalize the result.

4. Watson Waterbed Works Inc. has an EBIT of $2.75 million, can borrow at 15% interest, and pays combined state and federal income taxes of 40%. It currently has no debt and is capitalized by equity of $12 million. The firm has 1.5 million shares of common stock outstanding that trade at book value.

a. Calculate Watson's EAT, ROE, and EPS currently and at capital structures that have 20%, 40%, 60%, and 80% debt.

b. Compare the EPS at the different leverage levels, and the amount of change between levels as leverage increases. What happens to the effect of more debt as leverage increases from a little to a lot?

5. The Canterbury Coach Corporation has EBIT of $3.62 million and total capital of $20 million, which is 15% debt. The 425,000 shares of stock outstanding sell at book value. The firm pays 12% interest on its debt and is subject to a combined state and federal tax rate of 40%. Canterbury is contemplating a capital restructuring to either 30%, 45%, 60%, or 75% debt.

a. At the current level of profitability, will more debt enhance results? Why?

b. Calculate the EAT, ROE, EPS, and the DFL at the current and proposed structures, and display your results in a systematic table.

c. In a short paragraph referring to your table, discuss the trade-off between performance and increased risk (reflected in the DFL) as leverage increases. Do some levels seem to make more sense than others?

What business characteristics would make the higher leverage levels less of a problem?

6. The Tanenbaum Tea Company wants to show the stock market an EPS of $3 per share, but doesn't expect to be able to improve profitability over what is reflected in the financial plan for next year. The plan is partially reproduced below.

Tanenbaum Tea Company
Financial Projection 20X1
($000)

EBIT	$18,750	Debt	$ 13,000
Interest (@ 12%)	1,560	Equity	97,000
EBT	$17,190	Capital	$110,000
Tax (@ 40%)	6,876		
EAT	$10,314	Number of shares = 3,700,000	

Tanenbaum's stock sells at book value. Will trading equity for debt help the firm achieve its EPS goal, and if so, what debt level will produce the desired EPS?

7. Balfour Corp. has the following operating results and capital structure ($000).

Revenue	$6,000	Debt	$1,200
Cost/expense	4,500	Equity	8,800
EBIT	$1,500	Total	$10,000

The firm is contemplating a capital restructuring to 60% debt. Its stock is currently selling for book value at $25 per share. The interest rate is 9% and combined state and federal taxes are 42%.

a. Calculate EPS under the current and proposed capital structures.

b. Calculate the DFL under both structures.

c. Use the DFLs to forecast the resulting EPS under each structure if operating profit falls off by 5%, 10%, or 25%.

d. Comment on the desirability of the proposed structure versus the current one as a function of the volatility of the business.

e. Is stock price likely to be increased by a change to the proposed capital structure? Discuss briefly.

8. Algebraically derive:

$$EPS = ROE \times (\text{book value per share}).$$

(*Hint:* Write the definitions of ROE, EPS, and book value, and then start substituting.)

9. You're a financial analyst at Pinkerton Interactive Graphic Systems (PIGS), a successful entrant in a new and rapidly growing field. As in most new fields, however, rapid growth is anything but assured, and PIGS's future performance is uncertain.

The firm expects to earn operating profits of $4 million next year, up from $1 million last year. To support this enormous growth the firm plans to raise $15 million in new capital. It already has capital of $5 million that is 40% debt.

PIGS can raise the new money in any proportion of debt and equity management chooses. The CFO is considering three possibilities: all equity, $8 million debt and $7 million equity, and all debt.

Interest on the current debt as well as on new borrowing is expected to be 10%, and the company pays state and federal income taxes at a combined rate of 40%. Equity will be raised by selling stock at the current market price of $10, which is equal to its book value.

The CFO has asked you to prepare an analysis to aid management in making the debt/equity decision. You are also to provide a recommendation of your own.

a. Prepare an EBIT–EPS analysis of the situation showing a line for the capital structure that results from each of the three options. (Calculate EPS under each new capital structure at EBIT levels of $1 million, $2 million, and $4 million. Then graph EBIT versus EPS for each option. Refer to Figure 13.3. Show last year's EPS on the graph.)

b. Discuss the effect the options might have on stock price.

c. Make a subjective recommendation under each of the following assumptions about the $4 million operating profit forecast. Support your position with words and references to your EBIT–EPS analysis.

1. The $4 million operating profit projection is a best case scenario. Anything from ($2) million to $4 million has an equal probability of occurring.

2. The $4 million is a fair estimate with about a 60% probability. However, performance better than $4 million is unlikely. Results could range anywhere from zero to $4 million.

3. The $4 million is an easy target. There's an even chance of anything between $4 million and $8 million.

10. Cranberry Wood Products Inc. spends an average of $9.50 in labor and $12.40 in materials on every unit it sells. Sales commissions and shipping amount to another $3.10. All other costs are fixed and add up to $140,000 per month. The average unit sells for $32.00.

a. What are Cranberry's contribution and contribution margin?

b. What is the firm's breakeven point in units?

c. Calculate the dollar breakeven point in two ways.

d. Sketch the breakeven diagram.

e. Calculate the DOL when sales are 20%, 30%, and 40% above breakeven.

11. Refer to the Cranberry company of Problem 10:

a. Suppose automated equipment is added that increases fixed costs by $20,000 per month. How much will total variable cost have to decrease to keep the breakeven point the same?

b. Calculate the DOL at the same output levels used in part e of Problem 10.

c. Comment on the differences in DOL with and without the additional equipment.

12. The Spitfire Model Airplane Company has the following modified income statement ($000) at 100,000 units of production.

Revenue	$10,000
Variable cost	6,500
Fixed cost	2,200
EBIT	$ 1,300
Interest (@ 10%)	500
EBT	$ 800
Tax (@ 40%)	320
EAT	$ 480
Number of shares	20,000

a. What are Spitfire's contribution margin and dollar breakeven point?

b. Calculate Spitfire's current DFL, DOL, and DTL.

c. Calculate the current EPS and estimate what it would become if sales declined by 25%. Use the DTL first and then recalculate the modified income statement. (Assume a negative EBT generates a negative tax.)

13. The Singleton Metal Stamping Company is planning to buy a new computer-controlled stamping machine for $10 million. The purchase will be financed entirely with borrowed money, which will change Singleton's capital structure substantially. It will also change operations by adding $1.5 million in fixed cost and eliminating $2 million in variable cost at the current level of sales. The firm's current financial position is reflected in the following statement ($000).

Revenue	$18,000		
Variable cost	10,000	Debt	$ 5,000
Fixed cost	5,000	Equity	15,000
EBIT	$ 3,000	Total	$20,000
Interest (@ 10%)	500		
EBT	$ 2,500	Number of shares	750,000
Tax (@ 40%)	1,000	EPS	$ 2.00
EAT	$ 1,500		

a. Restate the financial statements with the new machine, and calculate the dollar breakeven points with and without it.

b. Calculate the DFL with and without the new machine.

c. Calculate the DOL with and without the new machine. (*Hint:* You don't need Q to use equation 13.11, because PQ is revenue and VQ is total variable cost.)

d. Calculate the DTL with and without the new machine.

e. Comment on the variability of EPS with sales and the source of that variability.

f. Is it a good idea to buy the new machine if sales are expected to remain near current levels? Give two reasons why or why not. What has to be anticipated for the project to make sense?

Internet Problem

14. Visit Fortune at http://www.fortune.com and click on Fortune 500. Click on the *Industry List* and then click on *Airlines* and note the top three companies. Click on the *Company Snapshot* of each to get their ticker symbol. Do the same for the *General Merchandisers* industry.

Next, visit HooversOnline at http://www.hoovers.com and click on Companies and Industries. Use each company's balance sheet to calculate their use of debt and equity financing. For each company list what percentage of their total assets is financed from debt and what percentage from equity.

Compare the use of debt versus equity financing both within each industry and between the two industries. What conclusions can you make from reviewing this data? Do they make sense?

CHAPTER 14

Dividends

Chapter Outline

In this chapter we'll concern ourselves with common stock dividends, the payments made by companies to equity investors.[1] Dividends present an interesting puzzle in modern finance. People are basically divided on their importance to investors and as to whether their payment has an influence on stock prices. Practitioners tend to think dividends are important to prices, while scholars feel that in theory they shouldn't make much difference. The debate is significant because of the central role dividends occupy in the fabric of finance. To understand the issues, we'll need to review a little background.

BACKGROUND

DIVIDENDS AS A BASIS FOR VALUE

● **Dividends** are the **basis of value** for stocks.

Dividends are a critical piece of the financial system because of their role in determining the value of stocks. Recall that in Chapter 7 we came to the conclusion that stock prices depended *entirely* on expected future dividends. We need to review those ideas and revise our focus slightly for the present discussion.

The relationship between dividends and value can be viewed from the perspective of an individual investor or from that of the market as a whole.

The Individual Perspective

An individual buys a stock because he or she expects an acceptable return from dividends and from the receipts when the shares eventually are sold. Today's price is the present value of those future cash flows discounted at the appropri-

---

1. Although payments made to preferred stockholders are also called dividends, we won't be dealing with them here.

ate rate for an equity investment in the company. If an investor plans to hold a stock for n years, these ideas can be written as follows.

$$(14.1) \quad P_0 = \frac{D_1}{(1+k)} + \frac{D_2}{(1+k)^2} + \cdots + \frac{D_n}{(1+k)^n} + \frac{P_n}{(1+k)^n}$$

where: P_0 = today's stock price

D_i = the dividend in the ith year (i = 1, 2, . . . , n)

P_n = the selling price of the stock in the nth year

k = the expected return on equity

This idea was developed in more detail in Chapter 7 in equation 7.5, page 226.

The Whole Market View

In Chapter 7 we went on to develop the whole market focus by replacing P_n with the present value of the remaining dividends stretching infinitely into the future. We argued that the buyer in year n would have a model in mind similar to equation 14.1, and replacing P_n with that model would conceptually push the selling price farther into the future. We could apply this mental process as many times as we liked to get the eventual selling price infinitely distant in time, at which point its present value would be zero. Hence we could work with a model that had an infinite dividend stream rather than a finite stream followed by a price.

Our Current Focus

● Valuation can be based on a series of dividends and an **eventual selling price.**

Both the finite and infinite stream models are valid expressions for valuation. In Chapter 7 we focused on the infinite stream. Here we'll make use of the individual model with a finite time horizon.

●UNDERSTANDING THE DIVIDEND DECISION

The dividend decision is simple on the surface. It relates to how much of its earnings a firm should pay out in dividends. The options range from nothing to everything. However, it's important that we understand all the implications involved in the choice, because some aren't entirely obvious.

The Discretionary Nature of Dividends

The Stock Center at Market Edge is a good source of dividend information:

● www.marketedge.com

We need to keep in mind the fact that dividends are legally discretionary. A company's board of directors has the authority to determine the amount of every dividend, including whether anything is paid at all.

This is a very significant point. In spite of the importance of dividends in the valuation process, they are never assured. The purchase of a share of stock includes no guarantee of future dividends, regardless of what has been paid in the past.

The Dividend Decision

A firm's earnings belong to its stockholders. The dividend decision is a choice made by management on behalf of those stockholders about what to do with their earnings. Theoretically, there are only two alternatives. Earnings can be paid out as dividends or retained for reinvestment in the business. Both options benefit stockholders, but in different ways.

The dividend option gives stockholders an immediate cash payment that they can spend or reinvest as they please. Retaining earnings, on the other hand, involves investing the money in business projects that are expected to enhance profitability. Those higher profits cause the stock price to increase, which means share owners hold more valuable financial assets. It's important to focus on the different characteristics of the benefits created by the two mechanisms.

A dividend gives stockholders *current income* they can spend immediately. Current income is important to some investors because they need to live on it. To others it's less significant because they don't need it immediately and would just reinvest it.

Stock price appreciation, on the other hand, can't be spent without selling the stock, which many people don't want to do right away. Hence retaining earnings produces *deferred income*.

● The **dividend decision** is whether to **pay cash dividends** or **retain earnings** for growth, both of which benefit stockholders.

The **dividend decision** is the choice between paying more or less in *near-term* dividends. That implies trading off between the two stockholder benefits. It is not a question of whether the stockholder gets a dividend or gets nothing.

THE DIVIDEND CONTROVERSY

The central issue about dividends is whether paying them or paying larger rather than smaller dividends has a positive, negative, or neutral effect on a firm's stock price. The question can also be stated in terms of stockholder preferences. Do shareholders prefer current or deferred income as just described? Presumably, doing what they prefer will make a stock more desirable, and its price will be bid up to some extent. In other words, we'd like to know whether it's generally possible for management to partially accomplish the goal of maximizing shareholder wealth by manipulating the firm's dividend-paying policy.

● The **dividend controversy** is whether paying or not paying **dividends** affects stock price.

There are three major arguments regarding investors' preferences for or against dividends and several lesser but related theories that tend to tie things together. None of them are entirely right or wrong.

● DIVIDEND IRRELEVANCE

The position endorsed by most theorists is that dividends should matter very little to stock price if they matter at all. The reasoning behind this idea can be seen from equation 14.1. In that equation, suppose early dividends such as D_1 and D_2 are reduced or eliminated, thereby increasing retained earnings. The additional income retained may cause the company to become more profitable and/or grow faster. That, in turn, will make the eventual selling price of the stock, P_n, higher, and may also make later dividends like D_n larger.

● Under **dividend irrelevance** the value of eliminated dividends is **offset by growth-created value** in the future.

The dividend irrelevance hypothesis is that the negative impact on P_0 of reducing or eliminating early dividends is offset by the positive effect of an increased selling price in period n as well as larger later dividends. Hence the current price of the stock, represented by P_0, is independent of changes in the early dividends.

Tailoring the Cash Flow Stream

The irrelevance argument clearly makes sense if investors don't have a preference for current income. If they do, we have to reason a little harder.

A preference for current income means people care about the pattern of cash flows from an investment as well as about the present value of the entire stream of payments (the security's price). For example, retirees who need a certain amount of current income from investments to live comfortably will be upset if a stock they hold reduces its dividends, regardless of the fact that the present value of the whole stream doesn't change.

Does this imply that if management reduces or eliminates dividends in the near term, investors who need current income have to get out of the stock? In theory the answer is no, because an investor in need of cash can always sell some of his or her stock for cash. The portion of the holding that isn't sold appreciates because of the retention of additional earnings, so the value of the original investment can be maintained in spite of the selloff, even though the number of shares owned decreases.

● Investors can **tailor** their income stream by selling off shares of a growing stock that doesn't pay dividends.

EXAMPLE 14.1

Jack and Wendy Winter are retirees who have most of their savings invested in 10,000 shares of Ajax Corporation. Ajax sells for $10 per share and pays a yearly dividend of $.50 per share. The firm hasn't grown for some time. The Winters depend on their Ajax dividends to supplement their retirement income.

This year Ajax discontinued the dividend, but began to grow at 5% per year because of the additional retained earnings. How can the Winters maintain their income and their position in Ajax? Assume there are no costs to buying and selling securities.

Solution: At $10 each, the Winters's 10,000 Ajax shares were originally worth a total of (10,000 × $10 =) $100,000. That's the principal amount of their investment that they want to maintain. At the same time, they have to generate a yearly income stream of (10,000 × $.50 =) $5,000 to replace the dividend that's no longer being paid.

After a year of growth at 5%, Ajax's shares are worth $10.50 each. The Winters can raise $5,000 in cash by selling

$$\frac{\$5,000}{\$10.50} = 476 \text{ shares} .$$

At the appreciated price, the remaining (10,000 − 476 =) 9,524 shares are worth

$$\$10.50 \times 9,524 = \$100,002.$$

Hence the gross amount of the Winters's investment is maintained. (The numbers aren't quite exact because we have to deal in whole shares.) As an exercise, calculate the required selloff in the second year.

It's easy to imagine the reverse situation in which a firm's dividend provides more cash than an investor currently needs. In such a case, some of the cash received can be used to buy more stock in the same company. That effectively reduces the dividend and expands the investor's stake in the firm.

Summarizing, it's theoretically possible to *tailor* one's current income from a stock investment in a growing company to any level by buying or selling shares.

Transaction Costs

All this works fine as long as trading in and out of the stock doesn't cost anything. Much of formal economic theory operates in a hypothetical world where this is the case. Capital markets are assumed to be *perfectly efficient,* which among other things implies that securities can be traded without incurring costs. In such a world people would truly be indifferent to the payment of dividends.

In reality, however, financial markets are burdened with imperfections, including transaction costs such as brokerage commissions. Consider the Winters from Example 14.1. If they have to pay commissions to sell stock, the process of tailoring a current income stream will have a cost. That may make it impossible for them to stay in the Ajax investment.

As a practical matter, if the commission rate is small, selling stock to generate current income can remain a reasonable thing to do. But if the rate is significant, selling off shares can become a prohibitively costly process. Then the discontinuation of the dividend would probably drive the Winters and others like them away from Ajax. If most of the firm's stockholders were affected that way, Ajax's market price would drop.

Clearly, the more significant the transaction costs, the less valid the irrelevance theory becomes.

Income Taxes

It's worth noting that the tax system plays a subtle part in the indifference theory. Notice that the idea depends on trading short-run dividend income for price appreciation in the longer run. We've described that trade-off in pretax terms with equation 14.1; however, the tax system can add a complication.

Dividends are taxed as ordinary income, while appreciation is taxed as a capital gain. Therefore the difference in the tax rates on those types of income should be included in the offsetting idea. This is conceptually easy to do. To the extent capital gains are taxed at lower rates than ordinary income, it takes a proportionately smaller increase in P_n to offset the value of a near-term dividend reduction than it would if the rates were the same.

The View from within the Company

From the perspective of the firm, dividends represent an outflow of cash that could be used for other things. Specifically, paying dividends reduces retained earnings, which are a source of funds for capital budgeting projects.

Recall that in Chapter 12 (page 399) we dealt with what happens when the firm runs out of retained earnings before it runs out of projects. We concluded that if more equity is needed after retained earnings are exhausted, the company raises it by selling additional stock. This means that a dividend paid may result in the need to sell new stock, because it reduces earnings retained.

This doesn't create a problem if the new stock is sold in a perfectly efficient market without incurring flotation costs.[2] In that case, the firm would be internally indifferent between paying and not paying dividends. The cash used for dividends would simply be replaced by selling stock as needed.

However, if there are flotation costs, an expense is associated with selling new stock. Then paying dividends leads to incurring extra cost, and the firm has a

● **Transaction costs** tend to make tailoring an income stream impractical.

● Firms **prefer not paying dividends** if it avoids selling new stock, because **retained earnings cost less** than new equity.

from the CFO

---

2. Recall that flotation costs are the transaction costs associated with issuing new securities.

definite internal preference for not paying dividends. This preference is shared by stockholders because more cost ultimately means less earnings.

Needless to say, flotation costs do exist in the real world, and they're quite significant.

DIVIDEND PREFERENCE

● Under **dividend preference** investors prefer immediate cash to **uncertain** future benefits.

The dividend preference theory maintains that generally stockholders prefer receiving dividends to not receiving them. The argument is based on the uncertainty of the future. It asserts that stockholders prefer current dividends to future capital gains, because something paid today is more certain to be received than something expected in the future. The idea can be put in somewhat cynical terms by saying that stockholders don't trust management to use the cash on hand today to grow the firm into something larger and more valuable later on.

Notice that this is not a time value of money argument. It doesn't say people prefer the dividend today because it's worth more. It says they'd rather have it now to be sure of getting it. The argument is often called the *bird in the hand theory* from the old cliché, "A bird in the hand is worth two in the bush" (because you may not catch either of those in the bush).

The reasoning has one rather substantial flaw. If stockholders are concerned about reinvesting dividend money in a firm because they're afraid it will be lost, why have they invested in that firm in the first place?

DIVIDEND AVERSION

The dividend aversion position asserts that investors generally prefer that companies not pay dividends in order to enhance stock prices later on. The argument is based on capital gains taxes, so its persuasiveness depends on current tax law.

● Under **dividend aversion** investors prefer future capital gains to current dividends because of lower **tax rates.**

The logic underlying the idea is that dividends are taxed at ordinary income rates, while capital gains are taxed at lower "capital gains rates." Notice that in equation 14.1 the dividend decision involves trading early dividends for a higher selling price in period n. The current dividend is ordinary income, but the appreciated price represents a capital gain when the stock is sold. Hence the trade-off between a dividend today and a higher price later has to be modified to reflect the fact that, after taxes, investors get to keep more of the appreciation than the dividends. That clearly makes the deferred gain more desirable.

Congress makes changes to the tax treatment of capital gains almost constantly. Most of the time tax rates on capital gains are set lower than the rates on ordinary income to provide an incentive for investing, which in turn stimulates the economy. But that hasn't always been the case. The Tax Reform Act of 1986, for example, eliminated favorable treatment of capital gains for several years until a favorable bias was gradually restored during the 1990s. As of 2001, capital gains enjoy a substantial tax advantage over ordinary income.

It's important to realize that Congress is capable of reversing itself again and reducing or eliminating capital gains benefits in the future. The issue is politically sensitive because capital gains largely accrue to the wealthy, so favorable rates are a break for the rich.

There are two other less obvious tax benefits associated with capital gains that support a dividend aversion argument. First, taxes on capital gains are deferred until stock is sold. Second, all taxes on capital gains are avoided if stock isn't sold when an investor dies. Then the shares pass to the heirs with a tax basis equal to their current market value, so the price appreciation up to that date is never taxed. (This benefit is scheduled to be eliminated in 2010.)

OTHER THEORIES AND IDEAS

After all this we're still not sure whether there ought to be a general preference for or against dividends. There are a few other ideas that can help us understand the overall picture.

The Clientele Effect

The clientele argument is that individual investors do have definite dividend preferences because of their needs for more or less current income. These preferences arise because transaction costs make tailoring a cash flow stream by buying and selling stock very expensive.

It's easy to visualize the kinds of people who have various preferences. Retirees living on fixed incomes, for example, are likely to need dividend income to supplement pensions and social security. Young professionals with plenty of disposable income, on the other hand, may be willing to bet on capital gains in the longer run if the expected return is higher. People tend to gravitate toward the type of company that meets their needs. The retirees are likely to prefer companies like public utilities that are stable and tend to pay regular dividends. The young professionals like high-tech start-ups that don't pay dividends at all but may offer huge price appreciation.

Each company develops a *clientele* of investors whose needs match its dividend-paying characteristics, hence the term **clientele effect.** The most significant implication of the effect is that once a clientele is established, it's unwise to change dividend practices. Such a change would be almost guaranteed to alienate shareholders who invested in the firm at least partially because they liked its dividend policy. It would cause them to migrate away from the stock, creating a general downward pressure on its price.

The Residual Dividend Theory

The **residual dividend theory** focuses on the firm's internal need for capital. Earlier we mentioned that dividends reduce retained earnings, and therefore can force the sale of additional stock when a company needs equity capital for projects. Further, we noted that equity from new stock is more expensive than retained earnings because of flotation costs.

Under the residual dividend concept, companies recognize the cost effectiveness of retained earnings, and fund the equity portion of all viable projects with earnings before paying any dividends. Anything left over is paid out as a dividend. The term "residual" comes from this *leftover* status of the dividend.

The residual theory has an intuitive appeal, but it isn't the way most companies work. Most managements see a value in dividends and set them aside first rather than last. Further, most companies can come up with a virtually unlimited number of capital projects that look good on paper. As a result, a firm that truly adhered to the residual theory might never pay a dividend.

The Signaling Effect of Dividends

Rightly or wrongly, financial markets have come to read a great deal of information into the payment or nonpayment of a dividend. Indeed, the dividend is

---

● The **clientele effect** maintains that investors choose stocks **for dividend policy,** so any **change** in payments is **disruptive.**

http://

Many investors rely on a company's dividend yield as a guide to selecting stocks. Go to

http://dogsofthedow.com/

to learn more about how the dogs are selected. List this year's dogs of the Dow. How does their performance compare to the DJIA?

● Under the **residual** view, dividends are paid from earnings only **after all viable projects are funded.**

from the CFO

viewed as a way for management to send a message to its shareholders. People seem to have more faith in the message carried by dollars and cents than in spoken words. The phenomenon is called the signaling or information effect of dividends, and is especially significant when earnings change.

If earnings turn down, the continuation of a regular dividend is viewed as a statement by management that the business is fundamentally sound and that the downturn is temporary. As a result, firms generally continue paying their normal dividends in the face of temporary decreases in earnings. The message to shareholders is, "EPS is off a little, but don't worry about it. Things will be fine. In the long run we expect to have plenty of money, so here's your regular dividend."

In the same vein, an increase in the dividend is a stronger statement of management's confidence in the future. An increase accompanying rising earnings is a statement that the earnings improvement is expected to be permanent, and signifies a generally bright future. An increase in the face of a downturn is a clear attempt to allay stockholders' fears.

○ Cash dividends signal **management's confidence** in the future.

On the other hand, a decrease in dividends is taken as terrible news. It generally comes after a sustained reduction in earnings, and tells the market that management doesn't expect the company to have the cash it had in the past. Investors usually react negatively and tend to sell off the stock, depressing its price. A decrease without an associated decline in earnings is a more mysterious but nevertheless dark message that isn't well received either.

As a result of all this, managements sometimes maintain or even raise dividends in an attempt to forestall negative investor reactions to serious problems. This practice is clearly inappropriate.

The signaling effect is very real and makes it difficult to tell what investor preferences for cash dividends really are. For example, suppose a firm has steady earnings but reduces its regular dividend, explaining to stockholders that it needs more money for capital projects. In spite of the explanation, the stock's price drops. Is the drop due to the fact that investors prefer a higher dividend, or is it because they don't quite believe management's explanation and suspect operating problems are coming? It's very difficult to tell.

The Expectations Theory

The *expectations theory* is a refinement of the signaling effect. It says that investors form expectations of what a company's next dividend will be and can become alarmed if those expectations aren't met, even if the dividend actually paid is steady or increasing.

○ Dividends that **fail** to fulfill stockholders' **expectations** send a **negative message** even if the payment is good.

For example, suppose a company whose dividend has been $2.00 per share achieves a substantial improvement in business, and people form the expectation that the next dividend should be $2.20. Then suppose the firm pays $2.10, an increase, but a smaller one than expected. The expectations theory says that investor reaction is likely to be negative because expectations weren't met, and that the stock's price may very well fall.

● CONCLUSION

The conclusion is that we don't really have a conclusion. No one knows with certainty whether paying more or less in dividends generally increases or decreases stock prices. Most practicing financial professionals feel dividends have a positive effect on prices. Scholars tend to say that notion can't really be proven.

As a practical matter, the overwhelming majority of companies do pay dividends. On the average, U.S. companies pay out about 50% of their earnings in dividends.

PRACTICAL CONSIDERATIONS

● LEGAL AND CONTRACTUAL RESTRICTIONS ON DIVIDENDS

Companies aren't always entirely free to pay whatever dividends they want. Restrictions are imposed by state law and contractual agreements.

Legal Restrictions

The laws governing corporate dividend practices differ from state to state, but two generalizations are possible.

First, dividends can't be paid out of capital; they must come from retained earnings. This rule protects creditors. Suppose Able starts a company, investing $1,000 of his own equity money, and convinces Baker to *lend* the firm another $1,000. As soon as the company is set up, Able, being the only shareholder, declares a $2,000 cash dividend which he pays to himself. The company now has no operating money, so it closes. Able has effectively stolen Baker's $1,000. To prevent this abuse, the law requires that firms earn some money before dividends are paid, and that dividends can be paid only to the extent of cumulative past earnings.

Second, a firm can't pay dividends if it is insolvent, meaning its liabilities exceed its assets. This rule is also designed to protect creditors. An insolvent company may face bankruptcy proceedings in which its assets may be sold to pay off as many of its liabilities as possible. A company anticipating proceedings could sell its assets and pay a dividend to stockholders with the cash received. This would take the assets out of the hands of the creditors at the last minute and leave them with a loss that should be the stockholders'.

- ● Dividends **can't be paid** by an in-solvent firm and must come from current or prior **earnings.**

Contractual Restrictions

DEBT CONTRACTS   Business loans and bond issues usually come with restrictions on the behavior of the borrowing company that are designed to ensure repayment. Such contractual agreements are called **indentures** (bonds) and **covenants** (loans). The restrictions are generally aimed at conserving cash and maintaining prudent, conservative business practices. (See Chapter 6, page 214.)

It isn't uncommon for indentures and covenants to restrict or prohibit the payment of common stock dividends under certain conditions. For example, a lender might stipulate that if EBIT falls below two times debt service (the sum of interest and principal payments) in any period, no cash dividends can be paid. This restriction would protect the interests of creditors by preventing cash from being siphoned off to stockholders when it looks like financial troubles might be approaching.

- ● Loan **indentures** and **covenants** may limit dividend payments to **protect creditors'** interests.

PREFERRED STOCK   Another common restriction on the payment of common stock dividends is the cumulative feature of preferred stock dividends. Recall that preferred stock pays a fixed dividend into the indefinite future, but that the payment isn't quite guaranteed. The *cumulative feature* generally specifies that if one or more preferred dividends are passed, no common stock dividends can be paid until they're caught up cumulatively. (See Chapter 7, page 241.)

- ● The **cumulative** feature of **preferred stock** limits dividend payments.

INSIGHTS

Practical Finance

The Painful Decision to Cut Dividends

Companies are reluctant to reduce dividends because of the signaling and clientele effects. They do it only when forced to by poor earnings or fundamental changes in their businesses. Two examples are worth noting.

IBM was a financial powerhouse from the 1960s until the late 1980s when it started having severe market problems associated with the general shift from mainframe to personal computers. The company experienced record losses in 1992. As a result, it cut its dividend from $4.84 to $1.00 in 1993. Notice that in spite of the fact that the company was in dire straits and losing money, the dividend was not entirely eliminated. This undoubtedly was a signal from management intended to convey long-term confidence in its ability to bring the company back. That did happen beginning in 1994, and during the mid-1990s IBM was an exceptional stock market performer. Dividends, however, have not been returned to their former levels.

The clientele effect is especially important to public utilities such as water and electric companies. Utilities are regulated monopolies, meaning they have no competitors, but the prices they can charge are limited by the government. As a result their performance is very stable, and they typically pay out most of their earning in dividends. Utilities attract investors like retirees who value stability and depend on receiving regular dividend income. These ideas are behind the clientele theory.

In the mid-1990s the electric utility industry was deregulated. Companies no longer enjoy government protection, and have had to learn to survive in more traditionally competitive markets. That means a policy of paying out nearly all earnings in dividends is no longer appropriate. The first electric utility to recognize that in its dividend policy was Florida Power and Light (parent company FPL). FPL cut its dividend by about a third in 1994 even though current earnings were good and the move broke a string of 47 straight annual increases. The stock market initially reacted negatively, dropping FPL's price, but later absorbed the logic behind the move. As a result the firm went on to become an outstanding performer.

DIVIDEND POLICY

Dividend policy refers to the rationale under which a firm determines what it will pay in dividends. The term encompasses both the amount paid and the pattern under which changes in the amount occur over time.

Before getting into different policies, we need two definitions. The dividend **payout ratio** is the ratio of the dividends paid to earnings. It can be thought of in total or in per-share terms.

● The **payout ratio** states dividends as a fraction of earnings.

(14.2)
$$\text{payout ratio} = \frac{\text{dividend}}{\text{earnings}} = \frac{\text{dividend per share}}{\text{EPS}}$$

For example, a payout ratio of 40% would mean the firm pays a cash dividend of 40 cents out of every dollar it earns. The concept contains a subtlety that's worth pointing out. The dividend is paid in cash, but the earnings figure doesn't represent cash availability. That's because net income (earnings) includes accrual accounting entries for both income and cost. Hence, in any particular year, more or less cash may be available to pay dividends than is implied by earnings. More significantly, a firm with even a modest payout ratio may have trouble paying the appropriate dividend if it has other substantial cash needs. These might include capital expenditures and debt repayment.

● A **stable dividend** is **nondecreasing.**

Stability refers to the constancy of dividends over time. A **stable dividend** is constant in amount from period to period but is usually increased occasionally. A dividend with a *stable growth rate* increases by a more or less constant percentage over time.

Recall that a decrease in dividends generally carries a bad signaling effect. Managements therefore try to keep dividends from ever going down. As a result, the term "stable" tends to imply a dividend that can go up or flatten out, but that doesn't decline.

Alternate Policies

Three dividend policies are common.

TARGET PAYOUT RATIO   A firm following this policy selects a long-run payout ratio with which it's comfortable. However, it doesn't apply that ratio blindly each year. To do so would result in dividends that fluctuate up and down with earnings. From what we've learned about signaling, that would have a negative effect on the stock's market price. The actual payout ratio is generally somewhat below the target to allow for variations in earnings without forcing a decrease in dividends.

● Typical policies include a **target payout ratio,** a **stable dividend,** and year-end extras.

STABLE DIVIDEND PER SHARE   A constant dividend is paid regardless of earnings unless business conditions deteriorate so badly that the firm's ability to continue paying comes into doubt. If things go well and the company grows, the dividend is raised from time to time. A stable dividend per share is by far the most common practice.

SMALL REGULAR DIVIDEND WITH A YEAR-END EXTRA IF EARNINGS PERMIT   With this policy management more or less assures stockholders of the regular dividend, but maintains the ability to either pay or forego the year-end extra. In theory this gives the firm the ability to lower its dividend level without a negative informational effect. In other words, the firm attempts to defeat the signaling effect of a reduction by keeping stockholders from counting on the extra payment. Unfortunately, people get used to the extra payment very fast.

● THE MECHANICS OF DIVIDEND PAYMENTS

In the work we've done so far, we've treated dividends as annual cash flows. In practice, however, virtually all companies make dividend payments quarterly.[3]

Key Dates

Every quarterly dividend has four key *dates* associated with it.

THE DECLARATION DATE   The amount of each quarterly dividend is authorized by the firm's board of directors. A separate authorization occurs every quarter even if the firm's policy is to pay the same amount repeatedly. The date on which the board authorizes the dividend is called the **declaration date.**

● Dividends are authorized on the **declaration date** for owners as of the **date of record** and are sent on the **payment date.**

THE DATE OF RECORD   Stocks are **registered securities,** meaning that a list is kept indicating the name of the *owner of record* of every share. When a share is

---

3. The annual figures people work with are generally the latest quarterly figure times four.

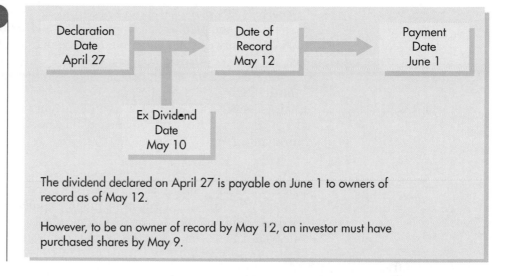

FIGURE 14.1

The Dividend Declaration and Payment Process

Declaration Date April 27 → Date of Record May 12 → Payment Date June 1

Ex Dividend Date May 10

The dividend declared on April 27 is payable on June 1 to owners of record as of May 12.

However, to be an owner of record by May 12, an investor must have purchased shares by May 9.

http://

Click on

www.e-analytics.com/splitd.htm

to find the most recent ex-dividend date for a stock as well as the amount of its annual dividend.

sold, ownership is transferred on the record from the seller to the buyer.[4] When the board authorizes a dividend, it stipulates a **date of record**. The dividend is payable to owners of record as of the date of record.

THE PAYMENT DATE   The board also stipulates the date on which the dividend check is to be mailed. This is the **payment date.**

THE EX-DIVIDEND DATE   When shares are sold, it can take a few days to update the ownership records, so a sale made shortly before the date of record might not be recognized for payment purposes. To allow for a paperwork lag, brokerage firms have agreed to cut off sales *for dividend purposes* two business days prior to the date of record. The cutoff is called the **ex-dividend date.**

Figure 14.1 is a graphic representation and some sample dates. The ex-dividend date is significant with respect to stock market activity. An investor who purchases the stock prior to the ex-dividend date receives the next dividend; one who purchases on or after that date does not. In the example, the stock trades without the dividend starting on the morning of May 10.

● An investor who buys a stock on or after the **ex-dividend date** does **not** receive the pending dividend.

As ex-dividend dates pass, stocks generally drop in price, reflecting the loss of the dividends to new purchasers. Interestingly, the drop tends to be 20% or 30% less than the full amount of the dividend. The difference is believed to be due to the fact that investors value the dividend after taxes rather than before.

Dividend Reinvestment Plans

Most large companies offer stockholders an optional dividend reinvestment plan under which the company keeps the dividends of participating stockholders and gives them additional shares instead.

● Large companies offer automatic **dividend reinvestment plans** to shareholders.

For example, if a firm paid a $.50 dividend and someone owned 100 shares, his or her dividend check would be for $50. If the stock was selling for $25 at the time, that person would receive two additional shares instead of the money.

4. Most large companies use specialized firms called transfer agents to do this record-keeping chore. See Chapter 7.

Reinvestment plan shares can come from either of two sources, depending on the nature of the plan. In one approach the undistributed dividends are pooled and used to buy existing shares on the open market. The shares are then distributed back to the participating stockholders. This kind of plan is just a service provided to stockholders and doesn't significantly benefit the company.

In the second kind of plan, the company issues new shares at a price that's usually slightly below market. This approach has two benefits. It avoids the brokerage fees associated with buying existing stock, and it provides the company with a source of new equity capital that's free of flotation costs.

TAX TREATMENT   It's important to understand the tax treatment of reinvested dividends. In the reinvestment process, stockholders *effectively* receive cash and use it to buy more stock. The company just administers the transaction on their behalf. For this reason, the Internal Revenue Service treats the reinvested dividend as taxable income even though the stockholder never had the cash in hand.

● STOCK SPLITS AND DIVIDENDS

Companies sometimes revise the number of shares of stock they have outstanding with stock splits and stock dividends. These transactions increase the count of shares in the hands of stockholders with no other real effect.

Stock Splits

● Stock **splits and dividends** issue new shares to **existing stockholders** in proportion to the number held.

A *stock split* issues new shares in numbers proportionate to those already outstanding. We'll illustrate the idea with a two-for-one split.

A firm with 100,000 shares outstanding executes a two-for-one split by issuing an additional share to all current stockholders for every share they already own. After the split there are 200,000 shares outstanding, and all stockholders hold twice as many shares as they held before.

It's important to realize that after a split, every stockholder has the same proportion of outstanding shares he or she had previously. Therefore the split doesn't result in any change in ownership or control.

● Stock splits and dividends **don't change ownership** or control and have **no real value** to shareholders.

Because there are twice as many shares after the split representing ownership of the same company, each share is worth half as much as it was before. But because each stockholder owns twice as many shares, there's no change in anyone's wealth. In effect, a split doesn't do anything but change the arithmetic involved in keeping track of shares.

A split doesn't have to be two-for-one; it can be made in any proportion. For example, a 1.5-for-one split implies that shareholders get one new share for every two they already own. A 1.25-for-one split would give one new share for every four owned. In any case, the effect is the same: The proportionate ownership of the company is unchanged, as is the wealth of stockholders.

Reverse splits are also possible. A company might, for example, call in all of its shares and reissue one new share for every two owned. This would halve the number of shares outstanding and generally double the price.

Stock Dividends

When additional shares are issued as we've just described, and the number of new shares is less than or equal to 20% of the original number of shares outstanding, the procedure is called a **stock dividend** rather than a stock split. For

http://

Visit the Equity Analytics, Ltd., web site at

www.e-analytics.com/index.htm

to learn more about stock splits and stock dividends.

example, a 1.1-for-one "split," in which one new share is received for every 10 owned, is called a 10% stock dividend.

Accounting Treatment of Stock Splits and Stock Dividends

A stock dividend is in reality just a small split. The two transactions are the same conceptually, and neither creates any real economic value. However, their respective accounting treatments differ substantially. Accounting for splits is very simple, while handling stock dividends is more complicated. We'll illustrate with an example after reviewing the standard equity accounts.

Recall that the equity section of the balance sheet is divided into the following three accounts.

- *Common stock* carries the par value of all outstanding shares.
- *Paid in excess* carries the amount by which the original price of all stock sold exceeded par.
- *Retained earnings* represents the sum of all past earnings that haven't been paid out in dividend.

The equity of Eagle Inc. is presented in Table 14.1. The firm sold 2 million shares of $3 par common stock at $4, and later earned $4 million.

● A **stock split** simply changes **par value** and the **number of shares.** The capital accounts are unaffected.

ACCOUNTING FOR A SPLIT   The impact of a split on the equity accounts is very simple. The number of shares is increased and the par value is reduced proportionately. If Eagle were to split two-for-one, the number of shares would double and par value would halve. The result is illustrated in Table 14.2.

Notice that the dollar amounts in the three accounts are unchanged. The changes appear in the number of shares outstanding, the par value, and the stock's book value per share. Also notice that no reference needs to be made to the current market price of the stock to account for a split.

TABLE 14.1	**Eagle Inc. Stockholders' Equity**

Common stock (2 million shares outstanding, $3 par)	$6,000,000
Paid in excess	2,000,000
Retained earnings	4,000,000
Total common equity	$12,000,000
Book value per share	$6.00

TABLE 14.2	**Eagle Inc. Stockholders' Equity after a Two-for-One Stock Split**

Common stock (4 million shares outstanding, $1.50 par)	$6,000,000
Paid in excess	2,000,000
Retained earnings	4,000,000
Total common equity	$12,000,000
Book value per share	$3.00

● In a **stock dividend** money is moved from RE into the stock accounts to give the **appearance of a sale** at market price.

ACCOUNTING FOR A STOCK DIVIDEND   In a stock dividend, new shares are issued but the stock's par value isn't changed. Therefore the common stock account has to be increased for the par value of the newly issued shares. In addition, the paid in excess account is increased as though the new shares had been sold at a price equal to the market value of the stock just before the stock dividend. The balancing entry reduces retained earnings by the sum of the additions to the common stock and paid in excess accounts.

We'll illustrate with a 10% stock dividend for Eagle Inc. that results in 200,000 new shares. Assume the stock is selling for $10 before the dividend.

The common stock account is increased by the par value of the new shares,

$$200{,}000 \times \$3 = \$600{,}000 \ .$$

As the stock's market price is $10, the excess over par is ($10 − $3 =) $7, so the paid in excess account increases by

$$200{,}000 \times \$7 = \$1{,}400{,}000 \ .$$

At the same time, retained earnings is reduced by $2,000,000, the sum of these entries.

Because the additions to the first two accounts are offset by the reduction to retained earnings, total equity doesn't change. Book value per share does change, however, because of the additional shares. The result is shown in Table 14.3.

The entries recording a stock dividend are said to capitalize the market value of the new shares into the two paid-in accounts. They seem to be an attempt to reflect the creation of new market value even though total equity doesn't change. This is misleading, because no new economic value is created by a stock dividend.

Rationale for Stock Splits and Stock Dividends

Because stock splits and dividends don't seem to have any real economic meaning, it's fair to ask why companies do them. The reasons make some sense.

THE TRADING RANGE ARGUMENT FOR SPLITS   Many financial professionals feel that a stock loses its appeal to small investors if the price of a single share gets too high. For example, suppose a share of IBM sold for $20,000. Then no one could invest in the company unless they had at least that much money. Most small investors would be out of the market for IBM.

● **Splits** keep stock prices in a **trading range.**

To keep the markets for their equity as broad as possible, companies split their stocks from time to time to keep prices in a **trading range.** Most people feel this is somewhere between $30 and $80.

TABLE 14.3	**Eagle Inc. Stockholders' Equity after a 10% Stock Dividend**

Common stock (2.2 million shares outstanding, $3 par)	$6,600,000
Paid in excess	3,400,000
Retained earnings	2,000,000
Total common equity	$12,000,000
Book value per share	$5.45

It can be argued that keeping the market for a stock broad in this manner puts an upward pressure on price, because it maximizes the number of potential buyers. Whether that's true is debatable. Nevertheless, virtually all companies use splits to keep prices in trading ranges. Check the listings in *The Wall Street Journal;* you'll find very few issues trading at prices over $100.

● **Stock dividends** are an attempt at signaling.

GIVING SOMETHING THAT DOESN'T COST ANYTHING   Stock dividends tend to be used as signaling devices. They're often employed when companies want to send a positive message, but for some reason can't give as large a dividend as they'd like.

For example, a firm might give a stock dividend in addition to its regular cash dividend if things are going exceptionally well but it needs to conserve cash for investment in projects. Conversely, a stock dividend might be offered if things are going poorly, and no money is available for cash dividends, but management wants to make a positive statement by giving stockholders something. The value of such practices is clearly questionable.

The Effect on Price and Value

Splits and stock dividends increase shares outstanding without changing the economic value of the underlying company. It's generally accepted by scholars and most professionals that the transactions result in proportionate drops in market price, so stockholders see no real financial gain.

However, there's an underlying sentiment among some investors that something is gained with a split or a stock dividend. This probably comes from the fact that the transactions, especially splits, usually come along when prices are rising. Hence the split or dividend takes on a positive information effect through a general association with rising prices.

The statistical studies that have been done seem to indicate that there is indeed no free lunch, and that prices do drop proportionately with splits and stock dividends.

A Potential Point of Confusion

It's important not to confuse a stock dividend with the dividend reinvestment plans we talked about in the last section. In a dividend reinvestment, stockholders are actually purchasing additional shares and, because everyone doesn't participate, the proportional ownership of the company changes.

STOCK REPURCHASES

From time to time companies buy up their own stock. There are several reasons for doing this, but the most important is that it's an effective substitute for a dividend.

● REPURCHASE AS AN ALTERNATIVE TO A DIVIDEND

A firm with the cash in hand to pay a dividend can use the money to buy some of its own stock instead. Doing that reduces the number of shares outstanding, thereby increasing the EPS of the remaining shares. If the market attaches the same price/earnings (P/E) ratio to the stock after the repurchase that it did before, the remaining shares will go up in price. As a result, the remaining stockholders will see an appreciation in the value of their shares in lieu of a cash dividend. A numerical illustration will make the idea clear.

Suppose the Johnson Company has after-tax earnings of $5 million and 2,500,000 shares of common stock outstanding. Also suppose the stock trades at a P/E ratio of 10. Then EPS and market price are as follows.

$$\text{EPS} = \frac{\text{EAT}}{\text{number of shares}} = \frac{\$5,000,000}{2,500,000} = \$2.00 \text{ per share}$$

$$\text{market price} = \text{EPS} \times \text{P/E} = \$2.00 \times 10 = \$20$$

Now suppose Johnson has $1 million that it can distribute in dividends. If it does so, the dividend per share will be

$$\text{dividend} = \frac{\$1,000,000}{2,500,000 \text{ shares}} = \$.40 \text{ per share .}$$

However, suppose the company uses the $1 million to buy its own shares instead of paying a dividend. Then it can purchase and retire

$$\frac{\$1,000,000}{\$20} = 50,000 \text{ shares .}$$

After the repurchase, there will be

$$2,500,000 - 50,000 = 2,450,000 \text{ shares}$$

left outstanding. If earnings don't change, EPS will then be

$$\text{EPS} = \frac{\$5,000,000}{2,450,000} = \$2.04 \text{ per share .}$$

Finally, if the P/E remains the same, the market price of the remaining shares will be

$$\text{market price} = \text{EPS} \times \text{P/E} = \$2.04 \times 10 = \$20.40 \text{ .}$$

Under these assumptions, buying back the shares results in a price appreciation in the remaining shares just equal to the dividend. The company has spent the available cash and stockholders have received value, but no dividend was paid.

Notice that the repurchase substitutes a potential capital gain for current cash income. Therefore, to spend the value they've received, stockholders would have to sell some of their shares.

● **Repurchasing** shares is an **alternative** to paying a **dividend.**

Methods of Repurchasing Shares

Stock can be repurchased in three ways. The first and simplest method is to buy the shares on the open market. However, this can be difficult to do quickly and without affecting the market price if a large number of shares are to be acquired.

The second method is to make a **tender offer** to buy shares at a set price from any stockholders interested in selling. In this approach, stockholders are invited to "tender" their shares for purchase at the proposed price, which is generally somewhat above the current market price. If too many shares are tendered, the firm buys a pro rata portion of all those offered.

In the third method, the firm makes a negotiated deal with a large investor who holds a big block of stock. Such investors are frequently institutions such as mutual funds, pension funds, or insurance companies. This approach can involve some risk, because the price negotiated with a large and powerful investor will generally be above the stock's market price. In essence the firm is buying one stockholder's shares at a premium with money belonging to all stockholders. It's easy to interpret this as unfair to those who aren't being bought out. Remaining stockholders have been known to sue management over the issue.

OTHER REPURCHASE ISSUES

The Opportunistic Repurchase

● Repurchases are appropriate when a stock is **temporarily undervalued** or the firm has **excess cash.**

If a company's stock is undervalued,[5] repurchasing shares can be beneficial to the remaining stockholders. This can happen if the market takes a sudden downturn that's expected to be temporary. Let's consider an example.

Suppose Catatonic Inc. has 100,000 shares outstanding that sell at their book value of $10. This means the market sees the firm as worth $1 million, the book value of its equity. Also suppose the firm has $100,000 in available cash. Then imagine that the stock market crashes, losing 30% of its value, and Catatonic shares fall to $7.00.

Assume management believes the market will recover within a reasonable period and the firm's shares will again sell at book value. The company therefore uses its cash of $100,000 to repurchase stock. At $7 per share it acquires

$$\frac{\$100,000}{\$7.00} = 14,286 \text{ shares}.$$

This leaves

$$100,000 - 14,286 = 85,714$$

shares outstanding.

Later, the market recovers and again values the firm at book equity, which is now $900,000 because $100,000 was spent on stock. Each share will then have a market value of

$$\frac{\$900,000}{85,714} = \$10.50.$$

This amount is $.50 more than the value of a share before the market downturn. Management earned the extra value for the remaining stockholders by taking advantage of the temporary drop in market price. Of course, it was earned at the expense of shareholders who sold at $7.

The situation described in the illustration is exactly what happened during a famous stock market decline in 1987. The market lost approximately 30% of its value in a few weeks, and then stabilized. Many corporate managements recognized the situation as a buying opportunity and rushed to repurchase shares. That turned out to be the right thing to do at the time, because the market subsequently recovered. Unfortunately, it's not easy to determine when a stock is *temporarily* undervalued.[6]

---

5. A security is said to be undervalued if it is selling in a financial market for less than its true worth. Clearly, this reflects a difference of opinion about that true worth.
6. This example is presented just to illustrate the effect of buying undervalued stock. The market doesn't price companies on the basis of their book values.

Repurchases to Dispose of Excess Cash

A period of high earnings that isn't expected to be repeated can leave the company with a one-time sum of money. If there aren't sufficient capital investment opportunities available to use up the funds, they should be distributed to stockholders.

Excess cash can be distributed by paying a one-time dividend. However, such a payment can create problems because of the signaling effect. Managers are reluctant to increase and then decrease dividends, because they anticipate a negative information impact from the decrease that more than offsets the positive effect of the extra money paid.

A stock repurchase can be a solution to the dilemma. It effectively distributes the money to the shareholders, but tends not to generate expectations of future distributions the way a dividend might.

Taxes

As we've demonstrated, a stock repurchase creates appreciation in the unredeemed shares. If the firm repurchases its stock occasionally, the appreciation is treated as a capital gain and is not taxed until the stock is sold.

However, if a firm repurchases its stock regularly and predictably, the IRS is likely to take the position that the transactions are effectively dividends. It could then tax the gains received by stockholders as current, ordinary income even though no cash was received.

As a result of this possibility, regular repurchase activity in lieu of dividends is not advisable. There is considerable uncertainty in this area of taxation.

Repurchases to Restructure Capital

It should be clear from our work in Chapter 13 that restructuring capital in the direction of debt involves repurchasing stock. Indeed, capital restructuring is a major reason for repurchases. In a transaction to restructure toward debt, the firm simply borrows money and uses the proceeds of the loan to buy back its stock.

DISCUSSION QUESTIONS

1. Dividends are said to be the basis for the value of stocks. If that's true, how do we explain the fact that companies that pay no dividends often have substantial market value? (Such companies are usually relatively young and in high-growth fields.) First explain the phenomenon in terms of the individual valuation model (a stream of dividends followed by a selling price, equation 14.1). Then reconcile the idea with the whole market model (an infinite stream of dividends). Can you explain cases in which managements claim their companies will never pay dividends? (*Hint:* Does such a claim make sense?)

2. Given the importance of dividends to the well-being of equity investors, why do they put up with the fact that dividends are discretionary?

3. Fully explain the choices implied by the dividend decision. Are the results of the choices known or uncertain?

4. There is said to be a controversy over dividends. What is it and why is it important?

5. You're the treasurer of SuperTech Inc., a high-technology firm in the fast-growing computer business. The management team has recently been trying to decide on a long-term dividend policy. Earnings are good, but the firm has far more investment opportunities than income.

There's no doubt that the company will need to sell more equity in the near future to fund its growth. Therefore management wants to do everything possible to maximize stock price, including making the right dividend decision.

This morning the chief engineer, Susan Mathematica, came into the meeting and professed to have the answer to the firm's problems. She said she's been taking a high-powered finance course at night, and that her instructor assured her that dividends don't matter to stock price. According to Susan, that's because investors are perfectly capable of tailoring their own income stream from any investment. Therefore she suggests not paying any dividends and using the money for projects.

How would you respond to Susan's suggestion? Do you think she's missed part of her instructor's message? Is it possible that her suggestion is right, but for the wrong reason? What would you recommend that SuperTech do?

6. You're an investment advisor and have several well-off older people among your clients. One of these individuals, Charlie Haverty, steadfastly refuses to invest in companies that pay significant dividends. A successful investment counselor advised him to avoid such stocks in 1965, and he's stuck to that view ever since. However, he never really did understand the reasoning behind the advice. How would you advise Charlie today? Include an explanation of why the advisor said what he did in 1965, and whether it was better advice then than it is now.

7. The Tanglefern Corporation has traditionally paid out 60% of its earnings in dividends. Recently some marvelous growth opportunities have arisen that involve only a little risk but require a lot of cash. Most of the executive team thinks the firm should do two things to raise the cash needed to take advantage of the opportunities. They want to (1) sell more stock and (2) suspend dividend payments for two to three years. The dividend suspension would be accompanied by an explanation to stockholders of what was going on. You're the company's CFO. Prepare a response to the others' suggestion. Do the two proposed actions taken together create a particular problem?

8. You're a financial analyst for a large mutual fund. You're doing an analysis of the Truebright Apparel Company, which makes stylish cotton clothes for teenagers. The company has recently been under attack by foreign competition and seems to have lost its edge in the fashion market. EPS fell from $2.00 to $1.80 to $1.20 over the past three years. Dividends were held steady at $1.00 per share in spite of the declining earnings for two years. Last year the dividend was raised to $1.50. Why do you think the dividend was maintained and then raised? How would this affect your recommendation?

9. You're a bank officer considering making a loan to a small family-owned company. The firm's principal owner is a hard-working, conservative woman who has built up the company over a number of years. However, two of her grown children are now active in the company's management. They're both bright and hard working, but have a reputation for taking business risks as well as for extravagant living. You'd like to make the loan, but are concerned about a potential change in the character of the company. How might you make the loan and still protect your bank's investment?

10. Your pal, Fred Flinderbinder, came into class this morning grinning from ear to ear. It seems a stock in which he advised his parents to invest is doing fabulously well. Fred said the firm usually pays a dividend of $2.00 a share, which is about 4% of its recent $50 market price. Yesterday, however, his folks got a letter that said the cash dividend was being passed, but instead the firm was issuing a stock dividend of one share for every 10 owned. Fred calculates that's worth the equivalent of $5 a share, two and a half times the normal cash dividend! Fred has told you all this knowing you're taking finance. He's asked you what you think, obviously expecting praise and approval. What would you say to Fred?

11. Blazingame Mill Works recently sold a tract of land it had owned for 30 years. All expenses and taxes have been paid, and the company has $10 million sitting in the bank as a result of the sale. As there aren't any pressing investment opportunities available, the board would like to distribute the money to shareholders. Most of the board members are high-income individuals and major stockholders themselves. Discuss the company's options for disposing of the money.

PROBLEMS

1. The Argo Pamphlet Company's dividend payout ratio is 35%. It is currently paying an annual dividend of $1.30.

a. What is Argo's EPS?

b. What is the market price of Argo's stock if its P/E ratio is 14?

c. How much current income per share will stockholders lose if Argo cuts its payout ratio to 20% and nothing else changes?

d. If the change in payout ratio does not affect the stock's price, approximately how many shares would a stockholder who owns 1,000 shares have to sell to make up her loss in current income? Ignore tax effects and transaction costs.

2. Randal Flapjack is a retired short-order cook living on a fixed income in the state of Utopia, where all financial markets are perfectly efficient. Randal has 20,000 shares of the Sugarcooky Corp., which pays an annualized dividend of $1.00 per share. Sugarcooky sells at a P/E of 10, has maintained a payout ratio of 50% for many years, and has not grown in some time. Management has recently announced that it will reduce Sugarcooky's payout ratio to 25% but expects earnings to grow at 5% from now on.

a. What is Sugarcooky's current price?

b. How much current income is Randal losing as a result of management's action?

c. If Randal keeps his money in Sugarcooky but needs to maintain his current income, how many shares will he have to sell in the first year?

d. What will be the value of his remaining shares at the end of a year if the P/E remains the same? Is his investment still growing? Why?

3. The Holderall Rope and Yarn Co. has 2 million common shares outstanding. Its capital structure is two-thirds equity. The firm expects earnings of $10 million next year and anticipates capital spending of $12 million on projects. Assume the projects will be funded with money raised in the debt/equity proportions of the existing capital structure. How much will the per-share dividend be next year if the firm adheres to a residual dividend policy?

4. The Montauk Company has a dividend reinvestment plan in which shareholders owning 25% of its common stock participate. Last year the firm's EPS was $4.20, and its payout ratio was 50%. There are 2 million shares of common stock outstanding. How much new capital did Montauk raise through the reinvestment program?

5. Segwick Petroleum Ltd. has a dividend reinvestment plan in which new stock is issued to participating investors. Segwick's payout ratio is 40%, and 30% of stockholders participate in the plan. The firm's ROE is 10%. What percentage increase in flotation-cost-free equity capital does the plan provide?

6. The Addington Book Company has the following equity position. The stock is currently selling for $3 per share.

Common stock (8 million shares outstanding, $2 par)	$16,000,000
Paid in excess	4,000,000
Retained earnings	12,000,000
Total common equity	$32,000,000
Book value per share	$4.00

a. What was the average price at which the company originally sold its stock?

b. Reconstruct the equity statement above to reflect a four-for-one stock split.

c. Reconstruct the statement to reflect a 12.5% stock dividend.

7. The Alligator Lock Company is planning a two-for-one stock split. You own 5,000 shares of Alligator's common stock, which is currently selling for $120 a share.

a. What is the total value of your Alligator stock now, and what will it be after the split?

b. Alligator's CFO says that the value of the shares will decline less than proportionately with the split because the stock is now out of its trading range. If the decline is 45%, how much will the split make you?

8. The Featherstone Corp. has $8 million in cash for its next dividend but is considering a repurchase instead. Featherstone has 10 million shares outstanding, currently selling at $40 per share. The P/E is 20 on EPS of $2.

a. If the dividend is paid, how large will it be per share?

b. If stock is repurchased, how many shares will remain outstanding and what will the new EPS be?

c. If the P/E holds at 20, what will be the new stock price and how much per share will continuing stockholders have gained? How does that compare with the dividend that could have been paid?

d. Are there other considerations (words only)?

9. Parnell Bolts Inc. has 20 million common shares outstanding and net income of $30 million. The stock sells at a P/E of 15. The company has $5 million available to pay the next quarterly dividend, but is considering a repurchase instead.

a. If Parnell pays the cash dividend, what will be its dividend yield on an annualized basis?

b. How many shares will be redeemed if the repurchase option is chosen and the stock is acquired at market value?

c. What will be the EPS after the repurchase if earnings remain unchanged?

d. What will be the new stock price if the P/E remains unchanged?

10. Tydek Inc. just lost a major lawsuit and its stock price dropped by 40% to $6. There are 3.5 million shares outstanding with a book value per share of $10. The company has $5 million in cash readily available. The CFO feels the decline in price is temporary and the firm's stock is an excellent investment at this time. If Tydek spends the entire $5 million on its own stock and the market to book value ratio returns to its former level, how much more will each remaining share be worth than it was before the temporary price decline?

Internet Problem

11. An excellent source of recent dividend news releases for major corporations is available at the web site of Corporate Financials Online at http://www.cfonews.com.

   Click on any of the companies preceded by a blue dot, and perform a search for the company's dividend announcements. Print the most recent announcement.

PART FIVE

Operations Issues— Working Capital Management and Planning

CHAPTER 15

The Management of Working Capital

Chapter Outline

Working capital consists of certain balance sheet accounts that arise from routine activities common to most companies. Working capital *management* refers to controlling the balances in the accounts, but more importantly to the way the underlying functions are run. In what follows we'll gain an understanding of the decisions involved in working capital management and the relationships it creates between finance and other departments.

WORKING CAPITAL BASICS

The term "working capital" refers to the assets and liabilities required to operate a business on a day-to-day basis. The assets include cash, receivables, and inventories, while the liabilities are generally payables and accruals.

It's important to distinguish these accounts from long-term items such as buildings and equipment on the asset side of the balance sheet and long-term debt and equity on the liabilities side. Long-term assets are held for extended pe-

Practical Finance

Going Broke Profitably

Can a company that's making a profit and has great prospects for the future fail? That sounds like a trick question, but it isn't. Profitable businesses, especially small ones, fail all the time. All that's necessary is a few mistakes with working capital.

Here's an example. Suppose an entrepreneur has a great idea for a product she wants to sell to a large company nearby. A unit sells for $1,000, costs $500 to make, and requires overhead of about $200. That means in the long run every unit makes $300, and the business looks like it will be solidly profitable.

Flushed with excitement, our entrepreneur leases space, hires workers, and buys a year's inventory. Then she operates for three months, shipping product to a delighted customer who promises to pay in 30 days.

But at the end of that time the receivable isn't paid and the business is out of cash. Calling the customer, the entrepreneur gets a long story about minor technical problems with the product, a confusing tale about invoices not matching purchase orders, and an assurance of payment after these problems are worked out.

However, after checking around, she finds that the customer is well known for paying bills slowly and using excuses to delay. It also turns out that they're in financial difficulty and have been especially bad about paying bills lately.

Notice that at this point the entrepreneur's income statement says she's doing great having made $300 on every unit shipped. But the balance sheet tells a different story. She's got a pile of inventory, a big receivable, and no cash. That means she can't pay the rent or her workers in the fourth month of operation. The new business will fail immediately unless a bank bails it out.

This entrepreneur's failure comes from two mistakes in working capital management. She bought too much inventory and didn't do a credit check on the customer. Those seemingly small oversights cost her everything. We'll learn how to avoid this kind of disaster in this chapter.

● **Working capital** accounts arise from **day-to-day operations** and include **cash, receivables, inventory, payables,** and **accruals.**

● The assets and liabilities in working capital accounts **turn over** regularly.

riods (at least a year) and tend to be financed or *supported* with liabilities that don't have to be paid off for similarly long periods of time.

Working capital items, on the other hand, are short term. Most *turn over* continually, meaning that items are held for only a little while. Inventory is a good example. Although firms always have inventory on hand, individual pieces are purchased and sold relatively quickly. The important point is that normal operating activities create and liquidate the elements of working capital on a regular basis.

● WORKING CAPITAL, FUNDING REQUIREMENTS, AND THE CURRENT ACCOUNTS

The assets associated with short-term operating activities in most companies are cash, accounts receivable, and inventory. Together, they're called *gross working capital*. The word "capital" refers to the idea that funds have to be committed to support these short-term assets, while the word "working" emphasizes the fact that they're associated with the day-to-day operation of the business.

It's important to realize that working capital is an absolute necessity to the operation of virtually all companies. Firms can no more do business without working capital than they can without buildings or equipment.

Working Capital Requires Funds

● Maintaining a working capital balance requires a **permanent** commitment of **funds.**

Providing working capital takes a more or less permanent investment of funds. For example, suppose a company operates with a $10 million inventory. Even though individual inventory items are constantly being bought and sold, approximately $10 million is always required to support the total. In effect, the firm buys an inventory *level* just as it buys a building or a machine.

The same is true of receivables, although it's a little more difficult to visualize. When product is sold on credit, a receivable is created that won't be realized in cash until the customer pays the bill. In the meantime the receivable represents money the company has recognized from the sale but doesn't have.

Keeping cash in the bank also takes funding. Even though money is constantly flowing in and out of a company's bank account, an average balance has to be maintained to pay bills and conduct business. That money has to come from somewhere and represents a funding requirement just like inventory or receivables. In effect, the company buys a cash balance in its bank account.

The Short-Term Liabilities—Spontaneous Financing

Operating activities also create payable and accrual liabilities. When inventory is purchased on credit, the payable represents material that can be used (temporarily) without payment. Similarly, labor that's been received but not yet paid is reflected in an accrual. (Review the definition of accruals in Chapter 2, page 34, if necessary.)

● The **liabilities** created by operations **spontaneously** offset the funding required to support the assets.

These liabilities provide an offset to the funding requirements discussed in the last section. It's important to notice that they come *automatically* with the associated assets and operating activities. In other words, the acts of buying inventory and building product lead directly to the related payables and accruals.

Because of the automatic nature of the liabilities arising from operating activities, they're referred to as *spontaneous financing*. They spontaneously reduce the need for funds to support gross working capital.

The term "net working capital" refers to the difference between gross working capital and spontaneous financing. *A firm's net working capital reflects the net amount of funds required to support routine operations.*

Working Capital and the Current Accounts

In Chapter 2 (pages 31 and 35) we defined current assets and current liabilities as items that are expected to generate or require cash within a year. The elements of working capital make up the bulk of the current accounts in most companies. For that reason, it's customary to define working capital as follows.

● In practice, **working capital** is the net of **current assets less current liabilities.**

$$\text{gross working capital} = \text{current assets}$$

$$\text{net working capital} = \text{current assets} - \text{current liabilities}[1]$$

---

1. There's a minor problem in this definition. Certain items are regularly classified as current that are not related to routine operating activities. For example, when the repayment date for a long-term loan is less than a year away, the loan is normally classified as a current liability. Similarly, a receivable due from the sale of something other than product (like real estate) will be a current asset, but has nothing to do with daily operations. Hence current assets and liabilities don't quite match the working capital concept. Nevertheless, it's common practice to define working capital in terms of the current accounts, ignoring any imprecision implied.

Usage

Common usage isn't particularly consistent in this area. People often use the term "working capital" for "net working capital." In practice it pays to be sure anyone you're talking with is using the same definition you are.

http://

Check out business solutions at ACCPAC at

www.accpac.com

THE OBJECTIVE OF WORKING CAPITAL MANAGEMENT

Good working capital management means running the company effectively with as little money tied up in the current accounts as possible. That involves an important series of cost/benefit trade-offs. The trade-offs arise because it's easier to run a business with more working capital than with less, but it's also more expensive. Let's briefly consider each working capital element to see why.

Inventory: Large inventories keep customers happy because firms always have what they want right away. Also, production delays due to running out of materials are minimized by carrying big stocks of parts. However, larger inventories cost more to finance; incur bigger losses from obsolescence, breakage, and theft; and take more storage space than smaller inventories.

Receivables: A large receivables balance means the firm grants credit to customers easily and is willing to wait a long time to be paid. That makes customers happy and tends to increase sales. However, it also means relatively large bad debt losses and big interest charges to finance the receivables balance.

Cash: More rather than less cash in the bank makes it easier to conduct business and minimizes the chance of running short, but it also increases financing costs.

Payables and Accruals: On the liabilities side, more net working capital means smaller payables and accruals balances. That comes from paying vendors and employees quickly, which keeps them happy. However, it also reduces spontaneous financing and thus increases the need for costly external funding.

In general, using more working capital increases sales and improves relations with customers and vendors, but costs extra money. There's no magic prescription for setting the right working capital level. The choice is a matter of policy, and involves trade-offs that are often hard to quantify. Therefore, working capital management requires judgment, experience, and an ability to work with others in the organization.

We'll look into the management of each working capital component in detail later in the chapter.

● **Working capital management** involves **trade-offs** between **easier operation** and the **cost of carrying** short-term assets.

OPERATIONS—THE CASH CONVERSION CYCLE

Current assets can be thought of as going through a series of transformations as a business operates. Cash "becomes" inventory and labor, which combine to become product. When product is sold, a receivable is created, which in turn becomes cash when collected.

The transformation process is conceptually important. In essence, the firm begins with cash, which it turns into things that eventually turn back into cash. This enables it to buy more inventory, which starts the cycle all over again. We referred to the process in our discussion of cash flows in Chapter 3, calling it the cash conversion cycle or the race track diagram (Figure 3.3, page 67). We'll repeat part of the diagram here for convenience as Figure 15.1.

FIGURE 15.1

The Cash Conversion Cycle

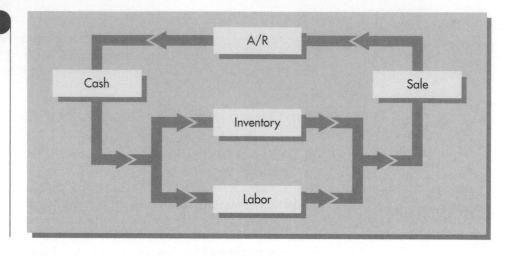

The Cash Conversion Time Line

Another way to look at the cash conversion cycle is by laying out its elements on a time line as illustrated in Figure 15.2. In this representation, events occur along the line and processes occupy intervals between the events.

It's important to notice how the two cycles are defined at the bottom of the diagram. A business's *operating cycle* is the period from the acquisition of inventory to the realization of cash from the sale of product. However, the cash conversion cycle is shorter by the period during which the firm holds a payable for the inventory. Cash conversion is the time from the disbursement to the receipt of cash.

Notice that Figure 15.2 doesn't show labor. Generally, production labor is continuously added to inventory during the conversion to product process, and is paid relatively quickly. Administrative labor is being performed and paid all the time.

The cash conversion concept is important because it contributes to our understanding of just how an ongoing business works. It's particularly enlightening in terms of the relationship between physical things and money.

● The **operating cycle** is the time from the **acquisition of inventory** until **cash is collected** from product sales.

PERMANENT AND TEMPORARY WORKING CAPITAL

A firm's need for working capital varies directly with its sales level. The more it produces and sells, the larger its inventories have to be and generally the more receivables and cash it has to carry.

Some businesses operate at relatively even sales levels year round, and therefore have more or less constant needs for working capital. In *seasonal* businesses, however, sales vary throughout the year, as do working capital needs.

Seasonally variable business gives rise to the ideas of permanent and temporary working capital. Working capital is permanent to the extent that it supports a constant or minimum level of sales. On the other hand, working capital that supports operations above the minimum level doesn't need to be maintained year round and can be viewed as temporary. Temporary working capital can be thought of as supporting *peak* sales levels. These ideas are portrayed graphically in Figure 15.3.

● **Temporary** working capital supports **seasonal peaks** in business.

FIGURE 15.2   **Time Line Representation of the Cash Conversion Cycle**

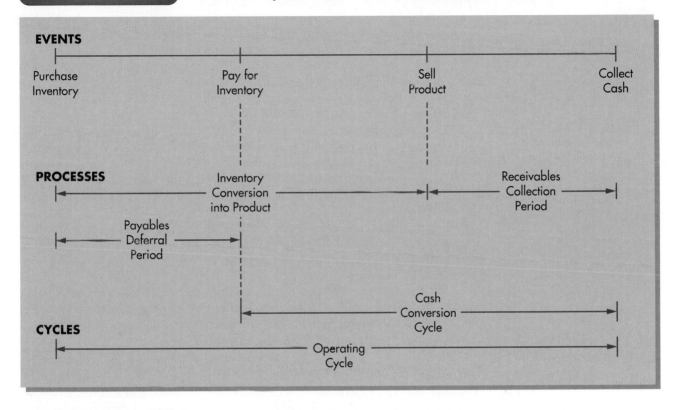

FIGURE 15.3

**Working Capital Needs
of Different Firms**

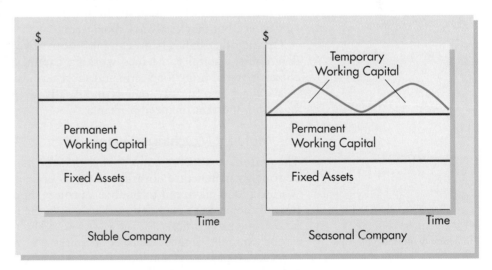

FINANCING NET WORKING CAPITAL

The fact that working capital differs from other assets because of its short-term nature leads to the idea that it may be appropriate to support it separately with short-term financing rather than using the firm's general pool of debt and equity capital. The idea arises almost naturally. Let's consider an illustration.

● Working capital tends to be **financed separately** with **short-term** debt.

Suppose a merchant who has a store but no money for inventory approaches a bank for a loan to buy merchandise that he'll sell through his store. He promises to repay the loan with the money from the sale as soon as the goods are sold. Banks are generally reluctant to lend to very small businesses because they're extremely risky. However, this proposal has some attractive features for the bank.

First, the loan is short term because it will be paid off as soon as the merchandise sells. Banks consider short-term loans safer than those made for longer periods because they don't allow much time for business conditions to deteriorate before repayment is made.

Second, the bank can see exactly where the money to pay off the loan will come from—the proceeds of the sale of the inventory purchased with the borrowed money. This is an important point. The loan is *self-liquidating*. The merchant is not at liberty to do anything else with the sale proceeds. Such an arrangement is more secure than depending on the business's general profitability for repayment.

● **Self-liquidating** debt is paid off when the **item financed becomes cash** in the borrower's hands.

Third, the bank can demand that the merchant pledge the inventory itself as security for the loan. Then if payment isn't made, it can repossess and sell the inventory, which should be easily marketable. A similar case can be made for a loan based on receivables.

These features enable banks to make working capital loans to businesses that wouldn't qualify for general unsecured loans. The point is that working capital lends itself to short-term financing by offering lenders elements of security that aren't available with loans for other purposes.

The Options Available to Most Companies

Although everyone's situation isn't exactly like the merchant's in our example, most companies have the option of financing at least some of their working capital needs on a short-term basis. In practice, the loans aren't always tied to specific assets, but they're always short term.

On the other hand, firms can just about always use some of their long-term debt/equity capital to finance working capital. Therefore management has a choice between using long-term and short-term funds.

We'll get into the advantages and disadvantages of each option after we review an important financial principle.

The Maturity Matching Principle

The *maturity matching* concept says that the maturity date of financing should be roughly matched to duration of the asset or project being financed. In other words, a loan taken out to finance a project should be repayable at roughly the time of the project's completion. This makes the loan/project combination a *self-liquidating* proposition.

● The **maturity matching** principle advises that the **term of financing** match the **duration** of the **item supported.**

For example, suppose a project requires a $1 million investment today and is expected to pay off $1.2 million in six months. Maturity matching implies that a firm should borrow the $1 million for about six months and use the project's proceeds to pay off the loan. Borrowing for a longer period will leave unused funds drawing interest after the project's end. Borrowing for a shorter period can result in a default.

To illustrate the danger of borrowing short, imagine a firm borrows $1 million for just three months with the intention of refinancing for the second three months. But suppose conditions change and the lender refuses to refinance after the first three-month period. The firm won't be able to pay off the loan at that time because the project will not yet have generated the expected cash. That can lead to default and potential bankruptcy.

Hence, in principle, it's a good idea to match the duration of short- and intermediate-term projects with the maturity of the financing supporting them. Very long-term projects should be financed with equity, which has an indefinite duration, or with long-term debt lasting 20 to 40 years.

It's also not a good idea to *overfinance* a project. For example, imagine that a new venture requires $6 million to get started, but the owner manages to raise $10 million. Investors will expect a high return on the entire $10 million, but will probably be disappointed because earning opportunities are available for only $6 million.

These guidelines shouldn't be interpreted too literally. Modest overfunding in both time and amount provides conservatism. In our first example, if the $1.2 million is late coming in, borrowing a little long avoids missing the six-month loan repayment date. In the second example, if the start-up is more expensive than anticipated, a slightly larger initial loan might save the trouble and embarrassment of going back to investors a second time.

Short- and Long-Term Working Capital Financing

> ● **Permanent** working capital can be financed **long or short** term, but **temporary** needs should be supported with **short-term** funds.

Now let's return to the choice between financing working capital with short- or long-term money. It's easy to see that maturity matching doesn't give us a clear prescription in the case of permanent working capital. Although the inventories and receivables financed are clearly short term, they're continuously replaced so the *level* of the working capital assets remains constant. In the context of maturity matching, the situation can be interpreted as appropriate for either short- or long-term financing. Temporary working capital, on the other hand, is more clearly of limited duration and therefore calls for short-term financing.

Firms clearly have a range of reasonable options for financing working capital. They can support it very largely with long-term sources using little or no short-term borrowing, or they can use short-term money extensively. Let's look at why a firm might prefer one or the other.

> ● **Long-term** financing is **safe but expensive**, while **short-term** money is **cheap but risky.**

Financing with long-term funds is safe but expensive.[2] It's safe because enough money is raised at the outset to cover anticipated working capital needs for a long time, and the firm is unlikely ever to run short. It's expensive because long-term rates of return are generally higher than short-term rates, and raising long-term money usually involves paying flotation costs.

On the other hand, financing with short-term funds is cheap but risky. It's cheap because short rates are generally lower than long rates, and the transaction costs of raising the money are relatively small. But borrowing short term is risky because every time a new loan is required, the firm has to face a new set of market conditions. For example, if interest rates rise over time, a company borrowing short term will have to pay increasing market rates. These may turn out to be higher than the long-term rate that was available initially.

There's also a possibility that money can become so tight[3] that financing isn't available at any rate. If that happens, the firm may not be able to finance working capital at all, which can seriously affect its survival.

2. Long-term funds are capital and may include equity, long-term debt, or preferred stock.
3. "Tight money" means there's little available to borrow, so lenders demand very high rates and may refuse credit to all but the highest-quality borrowers.

Alternative Policies

The result of all this is that the degree to which a firm uses short-term financing to support working capital is an issue of policy. Two possible options are illustrated graphically in Figure 15.4 for a firm that has both permanent and temporary working capital.

We say a working capital financing policy is conservative if long-term funding is used predominantly as illustrated in Figure 15.4(a). Notice that short-term funding supports only the peaks of temporary working capital. When temporary working capital is low and the total funding requirement is below the long-term level, the excess funds are invested in short-term marketable securities. This pol-

● The **mix** of short- or long-term working capital financing is a matter of **policy.** Use of **longer-term** funds reflects **conservatism.**

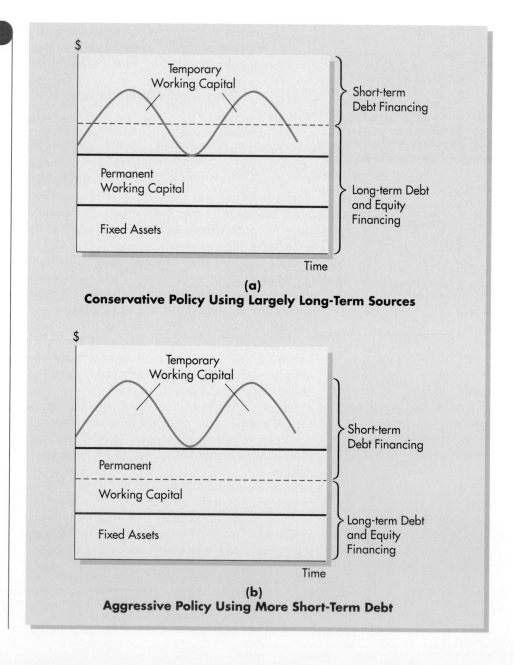

FIGURE 15.4

Working Capital Financing Policies

(a)
Conservative Policy Using Largely Long-Term Sources

(b)
Aggressive Policy Using More Short-Term Debt

icy is conservative in that there's very little risk of being unable to fund ups and downs in working capital. However, its cost tends to be fairly high.

We say a working capital financing policy is aggressive if relatively more short-term funding is used as illustrated in Figure 15.4(b). Here short-term funds support all of temporary and a good part of permanent working capital. The policy is aggressive in the sense that some risk is being taken to reduce cost. The illustration makes it easy to see that a sudden rise in short-term rates will substantially increase the firm's interest costs. Further, a drying up of the availability of short-term funds could make normal business operations very difficult.

WORKING CAPITAL POLICY

Working capital policy refers to the firm's policies on four subissues.

1. How much working capital is used
2. The extent to which working capital is supported by short- versus long-term financing
3. The nature/source of any short-term financing used
4. How each component of working capital is managed

We've already discussed the first and second of these subissues; we'll consider the third and fourth next.

SOURCES OF SHORT-TERM FINANCING

Working capital is the major reason most firms seek short-term loans. It's worth noting explicitly that short-term financing is always debt of one form or another.

We'll divide the sources of short-term financing into the following four categories and review each in some detail.

1. Spontaneous financing consisting of accounts payable and accruals
2. Unsecured bank loans
3. Commercial paper
4. Secured loans, which may be from banks or other sources

SPONTANEOUS FINANCING

Spontaneous financing consists of accounts payable and accruals. We'll consider accruals first.

Accruals

Accruals arise because firms receive services continually, but make payments at fixed intervals. (Review Chapter 2, pages 34-35.) A payroll accrual is relatively easy to understand. Suppose employees working a normal week are paid on Friday afternoon. At any time after the start of work on Monday until paychecks are handed out on Friday, the firm owes its employees for services performed so far that week. The obligation is represented by a balance sheet accrual if the books are closed any time other than Friday.

Accruals are made for any number of other services and obligations such as property taxes, insurance, and rents. Effectively, they're interest-free loans from whoever provides the service.

● **Payables and accruals** arise in the normal course of business and represent **spontaneous financing**.

Accruals, especially for labor, tend to be very short term. In most companies they're liquidated every week or two on payday. They're also not very controllable. Labor market practices and tax laws dictate when payments have to be made with little or no flexibility. In other words, accruals provide a modest financing advantage, but they're not a policy issue.

Accounts Payable—Trade Credit

Most sales between companies are made on credit. The buying firm receives the goods and is expected to pay for them at a specified later date. Effectively, the selling company *lends* the buyer the purchase price, without interest, from the time the goods are shipped until payment is made. The practice is called extending *trade credit* to the customer.

There's typically no security and very little contractual support for trade credit. The contract between the parties is limited to the terms written on the buyer's purchase order and the seller's invoice.

Trade credit is an attractive source of financing because it's free. However, it typically isn't extended for very long periods of time.

CREDIT TERMS   A vendor's terms of sale specify the number of days after delivery that payment is expected. In most cases, a discount is offered for earlier payment. Typical terms are specified as

2/10, net 30 .

This expression means that the net amount of the invoice is due within 30 days, but a 2% prompt payment discount may be taken if payment is made in 10 days or less. Any combination of discount period, net period, and discount is possible.

You can also interpret terms like these as meaning the true price of the goods is 98% of the invoiced amount, and 2% is a penalty for not paying quickly.

THE PROMPT PAYMENT DISCOUNT   The early payment discount is typically a very generous offer on the part of the vendor. We'll illustrate with the 2/10, net 30 case.

● **Passing prompt payment discounts** is generally a very **expensive** source of financing.

Because payment is due in 30 days and the discount can be taken within 10, foregoing the discount buys the customer an additional 20 days of trade credit. We can think of this as paying 2% interest for 20 days' use of money. That rate can be converted to an annual figure by multiplying by the number of 20-day periods in a year as follows.[4]

$$\frac{365}{20} \times 2\% = 36.5\%$$

---

4. The calculation shown is a simplification in two respects. First, the money made available by not taking the discount isn't the invoiced amount, but 98% of that amount. The extra 2% is interest. That means the cost of the 20 days' use of the funds isn't 2% but 2%/.98 = 2.04%.

Second, we should really compound the 20-day rate into a year rather than multiplying it. Because there are (365/20 =) 18.25 20-day periods in a year, the effective interest rate implied by not taking the discount is

$$[(1.0204)^{18.25} - 1] = .446 = 44.6\%.$$

Although this is the more technically correct calculation, most people think in terms of the simpler approach.

The implication is that by not taking the prompt payment discount, the firm is effectively borrowing at 36.5%, clearly a very high rate. It's apparent that when such a discount is offered, early payment should be made and the discount taken.

Most prompt payment discounts, like the illustration, are quite attractive. Therefore many companies have simply ordered their payables departments to take all discounts offered. This has prompted some vendors to offer discounts that aren't such a good deal. As an exercise, calculate the approximate interest cost of ½/15, net 30. Is it clearly a good idea to take the discount?

Abuses of Trade Credit Terms

On its face, trade credit is purely an accommodation to customers. In fact, however, the practice has become so ingrained in industry that it's come to be expected. In other words, vendors offer credit because they have to rather than because they want to.

In that context, the trade credit relationship can become somewhat adversarial, with customers abusing credit privileges when they can. Paying late, beyond the net date specified in a vendor's invoice, isn't uncommon at all. The practice is called **stretching payables** or **leaning on the trade.** It's probably safe to say that most firms do at least a little stretching if they can. Another common practice involves taking the prompt payment discount after the specified period has elapsed.

Vendors will tolerate a limited amount of abuse because they want to keep the customer's business. But if the practice becomes excessive the customer is labeled a slow payer and can find itself with problems. Slow-paying customers can be cut off from further shipments until debts are caught up or can be refused product unless payment is made in advance.

In addition, vendors usually report slow payers to a **credit agency** (also known as a **credit bureau**). Credit agencies prepare *credit reports* on virtually all companies doing business in the country. When new customers approach vendors asking for trade credit, it's customary to consult an agency about the applicant's record. A bad *credit rating* from a credit agency generally prevents a firm from getting trade credit.

● **Stretching payables** is a common **abuse** of trade credit.

from the **CFO**

● **Slow paying** companies receive poor **credit ratings** in **credit reports** issued by **credit agencies.**

● UNSECURED BANK LOANS

Bank loans are the primary source of short-term financing for most companies, and are the primary business of commercial banks.[5] They come in a variety of forms and may be secured or unsecured.[6]

Promissory Note

A *promissory note* is the traditional bank lending arrangement. A note is signed promising to repay the amount borrowed at a definite future date along with a specified amount of interest. Sometimes a schedule of several repayments is stipulated. The note also stipulates the nature of supporting collateral if there is any, and any other terms and conditions that may have been agreed on.

http://

The Federal Deposit Insurance Corporation provides access to consumer information, press releases, and banking statistics at
● www.fdic.gov

---

5. Although commercial banks do make longer-term loans, about two-thirds of their lending activity entails maturities of less than a year.
6. A secured loan is backed by a specific asset. If the borrower defaults, the bank gets the asset, which it can sell to repay the debt.

When the agreement is signed, the bank generally credits the amount borrowed directly into the borrowing firm's checking account.

Line of Credit

A **line of credit** is a relatively informal, nonbinding agreement between the bank and the borrowing firm that specifies the maximum amount that can be borrowed during a particular period, usually a year.

> ● A **line of credit** is an informal, re-vocable borrowing limit offered by banks.

For example, a firm with a $100,000 line of credit could have up to five $20,000 promissory notes outstanding at any time during a year. However, because the agreement is nonbinding, the bank could reduce the line at any time. For example, it could decide that the firm's condition had deteriorated somewhat after $80,000 had been advanced, and refuse to make the last loan. It could not, however, shorten the term of any note that had already been signed. An amount borrowed under a line of credit is said to *take down* the line by that amount.

Under a line of credit agreement, the borrower pays interest only on the amounts actually borrowed.

Credit lines are generally *unsecured,* meaning the loans are not backed by specific assets and the bank relies only on the general creditworthiness of the borrower for repayment.

●REVOLVING CREDIT AGREEMENT

> ● A **revolving credit agreement** is an **irrevocable** borrowing limit requiring a **commitment fee** on the unused amount.

A **revolving credit agreement** is similar to a line of credit except that the bank guarantees the availability of funds up to a maximum amount during the specified period. In other words, a *revolver* is essentially a *binding* line of credit. It is also generally unsecured.

The bank's commitment to advance funds up to a maximum in a revolver isn't free. The borrower is required to pay a **commitment fee** on the unborrowed balance of the agreement whether it's used or not. Commitment fees are in the neighborhood of one quarter of one percent per year.

The interest rates on revolving credit agreements are generally variable. They're usually specified relative to the bank's **prime rate,** which is the rate it charges its largest and most creditworthy corporate customers. Most banks follow the lead of the major New York banks in setting their prime rates. The interest rate on a smaller firm's revolving debt is likely to be stated as prime plus two or three percent.

EXAMPLE 15.1

The Arcturus Company has a $10-million revolving credit agreement with its bank at prime plus 2.5% based on a calendar year. Prior to the month of June, it had taken down $4 million that was outstanding for the entire month. On June 15, it took down another $2 million (assume the funds were available on June 16). Prime is 9.5% and the bank's commitment fee is .25% annually. What bank charges will Arcturus incur for the month of June?

Solution: Arcturus's payment will consist of the interest on money actually borrowed and the commitment fee for the unused balance of its revolving credit agreement. Its monthly interest rate is

$$(\text{prime} + 2.5\%)/12 = (9.5\% + 2.5\%)/12 = 1\%$$

and the monthly commitment fee is

$$.25\%/12 = .0208\% \,.$$

In June a loan of $4 million was outstanding for the entire month and an additional $2 million was outstanding for 15 days. Hence the interest charge is

$$(\$4,000,000 \times .01) + \left(\$2,000,000 \times .01 \times \frac{15}{30}\right) = \$50,000 \,.$$

The unused balance of the revolver was $6 million for 15 days and $4 million for 15 days for an average of $5 million. The commitment fee is then

$$\$5,000,000 \times .000208 = \$1,040 \,.$$

Thus, the total interest payment is $51,040.

http://

Information about banking services from the American Savings Education Council can be found at

● www.aba.com

● A **compensating balance** requires leaving a **portion of the loan on deposit** raising the effective interest rate.

Compensating Balances

Short-term bank loans often come with a feature that seems outrageously unfair to the borrower, but is actually just a roundabout way of compensating the bank for its services. A **compensating balance** is a minimum percentage of the loan amount that has to be left in the borrower's account and is therefore unavailable for use.

For example, if a firm borrows $100,000 subject to a 20% compensating balance, the bank will deposit $100,000 in the company's account, but only $80,000 can be drawn out and used.

Compensating balances increase the effective interest rate on the loan. Suppose the rate in our example was 12%. That would mean the borrower would pay 12% of $100,000 in interest, but would have actually borrowed only $80,000. In a year, that means the interest would be

$$\frac{\$12,000}{\$80,000} = 15\% \,.$$

There are two kinds of compensating balance. One is the *minimum balance requirement* we've just described. The other is an *average balance requirement,* which may not have as severe an effect. In this arrangement the average daily balance over a month cannot fall below a specified level. That means the entire loan can be used, but not all the time.

Firms typically maintain positive cash balances in their checking accounts most of the time anyway, so an average balance requirement may not present much of a problem. If that's the case, the effective interest rate on the loan isn't necessarily raised by very much.

Compensating balances are typically between 10% and 20% of amounts loaned.

EXAMPLE 15.2

What is the effective interest rate on a $50,000 loan at 9% for 90 days if a 15% minimum compensating balance requirement is imposed? What is the effective rate if a 15% average compensating balance is required?

Solution: First note that we don't need the loan amount or the term to solve the problem. We can adjust the nominal interest rate directly by dividing by one minus the minimum compensating balance requirement stated in decimal form. In this case, the calculation is

$$\text{effective rate} = \frac{9\%}{(1 - .15)} = \frac{9\%}{.85} = 10.6\% \,.$$

There isn't an answer to the second question because we can't say by how much the average balance requirement will reduce the borrower's use of the money without knowing what the firm's average balances would have been anyway.

Clean-Up Requirements

● Most banks require that borrowers **clean up** short-term loans once a year.

Theoretically, a firm can maintain a balance of short-term debt all the time by borrowing on a new note to pay off each old one as it comes due. Doing that makes it possible to fund long-term projects with short-term money, refinancing the debt again and again throughout the life of the project.

This procedure is rather risky for two reasons. If short-term rates rise, interest expense can increase quickly, putting a strain on the firm's profitability. Worse, if refinancing funds become unavailable, a default on the short-term notes is likely as they come due.

This kind of risk for a borrowing company is also risk for the bank, because a defaulted customer is likely to mean a lending loss. Therefore banks try to keep customers from falling into the trap of using short-term funds to support long-term projects.

Their approach is the clean-up requirement. Banks simply require that borrowers pay off all unsecured short-term debt periodically and remain out of debt for a specified period. Most clean-up requirements stipulate that borrowers be out of short-term debt for 30 to 45 days once a year.

● COMMERCIAL PAPER

Commercial paper refers to notes issued by large, strong companies to borrow money from investors for relatively short periods. The paper itself is simply a promise to repay the money borrowed at a given date. Conceptually, commercial paper is simply a very short-term corporate bond, but there are a number of administrative differences.

Buyers and Sellers

● **Commercial paper** is **short-term borrowing** done by the largest corporations.

Commercial paper is *unsecured* debt issued by a limited number of the nation's largest and strongest companies. It tends to be purchased by other large organizations that have excess funds to invest for short periods. Typically buyers are insurance companies, money market mutual funds, banks, and pension funds. The notes are generally placed with buyers by dealers for a fee.

Maturity and Terms

Commercial paper is actually a debt security of the issuing corporation. However, it can be sold without SEC registration as long as its maturity is under 270 days and the buyers are "sophisticated" investors. Maturities generally range from one to nine months, averaging five or six.

Commercial paper is considered a very safe investment because of its short maturity and the strength of the borrowing organizations. It therefore pays a relatively low interest rate, typically about a half point above the three-month treasury bill rate. Rather than bearing interest, the notes are generally discounted like treasury bills. That means the interest is taken out of the price when the note is sold. For example, a six-month, $1 million note paying an annual rate of 6% would sell for approximately ($1M/1.03 =) $970,874.

Commercial paper has one drawback even for the large, strong companies that issue it. The commercial paper market is very rigid and formal. If a company is a little short of cash when a note is due, there's no flexibility in repayment terms. Banks, on the other hand, are generally willing to bend a little to accommodate to business ups and downs.

SHORT-TERM CREDIT SECURED BY CURRENT ASSETS

> Several **short-term financing** arrangements are available in which the **debt is secured by the current asset financed.**

Several common arrangements enable firms to borrow to fund working capital using the value of the current assets themselves to guarantee the loan. The assets that provide such credit security are accounts receivable and inventories. The funding sources are often banks, but can also be other financial institutions.

Borrowing against receivables and inventories tends to be more popular in some industries than in others. It's especially common in seasonal businesses where temporary working capital needs are substantial.

The commitments, rules, and procedures vary considerably between different arrangements. We'll consider receivables financing first and then inventory financing.

Receivables Financing

Under normal circumstances, accounts receivable represent cash that is to be received in the near future. Lending institutions are generally willing to recognize the value of this about-to-be-received money, and will extend credit backed by that value where they otherwise would not. A key lending issue is the collectibility of the receivables, which relates to the creditworthiness of the firm's customers rather than to its own creditworthiness. Two receivables arrangements are common, pledging and factoring.

> A borrowing firm can **pledge receivables** by agreeing to use the **cash collected** only to **pay off** the loan.

PLEDGING ACCOUNTS RECEIVABLE   **Pledging receivables** involves using their cash value as collateral for a loan. The borrower signs a binding agreement stating that the money collected from pledged receivables will be used to satisfy the loan.

The distinguishing feature of the arrangement is that the receivables continue to belong to the borrowing firm, which receives the cash directly from its customers as it would in the absence of the pledging agreement. In fact, the company's customers are generally unaware that their obligations have been pledged.

> **Uncollectible** accounts remain the **responsibility of the borrower** if the pledging agreement is **with recourse.**

Under a pledging arrangement, if a particular receivable proves uncollectible, the borrowing firm is not relieved of its obligation to the lender. This feature is known as **recourse**. The lender is said *to have recourse* to the borrowing firm for the value of a defaulted receivable.

Pledging can be accomplished in two ways with respect to the receivables offered as security. A lender can provide a *general line of credit* tied to all of the firm's receivables without reviewing individual accounts in detail. In such a case, the lender is unlikely to advance much more than 75% of the receivables balance because of the risk that some accounts may not pay.

In the other approach, the lender reviews each receivable individually, considering the creditworthiness of the customer owing the money. Then funds are advanced only on the basis of acceptable accounts. In this approach, the lender is likely to advance as much as 90% of the balance of accounts accepted.

Under a straight pledging of receivables, the borrowing company continues to do all of its own credit and collection functions. Hence the lender is relying on the borrower to a great extent for the quality of the assets securing the loan. Some banks offer billing and collection services that the borrower can use for an additional fee.

Pledging receivables is a relatively expensive form of financing. Financing sources generally charge interest at rates 2% to 5% over prime plus an administrative fee of another 1% or 2% of the face value of all the receivables pledged.

EXAMPLE 15.3

The Kilraine Quilt Company has an average receivables balance of $100,000 that turns over once every 45 days. It generally pledges all of its receivables to the Kirkpatrick County Cooperative Finance Company, which advances 75% of the total at 4% over prime plus a 1.5% administrative fee. If prime is 11%, what total interest rate is Kilraine effectively paying for its receivables financing?

Solution: Because the finance company advances 75% of the receivables balance, the average loan outstanding is $75,000. Traditional interest of (11% + 4% =) 15% is charged on this amount.

The administrative fee is 1.5% of all new receivables. The $100,000 balance turns over every 45 days or (360/45 =) eight times a year. That means ($100,000 × 8 =) $800,000 in new receivables is pledged each year. The administrative fee is 1.5% of this total, or ($800,000 × .015 =) $12,000, which can be stated as a percentage of the average loan balance,

$$\frac{\$12,000}{\$75,000} = 16\% \ .$$

Hence the total financing cost including traditional interest and administration is

$$15\% + 16\% = 31\% \ ,$$

a high rate indeed.

FACTORING RECEIVABLES   Factoring differs from the kinds of short-term financing we've considered so far because it doesn't involve borrowing. **Factoring receivables** means *selling them at a discount* to a financial organization called a *factor,* which can be a commercial bank or a finance company.[7] The cash from the sale of the receivable provides financing to the selling company.

When a receivable is factored, the factor takes possession of the obligation and generally becomes responsible for its collection. In most cases, the customer owing the money is notified to make payment directly to the factor rather than to the sell-

---

7. The word "customer" can be a little confusing with respect to factoring. The company selling its receivables has customers, and is at the same time the customer of the factor. We'll use the word to mean the customer of the firm selling the receivable. That's the party actually owing the money that gives the receivable value. We'll call the firm selling the receivable the selling firm.

Factoring means **selling receivables** to a finance company, which then becomes responsible for collection.

ing company. The factor covers its expenses and makes a profit from the difference between the face value of the receivable and what it pays the selling company. This can be in the neighborhood of 10%, depending on the services provided.

Factors generally review the credit standing of the customers whose receivables they buy, and don't accept everything offered by the selling firm. Rejected accounts have to be handled by the selling firm on its own.

Companies that factor their receivables generally do so continually. That means a routine procedure is set up under which incoming orders are submitted directly to the factor and funded on an ongoing basis.

The procedures just described are the basic factoring function. In practice, factors offer a wide range of services with respect to receivables. They are willing to virtually take over a firm's credit and collection function. However, it isn't necessary to use everything they offer. Firms can select from a menu of services and tailor an arrangement to suit their needs.

The companies that use the other services offered by factors do so because it can save them money. It can be cheaper to hire an expert to do a specialized administrative function than to gear up and do it yourself. This is especially true for smaller firms.

In general, a factor is willing to do any or all of the following things for the appropriate fees.

1. Perform credit checks on potential customers.

2. Advance cash on accounts it accepts or remit cash after collection.

3. Collect cash from customers.

4. Assume the bad-debt risk when customers don't pay.

Item 2 requires a little explanation. Cash advances can be done in either of two ways. The factor can pay the selling firm for a receivable when it's sold or when the underlying cash is collected from the customer. If payment is made when the receivable is taken over, the factor is out the cash until it collects from the customer. Its fee therefore includes interest despite the fact that the receivable has been purchased and there really isn't a loan outstanding.

If payment to the selling firm is delayed until cash is received from the customer, the factor doesn't charge any interest. Notice that in this arrangement the factor isn't really *financing* the receivable—it's just administering collections.

If the selling firm chooses not to pass the bad debt risk to the factor, we say the factoring arrangement is done with recourse. In that case, bad debts are charged back to the seller.

Inventory Financing

Inventory financing uses a firm's inventory as security for a short-term loan. The method is popular, but is subject to a number of problems that can make it expensive and difficult to administer.

Financing secured by inventory is difficult because specialized or perishable items are **hard to sell.**

A basic problem is the marketability of the inventory in the hands of a lender. Unlike receivables, inventory doesn't turn to cash by itself. It has to be sold, and lenders aren't generally equipped to do that well. That means they have to dispose of defaulted inventory at bargain prices, which reduces the amount they can lend on it.

In particular, specialized inventories such as unique or unusual parts have little collateral value because they're difficult for a lender to sell. Perishable goods have a similar problem in that their value is lost by the time a lender can take possession. Other commodity-type inventories are quite marketable and make good loan collateral. Canned foods are a good example.

If an inventory does have an acceptable collateral value, its availability in the event of a default must somehow be guaranteed to the lender. This is difficult, because the borrowing firm is continuously using and replacing inventory in running its business. Several methods are used that involve varying amounts of administrative attention and cost.

BLANKET LIENS[8]   A blanket lien gives the lender a lien against all inventories held by the borrower. However, the borrower remains in complete physical control of the inventory, and can draw it down to any level without consulting the lender.

For example, suppose a firm borrows $600,000 collateralized by a blanket lien on an inventory of $1 million verified by a bank representative on the date the loan is disbursed. As long as the lender does not inspect the operating facility, nothing prevents the borrower from suspending inventory purchases while continuing to sell the existing stock until its level has reached, say, $200,000. This can easily put the lender in an unsecured position unless it spends an inordinate amount of time and effort monitoring the borrower's activities.

TRUST RECEIPT OR CHATTEL MORTGAGE AGREEMENT   In this arrangement, financed inventory is identified by serial number and cannot be sold legally without the lender's permission. When the items are sold, the proceeds must be used to repay the lender. The arrangement is legally binding, but the borrower is still in control of the inventory and might sell it without paying the lender. Guaranteeing that the borrower is in compliance requires inspection by representatives of the lender.

● **Warehousing companies** control secured inventories for the **benefit of lenders.**

WAREHOUSING   Under a **warehousing** arrangement, financed inventory is placed in a warehouse and the borrower's access to it is controlled by a third party. When the borrower draws a piece of inventory, paperwork is created that signals the lender to look for repayment of the money lent to finance that inventory. *Warehousing companies* specialize in administering such arrangements.

There are two kinds of warehousing arrangements. A *field warehouse* is a secured area within the borrower's own facility that's accessible only to employees of the warehousing firm. A floor-to-ceiling chain-link fence can be built to segregate open factory space for the purpose. Employees of the warehousing firm make themselves available during designated hours each week.

A *public warehouse* is operated by the warehousing firm at a site physically removed from the borrower's facility. This arrangement provides the lender maximum security because the material is completely out of the borrower's control.

Warehousing gives lenders excellent security, but tends to be expensive because of the administrative cost of operating the warehouse and tracking individual inventory items.

CASH MANAGEMENT

Although good cash management can improve financial results, it isn't likely to make a weak business strong. Bad cash management, on the other hand, can make a strong company weak to the point of failure. Especially among small

---

8. A lien is a legal money claim attached to specific property. The proceeds of the sale of the property must be used to satisfy the lien.

firms, it isn't uncommon for companies to be simultaneously profitable and bankrupt. In other words, a firm that doesn't have the cash to pay its bills and meet its payroll goes out of business, regardless of how good its long-term prospects are. For that reason, it pays to understand how cash oils the gears of business and how firms can get the most out of it.

DEFINITIONS AND OBJECTIVES

A firm's *cash* is the money it has on hand in currency and in bank *checking accounts.*[9] The overwhelming bulk of business cash is in checking accounts, because very little commercial activity is transacted in currency.

The Motivation for Holding Cash

Firms have to have cash on hand for three economic and one administrative reason. The economic reasons are transactions demand, precautionary demand, and speculative demand. The administrative reason for holding cash has to do with compensating banks for the services they perform.

TRANSACTIONS DEMAND   Firms need money in the bank to pay bills for the goods and services they use. Payments are made to employees, vendors, utility companies, and taxing authorities, to name just a few. At the same time, most receipts come in the form of checks that are deposited in the bank. The constant flow of money in and out of the bank gives rise to an average account balance that we associate with transactions.

> Firms **hold cash** to make **transactions,** as a **precaution,** for **speculative** opportunities, and to maintain **compensating balances.**

If firms had perfect knowledge of when cash would come in and when it should go out, transactions balances could be kept very low. However, we don't generally have such knowledge, especially with respect to receipts. It's therefore necessary to keep the balance high enough to support routine operations. It's especially important to have enough cash on hand to take advantage of prompt payment discounts offered by vendors.

PRECAUTIONARY DEMAND   Sometimes emergencies arise with little warning. For example, suppose a shipment intended for a demanding customer is accidentally damaged on the loading dock, and a new shipment has to be produced immediately. That could require extra labor at overtime rates and the quick acquisition of new raw materials. Firms keep cash on hand to pay for such emergency needs.

SPECULATIVE DEMAND   Firms also keep cash available to take advantage of unexpected opportunities. For example, suppose the price of a particular input drops suddenly, but is expected to go up again quickly. If cash is available, a bargain can be had; if not, it has to be passed up. Firms keep money on hand to take advantage of such opportunities.

COMPENSATING BALANCES   Banks stay in business by investing the money individuals and companies deposit with them for a return. It is therefore customary for banks to require that depositors receiving certain services maintain

---

9. A bank checking account is known more formally as a demand deposit. The bank pays money out of the account to third parties on the basis of checks that represent demands of the account owner. In the normal course of business, when buyers and sellers know each other well, checks are accepted as readily as currency. Therefore, the money available in the economy is defined to include checking account balances. The financial definition of cash follows the same principle.

minimum *compensating balances* to partially offset the cost of those services. This arrangement is equivalent to charging fees for services. We've already discussed the compensating balances associated with loans. Banks also require them for cashing checks and conducting a variety of transactions.

The four reasons for holding cash aren't entirely additive. Money available for transactions also provides some speculative and precautionary capability, and certainly contributes to meeting compensating balance requirements.

The Objective of Cash Management

The problem with cash in the bank is that it doesn't earn a return. Banks don't pay interest on the balances in commercial checking accounts. That means companies have to devote a certain amount of their financial resources to maintaining cash in the bank, but receive no return on those resources. For this reason, it's desirable to operate with as little cash as possible.

> Good **cash management** implies maintaining adequate **liquidity** with **minimum cash** in the bank.

At the same time, it's clearly easier to run a business with more cash than with less. A firm with a substantial bank balance will never be embarrassed by running out of money. This is described as *liquidity*. An adequately liquid firm will always be able to pay its bills on time, take the appropriate discounts, and take emergencies and opportunities in stride.

Cash management involves striking a balance between these conflicting objectives. Good cash management minimizes the amount of cash in the bank, but at the same time assures there's enough available to operate efficiently. We'll see shortly that there are several relatively standard techniques for doing that.

MARKETABLE SECURITIES

Notice that the precautionary and speculative motives call for having cash on hand that isn't used very often. These demands can be largely satisfied by assets that are only slightly less liquid than cash but do earn a return.

> **Marketable securities** are **liquid** investments that can be held **instead of cash** and earn a **modest return**.

For example, suppose a firm invests some of its cash in short-term treasury bills, and then has an emergency need for funds. Because there's a ready market for government debt, the securities can be sold within a day and the proceeds used to satisfy the emergency need. In the meantime, the treasury bills pay a modest return on the funds invested. This compromise is known as investing in *marketable securities*. It sacrifices a little liquidity for a modest but significant return.

Marketable securities are short-term obligations of very strong organizations, including treasury bills and commercial paper. The fact that the securities are short term is important. That insulates them from changes in value due to interest rate fluctuations. The word "marketable" implies that the issues can be sold quickly. Marketable securities are also referred to as *near cash* or *cash equivalents*.

Investing excess cash in marketable securities is a specialized function carried out within the treasury departments of larger firms. People who work in the area develop considerable expertise about the pros and cons of the various investment vehicles available. We won't delve into the operating details here, but the concept of marketable securities and the fact that most large companies invest in them regularly are very important.

CHECK DISBURSEMENT AND COLLECTION PROCEDURES

The amount of cash companies need is related directly to the method by which the *financial system* gets money from a paying organization (the *payer*) to the receiving party (the *payee*). Understanding the rudiments of this system is key to understanding cash management.

The Basic Procedure for Transferring Cash

Let's look at the routine procedure through which one party pays another with a check through the banking system. The procedure is written out below and portrayed graphically in Figure 15.5. In both, typical elapsed time requirements are indicated in parentheses near each step.

1. The payer writes a check on its bank and mails it to the payee. (2–3 days)

2. The payee receives the check, records it, and processes it internally for deposit.

3. The payee then deposits the check in its own bank. (2 days—items 2 and 3)

4. The payee's bank sends the check into the Federal Reserve's interbank *clearing system* at a Federal Reserve office.

5. The clearing system processes the check. This transfers money from the payer's account at its bank into the payee's account at its bank. The funds are now available for the payee's use. The canceled check is returned to the payer through its bank. (2 days—items 4 and 5)

● **Float** is money **tied up** in the check-clearing process.

It's important to pay particular attention to the length of time taken by each step. Money tied up in the process is called **float**. During the time checks are in the mail they're part of *mail float*, when they're being processed at the payee's office they're in *processing float*, and when they're in the Federal Reserve system they're in *transit float*. Collectively the money in the entire process is called *check-cashing float* or just *float*.

Notice that there are two important geographic variables in the process we've described. The farther the payer is located from the payee, the longer will be the mail float. And if the payee's bank is far from a Federal Reserve office, extra time may be required to get checks into the clearing system. We'll return to these factors later.

FIGURE 15.5

The Check-Clearing Process

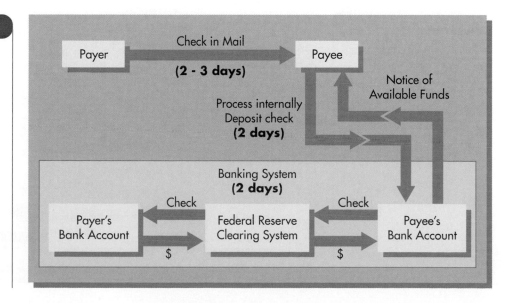

Objectives in Managing Use of the Check-Clearing Process

The check-clearing process normally takes six or seven days. During that time the payee doesn't have the use of the cash even though the payer has written and mailed the check. In fact, funds remain in a payer's account balance and are technically usable until the check clears through the banking system.

This leads to two important cash management ideas. First, from the perspective of a payee receiving money, speeding up the collection of checks *after they've been mailed* gets the cash in faster. Second, from the perspective of a payer sending money to someone else, slowing down the payment of checks *after they've been mailed* gives a company use of its cash longer.

All companies are simultaneously payers and payees, so any firm can use both ideas to reduce the funds that need to be committed to cash balances.

> ● **Payees** are interested in **speeding** the check-clearing process, while **payers** want to **slow** it down.

● ACCELERATING CASH RECEIPTS

In this section, we'll take the point of view of the payee, the party receiving money, and examine approaches to accelerating the receipt of cash.

Lock Box Systems

Lock box systems are services provided by banks to accelerate the collection of cash once a check has been mailed to a payee. The idea behind the system is very simple.

Notice that in Figure 15.5 the first step of the payment process involves the payer mailing a check, which is processed and deposited by the payee in the second step. Together, these steps take four to five days. A lock box system reduces this float period by moving the check directly from the payer to the bank, eliminating the stop at the payee's office.

In a lock box system, the payee rents a post office box near its bank. It then orders payers to mail their checks to the post office box rather than to its own headquarters. The bank opens the box several times a day, collects the checks received, and deposits them in the payee's account. This cuts an average of two or three days out of the whole process. The idea is illustrated in Figure 15.6.

FIGURE 15.6

A Lock Box System in the Check-Clearing Process

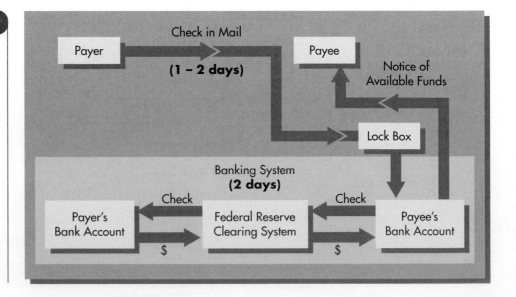

● **Lock boxes** are located near customers and **shorten mail** and **processing float.**

After the bank deposits the checks, copies are sent to the payee's office. Its internal processing is based on those copies after the deposit has been made and the clearing process has begun.

FINE TUNING THE LOCK BOX SYSTEM   Two geographic details can make lock boxes especially effective. Suppose a payer is on the West Coast and the payee and its primary bank are on the East Coast. That means the payer's checks have to make a time-consuming trip across the country before they're received.

The payee can accelerate the process by establishing a lock box at a bank on the West Coast, thus eliminating much of the mail float. When funds clear into the West Coast bank, they're electronically transferred to the payee's primary bank on the East Coast.

The payee can also speed things up by choosing banks that are close to Federal Reserve branches. That minimizes the time required to get checks from the bank into the central clearing system.

Big companies that receive payments from all over the country maintain lock boxes in all the areas in which their customers are concentrated.

Concentration Banking

● **Concentration banks** sweep excess balances in **distant depository** accounts into **central locations** daily.

Large companies often have a great many *depository*[10] bank accounts spread around the country. This is a result of the multiple lock box systems we described in the last section. It also happens when firms have widespread retail outlets, because each store has to deposit its receipts in a local bank every day.

Holding cash in a number of small accounts tends to be administratively inefficient because of duplicated effort and lack of central control. It also makes it difficult to invest in marketable securities, which tend to be traded in large sums. When cash is separated into a number of small bundles under the control of local divisions, no one has enough to take advantage of short-term investment opportunities.

Concentration banking is a system in which a single *concentration bank* manages the balances in remote accounts to target levels, and *sweeps* excess cash into its own central location. Special documents called *depository transfer checks* are used to move funds from one bank to another within a concentration network. Funds can also be moved electronically.

Wire Transfers

● **Wire transfers** move money electronically.

The fastest way of moving money from one bank to another is an electronic wire transfer. Two wire transfer networks are in use by banks. The Federal Reserve Wire System is available to member banks and their correspondents. Bank Wire is a private network supporting about 250 U.S. banks.

Wire transfer is quick and secure, but the fees involved make it too expensive for regular use with small sums.

Preauthorized Checks

When there's a very good working relationship between a payer and a payee, preauthorized checks can eliminate mail float entirely. In this arrangement the

---

10. A large company's working bank accounts are usually of two kinds for administrative purposes. The depository account receives incoming cash, while outgoing checks are written on the disbursing account.

payer, a customer, gives the payee, a vendor, a number of signed check-like documents in advance. When the vendor (payee) ships product to the customer (payer), it simply deposits a preauthorized check in its bank account. Clearly this arrangement requires a certain amount of trust on the part of the payer.

MANAGING CASH OUTFLOW

We'll look at managing outflows briefly from the perspective of the payer. There are two goals, maintaining control of disbursements and slowing checks in the clearing process.

Control Issues

Most large companies are decentralized, meaning they have operating divisions in locations remote from headquarters. There are benefits to central control of cash, but there are also benefits associated with decentralized control.

In large companies, most agreements with customers and vendors are made at the division level. Because cash payments are a key element in the process of managing such agreements, it makes sense to place disbursing authority in the hands of division management. However, that results in at least one disbursing account at every division, which in turn leads to an undesirable distribution of cash balances around the country.

Zero Balance Accounts (ZBAs)

Zero balance accounts solve this control problem. They are empty disbursement accounts established at the firm's concentration bank for its various divisions. Divisions write checks on their ZBAs that are automatically funded as they're presented for payment. The funds come out of a master account at the concentration bank. In essence, ZBAs are subdivisions of the master account. Although the ZBA never has a positive balance, it has a number and receives statements that enable the division to use it to manage its business just like any other checking account.

Remote Disbursing

> Payers sometimes **disburse** checks from **remote banks** to lengthen float and **slow** cash outflow.

Look back at Figures 15.5 and 15.6 and take the perspective of the payer. Payers would like to slow the check-collection processes and expand float as much as possible to prolong the time cash remains in their bank accounts.

Remote disbursing is a way to keep checks in the bank clearing system. If a check is written on a bank in a distant city or in a small city that isn't the site of a Federal Reserve branch, it will take a day or two longer to leave the bank and get back to it. This delay has the effect of increasing transit float, keeping money in the payer's account longer. For this reason, it isn't uncommon for checks from large companies located in big cities to be drawn on small banks in out-of-the-way places.

EVALUATING THE COST OF CASH MANAGEMENT SERVICES

> To be **effective** a **cash management** system must lower balances enough to **save more** in interest than it **costs.**

Cash management, especially acceleration of receipts, can reduce the financial resources firms have tied up in their cash accounts. The general implication is that a firm can borrow less money by the amount of the reduction in its cash balance, and pay commensurately less interest. This saving has to be measured against the cost of the cash management system to see if it's worthwhile. The calculations are relatively straightforward.

Ethics **Ethical Cash Management**

Is remote disbursing ethical? Is it in general right to take advantage of mail float to keep cash longer? Isn't the payer who uses the practice essentially stealing a little interest from the recipient on each check?

Is the situation more sensitive to ethical issues if the payer is a financial institution with a "fiduciary" duty to the payee client? A fiduciary relationship is one of trust and confidence in which one party relies on the professional integrity of the other. It usually exists between certain professionals and their clients where money is involved. Banks, brokers, accountants, and lawyers may be fiduciaries.

In other words, is it less appropriate to take advantage of the other party in a transaction when that party is trusting you to look after their interests? Most people would say that it is.

Courts have held that remote disbursing is indeed a violation of the trust implied in relationships between parties, like stockbrokers and clients, and have disallowed the practice in that context. In that way the courts have made something unethical also illegal.

EXAMPLE 15.4

Kelso Systems Inc. operates primarily on the East Coast, but has a cluster of customers in California that remit about 5,000 checks a year. The average check is for $1,000. West Coast checks currently take an average of eight days from the time they're mailed by customers to clear into Kelso's East Coast account. A California bank has offered Kelso a lock box system for $2,000 a year plus $.20 per check. The system can be expected to reduce the clearing time to six days. Is the bank's proposal a good deal for Kelso if it borrows at 12%?

Solution: The checks represent revenue of $5 million per year. The average amount of West Coast revenue tied up in cash is

$$\frac{8}{365} \times \$5,000,000 = \$109,589 \ .$$

The proposal will reduce this to

$$\frac{6}{365} \times \$5,000,000 = \$82,192 \ .$$

The difference, $27,397, is the amount of cash freed by the lock box system. If Kelso installs the system, it should be able to borrow an average of this much less money all the time. The interest savings at 12% is

$$\$27,397 \times .12 = \$3,288 \ .$$

However, the cost of the system is the annual fee plus the per-check charge.

$$\$2,000 + \$.20(5,000) = \$3,000$$

Hence the bank's proposal is only marginally worth doing.

Cash management systems are subject to significant economies of scale, so larger companies benefit more clearly from having sophisticated systems than do smaller firms.

MANAGING ACCOUNTS RECEIVABLE

A firm's accounts receivable represent the obligations of customers for future payments that arise when sales are made on credit. The management of receivables is a relatively unique function in finance in that it involves an interface with customers, something usually reserved for the sales department.

● OBJECTIVES AND POLICY

● Higher **receivables** improve **sales and customer relations,** but lead to more **bad debts** and **interest expense.**

In general, companies like to operate with as little tied up in receivables as possible. There are basically two reasons for that preference. First, carrying fewer receivables minimizes the interest cost of supporting the receivable asset. Second, it minimizes bad debt losses because whenever money is owed, there's a chance that it will never be collected.

There are trade-offs, however. For several reasons we'll point out shortly, a higher level of receivables generally increases sales and leads to better customer relations.

Managing accounts receivable means striking a balance between these effects. As receivables increase, sales tend to go up, which increases profit. At the same time, interest cost and collection losses increase, which depresses profit.

● **Receivables policy** involves **credit** standards, **terms,** and **collection** procedures.

It's important to notice that the focus of the trade-off is at the EBT level. Managing receivables means finding the point at which *profitability* is maximized as a result of the opposing forces, not the point at which sales are maximized.

The things firms do to influence profitability through receivables management are collectively called *receivables policy* or *credit and collections policy.* Three broad issues are involved.

1. *Credit policy:* How financially strong must a customer be for the firm to sell to it on credit?

2. What *terms of sale* (due dates and discounts) should be offered to credit customers?

3. *Collections policy:* How should customers whose bills aren't paid on time be handled?

Who Is Responsible for Receivables Policy?

Although receivables policy is under the control of financial management in most companies, it has a major effect on sales. Therefore most policy decisions are joint efforts between financial and sales/marketing management. As a practical matter, it's not unusual for this shared area of responsibility to create quite a bit of conflict between the two organizations. We'll understand why this happens as we go along.

● DETERMINANTS OF THE RECEIVABLES BALANCE

The size of a firm's receivables balance is determined primarily by the level of its credit sales. The more it sells for cash, the smaller will be its receivables and the fewer associated problems it will have. It is axiomatic that everyone prefers to sell for cash when they can. However, industrial custom doesn't permit many inter-business cash sales, and receivables are about 25% of total assets for most firms.[11]

Credit Policy

Credit policy is the most important decision variable available for influencing the level of receivables. It determines the customers to which a company is willing to make credit sales.

Most firms have *credit departments* staffed by credit specialists. When an order is received from a new customer, or an old customer wants to buy more on credit than it has previously, the credit department has the responsibility of approving or disapproving the request.

To make its decision, the department investigates the creditworthiness of the customer by using a number of information sources. These sources include the reports of *credit agencies* (also called *credit bureaus*), the customer's own financial statements, bank references, and the customer's reputation among other vendors.

The primary source of information is usually the report of a credit agency, an organization that keeps files on the financial condition and bill-paying records of vast numbers of companies. For a fee, the credit agency will provide a vendor with a report on any customer or potential customer.

A company's credit policy revolves around how good a risk a customer has to be before it will be extended credit. A typical policy might require that a customer

- be in business at least three years,
- have a net worth of three times the amount of credit requested,
- have a current ratio of 2.5:1 or higher, and
- have no adverse comments on its credit report from other vendors.

If the conditions aren't met, the firm will sell to the customer only on a cash basis.

It's important to understand that customers whose credit applications are disapproved generally do not buy from the firm. They either can't because they don't have the cash, or they can find another vendor with a more liberal policy.

Hence a *tighter* credit policy, meaning higher quality requirements for credit customers, generally has the effect of reducing sales. On the other hand, a *looser* credit policy accepts lower-quality customers and increases sales. However, some of the incremental customers brought in by a looser policy generally prove unable or unwilling to pay their bills. The result is a *credit loss* (also called a *bad debt loss*) of the value of their receivables. The frequency of bad debt losses tends to increase substantially as credit policy is relaxed.

Clearly, setting credit policy requires striking a balance between these effects. We want to find the policy that maximizes *profit*. Unfortunately, there's no formula for doing this; it's a matter of judgment and experience.

THE CONFLICT WITH SALES OVER CREDIT POLICY   The job of the sales department is generally to sell as much product as it can. When salespeople's compensation is based on commissions, the task becomes a very personal challenge.

---

http://

Credit law information can be found at

www.ftc.gov

and

● **www.pirg.org**

● A firm's **credit policy** is a statement of the **minimum customer quality** it will accept for **credit sales.**

● There are often **conflicts** between the **sales** and **credit** departments.

---

11. The custom is reversed in consumer markets where retailers usually demand cash at the time of sale, either from the customer or from a credit card company.

A Practical Management Warning

It's clearly easy to increase sales by easing credit and collections policies, but receivables balances and credit losses go up at the same time. This situation can be dangerous for the senior financial manager. The applause for the increased sales tends to be given to the marketing department, but the blame for a high receivables balance and the associated losses belongs exclusively to the finance department. This can be a political no-win situation for the executive in charge of finance.

It's important to make sure the CEO (president, general manager) understands that while receivables are financial, creating them is a joint effort with sales and that problems need to be owned by both organizations.

The philosophy in most companies is that the salesperson delivers a willing buyer to the credit department, which then approves or disapproves a credit sale.

If the sale is approved, the customer gets product on credit, the salesperson gets his or her commission, and everyone is happy. If the credit sale is disapproved, it is generally lost. That means the salesperson doesn't get a commission and has wasted whatever work has gone into the account. This understandably creates a good deal of resentment on the part of the salesperson toward the credit department, especially if the customer's credit quality was marginal.

But what happens if a credit sale is approved and the customer eventually fails to pay? It's logical to assume that the salesperson in such a case would be charged back his or her commission. *However, most companies don't operate that way. The credit decision is viewed as strictly the responsibility of the credit department, so the blame for a bad debt loss is laid at its door alone and the salesperson gets to keep the commission.*

This practice can create a counterproductive conflict of interest. Salespeople are generally in close contact with customers and may be aware of things no one else knows about. But if those things are negative, the commission system motivates them not to share the information with the credit department. Credit personnel therefore may harbor some resentment toward salespeople when receivables go sour.

from the CFO

The Terms of Sale

Recall that credit sales are made on terms that specify the number of days after which the net payment is due and a period during which a prompt payment discount may be taken. For example, terms of 2/10, net 30 mean a 2% discount can be taken if payment is made within 10 days; otherwise the entire amount is due in 30.

● The **prompt payment discount** is usually an effective tool for **managing receivables.**

Terms can have an effect on receivables in two ways. First, shortening or extending the net period tends to affect the length of time a nondelinquent customer takes to pay its bill. It would therefore seem that shortening the term would reduce the receivables balance. As a practical matter, however, companies don't have a great deal of latitude in making the net period shorter than whatever is customary in the industry.

The prompt payment discount tends to be a more effective policy variable. A generous discount usually reduces receivables balances because customers pay quickly to save money. As we've said before, however, discounts are expensive for the firm giving them.

Occasionally prompt payment discounts don't help to reduce receivables at all. That happens when a firm's customers are too cash poor to take the discount regardless of how attractive it is. That's often the case when the customers are struggling small businesses. In such situations, increasing the discount in an effort to reduce receivables can backfire and cost money. The reason is that only customers who are already paying promptly take the increased discount.

Collections Policy

A firm's credit department is usually closely connected with its *collections department*. The function of the collections department is to follow up on overdue receivables to get delinquent customers to pay their bills. The process is known as **dunning** the debtor.

The normal procedure begins with mailing a polite reminder that payment is overdue a few days after the net date on the invoice. If payment isn't received, two or three additional *dunning letters* follow using progressively stronger language. After that, phone calls are made first to the customer's payables department and then to responsible executives. If a customer is substantially in arrears, further shipments usually are stopped until some payment is received.

In the majority of cases, unpaid bills are the result of some product or administrative problem. For example, if the product purchased doesn't work as expected, many firms don't pay the bill. In such a case the collections department gets the customer together with the firm's sales and service personnel to try to straighten out the problem.

Another common problem involves mismatches between the firm's invoice and what the customer's records show as having been ordered and received. If these don't match exactly, many organizations don't pay. In such cases the collections department works to reconcile the paperwork and get the bill paid.

In other cases, customers don't pay because they don't have the cash or are disreputable and just don't pay bills until they're forced to. When that happens, letters and phone calls don't work and the account is eventually turned over to a **collection agency.** Collection agencies are companies that specialize in dunning and collecting overdue accounts for a percentage of the amounts collected. They use the same techniques as the selling firm, but tend to be more persistent, aggressive, and threatening.

If the agency isn't successful, a lawsuit can be filed against the delinquent customer. The filing can be handled by either the company or the collection agency. If the suit is successful the firm is awarded a judgment, which still may not be collectible if the customer is missing or bankrupt.

A company's *collections policy* determines how quickly and aggressively it pursues overdue accounts. There's a great deal of difference, for example, between a firm that sends polite letters and calls for several months and one that threatens a lawsuit when a bill is 30 days overdue.

COLLECTIONS AND CUSTOMER RELATIONS   Overly aggressive collection efforts can damage customer relations. For example, imagine that a particular shipment has become very confused because of malfunctioning product and

Dunning is the process of following up on **overdue** receivables.

Collection agencies specialize in **pursuing overdue accounts,** and are usually very **aggressive.**

Collection policy is the **manner** and **aggressiveness** with which a firm **pursues payment** from delinquent customers.

INSIGHTS

Real Applications

How Lafarge's Western Region Controls Receivables Sharing Responsibility for Collections with Sales

Lafarge Group, a giant French company, is a dominant player in the international construction materials business. The firm, with over 85,000 employees worldwide, generates annual sales of about $12 billion from operations in 75 countries. Lafarge North America, a 54% owned subsidiary, is headquartered in Virginia, and is this continent's largest diversified supplier of construction materials. It operates out of regional offices throughout the United States and Canada.

CFO, The Magazine for Senior Financial Executives, posts the *Working Capital Scoreboard*, which ranks 1,000 public companies on the efficiency of their working capital management. Recently, Lafarge North America's Western Region, based in Calgary, Alberta, racked up an impressive 36-place advance in its scoreboard position largely due to shortening its average collection period by eleven days. The region's vice president and controller listed 12 fundamentals behind this improvement in collections including the following points.

- Focus all management on collections; it's not just a finance responsibility.

- Assign ownership of customer accounts among the sales staff to prevent passing the buck on delinquent accounts

- Clearly define Lafarge's responsibilities to customers including terms and conditions of sale.

- Establish monthly collection targets by salesperson.

- Train salespeople to focus on customer profitability (rather than just on sales volume).

- Engage in weekly credit and collections meetings with the sales team, the credit and collections manager, and the general manager

The message should be clear. Excellence in receivables management depends on making sure the sales department recognizes that it shares the responsibility for collections with finance. At Lafarge, the responsibility is made explicit by holding sales people accountable for delinquent customer accounts, and engaging in constant management review of overall collections activity.

Sources: Steven L. Mintz, "Dollars in the Details, Winners Sweat the Small Stuff in the Third Annual Analysis of Working Capital," *CFO, The Magazine for Senior Financial Executives* (July 1999): 55. http://www.lafarge.fr www.lafargenorthamerica.com

mistakes in shipping, receiving, and invoicing. Also suppose the customer and the firm's sales and service departments are working reasonably diligently to straighten out the problems. Now imagine that in the middle of all this the customer is served with a lawsuit initiated by the collections department for payment of the disputed bill.

Clearly, that would create a tendency for the customer to buy from another vendor in the future. It would also upset the sales department, because it wants to continue selling to the customer. On the other hand, it isn't unusual for salespeople to attempt to placate the collections department in order to sell more commissionable product to a customer they know is a payment risk.

INVENTORY MANAGEMENT

Inventory is product held for sale to customers. Its significance and the complexity of managing it vary tremendously between businesses. For example, in retailing operations inventory management is critically important but relatively simple, while in manufacturing it can be as complex as it is crucial. At the other extreme, most services businesses carry only incidental inventories, so the issue is relatively minor.

It's important to realize that in any business in which inventory is significant, its mismanagement has the potential to ruin the company.

WHO IS RESPONSIBLE FOR INVENTORIES?

Unlike cash and receivables, inventory is virtually never the direct responsibility of the finance department. It is usually managed by a functional area such as manufacturing or operations. The executives in charge of those areas generally have broad latitude in choosing inventory levels and management methods.

● Finance has an **oversight** responsibility for inventory management.

Finance gets involved in an oversight or policing way. If inventory levels become too high, it's the job of financial management to call attention to the fact that things might be run more efficiently. Financial people generally monitor the level of lost or obsolete inventory that has to be written off and ensure that it doesn't become excessive. They also supervise periodic *physical inventories* (counts) that reconcile quantities actually on hand with the firm's records.

In short, although the finance department does not itself manage the typical firm's inventory, it has a responsibility to ensure that those who do manage it act cost effectively.

THE BENEFITS AND COSTS OF CARRYING INVENTORY

As might be expected, for firms to which inventory is important, it's easier to operate with more usable inventory than with less. However, carrying the extra material costs money, so there's a trade-off between cost and benefit. The idea behind inventory management is to find a level that's close to optimal in balancing the pluses against the minuses.

The Benefits of Carrying Adequate Inventory

In manufacturing, inventory separates and smooths out the work of different production departments. For example, suppose departments A and B work on product sequentially. If product moves directly out of department A into B, everything runs smoothly as long as there are no delays in A's operation. However, if some defect or accident causes a delay in A, department B will run out of work and be idle until the problem is fixed. Clearly, time and money will be wasted. But if some product is inventoried between the two departments, B can avoid idle time by working on it while department A is fixing its problem.

In any business, carrying more inventory rather than less reduces **stockouts** and **backorders.** A stockout occurs when something the company doesn't have on hand is needed in production or by a customer. The firm is out of stock on the item and places a backorder with its supplier to get it. The term "backorder" implies the order is remedial in the sense that the item is currently needed, and usually implies a request for expedited handling.

In manufacturing, stockouts disrupt operations and cause idle time and missed schedules, which cost money. At the point of sale, stockouts mean customers don't get what they want right away. That causes dissatisfaction and can drive customers to other suppliers, which means lost sales. Too many stockouts can drive customers away permanently.

All in all, carrying more active, usable inventory makes operations run more smoothly, improves customer relations, and increases sales.[12]

The Cost of Carrying Inventory

Keeping inventory on hand takes money. The reasons can be separated into traditional costs of the inventory and potential losses in its value. In general, both increase with the amount of inventory carried.

The following traditional costs are associated with holding inventory.

- Interest: Firms have to pay a return on the funds used to acquire inventory just as they do on any other asset.

- *Storage and security:* Inventory takes up space and is often subject to pilfering. Storage space has to be provided along with security to prevent theft.

- *Insurance:* Firms generally buy insurance to protect themselves against large inventory losses due to fire, theft, or natural disaster.

- *Taxes:* Many states and localities levy a tax on the value of inventory.

Several phenomena cause inventory to lose value. In general, the more inventory a firm carries, the more it exposes to a risk of loss from each of the following causes and the higher is its overall loss.

- *Shrinkage:* In spite of security measures, some inventory inevitably disappears. Such vanishing, presumably due to theft, is known as shrinkage.

- *Spoilage:* Many items have a limited shelf life, after which they lose their value partially or entirely. Even when inventory is monitored carefully, some spoilage of perishable items is expected.

- *Breakage:* Inventory in stock can be run over, stepped on, leaked on or into, or broken in any number of ways.

- *Obsolescence:* New products often do jobs better, faster, or cheaper than their predecessors. When that happens, the old products lose value rapidly because no one wants them unless their prices are heavily discounted.

The costs and losses together can be called the *carrying cost* of inventory.

● More inventory means fewer **lost sales** and production **delays,** but more **carrying cost.**

ORDERING COSTS   The process of ordering and receiving goods generates a different sort of inventory-related expense. The carrying costs we've talked about so far depend on the amount of inventory on hand during a period. *Ordering costs* reflect the expenses of placing orders with suppliers, receiving shipments, and processing materials into inventory. These costs are related to the number of orders placed rather than to the amount of inventory held.

---

12. It should be obvious that carrying extra obsolete or damaged inventory doesn't convey these benefits. Hence we have to look beyond the dollar inventory figure on the balance sheet to see whether the firm has enough or too much.

We'll see shortly that ordering costs and carrying costs tend to vary inversely with one another.

INVENTORY CONTROL AND MANAGEMENT

Companies develop elaborate systems for tracking and controlling their inventories. The cost of such systems and the people to run them are additional expenses associated with inventory. This kind of cost doesn't necessarily increase with incremental inventory or orders. Rather, it's tied to the number of different pieces carried and the way they're used.

● **Inventory management** refers to the **overall** way a firm **controls inventory** and its cost.

Inventory management refers to the overall way a company oversees its inventory and uses its control system to manage the benefits of carrying inventory against the cost. You can think of the process as defining an acceptable level of operating efficiency in terms of stockouts, backorders, and production problems, and then trying to achieve that level of efficiency with the minimum inventory cost.

There's no single, all-encompassing approach to managing inventory. Success is achieved through frequent reviews, attention to detail, and the use of a variety of mechanized and manual systems. In the rest of this section we'll review some well-known ideas that address pieces of the inventory management process.

THE ECONOMIC ORDER QUANTITY (EOQ) MODEL

We've defined carrying and ordering costs as being related to inventory in different ways. Carrying costs increase with the amount of inventory held, while ordering costs increase with the number of orders placed to replenish depleted stocks. The total cost of having inventory is the sum of the two. The **economic order quantity (EOQ) model** is an approach to minimizing total inventory cost by recognizing that under certain conditions there's a trade-off between carrying cost and ordering cost.

Imagine that an inventory item is used evenly during the year and is periodically reordered in quantity Q. For the moment we'll ignore time lags in ordering and delivery. We'll assume the item is used steadily until none are left, then immediately restocked by a delivery of Q units. Figure 15.7 is a plot of the number of units on hand over time under these assumptions.

FIGURE 15.7

Inventory on Hand for a Steadily Used Item

Notice that inventory in stock decreases steadily along the diagonal lines until it is replenished. Under these conditions, the average quantity on hand is Q/2 units and the number of reorders is the annual usage divided by Q.

The model assumes that carrying costs vary directly with the average inventory balance and that ordering costs are fixed on a per-order basis. If C represents yearly carrying cost per unit, total carrying cost can be written as

(15.1) $$\text{carrying cost} = C\,(Q/2)\,.$$

It's clear from equation 15.1 and the diagram that total carrying cost can be reduced by ordering more frequently in smaller quantities. If Q was smaller, Figure 15.7 would have more sawtoothed peaks, but each would be lower and the average quantity on hand (Q/2) would be lower.

However, ordering more frequently will increase the number of orders placed each year. Because each order costs a fixed amount, this increases total ordering cost. If annual demand is D, the firm places

(15.2) $$N = D/Q$$

orders per year. Then if the fixed cost per order is F, total ordering cost will be

(15.3) $$\text{ordering cost} = FN = F\,(D/Q)\,.$$

This expression clearly increases as order size decreases because Q appears in the denominator.

Total inventory cost, which we'll call TC, is the sum of carrying cost and ordering cost. Adding equations 15.1 and 15.3 gives

(15.4) $$TC = C\,\frac{Q}{2} + F\,\frac{D}{Q}\,.$$

These ideas are represented graphically in Figure 15.8. The diagram shows carrying cost increasing and ordering cost decreasing with order size, Q. Notice that the sum of these costs, total cost, first decreases and then increases as Q gets larger. Hence it's possible to choose an optimal order size that minimizes the cost of inventory. That value of Q is known as the economic order quantity, abbreviated EOQ. On the diagram, it is directly below the minimum point on the total cost line.

A technique for finding the minimum value of an expression like equation 15.4 is available using calculus. We'll accept the following result without getting into the math.[13]

(15.5) $$EOQ = \left[\frac{2FD}{C}\right]^{1/2}$$

---

13. The mathematically inclined will recognize the EOQ as a straightforward minimization problem with respect to the variable Q. Differentiate equation 15.4 with respect to Q, and set the result equal to zero to get

$$0 = \frac{C}{2} - \frac{FD}{Q^2}\,.$$

Then solve for Q to get equation 15.5.

FIGURE 15.8

Inventory Costs and the EOQ

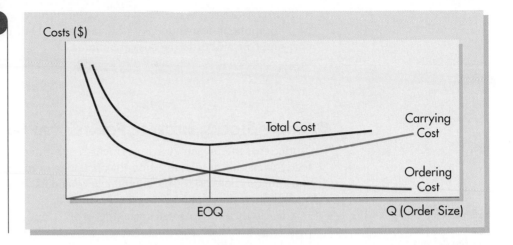

EXAMPLE 15.5

The Galbraith Corp. buys a part that costs $5. The carrying cost of inventory is approximately 20% of the part's dollar value per year. It costs $45 to place, process, and receive an order. The firm uses 1,000 of the $5 parts a year. What ordering quantity minimizes inventory costs and how many orders will be placed each year if that order quantity is used? What inventory costs are incurred for the part with this ordering quantity?

Solution: First note that the unit carrying cost per year is 20% of the part's price, so

$$C = (.2)(\$5) = \$1 \ .$$

Next write equation 15.5 and substitute from the information given.

$$EOQ = \left[\frac{2FD}{C}\right]^{1/2}$$

$$= \left[\frac{2(\$45)(1,000)}{\$1}\right]^{1/2}$$

$$= [90,000]^{1/2}$$

$$= 300 \text{ units}$$

The annual number of reorders is

$$1,000/300 = 3.3333 \ .$$

Carrying costs are

$$(300/2) \times \$5 \times .2 = \$150$$

and ordering costs are

$$\$45 \times 3.3333 = \$150 \ .$$

Hence the total inventory cost of the part is $300.

As an exercise, demonstrate that this is a minimum by calculating the cost at several different ordering quantities around 300 units.

Notice from the diagram that the minimum total cost is achieved where the two component cost lines cross one another. That means at the optimal point, carrying cost and ordering cost are equal.

SAFETY STOCKS, REORDER POINTS, AND LEAD TIMES

Notice that the inventory arrangement represented in Figure 15.7 assumes a perfectly even and predictable flow of parts out of inventory. It also assumes an instantaneous delivery of parts whenever needed. In reality, usage rates vary and restocking orders don't always arrive on time.

> **Safety stock** provides a **buffer** against **unexpectedly** rapid use or delayed delivery.

Clearly these factors can cause the firm to run out of inventory and suffer the problems associated with stockouts we described earlier. Such outages can be largely avoided by carrying a **safety stock** of inventory for emergencies. A safety stock is simply an additional supply of inventory that is carried all the time to be used when normal working stocks run out.

The EOQ model of Figure 15.7 can be modified conceptually to include safety stocks by placing the sawtoothed lines on top of a safety stock as shown in Figure 15.9.

Lead Times and Reorder Points

As a practical matter, a restocking order has to be placed in advance of the time at which it's needed. The advance period, known as an *ordering lead time,* is generally estimated by the item's supplier.

Referring to Figure 15.9, we see that as time passes the quantity on hand diminishes along one of the diagram's diagonal lines until the *reorder point* (indicated on the vertical axis) is reached. At that time an order for resupply is placed with the supplier of the item. The reorder point is calculated so that the expected

---

FIGURE 15.9

Pattern of Inventory on Hand Including Safety Stock Showing Reorder Point, Lead Time, and the Effects of High Usage and Delayed Delivery

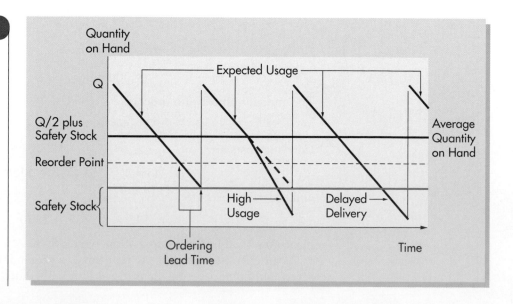

usage during the ordering lead time will bring the stock to its lowest planned level just as the new supply is delivered.

However, if the usage rate increases after an order is placed, the stock will diminish faster than planned and the inventory balance will dip into the safety stock range. That situation is depicted under the third peak in the diagram. If there was no safety stock, the increased usage would result in a stockout.

It is also easy to see that a delay in delivery after a reorder will cause a dip into safety stock. This situation is depicted under the last peak, and would also result in a stockout if there was no safety stock.

SAFETY STOCK AND THE EOQ   The inclusion of safety stocks does not change the EOQ. It just increases the total cost of inventory by the carrying cost of the safety stock. In effect, the EOQ model sits on top of a safety stock level as shown in Figure 15.9.

THE RIGHT LEVEL OF SAFETY STOCK   Choosing a safety stock level involves another cost trade-off. The extra inventory increases carrying cost but avoids losses from production delays and missed sales. These opposing effects have to be balanced in the choice of an appropriate level of safety inventory. The choice can be difficult because the savings aren't visible. They're the result of problems that didn't happen, so they don't appear anywhere on financial statements. The carrying cost, on the other hand, is quite visible and measurable.

It's rarely advisable to carry so much safety inventory that stockouts are avoided entirely. Under most conditions, that would require a huge amount of inventory at an excessive cost. It's generally best to tolerate an occasional outage to keep inventory levels reasonable. In some businesses, backorders are filled quickly and outages don't cause a lot of trouble. In such cases, safety stocks can be minimal.

TRACKING INVENTORIES—THE ABC SYSTEM

The amount of attention that should be given to controlling inventories of particular items varies with the nature and cost of the item. Some pieces are very expensive, and for that reason alone warrant a great deal of attention. Some items are critical to the firm's processes or to those of customers, and therefore are important whether they cost a lot or not. On the other hand, some items are cheap and easy to get, so spending a lot of effort to control them isn't worthwhile. Common nuts and bolts are a good example.

● An **ABC system** segregates items by **value** and places **tighter control** on **higher cost** pieces.

Most companies recognize this fact and use a variant of the **ABC system** in their inventory control systems. Items designated A are important because of their value or the consequences of running out, and are carefully controlled. They're usually serialized, kept under lock and key, and signed out to a responsible individual when used. C items are cheap and plentiful, kept in a bin accessible to anyone, and reordered when the bin gets low. B items are between As and Cs and are handled accordingly.

Recognizing that inventory items differ in importance enables companies to keep control costs low.

JUST IN TIME (JIT) INVENTORY SYSTEMS

In recent years, a manufacturing inventory concept developed by the Japanese has received a lot of publicity. In theory, the **just in time (JIT)** system virtually

● **JIT** eliminates manufacturing inventory by pushing it **back on suppliers.**

eliminates factory inventory. Under JIT, suppliers deliver goods to manufacturers just in time (within a few hours) to be used in production. The idea requires a great deal of faith and cooperation between a manufacturer and its suppliers, because a late delivery can stop a factory's entire production line.

Under JIT the manufacturer is essentially pushing the task of carrying inventory back onto its suppliers. Conceptually the supplier will push its inventory back onto its suppliers, which do the same to their suppliers. Ultimately the entire production chain works in a coordinated manner, largely eliminating inventories.

The idea sounds good in theory, and does work under certain conditions, but hasn't proven as successful as its proponents originally hoped. In many situations it doesn't work at all.

JIT works best when the manufacturer is very large and powerful with respect to the supplier and buys most of the supplier's output. In such cases the supplier is willing to do almost anything to keep the manufacturer's business, including orchestrating JIT deliveries. Even then the concept works really well only when the supplier is located near enough to the manufacturer that shipping delays aren't a problem. The automobile industry tends to be organized like that, and has had some success with JIT. The idea was originally developed by Toyota in Japan.

For smaller companies that don't have any particular clout over suppliers that may be located far away, the idea may not be practical. In such cases suppliers have little incentive to go to the trouble and expense of making the precise and timely deliveries that JIT requires.

DISCUSSION QUESTIONS

1. Explain the differences between short-term and long-term money used by businesses with respect to both the uses and sources of the funds.

2. Because companies always have inventory and accounts receivable, most banks are happy to make long-term loans to support those assets. Either refute or support that statement.

3. Describe the maturity matching principle. What are the risks of not matching maturities? How would you characterize a firm that ignores the principle? Can you think of situations in which it would be advisable for an otherwise prudent firm to deviate from the principle?

4. Working capital spontaneously finances itself because it's being turned over all the time. Is this statement true, false, or a little of both? Exactly what is meant by spontaneous financing? Does working capital require funding? Why?

5. Working capital is generally defined as the difference between current assets and current liabilities. Is this definition precisely correct? Why?

6. Support or challenge each of the following statements individually.

a. Because accounts receivable aren't purchased like inventory or fixed assets, they don't require financing.

b. Cash represents a pool of available money, so it actually reduces financing needs.

7. You're a supervisor in the treasury department of Big Corp. Recently there's been increasing concern about the firm's rising interest expense. Fred Eyeshade is an analyst in your group who transferred from the accounting department a short time ago. He has suggested that senior management mandate a 50% across-the-board cut in cash, inventory, and receivables along with a doubling of payables to reduce the firm's financing needs for net working capital. Explain why this might not be a good idea with respect to each of these elements of net working capital (four accounts).

8. Things tend to run more smoothly and efficiently with more working capital. With respect to each working capital account (four, exclude accruals), explain why this statement isn't absolutely true. In other words, why might a very large inventory or receivables balance not do much good at all?

9. How does a firm's operating cycle differ from its cash conversion cycle? Explain fully.

10. You work in the finance department of a manufacturing company. Over lunch, a friend in the engineering department said she'd heard that the firm used a lot of temporary working capital. Because temporary equipment is usually of lower quality than permanent material, she wonders why the company, which is quite prosperous, doesn't buy the best and store it when it isn't needed.

What misconceptions does your friend have? Write a brief explanation for someone who knows nothing about finance to straighten out her understanding.

11. Why does it make sense to finance net working capital separately from fixed assets?

12. You work in the finance department of HiTech Inc. The firm's owner and CEO, Charlie Dollars, is very profit oriented. He understands that short-term interest rates are quite low at the moment, and has suggested that the firm finance all of its working capital needs with short-term loans. The CFO has asked you to prepare a memo for his signature outlining why this may not be the best strategy. In your memo, outline the working capital financing options available to most firms and discuss the trade-offs involved in using long-term versus short-term financing.

13. What are the advantages and disadvantages of stretching payables? If you owned your own business, would you do it? Why or why not?

14. What's the difference between a promissory note, a line of credit, and a revolving credit agreement? Are they mutually exclusive? That is, might one be part of the other?

15. You and your friend Harry have started a business. Harry is a technical whiz, but doesn't know much about business or finance. After several months you've been approved for a $100,000 bank loan at what seems to be a rather high interest rate, 16%. Harry is especially bothered by the rate. He thinks banks shouldn't get any more than 4 or 5%, but doesn't really know why he feels that way. When you both were about to sign the loan papers, the banker mentioned that a minimum balance of $20,000 would have to remain in the bank. Hearing this, Harry pulled out his calculator and made a calculation at which he became outraged. He then stormed out of the meeting.

Why is Harry so upset? What calculation did he make? Write a short memo explaining banking practices to calm Harry down. Is there a kind of minimum balance requirement that might make Harry's calculation invalid?

16. Explain the difference between pledging and factoring receivables. Which is likely to be a more expensive source of financing? Is factoring the same kind of financing as pledging?

17. Factoring may involve interest even though it isn't a loan. How can this come about?

18. What is the biggest problem associated with financing secured by inventory? How is it addressed in practice?

19. Outline the reasons for holding cash and the big cost associated with it. How do these lead to the objective of cash management? How do marketable securities help or hinder achievement of the objective?

20. The Medco Supply Co. operates out of Waco, Texas, and has a number of customers around Portland, Maine. It seems to take a particularly long time for the Portland customers' payment checks to reach Medco. What can the company do to speed things up? Explain how your solution would work.

21. Sally Johnson lives in Baltimore and does business with a large, national brokerage firm. When she sends the broker a check, she mails it to a local address in Baltimore. However, when she receives a check from the broker, it comes from San Francisco. Her sister Joan lives in Los Angeles and uses the same firm. She mails payments to an office a few blocks from her home, but receives checks from an office in Miami. What's going on? Should the Johnson sisters be upset?

22. You're the cash manager for Huge Inc., which has factories and stores all over the country. Each operation has several bank accounts to receive deposits and pay vendors, so the company's cash is spread all over the country under the control of divisional CFOs. It's essential that those divisional executives have control of their cash to run their operations effectively. However, the rather substantial cash total isn't earning anything because it's too dispersed to be invested in marketable securities. Suggest a way to fix this problem and explain how it will work.

23. Every company should take full advantage of the sophisticated cash management services offered by today's banking industry. Right or wrong? Explain.

24. Outline the costs and benefits involved in the trade-off between a tighter versus a looser receivables policy.

25. You're the CFO of the Wachusett Window Company, which sells windows to residential builders. The firm's customers tend to be small, thinly capitalized construction companies that are frequently short of cash. Over the past year, there's been a slump in the housing industry and Wachusett's sales have slowed. Several months ago the marketing department initiated a program to attract new customers to counteract the downward sales trend. The VP of marketing and the president agreed that the firm would have to deal with even smaller, newer builders if it was going to keep sales up. At the time the president overruled your concerns about the credit quality of such customers. He personally approved a number of accounts brought in by the sales department that ordinarily wouldn't have qualified for credit.

More recently receivables have gone up substantially, and collection efforts have been less successful than usual. Collectors have asked for help from sales representatives in chasing down delinquent customers, but the VP of marketing says they don't have time because "reps have to be out on the street selling."

The president has suddenly become concerned about the receivables increase, and has demanded to know why finance has let it happen. Prepare a memo explaining the processes behind the creation and management of receivables and explain what's behind the increase. Tactfully explain why the blame should not be placed solely on the finance department. Can you argue that finance is completely without fault in this matter?

26. In the situation at Wachusett Window outlined in the last question, do you think a higher prompt payment discount alongside the new sales program would have kept receivables down? Why?

27. Speculate on the nature of the relationship between the credit and collections department and the sales department at Wachusett Window in questions 25 and 26.

28. Inventory management is a shared responsibility between finance and manufacturing just as receivables management involves both sales and finance. Right or wrong? Explain.

29. Because of the advances in computer technology, inventory management is a precise science, and there's no excuse for not having the optimal quantity on hand at all times. Is that statement true or false? Explain.

30. Does the EOQ model properly applied prevent stockouts? Does it address stockouts at all? Do you think the EOQ model solves very many of management's inventory problems?

31. Wildebrant Inc. runs out of inventory all the time both in the factory and at the point of sale. However, the company is profitable, and no one worries about it much. Is this OK? What's probably going on that management doesn't see? Why don't they see it? What would you suggest to fix the problem? How would it work?

32. The Philipps Lighting Company manufactures decorative light fixtures. Its revenues are about $100 million a year. It purchases inputs from approximately 20 suppliers, most of which are much larger companies located in various parts of the country. Sam Spade, the vice president of manufacturing, is a sophisticated executive who has always been impressed by the latest innovative techniques in management.

Last week Sam came into a meeting of the executive team with a proposal to cut inventory costs to almost nothing. Just in time (JIT) is the wave of the future, he said, and proposed that Philipps enter into negotiations with all of its suppliers to implement the concept immediately.

You're the CFO and tend to be more skeptical about new methods. Prepare a memo to the team, tactfully outlining the problems and risks involved in Sam's proposal.

PROBLEMS

1. Thompson Inc. has a $10 million revolving credit agreement with its bank. It pays interest on borrowing at 2% over prime and a $\frac{1}{4}$% commitment fee on available but unused funds. Last month Thompson had borrowings of $5 million for the first half of the month and $10 million for the second half. Calculate its interest charges for the month. The bank's prime rate is 6%.

2. The Conejo Corp. borrows from its bank under an $8 million revolving credit arrangement. It pays a base rate of 9% on its outstanding loan plus a $\frac{1}{4}$% commitment fee on the unused balance. The firm had borrowed $2 million going into April and borrowed an additional $4 million on April 11. No further borrowing or repayment was made during the month. Calculate Canejo's interest charges for April.

3. The Grass Ridge Company has the following current asset accounts.

Cash	$1,900,000
Accounts receivable	$4,600,000
Inventory	$5,500,000

Its current ratio is 2.5:1. The bank is willing to lend the company enough to finance its working capital needs under a $10 million revolving credit arrangement at a base rate of 12% with a 3/8% commitment fee on the unused balance. If the current accounts stay relatively constant throughout the year, what will Grass Ridge pay the bank for working capital financing?

4. Bridgeport Inc. has a $30 million revolving credit agreement with its bank at prime plus 3.2% based on a calendar year. Prior to the month of April, it had taken down $15 million that was outstanding for the entire month. On April 10, it took down another $5 million. Prime is 8.2%, and the bank's commitment fee is .25% annually. Calculate the charges associated with Bridgeport's revolving credit agreement for the month of April.

5. Southport Inc. has an inventory turnover of 10×, an ACP of 45 days, and turns over its payables once a month. How long are Southport's operating and cash conversion cycles? (Use a 360-day year.)

6. The Langley Corporation is in a seasonal business. It requires a permanent base of net working capital of $10 million all year long, but that requirement temporarily increases to $20 million during a four-month period each year. Langley has three financing options for net working capital.

1. Finance the peak level year round with equity, which costs 20%, and invest temporarily unused funds in marketable securities, which earn 6%.

2. Finance permanent net working capital with equity and temporary net working capital with a short-term loan at 12%.

3. Finance all net working capital needs with short-term debt at 12.5%.

Calculate the cost of each option. Which would you choose? Why?

7. Calculate the effective interest rate implied by the following terms of sale. (Use a 365-day year.)

> 2/10, net 30
>
> 1/5, net 15
>
> .5/10, net 30
>
> 2.5/10, net 25
>
> 1/5, net 20

8. What is the effective interest rate on a $750,000 loan at 8% for 120 days if a 20% minimum compensating balance is required?

9. DeSquam Inc. pledges receivables of $250 million per year to the Sharkskin Finance Company, which advances cash equal to 80% of the face value of the accounts pledged. DeSquam's receivables are usually collected in about 36 days, so 10% of the annual amount advanced is generally outstanding at any time. (Thirty-six days is one-tenth of a year, so receivables "turn over" ten times a year.) Sharkskin charges 14% interest plus an administrative fee of 1.6% of the amount pledged. What is DeSquam's cost of receivables financing? State the result in dollar terms and as a rate.

10. The York Company has an average receivables balance of $55,000, which turns over once every 30 days. It offers all of its receivables to its bank as collateral for short-term borrowing (pledging). The bank generally accepts 60% of the accounts offered and advances cash equal to 85% of those. Interest is 3% over prime and the bank charges a 1% administrative fee on the gross value of all accounts offered. The prime rate is currently 9.5%. What effective rate is York paying for its receivables financing?

11. Southern Fabrics Inc. factors all of its receivables. The firm does $150 million in business each year and would have an ACP of 36.5 days if it collected its own receivables. The firm's gross margin is 35%. The factor operates without recourse and pays immediately upon taking over the accounts. It discounts the gross amount factored by 10% and pays Southern immediately. Because the factor doesn't collect from customers until they pay, it charges interest at 10% in the interim.

a. Calculate the gross cost of factoring to Southern Fabrics if all receivables are collectible.

b. What interest rate is implied by the arrangement?

c. Suppose Southern is considering giving up the factoring arrangement and handling its own collections. Should the firm do it if bad debt losses are expected to average 3% of gross sales and running a collections department will cost about $1.5 million per year? Assume the interest cost of carrying the receivable balance is also 10%.

d. What is the implied interest rate in the factoring arrangement if the costs in part c are taken into account?

12. Central City Bank will lend Williams Inc. 60% of the value of its inventory at 12% if Williams will pledge the inventory as collateral for the loan. The bank also insists that Williams employ a warehousing company to monitor and control the inventoried material. Blyth Warehousing will do the job for an annual fee of $150,000 plus 2% of the value of all the inventory it handles. Williams moves inventory valued at about $15 million through its plant each year at a turnover rate of 5 times. What will the cost of financing be under this proposal? State the result in both dollar and percentage (of amount borrowed) terms.

13. The Shamrock Company has a raw materials inventory of $20 million, which is completely replaced approximately 10 times a year. The Bridgewater Bank is willing to advance financing of 75% of the value of Shamrock's inventory at an interest rate of 12%. However, it requires a warehousing system to secure its interests. A warehousing company will install and operate the system for $800,000 a year plus .5% of the value of materials entering the system. What is the effective cost of this financing to Shamrock?

14. Tambourines Inc. collects $12 million per year from customers in a remote location. The average remittance check is $1,200. A lockbox system would shorten the overall float on these receipts from 8 days to 7 days, but would cost $2,500 per year plus $.20 per check. The relevant interest rate is 9%. Should Tambourines install the system? Use a 360-day year.

15. The Hadley Motor Company is located in Florida but has a number of customers in the Pacific Northwest. Sales to those customers are $30 million a year paid in checks that average about $1,500. The checks take an average of nine days to clear into Hadley's Florida bank. A bank in Oregon will operate a lock box system for Hadley for $8,000 a year plus $.50 per check. The system can be expected to reduce the clearing time to six days.

a. Is the lock box system worthwhile if Hadley borrows at 13.5%?

b. What is the minimum number of days of float time the system has to save (to the nearest tenth of a day) to make it worthwhile?

16. The Bailey Machine Tool Company thinks it can increase sales by $10 million by loosening its credit standards somewhat. The firm normally experiences bad debts of about 2% of sales, but marketing estimates that the incremental business would be from financially weaker customers who would not pay about 5% of the time. The firm's gross margin is 35% (production-related costs are 65% of revenue).

a. Should Bailey lower its credit standards to get the new business?

b. Would your answer change if taking on the new business also involved incremental collection expenses of $50,000 per year?

17. The Kranberry Kids Klothing Kompany is in the volatile garment business. The firm has annual revenues of $250 million and operates with a 30% gross margin on sales. Bad debt losses average 3% of revenues. Kranberry is contemplating an easing of its credit policy in an attempt to increase sales. The loosening would involve accepting a lower quality customer for credit sales. It is estimated that sales could be increased by $20 million a year in this manner. However, the collections department estimates that bad debt losses on the new business would run four times the normal level, and that internal collection efforts would cost an additional $1 million a year.

a. Is the policy change a good idea?

b. Is it likely that coupling an increased prompt payment discount with the looser guidelines would reduce the bad debt losses?

c. Is it possible that the idea in part b could have a net negative impact? How?

18. Sharon's Sweater Shop orders 5,000 sweaters per year from a supplier at a wholesale cost of $65 each. Carrying costs are 22% of inventory, and it costs $52 to place and receive an order. How many orders should Sharon place with the supplier each year, and how large should each be?

19. Smithson Hydraulics Inc. carries an inventory of valves that cost $25 each. The firm's inventory carrying cost is approximately 18% of the value of the inventory. It costs $38 to place, process, and receive an order. The firm uses 20,000 valves a year.

a. What ordering quantity minimizes the inventory costs associated with the valves? (Round to the nearest unit.)

b. How many orders will be placed each year if the EOQ is used?

c. What are the valves' carrying and ordering costs if the EOQ is used?

 Internet Problem

20. Go to the *Business Owner's Toolkit* at http://www.toolkit.cch.com for information on how to more effectively manage accounts receivable. First click on *Managing Your Business Finances,* then on *Credit and Collections.* Read the introduction and the following sections: *Building a Credit Policy That Works, Improving Your Collection Cycles,* and *Accounting For Bad Debts.* Prepare a one-page report summarizing what you found.

CHAPTER 16

Financial Planning

Chapter Outline

Planning is a big part of modern corporate life, especially in large companies. Firms plan their futures constantly, addressing everything from cash flow and short-term profitability to long-run strategy.

Generally, the higher in management people are, the more time they devote to planning. It isn't unusual for top executives to spend 80% of their time thinking about the future. At the same time, some planning functions involve virtually everyone in management. For example, one thing you can be sure you'll do in your first management job is prepare a budget.

This chapter deals primarily with *financial planning.* Simply put, that means projecting a company's financial statements into the future. However, financial planning is a part of a broader activity known as *business planning.* To really appreciate financial planning, we have to understand the nature and purpose of business planning, and see how the financial element fits into the broader concept.

BUSINESS PLANNING

The easiest way to describe business planning is in terms of its result. The process produces a document called a **business plan,** which can be thought of as a picture or model of what a business unit is expected to become in the future. The business plan generally looks like a magazine (with graphs and diagrams rather than pictures), and consists of a combination of words and numbers that describe the business.

● A **business plan** is a model of what management expects a business to become in the future expressed in **words** and **financial projections.**

The numbers in a plan are largely projected financial statements. That is, they're estimates of what the firm's statements will look like in the future if the assumptions about the business made by the planners come true. Such statements based on hypothetical circumstances are called *pro forma,* meaning they are cast "as if" the planning assumptions are true.

The words in a business plan describe the operation in a realistic yet concise way. They discuss broad strategic issues, detail the handling of short-term tactical questions, and amplify the financial projections.

The overall image conveyed by a good business plan is very comprehensive. It includes information on products, markets, employees, technology, facilities, capital, revenue, profitability, and anything else that might be relevant in describing the organization and its affairs.

● COMPONENT PARTS OF A BUSINESS PLAN

Although the detail within business plans varies a great deal from company to company, most follow a fairly standard overall format. A typical outline follows.

A. Contents

B. Executive Summary

C. Mission and Strategy Statement

D. Market Analysis

E. Operations (of the business)

F. Management and Staffing

G. **Financial Projections**

H. Contingencies

The first two sections are introductory. The table of contents is just that, and the executive summary is a one-page overview of everything that follows.

The mission and strategy section lays out the basic charter of the business and establishes its long-term direction. The market analysis attempts to demonstrate why the business will succeed against its competitors. The chapter on operations describes how the firm creates and distributes its product or service. The management and staffing chapter details the firm's projected personnel needs and in some cases lays out the credentials of key managers.

● A firm's **financial plan** is a projection of its financial statements into the **future.**

The financial section of the business plan projects the company's financial results into the future, and is the firm's **financial plan.** How that projection is put together will be our main focus in this chapter. The section on contingencies tells what the company will do if things don't go as planned.

● THE PURPOSE OF PLANNING AND PLAN INFORMATION

The two major audiences for a firm's business plan and the information it contains are the firm's own management and outside investors.

The Managerial Value of Planning

Business planning has several managerial benefits. One has to do with the process of creating the plan, while the others are related to using the finished product.

> ● The **planning process** helps to pull the management team together.

THE PLANNING PROCESS   The planning process can pull a management team into a cohesive unit with common goals. It helps everyone understand what the objectives of the organization are, why they're important, and how the organization intends to achieve them. Creating a plan forces the team to think through everything that has to be done in the coming period, making sure everyone understands what they have to do.

A ROAD MAP FOR RUNNING THE BUSINESS   A business plan functions as a road map for getting an organization to its goal. Comparing the details of operating performance with the plan and investigating deviations is an important management process. When a business goes off course, such a comparison is the best way to understand the firm's problems and come up with solutions. The idea is illustrated in Figure 16.1.

> ● A completed plan serves as a **road map** for guiding a business toward the goals stated in the plan.

A STATEMENT OF GOALS   A business plan is a projection of the future that generally reflects what management would like to see happen. Accordingly, it can be viewed as a set of goals for the company as a whole and for its individual departments.

A plan contains revenue targets, departmental expense constraints, and various development goals for products and processes. Different people are responsible for different goals, and performance against them can be measured and evaluated.

FIGURE 16.1

Using a Plan to Guide Business Performance

It's especially common to tie executive bonuses to the achievement of goals within business plans. We'll have more to say about goals within plans later in the chapter.

● The financial plan is especially important for anticipating **financing needs.**

PREDICTING FINANCING NEEDS   Financial planning is extremely important for companies that rely on outside financing. Only through accurate financial planning can a corporate treasurer predict when he or she will need to turn to financial markets to raise additional money to support operations.

Communicating Information to Investors

● The business plan is a vehicle for communicating with potential **investors.**

A business plan is management's statement about what the company is going to be in the future, and can be used to communicate those ideas to investors. A plan predicts the future character of the enterprise. It makes an estimate of profitability and cash flow. The financial information tells equity investors what returns they can expect and debt investors where the firm will get the money to repay loans.

Small firms use the business plan document itself in dealing with investors. Large companies convey selected plan information to securities analysts who use it and past performance as a basis for recommendations to clients.

Business Planning in Divisions of Large Companies

Large companies are usually organized into decentralized operating divisions that function more or less like independent companies. Most large firms engage in a nearly continuous planning process. Divisions produce their own plans, which are consolidated to create overall corporate plans.

The business planning process is an important vehicle through which divisions communicate with corporate managements. A division's final business plan is a statement of its goals that reflects the parent company's expectations as well as its own. Divisional plans are generally approved by corporate management after lengthy reviews, and nearly everything a division does is compared with its plan.

Success and failure at the division are defined relative to the business plan.

● CREDIBILITY AND SUPPORTING DETAIL

Predictions of the future may not come true. Everyone knows that, so there's always an issue of believability surrounding business plans. Financial plans are especially subject to skepticism because it's usually hard to tell how the planners developed the numbers in the projected statements. Let's consider a simplified example to illustrate the idea.

Suppose Poorly Inc. has revenue of $100 million and profit of $1 million this year. The board of directors is pressuring management for better performance and has demanded a plan showing an improvement. In response, management submits the following.

● A good business plan shows enough **supporting detail** to indicate that it is the product of **careful thinking.**

Poorly Inc.
Financial Plan

	This Year	Next Year
Revenue	$100M	$120M
EAT	$ 1M	$ 12M

Technically, this projection satisfies the board's request for a plan showing improvement, but the obvious question is why should the board members believe it. In the situation described, they probably would not.

The problem is that this "plan" as presented lacks *supporting detail*. A reader doesn't know whether it's something made up just to satisfy the board's demand or represents the summarized product of a great deal of analysis. In other words, it doesn't tell the reader enough about the thinking behind the financial figures to make them believable.

A competent plan may display summarized financial projections, but the figures are supported by enough detail to show that they're the product of logical thinking. For example, revenue projections are usually supported by schedules showing the products and quantities to be sold, their prices, and which sales organizations are expected to do the selling. These schedules in turn are backed up by reasoning that tells why certain products are expected to sell more than others and why some salespeople will outsell their rivals. The point is that a planner can't just write down a revenue figure that's plucked out of thin air and expect people to believe it.

Supporting detail shows how the numbers in the financial plan were developed. The detail doesn't all have to be included in the plan document itself, but should be available if a reader has questions.

As we proceed, we'll see that financial plans are constructed with varying levels of supporting detail depending on their use. It's important to match the level of detail to the purpose of the plan.

FOUR KINDS OF BUSINESS PLAN

There are as many as four variations on the basic idea of business planning. Each serves a different purpose and results in a separate document. Large, sophisticated companies tend to do all of these different kinds of planning. Small firms usually do only one plan that combines features of the four variations.

The four kinds of planning are (1) strategic planning, (2) operational planning, (3) budgeting, and (4) forecasting.[1, 2] They differ according to three attributes: the length of the planning period (the **planning horizon**), the kinds of issues addressed, and the level of financial detail projected.

Strategic Planning

Strategic planning involves broad, conceptual thinking about the nature of a business, who it serves, and what it does. It's generally a long-term exercise in which managers try to predict in rough terms what the business will do and become over a period of several years. A five-year horizon is the most common.

Strategic planning begins by questioning the company's very existence. Why is the firm doing what it does? Would it be better off doing something else? What customer need does it serve? How? What opportunities are present in the marketplace?

• The **strategic plan** addresses broad, long-term issues, and contains only summarized, **approximate financial projections.**

---

1. Planning terminology isn't consistent between companies. In some firms, people talk about an annual operating budget, while others make a long-term forecast. The words "outlook" and "view" are also common. The important distinction is the length of the planning horizon: Multi (usually 5) year—long-term, strategic. One year—intermediate term, operating. Three to six months—short-term, budgetary. Two weeks to three months—very short-term, forecast.

2. Budgets and forecasts are abbreviated business plans and often don't have all the parts described earlier. They are predominantly financial projections.

What threats? Strategy demands that a company develop a mission and a charter, that it define what it does and why, while stating its loftiest goals.

Once that base is established, strategic planners look forward over several years and consider broad, sweeping issues. At the end of five years, will the firm be in the same lines of business? In the same geographic areas? How large will it have grown? Who will be its competitors, and how will it fight them? And so on.

Strategic planning deals with concepts and ideas expressed mostly with words rather than numbers. The numbers used tend to be simple and approximate. For example, a firm's strategic plan might establish a goal of being the number one or two rated company in its industry based on some measure such as sales or market share. Or a firm might set a sales goal of about $500 million a year, stating that revenue figure without a lot of supporting detail.

Strategic plans include projected financial statements, but they're approximate and ideal, and usually not supported by much detail. The plan's last (usually fifth) year generally shows financial results that reflect the best the business could ever be expected to do.

Strategic plans are often called long-range plans or five-year plans.

In a nutshell, systematic strategic thinking says that a business must first analyze itself, its industry, and the competitive situation. Then it must construct an approach to doing business that takes advantage of its strengths and minimizes the vulnerabilities created by its weaknesses. A strategic plan is a vehicle for documenting this kind of thinking.

Operational Planning

Operational planning involves translating business ideas into concrete, shorter-term projections usually encompassing about a year. Projections are a great deal more detailed here than in strategic planning.

Among other things, operational plans specify how much the company will sell, to whom, and at what prices. They also spell out where the firm will get its inputs and equipment, what those things will cost, and what the firm expects to earn.

● The **annual operating plan** projects the business **in detail** over a year, and is the **most important** planning exercise.

The word "operational" or "operating" means having to do with the day-to-day running of the business. Major short-term goals are generally set up in the operating plan. Revenue targets are established along with profit objectives. Sales quotas and product development milestones are laid out. Compensation and bonus systems are also specified. Most companies do an annual plan that is an operational plan.

A typical annual **operating plan** is conceptually an almost even mix of words and numbers. The document explains what's going on verbally, but backs the explanation up with financial projections containing substantial supporting detail.

Budgeting

In many industries, business conditions change rapidly and an annual operating plan can be badly out of date by the second half of the year it covers. Budgets are essentially short-term updates of annual plans, typically covering three-month quarters. In addition, they usually contain supporting detail beyond that found in the annual plan.

● **Budgets** are short-term updates of the annual plan when business **conditions change** rapidly.

A budget ties down exactly how much money, material, and labor will flow through the organization and fixes responsibility on specific people for making it happen. The budgeting process involves trying to predict exactly how much of which products will be sold and at what cost. Along with that it attempts a precise estimate of how many dollars will be spent in each department, on exactly what items: salary, material, travel, and so on.

It's important to realize that the budgetary time frame is too short to make major conceptual changes in the businesses. Policy issues and long-term direction aren't usually discussed, so budgets have relatively fewer words and more financial detail than annual plans. Clearly, a budget can also be considered an operating plan because it details the day-to-day operation of the business.

Forecasting

Forecasts are quick estimates of short-term financial results. They're essentially projections of where the *financial momentum* of a business will carry it over a short period. They usually consist almost entirely of numbers with very little supporting verbiage.

Forecasts are generally made either to estimate cash flows or when management gets worried about how the company will close out a period in terms of profits.

Short-term forecasting is especially important with respect to cash requirements. If a company is to pay its bills and make its payroll, it has to have an accurate picture of the cash ins and outs that can be expected over the next few weeks and months. If a temporary shortage is predicted, bank borrowing has to be arranged to keep the firm running until collections catch up with disbursements.

A *cash forecast* is a financial projection made with the explicit purpose of predicting short-term cash needs. Most large firms do *monthly* cash forecasts.[3]

● Forecasts are **very short-term** projections of **profit** and **cash** flow.

The Business Planning Spectrum

It helps one's understanding of planning to imagine the different kinds of plan arrayed along a spectrum. The broad, conceptual thinking of long-term strategic planning is on one end, while the numerical detail of short-term forecasting is on the other. The idea is illustrated in Figure 16.2. As we move from left to right, the planning horizon (time covered) gets shorter, and the documents progress from qualitative to quantitative—that is, from being mostly words to mostly numbers.

Ideally, companies practice the whole spectrum of planning. That's the way most large companies operate, producing all the different documents. In such an environment, the strategic plan and the annual operating plan are each produced once a year about six months apart.[4] In addition, there are usually four quarterly budgets and any number of forecasts.[5]

3. The words "plan" and "forecast" have slightly different implications when used as nouns and verbs. A forecast (noun) tends to mean a short-term projection. A plan (noun) has a longer-term implication. The verbs are used more generally and don't tend to be tied to the length of the planning horizon. Hence we routinely talk about *forecasting* the numbers within a plan or *planning* the numbers within a forecast.
4. It's important to notice that even though the strategic plan covers five or more years, it is revised annually.
5. Companies in very stable businesses may omit the budget segment of the spectrum. Public utilities are good examples. Their revenues are based on the number of households in an area, which doesn't change rapidly. Therefore it may not be necessary to rebudget quarterly to keep up with changing business conditions. High-tech industries represent the opposite extreme. Technology and the markets for it change rapidly, and the companies constantly engage in replanning.

FIGURE 16.2

The Business Planning Spectrum

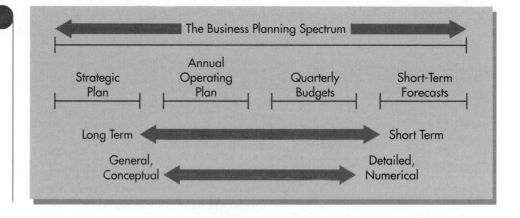

FIGURE 16.3

Relating Business Planning in Large and Small Companies

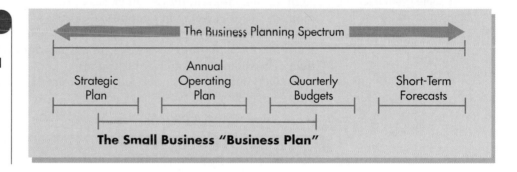

● **Small businesses** tend to do a single **business plan** when in need of funding that contains both strategic and operating elements.

http://

The Small Business Administration offers some helpful tips and information on running a small business including financial guidance at

● **www.sba.gov**

Relating Planning Processes of Small and Large Businesses

In the small business world, the planning spectrum is usually compressed into one document known simply as the company's "business plan." It tends to be produced when the firm is getting started and updated later when money is needed from a bank or another outside source.

The business plan produced by small companies can be related to the full planning spectrum found in larger firms. The idea is illustrated in Figure 16.3. The (small) business plan overlaps three of the exercises along the spectrum. It includes everything we normally think of as operational (annual) planning, as well as elements of both strategic planning and budgeting.

The entrepreneur's plan must do everything the big corporation's annual operating plan does. It has to provide a thorough rationale for the concrete actions planned in the next year and make some fairly detailed projections of quantities, staffing, and dollars over that period.

With respect to strategy, however, the small business plan doesn't need to cover the broadest issues. For example, it doesn't have to discuss why the entrepreneur chose this business over others because that decision has already been made. The plan does have to establish that a market clearly exists and that it can be served by the business. The small business plan must also make longer-term strategic projections of what the business will be three to five years in the future.

● The **financial plan** is an integral part of the overall **business plan**.

Finally, a small business plan has to get under an operating plan and project at least the first year in budget-like detail. Investors generally demand at least this much precision from entrepreneurs.[6]

THE FINANCIAL PLAN AS A COMPONENT OF A BUSINESS PLAN

A financial plan is simply the financial portion of any of the business plans we've been talking about. It is a set of pro forma financial statements projected over the time period covered by the plan.[7]

It's important to appreciate the role of the financial plan in each of the four planning documents we discussed earlier. No business plan is complete without a financial projection, but it's of secondary importance in the strategic plan. That document is an exposition of thoughts and ideas that discusses the how and why of a business. The *financials* are a piece of the projection, but generally aren't central to the presentation.

In an annual plan, on the other hand, the financial projection is the center-piece of the document. In operational terms, a company's financial plan is its business plan. There are usually a great many words in an annual plan, but they tend to be explanations of how the operating figures are to be achieved rather than discussions that stand by themselves.

Budgets and forecasts, especially the latter, are almost entirely financial planning exercises.

http://

The Business Toolkit at **www.toolkit.cch.com/tools/tools.asp** offers some great financial planning ideas for small businesses.

MAKING FINANCIAL PROJECTIONS

Projecting financial statements involves translating planned physical and economic activity into dollars. That generally means making a sales forecast first, and then developing what the rest of the company needs to do to support the activity implied. Those physical projections lead to the dollar figures in the financial statements.

PLANNING FOR NEW AND EXISTING BUSINESSES

Financial plans are constructed for both new and ongoing businesses. The processes are conceptually similar, but as a practical matter it's a good deal harder to plan for an operation that's either very new or has yet to be started.

It's difficult to forecast how much a new business will sell or how much support it will need, because there's no history on which to base projections. That means everything has to be developed from the ground up. Forecasting for an established business is much easier, because recent results and the existing base of assets and liabilities can be used as points of departure for the projection.

---

6. For a comprehensive treatment of business planning in the context of small business, see *The Perfect Business Plan Made Simple* by William Lasher (New York: Doubleday, 1994).
7. The terms "financial plan" and "financial planner" have a common meaning that shouldn't be confused with their use in this chapter. Personal financial advisors who set up investment programs (financial plans) for clients are known as financial planners. The field has nothing to do with business planning or projecting financial statements.

The Typical Planning Task

Most financial planning is done for existing businesses. Basically, it involves forecasting changes to what's been going on in the past. The changes are generally referred to as **planning assumptions**. Anything about which an explicit assumption isn't made is implicitly assumed to remain unchanged from the previous year. (For a new business, everything has to be explicitly assumed.)

For example, an existing business might plan next year's operations assuming the following changes.

- A 10% growth in unit sales
- A 3% reduction in product price
- A $2 per unit increase in the cost of materials
- Overall labor cost increases of 4%
- An improvement in inventory turnover from 5× to 6×
- An improvement in the ACP from 45 to 40 days
- An increase in interest rates from 9% to 11%
- And so on.

The financial planner's task is to put together a plan, benchmarking from last year's performance, that reflects these changes in the projected financial statements.

⬤**THE GENERAL APPROACH, ASSUMPTIONS, AND THE DEBT/INTEREST PROBLEM**

In this section we'll outline how any financial planning problem is tackled, and consider the peculiar problem of forecasting debt and interest. We'll begin by establishing exactly what we're trying to forecast and exactly what we have to start with.

What We Have and What We Need to Project

Every financial planning problem involves forecasting future financial statements beginning with the next period given the results of the last period.[8,9] Only the income statement and balance sheet have to be forecast. The statement of cash flows is developed from those two without any additional projections.

Figure 16.4 shows the planner's task conceptually. The current (this) year's income statement is available, as is the ending balance sheet (which is next year's beginning balance sheet). These items are indicated by $XX in the figure. Using those as references, next year's income statement and ending balance sheet must be forecast incorporating the physical and economic assumptions made in the plan.

If the plan is for a new business, the $XXs are simply all zeros.

Planning Assumptions

We introduced the idea of an assumption briefly in the last section. At this point we'll define the concept more precisely and illustrate how it works.

⬤ Most financial planning involves forecasting changes in ongoing businesses based on **planning assumptions.**

---

8. For discussion purposes, we'll assume yearly time periods.

9. Most of the time, planning for a particular year is done toward the end of the preceding (current) year. That means planners don't have actual financial results for the current year with which to work. However, because year end is close, they generally have relatively good estimates of the year's actual results.

FIGURE 16.4

The Planning Task

INCOME STATEMENTS

	This Year	Next Year
Revenue	$XX	$?
COGS	XX	?
Gross margin	$XX	?
Expense	XX	?
EBIT	$XX	?
Interest	XX	?
EBT	$XX	?
Tax	XX	?
EAT	$XX	?

BALANCE SHEETS

	Next Year	
	Beginning	Ending
ASSETS		
Current	$ XX	$?
Fixed	XX	?
Total assets	$XXX	?
LIABILITIES		
Current	$ XX	?
Debt	XX	?
Equity	XX	?
Total L&E	$XXX	?

● A **planning assumption** is an **expected condition** that dictates the size of one or more **financial statement items.**

A *planning assumption* is some physical or economic condition that is expected to exist during the planning period. Assumptions can reflect any of the forces that influence a firm's financial results. Some things originate outside the company, like interest rates and taxes. Others come from planned management actions, like pricing or cost control. Still others come from customer behavior, like the volume response to a price change.

In general, each line on a projected set of financial statements is forecast on the basis of one or more assumptions about the business. Here's a simplified example to illustrate the idea.

EXAMPLE 16.1

This year Crumb Baking Corp. sold 1 million coffee cakes per month to grocery distributors at $1 each for a total of $12 million. The firm had year-end receivables equal to two months of sales or $2 million. Crumb's operating assumptions with respect to sales and receivables for next year are:

1. Price will be decreased by 10% in order to sell more product.

2. As a result of the price decrease, unit sales volume will increase to 15 million coffee cakes.

3. Collection efforts will be increased so that only one month of sales will be in receivables at year end.

Forecast next year's revenue and ending receivables balance on the basis of these assumptions. Assume sales are evenly distributed over the year.

Solution: There are three interrelated planning assumptions in this example. The first reflects a management action with respect to pricing, and the second defines the expected customer response to that action. Together, they establish the revenue forecast: Next year, 15 million coffee cakes will be sold at $.90 each, so total revenue will be

$$\text{revenue} = 15,000,000 \times \$.90 = \$13,500,000.$$

The third assumption is that the company's credit and collection activities will be more effective next year. This will be reflected by a decrease from two to one in the number of months of revenue that remain uncollected in accounts receivable at year end.

$$A/R = \$13,500,000/12 = \$1,125,000$$

Notice that the receivables calculation depends on all three assumptions, because it uses the revenue projection developed from the first two as well as the third assumption about the effectiveness of credit and collections.

The Procedural Approach

Financial plans are built by attacking line items one at a time starting with revenue, doing the kind of thing illustrated in Example 16.1.

The substance of financial planning is the logical translation of assumptions into the forecast figures they imply. It's important to realize that the calculations required for that translation differ, depending on the line item and the nature of the assumption. Some are very simple while others can become involved. We'll go through some more examples shortly.

The procedure moves down the income statement through cost and expense, stopping just *before* the interest expense line. Then the balance sheet projections are addressed. All the asset and liability accounts other than long-term debt and equity are forecast. At that point the planning procedure encounters a problem.

The Debt/Interest Planning Problem

● The **debt/interest** dilemma: Planned **debt is required to forecast interest**, but **interest is required to forecast debt.**

The next items needed to complete the financial statements are interest expense on the income statement and debt on the balance sheet. The problem is that each depends on the other, so a straightforward forecast is impossible.

It's important to understand the reason for this difficulty, but the explanation can be a little hard to follow. The problem is described in the following paragraphs and illustrated in Figure 16.5. Read the explanation carefully, referring to the illustration at the same time.

Start by examining Figure 16.5. $XXs imply dollar forecasts have already been made and question marks (?) indicate they haven't. Notice that on the income statement we lack a forecast of interest expense and everything below it, including earnings after tax (EAT). On the balance sheet we have forecasts for all the asset and liability accounts other than debt and equity. Notice that we do have the total liabilities and equity figure, because it's equal to total assets.

To complete the income statement, we need a forecast of interest expense. But interest is calculated by applying the interest rate to the average projected debt balance during the coming year. We know the beginning debt balance, but we have to forecast the ending figure to get an average.

Forecasting ending debt requires that we complete the ending balance sheet, which requires that we forecast ending equity. Ending equity is computed by adding the year's EAT from the income statement, less any dividends to be paid, to beginning equity.

But we don't have a forecast for EAT because we weren't able to complete the income statement without interest expense, which we don't have because we don't have a forecast for ending debt. In other words, the problem is circular. We need debt to calculate interest, but we have to have interest to calculate debt (through EAT and equity).

All this means we can't make a direct forecast of either debt or interest expense. Therefore we can't complete the financial plan with the direct line-by-line approach we've been using so far. Every financial plan runs into this technical impasse.

FIGURE 16.5

The Debt/Interest Planning Problem

INCOME STATEMENTS		BALANCE SHEETS		
			Next Year	
	Next Year		*Beginning*	*Ending*
Revenue	$XX	ASSETS		
COGS	XX	Current	$ XX	$ XX
Gross margin	$XX	Fixed	XX	XX
Expense	XX	Total assets	$XXX	$XXX
EBIT	$XX	LIABILITIES		
Interest	?	Current	$ XX	$ XX
EBT	?	Debt	XX	?
Tax	?	Equity	XX	?
EAT	?	Total L&E	$XXX	$XXX

EAT (less dividends) is added to beginning equity to arrive at ending equity, which is required to compute ending debt

Ending debt is averaged with beginning debt and multiplied by the interest rate to calculate interest expense

An Iterative Numerical Approach

The problem is solved using a numerical technique that begins with a guess at the solution. The guess is usually wrong, but it gives us a starting point from which we can work toward the correct answer.

The procedure works as follows.

1. *Interest:* Guess a value of interest expense.

2. *EAT:* Complete the income statement.

3. *Ending equity:* Calculate ending equity as beginning equity plus EAT (less dividends plus new stock to be sold if either of these exist).

● An **iterative, numerical approach** solves the debt/interest problem.

4. *Ending debt:* Calculate ending debt as total L&E (= total assets) less current liabilities less ending equity.

5. *Interest:* Average beginning and ending debt. Calculate interest by multiplying average debt by the interest rate.

6. *Test results:* Compare the calculated interest from step 5 to the original guess in step 1.

   a. If the two are significantly different, return to step 1, replacing the guess at interest with the value just calculated and repeat steps 2 through 6.

   b. If the calculated value of interest is close to the guess, stop.

Procedures like this one that find solutions to problems though a repetitive series of calculations are known as *numerical methods* or *iterative techniques*. Each pass through the procedure is an iteration. It rarely takes more than two or three iterations to arrive at an acceptable solution regardless of the initial guess. An example will make the method clear.

EXAMPLE 16.2

The following partial financial forecast has been done for Graybarr Inc. Complete the financial plan, assuming that Graybarr pays interest at 10% and has a flat income tax rate of 40% including federal and state taxes. (We'll generally assume a simple, flat tax rate in our examples.) Also assume no dividends are to be paid and no new stock is to be sold.

Financial Plan for Graybarr Inc. ($000)

INCOME STATEMENTS		BALANCE SHEETS		
			Next Year	
	Next Year		Beginning	Ending
Revenue	$10,000	ASSETS		
Cost/Expense	9,000	Total assets	$1,000	$3,000
EBIT	$ 1,000	LIABILITIES		
Interest	?	Current Liabilities	$ 300	$ 700
EBT	?	Debt	100	?
Tax	?	Equity	600	?
EAT	?	Total L&E	$1,000	$3,000

Solution:
First notice that we're assuming a rather large growth rate in this illustration. Graybarr's assets are forecast to triple in one year. That's possible, but unusual. In this case, it will cause the company's debt to increase rather dramatically in the coming year.

We'll complete the forecast using the procedure outlined above, considering each step in turn.

1. *Guess at interest:* In most practical situations, the interest paid last year makes a good starting guess for next year's interest. Since we don't have that here, we'll make an arbitrary guess of $200,000.

The forecast is completed in the next three steps. We'll display the result now, and then show the detail of steps 2 through 4. The bottom of the income statement and the liabilities and equity portion of the balance sheet based on our interest guess are as follows.

First Iteration ($000)

EBIT	$1,000	LIABILITIES & EQUITY		
Interest	200	Current Liabilities	$ 300	$ 700
EBT	$ 800	Debt	100	1,220
Tax	320	Equity	600	1,080
EAT	$ 480	Total L&E	$1,000	$3,000

The following steps get us to this result.

2. *Compute EAT:* Assuming interest expense of $200,000, EAT is $480,000 calculated as follows.

EBIT	$1,000,000
Interest	200,000
EBT	$ 800,000
Tax (@ 40%)	320,000
EAT	$1,480,000

3. *Ending equity:* Ending equity is beginning equity plus EAT less dividends, which in this case are zero.

Beginning equity	$ 600,000
EAT	480,000
Ending equity	$1,080,000

4. *Ending debt:* Ending debt is total L&E less ending equity less ending current liabilities.

Total L&E	$3,000,000
Ending equity	(1,080,000)
Current liabilities	(700,000)
Ending debt	$1,220,000

At this point we have a set of financial statements based on our guess at interest expense. Next we test to see whether the calculated debt and the implied interest are consistent with that guess.

5. *Interest:* The interest implied by our calculated debt is the product of average debt and the interest rate.

$$\frac{\text{average}}{\text{debt}} \times \frac{\text{interest}}{\text{rate}} = \frac{\$100,000 + \$1,220,000}{2} \times .10 = \$66,000$$

6. *Test results:* Our next step is to test the calculated interest from step 5 against the original guess. As is usually the case, the two aren't very close. The original guess of $200,000 is much higher than the calculated interest of $66,000.

We begin the next iteration of the procedure by using the calculated interest figure ($66,000) in place of the guess. Verify that steps 2 through 4 result in the following figures (rounded to the nearest thousand dollars).

Second Iteration ($000)

EBIT	$1,000	LIABILITIES & EQUITY		
Interest	66	Current Liabilities	$ 300	$ 700
EBT	$ 934	Debt	100	1,140
Tax	374	Equity	600	1,160
EAT	$ 560	Total L&E	$1,000	$3,000

Given these results, average debt is

$$\frac{\$100,000 + \$1,140,000}{2} = \$620,000$$

and interest is

$$\$620,000 \times .10 = \$62,000.$$

Thus, the second guess and the calculated result are off by only $4,000 out of $62,000.

As an exercise, demonstrate that one more iteration gives a result that's accurate to within a thousand dollars with interest of $62,000 and ending debt of $1,143,000.

PLANS WITH SIMPLE ASSUMPTIONS

Financial plans can be constructed roughly or with great precision. The difference lies in the amount of thought and detail put into the assumptions on which the plans are based. A rough plan is based on just a few assumptions about the future, while a detailed plan can involve a great many. In this section we'll look into creating a financial plan for an existing business in simple, rough terms.

The Quick Estimate Based on Sales Growth

Percentage of sales methods assume most financial statement line items **vary directly** with **revenues**.

The *percentage of sales method* is a simple, approximate approach to forecasting financial statements for an existing business. The method involves estimating the company's sales growth rate, and assuming that all income statement and balance sheet line items grow at the same rate. The technique implicitly assumes that the firm's efficiency and all of its operating *ratios* (Chapter 3) stay the same through the growth period.

from the CFO

   The assumption that everything varies proportionately with (grows at the same rate as) sales is an oversimplification that's of theoretical interest, but isn't usually applicable in practice. Most of the time, the method is modified to assume that most, but not all, things vary directly with sales. We'll call such an approach the **modified percentage of sales method**. Here's an example.

EXAMPLE 16.3

The Overland Manufacturing Company expects next year's revenues to increase by 15% over this year's. The firm has some excess factory capacity, so no new fixed assets beyond normal replacements will be needed to support the growth. This year's income statement and ending balance sheet are estimated as follows.

Overland Manufacturing Company This Year ($000)

INCOME STATEMENT		BALANCE SHEET	
Revenue	$13,580	ASSETS	
COGS	7,470	Cash	$ 348
Gross margin	$ 6,110	Accounts receivable	1,698
Expense*	3,395	Inventory	1,494
EBIT	$ 2,715	Current assets	$3,540
Interest	150	Net fixed assets	$2,460
EBT	$ 2,565	Total assets	$6,000
Tax	1,077	LIABILITIES & EQUITY	
EAT	$ 1,488	Accounts payable	$ 125
*Includes marketing, engineering, and administration.		Accruals	45
		Current Liabilities	$ 170
		Debt	$1,330
		Equity	4,500
		Total L&E	$6,000

   Assume the firm pays state and federal income taxes at a combined flat rate of 42%, borrows at 12% interest, and expects to pay no dividends.

Project next year's income statement and balance sheet by using the modified percentage of sales method.

Solution: In this problem we'll grow everything except net fixed assets by 15%. That means we'll multiply the following items by 1.15: revenue, COGS, expense, all current assets, and all current liabilities. Then we'll hold net fixed assets constant because of the assumption that the firm has excess capacity, and will just replace equipment that wears out. The result is reflected in the following incomplete statements.

Incomplete Statements for Next Year ($000)

INCOME STATEMENT		BALANCE SHEET	
Revenue	$15,617	ASSETS	
COGS	8,591	Cash	$ 400
Gross margin	$ 7,026	Accounts receivable	1,953
Expense*	$ 3,904	Inventory	1,718
EBIT	$ 3,122	Current assets	$4,071
Interest	$ —	Net fixed assets	$2,460
EBT	$ —	Total assets	$6,531
Tax	$ —	LIABILITIES & EQUITY	
EAT	$ —	Accounts payable	$ 144
*Includes marketing, engineering, and administration.		Accruals	$ 52
		Current Liabilities	$ 196
		Debt	$ —
		Equity	$ —
		Total L&E	$6,531

At this point we're at the debt/interest impasse. To complete the projection, we have to guess at interest and work through the procedure illustrated in the last section. This time, however, we have last year's interest of $150,000 to use as a starting guess. That and Overland's other projected figures result in the following first iteration.

Debt/Interest Calculation—First Iteration ($000)

INCOME STATEMENT		BALANCE SHEET		
	Next Year		This Year	Next Year
EBIT	$3,122	Total assets	$6,000	$6,531
Interest	150	LIABILITIES & EQUITY		
EBT	$2,972	Current Liabilities	$ 170	$ 196
Tax	$1,248	Debt	$1,330	$ 111
EAT	$1,724	Equity	$4,500	$6,224
		Total L&E	$6,000	$6,531

Taking the average debt at 12% yields a calculated interest of approximately $86,000, which is considerably less than the $150,000 assumed. Two more iterations yield the following complete financial projection.

Overland Manufacturing Company Next Year ($000)

INCOME STATEMENT		BALANCE SHEET	
Revenue	$15,617	ASSETS	
COGS	8,591	Cash	$ 400
Gross margin	$ 7,026	Accounts receivable	1,953
Expense*	3,904	Inventory	1,718
EBIT	$ 3,122	Current assets	$4,071
Interest	84	Net fixed assets	$2,460
EBT	$ 3,038	Total assets	$6,531
Tax	1,276	LIABILITIES & EQUITY	
EAT	$ 1,762	Accounts payable	$ 144
*Includes marketing, engineering, and administration.		Accruals	52
		Current liabilities	$ 196
		Debt	$ 73
		Equity	6,262
		Total L&E	$6,531

Forecasting Cash Needs

Recall that a key reason for doing financial projections is to forecast the firm's external financing needs. We can observe that need quickly in the preceding example by comparing Overland's beginning and ending debt balances for the forecast year. If the balance increases, the plan implies the firm will need more cash than it is generating through operations, and will have to borrow more. A decrease in debt implies that cash will be generated beyond the firm's immediate needs, so debt can be paid down.[10] In this example, Overland is planning to generate $1,255,000 in cash, enough to pay down its debt from $1,330,000 to $73,000.

When a plan shows increasing debt, the implication is that additional external financing will be needed during the forecast year. Of course, the funds could be acquired by selling additional stock (equity) rather than borrowing. That would be reflected as an increase in the ending equity account beyond the addition of EAT to retained earnings, which in turn would reduce the amount of ending debt required to balance the balance sheet.

● THE PERCENTAGE OF SALES METHOD—A FORMULA APPROACH

In Example 16.3 we used a modified percentage of sales method to create a financial projection based on an assumed growth in revenue and a separate assumption about fixed assets. If we're willing to assume that net fixed assets also grows proportionately with revenue, the percentage of sales method can be condensed into a single formula for the purpose of estimating external funding requirements. We'll call the formula the *EFR* relationship for *external funding requirement*.

---

10. A negative figure for ending debt is possible and implies that cash will be generated beyond the firm's beginning debt level.

The idea behind the EFR relationship is very simple: A growing firm must have enough money on hand to purchase the new assets it needs to support its growth. However, that funding requirement is reduced by two automatic sources, (1) the amount by which current liabilities grow[11] and (2) the amount the firm earns during the year but doesn't pay out in dividends.[12] In other words, for the year being planned (next year):

(16.1)

$$\begin{array}{l} \text{growth in assets} \\ - \text{ growth in current liabilities} \\ \underline{- \text{ current earnings retained}} \\ = \text{ external funding requirement} \end{array}$$

Expression 16.1 is true for any financial projection, but can be written in simple terms when sales, earnings, assets, and current liabilities are all assumed to grow at the same rate, which we'll call g.

We generally define g in terms of sales growth. That is,

$$g = \frac{\text{increase in sales}}{\text{sales}_{\text{this year}}}.$$

For example, if this year's sales are \$100,000 and next year's are projected to be \$115,000, g = .15 or 15%.

In terms of expression 16.1, the assumption that assets and current liabilities grow at rate g means

(16.2) $$\text{growth in assets} = g \times \text{assets}_{\text{this year}}$$

and

(16.3) $$\text{growth in current liabilities} = g \times \text{current liabilities}_{\text{this year}}.$$

To develop an expression for current earnings retained in terms of profits and dividends, begin by recalling the expression for return on sales (ROS) (Chapter 3, page 83).

$$\text{ROS} = \frac{\text{EAT}}{\text{sales}}$$

Solve for EAT in terms of ROS and sales.

$$\text{EAT} = \text{ROS} \times \text{sales}$$

Notice that since we're assuming both EAT and sales grow at the same rate, ROS will remain constant from year to year. Then next year's EAT can be written as the constant ROS times next year's sales, which are just $(1 + g)$ times this year's sales. So

(16.4) $$\text{EAT}_{\text{next year}} = \text{ROS} \times (1 + g)\text{sales}_{\text{this year}}.$$

● The **EFR** relationship provides an **estimate of funding** needs assuming all financial items **vary directly** with sales.

---

11. Current liabilities are said to provide spontaneous financing, because they reflect the acquisition of assets that don't have to be paid for immediately. We examined this idea in more detail in our discussion on working capital in Chapter 15.

12. In the *unmodified* percentage of sales method, we shortcut the iterative debt/interest procedure by assuming EAT grows at the same rate as sales. This is equivalent to assuming that the return on sales ratio (ROS) stays constant.

Next write the *dividend payout ratio,* which is defined as the ratio of dividends paid to EAT.

$$d = \frac{\text{dividends}}{\text{EAT}}$$

From that definition, earnings (EAT) are split between those paid out as dividends, d(EAT), and those retained, $(1 - d)$EAT. We can call $(1 - d)$ the *earnings retention ratio.*

For next year,

$$\text{current earnings retained} = (1 - d)\text{EAT}_{\text{next year}}.$$

Substituting for $\text{EAT}_{\text{this year}}$ from expression 16.4 yields

(16.5) current earnings retained $= (1 - d)\text{ROS} \times (1 + g)\text{sales}_{\text{this year}}.$

Now, to get the EFR relation, rewrite expression 16.1 as an equation, substituting from 16.2, 16.3, and 16.5.

$$\text{EFR} = g(\text{assets}_{\text{this year}})$$

(16.6) $$- \; g(\text{current liabilities}_{\text{this year}})$$

$$- \; [(1 - d)\text{ROS}][(1 + g)\text{sales}_{\text{this year}}]$$

Although equation 16.6 looks messy, it's easy to use because everything on the right side comes from this year's financial statements and the growth rate assumption.

EXAMPLE 16.4

Reforecast the external financing requirements of the Overland Manufacturing Company of Example 16.3, assuming net fixed assets and EAT grow at the same 15% rate as sales. However, also assume the firm plans to pay a dividend equal to 25% of earnings next year.

Solution: First note Overland's sales, assets, and current liabilities for this year (page 553) as well as its payout ratio. Then calculate its return on sales. (Omit $000 as before.)

$$\text{sales}_{\text{this year}} = \$13,580$$

$$\text{assets}_{\text{this year}} = \$6,000$$

$$\text{current liabilities}_{\text{this year}} = \$170$$

$$d = 25.0\%$$

$$\text{ROS} = \frac{\text{EAT}}{\text{sales}} = \frac{\$1,488}{\$13,580} = 11.0\%$$

Next write equation 16.6 and substitute.

$$\text{EFR} = g(\text{assets}_{\text{this year}})$$

$$- \; g(\text{current liabilities}_{\text{this year}})$$

$$- \; [(1 - d)\text{ROS}][(1 + g)\text{sales}_{\text{this year}}]$$

$$\text{EFR} = .15(\$6,000) - .15(\$170)$$

$$- [(1 - .25)(.11)][(1.15)(\$13,580)]$$

$$\text{EFR} = -\$413.9$$

This result says that Overland will generate enough funds during the projected year to reduce its debt by about $414,000. As an exercise, compare this with the result in Example 16.3 and identify where the differences come from.

It's important to keep in mind that the EFR approach and the related unmodified percentage of sales method are of limited value because of the general impracticality of the assumption that everything varies directly with sales.

THE SUSTAINABLE GROWTH RATE

A firm's **sustainable growth rate** is a theoretical measure of its strength. It is the rate at which the firm can grow if none of its financial ratios change and if it doesn't raise any new equity by selling stock. These conditions are equivalent to the assumptions of the unmodified percentage of sales method.

Sustainable growth is simply the growth in equity created by profits. We can develop an expression for the rate by noticing that business operations create new equity equal to the amount of current earnings retained. In the last section we showed that to be equal to

$$(1 - d)\text{EAT} ,$$

where d is the dividend payout ratio.

This implies a sustainable growth rate in equity, g_s, equal to the amount of new equity created divided by equity itself.

(16.7a)
$$g_s = \frac{\text{EAT}(1 - d)}{\text{equity}},$$

from which

(16.7b)
$$g_s = \text{ROE}(1 - d)$$

because ROE = EAT/equity.

Notice that although the idea of sustainable growth implies that no new equity is raised through the sale of stock, it does require new borrowing to keep the debt/equity ratio constant as equity grows through retaining earnings.

> A firm can grow at its **sustainable growth rate** without selling new stock if its financial ratios remain constant.

The value of the sustainable growth concept is largely theoretical. It gives an indication of the determinants of a firm's inherent growth capability. Recall from our study of Du Pont equations (Chapter 3, pages 85–87) that ROE can be written as

$$\text{ROE} = \text{ROS} \times \text{total asset turnover} \times \text{equity multiplier}.$$

Substituting this expression for ROE into 16.7b, we have

$$g_s = (1 - d)[\text{ROS} \times \text{total asset turnover} \times \text{equity multiplier}],$$

which can be written more explicitly as

(16.8)
$$g_s = (1 - d) \times \frac{\text{EAT}}{\text{sales}} \times \frac{\text{sales}}{\text{assets}} \times \frac{\text{assets}}{\text{equity}} .$$

Equation 16.8 says a firm's ability to grow depends on four fundamentals:

1. Its ability to earn profits on sales as measured by its ROS (EAT/sales)

2. Its talent at using assets to generate sales as measured by its total asset turnover (sales/assets)

3. Its use of leverage (borrowed money) as measured by the equity multiplier (assets/equity)

4. The percentage of earnings it retains as measured by $(1 - d)$, the earnings retention ratio

These ideas can be used to analyze why a particular firm's growth has been good or bad in relation to that of other firms. For example, after having lower than average growth, Slowly Inc. might compare its sustainable growth rate with an industry average as follows.

	g_s	=	$(1 - d)$	×	ROS	×	total asset turnover	×	equity multiplier
Industry	13.5%		.75		6%		1.2		2.5
Slowly Inc.	4.8%		.40		8%		1.0		1.5

Notice that Slowly's sustainable growth rate is much lower than the average. The question is why. The comparison immediately shows that profitability is not the problem, as Slowly's ROS is better than average. It's also apparent that total asset turnover is a bit low, but not enough to make much difference.

Slowly's growth problem seems to be associated with its modest use of leverage. The firm's equity multiplier is substantially lower than average, meaning it is financed with proportionately less debt and more equity than other firms. Its *earnings retention ratio*, $(1 - d)$, is also lower than average.

These things may explain why the firm isn't growing rapidly. It's paying most of its earnings out in dividends rather than reinvesting them in growth opportunities. At the same time, it's constrained not to raise much money by borrowing. This is a low-risk strategy but it doesn't lead to rapid growth.

● PLANS WITH MORE COMPLICATED ASSUMPTIONS

The percentage of sales methods (modified and unmodified) are appropriate for quick estimates, but aren't generally used in formal plans because they gloss over too much detail.

It's usually possible to make intelligent estimates of a large number of individual items within a financial plan. Putting those separate pieces of intelligence into the projections clearly makes sense. That's done by incorporating a series of detailed assumptions into the process. Each assumption is worked into the plan in a manner that depends on the way the related item is managed and on its accounting treatment. As an illustration, let's take a closer look at the treatment of fixed assets for the Overland Manufacturing Company of Example 16.3.

In that example we made the assumption that the firm had excess factory capacity, which implied that a certain amount of growth could be accommodated in the plant without adding new assets. Hence net fixed assets could be expected to remain roughly constant. That assumption is reasonable but somewhat simplistic. It would rarely be used in a serious operating plan.

Fixed asset accounts reflect the kinds of things we studied under the topic of capital budgeting. Such items require the commitment of large amounts of

● **Real plans** generally incorporate **complex assumptions** about important financial items.

money, and tend to be analyzed very carefully. That means a great deal of information about fixed assets is usually available.

In fact, the business planning process generally includes a *capital plan*, a list of the assets and projects on which the firm intends to spend money during the coming period.

In the next example, we'll assume a capital plan has been done for Overland, and show how some of the information it contains can be worked into the financial plan.

EXAMPLE 16.5

Assume the following for the Overland Manufacturing Company of Example 16.3.

1. The ending balance sheet for the current year contains the following fixed asset accounts.

Gross	$5,600,000
Accumulated depreciation	(3,140,000)
Net	$2,460,000

2. Next year's depreciation on the assets owned at the end of this year is $450,000, and there are no plans to dispose of old assets.

3. The capital plan indicates that assets will be acquired next year at an estimated total cost of $1.2 million.

4. The average depreciation life of the new equipment will be five years. Straight line depreciation will be used. Assume one-half year of depreciation will be taken on new assets in the first year to reflect less than a full year's use.

Notice that items 1 and 2 are not planning assumptions. They're financial facts available from the company's accounting records. Items 3 and 4 are planning assumptions summarizing the information contained in Overland's capital plan.

Forecast Overland's fixed asset accounts for next year.

● **Fixed assets** are forecast by projecting the **gross** account using the **capital plan** and handling **depreciation** separately.

Solution: Gross fixed assets will grow by the amount of new capital expenditures.

Beginning gross fixed assets	$5,600,000
Planned additions	1,200,000
Ending gross fixed assets	$6,800,000

Depreciation during the year will come from two sources, the old assets already on board at the beginning of the year and the new additions. We've already established that the old depreciation will be $450,000. New depreciation based on the five-year/straight line assumption factored down by one half for a partial year of service is

$$\text{depreciation on new assets} = \frac{\$1,200,000}{5} \times \frac{1}{2} = \$120,000.$$

Then total depreciation next year is as follows.

Old assets	$450,000
New assets	120,000
Total	$570,000

With this information, the balance sheet fixed asset accounts at year end are forecast as follows. (Review the accounting for fixed assets, Chapter 2, pages 31–33 if necessary.)

	Actual Beginning	Planned Additions	Planned Ending
Gross	$5,600,000	$1,200,000	$6,800,000
Accumulated depreciation	(3,140,000)	(570,000)	(3,710,000)
Net	$2,460,000	$ 630,000	$3,090,000

It's important to notice that this approach produces the following fixed-asset-related items for the projected financial statements.

1. The year-end balance sheet account detail

2. An estimate of the use of cash for capital spending for the cash flow statement

3. An estimate of total depreciation for the income statement and the cash flow statement

The approach in Example 16.3, on the other hand, gave us no information beyond the net fixed asset figure, which was not very accurate.

Two Kinds of Planning Assumption—Direct and Indirect—Management by Ratios

> **Indirect** planning assumptions are made about financial **ratios,** which in turn lead to line item values.

A financial planning assumption can be made directly about the financial item to which it's related or indirectly about a derivative of the item, usually a ratio. In Example 16.5 we made direct assumptions about capital expenditures to forecast items related to fixed assets.

An indirect planning assumption is usually based on the use of financial ratios. Instead of forecasting a particular item, we forecast a related ratio. Accounts receivable is a good example. Managers generally think of receivables in terms of the average time it takes to collect cash from customers rather than in terms of the magnitude of the receivables account on the balance sheet. In other words, receivables are managed through the average collection period (ACP) ratio. (See Chapters 3 and 15, pages 78 and 518.) This means that financial planning assumptions about receivables tend to be made in terms of the ACP. Projected statements are then put together using receivables balances calculated from those assumptions.

EXAMPLE 16.6

The Mylar Corporation currently has receivables of $1.2 million on revenues of $7.2 million for an ACP of 60 days calculated as follows.

$$ACP = \frac{A/R}{\text{average daily sales}}$$

$$= \frac{A/R}{\text{sales}} \times 360 = \frac{\$1.2M}{\$7.2M} \times 360 = 60 \text{ days}$$

A review of individual accounts has revealed that there are no very old or plainly uncollectible accounts in the receivables balance.

Management feels that a 60-day ACP represents unacceptably slow payment by customers, and plans to tighten credit and collection policy enough to reduce it to 40 days in the coming year. Next year's revenue projection reflects a growth of approximately 10% to $7.9 million after consideration of the credit and collections policy change.

What balance sheet figure for receivables should be included in the financial plan to reflect this assumption about ACP?

● **Accounts receivable** are generally forecast by making an assumption about the **ACP** and calculating the implied balance.

Solution:
The indirect planning assumption is that the ACP will be 40 days next year. To put together a financial plan consistent with that assumption, we calculate the year-end receivables balance that results in a 40-day ACP. Begin by rewriting the ACP formula.

$$\text{ACP} = \frac{\text{A/R}}{\text{sales}} \times 360$$

Then substitute next year's figures, treating A/R as an unknown.

$$40 \text{ days} = \frac{\text{A/R}}{\$7,900,000} \times 360$$

Solve this expression for the A/R balance implied by the ACP assumption.

$$\text{A/R} = \$877,777.[13]$$

A COMPREHENSIVE EXAMPLE—A COMPLEX PLAN FOR AN EXISTING BUSINESS

In this section we'll take an ongoing business and make a projection for next year based on a fairly broad set of assumptions. Notice that most of the assumptions are based on changes from last year.

---

13. In practice, the calculation would usually be somewhat more complicated. Most people calculate ACPs on the basis of an average A/R balance over the year using the following formula.

$$\text{ACP} = \frac{(\text{beginning A/R} + \text{ending A/R})/2}{\text{sales}} \times 360$$

Next year's beginning A/R balance is this year's ending balance, $1.2 million in this case. Substituting yields

$$40 \text{ days} = \frac{(\$1,200,000 + \text{ending A/R})/2}{\$7,900,000} \times 360,$$

From which

$$\text{ending A/R} = \$555,556.$$

Notice that this figure is unrealistically low because of the inclusion of the high ending balance from last year. If the ACP calculation is based on average A/R balances, the target ACP should be raised in a transitional year to reflect that fact. In this case, a 50-day target over the entire year would be appropriate to get the firm operating at a 40-day level by year end.

EXAMPLE 16.7

The Macadam Company is developing its annual plan for next year. The company expects to finish this year with the following financial results.

Macadam Company Income Statement This Year ($000)

	$	%
Revenue	$14,200	100.0
COGS	7,810	55.0
Gross margin	$ 6,390	45.0
Expenses		
Marketing	$ 2,556	18.0
Engineering	1,065	7.5
Finance & administrative	1,349	9.5
Total expenses	$ 4,970	35.0
EBIT	$ 1,420	10.0
Interest	568	4.0
EBT	$ 852	6.0
Income tax	341	2.4
EAT	$ 511	3.6

Macadam Company Balance Sheet This Year ($000)

ASSETS		LIABILITIES & EQUITY	
Cash	$ 1,560	Accounts payable	$ 716
Accounts receivable	3,550	Accruals	230
Inventory	2,603	Current liabilities	$ 946
Current assets	$ 7,713	Long-term debt	$ 4,000
Fixed assets		Equity	
Gross	$12,560	Stock accounts	6,000
Accumulated depreciation	(3,620)	Retained earnings	5,707
Net	$ 8,940	Total equity	$11,707
Total assets	$16,653	Total L&E	$16,653

(The income statement is presented with a common size statement, because certain planning assumptions are commonly based on projected percentages of revenue. See Chapter 3, pages 74–75.)

The current values of Macadam's ACP and inventory turnover ratio can be calculated from the statements. (We'll use ending balances only.)

The ACP is

$$\text{ACP} = \frac{\text{A/R}}{\text{sales}} \times 360 = \frac{\$3,550}{\$14,200} \times 360 = 90 \text{ days},$$

and the inventory turnover based on COGS is

$$\text{inventory turnover} = \frac{\text{COGS}}{\text{inventory}} = \frac{\$7,810}{\$2,603} = 3.0.$$

The following facts (not assumptions) are also available about the firm's operations.

FACTS

- Virtually all payables are due to inventory purchases, and the COGS is approximately 60% purchased material.

- Assets currently on the firm's books will generate depreciation of $510,000 next year.

- The only balance sheet accrual represents unpaid wages. Preliminary estimates indicate that next year's payroll will be about $6.1 million. Next year's closing balance sheet date will be nine working days after a payday.

- The combined state and federal income tax rate is 40%. (Assume a flat rate.)

- Interest on current and future borrowing will be at a rate of 10%.

The management team has met and agreed upon the following assumptions under which the plan will be developed.

PLANNING ASSUMPTIONS

Income, Cost, and Expense

1. During the coming year, the firm will mount a major program to expand sales. The expected result is a 20% growth in revenue. Pricing and product mix will remain unchanged.

2. The revenue growth will be accomplished by increasing efforts in the marketing/sales department. The increased expenses generated will be accommodated by planning marketing department expenses at 19% of the expanded revenue rather than the current 18%.

3. A major cost-reduction effort is under way in the manufacturing department, which is expected to reduce the *cost ratio* (COGS/revenue) to 53% from its current level of 55%.

4. The engineering department will be unaffected by the expansion in sales. Its dollar expenses will increase by normal inflation at a 4% rate over last year's level.

5. Finance and administrative expenses will need to expand to support the higher volume, but because of scale economies the expansion will be at a lower rate than the growth in sales. A target growth of 10% is planned for those expenses.

Assets and Liabilities

6. A new lock box system will reduce the cash balance by 20%.

7. The current 90-day collection period (ACP) is considered unacceptable. Increased attention to credit and collections in both finance and sales is expected to bring the ACP down to 65 days.

8. Top management feels that the firm is operating with more inventory than it needs. Manufacturing management has been challenged to increase the inventory turnover ratio based on COGS to 5.0 from its present level of 3.0.

9. The capital plan has been put together in preliminary form, and indicates capital spending of $5 million. The average depreciation life of the assets to be acquired is 10 years. Straight line depreciation will be used, and a convention of taking one-half year's depreciation in the first year will be followed.

10. Vendors are complaining because the firm pays its bills in 55 days even though most terms call for payment within 30 days. Fearing that inventory and supplies will be cut off, management has decided to shorten the payment cycle to 45 days.

11. No dividends will be paid next year, and no new stock will be sold.

Construct a financial plan for next year for Macadam based on last year's statements and these assumptions. To keep the computation simple, we'll assume all balance sheet ratios are calculated by using ending balances (not averages).

Solution: We'll begin Macadam's plan by projecting each operating line of the income statement and balance sheet. Then we'll complete those statements by iterating for debt and interest. Finally, we'll construct a projected statement of cash flows from the completed income statement and balance sheet.

Notice as we go along that each line item is handled differently. Some are very simple, while others take some calculation. We'll omit the $000 and round all results to the nearest thousand dollars for convenience.

Revenue: Our revenue forecast is based on the direct assumption of a 20% growth rate on last year's figure.

$$\text{revenue} = \$14,200 \times 1.20 = \mathbf{\$17,040}$$

Cost of goods sold (COGS): The forecast of COGS is based on an assumed improvement in manufacturing efficiency, which is reflected in an improvement (lowering) in the *cost ratio* from last year's 55% to 53% next year. The cost ratio is the ratio of COGS to revenue and appears on the COGS line of the common size income statement. Because we know next year's cost ratio as well as its revenue, we can multiply to project COGS.

$$\text{COGS} = \$17,040 \times .53 = \mathbf{\$9,031}$$

Marketing expense: Departmental expenses are frequently managed to a first level of approximation in common size terms. This implies comparing those expenses as percentages of revenue to industry averages to keep them in reasonable ranges. In this case, Macadam's top management is permitting spending in marketing to increase from 18% to 19% of sales to allow for an expanded effort in sales. The figure is easily forecast as 19% of next year's sales.

$$\text{marketing expense} = \$17,040 \times .19 = \mathbf{\$3,238}$$

Notice that this represents a very substantial growth (27%) over last year's spending in dollar terms.

Engineering expense: Engineering is a long-term development function that isn't directly related to the current year's sales. Hence there's no reason to assume it has to grow a great deal to support the marketing expansion. The assumption of a 4% growth in spending over last year just keeps up with normal inflation.

$$\text{engineering expense} = \$1,065 \times 1.04 = \mathbf{\$1,108}$$

Finance and administrative expense: Finance and administrative expenses pay for things like accounting, treasury, personnel, and executive management. These functions grow with revenue, but economies of scale tend to make them more efficient as size increases, implying that they should grow less rapidly than sales. In this case management has assumed a growth of 10%, half the rate assumed for sales.

$$\text{finance and administrative expense} = \$1,349 \times 1.10 = \mathbf{\$1,484}$$

The next line on the income statement is interest, which we can't address until we've completed the balance sheet down to debt. Therefore we'll move on to current assets at this point.

Cash: A lock box system is forecast to improve Macadam's cash management, resulting in a 20% decrease in the balance from its current level. This assumption is quite aggressive in the face of an increase in business.

$$\text{cash} = \$1,560 \times (1 - .20) = \mathbf{\$1,248}$$

Accounts receivable: Macadam manages its receivables indirectly by addressing the ACP, which it has forecast at 65 days for next year.

$$\text{ACP} = \frac{\text{A/R}}{\text{sales}} \times 360$$

from which

$$65 = \frac{\text{A/R}}{\$17,040} \times 360$$

And

$$\text{A/R} = \mathbf{\$3,077}$$

Notice that this forecast represents a decrease in A/R in spite of the planned increase in revenue, which would normally be expected to raise receivables. That's because the improvement in collections is forecast to have a bigger effect than the growth in revenue. This too is a very aggressive assumption.

Inventory: Management has assumed an improvement in inventory utilization, which is reflected by an increase in the inventory turnover ratio to 5.0 from its current level of 3.0. This (indirectly) implies an inventory level through the equation defining the turnover ratio.

● **Inventory** is generally forecast **indirectly** through the **inventory turnover** ratio.

$$\text{inventory turnover} = \frac{\text{COGS}}{\text{inventory}}$$

from which

$$5.0 = \frac{\$9,031}{\text{inventory}}$$

and

$$\text{inventory} = \mathbf{\$1,806}$$

Here again it's important to notice the aggressiveness of management's planning assumption. A 20% volume increase would normally lead to larger inventories, but this forecast is for a substantial decline due to the projected efficiency improvement.

Fixed assets: The fixed asset forecast is handled exactly as illustrated in Example 16.5. Additions and depreciation are as follows.

Gross fixed asset additions = $5,000
Depreciation
New Equipment = [$5,000/10] × 1/2 =   250
Old equipment =   510
                                                 $760

From these and the beginning balances in the fixed asset accounts, the ending balances are forecast as follows.

	Beginning	Additions	Ending
Gross	$12,560	$5,000	$17,560
Accumulated depreciation	(3,620)	(760)	(4,380)
Net	$ 8,940	$4,240	$13,180

Accounts payable: Macadam is currently slow-paying vendors in 55 days, probably to conserve cash. The practice is an abuse of most credit terms, which demand payment in 30 days, and the firm is getting a bad reputation among its suppliers. That can lead to production problems if suppliers hold up delivery. Management has decided to adjust its policy by paying in 45 days. This is still a violation of most 30-day terms, but it's less flagrant and more likely to be tolerated by vendors over the long run. Our problem is to calculate the payables balance implied by the policy.

Payables are generated almost entirely by inventory purchases, which are 60% of product cost. Hence the total amount passing through the payables account in a year is 60% of COGS. If bills are paid in 45 days, the unpaid amount at any time is 45/360 of that annual total. This thinking leads to the following calculation.

$$\text{accounts payable} = \text{purchases} \times \frac{45}{360} = .60 \times \text{COGS} \times \frac{45}{360}$$

$$= .60 \times \$9,031 \times \frac{45}{360} = \$677$$

(As an exercise, demonstrate that this year's payables balance represents a 55-day payment policy.)

Accruals: Macadam's only accrual reflects unpaid wages. Recall that the amount of such an accrual represents wages earned between the year's last payday and its closing date. (See Chapter 2, pages 34–35.) The amount can be estimated by examining a calendar to determine the ending date of the year being planned and the date of the immediately preceding payday. The period between the two dates represents the time for which wages have to be accrued. In this case there are nine working days between the two dates, which represent 1.8 (= 9/5) normal five-day workweeks. Hence the accrual must be for 1.8/52 of the total amount paid to employees in a year. Next year's annual payroll is estimated at $6,100, so the amount that will be accrued is

$$\text{accruals} = \$6,100 \times \frac{1.8}{52} = \$211.\text{[14]}$$

---

14. In practice, accrual calculations tend to be more complex than this. Firms often have different payrolls for different types of employees, and everyone isn't always fully paid off as of payday. In addition, a number of things besides wages are generally accrued.

This completes the forecast of the operating items in Macadam's income statement and balance sheet. To complete those statements we have to go through the iterative procedure illustrated previously to determine debt and interest. That's readily accomplished by starting with this year's interest as a guess for next year. Three iterations result in the statements below. The figures that come from the iterative procedure are shown in italics.

Notice the side-by-side (comparative) format in which the statements are presented. This year and next year are shown together for both statements, and a common size presentation is included for the income statement. This format is highly recommended for planning work because it makes it easy to work with the year-to-year changes that are the essence of most planning exercises.

Macadam Company Projected Income Statement ($000)

	This Year		Next Year	
	$	%	$	%
Revenue	$14,200	100.0	$17,040	100.0
COGS	7,810	55.0	9,031	53.0
Gross margin	$ 6,390	45.0	$ 8,009	47.0
Expenses				
Marketing	$ 2,556	18.0	$ 3,238	19.0
Engineering	1,065	7.5	1,108	6.5
Finance & administrative	1,349	9.5	1,484	18.7
Total expenses	$ 4,970	35.0	$ 5,830	34.2
EBIT	$ 1,420	10.0	$ 2,179	12.8
Interest	568	4.0	485	2.8
EBT	$ 852	6.0	$ 1,694	10.0
Income tax	341	2.4	678	4.0
EAT	$ 511	3.6	$ 1,016	6.0

Macadam Company Projected Balance Sheet ($000)

ASSETS	This Year	Next Year	LIABILITIES & EQUITY	This Year	Next Year
Cash	$ 1,560	$ 1,248	Accounts payable	$ 716	$ 677
Accounts receivable	3,550	3,077	Accruals	230	211
Inventory	2,603	1,806	Current liabilities	$ 946	$ 888
Current assets	$ 7,713	$ 6,131	Debt	$ 4,000	$ 5,700
Fixed assets			Equity		
Gross	$12,560	$17,560	Stock	$ 6,000	$ 6,000
Accumulated			Retained		
depreciation	(3,620)	(4,380)	earnings	5,707	6,723
Net	$ 8,940	$13,180	Total equity	$11,707	$12,723
Total assets	$16,653	$19,311	Total L&E	$16,653	$19,311

Macadam's financial plan is completed by constructing a projected statement of cash flows. That is readily done by using the procedures we studied in Chapter 3. No new projecting is required because the cash flow statement comes entirely from the income statement and balance sheet, which have already been forecast. The comparative format we're using makes constructing a cash statement particularly convenient. We begin with a summary of the planned changes in working capital items.

Macadam Company Projected Changes in Working Capital ($000)

	Beginning	Ending	Change
Accounts receivable	$3,550	$3,077	$ 473
Inventory	2,603	1,806	797
Accounts payable	716	677	(39)
Accruals	230	211	(19)
Decrease/(increase) in working capital	$5,207	$3,995	$1,212

The projected statement of cash flows follows immediately.

Macadam Company Projected Statement of Cash Flows ($000)

OPERATING ACTIVITIES

EAT	$1,016
Depreciation	760
Decrease in working capital	1,212
Cash from operating activities	$2,988

INVESTING ACTIVITIES

Increase in gross fixed assets	($5,000)
Cash from investing activities	($5,000)

FINANCING ACTIVITIES

Increase in debt	$1,700
Cash from investing activities	$1,700
NET CASH FLOW	($312)

RECONCILIATION

Beginning cash	$1,560
Net cash flow	(312)
Ending cash	$1,248

● PLANNING AT THE DEPARTMENT LEVEL

The financial plan we developed for the Macadam Company in Example 16.7 includes an income statement that shows the total expenses of three major departments: marketing, engineering, and finance/administration.

It's important to understand that in operational plans (annual plans and quarterly budgets) projections of departmental expenses are much more detailed and complex than the single numbers appearing on the income statement. The statement numbers are simply departmental totals. They're *supported* by documentation that details the nature of the expenses and when during the planning period they'll occur.[15]

● **Departmental detail** supports the expense entries on the planned income statement.

The format for departmental detail is usually a spreadsheet with time periods across the top and expense categories down the side. In an annual plan, the time periods are usually quarterly. The idea is illustrated in Figure 16.6.

The illustration shows expense detail for a single subdepartment within the larger marketing department. Every subdepartment has such a sheet, all of which consolidate into a single detail sheet for marketing as a whole. The total expense figure in the lower right corner of the consolidated sheet must match the marketing expense figure on the plan's income statement.

Manufacturing Departments

Spending detail in expense areas like marketing, engineering, and administration is relatively straightforward and easy to understand. In manufacturing departments, the way in which departmental plans are reflected in the income statement is quite a bit more complex.

Spending in manufacturing becomes incorporated in the cost of product through cost accounting procedures. Money spent is absorbed into inventory and then moves onto the income statement as COGS to the extent that product is sold. Therefore a fully developed manufacturing plan must assume spending levels in factory departments, production quantities, and inventory levels at the beginning and end of the year.

FIGURE 16.6

Supporting Detail for Annual Planning at the Department Level

Department: Sales Training — Annual Plan 20x1					
Item	**1Qtr**	**2Qtr**	**3Qtr**	**4Qtr**	**Total**
Headcount	35	36	38	38	
Wages	$350K	$360K	$382K	$383K	$1,475K
Overtime	$ 78K	$ 86K	$ 38K	$ 40K	$ 242K
Travel	...	...	...	...	...
Depreciation	...	...	...	...	...
Telephone	...	...	...	...	...
Supplies	...	...	...	...	...
Advertising		...	...	...	...
⋮	⋮	⋮			⋮
Misc. Expenses	...	...	...	...	...
Total	$XXX	$XXX	...	...	$X,XXX

---

15. In a long-range strategic plan such supporting detail generally doesn't exist.

● The **cost ratio** assumption summarizes **enormous detail** in manufacturing departments.

Comparing actual manufacturing performance with plan involves breaking variations in product cost into those caused by spending differences and those caused by differences in production quantities, and comparing each with plan. The approach we've taken in the Macadam example is something of a shortcut in that we're working with the overall cost ratio, which is a top-level summary of a great deal of cost detail. The approach is an effective way for senior management to overview factory cost, but has to be backed up by analysis at the department level.

Our purpose here is to give readers an overview of planning processes. For that we can stay at the summary level implied by cost ratios as long as we understand that real business plans are supplemented with considerably more detail.

●THE CASH BUDGET

Forecasting cash is an especially important part of financial planning. Companies need to be able to predict cash balances accurately, because running out can be a complete disaster. For example, even if everything else is going well, a firm without the cash to meet its payroll is likely to fail quickly. Hence well-managed companies pay a lot of attention to cash.

● The **cash budget** is a detailed projection of **receipts and disbursements** of cash.

There are two ways to forecast cash. We've already looked at the first, which involves forecasting the income statement and balance sheet and deriving a projected statement of cash flows from those documents.

The second approach, known as **cash budgeting,** is more detailed. It involves forecasting cash receipts and disbursements on the dates they're likely to occur. Then the ins and outs are summed in each planning period, usually months, to get net cash flows.

Receipts generally come from cash sales, collecting receivables, borrowing, and selling stock. Disbursements include paying for purchases, wages, taxes, and other expenses such as rent, utilities, supplies, and outside services.

Receivables and Payables—Forecasting with Time Lags

Forecasting the collection of receivables is difficult, because it's hard to know exactly when customers will pay their bills. Some pay within the terms of sale, usually 30 days, but others lean on the trade and don't pay for 50 or 60 days. A few never pay at all.

However, firms generally have historical information on the percent of revenues that tend to be collected in each month following sales. For example, on the average a firm's collections may behave according to the following *time lagged* pattern.

Months after sale	1	2	3
% collected	60%	30%	8%

Notice that the total collected is 98%, which recognizes that on the average 2% of sales turn out to be bad debts.

Applying the pattern to each month's forecast of sales revenue lets us build up a projection of collections. Here's an illustration showing how first quarter sales might be collected.

	Jan	Feb	Mar	Apr	May	Jun
Sales	$500	$600	$700			
Collections from sales made in						
Jan		$300	$150	$ 40		
Feb			360	180	$ 48	
Mar				420	210	$56
Total collections		$300	$510	$640	$258	$56

There's an added complication if a prompt payment discount is offered. In that case first month collections are reduced to reflect some customers taking the discount.

Payables are handled similarly but with more precision, because the firm knows its own payment policy. For example, if a company pays its bills 30 days after receipt of product, it simply lags forecast inventory receipts by one month to predict disbursements. If the policy is to pay in 45 days, split the payment evenly between the first and second month after receipt.

Debt and Interest

Forecasting short-term debt and interest can be a little tricky if a company is funding current cash needs directly by borrowing, which isn't unusual. Under that arrangement the current month's interest payment is based on the loan balance at the end of the last month. But that balance changes depending on whether the month's cash flow is positive or negative. That means we have to work our way through a forecast, month by month, to calculate the interest payments.

Consider the following illustration in which interest is charged at 1% per month. Assume the forecast of everything but interest has been completed and is summarized in the first line, and that there's no debt at the beginning of the year (end of December). Interest is charged/earned on cumulative cash flow, which is debt when negative and money in the bank when positive.

	Dec	Jan	Feb	Mar	Apr
Cash flow before interest		($500)	($800)	($700)	$900
Interest		0	5	13	20
Net cash flow		($500)	($805)	($713)	$880
Cumulative cash flow at month end	0	($500)	($1,305)	($2,018)	($1,138)

Working from left to right, there's no interest payment in January, but cash flow is negative, so there's a $500 debt at the end of the month. Five dollars interest is charged on that balance in February. That adds to the month's negative cash flow making the cumulative debt $1,305. That generates $13 interest in March, which adds to that month's cumulative outflow bringing it to $2,018, and so on.

Other Items

Forecasting most other items is fairly straightforward. Payroll dates are known so wages area easy to forecast. The payment dates for interest and repayment on long-term debt are also generally easy to predict as are big disbursements for things like taxes and projects.

EXAMPLE 16.8

The Pulmeri Company's revenues tend to go through a quarterly cycle. It's now mid-March and management expects the first quarter's pattern to be repeated in the second quarter. The six-month period is as follows ($000).

	Jan	Feb	Mar	Apr	May	Jun
Revenue	$5,000	$8,000	$9,000	$5,000	$8,000	$9,000

Historically, Pulmeri collects its receivables according to the following pattern.

Months after sale	1	2	3
% collected	65%	25%	10%

No prompt payment discount is offered, and there are virtually no bad debts. The firm purchases and receives inventory one month in advance of sales. Materials cost about half of sales revenue. Invoices for inventory purchases are paid 45 days after receipt of material.

Payroll runs a constant $2.5M per month, and other expenses such as rent, utilities, and supplies are a fairly steady $1.5M per month. A $0.5M tax payment is scheduled for mid-April. Pulmeri has a short-term loan outstanding that is expected to stand at $5M at the end of March. Monthly interest is 1% of the previous month end balance.

Prepare Pulmeri's cash budget for the second quarter.

Solution: First lay out revenue and lag in collections according to the historical pattern.

	Jan	Feb	Mar	Apr	May	Jun
Revenue	$5,000	$8,000	$9,000	$5,000	$8,000	$9,000
Collections from sales made in						
Jan		$3,250	$1,250	$500		
Feb			5,200	$2,000	$ 800	
Mar				5,850	2,250	$ 900
Apr					3,250	1,250
May						5,200
Second quarter collections				$8,350	$6,300	$7,350

Next, lag inventory purchases (half of sales dollars) *back* one month from the date of sale and then lag the payment two months *forward* in two equal parts.

	Jan	Feb	Mar	Apr	May	Jun
Purchases		$4,500	$2,500	$4,000	$4,500	
Payment						
Feb			$2,250	$2,250		
Mar				1,250	$1,250	
Apr					2,000	$2,000
May						2,250
Payment for materials				$3,500	$3,250	$4,250

Next, summarize these results along with payroll and other disbursements and work through the interest charges.

Pulmeri Company
Cash Budget
Second Quarter 20x1
($000)

	Jan	Feb	Mar	Apr	May	Jun
Revenue	$5,000	$8,000	$9,000	$5,000	$8,000	$9,000
Collections				$8,350	$6,300	$7,350
Disbursements						
Materials purchases				$3,500	$3,250	$4,250
Payroll				$2,500	$2,500	$2,500
General expenses				$1,500	$1,500	$1,500
Tax payment				$ 500		
Disbursements before interest				$8,000	$7,250	$8,250
Cash flow before interest				$350	($950)	($900)
Interest				($50)	($47)	($57)
Net cash flow				$300	($997)	($957)
Cumulative cash flow (loan)			($5,000)	($4,700)	($5,697)	($6,654)

MANAGEMENT ISSUES IN FINANCIAL PLANNING

Financial plans and their use in business create a number of potential managerial problems. It's a good idea to be aware of these problems before you run into them at work.

THE FINANCIAL PLAN AS A SET OF GOALS

Example 16.7 can be used to illustrate an important practical use of a financial plan. Look back at the way the ACP and the inventory turnover ratio have been used to construct next year's financial statements, and notice the large size of the forecast improvements. In essence, the ratios and the associated balance sheet accounts are set up as *targets* to be achieved by the responsible managers.

In most companies, executive pay is part salary and part bonus. In well-managed companies, executive bonuses are tied to the achievement of measurable goals like the ACP and inventory turnover in this example. In the Macadam Company, it's quite likely that the CFO's bonus will be in some part dependent on lowering the ACP to the planned level and that the VP of manufacturing's will depend on increasing the inventory turnover ratio.

Seen in this context, the financial plan becomes a tool with which to manage the company and motivate desirable performance. It's easy to identify several bonusable features and the responsible departments in the Macadam plan:

- 20% growth in revenue—marketing/sales
- Inventory turnover—manufacturing
- 53% cost ratio—manufacturing
- ACP—finance and marketing/sales
- Reduction in vendor complaints—finance
- Control cash balance—finance

- Overall profitability and cash flow—general manager and staff VPs
- Operating departments within planned expense levels—all departments.

Inherent Conflicts

Financial plans are used as management goals all the time. A problem sometimes arises, however, when top management puts in what may be described as stretch goals. A stretch goal serves as a target toward which the organization strives, but isn't likely to be achieved.

In the Macadam example, inventory turnover is probably a stretch goal. Notice that the plan calls for a 67% improvement, from 3× to 5×. In most factories, that would be a herculean achievement in one year. Top management probably wants the organization to work hard on turnover, but doesn't really expect it to achieve the goal in a year.

A stretch goal can sometimes backfire in terms of motivation. Instead of stretching toward the goal, people may give up on it if they consider it impossible.

from the CFO

Another problem arises if someone else uses the plan and assumes it's an accurate estimate of what's going to happen in the future. To understand this issue, let's evaluate the cash flow implication of the assumption that inventory turnover will increase to 5.0.

Notice that in the statement of changes in working capital, the source of cash resulting from the decrease in inventory is $797,000. However, that's after a 20% volume increase. If there were no improvement in turnover, instead of shrinking, inventory would actually grow by $407,000 [($9,031/3) − $2,603]. That means the cash flow effect of the turnover assumption is a *source* of roughly $1.2 million.

● **Stretch goals** can lead to confusion. Is the plan a reliable prediction or an unreachable goal?

Now suppose Macadam uses the plan's cash flow projection as a basis for arranging next year's bank borrowing. If the turnover assumption doesn't come true, the firm will have understated its borrowing requirements by up to $1.2 million. That means the arrangement it makes with the bank is unlikely to provide enough cash to get it through the year.

Obviously, the CFO should take a modified plan to the bank.

● RISK IN FINANCIAL PLANNING IN GENERAL

Let's pursue this idea a little further. We'll begin by reexamining Macadam's overall plan with an eye toward judging whether it's likely to come true. In doing that, it's important to keep in mind that what a plan says about a business's future flows directly from the *assumptions* made by the planners. Therefore the impression conveyed may or may not be realistic.

Look back at Macadam's list of assumptions. Everything is marvelously positive. Revenue is going to grow by a whopping 20%, the cost of production will decrease by 2% (that's a lot in an established factory), and asset management will be terrifically successful. We have to ask ourselves if *all* of these positive things are likely to come true without any offsetting negatives. The answer is generally no.

● Stretch planning and **aggressive optimism** can lead to **unrealistic plans** that have little chance of coming true.

The situation depicted for Macadam is typical of corporate business plans. Everything is routinely forecast to improve in the future, regardless of whether recent performance has been good or bad. The positive assumptions made by managements tend to be a combination of stretch planning and what might be called aggressive optimism. This is a condition in which people allow what they want to happen to overshadow their forecast of what's likely to happen.

from the CFO

For example, suppose a business operation is planning for next year after having had sales of $100 million and profits of $6 million last year. The chances are that the performance of the organization's top management is measured primarily by growth in revenue and profit. An "A" report card might be revenue of $120 million and profit of $8 million next year. In such a situation, it is very common for top management to define its expectations about next year's performance in terms of the "A" report card. It is then likely to force the organization into a plan that shows those goals being met even if market conditions are such that they're unrealistic.

● **Top-down** plans are forced on the organization by management and are often **unrealistically optimistic.**

The practice is called **top-down planning** because top executives force a plan on the rest of the organization. Middle and lower-level managers often feel that such plans are unrealistic. The risk in financial planning is that a great many plans overstate achievable performance because of the top-down phenomenon.

Excessive optimism in business planning can be a major problem because important operating and investment decisions are based on the information in plans. If an optimistic future is projected, resources tend to be committed in ways that will take advantage of that success. If it doesn't materialize, there is generally considerable loss.

The issue can be stated another way. It's never quite clear whether a company's plan (for periods of a year or longer) is a candid statement of what's likely to happen in the future or a set of desirable goals. All plans are ultimately a little of each, but which idea predominates and the extent of the diversion between the two is generally a bit of a mystery.

Underforecasting—The Other Extreme

● **Bottom-up** plans are consolidated from lower management's inputs, and tend to understate what the firm can do.

The opposite phenomenon can also occur when people know their performance is going to be graded relative to a plan. Underforecasting sets up a goal that's easy to meet and ensures success in the future. The practice is especially common when department managers submit their expense requirements as inputs to the planning process. The philosophy is "ask for more than you need, because you won't get everything you ask for." This is especially true in operational planning where targets are set that are tied to compensation.

Bottom-up planning puts together the requests and forecasts of lower and middle management without judgment by top-level executives. Bottom-up plans have a tendency to understate achievable performance.

Underforecasting is a less serious problem in that it results in plans that are beaten by actual performance. That's a pleasant problem in comparison to significantly underperforming a widely published estimate.

The Ideal Process

● Planning ideally **combines** top-down and bottom-up processes.

Ideally the financial planning process is a combination of top-down and bottom-up elements. Healthy planning begins with a completely bottom-up pass at a plan to which top management applies its judgment in a give-and-take process. The end result is a realistic compromise that stretches the organization's abilities, but can be achieved.

from the CFO

In well-run companies, it's common for financial management to assume an important role in addressing the problem of unrealistic forecasting in either direction. Led by the CFO, the finance staff acts as a voice of reason in reviewing planning assumptions. Unrealistic assumptions should be challenged and sent back to the responsible departments for justification or revision.

Scenario Analysis—"What If"ing

Many companies address the risk issue by producing a number of plans reflecting different *scenarios,* each of which is a variation on the assumptions underlying the plan. The term "what if"ing means the same thing, analyzing what would happen if an assumption takes on one value rather than another.

In scenario analysis, assumptions can be varied singly or several can be changed at a time. In Example 16.7, Macadam's management might be concerned that the assumption of a 20% growth in revenue is too aggressive. It would then be appropriate to construct another plan based on the assumption of only a 10% growth.[16]

On the other hand, there might be concern about several issues. Then a scenario could be constructed varying all of the questionable assumptions at once. For example, the implication of lower revenue growth coupled with a less significant improvement in asset management could be investigated. This might be achieved by constructing a plan based on a 15% revenue growth, an ACP of 75 days, and an inventory turnover ratio of 4.0.

Scenario analysis gives planners a feel for the impact of their assumptions not coming true. It produces a range of values within which the important results of a plan can be expected to fall.

We talked about scenario analysis in the context of estimating cash flows for capital budgeting projects in Chapter 11 (page 359). The idea here is essentially the same, but the result is a complete financial plan rather than a single cash flow estimate.

● Some companies plan for several **scenarios** representing **variations** in their **assumptions** about the future.

Communication

Perhaps the biggest problem related to risk in planning is communication. A business unit is expected to have a financial plan that management is confident it will achieve. Holding more than a brief discussion with outsiders about how likely the plan is to come true casts doubt on management's confidence in its own ability to steer the company. As a result, a single plan tends to be published with the attendant risks we've been discussing.

● FINANCIAL PLANNING AND COMPUTERS

Today, virtually all financial planning is done with the aid of computers. It's important to understand what computers do for planning and what they don't do.

Computers make repetitive calculations easy, but don't do our thinking for us. In other words, computers help us create plans once we've made judgments about the underlying business assumptions, but they don't help us with those judgments. It's very important to realize that the heart and substance of financial planning lies in making assumptions, not in cranking out numbers. Hence computers have made us quicker planners, but not necessarily better planners.

● **Computers** make planning **quicker** and more thorough, but **don't improve the judgments** at the heart of the process.

Repetitive Calculations

Repetitive planning calculations come from two sources. One is multiyear forecasts. Calculations beyond one year tend to be repetitive of the first year's.

---

16. It's important to realize that many assumptions are interrelated, so changing one implies some change in others. This is especially true of revenue, which tends to drive the whole plan. For example, the assumption of an improved cost ratio in the Macadam example is probably partially dependent on spreading overhead over the larger production volume implied by the revenue growth assumption. Therefore changing the revenue assumption is likely to require modifying the cost ratio improvement assumption to a less aggressive figure.

INSIGHTS

Ethics   **Judgment Calls and Ethics in Business Planning**

It's common for the planning system to put financial executives in uncomfortable ethical positions. Plans are vehicles for communications to outsiders and they are usually put together by the finance department. But outside communications are ultimately the responsibility of the Chief Executive Officer (CEO). That means if the CEO doesn't like what a plan says, he can apply his "judgment" and tell outsiders something else.

Problems arise when CEOs use judgment to further their personal ends or just refuse to accept unpleasant realities. Chief Financial Officers (CFOs) get caught in the middle, because although they work for CEOs, they're supposed to have an overriding responsibility for truth and fairness in financial representations. They also have to stand up next to the CEO when the message is delivered and at least act as if they support every word.

Here's an illustration. Suppose the planning process at a division of a large corporation reveals that it's likely to lose market share and a great deal of money in the future. If the information is revealed to parent company executives in an upcoming meeting, they're likely to replace the division's president whose strategy is probably responsible for the poor performance. On the other hand, if a falsely optimistic plan is presented, the current president and his policies will continue in place, but the eventual loss is likely to be much larger.

The president plans to present the optimistic version of the plan. The division CFO feels this constitutes misleading corporate management. What is her ethical responsibility?

To appreciate this dilemma, it's crucial to understand that all plans are to some extent matters of opinion. No one cay say with certainty that the executive is proposing to lie. He's just supporting a planning position that most people would find very unrealistic if they knew all the details. The fact that it serves his own personal ends makes him suspect, but it doesn't prove he doesn't believe in the better plan. Optimistic people believe what they want to in spite of overwhelming evidence to the contrary all the time!

If the CFO refuses to go along and insists on presenting the more likely plan herself, she'll be setting up a confrontation with her boss in front of senior management. That will probably destroy her relationship with the president forever. And she may not win. Remember that the corporate managers put the president in charge because they valued his judgment above that of others. They may still do that in spite of strong evidence that he's wrong. The fact that the CFO may eventually be proven right doesn't help, because the damage will be done, and she'll be long gone by then.

On the other hand, if the CFO doesn't stand up and give her opinion, there's no doubt the unduly optimistic plan will be accepted. That will probably mean deeper losses for the company, which might lead to closing the division and laying off its employees. At that time the corporate people will probably want to know why the division's management team didn't see the problem coming.

What are the CFO's options? What would you do?

The second and more important source is changes. The normal planning process involves making a set of assumptions, developing a plan from those assumptions, and evaluating its implications. If the plan isn't satisfactory, the assumptions are changed and everything is recomputed and reevaluated. This can go on literally dozens of times until a satisfactory plan is reached.

Before the advent of computers, recomputing a plan was a time-consuming, labor-intensive process that seriously limited the number of things that could be evaluated. Today that's changed. With the help of a personal computer and spreadsheet software, any number of assumption sets can be tried quickly and easily. That's been an enormously positive development in planning.

DISCUSSION QUESTIONS

1. Ed Perez has always wanted to run his own restaurant. He worked part time in the food service business during high school and college and has worked for a large restaurant chain since graduating from college four years ago. He's now ready to open a franchised family-style restaurant. However, a large investment is required to get started. Ed has saved some money, but will also have to secure a substantial loan.

Fortunately, Ed's old college roommate, Joe Dixon, is now a loan officer with the local bank. Besides being a good friend, Joe knows that Ed is a stable, hard-working businessman and an excellent credit risk.

Ed is now meeting with Joe to apply for the loan. After exchanging pleasantries, Joe asks to see Ed's business plan. In response, Ed tells him all about the idea and shows him the written information from the franchisor, which Joe glances at briefly.

Joe listens politely, leans back in his chair, and says, "Ed, I've known you for years. I'm sure this is a great idea, and that you'll make a terrific restaurateur, but we can't even begin to consider a loan until we see a fully developed business plan that looks at least five years into the future."

a. Why is Joe (the bank) insisting that Ed prepare a business plan?

1. What will it show the bank?

   i. List some specific concerns the bank might have that a plan would answer outside of the financial section.

   ii. List several concerns that the financial plan might answer for the bank.

   iii. Why is the bank insisting on such a long planning horizon? Does that imply the bank is looking for a strategic plan?

2. What will preparing a business plan do for Ed?

   i. Before he gets started.

   ii. After he gets started.

   iii. What will he learn by doing the financial plan?

b. What kind of thinking is the bank looking for in Ed's plan? That is, should the plan be strategic or operational or short term?

2. You're the CFO of the Ramkin Company, which makes and sells electronic equipment. The firm was originally an independent business, but was acquired by the larger BigTech Inc. 10 years ago and is now operated as a division. BigTech has an elaborate planning system requiring all divisions to produce a strategic plan and an annual operating plan once a year, a budget each quarter, monthly cash forecasts, and several quick forecasts near the end of each quarter

The forecasts are done primarily by the finance department and don't require much of anyone else's time. However, the strategic plan takes a good deal of executive effort, while budgets and the annual operating plan demand a great deal of management effort at all levels.

It's eight o'clock on a morning in mid-October, and the executive team is about to start a meeting to kick off the preparation of the annual operating plan for the next calendar year. As the meeting convenes, Charlie Goget-ter, the VP of marketing, is clearly upset. He takes the floor and makes the following statement.

"I'm tired of spending all this time on these silly plans! We just finished a strategic plan in June that must've taken a month of my time while the western sales region got inself into big trouble. We also did a third quarter budget in June, and a fourth quarter budget in September. Now we're starting another plan that will probably tie up half of my sales managers' time until Christmas.

"On top of that it seems whenever we're not planning, we're putting together reviews comparing actual performance to plan. Before we were acquired by BigTech, we hardly ever planned and we did just fine! It's true we're a lot larger and more complex now, but I don't think we can spend this much time planning rather than doing!

"I suggest that the CFO (he gestures toward you) be assigned to throw together something we can submit to BigTech, and that the rest of us get on with our work."

Other members of the group to some extent share Charlie's feelings, and his comments have created some unrest among the executive team about the company's management style. Prepare a response to his state-ment and proposal. Don't rule out the possibility that BigTech is overdo-ing planning.

3. A financial plan has to be either a prediction about the future or a state-ment of goals; it can't be both. Explain this statement and comment on its validity.

4. You've just been hired as CFO of the Gatsby Corp., a new company in the high-tech computer business. Shortly after your arrival you were amazed to find that the firm does virtually no planning. An extensive business plan was put together when it was started with venture capital eight years ago, and revised when another round of funding was needed four years later. Other than on those occasions, no planning seems to have been done at all.

The firm was founded by its entrepreneur president, Harvey Gatsby, based on a new technical product he'd invented. Initial demand for the gadget was overwhelming and the firm grew rapidly if chaotically until about a year ago, when competitive devices started to affect its business. The following conditions exist today.

- Sales of the original product are beginning to decline.

- The organization seems to have a number of people and departments whose function and value aren't clear.

- The engineering department is pursuing several new developments that have commercial possibilities, but progress has been haphazard and no one seems to have thought through how any money will be made from the ideas.

- Additional funding is required to get any new products that might be developed to market. Harvey has suggested that you dust off the old business plan for another run at investors.

You feel that the company is in real danger, and that the source of the problem is that management hasn't done any real forward planning in years. In your opinion the first step toward recovery is to install a competent planning system. Write a memo to Harvey outlining your concerns and suggestions. Include:

a. The problem—why the happy chaos of the past may be about to come to an end, and what that may mean.

b. How management's approach has to change if the firm is to survive. In other words, it will have to do a good deal of forward thinking and structured planning.

c. A statement of how planning systems differ between small and larger companies.

d. The benefits Gatsby can expect to realize by planning in a careful, structured way.

e. The need for a well-defined financial plan.

5. The following issues are related to the accuracy and reliability of financial plans. Explain the process/issues related to each.

- Top-down versus bottom-up planning

- Plans as statements of goals versus plans as predictions of what's going to happen.

- Planning assumptions

- Aggressive optimism versus underforecasting

- Scenario analysis

6. Why is it important that physical assumptions precede financial results in the planning process? For example, what's wrong with assuming you want a business that sells $50 million a year earning a profit of $5 million, and then building a revenue and cost plan to fit those goals?

7. Why is planning for a new business harder than planning for an established operation? In which do you have to make more assumptions? Why? What implicit assumption provides a shortcut in one situation?

8. Briefly describe the debt/interest planning problem and the approach that leads to its solution. (Use a few brief sentences. Don't list the procedural steps or give a numerical example.)

9. How are planning assumptions reflected in projected financial statements? Is there a standard computational procedure for incorporating assumptions into planned numbers? What's the difference between simple, estimated plans and more complex, precise plans? Can a plan be precise, complex, and inaccurate at the same time? How?

10. Comment on the value of the formula (EFR) approach to estimating funding requirements. Could it create more problems than it solves?

11. Financial planning is no longer a problem in business because of the advent of personal computers. Armed with a PC and the appropriate software, anyone can do a plan for even the largest and most complicated company. Evaluate this statement.

12. You're a new member of the planning staff within the finance department at Bertram Enterprises, a large manufacturer of household goods. The firm does an annual operating plan and a long-range plan every year. You've just received a note from the CFO asking you to help him prepare for a meeting with the firm's investment bankers to discuss issuing new securities in the future. The note asks you to prepare an estimate of the company's funding needs and suggests that you "start with" the most recent annual and long-range plans. You're confused by the term "start with," since the plans clearly indicate future funding needs. What might the CFO be getting at, and how would you approach the assignment?

PROBLEMS

1. The Cambridge Cartage Company has partially completed its forecast of next year's financial statements as follows.

Financial Plan Cambridge Cartage Company ($000)

INCOME STATEMENT		BALANCE SHEET		
	Next Year		Beginning	Ending
Revenue	$17,220	ASSETS		
Cost/expenses	14,120	Total assets	$12,540	$18,330
EBIT	$ 3,100	LIABILITIES & EQUITY		
Interest	?	Current liabilities	$ 410	$ 680
EBT	?	Debt	5,630	?
Tax	?	Equity	6,500	?
EAT	?	Total L&E	$12,540	$18,330

The firm pays interest at 10% on all borrowings and pays a combined state and federal tax rate of 40%. Complete the forecast income statement and balance sheet. Begin by guessing at interest expense as 10% of beginning debt.

2. The Libris Publishing Company had revenues of $200 million this year and expects a 50% growth to $300 million next year. Costs and expenses other than interest are forecast at $250 million. The firm currently has assets of $280 million and current liabilities of $40 million. Its debt to equity ratio is 3:1. (That is, capital is 75% debt and 25% equity.) It pays 12% interest on all of its debt, and is subject to federal and state income taxes at a total effective rate of 39%.

Libris expects assets and current liabilities to grow at 40%, 10% less than the revenue growth rate. The company plans to pay dividends of $10 million next year.

a. What is the planned debt to equity ratio at the end of next year?

b. Do these results indicate a problem?

3. Larime Corp. is forecasting 20X2 near the end of 20X1. The estimated year-end financial statements and a worksheet for the forecast are shown here.

Larime Corp. Projected Income Statement ($000)

	20X1		20X2	
	$	%	$	%
Revenue	$245,622	100.0		100.0
COGS	142,461	58.0	___	___
Gross margin	$103,161	42.0		
Expenses	$ 49,124	20.0		
EBIT	$ 54,037	22.0		
Interest (12%)	9,642	3.9	___	___
EBT	$ 44,395	18.1		
Income tax (43%)	19,090	7.8	___	___
EAT	$ 25,305	10.3		

Larime Corp. Projected Balance Sheet ($000)

	20X1	20X2		20X1	20X2
ASSETS			LIABILITIES & EQUITY		
Current assets	$178,106		Current liabilities	$ 85,700	
Fixed assets	142,128		Debt	78,178	
Total	$320,234	___	Equity	156,356	___
			Total	$320,234	

Management expects the following next year.

- An 8% increase in revenue.
- Price cutting will cause the cost ratio (COGS/Sales) to deteriorate (increase) by 1% (of sales) from its current level.
- Expenses will increase at a rate that is three quarters of that of sales.
- The current accounts will increase proportionately with sales.
- Net fixed assets will increase by $5 million.
- All interest will be paid at 12%.
- Federal and state income taxes will be paid at a combined rate of 43%.

Make a forecast of Larime's complete income statement and balance sheet. Work to the nearest thousand dollars.

4. The Winthrop Company is constructing a five-year plan. The firm's ACP is currently 90 days, while its inventory turnover ratio is 3× based on COGS. The company has forecast aggressive revenue growth along with efficiency improvements in manufacturing and credit and collections as follows. (Year 0 is the current year.)

	Year					
	0	1	2	3	4	5
Revenue ($000)	$50.0	$57.5	$66.0	$76.0	$87.5	$100.0
Cost ratio	60%	59%	58%	57%	56%	55%
ACP (days)	90	70	60	50	45	40
Inventory turnover	3×	4×	5×	6×	6.5×	7×

For each planned year:

a. Calculate the COGS.

b. Calculate the A/R balance at year end.

c. Calculate the inventory balance at year end.

5. The Eagle Feather Fabric Company expects to complete the current year with the following financial results ($000).

INCOME STATEMENT		BALANCE SHEET	
Revenue	$36,100	Assets	
COGS	14,440	Cash	$ 1,000
GM	$21,660	Accounts receivable	5,000
Expenses	12,635	Inventory	2,888
EBIT	$ 9,025	Current assets	$ 8,888
Interest (11%)	625	Net fixed assets	7,250
EBT	$ 8,400	Total assets	$16,138
Tax (42%)	3,528	Liabilities & equity	
EAT	$ 4,872	Accounts payable	$ 1,550
		Accruals	530
		Current liabilities	$ 2,080
		Debt	5,598
		Equity	8,460
		Total L&E	$16,138

Forecast next year using a modified percentage of sales method assuming no dividends are paid and no new stock is sold along with the following:

a. A 20% growth in sales and a 40% growth in net fixed assets.

b. A 15% growth in sales with a 10% growth in expenses and a 20% growth in net fixed assets. (Negative debt means the business will generate more cash than is currently owed.)

6. Assume we're at the end of "this year" planning "next year's" financial statements. Calculate the following using indirect planning assumptions as indicated. (To keep the calculations simple, formulate ratios using ending balance sheet figures only.)

a. Sales are forecast to be $58,400,000. Management wants to plan for a 45-day ACP next year. What ending receivables balance should be planned for next year?

b. What ending inventory should be planned if revenue is expected to be $457,000 and the cost ratio is 53% (cost of goods sold as a % of revenue) and management wants to forecast an inventory turnover of 5×.

c. Normal credit terms from suppliers request payment within 30 days. In an effort to conserve cash, management has decided to pay in 50 days. Nearly all payables come from purchases of inventory. Materials makes up 60% of the Cost of Goods Sold. Next year's revenue is forecast to be $378 million. The firm's cost ratio is expected to be 56%. What figure should be included in next year's ending balance sheet for Accounts Payable?

7. The Dalmation Corporation expects the following summarized financial results this year ($000).

INCOME STATEMENT		BALANCE SHEET	
Revenue	$10,500	Assets	
Cost/expenses	9,100	Current assets	$ 5,500
Tax	560	Net fixed assets	6,900
EAT	840	Total assets	$12,400
Dividends	420	Liabilities & equity	
		Current	$ 320
		Debt	5,080
		Equity	7,000
		Total L&E	$12,400

Use the EFR relation to estimate Dalmation's external funding requirements under the following conditions.

a. Sales growth of 15%.

b. Sales growth of 20% and a reduction in the payout ratio to 25%.

c. Sales growth of 25%, elimination of dividends, and a 4% improvement in ROS.

8. The Bubar Building Co. has the following current financial results ($000).

Revenue	$45,000	Assets	$37,000
EAT	$ 3,600	Equity	$28,580
Dividends	$ 1,800		

On the average, other building companies pay about one quarter of their earnings in dividends, earn about six cents on the sales dollar, carry assets worth about six months of sales, and finance one-third of their assets with debt.

Use the sustainable growth rate concept to analyze Bubar's inherent ability to grow without selling new equity versus that of an average building company. Identify weak areas and suggest further analyses.

9. The Haverly Company expects to finish the current year with the following financial results, and is developing its annual plan for next year.

Haverly Company Income Statement This Year ($000)

	$	%
Revenue	$73,820	100.0
COGS	31,743	43.0
Gross margin	$42,077	57.0
Expenses		
Marketing	$17,422	23.6
Engineering	7,087	9.6
Finance & administrative	7,603	10.3
Total expenses	$32,112	43.5
EBIT	$ 9,965	13.5
Interest	2,805	3.8
EBT	$ 7,160	9.7
Income tax	3,007	4.1
EAT	$ 4,153	5.6

Haverly Company Balance Sheet This Year ($000)

ASSETS		LIABILITIES & EQUITY	
Cash	$ 8,940	Accounts payable	$ 1,984
Accounts receivable	12,303	Accruals	860
Inventory	7,054	Current liabilities	$ 2,844
Current assets	$28,297	Long-term debt	$22,630
Fixed assets		Equity	
Gross	$65,223	Stock accounts	18,500
Accumulated depreciation	(23,987)	Retained earnings	25,559
Net	$41,236	Total Equity	$44,059
Total assets	$69,533	Total L&E	$69,533

The following facts are available.

FACTS

- Payables are almost entirely due to inventory purchases and can be estimated through COGS, which is approximately 45% purchased material.

- Currently owned assets will depreciate an additional $1,840,000 next year.

- There are two balance sheet accruals. The first is for unpaid wages. The current payroll of $32 million is expected to grow by 12% next year. The closing date of the year will be six working days after a payday. The second accrual is an estimate of the cost of purchased items that have arrived in inventory, but for which vendor invoices have not yet been received. This materials accrual is generally about 10% of the payables balance at year end.

- The combined state and federal income tax rate is 42%.

- Interest on current and future borrowing will be at a rate of 12%.

The plan will be based on the following assumptions.

PLANNING ASSUMPTIONS

Income Statement Items

1. Revenue will grow by 13% with no change in product mix. Competitive pressure, however, is expected to force some reductions in pricing.

2. The pressure on prices will result in a 1.5% deterioration (increase) in the next year's cost ratio.

3. Spending in the marketing department is considered excessive and will be held to 21% of revenue next year.

4. Because of a major development project, expenses in the engineering department will increase by 20%

5. Finance and administration expenses will increase by 6%.

Assets and Liabilities

6. An enhanced cash management system will reduce cash balances by 10%.

7. The ACP will be reduced by 15 days. (Calculate the current value to arrive at the target.)

8. The inventory turnover ratio (COGS/inventory) will decrease by .5×.

9. Capital spending is expected to be $7 million. The average depreciation life of the assets to be acquired is five years. The firm uses straight line depreciation, and takes a half year in the first year.

10. Bills are currently paid in 50 days. Plans are to shorten that to 40 days.

11. A dividend totaling $1.5 million will be paid next year. No new stock will be sold.

Develop next year's financial plan for Haverly on the basis of these assumptions and last year's financial statements. Include a projected income statement, balance sheet, and statement of cash flows.

10. Lapps Inc. makes a gift product that sells best during the holiday season. Retailers stock up in the fall so Lapps's sales are largest in October and November and drop dramatically in December. The firm expects the following revenue pattern for the second half of this year ($000). The third quarter figures are actual results, while the fourth quarter is a projection.

	Jul	Aug	Sep	Oct	Nov	Dec
Revenue	$5,500	$6,000	$7,500	$8,000	$9,500	$4,000

Historically Lapps collects its receivables according to the following pattern.

Months after sale	1	2	3
% collected	60%	30%	9%

The firm offers a 2% prompt payment discount, which is taken by about half of the customers that pay in the first month.

Lapps receives inventory one month in advance of sales. The cost of material is 40% of revenue. Invoices are paid 45 days after receipt of material.

The firm uses temporary labor to meet its seasonal production needs, so payroll can be estimated at 35% of the current month's sales. Other expenses are a constant $1.8M per month. A $.7M tax payment is scheduled for November, and an expansion project will require cash of $.5M in October and $.8M in December. Lapps has a $6M short-term loan outstanding at the end of September. Monthly interest is 1% of the previous month-end balance.

Prepare Lapps's cash budget for the fourth quarter.

 Internet Problem

11. The Business Owner's Toolkit at **http://www.toolkit.cch.com/tools/tools.asp** offers a series of comprehensive training modules that will help you learn how to market, manage, promote, and grow your business. Go to the section on Business Finance and read about the Cash Flow Budget Worksheet Template. Why is it so important for businesses to prepare a cash budget monthly? What is the purpose of comparing the monthly cash budget to the actual figures reported?

PART SIX

Current Topics in Financial Management

CHAPTER 17

Corporate Restructuring

Chapter Outline

Corporate restructuring is a broad term that describes a number of the ways in which firms are reorganized. It refers to changes in capital structure (Chapter 12), changes in ownership, merging companies together or breaking them apart (divestitures), modification of asset structures, and certain changes in methods of doing business. In addition, business failure and bankruptcy usually result in some kind of restructuring.

In recent years, corporate mergers have been the most publicized restructuring activities. They occur when two or more firms combine under one ownership.

In this chapter, we'll examine several of the ways in which companies restructure, beginning with a fairly detailed look at mergers.

MERGERS AND ACQUISITIONS

Mergers are an important force in modern business. They've reshaped American industry several times in the last century, and continue to have a significant effect on companies and financial markets.

● BASIC DEFINITIONS, TERMINOLOGY, AND PROCEDURE

The terms "merger," "acquisition," and "consolidation" all mean the *combination* of two (or more) business units under a single controlling ownership. In day-to-day practice, the word "merger" is loosely used to mean any business combination, but technically each term refers to a particular type of transaction.

A **merger** is a combination of two or more businesses in which all but one legally cease to exist, and the combined organization continues under the original name of the one surviving firm. A **consolidation** occurs when *all* of the combining legal entities dissolve, and a new one with a new name is formed to continue into the future. These ideas are illustrated in Figure 17.1 for combinations involving two firms. The left side illustrates a merger of company B into company A, while the right side shows A and B consolidating into C.

The merger situation is also called an **acquisition,** because the stock of the firm that goes out of existence is usually acquired by the continuing firm. In the left diagram, A is the *acquiring firm* and B is the **target** of the acquisition. The word "takeover" is sometimes used to describe the combination, because most of the time company A literally takes over company B. That term tends to have a hostile meaning, implying that A takes over B against the wishes of B's management.[1]

An important subtlety in all this is that the size of combining companies doesn't determine the nature of the combination. As a general rule, A would be larger than B in the merger/acquisition shown on the left and the two would be about the same size in the consolidation shown on the right. However, that isn't a requirement or always the case. There are many examples of smaller firms taking over larger ones.

> ● A **merger** is loosely defined as any **combination** of two or more businesses under **one ownership.**

> ● In an **acquisition** or **takeover,** one firm acquires the stock of another called the **target.**

Relationships

It's important to understand the relationships that come about when firms join together regardless of what the combination is called legally. In one situation, firms combine willingly, more or less as equals, even if there's a difference in their sizes. This is the general situation implied by a consolidation.

http://

Visit the M&A Marketplace at

www.mergernetwork.com

for the latest developments in mergers and acquisitions.

FIGURE 17.1

Basic Business Combinations

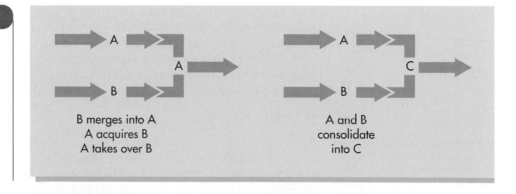

B merges into A
A acquires B
A takes over B

A and B
consolidate
into C

---

1. "Takeover" is a fairly general term, simply implying that one group takes control from another. This can occur outside of a merger if one group of stockholders takes over control from another within a single company.

In the other situation, one firm dominates the resulting relationship because it *acquires* the other's stock. That's the usual case in an acquisition or merger. The management of the acquired firm generally works for the management of the acquiring firm after the merger. It's important to note that a merger can be accomplished with the friendly approval of the acquired firm's management or against its wishes.

Stockholders

Any merger or consolidation represents a change in ownership. In the merger shown on the left of Figure 17.1, company B goes out of existence. That means its stockholders give up their shares (in B) for something else, usually either cash or stock in A. In the consolidation shown on the right, the stockholders of both A and B give up their shares for stock in C.

> ● A **majority** of the **target's stockholders** must accept the price offered by the acquiring company.

No one can force the shareholders of a corporation *as a group* into a business combination. They have to be willing to give up their shares for the price offered in the deal. In the context of an acquisition, this means that a majority of the stockholders of the target (acquired) company must approve the price offered for their shares. (If a majority approves, dissenters may be forced to go along.)

The major issue in the analysis of mergers is the value given for the shares of the companies that go out of existence. For example, consider a merger (left diagram) in which A's stock was selling for $10 a share and B's for $5 just before merger talks began. Negotiations would have to start with an offer of at least $10 or one share of A for every two shares of B. Anything less wouldn't interest B's shareholders.

The Friendly Merger Procedure

In what follows we'll be primarily concerned with the merger (acquisition) situation shown on the left in Figure 17.1. The merger process generally begins with the would-be acquirer's management contacting the target's management and proposing the deal.

> ● In a **friendly** merger the target's management approves of the deal and **cooperates** with the acquiring company.

A *friendly merger* takes place when the management (and board of directors) of the target company agrees that the combination would be a good idea and cooperates with the acquirer. In such a case negotiations between the two management groups on the price to be paid for the target's stock and other issues proceed until an agreement is reached. After that the proposal is submitted to the stockholders for a vote, with a recommendation by the target's board for approval. The percentage required for approval depends on the corporate charter and state law.

If the stockholders approve the merger, each firm files the appropriate papers with the state in which it's incorporated, cash or new stock certificates are issued to the stockholders of the acquired company, and the deal is consummated.

The Unfriendly Procedure

> ● In an **unfriendly merger,** the target's management resists and may take **defensive** measures to stop the deal.

When a target firm's management and board are opposed to a merger, they refuse to take it to their stockholders. If the acquiring firm doesn't accept the refusal, it can approach the target's stockholders directly. The merger then becomes *hostile* or *unfriendly*. Sometimes the acquiring firm doesn't even try to deal with the target's management, but approaches its stockholders immediately in an effort to take the company's management by surprise.

In an unfriendly merger, the acquiring firm makes a *tender offer* to the target's shareholders. This is a special kind of a proposal made to buy stock. It offers to

● An acquiring firm can bypass a target's management by making a **tender offer** directly to shareholders.

pay stockholders a fixed price for shares, but contains a provision stating that if the price isn't accepted on enough shares to gain control of the company, the deal is off. If the tender price is right, enough shares to gain control are offered and the acquiring firm takes over by purchasing them.

While all this is going on, the target company's management is likely to be contesting the proposal with what are known as *defensive measures*. Once an acquisition attempt is under way, these measures usually consist of efforts to convince shareholders not to sell to the acquirer. They generally have a limited effect if the price offered is fairly high. The target's management can also seek a preemptive merger with another acquirer it feels is more desirable. We'll talk more about these tactics later, along with defensive measures that managements can take before an acquirer comes along.

It's important to realize that the hostility in an unfriendly merger is between the managements or boards of directors of the two companies, not the stockholders. To most stockholders the target company is just an investment. If someone offers a high enough price for their stock, they'll sell without a second thought.

Why Unfriendly Mergers Are Unfriendly

Mergers usually come up when an acquiring company shows an interest in a target. They can be congenial affairs or outright battles between the managements of the two companies.

To understand the difference, recall that most companies are run by professional managers, *theoretically* for the sole benefit of stockholders. In fact, however, managers run companies for their own benefit *as well as* for the good of stockholders. (Recall the agency problems discussed in Chapter 1, pages 17–18.)

● A target's **management may resist** a merger in its own **self-interest** or because the price offered is too low.

There are two basic reasons why a target's management might resist a merger. One is that the deal offered by the acquiring firm doesn't give the target's stockholders enough value. The argument is that the market price of the company's stock is temporarily depressed, and the offer, which is always above the market price, doesn't represent what the stock is really worth. This reason is generally given publicly.

The other reason is more self-serving. After mergers, it's common for the managements of acquired companies to lose a good deal of power and influence. In fact, key executives of target companies often lose their jobs within a short time. This phenomenon is a great incentive to resist being acquired, especially by a company with a history of treating its acquisitions ruthlessly.

from the CFO

Economic Classification of Business Combinations

A common method of classifying mergers[2] describes the relationship between the businesses of the merging firms. This relationship is important because it helps to define the economic impact of the transaction.

VERTICAL MERGER When a firm acquires one of its suppliers or one of its customers, the merger is said to be **vertical.** The idea is that the companies are at different stages along a vertical production process from raw materials to end product. An automobile manufacturer acquiring a steel mill, or a cereal maker acquiring a grocery distributor, would be an example of a vertical merger.

---

2. In the rest of this chapter, we'll use the term "merger" loosely to mean either a merger or a consolidation.

● Merger relationships:
vertical—suppliers and customers;
horizontal—competitors;
conglomerate—unrelated.

HORIZONTAL MERGER   A merger is said to be **horizontal** if the merging firms are in the same kind of business, usually as competitors. This kind of merger has the effect of reducing competition in the industry. For example, if one maker of personal computers acquired another, the merger would be horizontal.

CONGLOMERATE MERGER   A **conglomerate merger** occurs when the lines of business of the merging companies have nothing to do with one another. If an electronics company acquires a potato chip maker, the merger is conglomerate. A company that is made up of a collection of unrelated businesses is known as a *conglomerate*.

The Role of Investment Banks

Recall that investment banks are organizations which help companies issue securities (Chapter 4, page 107). They function between investors and companies issuing securities by undertaking the sale of the securities to the investing public.

Investment banks are also instrumental in mergers and acquisitions, typically acting as advisors to acquiring companies. They generally assist in establishing a value for the target company and help the acquiring firm raise the money to pay for the target's stock when that's necessary.

Investment banks also advise reluctant targets on defensive measures.

● THE ANTITRUST LAWS

The United States is committed to the maintenance of a *competitive economy* in which most industries consist of at least a few competing firms.

A competitive economy is characterized by opportunity and fair dealing. Opportunity exists because anyone with the right resources can enter any industry and compete with established firms. Fair dealing comes from the notion that consumers are assured of reasonable treatment because no single firm can raise its prices too high without losing business to rivals.

These ideas have been endorsed by the government to a much greater extent in the United States than in other industrialized nations, and are reflected in a body of legislation known as the antitrust laws.[3]

The antitrust laws were enacted between 1890 and the 1930s and have been amended from time to time since then. Their objective is to prohibit certain activities that can reduce the competitive character of the economy.

The Antitrust Laws and Mergers

When the number of firms in an industry shrinks, the remaining firms become more powerful and competition is reduced. When that happens we say the industry becomes more *concentrated*. Because mergers combine two or more firms into a single unit, they clearly have the potential to increase concentration and reduce competition. As a result, they come under the purview of the antitrust laws.

● The **antitrust** laws prohibit mergers that significantly **reduce competition.**

It's fairly obvious that horizontal mergers combining two or more competitors have an anticompetitive effect, but vertical mergers can also be anticompetitive. They can act indirectly, doing things like locking an acquiring firm's competitors

---

3. A trust is a group of companies under a single control that acts like a monopoly. Therefore antitrust means against monopoly or against the excessive concentration of economic power.

out of sources of supply.[4] Conglomerate mergers don't generally have significant anticompetitive effects.

The antitrust laws limit the freedom of companies to merge. Proposed mergers over a certain size must be reviewed by the federal government's Justice Department, which evaluates whether or not they constitute an excessive reduction in competition. If a court decides a merger's effect is too detrimental, the merger will be blocked by the government.

THE REASONS BEHIND MERGERS

Most mergers don't turn out to be as successful as expected when they're undertaken. That poor record makes it important to take a hard, critical look at why people put companies together in the first place.

Synergies

The most persuasive reason for a merger is that for some reason the merged organization will perform better than the sum of the performances of the unmerged businesses. This means some extra value is available in the combination that can be shared by the owners of the two (or more) merging companies. This phenomenon is called **synergy**. It means that the whole is more than the sum of its parts. Here's an example.

- A **synergy** exists when performance together is better than the sum of separate performance.

Suppose one company makes lawnmowers and another makes snowblowers.[5] The lawnmower factory produces in the winter (for sale in the summer) and is idle in the summer. The snowblower plant produces in the summer (to be ready for the winter) and is idle in the winter. If these companies merge, their similarly manufactured products can be produced in one factory that operates year round, thus saving the cost of the second factory. This saving is a synergy available by combining the two businesses.

Synergies are usually cost-saving opportunities like the one we've just described. Less frequently they take the form of an enhancement of some kind. For example, suppose a breakfast cereal manufacturer with a recognized brand name acquires the maker of an unknown pancake mix. Marketing the acquired product under the cereal company's name might accelerate its success dramatically because of the recognition and acceptance accorded to the brand name.

Synergies sound good, but in practice have proven difficult to find and harder to implement.

from the CFO

Growth

- **External** growth through acquisition is usually much faster than **internal** growth.

Companies can grow either internally or externally. *Internal growth* occurs when firms get larger by selling more in current businesses or starting new ventures. *External growth* refers to getting larger by acquiring other companies.

---

4. Suppose two competing firms buy a critical input from a low-cost supplier. Then one firm acquires the supplier and refuses to sell the cheap input to the other. The second firm has to use a more expensive substitute and is forced to raise prices to cover the increased cost. This gives the first firm a price advantage that could drive the second out of business.

5. For the benefit of our southern readers, we should explain that a snowblower is essentially a power snow shovel. It operates like a lawnmower, but instead of cutting grass it throws snow off sidewalks and driveways. The parts and processes used to manufacture snowblowers are similar to those used to make lawnmowers.

External growth is much faster than internal growth. A firm can become large in its own industry by acquiring a rival much more quickly than by taking market share from others in competitive battles. Similarly, a company can get into a new industry much more quickly by acquiring a firm already in that business than by starting its own entry from scratch. The quest for rapid growth is therefore a major reason for undertaking acquisitions.

Diversification to Reduce Risk

A company that acquires other firms which aren't in exactly the same business is said to *diversify* itself. It becomes a collection of diverse businesses merged together under one control. Such a firm is generally less risky than a company in just one business when risk is defined as variation in financial performance.

The reasoning behind this phenomenon is identical to the logic that leads us to diversify a portfolio of stocks (see Chapter 8). Each business unit's performance moves up and down over time, but they don't move entirely together. Variations tend to offset, and the organization's combined performance remains fairly steady.

This kind of stability is sometimes given as a reason to justify mergers. However, it isn't obvious that the logic is appropriate in that context. In fact, a strong counterargument can be summarized as follows.

When a company acquires another firm, it effectively diversifies the portfolios of its shareholders. The acquiring company becomes a combination of what it was before and the newly acquired business, so its stockholders have an interest in both firms and are exposed to the risks and returns associated with both.

But shareholders don't need or want the firms in which they've invested to do that. Suppose A is thinking about acquiring B. If A's stockholders want to invest in B, they can just sell some shares of A and buy B. In other words, shareholders can diversify their own portfolios. They don't need or want the companies in which they've invested to do it for them.

This logic leads to the conclusion that managements diversify through acquisition to stabilize their own positions rather than their stockholders' interests.

● A firm with **diversified** operations is **more stable** than a company that does a single thing.

Economies of Scale

Horizontal mergers can lead to a larger company that produces at a lower cost than any of the merging organizations do individually. Scale economies are a variation on the synergy idea.

Guaranteed Sources and Markets

Vertical mergers can lock in a firm's sources of critical supplies or create captive markets for its product.

Acquiring Assets Cheaply

A firm in need of certain assets can sometimes get them by buying a company that already owns them. This can occasionally be cheaper than purchasing the assets alone, either new or used. It usually occurs when the target firm isn't doing well and its stock is selling below book value.

Tax Losses

A firm that's making a profit pays taxes on its earnings, but a firm that's losing money doesn't get a credit for its losses. In such a case merging the companies saves on total taxes paid. For example, consider the following possible combination of Rich Inc. and Poor Inc.

● Acquiring a firm with a **tax loss** can **shelter** the acquirer's **earnings.**

	Rich Inc.	Poor Inc.	Merged
EBT	$2,000	($1,000)	$1,000
Tax (35%)	700	-0-	350
EAT	$1,400	($1,000)	$ 650

Operating independently, Rich pays tax of $700 and Poor pays nothing for a total of $700. Merged, however, Poor's loss can offset Rich's profit *before* the tax calculation is made, so the combined company pays only $350 in tax. *However,* the IRS won't allow the offset if the primary reason for the merger is tax avoidance. There have to be other demonstrable business reasons behind the combination for the favorable treatment to be allowed.

Ego and Empire

● Critics maintain that **empire building** is behind many mergers that don't seem to make sense otherwise.

Although it's impossible to prove, powerful people at the top of large organizations sometimes seem to make acquisitions for the sake of making their empires larger. Part of the reason may be that executive pay tends to be more a function of the size of the organization managed than of its success. It is argued that the ego/empire phenomenon has led to a number of acquisitions in which the prices paid for target companies were inflated far above what the firms were reasonably worth.[6] This phenomenon is a windfall for the stockholders of the target at the expense of the acquirer's owners.

● HOLDING COMPANIES

Holding company is a general term for a corporation that owns other corporations known as *subsidiaries*. The holding company is also called the *parent* of the subsidiaries, which are legally separate companies. When one firm is acquired by another, it can be integrated into the acquirer's operations or be held as a subsidiary.

The holding company/subsidiary form of organization can be advantageous if it makes sense to keep two or more business operations separate and distinct. For example, it's generally possible to keep the liabilities of different subsidiaries separate, so the failure of one doesn't financially affect the parent or the other subsidiaries.

● **Parent** or **holding companies** own **subsidiaries** as legally separate entities.

The holding company organization has another advantage in that it can control a subsidiary without owning all of its stock. An interest as small as 10% can sometimes effectively control a widely held company in which no other single shareholder owns more than 1% or 2%. As a general rule, 25% ownership virtually guarantees control. This means that an "acquiring" company can in some ways control a target without expending the resources necessary to acquire it entirely.

On the other hand, holding companies don't make sense if the benefits of a merger depend on realizing synergies from combined operations.

Businesses acquired in conglomerate mergers are typically held as subsidiaries of a holding company.

---

6. Roll, Richard, "The Hubris Hypothesis of Corporate Takeovers." *Journal of Business,* 59, No. 2 (April 1986): 197–216.

THE HISTORY OF MERGER ACTIVITY IN THE UNITED STATES

There have been four periods of intense merger activity in the United States in the last 100 years. They're often referred to as *merger waves*.

Wave 1: The Turn of the Century, 1897–1904

● At the turn of the century a wave of **horizontal** mergers transformed the U.S. into a nation of industrial **giants.**

The mergers at the turn of the century had a profound effect on the structure of American industry. They were largely horizontal and occurred in primary industries such as mining, metals production, food products, transportation, and energy.

The first merger wave transformed the country from a nation of small companies to one of industrial giants, which were in many cases virtual monopolies. For example, U.S. Steel was formed by the combination of 785 separate companies led by Carnegie Steel. Other emerging giants included Standard Oil, Eastman Kodak, American Tobacco, and General Electric.

The mergers of the first wave were characterized by large companies absorbing small ones, sometimes by means of unfair and even violent tactics. Large firms often used their power and wealth to force smaller rivals out of business, and then bought the ruined companies at a fraction of their original worth.

Wave 2: The Roaring Twenties, 1916–1929

The second merger wave began during the First World War and ended with the stock market crash of 1929. It was fueled by postwar prosperity and the general boom climate of the 1920s. Mergers in this period also tended to be horizontal and resulted in the concentration of several industries into *oligopolies*.[7]

Wave 3: The Swinging Sixties, 1965–1969

The late 1960s was the era of the *conglomerate merger*. Companies like ITT, Litton Industries, and LTV acquired firms in totally diverse fields that had absolutely nothing to do with one another.

● Many of the **conglomerate** mergers of the 1960s were **stock market** phenomena without economic substance.

The conglomerate mergers of the 1960s were financial phenomena rather than actions driven by operating business considerations. When a large company with a high P/E ratio (see Chapter 3, page 84) acquires a smaller firm with a lower P/E ratio, paying for the target with its own stock, the result can be an increase in the earnings per share (EPS) of the merged company. If the stock market attaches the same P/E to the acquiring firm after the acquisition that it did before, its stock price will rise even though there's no expectation of improved performance by either company. This happened a great deal in 1960s and led to a large number of business combinations motivated by stock market games rather than by sound economic reasoning.

Because so much of this period's merger activity was conglomerate in nature, there was relatively little increase in concentration within industries. That is, the number of firms competing in particular industries didn't change much as a result of mergers. This was a contrast with the first two merger waves in which concentration increased substantially.

An Important Development during the 1970s

Prior to the 1970s, hostile takeovers were viewed as somewhat unethical and large, reputable companies did not undertake them. If a large firm's merger

---

7. An oligopoly is an industry dominated by a few powerful firms (as opposed to a monopoly, an industry in which there's only one seller). The automobile industry is an oligopoly.

overture was rejected by a target's board of directors, the effort was generally dropped. Further, reputable investment banks didn't participate in financing hostile takeovers.

All of that began to change in 1974 with the acquisition of ESB, the world's largest maker of batteries, by the Toronto-based International Nickel Company (INCO) assisted by Morgan Stanley, perhaps the most prestigious name in investment banking at the time.

That transaction and a few others established the *hostile takeover* as an acceptable financial maneuver.[8]

- The **hostile takeover** became an acceptable **financial** maneuver during the 1970s.

Wave 4: Bigger and Bigger, 1981–?

Merger activity slacked off somewhat during the 1970s but resumed in the 1980s, 1990s, and 2000s. This most recent period of intense merger activity has several distinguishing characteristics.

SIZE   Very large mergers have become more common, often involving the leading firms in their respective industries.

HOSTILITY   After the attitude change in the 1970s, hostile takeovers became common. The proportion of hostile actions is still small but has increased, especially at the large end of the spectrum. More important, the threat of hostile takeover now pervades corporate life. Few decisions are made at the tops of today's large corporations that don't include consideration of the risk of being taken over.

RAIDERS   The *corporate raider* emerged as a new kind of player in high finance. A raider is a financier who makes his or her living (a very good one!) by mounting hostile takeovers. Raiders can make money whether the takeover is successful or not.

DEFENSES   Defensive measures have emerged as a new field because of the prevalence of hostile takeover activity. They are things the target of a hostile takeover can do to avoid losing control. We'll discuss them in some detail later.

ADVISORS   Investment bankers and lawyers have aggressively expanded their roles as merger advisors, earning very substantial fees in the process. Indeed, they're probably responsible for instigating much of the current merger activity. They advise acquiring companies as well as reluctant targets on defensive measures.

FINANCING   The infamous junk bond market was developed by the now-defunct investment bank Drexel Burnham Lambert at least partially as a source of financing for takeovers.

Some Detail about Wave 4

It's worthwhile to be aware of a little detail about the current merger wave. Merger activity rose steadily during the 1980s, peaking at the end of the decade. It then declined in the early 1990s, probably because of the collapse of

8. For a detailed treatment of the important developments of the 1970s, see Gaughan, Patrick A. 1991. *Mergers and Acquisitions*. New York: Harper Collins.

the junk bond market in the 1989–1990 time frame. (We'll describe junk bonds and their relation to mergers in more detail shortly.) However, in the mid-1990s merger activity picked up again, especially with respect to very large transactions.

● Recent merger activity has been characterized by **very large** combinations frequently involving **industry leaders.**

The large mergers of the latest wave have some disturbing social and economic implications regarding the concentration of power and influence. The mega-mergers of the fourth wave have tended to involve major companies, often combining two or more of the top firms within an industry. Beyond the anticompetitive effect of such combinations, it's difficult to argue that they do not concentrate economic power into the hands of a few people who then have an inordinate level of influence over the direction of our society.

A more subtle characteristic of recent large mergers has been a tendency toward combinations among leading firms in *related* industries. For example, in 1995 the Disney organization, which makes movies (in addition to running theme parks), acquired the American Broadcasting Company (ABC), a major television network. Although these companies didn't compete directly, they both influence the viewing material placed before the public. The merger, therefore, puts a great deal of power over public opinion in the hands of the executives in charge of the combined company.

The long-term economic and political implications of today's megamergers are as yet unclear. On the one hand, it can be argued that the large and powerful companies being created are more efficient than the sum of the unmerged organizations would ever be, and therefore are better able to compete in an increasingly global marketplace. On the other hand, the massive accumulation of economic power currently taking place can be seen as having the potential to change the open and competitive nature of the economy for the worse. We won't know the bottom line for quite some time.

http://

Broadview is an investment banking firm specializing in mergers and acquisitions in the IT, communications, and media industries. Review a recent notable transaction at

● www.broadview.com

● MERGER ANALYSIS AND THE PRICE PREMIUM

The question of price comes up immediately in any acquisition. In other words, what should an acquiring company be willing to pay for a particular target? The question is answered by a *merger analysis* that attempts to pin down what an acquisition is worth to an acquiring company.

In theory, merger analysis is a straightforward capital budgeting exercise. The acquiring firm makes a projection of the cash flows the target is expected to generate over the indefinite future, and does a standard capital budgeting analysis to determine whether the acquisition viewed as a project has a positive NPV.

As in any capital budgeting analysis, two estimating issues are involved. First, the project's cash flows have to be forecast. Second, an appropriate discount rate has to be chosen.

Estimating Merger Cash Flows

Estimating the cash flows associated with a proposed merger should be a straightforward financial planning exercise with respect to the target company with two exceptions. The first exception involves making a provision in the analysis for any synergies that are expected as a result of the acquisition. The second requires that the cash flows recognized by the acquiring company be stated net of funds that will need to be reinvested in the business to provide for whatever growth is expected. We'll demonstrate these ideas in an example shortly.

In practice, however, estimating cash flows in a merger context is especially difficult. Remember all the things we said in earlier chapters about the accuracy of financial plans (Chapter 16) and cash flow estimates (Chapters 10 and 11). Our conclusion was that it's hard to project financial statements because of the inherent uncertainty of the future and because of the biases of the people making the estimates.

These problems are especially acute in a merger. The acquiring company has to do the analysis, but it generally doesn't have easy access to detailed information about either the target's future prospects or its past history. In a friendly merger, the target's management tends to be interested in pumping up the price, so information shared with the potential acquirer is biased optimistically. In an unfriendly merger, management won't share any internal data at all.

● **Merger pricing** is a **capital budgeting** exercise, but cash flows are **hard to estimate,** and there's a tendency to **overpay.**

It's not unusual for these conditions to lead to terribly inaccurate cash flow estimates. The tendency is to overstate the value of the target. That mistake can turn an acquisition into a financial disaster for the acquiring company, because it pays too much for the acquired firm. Of course, the same transaction is a financial windfall for the stockholders of the target who get an unrealistically high price for their stock.

The Appropriate Discount Rate

Because an acquisition is an equity transaction, it should be evaluated using a discount rate that reflects the cost of equity funds. Further, the target's equity rate should be used, not the acquiring firm's. That's because the risk in the project viewed from the perspective of the acquiring firm is inherently that of the target company.

The Value to the Acquirer and the Per-Share Price

The acquiring firm's analysis yields a value (an NPV) for the target company. That value divided by the number of shares of stock the target has outstanding is an indication of the amount the acquiring company should be willing to pay, per share, to make the acquisition. Anything less indicates a bargain for the acquirer and its stockholders; anything more represents an irrational transfer of wealth from the shareholders of the acquirer to those of the target.

The Price Premium

It's important to realize that whether a merger is friendly or hostile, the price offered to the target's shareholders is generally higher than the stock's market price. To understand this point, consider that any firm's stockholders always have the option of selling their shares at the market price, but at any particular time only a few actually do sell. Most shareholders don't sell on any given day because the market price is less than the value of the stock *to them* at that time.

In an acquisition, the acquiring firm has to offer a price that will cause the owners of a majority of the shares outstanding to sell at once. That price obviously has to be above the current market price. The amount by which the price offered exceeds the target's market price before word of the acquisition gets out is called the *premium*. A major issue in acquisitions is choosing a price that's just high enough to attract a majority of shares but no higher. Anything above that level represents a waste of the acquirer's money.

It should be clear from this that for a merger to make financial sense, the value of the target *to the acquiring firm* must exceed the company's market value at that time.

● Most acquisitions are made at **price premiums,** which leads to speculation on **in play** stocks, which drives prices up.

THE EFFECT ON MARKET PRICE The fact that a premium over market price is virtually always paid for the stock of an acquired firm creates a speculative opportunity. If an investor buys the stock of a company that is acquired shortly afterward, he or she is virtually assured of a quick profit because of the premium that will be associated with the acquisition.

This opportunity causes the market price of a company's stock to increase rapidly as soon as the fact that the firm is an acquisition target becomes known. Such a firm is said to be **in play.** The phenomenon clearly makes it advisable for the acquiring firm to keep merger negotiations secret.

● It is **illegal** for **insiders** to make short-term profits on **price movements** from the **acquisition** process.

Two other facts are important. First, it is illegal *insider trading* for people in any way associated with merger negotiations to make a short-term profit on price increases that come about as a result of the merger. This includes executives of the firms involved as well as peripheral players like the investment bankers and lawyers who advise on the transactions.

Second, an investment strategy has emerged in which people buy the stocks of firms that are likely acquisition targets, without knowledge of specific merger initiatives. Investors using this strategy are hoping that some of the firms whose stocks they buy will be placed in play in the near future.

THE POINT OF NEGOTIATIONS If a target company is indeed worth more than its market value to an acquiring company, a gain is available to the extent of the difference between the two values. Merger negotiations involve determining how that gain is to be distributed between the shareholders of the acquiring firm and those of the target.

The target's shareholders get their portion immediately in the form of the price premium paid for their stock. The remainder of the gain becomes incorporated into the value of the acquiring firm, and thereby accrues to its shareholders.

This means that in a friendly merger, the negotiations basically represent the dividing up of the gain between the two shareholder groups. In a hostile merger, the acquiring firm estimates the gain and offers a share of it to the target's stockholders in its tender offer price.

Keep in mind through all this that the gain is very difficult to estimate and particularly easy to overstate.

Calculating a Price and the Problem of Terminal Values

From the acquirer's perspective, merger analysis is a capital budgeting exercise using the NPV technique which we studied in Chapter 9. Recall Equation 9.1, the definition of NPV, which we'll repeat here for convenience.

(9.1) $$\text{NPV} = C_0 + \frac{C_1}{(1 + k)} + \frac{C_2}{(1 + k)^2} + \ldots + \frac{C_n}{(1 + k)^n}$$

A project's NPV is simply the sum of the present values of all the associated cash flows represented by $C_0, C_1, C_2 \ldots, C_n$. Recall that C_0 is the initial cash outlay required to get the project started. As an outflow, it is represented as a negative number. The subsequent Cs are generally positive and represent the project's cash inflows over the next n years. (Division by the $(1 + k)^i$ factors just takes the present value of each C.)

In a merger analysis, C_0 is the total amount the acquirer will pay for the target's stock. The subsequent Cs are the sums of the yearly cash flows expected to be generated by the target plus any synergies management thinks will come from the combination of the companies.

Any project is only worth doing if it has a positive NPV. In a merger context, that means C_0 must be less than the sum of the present values of the other Cs. Hence that sum is the *most* an acquiring company should be willing to pay for the target's stock. Dividing by the number of shares of stock the target has outstanding gives the maximum per share price the acquirer should be willing to pay to make the acquisition.

EXAMPLE 17.1

Alpha Corp is analyzing whether or not it should acquire Beta Corp. Alpha has determined that the appropriate interest rate for the analysis is 12%. Beta has 12,000 shares of stock outstanding, and its cash flows including synergies over the next three years are estimated to be ($000) as follows.

Year	1	2	3
Cash flow	$200	$220	$250

Alpha's management is fairly conservative and feels the acquisition should be justified by cash flows projected over no more than three years. Management believes projections beyond that are too risky to be considered reliable. What is the maximum Alpha should pay for a share of Beta's stock?

Solution: The present value of Beta's positive cash flows is calculated as follows:

Year	Cash Flow	$PVF_{12,i}$	Present Value
1	$200,000	.8929	$178,580
2	$220,000	.7972	$175,384
3	$250,000	.7118	$177,950
			$531,914

Hence the maximum Alpha should pay for all of Beta's stock is $531,914. This is the initial outlay (C_0) in the NPV equation and would result in a zero NPV. At that price, Alpha would be indifferent to the acquisition.

Dividing by the number of shares outstanding gives the maximum per share price Alpha should be willing to pay.

Maximum Acquisition Price = $531,914 / 12,000 = $44.33

Notice that in Example 17.1, the acquirer's management was financially conservative, and based the target's value on only three years of forecast cash flows. Unfortunately, acquirers are often not financially conservative, and are willing value targets based on long-term forecasts. This creates what can be called the *terminal value problem.*

As a merger analysis proceeds, detailed cash flow projections are generally made for a finite number of years, usually three to five. But most acquisitions are envisioned to last forever, and there's a tendency to project a stream of cash flows that goes on indefinitely after the three- to five-year detailed forecast, and to include it in the analysis. This tends to produce results that strongly favor doing the acquisition. The question is, how real are those results? A more realistic (and therefore more complex) example will make these ideas clear.

EXAMPLE 17.2

The Aldebron Motor Company is considering acquiring Arcturus Gear Works Inc. and has made a three-year projection of the firm's financial statements, including the following revenue and earnings estimate. Period 0 is the current year and not part of the forecast. Figures are in millions of dollars.

| | **Year** | | | |
	0	1	2	3
Revenue	$1,500	$1,650	$1,815	$2,000
EAT	95	106	117	130

Aldebron expects that synergies will net $10 million after tax per year. It also expects that cash equal to depreciation will have to be reinvested to keep Arcturus's plant operating efficiently, and that 60% of the remaining cash generated by operations will need to be invested in growth opportunities. Otherwise the balance sheet will remain relatively unchanged.

Results beyond three years become increasingly difficult to forecast in any detail, so Aldebron's plan simply assumes a 6% annual growth in all of the target's figures after the third year.

Currently 90-day treasury bills are yielding 8% and the market returns 13% on an average stock. Arcturus's beta is 1.8 and the firm has 20 million shares of stock outstanding, which closed at $19 a share yesterday.

How much should Aldebron be willing to pay for Arcturus's stock? Discuss the quality of the estimate.

Solution: First we'll compute the appropriate discount rate for the present value calculations. Recall that the target's return on equity is the appropriate rate (page 600). We'll estimate that using the capital asset pricing model (CAPM) approach (see Chapter 8, page 278). The SML yields the following.

$$k_x = k_{RF} + (k_M - k_{RF})b_x$$
$$= 8\% + (13\% - 8\%)1.8$$
$$= 17\%$$

Next we complete the rough cash flow estimate for the target for the first three years, using the information given.

Arcturus Gear Works, Inc. Estimated Cash Flows ($M)

| | **Year** | | | |
	0	1	2	3
Revenue	$1,500	$1,650	$1,815	$2,000
EAT (unmerged)	95	106	117	130
Synergies	10	10	10	10
EAT/cash flow (merged)*	$ 105	$ 116	$ 127	$ 140
Reinvested (60%)	63	70	76	84
Cash flow to Aldebron	$ 42	$ 46	$ 51	$ 56

*We haven't added back depreciation because of our assumption that cash equal to that amount must be reinvested to maintain the plant.

Cash flows after the periods planned in detail are often summarized in a single *terminal value* assumption.[9] In this case, Aldebron is assuming that the last year's flow, $56 million, will grow at 6% per year indefinitely. The value of a known payment that will grow at a known rate can be calculated by using the constant growth (Gordon) stock valuation model we studied in Chapter 7 (page 229). Recall Equation 7.10.

$$P_0 = \frac{D_0(1 + g)}{k - g}$$

In this application, we'll rewrite the equation replacing P_0 with the terminal value (TV) we're looking for while D_0 becomes the year 3 cash flow, which we'll call C_3. We've already calculated the discount rate, k, and g is the growth rate assumed after year 3.

$$TV = \frac{C_3(1 + g)}{k - g} = \frac{\$56M\ (1.06)}{.17 - .06}$$

$$= \$540M$$

Hence, the cash flow stream in our capital budgeting calculation is as follows ($M).

	Year		
	1	*2*	*3*
Operating cash flow	$46	$51	$ 56
Terminal value			540
Total	$46	$51	$596

Notice how large the terminal value is compared to the three annual cash flows. This is not unusual. Next we'll take the present value of the entire stream at the discount rate we calculated earlier. To make a point later on, we'll keep the three-year forecast and the terminal value calculation separate.

$$PV = \frac{\$46M}{1.17} + \frac{\$51M}{(1.17)^2} + \frac{\$56M}{(1.17)^3} + \frac{\$540M}{(1.17)^3}$$

$$PV = \$112M + \$337M$$

$$PV = \$449M$$

This procedure indicates that Arcturus is worth about $449 million to Aldebron. Notice that approximately three quarters of this figure comes from the terminal value assumption.

In other words, the absolute maximum that Aldebron should consider paying for Arcturus is $449 million, which if there are 20 million shares outstanding is $22.45 per share.

If the stock is currently selling at $19.00, this represents an 18.2% premium over its market price calculated as follows.

$$(\$22.45 - \$19.00)/\$19.00 = 18.2\%$$

---

9. We discussed terminal values in Chapter 10, page 338.

from the **CFO**

THE QUALITY OF THE ESTIMATE   *It's important to understand how arbitrary the valuation process we've just illustrated can be, especially the terminal value calculation. Even though it represents the period about which we know the least (the distant future), the terminal value accounts for fully three quarters of the final valuation. That means our results are highly sensitive to the assumptions made about the long-term future. In other words, modest changes in those assumptions can make huge differences in total value.*

For example, suppose a more optimistic person did the forecast and decided that a 9% long-term growth rate was more appropriate for Arcturus. Under that assumption the terminal value is $763 million and has a present value of $476 million. The total value of the firm is then

$$PV = \$112M + \$476M = \$588M .$$

Notice that under this more aggressive but still reasonable assumption, the terminal value represents 81% of the target's final calculated value. The maximum acquisition price is then ($588M/20M =) $29.40, which implies a premium of [($29.40 − $19.00)/$19.00 =] 54.7%.

This means an enormous range of values can be calculated for the offering price in an acquisition like this one. Good judgment is called for to avoid basing a multimillion-dollar deal on too high a price.

Although premiums this big have been paid in some large and sophisticated acquisitions in recent years, it's hard to believe a company can be worth so much more than its market value. The implication is that something else must be motivating the deal. Many observers have attributed such actions to sheer ego on the part of the executives in charge of the acquiring firms.

Paying for the Acquisition—The Junk Bond Market

Acquiring a company involves giving its stockholders something of value in return for their shares. That something is generally one or a combination of three things: cash, stock in the acquiring firm, or debt of the acquiring firm.

For example, suppose the firms in Example 17.2 agreed to a price of $25 for Arcturus's stock. At the same time suppose Aldebron's stock was selling for $10 a share. The following are a few of the combinations that might be offered for 100 shares of Arcturus.

Cash	Aldebron Stock	Bond
$2,500	—	—
—	250 shares	—
$1,000	50 shares	$1,000
$1,500	100 shares	—

To the extent that cash is offered, the acquiring firm must either have it or be able to raise it. Investment banks have played an important role in the most recent merger wave by helping companies raise money to pay for acquisitions. In particular, the *junk bond market* was a product of the period.

Junk bonds are low-quality bonds that pay high yields because the firms that issue them are risky. Prior to the 1980s, it was virtually impossible for any small, risky company to borrow regardless of the interest rate it offered on its bonds.

INSIGHTS

Practical Finance

How a Trendy Soft Drink Gave Cereal Giant Quaker Oats a $1.4 Billion Case of Indigestion

On March 28, 1997, *The Wall Street Journal* carried the modest headline "Quaker Oats to Sell Its Snapple Business." The article announced the end of a story that may be the most flagrant example *ever* of overpaying for an acquisition.

Only 2½ years earlier Quaker paid $1.7 billion for Snapple, a leader in "new age" soft drinks. The *WSJ* article reported that the business was being sold for a mere $300 million, a loss of *$1.4 billion*.

The loss amounted to $8.40 per share of Quaker stock. To indicate its magnitude the newspaper noted that in the same quarter a year earlier Quaker's earnings were about $0.23 per share. This might suggest that the Snapple disaster wiped out about ($8.40/$.23 =) 36 quarters or nine years of earnings!

Snapple caught on in the early 1990s with sales growing from $95M in 1991 to $516M in 1993. This blistering growth caught Quaker's eye, and probably fueled the acquisition price of 20 times earnings, which was twice the P/E ratio of other beverage companies. Further, Quaker already marketed Gatorade, and probably expected big synergies with Snapple.

But there was trouble from the very beginning that Quaker should have anticipated. First, the long-term growth rate of the beverage industry was only about 3%. That meant Snapple's supernormal growth couldn't last forever. Second, other firms including Coke and Pepsi had aggressively entered the new age market. By the time of the acquisition, Snapple's growth had stalled and its earnings estimates were dropping sharply.

It's hard to imagine how Quaker could have made so great an error. Snapple's 1993 earnings were about $68M. Quaker could have used the techniques of Example 17.2 to derive the kind of growth rate assumptions that would have been necessary to support an acquisition price of $1.7 billion. For example, if Quaker's required rate of return on the deal was only 15%, Snapple had to have been forecast to grow at about 11% *forever* to justify the price. That was incredibly optimistic when the overall beverage market was growing at just 3% and the competition included market savvy giants like Coke and Pepsi!

So why was Quaker willing to pay so much for Snapple? It's hard to say. A *Business Week* article published about six months earlier observed that some investors felt it may have had something to do with the "excitement of a splashy deal."

Sources: *Wall Street Journal* (28 March, 1997); *Business Week* (23 September, 1996); Thompson, Arthur J., and Strickland, A. J. 1996. *Strategic Management: Concepts and Cases*, 9th ed. Chicago: Richard D. Irwin.

During that period, however, investment banks started pooling risky bonds into funds, claiming that the failure rate of risky companies was only a little higher than that of more reputable firms. Then it was argued that if the failure rate of risky companies is only 1% or 2% higher than that of stable companies, but the pool of their bonds pays 5% or 6% more interest, an investor is better off with a share of the risky pool than with a stable firm's bond.

Investors bought the idea, and suddenly high-risk ventures could borrow substantial sums of money. A prime use of that money was paying for the stock of target companies in risky acquisitions. In other words, the acquiring company would issue junk bonds and use the borrowed money to make acquisitions.

It turned out that the basic premise on which the junk bond market was founded wasn't true. Risky firms failed only slightly more often than higher rated firms *in good economic times*. In bad times, however, they failed a lot

● **Junk bonds** are issued by **financially weak** firms and pay high interest rates. They are frequently used to **fund high-risk acquisitions.**

more often. A recession came along in the late 1980s, and the junk bond market collapsed.

The junk bond market was pioneered by an individual named Michael Milken who worked for the firm of Drexel Burnham Lambert. The firm later failed, and Milken spent some time in jail for his activities during the period.

The Capital Structure Argument to Justify High Premiums

Recall that we came to the conclusion in Chapter 13 (page 430) that capital structure can affect the market price of stock. In particular, we said that replacing equity with debt where there was little or no debt to begin with can sometimes cause the company's stock price to rise.

When the money used to buy out a target's shareholders is raised by borrowing, the result is frequently a more leveraged firm with new owners. If this results in a market value increment, the increment is argued to be a justification for paying a high premium for the acquisition's stock.

Even when this happens, it's hard for a reasonable person to justify premiums in the neighborhood of 50% over market value.

The Effect of Paying Too Much

An acquiring company that pays too much for an acquisition with either its stock or cash on hand transfers wealth from its own stockholders to those of the target. This represents a violation of the acquiring management's responsibility to act in the best interest of its stockholders, but isn't likely to cause problems beyond that.

On the other hand, paying too much with borrowed money results in a company that's heavily burdened with debt and the associated interest payments. That can cause the combined firm to perform poorly or fail in the future.

In the context of Example 17.2, if Aldebron borrows as much as $592 million to buy Arcturus, and Arcturus's cash flows turn out to be less than expected, there won't be enough money available to service the debt. That can spell bankruptcy.

● DEFENSIVE TACTICS

Defensive tactics are things management can do to prevent a company from being acquired. They can be divided into two categories, things that can be done after a takeover attempt is under way and things that can be done in anticipation of such an attempt.

Tactics after a Takeover Is Under Way

● A reluctant target's management can use **defensive tactics** to **avoid** being acquired.

After an acquiring firm has announced its intentions, a target's management can take the following actions.

CHALLENGE THE PRICE   By this tactic, management attempts to convince the stockholders that the acquirer's price is too low. This usually amounts to arguing that the market has temporarily undervalued the stock, and that the shareholders will do a lot better by holding on until the price rises above the amount offered.

CLAIM AN ANTITRUST VIOLATION   Management can approach the Justice Department and claim the merger is anticompetitive, hoping that the government will intervene.

ISSUE DEBT AND REPURCHASE SHARES This tends to drive up the stock's price, making the price offered by the acquirer less attractive. It also increases the firm's leverage, making the company less desirable from a capital structure point of view.

● A **white knight** is an alternate acquirer with a **better reputation** for its treatment of acquired firms.

SEEK A WHITE KNIGHT Some acquirers are particularly unattractive because they have a history of treating the management and employees of acquired companies poorly. A target's management will sometimes try to find an alternate acquirer with a better reputation. Such an alternative suitor is known as a **white knight.**

GREENMAIL Mergers are sometimes initiated when a powerful group acquires a substantial but minority interest in a company. This can signal its intention to acquire a controlling interest later. Managements have eliminated such threats by buying the group's shares at a price in excess of the stock's market value. Essentially management buys off the attacker with the company's money in a process known as paying **greenmail.** Other stockholders have been known to become upset over this practice and sue the board.

Tactics in Anticipation of a Takeover

Several things can be written into a corporation's charter and bylaws that make it difficult to acquire without the cooperation of management.

STAGGERED ELECTION OF DIRECTORS Companies are run by boards of directors which are normally elected annually by stockholders. The annual election of directors implies that if an outside party gains a controlling interest in the firm's stock, it can elect a new board and begin running the firm relatively promptly. However, if the elections of board members are staggered so that only, say, one-third are elected each year, it will take some time for a new controlling interest to take over the board and thereby control the company. That makes the acquisition less attractive.

APPROVAL BY A SUPERMAJORITY Mergers have to be approved by shareholders owning a majority of the firm's stock. However, the definition of the majority required is written into the corporation's bylaws. Requiring approval by a super-majority, say 80%, of shareholders makes taking control of the company more difficult.

POISON PILLS **Poison pills** are legal devices embedded in corporate bylaws that are designed to make it prohibitively expensive for outsiders to take control without the support of management. Conceptually, the acquirer commits financial suicide by swallowing the target along with its poison pill.

There are any number of poison pill arrangements, but there's also some uncertainty surrounding them. Some ideas can prove to be illegal and therefore aren't binding. Other arrangements can be discriminatory against certain groups of stockholders or can be shown to be an irresponsible squandering of the firm's resources. In such cases, the directors who approve the arrangements can be exposed to personal lawsuits by unhappy stockholders. The following are a few of the more common poison pill arrangements.

● **Golden parachutes** are exorbitant severance packages for a target's management.

GOLDEN PARACHUTES *Golden parachutes* are contracts between a company and its senior managers that guarantee exorbitant severance packages if those managers are fired after a takeover. In addition to making the managers rich, the cash drain can debilitate the company.

ACCELERATED DEBT   A firm can include a provision in its debt contracts that requires the principal amounts to become due immediately if the firm is taken over. Most firms don't have the cash available to make such a payment, so a takeover would put them into default. If that happens, the acquirer is forced to come up with enough cash to pay off all of the acquired firm's debt immediately after the acquisition. This is generally distasteful to acquiring firms.

SHARE RIGHTS PLANS (SRPS)   A share rights plan is a complicated arrangement in which current shareholders are given *rights,* which are securities that enable them to buy shares in the merged company at a reduced price after a takeover. That means an acquiring company has to be willing not only to buy the stock of a target, but also to turn over a number of its own shares to the target's stockholders at, say, half price. This doesn't prevent an acquisition, but can make it very expensive.

OTHER KINDS OF TAKEOVERS—LBOS AND PROXY FIGHTS

So far we've associated takeovers with acquisitions of one firm by another. However, changes in ownership and control can occur outside of business combinations.

LEVERAGED BUYOUTS (LBOS)

A **leveraged buyout** (**LBO**) is a transaction in which a publicly held company's stock is purchased by a group of investors through a negotiated deal or a tender offer. The company is then no longer publicly traded, but becomes a *private* or *closely held* firm owned by the group of investors, who are frequently the firm's management.

The investor group gets the money to buy the stock by contributing a relatively small amount of their own equity and borrowing the rest. The amount borrowed can turn out to be more than 95% of capital—hence the term "leveraged" buyout. The borrowed funds usually come through *asset-based* financing, meaning the loans are secured by the firm's own assets.

LBOs tend to be very risky because of the high debt burden placed on the firm after the change in ownership. For example, imagine a firm that has no debt and $100 million in equity whose stock is selling at book value. That is, the market value of the stock is also $100 million. Now suppose the management team purchases the stock at book value, contributing $5 million of its own money and borrowing the rest. The firm's capital structure before and after the LBO is as follows.

> In a **leveraged buyout (LBO)** investors **take a company private** by buying its stock with borrowed money.

	Before LBO	After LBO
Debt	$0	$95M
Equity	100M	5M
Capital	$100M	$100M

It's important to understand that nothing has changed with respect to the operating ability of the company to generate money. However, the post-LBO firm has to pay interest on debt of $95 million, making it a very risky company.

Notice that the LBO is a *takeover but not a merger.* The company has been taken over by a group of investors, but it hasn't been merged with anything.

● The **result** of an **LBO** is usually a **risky, debt-laden** company.

Specialized LBO companies help put together LBOs and assist in borrowing the necessary money. The best known of these is Kohlberg, Kravis, & Roberts (KKR), which is famous for its 1988 LBO of RJR Nabisco, a combined tobacco and food products company. Prior to the LBO, the firm's stock was trading at about $55 per share. The deal was finally done at $106 per share for a total of more than $25 billion.

After an LBO is completed, the object is to reduce the debt load as quickly as possible. This can sometimes be accomplished by selling off divisions or assets and using the proceeds to pay down the debt.

LBOs have been criticized as profit-driven financial manipulations that can destroy sound companies. Our numerical illustration gives an indication of what is meant by this accusation. Before the LBO, the company was a conservatively financed firm, presumably with good operating prospects (otherwise the acquiring group wouldn't have been interested). After the LBO the same firm was in serious danger of collapse under the weight of its debt.

LBOs are less common today than they were in the mid-1980s, presumably because a number have failed as a result of their debt burden.

● PROXY FIGHTS

● In a **proxy fight,** opposing groups solicit shareholders' **proxies** for the election of directors.

A *proxy* is a legal document that gives one person the right to act for another on a certain issue. When corporations elect boards of directors, management usually solicits stockholders for their proxies to use in voting for directors. In other words, management asks stockholders for their proxies to vote for the board members it has proposed. There's generally no opposition, and the proxies are willingly granted by most of the shareholders.

However, sometimes a group of shareholders becomes dissatisfied with management and seeks to gain control of the board. Such a dissident group can also solicit the proxies of the other shareholders for the election of board members. If the dissidents win, they can elect their representatives to the board and take control of the firm.

A *proxy fight* occurs when more than one group simultaneously solicits shareholders' proxies for the election of directors. A takeover is said to occur if the dissident group wins.

Notice that no change in ownership is associated with a proxy fight. The same stockholders own the firm before and after the battle, but the controlling interest on the board changes.

DIVESTITURES

A **divestiture** is the opposite of an acquisition. A company decides that for some reason it would be better off without a particular business operation, and gets rid of it in one of several ways.

● THE REASONS FOR DIVESTITURES

There are several reasons for divestitures.

CASH   The most straightforward reason to sell anything is a *need for cash*. A firm can simply sell off a noncritical piece of itself because it needs the money for something else.

● Companies **divest** operations to **raise money,** or because of poor **performance** or lack of **strategic fit.**

After LBOs, firms tend to have huge debt burdens which can sometimes be partially paid down by selling assets or noncritical operations for cash.

Acquisition targets sometimes have operations which acquirers don't want but which can't be separated from the things they do want before the merger. It's relatively common to divest unwanted divisions shortly after the acquisition and use the money received to reduce the expense of the original takeover.

STRATEGIC FIT   Sometimes companies have divisions or subsidiaries that don't fit into their long-term plans. This can be especially true if there's been a change in the firm's strategic thinking.

POOR PERFORMANCE   Certain operations just never become acceptably profitable. Eventually even the most patient of managements will want to get rid of them.

● METHODS OF DIVESTING OPERATIONS

There are basically three ways to divest a business unit: sale, spinoff, and liquidation.

SALE FOR CASH AND OR SECURITIES   An operation can be sold to another company or to an investor group. The first situation is a friendly acquisition of the operation by the other company. The second is an LBO.

● A **spinoff** creates a **new company** owned by the same shareholders that can be **separately traded.**

SPINOFF   A spinoff occurs when two parts of a firm are recognized to be strategically incompatible, but there's no desire to get rid of either. In other words, management believes that it's in the stockholders' best interest to keep both pieces, but it's operationally better to separate them completely. A spinoff is accomplished by setting up the operation to be divested as a separate corporation and giving shareholders of the original company a share of the new firm for every share of the old firm they own.

After the spinoff the two companies are owned by exactly the same shareholders, who are then free to trade the shares separately. After a relatively short time, the ownership is usually no longer identical.

Here's an example. Suppose a stable company begins to acquire and develop a few riskier business divisions. After a few years the firm has two distinct sides, one conservative and one risky. However, many of the original stockholders invested in the company because it was stable, so they're not comfortable with its new risky side. It makes sense to spin off the risky section and let the unhappy stockholders sell their shares in it while maintaining or increasing their holdings in the conservative business.

LIQUIDATION   In a liquidation, the divested business is simply closed down and its assets are sold off piecemeal. Liquidation is generally a last resort to dispose of businesses that have failed badly.

BANKRUPTCY AND THE REORGANIZATION OF FAILED BUSINESSES

Failure is an unpleasant but real fact of business life. More than 50,000 businesses fail each year, including some very substantial firms. We'll begin our discussion of the subject by defining exactly what is meant by failure.

FAILURE AND INSOLVENCY

Business failure can be defined economically in a long-run sense or in more immediate commercial terms. We're primarily concerned with the commercial concept and its implications, but it's important to understand the economic idea and appreciate the distinction between the two.

A business fails economically if it is unable to provide an adequate return to its owners. For example, suppose a company consistently pays its bills and earns a profit, but never makes more than a 1% or 2% return on the equity invested by its stockholders. After a while, investors will seek to get their capital out of such a company, and it will be closed as a failure.

● A firm is **insolvent** and a **commercial failure** if it can't pay its near-term debts.

The economic failure we've just described is an issue between a business and its owners. Commercial failure, on the other hand, is an issue between a business and its *creditors*. A business fails commercially when it can't pay its debts. The condition is described by the term "insolvent." A firm is said to be *technically insolvent* when it can't meet its short-term obligations as they come due. It is *legally insolvent* if its liabilities exceed its assets.

A commercial failure is generally also an economic failure, but a business can be an economic failure without ever failing in the legal or commercial sense.

Potential Actions by Creditors against an Insolvent Company

Imagine that an insolvent company owes money to a number of creditors. Then suppose one creditor sues and manages to take possession of the firm's producing assets to satisfy its debt.

This would be good for the suing creditor, but would be very bad for everyone else involved. If the insolvent firm loses its production equipment, it probably goes out of business immediately. In most cases that means all the employees lose their jobs and the firm's stockholders lose their entire investments. Further, because the company no longer has the ability to earn money, none of the other creditors are likely to be paid anything.

In most cases it would be better for the firm to continue in business and use its earnings to pay off its debts slowly. That implies it has to stop doing whatever made it insolvent in the first place if that's possible. The problem is that each creditor is looking out for itself and wants to have its debts satisfied out of the firm's assets before they're paid out to someone else.

BANKRUPTCY—CONCEPT AND OBJECTIVES

Bankruptcy is a legal proceeding designed to preclude the situation we've just described. When an insolvent firm goes into bankruptcy, the court protects it from suit by its creditors and at the same time determines whether it should be kept running or closed down.

A firm can be insolvent because its business has gone bad to the point of failure or it has too much debt in an otherwise survivable situation. In the first case it's better to shut the company down before it loses any more money, and salvage as many of its assets as possible to pay off its debts. In the second case, the firm may be able to make good on all of its debts if it's given enough time, so it may be appropriate to keep it running if whatever made it insolvent in the first place can be changed. Of course, some situations are a combination of both conditions, which makes the judgment a tough call.

If an insolvent company appears to be worth more as a going concern than the value of its assets, it goes through a *reorganization* under the supervision and protection of the court. This involves a *restructuring* of its debt and a plan to pay everyone off as fairly as possible.

> ● A **bankruptcy** proceeding protects a failing firm from creditors until a resolution is reached to close or continue it.

If the court decides that the company is a lost cause, worth more dead than alive, it orders a *liquidation*. In a liquidation, the firm's assets are sold under the court's supervision and the proceeds are used to pay creditors in accordance with a schedule of priorities included in the bankruptcy laws.

In summary, bankruptcy is a federal legal procedure designed to save as much pain and loss as possible when firms fail. A firm isn't *bankrupt* or *in bankruptcy* until the action is filed in court. Until that time it's just insolvent. A bankrupt firm *emerges from* or *comes out of* bankruptcy after a reorganization in which its creditors agree to some settlement of their claims.

● BANKRUPTCY PROCEDURES— REORGANIZATION, RESTRUCTURING, LIQUIDATION

> ● A **trustee** oversees the operation of a firm in bankruptcy to **protect** the interests of **creditors.**

A *bankruptcy petition* can be initiated by either the insolvent company itself or by its creditors. When the debtor firm itself files the petition, the bankruptcy is said to be *voluntary*. When creditors do the filing the action is *involuntary*. It takes only a group of three unsecured creditors who are owed a total of $5,000 to place a firm in involuntary bankruptcy. Once either petition is filed, the firm is protected from creditors' further legal actions related to its debts until the bankruptcy is resolved.

Normally, a firm in bankruptcy is permitted to continue in business. To prevent it from doing so would usually cause the kinds of losses described in the last section. However, there may be a concern that the company's management will cause a further deterioration in its financial position during the proceedings. There's also a concern that assets will be removed during this period, leaving an empty shell to satisfy creditors. To guard against these dangers, the court may appoint a **trustee** to oversee the company's operation while it's in bankruptcy.

Reorganization

> ● A **reorganization** is a plan under which an insolvent firm **continues to operate** while attempting to pay off its debts.

A **reorganization** is a business plan under which the firm can continue to operate and pay off its debts. Management and the company's stockholders invariably favor reorganization over liquidation, because there's generally little or nothing left for stockholders after a liquidation. Once the bankruptcy petition is filed, management has 120 days to come up with an acceptable reorganization plan.

Reorganization plans are judged on two general criteria, *fairness* and *feasibility*. Fairness implies that claims are satisfied in accordance with an order of priorities that's part of the bankruptcy laws. We'll talk about those priorities later. Feasibility refers to the likelihood that the plan will actually come true. It's important to realize that a reorganization plan is a business/financial plan just like those we discussed in Chapter 16. As such it's based on a set of assumptions that may or may not be realistic. A court is unlikely to approve a plan that's based on unrealistic assumptions.

To be accepted, a reorganization plan has to be approved not only by the bankruptcy court, but also by the firm's creditors and its stockholders. Once a reorganization plan is accepted, the firm can emerge from bankruptcy. Then it's generally the responsibility of the court-appointed trustee to oversee the plan's implementation.

Debt Restructuring

The heart of most reorganization plans is a **restructuring** of the firm's debt. Keep in mind that insolvent firms are bankrupt because they couldn't pay their debts. Therefore they aren't likely to be able to work themselves out of their troubles under the debt payment schedules that existed before the bankruptcy petition was filed. What's generally necessary is some kind of a reduction in payments. Restructuring the firm's debt makes such a reduction possible.

● **Debt restructuring** involves concessions that **lower** an insolvent firm's **payments** so it can continue in business.

Debt restructuring can be accomplished in two ways. The simplest is an *extension* whereby creditors agree to give the firm a longer time to repay its obligations. A temporary deferral of principal and sometimes interest payments is quite common. The second approach is a *composition* in which creditors agree to settle for less than the full amount owed them.

It's important to understand the position of creditors in a bankruptcy case. If they demand immediate payment of the full amounts of their debts, the bankrupt firm will fail and they'll receive only a small fraction of what they're owed. On the other hand, if they accept less in terms of either the amount paid or its timing, they may stand to get a great deal more money in the long run. Therefore they have an incentive to compromise and make concessions.

● **Extensions, compositions,** and **debt to equity** conversions are common approaches to **restructuring.**

A common method of accomplishing a debt restructuring is the conversion of debt into equity. Creditors give up their debt claims (loans, bonds, accounts receivable) in return for stock in the bankrupt company. This immediately reduces the debt service burden on the company in trouble and eases its cash flow problems (assuming it doesn't pay dividends on the new equity).

After such a conversion, creditors have equity positions in the troubled company. These aren't worth much initially, but if the firm survives and perhaps prospers, they can be worth more in the long run than the debt given up. Notice that in a conversion the original stockholders receive a benefit in terms of the forgiveness of some of their company's debt. In return their ownership is diluted.

EXAMPLE 17.3

The Adcock Company has 50,000 shares of common stock outstanding at a book value of $40, pays 10% interest on its debt, and is in the following financial situation.

Adcock Company Selected Financial Information ($000)

Income and Cash Flow		Capital	
EBIT	$200	Debt	$6,000
Interest	600	Equity	2,000
EBT	($400)	Total capital	$8,000
Tax	—		
EAT	($400)		
Depreciation	200		
Principal repayment	(100)		
Cash flow	($300)		

Notice that although the company has a positive EBIT, it doesn't earn enough to pay its interest let alone repay principal on schedule. Without help of some kind it will fail shortly. Devise a composition involving a debt for equity conversion that will keep the firm afloat.

Solution: Suppose the creditors (perhaps a number of bondholders) are willing to convert $3 million in debt to equity at the $40 book value of the existing shares. This would require the firm to issue 75,000 new shares, resulting in the following financial situation.

Adcock Company Selected Financial Information After Debt to Equity Conversion ($000)

Income and Cash Flow		Capital	
EBIT	$200	Debt	$3,000
Interest	300	Equity	5,000
EBT	($100)	Total capital	$8,000
Tax	—		
EAT	($100)		
Depreciation	200		
Principal repayment	(50)		
Cash flow	$50		

Notice that the company now has a slightly positive cash flow and can at least theoretically continue in business indefinitely. *However,* the creditors now own a controlling interest in the firm.

Liquidation

● **Liquidation** involves **closing** a troubled firm and selling its assets.

When the court decides that a bankrupt business isn't worth continuing it orders a **liquidation,** which involves selling off the firm's assets and using the proceeds to pay off as many of its debts as possible. The process is conceptually simple but can be administratively involved.

The liquidation is accomplished by a court-appointed trustee who first looks for and attempts to recover any unauthorized transfers out of the firm around the time of the bankruptcy filing. This is an important step. When business owners anticipate bankruptcy they frequently try to remove assets from the company. Doing that is illegal because those assets should rightly be used to satisfy creditors' claims. It's the trustee's job to find and recover such articles and payments.

● Unauthorized **transfers out** of a bankrupt firm can be **recovered** by the trustee.

Next the trustee supervises the sale of the business's assets, gathering the proceeds into a pool of funds that can be used to satisfy creditor's claims. Finally the trustee distributes the available funds to the various claimants.

It's important to realize that claimants aren't just lenders in the traditional sense. They include vendors who sold to the company on credit, employees who are owed wages, customers who may have put down deposits on merchandise, the government which may be owed taxes, and the people and organizations that are part of the bankruptcy proceeding. This last group includes lawyers and the court itself, which are owed fees for their services. In addition, the company's stockholders are claimants to the extent of whatever is left over after everyone else is satisfied.

INSIGHTS

Ethics

Is Bankruptcy Too Easy?—What about Ethics?

It's a question that's been around as long as the bankruptcy laws. Do courts and the bankruptcy code make it too easy to get out from under debts? The question applies to both companies and individuals in financial trouble. Creditors, especially credit card companies, think the answer is yes. They decry "bankruptcies of convenience," and popular guide books on how to use court procedures to escape debts. They claim bankruptcy has become a "first stop, not a last resort," and that it's being used as a "financial planning tool."

There's undoubtedly an ethical issue in bankruptcy. Is it right to allow people or companies to completely escape the repayment of substantial debts and start over scot-free? Creditors claim it isn't. Further, they assert that bankruptcies cost the economy $44 billion each year, which is passed on to consumers through higher prices and credit costs. This amounts to about $400 per American family per year. The creditors claim the bankruptcy procedures are too easy, and that many bankrupts could pay all or part of their debts if they were forced to try harder.

On the other hand, a two-year study by a government-appointed commission of bankruptcy judges and lawyers found no reason to change the current law. Further, there's a strong argument that creditors in the consumer area share a good deal of the blame for bankruptcies due to their aggressive marketing practices.

Despite these counterarguments, creditors have been lobbying Congress to toughen bankruptcy laws for years. Their efforts appear to have been successful. In 2001 the House of Representatives and the Senate each passed slightly different versions of a "Bankruptcy Reform Act," which would make bankruptcy more difficult and less forgiving. However, the House and Senate versions were not reconciled and passed into law because of shifts in legislative priorities toward the end of the year. Congress is likely to reconsider the issue before long.

Source: Schlesinger, Jacob M. "As Bankruptcies Surge, Creditors Lobby Hard to Get Tougher Laws," *Wall Street Journal* (27 June 1998): pp. A1-A9. Morgan D. King, "Bankruptcy Reform in a Nutshell," Bankruptcy Reform News, King Bankruptcy Media, 2001. **http:www.bankruptcyfinder.com/nutshellking.html**.

● The **bankruptcy code** contains **priorities** for the **distribution** of assets among claimants.

Distribution Priorities

The distribution of funds in bankruptcy follows an order of priority laid down by the bankruptcy code. This order is used to determine the sequence of payment in liquidation and as the basis for the fairness judgment in evaluating reorganization plans. Basically the priority rule says that all claimants are not equal in the eyes of the law.

It's important to understand the implications of this rule. The funds available from liquidation usually amount to a fraction of the value of the claims against the company. For example, a firm with total claims of $1 million might end up with a pool of funds from liquidation of $300,000. The priority rule says that the claimants do not all get 30 cents on the dollar for their debt. Some get more and some get less.

SECURED DEBT   The first distinction made among claimants is between *secured* and *unsecured creditors*. A secured creditor's debt is guaranteed by a specific asset. For example, when money is borrowed to buy a car, the loan is generally secured by the automobile itself. That means if the loan isn't paid, the car is sold and the money from the sale must be used to satisfy that debt before any other.

Unsecured debts aren't tied to particular assets and just rely on the general creditworthiness of the borrower.

● **Secured creditors** are paid out of the proceeds of the sale of **pledged assets.**

Secured obligations are each paid out of the proceeds of the sale of the related assets before the liquidation pool is established. To the extent that any individual secured debt is more or less than the value of its securing asset, the difference becomes unsecured debt or an addition to the pool, depending on whether the debt or the value of the asset is larger.

PRIORITIES FOR PAYMENT OF CLAIMS   After all secured debts are paid, unsecured claims are paid out of the remaining pool of funds in the following order.

1. Administrative expenses of the bankruptcy proceedings
2. Certain business expenses incurred *after* the bankruptcy petition is filed[10]
3. Unpaid wages up to $2,000 per employee
4. Certain unpaid contributions to employee benefit plans
5. Certain customer deposits up to $900 per individual[11]
6. Unpaid taxes
7. Unsecured creditors
8. Preferred stockholders
9. Common stockholders.

Clearly common stockholders receive only the bankrupt firm's residual value after all other obligations have been paid. That's often nothing at all.

Terminology—Bankruptcy Code Chapters 7 and 11

The federal bankruptcy code is divided into chapters. Reorganization is governed by **Chapter 11** and liquidation by Chapter 7.

People frequently refer to firms in reorganization proceedings as being "in Chapter 11." When firms voluntarily enter bankruptcy, it's common to say that they've "declared Chapter 11" or "gone into Chapter 11." References to other chapters aren't as common in everyday language.

DISCUSSION QUESTIONS

1. The Highland Instrument Company has revenues of about $300 million per year. Its management is interested in expanding into a new type of product manufactured primarily by Lowland Gauge Inc., a firm with sales of about $200 million annually. Both firms are publicly held with a broad base of stockholders. That is, no single interest holds a large percentage of the shares of either firm. Describe the types of business combination that might be available for the two firms. Include ideas like merger, consolidation, acquisition, friendly, and hostile. How would Highland's management

---

10. The high priority of postfiling expenses is aimed at keeping bankrupt firms in business until the proceedings are resolved. Without it, no one would do business with a firm in bankruptcy without being fully paid in advance.

11. Claims 3 through 5 clearly reflect a legislative intent to protect individuals over companies.

get started? Do the relative sizes of the two firms have any implications for the kinds of combination that are possible or likely?

2. The Cranston Company would like to acquire the Lamont Company, but overtures made to management have been emphatically rebuffed. Forty-five percent of Lamont's stock is owned by five investors who were involved in the company's founding and continue to be active in its management. Charlie Hardnose, Cranston's director of corporate development, has suggested a hostile takeover that would bypass Lamont's management. Could this work and does it seem to be a very good idea in this situation?

3. Hostile acquisitions create animosities between the stockholders of the acquired and acquiring companies. Comment on the truth of this statement.

4. You're a seasoned financial executive who's recently been hired as the CFO of the Pilaster Corporation. The firm has just finished two years in which its financial performance has been clearly below par. The company isn't in danger of failing, but it's clear that earnings and growth could be much better. The market price of Pilaster's stock reflects this lukewarm performance. It is currently selling for $32, down substantially from its peak of $48 a little over two years ago. (The market has been generally flat in the last two years.)

Several observers have blamed the lackluster performance on the firm's CEO, Gerald Beanweather, and his top assistants. This team installed some new technological and managerial methods several years ago that haven't worked out well. Recently, they've been talking about returning to the old, time-tested methods that most people feel will bring the firm back to its usual performance levels. In fact, your hiring was part of the turnaround effort.

It's currently seven o'clock on a cold, bleak Monday morning in February. On the previous evening the CEO's secretary phoned the entire executive team to tell them an emergency meeting was set for this morning. The group is now assembled waiting to hear what's going on.

At 7:01 Gerry walks into the room, obviously upset. He says that yesterday afternoon he received a call from Harvey Highroller, the CEO of Marble Inc., the leading firm in the industry. Marble is interested in acquiring Pilaster and is willing to offer $37 a share for its stock, a premium of more than 15%. Marble has a history of making both friendly and unfriendly acquisitions.

a. What kind of combination is Marble currently proposing?

b. What is likely to happen if Pilaster's management rejects Marble's offer?

c. Is Marble likely to be successful over management's objections?

d. Why is Gerry so personally upset?

e. Should you be personally upset?

f. Is Marble's offer a good deal for Pilaster's stockholders?

g. What should Pilaster's management do to avoid acquisition by Marble?

h. Do you think Marble is likely to be successful in an unfriendly merger attempt over Pilaster's defenses?

i. If Marble is not successful, what can the Beanweather team do to reduce the chances of a similar attack in the future?

5. Define vertical, horizontal, and conglomerate mergers and describe the economic effects of each.

6. Industry A is dominated by 10 large firms, each with sales of approximately $500 million per year. A proposal to merge two of these firms was approved by the Justice Department as not violating the antitrust laws. Industry B is locally defined and much smaller. It is dominated by three small firms, each selling about $50 million per year. A merger between two of these companies was prohibited under the antitrust laws. Explain the logic under which the merger of two $500 million giants can be allowed while the relatively insignificant merger of two small companies is disallowed.

7. Suppose an industry is dominated by three firms, one of which is twice as large as the other two, which are about the same size. Could a merger of the two smaller firms actually increase competition in the industry?

8. The Blue Tag Company and the Pink Label Corporation both make packaging and labeling equipment. The following facts are relevant.

  - Both firms use similar production and sales methods.
  - Pink Label has been losing money for years, while Blue Tag has been and is expected to continue to be profitable.
  - There is a great deal of overhead in label making.
  - The industry is dominated by the much larger Yellow Marker Co., which is difficult to compete with because of its size advantage.

  The managements of the two companies are considering a merger. What arguments can be made in favor of such a combination?

9. The Phlanders Flange Company has been doing quite well lately and would like to accelerate its growth within the flange industry. Harry Flatiron, the firm's CEO, has become interested in growth through acquisition because of some exciting articles in the business press. In particular he's interested in a friendly acquisition of the Framingham Flange Factory whose general manager, Jack Daniels (a major stockholder in Framingham), he's known for some time.

  Harry is prone to quick action based on brief analyses that he does himself. In the past his instincts have been pretty good, and this style has not as yet caused any major mistakes. Harry has taken Framingham's own estimate of its future cash flows and long-term growth rate along with synergies he and Jack have estimated to come up with a projected value for the company. All this has led to a proposal to offer Framingham's stockholders a 60% premium on the price of their stock.

  You're Phlanders's CFO, but Harry has done all this on his own. He's about ready to make a verbal offer to Framingham's management, and has asked you to check over his figures. His arithmetic is correct, but you're very concerned about the validity of his assumptions.

  Prepare a short memo to Harry outlining the risks associated with value estimates in mergers and the consequences of a mistake. Include advice on how to proceed.

10. You're the CFO of the Littleton Lighting Company. Joan Brightway, the president, has approached you and the firm's other senior executives with a proposal to take the company private through an LBO. She says that this is a good time to do it because the economic outlook is shaky and the firm's stock price is depressed, so it will take less money to acquire control. You agree that the weak outlook has depressed the stock's price, but aren't sure that this doesn't argue against an LBO at this time. You also suspect that some fundamental weakness is developing in the demand for the firm's product.

Certain successful LBOs have received a lot of favorable press lately, and you're concerned that Joan and the other nonfinancial executives may not appreciate the risks involved in the procedure. Prepare a memo outlining what's involved in an LBO and why the maneuver is risky, especially with respect to the business's performance in the immediate future. Make a recommendation on the analyses that should be undertaken prior to going forward.

11. Clarington Corp. has a division that's been performing well but doesn't fit into the company's current long-term strategic plans. Describe the methods through which it can divest the operation.

12. The Blivitt Company has been losing money and experiencing serious cash flow problems lately. The main problem is a large debt to the First National Bank that was incurred to purchase a computer that's now obsolete. Bill Blivitt, the firm's owner, has stated his intention to declare bankruptcy to rid the company of the loan. He expects to go in and out of Chapter 11 in a few weeks and emerge essentially as before but without the loan. Write a note to Bill explaining bankruptcy procedures and why this is probably an unrealistic approach on his part.

PROBLEMS

1. The target of an acquisition generates cash flows of $8 million per year with a risk level consistent with a return on equity of 16%.

   a. How much should an acquirer be willing to pay if it won't consider more than five years of future earnings in setting a price?

   b. What is the per share price if the target has 300,000 shares of common stock outstanding?

   c. Assume the acquirer intends to pay for the acquisition with its own stock, which is currently selling for $36 per share. How many shares must be offered for each share of the target's stock?

2. The Johnson Machine Tool Company is thinking of acquiring Lansing Gear Works Inc. Lansing's is a stable company that produces cash flows of $525,000 per year. That figure isn't expected to change in the near future, and no synergies are expected from the acquisition. Johnson's management has estimated that the appropriate risk adjusted discount rate for pricing calculations is 15%. Lansing has 200,000 shares of common stock outstanding.

a. What is the most Johnson should be willing to pay for Lansing if management is financially conservative and insists that an acquisition must justify itself within ten years? State the price in total and per share.

b. How much should Johnson be willing to pay, in total and per share, if management takes a more aggressive position and will consider Lansing's income as continuing forever? (*Hint:* Estimate Lansing's value as a perpetuity starting immediately.)

c. What total and per share prices are implied if Johnson's executives are financially very aggressive and assume that their management will transform Lansing into a better company that will grow at 3% per year indefinitely?

d. Comment briefly on the differences in your answers to a, b, and c.

3. Grandma's Cookies Inc. is considering acquiring Mother's Baked Goods Inc. After consideration of all benefits, synergies, and tax effects, Grandma (originally a finance major) has estimated that the incremental cash flows from the acquisition will be about $150,000 per year for 15 years. (Grandma is financially conservative and reluctant to base decisions on benefits projected farther into the future.) She has also estimated the project's discount rate, appropriately adjusted for risk, at 12%.

Mother's is a privately owned firm with 20,000 shares of stock outstanding. Grandma is confident that the owners will sell for $50 a share, but not for less. Should Grandma acquire Mother's?

4. Benson's Markets is a five-store regional supermarket chain that has done very well by using modern management and distribution techniques. Benson competes with Foodland Inc., a larger chain with ten stores. However, Foodland has not kept pace with technological and merchandising developments, and has been losing money lately. Foodland's owners are interested in retiring and have approached Benson's with a proposal to sell the chain for $50 million.

Within each chain, individual stores perform uniformly. Typical results for an average store in each company are as follows.

Typical Single-Store Results Benson's and Foodland Supermarkets ($000)

	Benson's	Foodland
Revenue	$45,000	$38,000
Cost of product	38,500	33,500
Store overhead: Depreciation	400	300
Other	4,600	4,700
EBT	$1,500	($500)
Tax	600	—
EAT	$ 900	($500)

If Benson were to make the acquisition, it would immediately close three of Foodland's stores that are located close to its own markets and sell the buildings for about $1 million each. The remaining stores would operate at their current loss levels for about two years, during which time they would be upgraded to Benson's operating standards. The upgrades would cost $3 million per store, spread over the first two years. After that, the acquired stores would have about the same operating performance as Benson's other stores. Benson's CFO feels that a discount rate of 12% is appropriate for the risk associated with the proposition. Benson's marginal tax rate is 40%.

a. Calculate the value of the acquisition to Benson's, assuming there is no impact on any of Benson's five original stores. Assume that the incremental cash flow from the acquired stores goes on forever but does not grow. Should Benson pay Foodland's price? If not, does the deal look good enough to negotiate for a better price? What is the most Benson should be willing to pay?

b. (No calculations—just ideas.) Are there reasons beyond the calculations in part a that argue in favor of the acquisition? (*Hint:* Think along two lines about the competitive situation. First, what will happen if Benson doesn't buy Foodland? Second, what effect will the acquisition have on Benson's existing stores?)

c. Could the ideas in part b be quantified into adjustments to the results in part a? Make your own estimate of the impact of such ideas on the price Benson should be willing to pay.

5. Frozen North Outfitters Inc. makes thermal clothing for winter sports and outdoor work. It is considering acquiring Downhill Fashions Corp., which manufactures and sells ski clothing. Downhill is about one quarter of Frozen's size and manufactures its entire product line in a small rented factory on a mountaintop in Colorado. It costs about $1 million a year in overhead to operate in that factory. Frozen produces its output in a less romantic but more practical southern location. Its factory has at least 50% excess capacity. Frozen's plan is to acquire Downhill and combine production operations in its southern factory, but otherwise run the companies separately.

Downhill's beta is 2.0, Treasury bills currently yield 5%, and the Standard and Poor's 500 Index is yielding 9%. The marginal combined federal and state income tax rate for both firms is 40%. Because Downhill will no longer be maintaining its own production facilities, only a minimal amount of cash will have to be reinvested to keep its equipment current and for future growth. This amount is estimated at $100,000 per year. Selected financial information for Downhill follows.

Revenue	$12,500,000
EAT	$ 1,300,000
Depreciation	$ 600,000

a. Calculate the appropriate discount rate for evaluating the Downhill acquisition.

b. Determine the annual cash flow expected by Frozen from Downhill if the acquisition is made (don't forget to include the synergy).

c. Calculate the value of the acquisition to Frozen assuming the benefits last for (1) 5 years, (2) 10 years, and (3) 15 years.

d. Downhill has 250,000 shares of stock outstanding. Calculate the maximum price Frozen should be willing to pay per share to acquire the firm under the three assumptions in part c.

e. If Frozen is willing to assume the benefits of the Downhill acquisition will last indefinitely but not grow, what should it be willing to pay per share?

6. In Problem 5, assume the cash flow from the Downhill acquisition grows at 10% from its initial value for one year and then grows at 5% indefinitely (starting in the third year). Calculate the value of the firm and the implied stock price under these conditions. Use a terminal value at the beginning of the period of 5% growth. What price premium is implied, in dollars and as a percentage, if Downhill's stock is currently selling at $62? Comment on the range of values in the results of Problems 3 and 4.

7. The Hamilton Corp. has 35,000 shares of common stock outstanding with a book value of $20 per share. It owes creditors $1.5 million at an interest rate of 12%. Selected financial results are as follows.

Income and Cash Flow		Capital	
EBIT	$ 80,000	Debt	$1,500,000
Interest	180,000	Equity	700,000
EBT	($100,000)		$2,200,000
Tax	0		
EAT	($100,000)		
Depreciation	50,000		
Principal repayment	(75,000)		
Cash flow	($125,000)		

Restructure the financial line items shown assuming a composition in which creditors agree to convert two-thirds of their debt into equity at book value. Assume Hamilton will pay tax at a rate of 15% on income after the restructuring, and that principal repayments are reduced proportionately with debt. Who will control the company and by how big a margin after the restructuring?

 Internet Problem

8. Using a search engine such as Yahoo or Alta Vista, look up bankruptcy and find out how many business bankruptcies occurred in the United States last calendar year. Then try to break down these bankruptcies by type (retail, restaurant, etc.). Finally, find out whether the trend for bankruptcies (both in absolute number and as a percent of businesses in existence) is up or down.

Chapter Outline

- The volume of **international business** is steadily **increasing** worldwide.

- International business has changed from import/export to **operating full-scale businesses** in other countries.

- Building a business in another country is a **direct investment**, while buying foreign securities is a **portfolio investment.**

In the last 40 years business has become increasingly international.[1] The change has occurred in two distinct ways. First, we do more business with other countries than ever before. In 1960, imports and exports were 3% and 4% of gross domestic product (GDP), respectively. In the 1990s, imports were about 10% of GDP, while exports were about 7.5%.

Second, the nature of international business has changed. In 1960 doing business with a foreign country generally just meant importing and exporting goods. Now, international business as often as not implies a **direct investment** in facilities and equipment in another country and the operation of a full-scale business there. Companies that have divisions and branches in other countries are known as **multinational corporations,** abbreviated MNCs.

Financial markets are also increasingly international. Forty years ago it was very unusual for an investor to buy the stock of a foreign company. Today people make **portfolio investments** in foreign stocks and bonds all the time.

---

1. The term "global" is often used to describe business's current international character. It implies that less developed countries are now included in the trading community along with industrially developed nations.

http://

For a listing of stock exchanges and major companies worldwide visit

www.euroyellowpages.com/bizlink/wldstock.html

International business is an increasingly large part of commercial activity in the United States. Virtually all companies of any size have some international dealings. It's clearly important, therefore, that we understand the basic financial principles of doing business with companies from other countries. Such business has all of the problems and challenges of operating domestically but includes several additional complications and risks. We'll begin by examining exchange rates in some detail.

CURRENCY EXCHANGE

Companies operate and expect to be paid in the currency of the countries in which they're located. That means anyone wanting to buy from a firm in another country has to acquire some of that country's currency first.

For example, if a U.S. company that operates department stores wants to buy expensive wool sweaters from a British manufacturer, it has to pay the bill in British pounds, not U.S. dollars. But the American firm has only dollars, not pounds. Clearly, to make the purchase, it has to *exchange* some dollars for pounds. We also say the firm *buys* pounds with dollars.

THE FOREIGN EXCHANGE MARKET

● Currencies are traded on **foreign exchange markets**.

The purchase is accomplished in the **foreign exchange market,** which is organized for the purpose of exchanging currencies.[2] The foreign exchange market operates much like other financial markets, but it isn't located in a specific place like a stock exchange. Rather, it's a network of brokers and banks based in financial centers around the world. Most commercial banks are able to access the market and provide exchange services to their clients.

EXCHANGE RATES

● An **exchange rate** states the price of one currency in terms of another.

Currencies are traded at an **exchange rate** that, in effect, is the price of each currency in terms of the other. In our illustration, the American firm needs to know how many pounds can be purchased for a dollar. That lets it calculate how many dollars it will need to pay the British firm's price in pounds.

The essence of the foreign exchange market is a table of exchange rates like Table 18.1. The table shows two reciprocal rates for each currency. For the moment ignore the *forward* rates in some currencies; we'll get to those shortly. Rates in the first column are called the *direct quote* and show the number of U.S. dollars required to buy one unit of the foreign currency. Rates in the second column are known as *indirect quotes* and represent the inverse relationship, how many units of the foreign currency it takes to buy one U.S. dollar. The direct and indirect quotes are reciprocals of one another.

Suppose the American company in our example wants to import 500 sweaters that cost a total of 35,000 pounds, written as £35,000 (where £ is used like the U.S. $). The exchange rate table indicates that one pound is worth $1.4259, so the American firm will have to exchange

---

2. The term **foreign exchange** is also used as a noun to refer to the foreign currency itself. We say a nation that wants to buy foreign goods needs foreign exchange.

TABLE 18.1

Exchange Rates, July 31, 2001

	Direct Quote ($ per unit of foreign currency)	Indirect Quote (foreign currency units per $)
Argentina (Peso)	1.0004	.9996
Australia (Dollar)	.5093	1.9633
⋮		
Brazil (Real)	.4044	2.4730
Britain (Pound)	1.4259	.7013
1-month forward	1.4241	.7022
3-months forward	1.4205	.7040
6-months forward	1.4152	.7066
Canada (Dollar)	.6521	1.5335
1-month forward	.6518	1.5342
3-months forward	.6513	1.5355
6-months forward	.6504	1.5374
⋮		
France (Franc)	.1335	7.4915
1-month forward	.1334	7.4967
3-months forward	.1332	7.5065
6-months forward	.1330	7.5179
Germany (Mark)	.4477	2.2337
1-month forward	.4474	2.2353
3-months forward	.4468	2.2382
6-months forward	.4461	2.2416
⋮		
Israel (Shekel)	.2374	4.2120
Italy (Lira)	.0004522	2211.36
Japan (Yen)	.007997	125.05
1-month forward	.008024	124.63
3-months forward	.008069	123.93
6-months forward	.008143	122.81
⋮		
Mexico (Peso)	.1090	9.1710
⋮		
Euro	.8756	1.1421
⋮		

Source: *Wall Street Journal,* 1 (August, 2001).

$$£35,000 \times \$1.4259/\text{pound} = \$49,907$$

to pay for the sweaters. In other words, the cost of the purchase is expected to be $49,907. Alternatively, the £35,000 could be divided by .7013 pounds per dollar to reach the same result.

The Effect of Exchange Rates on Prices and Quantities

It's important to notice that the exchange rate is part of the cost of product to a firm importing foreign goods. To illustrate, let's continue the sweater example we began in the last section. The expected cost per sweater at the time of ordering is

$$\$49,907/500 = \$99.81$$

● The exchange rate is **part of the cost** of product paid by an **importing** firm.

plus shipping and handling. Hence, a reasonable retail price would probably be about $200 (assuming roughly a 100% retail markup).

But what would happen if the exchange rate was less favorable? Suppose, for example, the direct quote is $1.95 per pound. Then the expected cost of the shipment would be

$$£35,000 \times \$1.9500/\text{pound} = \$68,250 \,,$$

a single sweater would cost

$$\$68,250/500 = \$136.50 \,,$$

and a reasonable retail price might be about $273.

In other words, the exchange rate has an influence on the domestic prices of imported goods. The more a foreign currency costs, the more expensive that nation's products are when offered to American buyers regardless of their cost in the country of origin.

● Exchange rates **affect the quantity of foreign product demanded** in an importing country.

It's an economic fundamental that when a product is more expensive, people buy less of it. For foreign goods that means higher prices due to less favorable exchange rates lead to decreased imports. In our illustration, the $1.95 pound implies a $73 higher retail price for a sweater. The American importer might well feel that the product won't sell at such a price and may order fewer than 500 or forgo the order entirely. Conversely, a more favorable exchange rate makes foreign products cheaper in the United States, causing larger quantities to be demanded leading to more imports. We'll come back to this important concept later.

Cross Rates

Given the information in the table, it's possible to develop an exchange rate between any two currencies without going through dollars. These are called *cross rates*. For example, the exchange rate between Brazilian reals and British pounds can be calculated from the direct quote column of Table 18.1 as follows.

$$\frac{1.4259 \text{ dollars per pound}}{.4044 \text{ dollars per real}} = 3.5260 \text{ reals per pound}$$

● CHANGING EXCHANGE RATES AND EXCHANGE RATE RISK

Exchange rates are constantly changing, sometimes quite rapidly and by significant amounts. We'll get into why they change in a little while, but first it's important to understand the implications of the fact that they do change.

Moving exchange rates give rise to **exchange rate risk**, a very important facet of international business. Exchange rate risk means that a firm can make or lose money on an international transaction because of rate movements aside from the business deal itself.

● **Exchange rate risk** is the chance of gain or loss from exchange rate movement that occurs **during** a transaction.

For example, imagine that the American company we've been talking about ordered its 500 sweaters on July 31, 2001, when the exchange rate was $1.4259 per pound. At that time it expected to pay the $49,907 we calculated earlier for the shipment. Also suppose the purchase is part of a contract that calls for payment three months after the order is placed.

When the U.S. firm returns to the foreign exchange market three months after ordering, the pound rate is unlikely to be the same. For the sake of illustration, suppose the direct quote has risen to $1.8500 per pound. That means paying the £35,000 bill will take

$$£35,000 \times \$1.8500/\text{pound} = \$64,750.$$

That's $14,843 more than was expected at the time the order was placed. The implication is that the profit made on the U.S. sale of the sweaters will be reduced by $14,843 just due to the fluctuation in the exchange rate.

Of course, the rate could have gone the other way. In that case, more profit than expected would be made. The point is that exchange rate variation throws an element of risk into the American firm's business that wouldn't be there if the sweaters were purchased domestically.

Transactions subject to exchange rate risk as well as the companies that do such transactions are said to have exchange rate *exposure*.

Spot and Forward Rates

The exchange rates we've described so far are *spot rates,* meaning that they're good for immediate, "on the spot" transactions.[3] Notice that the major currencies also have quotes on *forward rates* for one, three, and six months. These rates are quotes for delivery of the currency the indicated number of months in the future. Notice that they're somewhat different from the spot rates. The difference reflects the movement that foreign exchange brokers expect in the future relationship between the two currencies.

● **Forward rates** quote prices for **future delivery** of currencies.

For example, Table 18.1 shows that on July 31, 2001, the British pound was expected to become slightly less valuable in terms of dollars during the next six months. To see this, notice the decrease in the direct quote from $1.4259 to $1.4152, which says that it will take a little less U.S. money to buy a pound in the future. The indirect quote shows the same thing looking from the dollar to the pound; a dollar is expected to buy slightly more pounds in the future, because the indirect quote rises from .7013 to .7066 pounds per dollar.

When a foreign currency is expected to become less valuable in the future, as in this case, the forward currency is said to be selling at a *discount* over the spot currency. In the reverse situation, when a future dollar will buy less of the foreign currency than a present dollar, the forward currency is said to be selling at a *premium*.

THE TERMINOLOGY OF EXCHANGE RATE MOVEMENTS   When a currency becomes or is expected to become more valuable in terms of dollars, we say that it is becoming *stronger* or *rising* against the dollar. The same idea can also be expressed by saying that the dollar is becoming *weaker* or *falling* against the foreign currency. On July 31, 2001, the pound was expected to weaken against the dollar, which was expected to strengthen against the pound.

Hedging with Forward Exchange Rates

As we've said many times, people avoid risk whenever they can, and exchange rate risk is no exception. Most companies prefer to operate without it and are willing to pay a premium to do so.

● Exchange rate risk can be eliminated by **hedging** with a forward contract.

The forward market provides a way to eliminate foreign exchange risk from international transactions with a process called **hedging**.[4] A firm that knows it

---

3. Delivery on spot transactions is made in two days.
4. "Hedge" is a general term applied to an arrangement that reduces or avoids risk.

will need foreign currency at some time in the future can lock in an exchange rate by contracting with a bank for future delivery at the appropriate forward rate.

In our illustration, the American firm can negotiate a three-month *forward contract* for pounds with a bank at the time it places the sweater order. The three-month forward rate is $1.4205 per pound, which is a little less expensive than the spot rate (this isn't always the case; as often as not the forward rate is higher), so the shipment will cost

$$£35,000 \times \$1.4205/pound = \$49,718 \,.$$

Once the forward contract is written, exchange rate risk is eliminated from the transaction, as £35,000 will be delivered in three months for $49,718. The firm is said to have *covered* its obligation with a *forward market hedge*. Forward contracts can be written between any two currencies, for any amount, and for any length of time. There is a cost, however, because brokers and banks charge fees for the service.

The forward market enables companies to transfer foreign exchange risk to professionals who are in the business of bearing such risks.

● EUROPEAN CURRENCIES IN THE TWENTY-FIRST CENTURY—THE EURO

On January 1, 2002, twelve European countries adopted a common currency known as the Euro (€). A single currency is expected to help to solidify Western Europe into an economic force better able to compete with the United States and Japan. It should also promote trade between the countries sharing the currency because the flow of goods between them will no longer be influenced by exchange rate fluctuations.

The twelve participating nations are Austria, Belgium, Ireland, Italy, Finland, France, Germany, Greece, Luxembourg, the Netherlands, Portugal, and Spain. Great Britain, conspicuous by its absence, is not going along with the new idea, at least for the time being.

Notice that the exchange rates shown in Table 18.1 are dated July 31, 2001, five months prior to the transition, and show both the old national currencies and the Euro. That's because both the old and new currencies were in use during a two year transition period immediately prior to the change-over. The old currencies were also accepted for a short period immediately after January 1, 2002.

As this book goes to print in early 2002, the transition to Euros has been accomplished smoothly. If all goes as planned, the old national currencies will disappear from the foreign exchange market shortly. Thereafter, trading in the participating countries will be done strictly in Euros.

● SUPPLY AND DEMAND—THE SOURCE OF EXCHANGE RATE MOVEMENT

Simply stated, an exchange rate is the price of a unit of foreign currency. For example, Table 18.1 tells us that on July 31, 2001, a British pound cost $1.4259.

We can think of the pound as a commodity offered for sale in a free market. Its price, like that of any commodity, is determined by the interaction of supply and demand, traditionally represented by supply and demand curves like those in Figure 18.1(a). The intersection of the two curves determines the market price of the commodity—in this case the direct quote exchange rate.

Figure 18.1(b) shows the supply and demand picture from the British side where the dollar is a commodity purchased with pounds. In this view the intersection is the exchange rate in terms of pounds per dollar, the indirect quote.

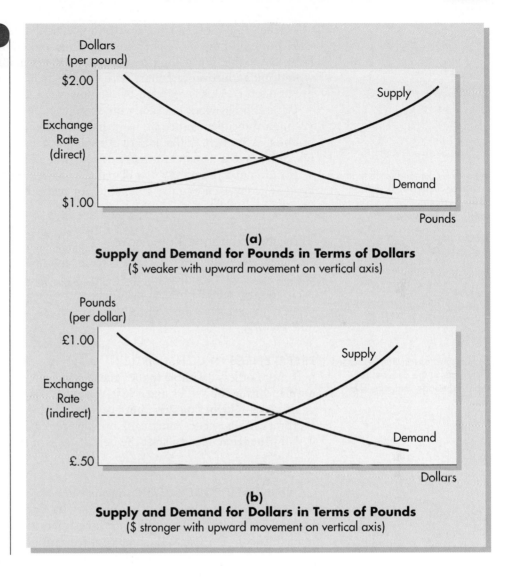

FIGURE 18.1

Foreign Exchange: British Pounds and U.S. Dollars

(a)
Supply and Demand for Pounds in Terms of Dollars
($ weaker with upward movement on vertical axis)

(b)
Supply and Demand for Dollars in Terms of Pounds
($ stronger with upward movement on vertical axis)

The Origins of the Supply and Demand for Foreign Exchange

The demand for and the supply of foreign exchange between any two nations stem primarily from trade and the flow of investment capital between those nations. First let's look at trade.

When companies in the United States want to buy things (import) from another country, say Britain, they also need to buy the currency to make their purchases. This sets up a demand for pounds. At the same time, British companies that want to buy American goods have to buy dollars with pounds. This sets up a supply of pounds.

Now look at Figure 18.1(a). As the direct exchange rate gets higher on the vertical axis—that is, as a pound becomes more expensive in terms of dollars—British goods get more expensive in the United States. That leads to a reduction in the quantity of those goods demanded by U.S. consumers and consequently to a reduction in the need for pounds. This is reflected by the downward slope of the demand curve in the diagram.

At the same time, moving up on the vertical axis of Figure 18.1(a) means a British pound buys more U.S. dollars. That makes U.S. goods cheaper in England, so people are willing to buy more of them. British importers therefore would like to buy more dollars with pounds, which increases the available supply of pounds. This is reflected by the upward slope of the supply curve.

Capital flows work in exactly the same way. A strong dollar makes British investments cheaper, so people want more of them, leading to a big demand for pounds. A weaker dollar makes American investments cheap for the British, which leads to a demand for more dollars and a larger supply of pounds.

● The supply/demand for foreign exchange is **derived** from each country's **demand** for the other's **goods** and investments.

In summary, the supply and demand curves that establish exchange rates are *derived* from each country's demand for the other country's trade goods and investments.

Why the Exchange Rate Moves

Movement in exchange rates results from shifts in the supply and demand curves for foreign exchange. Because the curves arise primarily from the demand within each country for the other's products and investments, anything that changes those demands affects the curves for currency. Let's examine several such changeable factors.

● Exchange rates move in response to **changes in the demand for imported goods** within the two countries.

PREFERENCES IN CONSUMPTION   Anything that makes one country's products more or less desirable to the other's population will move the curves. For example, during the 1970s and 1980s Japanese car manufacturers were perceived as producing higher quality, more cost effective products than American manufacturers. As a result, Americans bought increasing numbers of Japanese cars. This influence tended to shift the demand curve for Japanese currency (yen) to the right.

GOVERNMENT POLICY   Governments can actively encourage or discourage imports by imposing quotas, charging tariffs and duties, and making import licenses difficult to obtain. Foreign investment can be similarly encouraged or made difficult. For example, some countries prohibit foreign ownership of a majority interest in companies operating within their borders. That makes foreign direct investment less attractive.

The trade relationship between Japan and the United States in the postwar period has been shaped by the policies of the Japanese government. The Japanese have consistently encouraged exports while limiting U.S. imports. At the same time, the U.S. government maintains a relatively open policy and has done little to inhibit imports from Japan. This has led to a significant imbalance in which we import a great deal more from Japan than we export to it.

ECONOMIC CONDITIONS   A number of economic conditions influence the foreign exchange market. Here are a few.

1. In general, more prosperous economies demand more imports than economies undergoing recession.

2. Economies that are growing rapidly have more investment opportunities than those that aren't and therefore attract more foreign investment.

3. Countries in which interest rates are relatively high attract foreign investment because their financial assets offer higher returns than are available

in other countries (if the high interest rates aren't accompanied by excessive inflation).

4. Countries with relatively high inflation rates make poor foreign investment targets. During periods of high inflation, a country's currency can lose value at a rate that's greater than the returns offered on most investments. Therefore the net effect of an investment is likely to be a loss.

SPECULATION   Changes in exchange rates create speculative opportunities just like changes in the prices of stocks. If a foreign currency is strengthening against the dollar, holding it results in a gain. Hence, some people trade in currencies for profit rather than to do international business. The transactions made by such speculators can be significant in size and sometimes have a noticeable effect on overall demand and supply.

DIRECT GOVERNMENT INTERVENTION   Governments sometimes buy and sell their own currencies for the express purpose of keeping exchange rates within desirable ranges. We'll discuss the reasons behind this activity shortly.

In the modern world, the factors that cause exchange rate movement change all the time. Hence the supply and demand curves for foreign exchange are constantly shifting, as is their intersection, the exchange rate.

GOVERNMENTS AND THE INTERNATIONAL MONETARY SYSTEM

Recall that earlier we said exchange rates influence the domestic prices of imported goods. Let's pursue that idea a little further.

● A strong dollar makes **imports cheaper**, but has a negative effect on **employment** because it reduces exports.

Suppose a nation's currency suddenly strengthens relative to the currencies of other countries. We'll use the U.S. dollar to illustrate, but the results are true for any currency. As a result of a strengthening dollar, two things happen, one good and the other bad. First, imported goods become cheaper, because a dollar buys more foreign exchange and hence more foreign product. That's generally good for consumers, and people like it.

At the same time, however, U.S. exports become more expensive in other countries. That means fewer are sold and the demand placed on U.S. manufacturers for exported product diminishes. The result is a reduction in industrial activity in the United States and eventually a loss of jobs, which, of course, is bad.

Conversely, if the dollar weakens, foreign products become more expensive here, which leads to a general lowering of our standard of living. However, our exports increase because they're cheaper in other nations, and the increased business creates jobs here.

Summarizing, we can say that exchange rates affect the domestic economy through two opposing forces: the cost of imported goods and the employment generated by producing goods for export.

Government Influence on Exchange Rates

It's important to recognize that these opposing forces need to be kept in balance. In other words, it isn't good for an economy if the exchange rate goes too far in either direction. Cheap imports aren't worth excessive unemployment, and low unemployment isn't worth a substantially higher cost of living. For that reason, governments occasionally intervene in foreign exchange markets to keep rates within what they feel are reasonable ranges.

● **Governments** sometimes **intervene** in foreign exchange markets to keep **exchange rates within desirable limits**.

Governments accomplish this intervention by buying and selling their own currencies in the foreign exchange market. For example, if the dollar is getting too weak, the U.S. Treasury will buy dollars. This action adds to other demands for dollars and pushes all dollar demand curves to the right in diagrams like Figure 18.1(b). It thus raises the exchange rate for dollars in terms of the other currencies (the indirect quote).

A government's ability to *support* a weakening currency in this way is limited because it has to pay for its purchases of its own money with either gold or foreign exchange already in its possession. Both of these are clearly of limited availability.

Conversely, if a currency is too strong, the government will sell its own currency. This action has the effect of increasing supply and lowering its cost in terms of other currencies.

The International Monetary System

The international monetary system is the set of rules by which countries collectively administer the exchange of currencies. The system in place at the present time, which we've been describing, is known as a *floating exchange rate system*. That means exchange rates are determined essentially by free market forces. Some government intervention does occur, but not much, and it's usually the result of an agreement between several nations to maintain economic stability.

● In a **floating exchange rate** system, **market forces** set rates with **little intervention** from governments.

The floating rate system has been in effect since the early 1970s. Between the end of World War II (1945) and that time the world was on a *fixed exchange rate system*, meaning rates were fixed by international treaty and administered by an organization known as the International Monetary Fund (the IMF still exists).

Under the fixed rate system, market forces tended to push rates around just as they do now, but each country had the responsibility of holding its exchange rate with the U.S. dollar nearly constant. The value of the dollar was fixed in terms of gold at $35 per ounce. Countries maintained the value of their currencies against the dollar by buying and selling in the foreign exchange market as we described in the last section.

As the economic status of nations changed during the post–World War II period, it sometimes became impossible to keep certain exchange rates constant. When that happened a nation could go through a *revaluation* to officially raise the value of its currency relative to the dollar or a *devaluation* to lower its value. As the West German economy strengthened, it went through two revaluations in the 1960s, while the British pound was devalued in 1967.

By the 1970s the dollar's tie to gold at $35 per ounce had become unrealistic as the market price of gold had risen to more than $100. At that time the fixed rate system was abandoned along with the fixed dollar price of gold, and the floating rate system was established.

Convertibility

Not all currencies are *convertible*. That is, many can't be exchanged in the way we've described in this chapter. For its currency to be convertible, a nation must allow it to be traded on foreign exchange markets and be willing to accept the resulting value. The currencies of Russia and China have traditionally not been convertible.

● A currency that isn't **convertible** cannot be exchanged for other currencies at **market-determined** rates.

Nonconvertibility doesn't mean there isn't an exchange rate. If you want to buy a Russian product, the Russian government will be glad to sell you the *rubles* you need at its official exchange rate. However, the system works only one way.

If you have rubles, there is generally no one willing to exchange them for dollars or any other major currency at the exchange rate set by the Russian government.

Inconvertibility is a significant impediment to international business. Suppose a Western company establishes a branch in Russia and makes a profit doing business there. The profit is in rubles, and because the currency isn't convertible it's very difficult to repatriate it back into the company's home country. To get value out of the country, it's generally necessary to buy something made in Russia with the ruble profit (like vodka), export it to the home country, and sell it there. Unfortunately, nations with nonconvertible money don't tend to have a great many things that people in other countries want to buy.

The Balance of Trade

Let's go back to the supply and demand diagrams of Figure 18.1. Unlike the supply and demand diagrams for other commodities, those for foreign exchange represent a reciprocal arrangement. That is, the supply of another nation's currency seen by Americans depends on the demand in that other country for U.S. dollars. In other words, the only place you can get pounds is England, and the English have to want to buy U.S. dollars or there won't be any pounds available.

The total money flow between countries includes trade, investing activities, and payments made directly between governments. The latter include loans, loan payments along with interest, and foreign aid.

The net flow between two countries from trade is known as the **balance of trade.** If the U.S. imports more from another country than we export to it, we say a *trade deficit* exists between the nations from the U.S. perspective. If we export more to a country than we import, we say a *trade surplus* exists.

● If we **import more** from a country than we export, a **trade deficit** exists and our currency accumulates in that country.

A consistent trade deficit or surplus with respect to a particular country can continue for a long time if it's offset by other financial flows between the two nations, or if the country with the trade surplus is willing to accumulate a store of the currency of the country with a deficit. When such an accumulation happens, the available pool of the deficit country's money tends to weaken the value of its currency. In Figure 18.1(b), it pushes the supply curve to the right, lowering the indirect exchange rate. That should make the deficit nation's exports cheaper in the surplus nation, thus bringing trade back in balance. However, that tendency toward balance doesn't happen if the surplus nation artificially restricts imports from the deficit nation.

That's what happened between the United States and Japan during the 1970s, 1980s, and early 1990s. A trade deficit existed from the U.S. perspective largely because of Japan's restrictions on U.S. imports. During the period the dollar fell by about 60% against the yen. Further, the surplus of dollars available to the Japanese coupled with the low exchange rate enabled them to make massive investments in real estate and productive capacity in the United States. This led many people to become concerned about the level of economic control the Japanese exercise in this country.

In the last few years the problem has been mitigated for several reasons—some of which were quite unexpected. Under U.S. government pressure, the Japanese did ease import restrictions somewhat. More significantly, however, the Japanese economy suffered a series of financial crises in the mid-1990s that weakened the nation's international position dramatically and led to a normalization of the trade relationship between the two nations.

Nevertheless, the Japanese have strong, established positions in many U.S. markets today at the expense of U.S. manufacturers. The most visible examples are automobiles and electronics. That gain to their economy and loss to ours can be traced to currency and trade balance issues from a decade or more ago.

INTERNATIONAL CAPITAL MARKETS

http://

Qualisteam provides information on worldwide markets at

www.qualisteam.com/
● eng/marche.shtml

Today it is common for individuals and businesses to make investments in countries other than their own. We've already discussed making a direct investment in facilities in another country and a portfolio investment in the securities of a business from another country. A portfolio investment can also be made in bonds issued by another government. These activities require the flow of capital funds among nations, and several institutional practices have arisen to assist in those flows. We'll have a brief look at the Eurodollar market and international bonds after a digression on the status of the American dollar.

The Unique Status of the U.S. Dollar

Since World War II, the U.S. dollar has been the world's leading currency. In a sense it functions as international money. The dollar has this unique role because people have more confidence in its continuing value than they have in the value of any other currency. This confidence no doubt stems from America's unique status as a superpower in both military and economic terms.

● The **U.S. dollar** is the world's leading currency and in some ways serves as **"international money."**

In any event, most international businesspeople are willing to take dollars in trade because they're confident that American money can be exchanged for their own currencies at any time and that its value isn't likely to fall suddenly. (The exchange rate is still needed to determine how many dollars something priced in another currency is worth.) In fact, a dollar may be preferable to their own currency, which may not be as stable.

Many international contracts are denominated in dollars even when none of the parties to the contract are American.

● THE EURODOLLAR MARKET

A **Eurodollar** is an American dollar deposited in a bank outside the United States. People deposit money in foreign banks because their interest rates on dollar deposits are somewhat higher than those offered by domestic banks.

● **Eurodollars** are dollar deposits in **foreign banks** that are loaned to international businesses in the **eurodollar market**.

The foreign banks create the **Eurodollar market** by lending the Eurodollars to international companies and foreign governments that have a need for American currency. The borrowers use Eurodollars for a variety of things, including payment for U.S. exports, portfolio investments in American stocks and bonds, and as a medium of exchange between parties that don't want to deal in their own currencies.

Eurodollar deposits don't have to be in European banks; they can be anywhere in the world. They're called **Euro**dollars simply because the practice started in Europe. The deposits are typically made for fixed periods that can range from a single day to approximately five years. They're also rather large, starting at about $500,000.

● THE INTERNATIONAL BOND MARKET

In earlier chapters, we talked about bonds issued by domestic corporations sold in the United States. (Keep in mind that selling a bond means the issuing company is borrowing money from the bond's buyer.) It is possible, however, for companies to borrow internationally by selling bonds outside their own

● An **international bond** is sold outside of the home country of the borrower.

countries. Any bond sold outside the home country of the borrower is called an **international bond.**

The idea of an international bond raises a question about the currency in which the bond's face value is stated. The bond can be *denominated* in the currency of the issuing company's home country, or in the currency of the country in which it is sold, or in some third currency.

● A bond issued by a foreign company but denominated in **local** currency is a **foreign bond**.

A bond denominated in the currency of the country in which it is sold, but issued by a foreign borrower, is called a **foreign bond.** For example, a Japanese auto manufacturer like Honda or Toyota might want to open an assembly plant in the United States financed in some part by borrowing. It could do that by issuing dollar-denominated bonds in the United States, registering them with the Securities and Exchange Commission (SEC), and selling them through American financial markets. To buyers, the bonds would be just like those of domestic companies except for the headquarters location of the issuing company. Importantly, they would be subject to all of the registration and disclosure requirements of U.S. securities law, which tend to be more stringent than the requirements of other nations.

A bond denominated in a currency other than that of the country in which it is sold is called a **Eurobond.** For example, Honda could sell bonds denominated in Japanese yen to Americans in the United States or to people in any other country. Once again, the term "Euro" is historically derived and doesn't imply that the issuing company is European. In fact, most Eurobonds are denominated in American dollars and sold to investors in other countries.

● A **eurobond** is denominated in a currency other than that of the country in which it is sold.

Eurobonds have several distinguishing features. First, securities regulations in most countries require a much lower level of disclosure for Eurobonds than for domestic or foreign bonds. This significantly lowers the cost of issuing them in comparison with the cost of issuing foreign or domestic bonds.

Second, Eurobonds are issued in *bearer* form, so the owner is not identified. Third, most governments don't withhold income tax on Eurobond interest payments. The second and third features make Eurobonds attractive to some investors, perhaps those who are interested in privacy and/or avoiding their own countries' taxes.

POLITICAL RISK

When capital is invested in another country, especially through direct investment, it becomes subject to the authority of the government of that country. **Political risk** refers to the probability that the value of a firm's investment in a foreign country will be reduced by political actions taken primarily by the country's government.

Nations have a unique set of powers described as *sovereignty* that aren't shared by companies or lower level government units regardless of their size. In the extreme, a sovereign nation can take human life and seize property located within its borders without compensating the owner. When property is taken by a foreign government it is said to be **expropriated.**

● **Political risk** is the chance that a foreign government will **expropriate** property or that **terrorists** will destroy it.

Expropriation is generally the worst-case scenario contemplated within the idea of political risk. It is relatively rare, but it has happened in a number of less developed countries including Chile, Bolivia, Cuba, Libya, Iraq, and Iran.

Although not as drastic as expropriation, certain other actions can reduce the value of a foreign venture substantially. They take the form of arbitrarily

Ethics

The Foreign Corrupt Practices Act—
A Legal/Ethical Dilemma for U.S. Companies

Corruption in government is a worldwide problem and has been throughout recorded history. Corrupt practices occur in every nation, but they're particularly flagrant in some less developed countries (LDCs), including many in Africa, Asia, and South America.

In international business, the corruption issue typically arises when a government official has control over the selection of a foreign company to perform some work and allows that choice to be influenced by bribes. Virtually all countries have laws against officials taking bribes, but in LDCs they're usually ignored. In fact, in many LDCs bribery is a common practice that everyone knows about and expects.

In the mid-1970s the fact that U.S. companies were making payments to foreign officials to obtain business came to light in a big way. Congress and the public were appalled by the level of corruption that existed in some countries and the extent to which American companies were taking part in it. Congress responded by passing the Foreign Corrupt Practices Act of 1977, which makes it *illegal* for U.S. companies to pay bribes to influence decision makers in foreign governments. Companies can be fined and executives can be jailed for violating the law.

However, the act creates a large problem for U.S. companies trying to compete against firms from other industrialized nations that don't have similar laws. For example, suppose an oil-rich Middle Eastern country wants to construct a $500 million building complex in its capital city and that contractors from the United States, Germany, and Japan submit bids. Profit on the job might be $100 million.

Also suppose local government officials expect gifts of $5 million from the winning bidder according to a long-standing practice that's accepted even though it's technically against local law. Notice that from a financial perspective, the bribe is a relatively minor cost that any of the bidders would be glad to pay to get the profitable contract.

The problem should be obvious. The German and Japanese companies can pay the bribe to get the business, but the American company can't. That may shut it out of the competition.

Are we doing the ethically right thing as a nation? Or are we stepping on our own toes over something no one else cares about, while other industrialized nations laugh at us behind our backs?

imposed rules and regulations on operations and ownership. For example, a host country government can:

- Raise taxes of all kinds on the business.
- Limit the amount of profit that can be taken out of the country, either directly or through controls on currency conversion.
- Require that key inputs be purchased from local suppliers at arbitrary prices.
- Limit the prices charged for product sold within the country.
- Require part ownership by citizens of the host country, forcing sale of an interest in the business at an unrealistically low price.

Political risk also includes potential losses due to the actions of politically motivated terrorist groups. In the past these have included sabotage and bombing of property, as well as the murder and kidnapping for ransom of key executives.

Political risk is quite small in industrialized nations with which the United States is on good terms, such as the Western European countries, Japan, Taiwan, and Australia. It can be substantial, however, in the Third World nations of Africa, Asia, and South America and in places where the political climate is unstable or free enterprise capitalism is new to the population and the government, like the former Soviet Union and the Eastern Bloc countries.

TRANSACTION AND TRANSLATION RISKS

Earlier we defined exchange rate risk as the potential gain or loss that arises from changes in the exchange rate between the time an international transaction is contracted and the time it's completed. This idea is also called *transaction risk* because it arises from transactions as they occur. **Transaction gains and losses** have real profit and cash flow impacts because they're *realized* in cash as they happen. For this reason, they're taxable events.

However, exchange rates also generate the risk of another type of gain or loss. **Translation risk** refers to the potential gain or loss that arises from translating the financial statements (especially the balance sheet) of a foreign subsidiary from the local currency into dollars for consolidation with the parent company's financial statements.[5]

● Translation gains/losses arise when assets and liabilities held in a foreign country are translated into dollars.

For example, suppose an American firm spends $2 million to build a factory in England when the exchange rate is two dollars to the pound (direct quote $2.00 = £1.00; indirect quote $1.00 = £.50). Immediately after the factory is built, the balance sheet of the English subsidiary shows an asset of £1 million representing the factory and an equity account of the same amount. The parent's balance sheet shows an asset of $2 million representing its investment in the foreign company.

When the parent company closes its *consolidated* books in dollars, the value of the British factory effectively replaces the account carrying the investment in its foreign subsidiary.[6] While the exchange rate remains at two dollars to the pound, the £1 million factory on the British books translates exactly into $2 million, which replaces the $2 million investment account, so there's no problem.

Now suppose the dollar strengthens so that a pound is worth only $1.75 (indirect quote $1.00 = £.57). On the British subsidiary's books, the factory is

---

5. Three sets of financial statements are used when one company owns another: the parent's, the subsidiary's, and the consolidated sum of the two. The parent's balance sheet carries an asset called investment in subsidiary that reflects its ownership of the subsidiary. That account's balance is equal to the balance in the equity account of the subsidiary.

When the parent's and the subsidiary's balance sheets are consolidated, like assets and liabilities are added together for companywide totals. However, the investment in subsidiary (a debit) on the parent's books is combined with the subsidiary's equity (a credit). Normally, the two accounts are equal in magnitude, so they eliminate one another, and the consolidated books look like one big company.

6. In this simplified example the subsidiary has only one asset and no liabilities other than equity. Hence the exchange rate changes on the asset will be mirrored in the equity account.

still valued at £1 million. However, translating at the new rate gives a dollar value of

$$£1,000,000 \times \$1.75/£ = \$1,750,000.$$

But the parent's investment account still carries a $2 million balance. The difference implies that the factory has lost $250,000 in value in dollar terms. That loss has to be recognized in the consolidation procedure. This is a *translation loss*.

In other words, because the factory in England is valued in pounds, and the pound lost value against the dollar, the factory also lost value. And that loss has to be reflected in the company's overall consolidated books. Of course, if the pound had strengthened against the dollar, the firm would have had a translation gain.

The Relevance of Translation Gains and Losses

Notice that a translation gain or loss isn't quite real; it's only on paper. In our example, the American firm still owns the English factory regardless of its value in pounds, so nothing's really changed. As long as the company doesn't sell the factory and attempt to repatriate the proceeds to the United States, the loss isn't *realized* in cash and is something of an abstraction.

Recognizing this, the accounting rules for consolidating international subsidiaries specify that translation gains and losses are not to be included in consolidated income statements. Rather they're shown cumulatively in an account that adds to or offsets stockholders' equity. And because they're not realized, they're not taxable.

DISCUSSION QUESTIONS

1. Describe the ways in which international business has changed during the last 40 years. Include the concepts of an MNC and the different types of foreign investment.

2. After World War II, the United States was the world's dominant economic power. We're still the largest economy, but the rest of the world has caught up significantly. In some areas we've lost the lead. The production of consumer electronic equipment, for example, is largely done in the Far East. Is this trend good or bad for Americans? Explain.

3. When you want to buy something from another country, you have to find a seller who's willing to take dollars, but that isn't too hard because the U.S. dollar is widely accepted. Comment on this statement.

4. Exchange transactions between two currencies, neither of which is the U.S. dollar, have to be made by changing one currency into dollars and then changing the dollars into the other currency. This procedure is necessary because the exchange tables are all set up to convert between other currencies and dollars, the world's leading currency. Are these statements true or false? Why? If false, how does the conversion work?

5. You're the treasurer of Warm Wear Inc., which imports wool sweaters from around the world. Kreploc, a company in the country of Slobodia, has a product your marketing department would like to carry, and doesn't require payment until 90 days after delivery. Unfortunately the Slobodian blivit tends to vary in value by as much as 30% over periods as short as three months. This makes you reluctant to do business with Kreploc because of exchange rate risk. The marketing department can't understand why you have any concerns at all. Prepare a brief explanation, including an illustration, of why you're concerned.

6. You're the CFO of the Overseas Sprocket Company, which imports a great deal of product from Europe and the Far East and is continually faced with exchange rate exposure on unfilled contracts. Harry Byrite, the head of purchasing, has a plan to avoid exchange rate losses. He suggests that the firm borrow enough money from the bank to buy a six-month supply of foreign exchange that would be kept in a safety deposit box until used. "We'd never have another unexpected exchange rate loss again," says Harry. Prepare a polite response to Harry's idea. Explain why you do or don't like it, and suggest an alternative if you feel one is appropriate.

7. What generates the supply of and the demand for foreign exchange? Why do the supply and demand curves have the shape they do? What makes the supply and demand curves and hence the exchange rate move around?

8. Why might the government be interested in influencing exchange rates from time to time? How would it go about moving the exchange rate?

9. Describe the difference between a floating and a fixed exchange rate system.

10. You're the CFO of the Kraknee Roller Skate Company, which sells roller skates worldwide and also builds and operates roller rinks. Some time ago Archie Speedo, the head of international marketing, proposed selling skates in Russia. Everyone thought he was crazy, but the idea turned out to be very successful. Archie lined up a talented Russian importer, who managed to sell more skates than anyone imagined possible. Now Archie has proposed a new Russian venture. He wants to open and operate a roller rink in Moscow. He says that since the breakup of the Soviet Union, Russians are interested in Western pastimes, and a roller rink in the capital city would make a fortune. Based on his earlier success in Russia, the rest of the executive team is in favor of the idea. You, however, have some concerns. Write a memo explaining how the roller rink proposal differs from exporting skates to Russia, and what problem is likely even if the venture is as commercially successful as the skates. What other risk is involved?

11. What is a trade deficit, and why does it hurt us to consistently run a deficit with another country?

12. How and why is the U.S. dollar unique among the world's currencies?

13. A British importer has to pay for American goods, but the exchange rate is temporarily very unfavorable from the British perspective. Describe the Eurodollar market and tell how it might help the importer.

PROBLEMS

Use the exchange rates in Table 18.1 on page 627 for Problems 1 and 2.

1. An American importer owes vendors the following sums.
   a. 140,560 Canadian dollars
   b. 392,000 Australian dollars
   c. 1,362,000 Mexican pesos
   d. 680,540 British pounds

   State each debt in American dollars.

2. A Japanese importer owes an American exporter $450,520.
   a. What is her bill in yen if she pays immediately?
   b. What would the bill be if the importer wanted to lock in an exchange rate today but pay in 3 months?

3. The following direct quote exchange rates are found on the spot market today.
   a. Euro: $.9347
   b. Israeli shekel: $.2586
   c. British pound: $1.6544
   d. Japanese yen: $.009423

   Calculate the price of a U.S. dollar in terms of each currency, the indirect quote.

4. Go to the *Wall Street Journal* and look up today's exchange rates for the currencies in Problems 1 and 2. Resolve the problems using today's rates. Analyze how the rates have changed since July 31, 2001.

5. The Cline family made a trip to Europe in 2001. They paid the following amounts in local currency for hotel, entertainment, and transportation.

England	£855
France	FF9,246
Germany	DM1,930
Italy	L1,456,320

   How much did the trip cost in U.S. dollars once they get to Europe? Use the exchange rates in Table 18.1.

6. Suppose a car manufactured in Japan in the mid-1980s, when there were 250 yen to the dollar, cost 2 million yen to produce and was marked up 25% for sale in the United States. Assume the car's cost in yen and markup are the same today, but the exchange rate is 100 yen to the dollar.
   a. What did the car sell for in dollars in the United States in the mid-1980s?
   b. What does it sell for now?

7. In 2001, the Greenbay Motor Company ordered six German-built engines at DM15,000 each (DM is the symbol for the German mark) when the direct exchange rate was $.7014 per mark and elected not to cover the obligation with a forward contract. When the bill was due three months later the rate was $.6843. Greenbay's marginal tax rate is 40%.

a. How much was the exchange rate gain or loss on the deal?

b. What kind of exchange rate gain or loss was it?

c. What was the tax impact?

8. Hampshire Motors Ltd., a British manufacturing company, wants to buy a production machine that isn't available in England. Comparable products are made by an American company and a French firm. The Americans have quoted Hampshire a price of $175,000, while the French want €192,000. (€ is the symbol for Euros and is used like our $.) How much is each price in British pounds? Calculate a cross rate to state the French quote in pounds. Use the exchange rates in Table 18.1.

9. The Latimore Company invested $8.5 million in a new plant in Italy when the exchange rate was 1.1500 euros to the dollar. At the end of the year, the rate was 1.2000 euros to the dollar.

a. Did Latimore make or lose money on the exchange rate movement? If so, how much?

b. What kind of exchange rate gain or loss was it?

c. What was the tax impact?

Internet Problem

10. Visit the CNN Financial Network at http://cnnfn.com/markets/currencies.html. List the exchange rate per U.S. dollar for each of the following currencies:

a. Japanese yen

b. Mexican peso

c. South African rand

d. Euro

APPENDIXES

APPENDIX A: FINANCIAL TABLES

| TABLE A-1 | | | | | $FVF_{k,n} = (1 + k)^n$ | | | | | | | | | |

INTEREST RATES

Periods	0.5%	0.67%	0.75%	1%	1.5%	2%	2.5%	3%	3.5%	4%	4.5%	5%	6%	7%
1	1.0050	1.0067	1.0075	1.0100	1.0150	1.0200	1.0250	1.0300	1.0350	1.0400	1.0450	1.0500	1.0600	1.0700
2	1.0100	1.0134	1.0151	1.0201	1.0302	1.0404	1.0506	1.0609	1.0712	1.0816	1.0920	1.1025	1.1236	1.1449
3	1.0151	1.0201	1.0227	1.0303	1.0457	1.0612	1.0769	1.0927	1.1087	1.1249	1.1412	1.1576	1.1910	1.2250
4	1.0202	1.0269	1.0303	1.0406	1.0614	1.0824	1.1038	1.1255	1.1475	1.1699	1.1925	1.2155	1.2625	1.3108
5	1.0253	1.0338	1.0381	1.0510	1.0773	1.1041	1.1314	1.1593	1.1877	1.2167	1.2462	1.2763	1.3382	1.4026
6	1.0304	1.0407	1.0459	1.0615	1.0934	1.1262	1.1597	1.1941	1.2293	1.2653	1.3023	1.3401	1.4185	1.5007
7	1.0355	1.0476	1.0537	1.0721	1.1098	1.1487	1.1887	1.2299	1.2723	1.3159	1.3609	1.4071	1.5036	1.6058
8	1.0407	1.0546	1.0616	1.0829	1.1265	1.1717	1.2184	1.2668	1.3168	1.3686	1.4221	1.4775	1.5938	1.7182
9	1.0459	1.0616	1.0696	1.0937	1.1434	1.1951	1.2489	1.3048	1.3629	1.4233	1.4861	1.5513	1.6895	1.8385
10	1.0511	1.0687	1.0776	1.1046	1.1605	1.2190	1.2801	1.3439	1.4106	1.4802	1.5530	1.6289	1.7908	1.9672
11	1.0564	1.0758	1.0857	1.1157	1.1779	1.2434	1.3121	1.3842	1.4600	1.5395	1.6229	1.7103	1.8983	2.1049
12	1.0617	1.0830	1.0938	1.1268	1.1956	1.2682	1.3449	1.4258	1.5111	1.6010	1.6959	1.7959	2.0122	2.2522
13	1.0670	1.0902	1.1020	1.1381	1.2136	1.2936	1.3785	1.4685	1.5640	1.6651	1.7722	1.8856	2.1329	2.4098
14	1.0723	1.0975	1.1103	1.1495	1.2318	1.3195	1.4130	1.5126	1.6187	1.7317	1.8519	1.9799	2.2609	2.5785
15	1.0777	1.1048	1.1186	1.1610	1.2502	1.3459	1.4483	1.5580	1.6753	1.8009	1.9353	2.0789	2.3966	2.7590
16	1.0831	1.1122	1.1270	1.1726	1.2690	1.3728	1.4845	1.6047	1.7340	1.8730	2.0224	2.1829	2.5404	2.9522
17	1.0885	1.1196	1.1354	1.1843	1.2880	1.4002	1.5216	1.6528	1.7947	1.9479	2.1134	2.2920	2.6928	3.1588
18	1.0939	1.1270	1.1440	1.1961	1.3073	1.4282	1.5597	1.7024	1.8575	2.0258	2.2085	2.4066	2.8543	3.3799
19	1.0994	1.1346	1.1525	1.2081	1.3270	1.4568	1.5987	1.7535	1.9225	2.1068	2.3079	2.5270	3.0256	3.6165
20	1.1049	1.1421	1.1612	1.2202	1.3469	1.4859	1.6386	1.8061	1.9898	2.1911	2.4117	2.6533	3.2071	3.8697
21	1.1104	1.1497	1.1699	1.2324	1.3671	1.5157	1.6796	1.8603	2.0594	2.2788	2.5202	2.7860	3.3996	4.1406
22	1.1160	1.1574	1.1787	1.2447	1.3876	1.5460	1.7216	1.9161	2.1315	2.3699	2.6337	2.9253	3.6035	4.4304
23	1.1216	1.1651	1.1875	1.2572	1.4084	1.5769	1.7646	1.9736	2.2061	2.4647	2.7522	3.0715	3.8197	4.7405
24	1.1272	1.1729	1.1964	1.2697	1.4295	1.6084	1.8087	2.0328	2.2833	2.5633	2.8760	3.2251	4.0489	5.0724
25	1.1328	1.1807	1.2054	1.2824	1.4509	1.6406	1.8539	2.0938	2.3632	2.6658	3.0054	3.3864	4.2919	5.4274
26	1.1385	1.1886	1.2144	1.2953	1.4727	1.6734	1.9003	2.1566	2.4460	2.7725	3.1407	3.5557	4.5494	5.8074
27	1.1442	1.1965	1.2235	1.3082	1.4948	1.7069	1.9478	2.2213	2.5316	2.8834	3.2820	3.7335	4.8223	6.2139
28	1.1499	1.2045	1.2327	1.3213	1.5172	1.7410	1.9965	2.2879	2.6202	2.9987	3.4297	3.9201	5.1117	6.6488
29	1.1556	1.2125	1.2420	1.3345	1.5400	1.7758	2.0464	2.3566	2.7119	3.1187	3.5840	4.1161	5.4184	7.1143
30	1.1614	1.2206	1.2513	1.3478	1.5631	1.8114	2.0976	2.4273	2.8068	3.2434	3.7453	4.3219	5.7435	7.6123
32	1.1730	1.2369	1.2701	1.3749	1.6103	1.8845	2.2038	2.5751	3.0067	3.5081	4.0900	4.7649	6.4534	8.7153
34	1.1848	1.2535	1.2892	1.4026	1.6590	1.9607	2.3153	2.7319	3.2209	3.7943	4.4664	5.2533	7.2510	9.9781
36	1.1967	1.2702	1.3086	1.4308	1.7091	2.0399	2.4325	2.8983	3.4503	4.1039	4.8774	5.7918	8.1473	11.4239
38	1.2087	1.2872	1.3283	1.4595	1.7608	2.1223	2.5557	3.0748	3.6960	4.4388	5.3262	6.3855	9.1543	13.0793
40	1.2208	1.3045	1.3483	1.4889	1.8140	2.2080	2.6851	3.2620	3.9593	4.8010	5.8164	7.0400	10.2857	14.9745
48	1.2705	1.3757	1.4314	1.6122	2.0435	2.5871	3.2715	4.1323	5.2136	6.5705	8.2715	10.4013	16.3939	25.7289
50	1.2832	1.3941	1.4530	1.6446	2.1052	2.6916	3.4371	4.3839	5.5849	7.1067	9.0326	11.4674	18.4202	29.4570
60	1.3489	1.4898	1.5657	1.8167	2.4432	3.2810	4.3998	5.8916	7.8781	10.5196	14.0274	18.6792	32.9877	57.9464
120	1.8194	2.2196	2.4514	3.3004	5.9693	10.7652	19.3581	34.7110	62.0643	110.663	196.768	348.912	1088.19	3357.79
180	2.4541	3.3069	3.8380	5.9958	14.5844	35.3208	85.1718	204.503	488.948	1164.13	2760.15	6517.39	35896.8	*
240	3.3102	4.9268	6.0092	10.8926	35.6328	115.889	374.738	1204.85	3851.98	12246.2	38717.7	*	*	*
300	4.4650	7.3402	9.4084	19.7885	87.0588	380.235	1648.77	7098.51	30346.2	*	*	*	*	*
360	6.0226	10.9357	14.7306	35.9496	212.704	1247.56	7254.23	41821.6	*	*	*	*	*	*

Periods	8%	9%	10%	11%	12%	13%	14%	15%	16%	18%	20%	24%	30%	36%
1	1.0800	1.0900	1.1000	1.1100	1.1200	1.1300	1.1400	1.1500	1.1600	1.1800	1.2000	1.2400	1.3000	1.3600
2	1.1664	1.1881	1.2100	1.2321	1.2544	1.2769	1.2996	1.3225	1.3456	1.3924	1.4400	1.5376	1.6900	1.8496
3	1.2597	1.2950	1.3310	1.3676	1.4049	1.4429	1.4815	1.5209	1.5609	1.6430	1.7280	1.9066	2.1970	2.5155
4	1.3605	1.4116	1.4641	1.5181	1.5735	1.6305	1.6890	1.7490	1.8106	1.9388	2.0736	2.3642	2.8561	3.4210
5	1.4693	1.5386	1.6105	1.6851	1.7623	1.8424	1.9254	2.0114	2.1003	2.2878	2.4883	2.9316	3.7129	4.6526
6	1.5869	1.6771	1.7716	1.8704	1.9738	2.0820	2.1950	2.3131	2.4364	2.6996	2.9860	3.6352	4.8268	6.3275
7	1.7138	1.8280	1.9487	2.0762	2.2107	2.3526	2.5023	2.6600	2.8262	3.1855	3.5832	4.5077	6.2749	8.6054
8	1.8509	1.9926	2.1436	2.3045	2.4760	2.6584	2.8526	3.0590	3.2784	3.7589	4.2998	5.5895	8.1573	11.7034
9	1.9990	2.1719	2.3579	2.5580	2.7731	3.0040	3.2519	3.5179	3.8030	4.4355	5.1598	6.9310	10.6045	15.9166
10	2.1589	2.3674	2.5937	2.8394	3.1058	3.3946	3.7072	4.0456	4.4114	5.2338	6.1917	8.5944	13.7858	21.6466
11	2.3316	2.5804	2.8531	3.1518	3.4785	3.8359	4.2262	4.6524	5.1173	6.1759	7.4301	10.6571	17.9216	29.4393
12	2.5182	2.8127	3.1384	3.4985	3.8960	4.3345	4.8179	5.3503	5.9360	7.2876	8.9161	13.2148	23.2981	40.0375
13	2.7196	3.0658	3.4523	3.8833	4.3635	4.8980	5.4924	6.1528	6.8858	8.5994	10.6993	16.3863	30.2875	54.4510
14	2.9372	3.3417	3.7975	4.3104	4.8871	5.5348	6.2613	7.0757	7.9875	10.1472	12.8392	20.3191	39.3738	74.0534
15	3.1722	3.6425	4.1772	4.7846	5.4736	6.2543	7.1379	8.1371	9.2655	11.9737	15.4070	25.1956	51.1859	100.713
16	3.4259	3.9703	4.5950	5.3109	6.1304	7.0673	8.1372	9.3576	10.7480	14.1290	18.4884	31.2426	66.5417	136.969
17	3.7000	4.3276	5.0545	5.8951	6.8660	7.9861	9.2765	10.7613	12.4677	16.6722	22.1861	38.7408	86.5042	186.278
18	3.9960	4.7171	5.5599	6.5436	7.6900	9.0243	10.5752	12.3755	14.4625	19.6733	26.6233	48.0386	112.455	253.338
19	4.3157	5.1417	6.1159	7.2633	8.6128	10.1974	12.0557	14.2318	16.7765	23.2144	31.9480	59.5679	146.192	344.540
20	4.6610	5.6044	6.7275	8.0623	9.6463	11.5231	13.7435	16.3665	19.4608	27.3930	38.3376	73.8641	190.050	468.574
21	5.0338	6.1088	7.4002	8.9492	10.8038	13.0211	15.6676	18.8215	22.5745	32.3238	46.0051	91.5915	247.065	637.261
22	5.4365	6.6586	8.1403	9.9336	12.1003	14.7138	17.8610	21.6447	26.1864	38.1421	55.2061	113.574	321.184	866.674
23	5.8715	7.2579	8.9543	11.0263	13.5523	16.6266	20.3616	24.8915	30.3762	45.0076	66.2474	140.831	417.539	1178.68
24	6.3412	7.9111	9.8497	12.2392	15.1786	18.7881	23.2122	28.6252	35.2364	53.1090	79.4968	174.631	542.801	1603.00
25	6.8485	8.6231	10.8347	13.5855	17.0001	21.2305	26.4619	32.9190	40.8742	62.6686	95.3962	216.542	705.641	2180.08
26	7.3964	9.3992	11.9182	15.0799	19.0401	23.9905	30.1666	37.8568	47.4141	73.9490	114.475	268.512	917.333	2964.91
27	7.9881	10.2451	13.1100	16.7386	21.3249	27.1093	34.3899	43.5353	55.0004	87.2598	137.371	332.955	1192.53	4032.28
28	8.6271	11.1671	14.4210	18.5799	23.8839	30.6335	39.2045	50.0656	63.8004	102.967	164.845	412.864	1550.29	5483.90
29	9.3173	12.1722	15.8631	20.6237	26.7499	34.6158	44.6931	57.5755	74.0085	121.501	197.814	511.952	2015.38	7458.10
30	10.0627	13.2677	17.4494	22.8923	29.9599	39.1159	50.9502	66.2118	85.8499	143.371	237.376	634.820	2620.00	10143.0
32	11.7371	15.7633	21.1138	28.2056	37.5817	49.9471	66.2148	87.5651	115.520	199.629	341.822	976.099	4427.79	18760.5
34	13.6901	18.7284	25.5477	34.7521	47.1425	63.7774	86.0528	115.805	155.443	277.964	492.224	1500.85	7482.97	34699.5
36	15.9682	22.2512	30.9127	42.8181	59.1356	81.4374	111.834	153.152	209.164	387.037	708.802	2307.71	12646.2	64180.1
38	18.6253	26.4367	37.4043	52.7562	74.1797	103.987	145.340	202.543	281.452	538.910	1020.67	3548.33	21372.1	*
40	21.7245	31.4094	45.2593	65.0009	93.0510	132.782	188.884	267.864	378.721	750.378	1469.77	5455.91	36118.9	*
48	40.2106	62.5852	97.0172	149.797	230.391	352.992	538.807	819.401	1241.61	2820.57	6319.75	30495.9	*	*
50	46.9016	74.3575	117.391	184.565	289.002	450.736	700.233	1083.66	1670.70	3927.36	9100.44	46890.4	*	*
60	101.257	176.031	304.482	524.057	897.597	1530.05	2595.92	4384.00	7370.20	20555.1	56347.5	*	*	*
120	10253.0	30987.0	92709.1	*	*	*	*	*	*	*	*	*	*	*
180	*	*	*	*	*	*	*	*	*	*	*	*	*	*
240	*	*	*	*	*	*	*	*	*	*	*	*	*	*
300	*	*	*	*	*	*	*	*	*	*	*	*	*	*
360	*	*	*	*	*	*	*	*	*	*	*	*	*	*

*$FVF_{k,n} \geq 100{,}000$

	TABLE A-2			$PVF_{k,n} = (1 + k)^{-n}$										
						INTEREST RATES								
Periods	0.5%	0.67%	0.75%	1%	1.5%	2%	2.5%	3%	3.5%	4%	4.5%	5%	6%	7%
1	0.9950	0.9934	0.9926	0.9901	0.9852	0.9804	0.9756	0.9709	0.9662	0.9615	0.9569	0.9524	0.9434	0.9346
2	0.9901	0.9868	0.9852	0.9803	0.9707	0.9612	0.9518	0.9426	0.9335	0.9246	0.9157	0.9070	0.8900	0.8734
3	0.9851	0.9803	0.9778	0.9706	0.9563	0.9423	0.9286	0.9151	0.9019	0.8890	0.8763	0.8638	0.8396	0.8163
4	0.9802	0.9738	0.9706	0.9610	0.9422	0.9238	0.9060	0.8885	0.8714	0.8548	0.8386	0.8227	0.7921	0.7629
5	0.9754	0.9673	0.9633	0.9515	0.9283	0.9057	0.8839	0.8626	0.8420	0.8219	0.8025	0.7835	0.7473	0.7130
6	0.9705	0.9609	0.9562	0.9420	0.9145	0.8880	0.8623	0.8375	0.8135	0.7903	0.7679	0.7462	0.7050	0.6663
7	0.9657	0.9546	0.9490	0.9327	0.9010	0.8706	0.8413	0.8131	0.7860	0.7599	0.7348	0.7107	0.6651	0.6227
8	0.9609	0.9482	0.9420	0.9235	0.8877	0.8535	0.8207	0.7894	0.7594	0.7307	0.7032	0.6768	0.6274	0.5820
9	0.9561	0.9420	0.9350	0.9143	0.8746	0.8368	0.8007	0.7664	0.7337	0.7026	0.6729	0.6446	0.5919	0.5439
10	0.9513	0.9357	0.9280	0.9053	0.8617	0.8203	0.7812	0.7441	0.7089	0.6756	0.6439	0.6139	0.5584	0.5083
11	0.9466	0.9295	0.9211	0.8963	0.8489	0.8043	0.7621	0.7224	0.6849	0.6496	0.6162	0.5847	0.5268	0.4751
12	0.9419	0.9234	0.9142	0.8874	0.8364	0.7885	0.7436	0.7014	0.6618	0.6246	0.5897	0.5568	0.4970	0.4440
13	0.9372	0.9172	0.9074	0.8787	0.8240	0.7730	0.7254	0.6810	0.6394	0.6006	0.5643	0.5303	0.4688	0.4150
14	0.9326	0.9112	0.9007	0.8700	0.8118	0.7579	0.7077	0.6611	0.6178	0.5775	0.5400	0.5051	0.4423	0.3878
15	0.9279	0.9051	0.8940	0.8613	0.7999	0.7430	0.6905	0.6419	0.5969	0.5553	0.5167	0.4810	0.4173	0.3624
16	0.9233	0.8991	0.8873	0.8528	0.7880	0.7284	0.6736	0.6232	0.5767	0.5339	0.4945	0.4581	0.3936	0.3387
17	0.9187	0.8932	0.8807	0.8444	0.7764	0.7142	0.6572	0.6050	0.5572	0.5134	0.4732	0.4363	0.3714	0.3166
18	0.9141	0.8873	0.8742	0.8360	0.7649	0.7002	0.6412	0.5874	0.5384	0.4936	0.4528	0.4155	0.3503	0.2959
19	0.9096	0.8814	0.8676	0.8277	0.7536	0.6864	0.6255	0.5703	0.5202	0.4746	0.4333	0.3957	0.3305	0.2765
20	0.9051	0.8756	0.8612	0.8195	0.7425	0.6730	0.6103	0.5537	0.5026	0.4564	0.4146	0.3769	0.3118	0.2584
21	0.9006	0.8698	0.8548	0.8114	0.7315	0.6598	0.5954	0.5375	0.4856	0.4388	0.3968	0.3589	0.2942	0.2415
22	0.8961	0.8640	0.8484	0.8034	0.7207	0.6468	0.5809	0.5219	0.4692	0.4220	0.3797	0.3418	0.2775	0.2257
23	0.8916	0.8583	0.8421	0.7954	0.7100	0.6342	0.5667	0.5067	0.4533	0.4057	0.3634	0.3256	0.2618	0.2109
24	0.8872	0.8526	0.8358	0.7876	0.6995	0.6217	0.5529	0.4919	0.4380	0.3901	0.3477	0.3101	0.2470	0.1971
25	0.8828	0.8470	0.8296	0.7798	0.6892	0.6095	0.5394	0.4776	0.4231	0.3751	0.3327	0.2953	0.2330	0.1842
26	0.8784	0.8413	0.8234	0.7720	0.6790	0.5976	0.5262	0.4637	0.4088	0.3607	0.3184	0.2812	0.2198	0.1722
27	0.8740	0.8358	0.8173	0.7644	0.6690	0.5859	0.5134	0.4502	0.3950	0.3468	0.3047	0.2678	0.2074	0.1609
28	0.8697	0.8302	0.8112	0.7568	0.6591	0.5744	0.5009	0.4371	0.3817	0.3335	0.2916	0.2551	0.1956	0.1504
29	0.8653	0.8247	0.8052	0.7493	0.6494	0.5631	0.4887	0.4243	0.3687	0.3207	0.2790	0.2429	0.1846	0.1406
30	0.8610	0.8193	0.7992	0.7419	0.6398	0.5521	0.4767	0.4120	0.3563	0.3083	0.2670	0.2314	0.1741	0.1314
32	0.8525	0.8085	0.7873	0.7273	0.6210	0.5306	0.4538	0.3883	0.3326	0.2851	0.2445	0.2099	0.1550	0.1147
34	0.8440	0.7978	0.7757	0.7130	0.6028	0.5100	0.4319	0.3660	0.3105	0.2636	0.2239	0.1904	0.1379	0.1002
36	0.8356	0.7873	0.7641	0.6989	0.5851	0.4902	0.4111	0.3450	0.2898	0.2437	0.2050	0.1727	0.1227	0.0875
38	0.8274	0.7769	0.7528	0.6852	0.5679	0.4712	0.3913	0.3252	0.2706	0.2253	0.1878	0.1566	0.1092	0.0765
40	0.8191	0.7666	0.7416	0.6717	0.5513	0.4529	0.3724	0.3066	0.2526	0.2083	0.1719	0.1420	0.0972	0.0668
48	0.7871	0.7269	0.6986	0.6203	0.4894	0.3865	0.3057	0.2420	0.1918	0.1522	0.1209	0.0961	0.0610	0.0389
50	0.7793	0.7173	0.6883	0.6080	0.4750	0.3715	0.2909	0.2281	0.1791	0.1407	0.1107	0.0872	0.0543	0.0339
60	0.7414	0.6712	0.6387	0.5504	0.4093	0.3048	0.2273	0.1697	0.1269	0.0951	0.0713	0.0535	0.0303	0.0173
120	0.5496	0.4505	0.4079	0.3030	0.1675	0.0929	0.0517	0.0288	0.0161	0.0090	0.0051	0.0029	0.0009	0.0003
180	0.4075	0.3024	0.2605	0.1668	0.0686	0.0283	0.0117	0.0049	0.0020	0.0009	0.0004	0.0002	0.0000	0.0000
240	0.3021	0.2030	0.1664	0.0918	0.0281	0.0086	0.0027	0.0008	0.0003	0.0001	0.0000	0.0000	0.0000	0.0000
300	0.2240	0.1362	0.1063	0.0505	0.0115	0.0026	0.0006	0.0001	0.0000	0.0000	0.0000	0.0000	0.0000	0.0000
360	0.1660	0.0914	0.0679	0.0278	0.0047	0.0008	0.0001	0.0000	0.0000	0.0000	0.0000	0.0000	0.0000	0.0000

Periods	8%	9%	10%	11%	12%	13%	14%	15%	16%	18%	20%	24%	30%	36%
1	0.9259	0.9174	0.9091	0.9009	0.8929	0.8850	0.8772	0.8696	0.8621	0.8475	0.8333	0.8065	0.7692	0.7353
2	0.8573	0.8417	0.8264	0.8116	0.7972	0.7831	0.7695	0.7561	0.7432	0.7182	0.6944	0.6504	0.5917	0.5407
3	0.7938	0.7722	0.7513	0.7312	0.7118	0.6931	0.6750	0.6575	0.6407	0.6086	0.5787	0.5245	0.4552	0.3975
4	0.7350	0.7084	0.6830	0.6587	0.6355	0.6133	0.5921	0.5718	0.5523	0.5158	0.4823	0.4230	0.3501	0.2923
5	0.6806	0.6499	0.6209	0.5935	0.5674	0.5428	0.5194	0.4972	0.4761	0.4371	0.4019	0.3411	0.2693	0.2149
6	0.6302	0.5963	0.5645	0.5346	0.5066	0.4803	0.4556	0.4323	0.4104	0.3704	0.3349	0.2751	0.2072	0.1580
7	0.5835	0.5470	0.5132	0.4817	0.4523	0.4251	0.3996	0.3759	0.3538	0.3139	0.2791	0.2218	0.1594	0.1162
8	0.5403	0.5019	0.4665	0.4339	0.4039	0.3762	0.3506	0.3269	0.3050	0.2660	0.2326	0.1789	0.1226	0.0854
9	0.5002	0.4604	0.4241	0.3909	0.3606	0.3329	0.3075	0.2843	0.2630	0.2255	0.1938	0.1443	0.0943	0.0628
10	0.4632	0.4224	0.3855	0.3522	0.3220	0.2946	0.2697	0.2472	0.2267	0.1911	0.1615	0.1164	0.0725	0.0462
11	0.4289	0.3875	0.3505	0.3173	0.2875	0.2607	0.2366	0.2149	0.1954	0.1619	0.1346	0.0938	0.0558	0.0340
12	0.3971	0.3555	0.3186	0.2858	0.2567	0.2307	0.2076	0.1869	0.1685	0.1372	0.1122	0.0757	0.0429	0.0250
13	0.3677	0.3262	0.2897	0.2575	0.2292	0.2042	0.1821	0.1625	0.1452	0.1163	0.0935	0.0610	0.0330	0.0184
14	0.3405	0.2992	0.2633	0.2320	0.2046	0.1807	0.1597	0.1413	0.1252	0.0985	0.0779	0.0492	0.0254	0.0135
15	0.3152	0.2745	0.2394	0.2090	0.1827	0.1599	0.1401	0.1229	0.1079	0.0835	0.0649	0.0397	0.0195	0.0099
16	0.2919	0.2519	0.2176	0.1883	0.1631	0.1415	0.1229	0.1069	0.0930	0.0708	0.0541	0.0320	0.0150	0.0073
17	0.2703	0.2311	0.1978	0.1696	0.1456	0.1252	0.1078	0.0929	0.0802	0.0600	0.0451	0.0258	0.0116	0.0054
18	0.2502	0.2120	0.1799	0.1528	0.1300	0.1108	0.0946	0.0808	0.0691	0.0508	0.0376	0.0208	0.0089	0.0039
19	0.2317	0.1945	0.1635	0.1377	0.1161	0.0981	0.0829	0.0703	0.0596	0.0431	0.0313	0.0168	0.0068	0.0029
20	0.2145	0.1784	0.1486	0.1240	0.1037	0.0868	0.0728	0.0611	0.0514	0.0365	0.0261	0.0135	0.0053	0.0021
21	0.1987	0.1637	0.1351	0.1117	0.0926	0.0768	0.0638	0.0531	0.0443	0.0309	0.0217	0.0109	0.0040	0.0016
22	0.1839	0.1502	0.1228	0.1007	0.0826	0.0680	0.0560	0.0462	0.0382	0.0262	0.0181	0.0088	0.0031	0.0012
23	0.1703	0.1378	0.1117	0.0907	0.0738	0.0601	0.0491	0.0402	0.0329	0.0222	0.0151	0.0071	0.0024	0.0008
24	0.1577	0.1264	0.1015	0.0817	0.0659	0.0532	0.0431	0.0349	0.0284	0.0188	0.0126	0.0057	0.0018	0.0006
25	0.1460	0.1160	0.0923	0.0736	0.0588	0.0471	0.0378	0.0304	0.0245	0.0160	0.0105	0.0046	0.0014	0.0005
26	0.1352	0.1064	0.0839	0.0663	0.0525	0.0417	0.0331	0.0264	0.0211	0.0135	0.0087	0.0037	0.0011	0.0003
27	0.1252	0.0976	0.0763	0.0597	0.0469	0.0369	0.0291	0.0230	0.0182	0.0115	0.0073	0.0030	0.0008	0.0002
28	0.1159	0.0895	0.0693	0.0538	0.0419	0.0326	0.0255	0.0200	0.0157	0.0097	0.0061	0.0024	0.0006	0.0002
29	0.1073	0.0822	0.0630	0.0485	0.0374	0.0289	0.0224	0.0174	0.0135	0.0082	0.0051	0.0020	0.0005	0.0001
30	0.0994	0.0754	0.0573	0.0437	0.0334	0.0256	0.0196	0.0151	0.0116	0.0070	0.0042	0.0016	0.0004	0.0001
32	0.0852	0.0634	0.0474	0.0355	0.0266	0.0200	0.0151	0.0114	0.0087	0.0050	0.0029	0.0010	0.0002	0.0001
34	0.0730	0.0534	0.0391	0.0288	0.0212	0.0157	0.0116	0.0086	0.0064	0.0036	0.0020	0.0007	0.0001	0.0000
36	0.0626	0.0449	0.0323	0.0234	0.0169	0.0123	0.0089	0.0065	0.0048	0.0026	0.0014	0.0004	0.0001	0.0000
38	0.0537	0.0378	0.0267	0.0190	0.0135	0.0096	0.0069	0.0049	0.0036	0.0019	0.0010	0.0003	0.0000	0.0000
40	0.0460	0.0318	0.0221	0.0154	0.0107	0.0075	0.0053	0.0037	0.0026	0.0013	0.0007	0.0002	0.0000	0.0000
48	0.0249	0.0160	0.0103	0.0067	0.0043	0.0028	0.0019	0.0012	0.0008	0.0004	0.0002	0.0000	0.0000	0.0000
50	0.0213	0.0134	0.0085	0.0054	0.0035	0.0022	0.0014	0.0009	0.0006	0.0003	0.0001	0.0000	0.0000	0.0000
60	0.0099	0.0057	0.0033	0.0019	0.0011	0.0007	0.0004	0.0002	0.0001	0.0000	0.0000	0.0000	0.0000	0.0000
120	0.0001	0.0000	0.0000	0.0000	0.0000	0.0000	0.0000	0.0000	0.0000	0.0000	0.0000	0.0000	0.0000	0.0000
180	0.0000	0.0000	0.0000	0.0000	0.0000	0.0000	0.0000	0.0000	0.0000	0.0000	0.0000	0.0000	0.0000	0.0000
240	0.0000	0.0000	0.0000	0.0000	0.0000	0.0000	0.0000	0.0000	0.0000	0.0000	0.0000	0.0000	0.0000	0.0000
300	0.0000	0.0000	0.0000	0.0000	0.0000	0.0000	0.0000	0.0000	0.0000	0.0000	0.0000	0.0000	0.0000	0.0000
360	0.0000	0.0000	0.0000	0.0000	0.0000	0.0000	0.0000	0.0000	0.0000	0.0000	0.0000	0.0000	0.0000	0.0000

TABLE A-3

$$FVFA_{k,n} = \sum_{i=1}^{n} (1 + k)^{n-i}$$

INTEREST RATES

Periods	0.5%	0.67%	0.75%	1%	1.5%	2%	2.5%	3%	3.5%	4%	4.5%	5%	6%	7%
1	1.0000	1.0000	1.0000	1.0000	1.0000	1.0000	1.0000	1.0000	1.0000	1.0000	1.0000	1.0000	1.0000	1.0000
2	2.0050	2.0067	2.0075	2.0100	2.0150	2.0200	2.0250	2.0300	2.0350	2.0400	2.0450	2.0500	2.0600	2.0700
3	3.0150	3.0200	3.0226	3.0301	3.0452	3.0604	3.0756	3.0909	3.1062	3.1216	3.1370	3.1525	3.1836	3.2149
4	4.0301	4.0402	4.0452	4.0604	4.0909	4.1216	4.1525	4.1836	4.2149	4.2465	4.2782	4.3101	4.3746	4.4399
5	5.0503	5.0671	5.0756	5.1010	5.1523	5.2040	5.2563	5.3091	5.3625	5.4163	5.4707	5.5256	5.6371	5.7507
6	6.0755	6.1009	6.1136	6.1520	6.2296	6.3081	6.3877	6.4684	6.5502	6.6330	6.7169	6.8019	6.9753	7.1533
7	7.1059	7.1416	7.1595	7.2135	7.3230	7.4343	7.5474	7.6625	7.7794	7.8983	8.0192	8.1420	8.3938	8.6540
8	8.1414	8.1892	8.2132	8.2857	8.4328	8.5830	8.7361	8.8923	9.0517	9.2142	9.3800	9.5491	9.8975	10.2598
9	9.1821	9.2483	9.2748	9.3685	9.5593	9.7546	9.9545	10.1591	10.3685	10.5828	10.8021	11.0266	11.4913	11.9780
10	10.2280	10.3054	10.3443	10.4622	10.7027	10.9497	11.2034	11.4639	11.7314	12.0061	12.2882	12.5779	13.1808	13.8164
11	11.2792	11.3741	11.4219	11.5668	11.8633	12.1687	12.4835	12.8078	13.1420	13.4864	13.8412	14.2068	14.9716	15.7836
12	12.3356	12.4499	12.5076	12.6825	13.0412	13.4121	13.7956	14.1920	14.6020	15.0258	15.4640	15.9171	16.8699	17.8885
13	13.3972	13.5329	13.6014	13.8093	14.2368	14.6803	15.1404	15.6178	16.1130	16.6268	17.1599	17.7130	18.8821	20.1406
14	14.4642	14.6231	14.7034	14.9474	15.4504	15.9739	16.5190	17.0863	17.6770	18.2919	18.9321	19.5986	21.0151	22.5505
15	15.5365	15.7206	15.8137	16.0969	16.6821	17.2934	17.9319	18.5989	19.2957	20.0236	20.7841	21.5786	23.2760	25.1290
16	16.6142	16.8254	16.9323	17.2579	17.9324	18.6393	19.3802	20.1569	20.9710	21.8245	22.7193	23.6575	25.6725	27.8881
17	17.6973	17.9376	18.0593	18.4304	19.2014	20.0121	20.8647	21.7616	22.7050	23.6975	24.7417	25.8404	28.2129	30.8402
18	18.7858	19.0572	19.1947	19.6147	20.4894	21.4123	22.3863	23.4144	24.4997	25.6454	26.8551	28.1324	30.9057	33.9990
19	19.8797	20.1842	20.3387	20.8109	21.7967	22.8406	23.9460	25.1169	26.3572	27.6712	29.0636	30.5390	33.7600	37.3790
20	20.9791	21.3188	21.4912	22.0190	23.1237	24.2974	25.5447	26.8704	28.2797	29.7781	31.3714	33.0660	36.7856	40.9955
21	22.0840	22.4609	22.6524	23.2392	24.4705	25.7833	27.1833	28.6765	30.2695	31.9692	33.7831	35.7193	39.9927	44.8652
22	23.1944	23.6107	23.8223	24.4716	25.8376	27.2990	28.8629	30.5368	32.3289	34.2480	36.3034	38.5052	43.3923	49.0057
23	24.3104	24.7681	25.0010	25.7163	27.2251	28.8450	30.5844	32.4529	34.4604	36.6179	38.9370	41.4305	46.9958	53.4361
24	25.4320	25.9332	26.1885	26.9735	28.6335	30.4219	32.3490	34.4265	36.6665	39.0826	41.6892	44.5020	50.8156	58.1767
25	26.5591	27.1061	27.3849	28.2432	30.0630	32.0303	34.1578	36.4593	38.9499	41.6459	44.5652	47.7271	54.8645	63.2490
26	27.6919	28.2868	28.5903	29.5256	31.5140	33.6709	36.0117	38.5530	41.3131	44.3117	47.5706	51.1135	59.1564	68.6765
27	28.8304	29.4754	29.8047	30.8209	32.9867	35.3443	37.9120	40.7096	43.7591	47.0842	50.7113	54.6691	63.7058	74.4838
28	29.9745	30.6719	31.0282	32.1291	34.4815	37.0512	39.8598	42.9309	46.2906	49.9676	53.9933	58.4026	68.5281	80.6977
29	31.1244	31.8763	32.2609	33.4504	35.9987	38.7922	41.8563	45.2189	48.9108	52.9663	57.4230	62.3227	73.6398	87.3465
30	32.2800	33.0889	33.5029	34.7849	37.5387	40.5681	43.9027	47.5754	51.6227	56.0849	61.0071	66.4388	79.0582	94.4608
32	34.6086	35.5382	36.0148	37.4941	40.6883	44.2270	48.1503	52.5028	57.3345	62.7015	68.6662	75.2988	90.8898	110.218
34	36.9606	38.0203	38.5646	40.2577	43.9331	48.0338	52.6129	57.7302	63.4532	69.8579	77.0303	85.0670	104.184	128.259
36	39.3361	40.5356	41.1527	43.0769	47.2760	51.9944	57.3014	63.2759	70.0076	77.5983	86.1640	95.8363	119.121	148.913
38	41.7354	43.0845	43.7798	45.9527	50.7199	56.1149	62.2273	69.1594	77.0289	85.9703	96.1382	107.710	135.904	172.561
40	44.1588	45.6675	46.4465	48.8864	54.2679	60.4020	67.4026	75.4013	84.5503	95.0255	107.030	120.800	154.762	199.635
48	54.0978	56.3499	57.5207	61.2226	69.5652	79.3535	90.8596	104.408	120.388	139.263	161.588	188.025	256.565	353.270
50	56.6452	59.1104	60.3943	64.4632	73.6828	84.5794	97.4843	112.797	130.998	152.667	178.503	209.348	290.336	406.529
60	69.7700	73.4769	75.4241	81.6697	96.2147	114.052	135.992	163.053	196.517	237.991	289.498	353.584	533.128	813.520
120	163.879	182.946	193.514	230.039	331.288	488.258	734.326	1123.70	1744.69	2741.56	4350.40	6958.24	18119.8	47954.1
180	290.819	346.038	378.406	499.580	905.625	1716.04	3366.87	6783.45	13941.4	29078.2	61314.4	*	*	*
240	462.041	589.020	667.887	989.255	2308.85	5744.44	14949.5	40128.4	*	*	*	*	*	*
300	692.994	951.026	1121.12	1878.85	5737.25	18961.7	65910.7	*	*	*	*	*	*	*
360	1004.52	1490.36	1830.74	3494.96	14113.6	62328.1	*	*	*	*	*	*	*	*

Periods	8%	9%	10%	11%	12%	13%	14%	15%	16%	18%	20%	24%	30%	36%
1	1.0000	1.0000	1.0000	1.0000	1.0000	1.0000	1.0000	1.0000	1.0000	1.0000	1.0000	1.0000	1.0000	1.0000
2	2.0800	2.0900	2.1000	2.1100	2.1200	2.1300	2.1400	2.1500	2.1600	2.1800	2.2000	2.2400	2.3000	2.3600
3	3.2464	3.2781	3.3100	3.3421	3.3744	3.4069	3.4396	3.4725	3.5056	3.5724	3.6400	3.7776	3.9900	4.2096
4	4.5061	4.5731	4.6410	4.7097	4.7793	4.8498	4.9211	4.9934	5.0665	5.2154	5.3680	5.6842	6.1870	6.7251
5	5.8666	5.9847	6.1051	6.2278	6.3528	6.4803	6.6101	6.7424	6.8771	7.1542	7.4416	8.0484	9.0431	10.1461
6	7.3359	7.5233	7.7156	7.9129	8.1152	8.3227	8.5355	8.7537	8.9775	9.4420	9.9299	10.9801	12.7560	14.7987
7	8.9228	9.2004	9.4872	9.7833	10.0890	10.4047	10.7305	11.0668	11.4139	12.1415	12.9159	14.6153	17.5828	21.1262
8	10.6366	11.0285	11.4359	11.8594	12.2997	12.7573	13.2328	13.7268	14.2401	15.3270	16.4991	19.1229	23.8577	29.7316
9	12.4876	13.0210	13.5795	14.1640	14.7757	15.4157	16.0853	16.7858	17.5185	19.0859	20.7989	24.7125	32.0150	41.4350
10	14.4866	15.1929	15.9374	16.7220	17.5487	18.4197	19.3373	20.3037	21.3215	23.5213	25.9587	31.6434	42.6195	57.3516
11	16.6455	17.5603	18.5312	19.5614	20.6546	21.8143	23.0445	24.3493	25.7329	28.7551	32.1504	40.2379	56.4053	78.9982
12	18.9771	20.1407	21.3843	22.7132	24.1331	25.6502	27.2707	29.0017	30.8502	34.9311	39.5805	50.8950	74.3270	108.437
13	21.4953	22.9534	24.5227	26.2116	28.0291	29.9847	32.0887	34.3519	36.7862	42.2187	48.4966	64.1097	97.6250	148.475
14	24.2149	26.0192	27.9750	30.0949	32.3926	34.8827	37.5811	40.5047	43.6720	50.8180	59.1959	80.4961	127.913	202.926
15	27.1521	29.3609	31.7725	34.4054	37.2797	40.4175	43.8424	47.5804	51.6595	60.9653	72.0351	100.815	167.286	276.979
16	30.3243	33.0034	35.9497	39.1899	42.7533	46.6717	50.9804	55.7175	60.9250	72.9390	87.4421	126.011	218.472	377.692
17	33.7502	36.9737	40.5447	44.5008	48.8837	53.7391	59.1176	65.0751	71.6730	87.0680	105.931	157.253	285.014	514.661
18	37.4502	41.3013	45.5992	50.3959	55.7497	61.7251	68.3941	75.8364	84.1407	103.740	128.117	195.994	371.518	700.939
19	41.4463	46.0185	51.1591	56.9395	63.4397	70.7494	78.9692	88.2118	98.6032	123.414	154.740	244.033	483.973	954.277
20	45.7620	51.1601	57.2750	64.2028	72.0524	80.9468	91.0249	102.444	115.380	146.628	186.688	303.601	630.165	1298.82
21	50.4229	56.7645	64.0025	72.2651	81.6987	92.4699	104.768	118.810	134.841	174.021	225.026	377.465	820.215	1767.39
22	55.4568	62.8733	71.4027	81.2143	92.5026	105.491	120.436	137.632	157.415	206.345	271.031	469.056	1067.28	2404.65
23	60.8933	69.5319	79.5430	91.1479	104.603	120.205	138.297	159.276	183.601	244.487	326.237	582.630	1388.46	3271.33
24	66.7648	76.7898	88.4973	102.174	118.155	136.831	158.659	184.168	213.978	289.494	392.484	723.461	1806.00	4450.00
25	73.1059	84.7009	98.3471	114.413	133.334	155.620	181.871	212.793	249.214	342.603	471.981	898.092	2348.80	6053.00
26	79.9544	93.3240	109.182	127.999	150.334	176.850	208.333	245.712	290.088	405.272	567.377	1114.63	3054.44	8233.09
27	87.3508	102.723	121.100	143.079	169.374	200.841	238.499	283.569	337.502	479.221	681.853	1383.15	3971.78	11198.0
28	95.3388	112.968	134.210	159.817	190.699	227.950	272.889	327.104	392.503	566.481	819.223	1716.10	5164.31	15230.3
29	103.966	124.135	148.631	178.397	214.583	258.583	312.094	377.170	456.303	669.447	984.068	2128.96	6714.60	20714.2
30	113.283	136.308	164.494	199.021	241.333	293.199	356.787	434.745	530.312	790.948	1181.88	2640.92	8729.99	28172.3
32	134.214	164.037	201.138	247.324	304.848	376.516	465.820	577.100	715.747	1103.50	1704.11	4062.91	14756.0	52109.8
34	158.627	196.982	245.477	306.837	384.521	482.903	607.520	765.365	965.270	1538.69	2456.12	6249.38	24939.9	96384.6
36	187.102	236.125	299.127	380.164	484.463	618.749	791.673	1014.35	1301.03	2144.65	3539.01	9611.28	42150.7	*
38	220.316	282.630	364.043	470.511	609.831	792.211	1031.00	1343.62	1752.82	2988.39	5098.37	14780.5	71237.0	*
40	259.057	337.882	442.593	581.826	767.091	1013.70	1342.03	1779.09	2360.76	4163.21	7343.86	22728.8	*	*
48	490.132	684.280	960.172	1352.70	1911.59	2707.63	3841.48	5456.00	7753.78	15664.3	31593.7	*	*	*
50	573.770	815.084	1163.91	1668.77	2400.02	3459.51	4994.52	7217.72	10435.6	21813.1	45497.2	*	*	*
60	1253.21	1944.79	3034.82	4755.07	7471.64	11761.9	18535.1	29220.0	46057.5	*	*	*	*	*
120	*	*	*	*	*	*	*	*	*	*	*	*	*	*
180	*	*	*	*	*	*	*	*	*	*	*	*	*	*
240	*	*	*	*	*	*	*	*	*	*	*	*	*	*
300	*	*	*	*	*	*	*	*	*	*	*	*	*	*
360	*	*	*	*	*	*	*	*	*	*	*	*	*	*

*$FVFA_{k,n} \geq 100,000$

TABLE A-4

$$PVFA_{k,n} = \sum_{i=1}^{n} (1 + k)^{-i}$$

INTEREST RATES

Periods	0.5%	0.67%	0.75%	1%	1.5%	2%	2.5%	3%	3.5%	4%	4.5%	5%	6%	7%
1	0.9950	0.9934	0.9926	0.9901	0.9852	0.9804	0.9756	0.9709	0.9662	0.9615	0.9569	0.9524	0.9434	0.9346
2	1.9851	1.9802	1.9777	1.9704	1.9559	1.9416	1.9274	1.9135	1.8997	1.8861	1.8727	1.8594	1.8334	1.8080
3	2.9702	2.9604	2.9556	2.9410	2.9122	2.8839	2.8560	2.8286	2.8016	2.7751	2.7490	2.7232	2.6730	2.6243
4	3.9505	3.9342	3.9261	3.9020	3.8544	3.8077	3.7620	3.7171	3.6731	3.6299	3.5875	3.5460	3.4651	3.3872
5	4.9259	4.9015	4.8894	4.8534	4.7826	4.7135	4.6458	4.5797	4.5151	4.4518	4.3900	4.3295	4.2124	4.1002
6	5.8964	5.8625	5.8456	5.7955	5.6972	5.6014	5.5081	5.4172	5.3286	5.2421	5.1579	5.0757	4.9173	4.7665
7	6.8621	6.8170	6.7946	6.7282	6.5982	6.4720	6.3494	6.2303	6.1145	6.0021	5.8927	5.7864	5.5824	5.3893
8	7.8230	7.7652	7.7366	7.6517	7.4859	7.3255	7.1701	7.0197	6.8740	6.7327	6.5959	6.4632	6.2098	5.9713
9	8.7791	8.7072	8.6716	8.5660	8.3605	8.1622	7.9709	7.7861	7.6077	7.4353	7.2688	7.1078	6.8017	6.5152
10	9.7304	9.6429	9.5996	9.4713	9.2222	8.9826	8.7521	8.5302	8.3166	8.1109	7.9127	7.7217	7.3601	7.0236
11	10.6770	10.5724	10.5207	10.3676	10.0711	9.7868	9.5142	9.2526	9.0016	8.7605	8.5289	8.3064	7.8869	7.4987
12	11.6189	11.4958	11.4349	11.2551	10.9075	10.5753	10.2578	9.9540	9.6633	9.3851	9.1186	8.8633	8.3838	7.9427
13	12.5562	12.4130	12.3423	12.1337	11.7315	11.3484	10.9832	10.6350	10.3027	9.9856	9.6829	9.3936	8.8527	8.3577
14	13.4887	13.3242	13.2430	13.0037	12.5434	12.1062	11.6909	11.2961	10.9205	10.5631	10.2228	9.8986	9.2950	8.7455
15	14.4166	14.2293	14.1370	13.8651	13.3432	12.8493	12.3814	11.9379	11.5174	11.1184	10.7395	10.3797	9.7122	9.1079
16	15.3399	15.1285	15.0243	14.7179	14.1313	13.5777	13.0550	12.5611	12.0941	11.6523	11.2340	10.8378	10.1059	9.4466
17	16.2586	16.0217	15.9050	15.5623	14.9076	14.2919	13.7122	13.1661	12.6513	12.1657	11.7072	11.2741	10.4773	9.7632
18	17.1728	16.9089	16.7792	16.3983	15.6726	14.9920	14.3534	13.7535	13.1897	12.6593	12.1600	11.6896	10.8276	10.0591
19	18.0824	17.7903	17.6468	17.2260	16.4262	15.6785	14.9789	14.3238	13.7098	13.1339	12.5933	12.0853	11.1581	10.3356
20	18.9874	18.6659	18.5080	18.0456	17.1686	16.3514	15.5892	14.8775	14.2124	13.5903	13.0079	12.4622	11.4699	10.5940
21	19.8880	19.5357	19.3628	18.8570	17.9001	17.0112	16.1845	15.4150	14.6980	14.0292	13.4047	12.8212	11.7641	10.8355
22	20.7841	20.3997	20.2112	19.6604	18.6208	17.6580	16.7654	15.9369	15.1671	14.4511	13.7844	13.1630	12.0416	11.0612
23	21.6757	21.2579	21.0533	20.4558	19.3309	18.2922	17.3321	16.4436	15.6204	14.8568	14.1478	13.4886	12.3034	11.2722
24	22.5629	22.1105	21.8891	21.2434	20.0304	18.9139	17.8850	16.9355	16.0584	15.2470	14.4955	13.7986	12.5504	11.4693
25	23.4456	22.9575	22.7188	22.0232	20.7196	19.5235	18.4244	17.4131	16.4815	15.6221	14.8282	14.0939	12.7834	11.6536
26	24.3240	23.7988	23.5422	22.7952	21.3986	20.1210	18.9506	17.8768	16.8904	15.9828	15.1466	14.3752	13.0032	11.8258
27	25.1980	24.6346	24.3595	23.5596	22.0676	20.7069	19.4640	18.3270	17.2854	16.3296	15.4513	14.6430	13.2105	11.9867
28	26.0677	25.4648	25.1707	24.3164	22.7267	21.2813	19.9649	18.7641	17.6670	16.6631	15.7429	14.8981	13.4062	12.1371
29	26.9330	26.2896	25.9759	25.0658	23.3761	21.8444	20.4535	19.1885	18.0358	16.9837	16.0219	15.1411	13.5907	12.2777
30	27.7941	27.1088	26.7751	25.8077	24.0158	22.3965	20.9303	19.6004	18.3920	17.2920	16.2889	15.3725	13.7648	12.4090
32	29.5033	28.7312	28.3557	27.2696	25.2671	23.4683	21.8492	20.3888	19.0689	17.8736	16.7889	15.8027	14.0840	12.6466
34	31.1955	30.3320	29.9128	28.7027	26.4817	24.4986	22.7238	21.1318	19.7007	18.4112	17.2468	16.1929	14.3681	12.8540
36	32.8710	31.9118	31.4468	30.1075	27.6607	25.4888	23.5563	21.8323	20.2905	18.9083	17.6660	16.5469	14.6210	13.0352
38	34.5299	33.4707	32.9581	31.4847	28.8051	26.4406	24.3486	22.4925	20.8411	19.3679	18.0500	16.8679	14.8460	13.1935
40	36.1722	35.0090	34.4469	32.8347	29.9158	27.3555	25.1028	23.1148	21.3551	19.7928	18.4016	17.1591	15.0463	13.3317
48	42.5803	40.9619	40.1848	37.9740	34.0426	30.6731	27.7732	25.2667	23.0912	21.1951	19.5356	18.0772	15.6500	13.7305
50	44.1428	42.4013	41.5664	39.1961	34.9997	31.4236	28.3623	25.7298	23.4556	21.4822	19.7620	18.2559	15.7619	13.8007
60	51.7256	49.3184	48.1734	44.9550	39.3803	34.7609	30.9087	27.6756	24.9447	22.6235	20.6380	18.9293	16.1614	14.0392
120	90.0735	82.4215	78.9417	69.7005	55.4985	45.3554	37.9337	32.3730	28.1111	24.7741	22.1093	19.9427	16.6514	14.2815
180	118.504	104.641	98.5934	83.3217	62.0956	48.5844	39.5304	33.1703	28.5130	24.9785	22.2142	19.9969	16.6662	14.2856
240	139.581	119.554	111.145	90.8194	64.7957	49.5686	39.8933	33.3057	28.5640	24.9980	22.2216	19.9998	16.6667	14.2857
300	155.207	129.565	119.162	94.9466	65.9009	49.8685	39.9757	33.3286	28.5705	24.9998	22.2222	20.0000	16.6667	14.2857
360	166.792	136.283	124.282	97.2183	66.3532	49.9599	39.9945	33.3325	28.5713	25.0000	22.2222	20.0000	16.6667	14.2857

Periods	8%	9%	10%	11%	12%	13%	14%	15%	16%	18%	20%	24%	30%	36%
1	0.9259	0.9174	0.9091	0.9009	0.8929	0.8850	0.8772	0.8696	0.8621	0.8475	0.8333	0.8065	0.7692	0.7353
2	1.7833	1.7591	1.7355	1.7125	1.6901	1.6681	1.6467	1.6257	1.6052	1.5656	1.5278	1.4568	1.3609	1.2760
3	2.5771	2.5313	2.4869	2.4437	2.4018	2.3612	2.3216	2.2832	2.2459	2.1743	2.1065	1.9813	1.8161	1.6735
4	3.3121	3.2397	3.1699	3.1024	3.0373	2.9745	2.9137	2.8550	2.7982	2.6901	2.5887	2.4043	2.1662	1.9658
5	3.9927	3.8897	3.7908	3.6959	3.6048	3.5172	3.4331	3.3522	3.2743	3.1272	2.9906	2.7454	2.4356	2.1807
6	4.6229	4.4859	4.3553	4.2305	4.1114	3.9975	3.8887	3.7845	3.6847	3.4976	3.3255	3.0205	2.6427	2.3388
7	5.2064	5.0330	4.8684	4.7122	4.5638	4.4226	4.2883	4.1604	4.0386	3.8115	3.6046	3.2423	2.8021	2.4550
8	5.7466	5.5348	5.3349	5.1461	4.9676	4.7988	4.6389	4.4873	4.3436	4.0776	3.8372	3.4212	2.9247	2.5404
9	6.2469	5.9952	5.7590	5.5370	5.3282	5.1317	4.9464	4.7716	4.6065	4.3030	4.0310	3.5655	3.0190	2.6033
10	6.7101	6.4177	6.1446	5.8892	5.6502	5.4262	5.2161	5.0188	4.8332	4.4941	4.1925	3.6819	3.0915	2.6495
11	7.1390	6.8052	6.4951	6.2065	5.9377	5.6869	5.4527	5.2337	5.0286	4.6560	4.3271	3.7757	3.1473	2.6834
12	7.5361	7.1607	6.8137	6.4924	6.1944	5.9176	5.6603	5.4206	5.1971	4.7932	4.4392	3.8514	3.1903	2.7084
13	7.9038	7.4869	7.1034	6.7499	6.4235	6.1218	5.8424	5.5831	5.3423	4.9095	4.5327	3.9124	3.2233	2.7268
14	8.2442	7.7862	7.3667	6.9819	6.6282	6.3025	6.0021	5.7245	5.4675	5.0081	4.6106	3.9616	3.2487	2.7403
15	8.5595	8.0607	7.6061	7.1909	6.8109	6.4624	6.1422	5.8474	5.5755	5.0916	4.6755	4.0013	3.2682	2.7502
16	8.8514	8.3126	7.8237	7.3792	6.9740	6.6039	6.2651	5.9542	5.6685	5.1624	4.7296	4.0333	3.2832	2.7575
17	9.1216	8.5436	8.0216	7.5488	7.1196	6.7291	6.3729	6.0472	5.7487	5.2223	4.7746	4.0591	3.2948	2.7629
18	9.3719	8.7556	8.2014	7.7016	7.2497	6.8399	6.4674	6.1280	5.8178	5.2732	4.8122	4.0799	3.3037	2.7668
19	9.6036	8.9501	8.3649	7.8393	7.3658	6.9380	6.5504	6.1982	5.8775	5.3162	4.8435	4.0967	3.3105	2.7697
20	9.8181	9.1285	8.5136	7.9633	7.4694	7.0248	6.6231	6.2593	5.9288	5.3527	4.8696	4.1103	3.3158	2.7718
21	10.0168	9.2922	8.6487	8.0751	7.5620	7.1016	6.6870	6.3125	5.9731	5.3837	4.8913	4.1212	3.3198	2.7734
22	10.2007	9.4424	8.7715	8.1757	7.6446	7.1695	6.7429	6.3587	6.0113	5.4099	4.9094	4.1300	3.3230	2.7746
23	10.3711	9.5802	8.8832	8.2664	7.7184	7.2297	6.7921	6.3988	6.0442	5.4321	4.9245	4.1371	3.3254	2.7754
24	10.5288	9.7066	8.9847	8.3481	7.7843	7.2829	6.8351	6.4338	6.0726	5.4509	4.9371	4.1428	3.3272	2.7760
25	10.6748	9.8226	9.0770	8.4217	7.8431	7.3300	6.8729	6.4641	6.0971	5.4669	4.9476	4.1474	3.3286	2.7765
26	10.8100	9.9290	9.1609	8.4881	7.8957	7.3717	6.9061	6.4906	6.1182	5.4804	4.9563	4.1511	3.3297	2.7768
27	10.9352	10.0266	9.2372	8.5478	7.9426	7.4086	6.9352	6.5135	6.1364	5.4919	4.9636	4.1542	3.3305	2.7771
28	11.0511	10.1161	9.3066	8.6016	7.9844	7.4412	6.9607	6.5335	6.1520	5.5016	4.9697	4.1566	3.3312	2.7773
29	11.1584	10.1983	9.3696	8.6501	8.0218	7.4701	6.9830	6.5509	6.1656	5.5098	4.9747	4.1585	3.3317	2.7774
30	11.2578	10.2737	9.4269	8.6938	8.0552	7.4957	7.0027	6.5660	6.1772	5.5168	4.9789	4.1601	3.3321	2.7775
32	11.4350	10.4062	9.5264	8.7686	8.1116	7.5383	7.0350	6.5905	6.1959	5.5277	4.9854	4.1624	3.3326	2.7776
34	11.5869	10.5178	9.6086	8.8293	8.1566	7.5717	7.0599	6.6091	6.2098	5.5356	4.9898	4.1639	3.3329	2.7777
36	11.7172	10.6118	9.6765	8.8786	8.1924	7.5979	7.0790	6.6231	6.2201	5.5412	4.9929	4.1649	3.3331	2.7777
38	11.8289	10.6908	9.7327	8.9186	8.2210	7.6183	7.0937	6.6338	6.2278	5.5452	4.9951	4.1655	3.3332	2.7778
40	11.9246	10.7574	9.7791	8.9511	8.2438	7.6344	7.1050	6.6418	6.2335	5.5482	4.9966	4.1659	3.3332	2.7778
48	12.1891	10.9336	9.8969	9.0302	8.2972	7.6705	7.1296	6.6585	6.2450	5.5536	4.9992	4.1665	3.3333	2.7778
50	12.2335	10.9617	9.9148	9.0417	8.3045	7.6752	7.1327	6.6605	6.2463	5.5541	4.9995	4.1666	3.3333	2.7778
60	12.3766	11.0480	9.9672	9.0736	8.3240	7.6873	7.1401	6.6651	6.2492	5.5553	4.9999	4.1667	3.3333	2.7778
120	12.4988	11.1108	9.9999	9.0909	8.3333	7.6923	7.1429	6.6667	6.2500	5.5556	5.0000	4.1667	3.3333	2.7778
180	12.5000	11.1111	10.0000	9.0909	8.3333	7.6923	7.1429	6.6667	6.2500	5.5556	5.0000	4.1667	3.3333	2.7778
240	12.5000	11.1111	10.0000	9.0909	8.3333	7.6923	7.1429	6.6667	6.2500	5.5556	5.0000	4.1667	3.3333	2.7778
300	12.5000	11.1111	10.0000	9.0909	8.3333	7.6923	7.1429	6.6667	6.2500	5.5556	5.0000	4.1667	3.3333	2.7778
360	12.5000	11.1111	10.0000	9.0909	8.3333	7.6923	7.1429	6.6667	6.2500	5.5556	5.0000	4.1667	3.3333	2.7778

APPENDIX B: ANSWERS TO SELECTED PROBLEMS

CHAPTER 2

1. $10,000
2. $15,940
3. $400,000
4. ROE changes from 8.3% to 9.5%
5. Borrow. $20,000 per year
8. 43%
9. $7,233
10. a. $60,000
    b. $9,800
    c. 18.1%
    d. 27.5%; Yes. 20% on capital gains
11. a. $5,550
    b. $9,250
    c. $18,340
    d. $26,150
    e. $1,827,500 (See example 2.4)
    f. $4,800,000
    g. $6,043,000
    h. $8,225,000
12. $527,000 (See example 2.4)
13. $2,798,200

CHAPTER 3

4. ($285,000)
5. $6,385,000
8. a. $4,375,000
   b. $625,000
9. a. $2.75 M
   b. 14.2 ×
10. $875,000
11. 80%
13. INV = $125
    A/R = $200
    C/A = $575
    T/A = $1,425
    C/L = $250
    DEBT = $450
    EQUITY = $725
    ROA = 11.2%
    ROE = 22.1%

CHAPTER 4

1. 6%
2. 5%
3. 3%
4. DR = 6%
5. 9% and 11%
6. a. 4%, 1%
   b. 11%, 12%

CHAPTER 5

1. a. $7,722
   b. $6,989
   c. $7,885
   d. $5,851
   e. $8,105.70
2. a. $8,273.25
   b. $8,081.55
   c. $6,686.55
   d. $14,851.80
3. a. 11%
   b. 6%
   c. 8%
   d. 18%
4. a. 4 years
   b. 4 years
   c. 3 years
5. a. 15%
   b. 7.9 years
   c. 6.6 years
6. a. 1) $18,900
      2) $18,573
      3) $18,264
      4) $17,972
7. a. $129.82
   b. $2,952.40
8. a. 5%
   b. 7.4%
9. a. $2,015.69
   b. $3,940.15
10. a. $7,994.81
    b. $6,913.79
    c. $6,433.38
11. $4,704.55
12. 12%
13. 13 years 9 months
14. $17,597.20

16. 18%
17. $6,784.04
18. 6 years 6 months, 5 months
21. 20 years
22. Principal $10,771.13
    Interest $7,743.91
23. $20,131.66
24. a. $5,675.57
25. a. $18,179.70
    b. $2,118.10
26. $3,199.82
27. $301.40

CHAPTER 6

1. a. $849.52
   b. $1,197.94
   d. $1,000.00
2. a. $1,153.75
   b. $816.00
   c. $1,385.94
   d. $1,515.96
   e. $859.23
3. a. $656.77
   b. $659.42
   c. $985.16
4. Old $824.36
   New $654.93
5. $1,815.93
6. a. $1,000.00
   c. Old $852.52
      New $515.42
7. a. 12%
   b. 6%
   c. 8%
8. a. $1,508.85
   b. $1,857.91
9. with call $1,347.52
   without call $1,718.39
11. as stock $1,300
    as bond $1,296.90

CHAPTER 7

1. $31.15
2. $69.92
3. $53.00
4. a. $78.75

5. a. $123.33, $93.25, $74.60
  d. (1) $92.95, $73.80, $61.50
    (2) $73.20, $61.00, $52.29
6. a. $405.00
7. $74.11
8. a. $72.97
  b. $96.86
9. $87.57
11. $63.64
12. 7.5%

CHAPTER 8

1. a. 23.3%
  b. 15.0%
  c. -12.7%
2. No. k = 20%
3. 11.0%, 13.0%, 3.6%, .33
4. 10%, 2.12%, .47
5. 10%
6. 36.98%
8. 9.4%
9. a. .67
  b. 7.2%
10. 1.1
11. a. 12%
12.

K_{RF}	k_m		
	10%	11%	12%
5%	9.0%	9.8%	10.6%
6%	9.2%	10.0%	10.8%
7%	9.4%	10.2%	11.0%

13. a. $34.46
14. a. $42.74
  b.

b_A	g		
	5%	6%	7%
1.2	$38.60	$45.69	$55.83
1.3	$36.53	$42.74	$51.54
1.4	$34.61	$40.15	$47.86

15. Current price $18.93
  Proposed price $18.06

CHAPTER 9

1. a. 2 years
  b. $52
  c. 1.07
2. 16%
3. a. Payback approximately
    2.5 years

  b. NPV = $628
  c. PI = 1.08
4. IRR = 12%
5. a. 2.6 years
  b. $3,803
  c. 16% (approx)
  d. 1.15
6. a. $3,363.72, 1.10
  b. 10%
  c. -$3,017.08, .91
  d. 5 years
7. a. 3.6 years
  b. 12%
  c. $3,871
8.

		NPV	PI	IRR
a.	8%	$467	1.09	11%
	12%	-$208	.96	
b.	8%	$3,201	1.07	11%
	12%	-$674	.98	
c.	8%	$8,665	1.11	10%
	12%	-$6,764	.91	
d.	8%	$4,721	1.13	12%
	12%	$168	1.00	

9. a. H: 5.4 years, L: 5.0 years
  b. H: 7%, L: 9%
  d. H: NPV = $34,038
      PI = 1.04
    L: NPV = $84,690
      PI = 1.11
  e.

k	H	L
2% NPV	$190,852	$221,688
PI	1.20	1.29
4% NPV	$108,020	$149,323
PI	1.11	1.19
6% NPV	$34,038	$84,690
PI	1.04	1.11
8% NPV	-$32,242	$26,786
PI	.97	1.03
10% NPV	-$91,823	-$25,263
PI	.90	.97

10. a. $844.35
  b. -$6,195.35
  c. -$5,818.51
11. a. 7%
  b. 4%
12.

	NPV	IRR
a.	-$5,437.29,	6%
b.	$3,207.98,	12%
c.	$2,583.05,	14%

13.

	NPV	IRR
a.	-$196.40	10%
b.	-$377.30	8%
c.	-$15.10	12%

14. a. $364
  b. 15%
15. a. A: 1.7 years B: 3.5 years
  b. A: $10,407 B: $12,385
  c. A: 35% B: 25%
  d. Chain A to 9 yrs. NPV = $23,088
  e. A: $4,333 B: $2,324

CHAPTER 10

1. $C_1 - C_4$ $21,000
  $C_5 - C_6$ $17,000
2. $89,000
3. $141,600
4.

C_0	C_1	C_2
($50,000)	$11,300	$11,300
C_4	C_5	
$11,300	$26,500	

5. ($000)

C_0	C_1	C_2	C_3
($80)	($16)	($4)	$14
C_4	C_5	C_6	C_7
$20	$26	$30	$30

6. a.

C_0	C_1
($500,000)	$100,000
$C_2 - C_5$	$C_6 - C_8$
$139,000	$104,000

  b. 3.9 years, $108,000, 1.22
7. a.

C_0	$C_1 - C_5$
($150,000)	$38,450
C_6	
$27,950	

  b. 3.9 years, $11,534
8. a.

C_0	C_1
($45,840)	$7,300
C_2	C_3
$7,430	$8,685
C_4	C_5
$8,815	$8,945
C_6	C_7
$4,875	$5,005
C_8	
$5,135	

  NPV = ($9,732)
  b. NPV = $6,413

9. a. ($000)

C_0	C_1	C_2
($270)	$12	$45

C_3	C_4	C_5
$61	$86	$106

C_6
$120

b. 4.6 yrs.
c. ($4,000)
e. $98,000
f. $503,000

10. a. ($000)

C_0	C_1	C_2
($2,256)	($62)	$338

C_3	C_4	C_5
$630	$996	$1,094

C_6
$1,027

b. 4.3 yrs, $380, 14%, 1.17
c. (3) 14%

CHAPTER 11

1. $867,500 to $2,114,100
2. ($26,980)
3. a. Most likely: $6,000, .125000
   b. Best: $52,000, .015625
      Worst: ($41,000), .015625
4. a.

Path	NPV	Prob.
1	$2,895	.18
2	$1,356	.42
3	($1,937)	.32
4	($2,399)	.08

   b. $279
5. a.

Path	NPV	Prob.
1	$2,895	.18
2	$1,356	.42
3	($398)	.40

   b. $931
6. b. ($ M)

Path	NPV	Prob.
1	$21.6	.42
2	$7.5	.18
3	($.6)	.28
4	($6.0)	.12

   c. $9.53
7. 0, $1.0 M
8. a. $4.73 M
   b. $.21 M

CHAPTER 12

1. Debt 34.8%, Preferred 17.3%, Equity 47.9%
2. 16.8%
3. Mkt 17.9%, Book 15.3%
4. Debt 62.3%, Preferred 7.1%, Equity 30.6%
5. Debt 41.5%, Preferred 6.9%, Equity 51.6%
6.

	Book	Market
Debt	23.5%	16.5%
Preferred	29.4%	21.2%
Equity	47.1%	62.3%

7. 7.44%
8. 15.91%
9. a. 22%
   b. 24.2%
10. a. 5.55%
   b. 1) 6.96%
      2) 6.11%
11. 12.39%
12. RE 16.3%
   New 17.3%
13. 13.2%
14. 12% to 14%
15. a. 16.2%
   b. $12.3 M
   c. 17.6%
   d. 18.6%
   e. $16 M

CHAPTER 13

1. a. 11.0%, $.55
4.

Debt	EAT	ROE	EPS
0	$1,650	13.8%	$1.10
20%	$1,434	14.9%	$1.20
40%	$1,218	16.9%	$1.35
60%	$1,002	20.9%	$1.67
80%	$786	32.8%	$2.62

5. a. ROCE = 10.86%
   b.

Debt	EAT	ROE	EPS	DFL
15%	$1,956	11.5%	$4.60	1.11
30%	$1,740	12.4%	$4.97	1.25
45%	$1,524	13.9%	$5.54	1.43
60%	$1,308	16.4%	$6.54	1.66
75%	$1,092	21.8%	$8.74	1.99

6. ROCE = 10.6%

Debt = $24,048

7.

	Current	Proposed
a. EPS	$2.29	$3.48
b. DFL	1.08	1.56

   c.

ΔEBIT	Current EPS	Proposed EPS
5%	$2.17	$3.21
10%	$2.04	$2.94
25%	$1.67	$2.12

10. a. $7, 21.9%
   b. 20,000
   c. $640,000
   e. 6.0, 4.3, 3.5
11. a. $1 per unit or $20,000
   b. 6.0, 4.3, 3.5
12. a. 35%, $6,285,714
   b. 1.625, 2.692, 4.375
   c. $24, ($2.26)
13.

	With	Without
a.	$11,701	$11,251
b.	1.75	1.20
c.	2.86	2.67
d.	5.0	3.2

CHAPTER 14

1. a. $3.71
   b. $51.94
   c. $.56
   d. 11 shares
2. a. $20
   b. $10,000
   c. 500
   d. $409,500
3. $1.00
4. $1.05 M
5. 1.2%
6. a. $2.50
7. a. $600,000, $600,000
   b. $60,000
8. a. $.80
   b. 9.8 million, $2.04
   c. $40.80, $.80
9. a. 4.44%
   b. 222,222
   c. $1.5169
   d. $22.75
10. $1.25

CHAPTER 15

1. $50,523.25
2. $35,695
3. $874,500
4. $176,594
5. 81 days, 51 days
6. 1) $3,600,000
   2) $2,400,000
   3) $1,666,667
7. 36.5%, 36.5%, 9.125%, 60.833%, 24.333%
8. 10%
9. $6.8 M, 34%
10. 36%
11. a. $16.5 M
    b. 110%
    d. 70.67%
12. $430,000, 28.7%
13. 24%
14. Savings $3,000
    Cost $4,500
15. a. Savings $33,288
       Cost $18,000
    b. 1.6 days
16. a. New contribution $350,000
       New bad debts $325,000
17. a. New constribution $5.3 M
       New cost/loss $2.4 M
18. 26, 191
19. a. 581
    b. 34.4
    c. $1,307

CHAPTER 16

1. Ending debt = $9,751
2. Debt $272
   Debt : Equity is 4.25 : 1
   Eq $64
4.

	1	2
a. COGS	$33,925	$38,280
b. A/R	$11,181	$11,000
c. Inven.	$8,481	$7,656

3	4	5
$43,320	$49,000	$55,000
$10,556	$10,938	$11,111
$7,220	$7,538	$7,857

6. a. $7,300,000
   b. $50,350
   c. $17.6 M
7. a. $1,329
   b. $1,660
   c. $1,445

CHAPTER 17

1. a. $26,194,400
   b. $87.31
   c. 2.4253
2. a. $2,682,120, $13.41
   b. $3,500,000, $17.50
   c. $4,375,000, $21.88
3. Value = $51.08 per share
4. a. $45,708,000
5. a. 13%
   b. $2,400,000
   c. $8,441,000, $13,023,000, $15,510,000
   d. $33.76, $52.09, $62.04
   e. $73.85
6. Price $125.30, Premium = 102.10%

CHAPTER 18

1. a. $91,659.18
   b. $199,645.60
   c. $148,458.00
   d. $970,381.99
2. a. 56,337,526 Japanese yen
   b. 55,328,361 Japanese yen
3. a. 1.0699 euros/$
   b. 3.8670 Israeli shekels/$
   c. 0.6044 British pounds/$
   c. 106.12 Japanese yen/$
5. $4,202
6. a. $10,000
   b. $25,000
7. a. $256.50 gain
   b. $102.60 additional tax
8. American quote: £122,728
   French Quote: £117,888
9. a. Loss of $354,167
   c. $0

GLOSSARY

A

ABC system A system of controlling inventory that recognizes the differing cost and importance of various items. *A* parts are expensive and/or important and are controlled carefully. *C* parts are cheap and plentiful, so little effort is expended to monitor them. *B* parts are between As and Cs.

Accelerated depreciation Any method that shifts depreciation forward in an asset's life. Accelerated methods increase early charges and reduce those that come later, keeping total depreciation constant.

Acquisition A merger in which one company acquires the stock of another. May be friendly or hostile (unfriendly). See *Merger.*

Agency A relationship between two parties in which one (the principal) employs the other (the agent) in a decision-making capacity.

Agency problem In corporations, managers are the agents of stockholders and are often able to take advantage of the relationship by diverting corporate resources to their own use. Excessive pay is the primary example. The general situation is described as the agency problem. Costs associated with controlling the agency problem are *agency costs.*

Amortized debt A debt in which the principal is repaid over the life of the loan rather than in a lump sum at the end.

Annual report A yearly report on a company's performance prepared by management. An annual report includes financial statements and generally contains verbal discussions of the firm's operations and prospects.

Annuity A finite series of equal payments at equal intervals of time. In an *ordinary annuity* the payments occur at the ends of the time periods. In an *annuity due* they occur at the beginnings.

Antitrust law A body of legislation aimed at maintaining the competitive nature of the economy. The antitrust laws can prohibit certain mergers on the basis that they reduce competition.

Average collection period (ACP) A financial ratio that measures how long it takes to collect on credit sales. Also called *days sales outstanding (DSO).*

Average tax rate A taxpayer's total tax bill divided by taxable income. A composite of the various bracket rates to which the taxpayer's income is subject.

B

Backorder An order to replenish an out-of-stock item, usually on an expedited basis.

Balance of trade The difference between imports from and exports to another country. If imports are larger a *trade deficit* exists. If exports are larger there is a *trade surplus.*

Bankruptcy A federal court procedure to protect a failing firm from its creditors until the best resolution to its problems can be found.

Bearer bond An unregistered bond, owned by the "bearer," the person in possession.

Beta The measure of market risk in portfolio theory. The degree to which a stock's return moves with the market's return.

Bill A security associated with very short-term debt.

Board of directors The governing body of a corporation, elected by common stockholders.

Bond A security reflecting a relatively long-term debt relationship between the issuer (borrower) and the buyer (lender).

Bond rating A measure of the likelihood of default on payment of interest or principal. Ratings are prepared by *rating agencies.* The best known agencies are Moody's and Standard and Poor's.

Book value For a company, the value of equity, equal to total assets minus total liabilities. Book value can be stated in total or per share. For an asset, book value is the net of original cost minus accumulated depreciation, and is generally referred to as *net book value.*

Bottom-up planning Business planning based on inputs from lower level management. The process tends to understate achievable performance because people set easily achievable goals for themselves.

Breakeven analysis A technique for finding the volume at which a firm breaks even financially—that is, earns zero profit.

Broker See *Stockbroker.*

Brokerage (House) A company of stockbrokers generally having the right to trade on an exchange.

Budget A short-term, financially detailed business plan, usually covering about a calendar quarter.

Business plan A document projecting a firm's physical and financial performance into the future. Business plans can be short or long range. Long-range plans are "strategic" and tend to be more verbal than financial. Shorter-term plans are described as "operational," and detail the more routine running of the business.

Business risk Variation in a company's financial performance caused by changes in business conditions.

Business-specific risk Variation in the return on a stock investment caused by things that affect specific businesses or industries.

C

Call provision (feature) A provision in a bond contract that allows the borrowing organization to "call" in the bond and pay it off early. Calls are generally exercised when interest rates have dropped substantially since the bond's issue. An additional payment known as the *call premium* must usually be made to the investor if the call is exercised. Most call features cannot be exercised during an initial *call protected* period.

Capital Long-term assets or the money used to support long-term assets and projects. Long-term debt and equity on the balance sheet.

Capital budgeting Analysis techniques concerned with justifying money spent on long-term assets and projects.

Capital component One of three sources of capital: debt, preferred stock, or equity.

Capital gain (loss) The difference between the sale and purchase prices of an asset held over a period of time.

Capital gains yield The capital gain on a stock divided by the price at which it was purchased.

Capital market A financial market in which longer-term (at least one year) debt and equity securities are traded.

Capital rationing In capital budgeting, the process of allocating available capital among projects to maximize total NPV.

Capital restructuring Changing a firm's capital structure intentionally by buying and selling stocks and bonds simultaneously.

Capital structure The mix of the three capital components (debt, preferred stock, and equity) used by a firm. The *optimal capital structure* is the structure at which stock price is maximized, all other things held equal. Also see *Target capital structure*.

CAPM Capital Asset Pricing Model. A statistical model of the investment world aimed at explaining how required returns are determined in financial markets and thereby how stock prices are set. Also see *SML*.

Cash budgeting A forecast of cash flows based on expected receipts and disbursements rather than on projections of income statement and balance sheet accounts.

Cash flows (statement of) One of a firm's financial statements. It details the movement of cash in and out of the company. Constructed from the Income Statement and Balance Sheet.

Cash forecast A projection of future cash flows over a specified planning period.

Chapter 11 The chapter of the bankruptcy code dealing with reorganization. Firms in bankruptcy proceedings are commonly said to be "in Chapter 11."

Chartists Technical analysts.

Chief Financial Officer (CFO) The executive in charge of the financial function.

Clean-up requirement The requirement that borrowers pay off all short-term debt for some period each year. Prevents funding long-term projects with short-term debt.

Clientele effect The theory that firms attract equity investors at least in part because of their dividend-paying policies. The firm has a "clientele" of stockholders whose need for current or deferred income matches the firm's dividend practices. The implication is that it isn't a good idea to change dividend policies because such a change is bound to displease most stockholders.

Closing price (close) The price of a security in the last trade of a business day.

Collateral An asset backing a loan. In the event of default the collateral becomes the property of the lender to satisfy the obligation. Also called *security* for the loan.

Collection agency A firm that specializes in collecting debts, especially overdue receivables, for a percent of the amount collected.

Commercial paper Very short-term debt issued by major companies.

Commitment fee A fee charged by a bank for guaranteeing to have loanable funds available. The fee is charged on unborrowed amounts up to the maximum of the guarantee. See *revolving credit agreement*.

Common size statement A firm's Income Statement with every line stated as a per-

cent of revenue. A balance sheet with every line stated as a percent of total assets. Used to compare companies of different sizes or to identify performance trends in a single company over time.

Common stock The security representing ownership of a corporation. Equity.

Compensating balance A portion of a loan that banks require borrowers to leave in their checking accounts. Effectively increases the bank's yield. A minimum balance required to compensate banks for their services.

Compound interest The concept of earning interest on previously earned interest. A sum earning compound interest grows exponentially over time.

Compounding period The period of time after which interest is credited to the depositor's account for purposes of computing subsequent interest.

Concentration banking Employing one bank to manage the balances in remote accounts. Balances are generally swept into the concentration bank daily.

Conglomerate merger A merger between companies in unrelated businesses.

Consolidation A combination of two or more businesses in which all of the old legal entities dissolve and a new one with a new name is formed to continue into the future.

Contribution (margin) In break-even analysis, contribution is the difference between price and variable cost per unit that is "contributed" toward profit and fixed costs. The contribution margin is the contribution expressed as a percent of price.

Controller The executive in charge of the accounting function in most companies. The controller generally reports to the CFO.

Convertible bond A bond that can be converted into a specified number of shares of stock at the owner's discretion.

Convertible currency A currency that can be exchanged for other currencies on foreign exchange markets.

Corporate restructuring A broad term describing a number of ways in which companies are reorganized. Includes capital restructure, mergers, and reorganizations in bankruptcy as well as charges in certain methods of doing business.

Cost Business spending for items closely associated with production. Contrast with expense.

Cost of capital The average rate a firm pays its investors for the use of their funds, adjusted for taxes and administrative costs. Also called the *WACC* for weighted

average cost of capital. Distinguish from the costs of individual capital components that are the adjusted rates paid on debt, preferred stock, and common equity. The component costs are (weighted) averaged to get the WACC.

Cost structure The mix of fixed and variable cost used by a firm.

Coupon rate, coupon payment The interest rate paid by a bond on its face value. The dollar amount of the interest payment, which is usually made semiannually.

(Restrictive) covenants Contractual agreements associated with loans that limit the activities of borrowing companies. The limitations are designed to reduce the risk that the firm won't be able to pay the loan's interest and principal.

Credit agency (bureau) An organization that maintains records of the bill-paying histories of most companies and assigns *credit ratings* to firms that indicate how well they've paid their bills in the past. The agency's subscribers can receive *credit reports* on companies with which they're considering doing business.

Cumulative feature of preferred stock A provision to enhance the safety of preferred stock. If preferred dividends are passed, no common dividends can be paid until preferred dividends are caught up cumulatively.

Cumulative voting A method of electing boards of directors in which stockholders can cast all of their votes for a single seat. Enables minority interests to get at least some representation on the board.

Current assets Assets expected to become cash in less than one year. Current assets are largely cash, receivables, and inventories.

Current liabilities Obligations expected to require cash in less than one year, usually payables and accruals.

Current ratio Current assets divided by current liabilities. A financial ratio that measures a firm's liquidity, the ability to pay its bills in the short run.

Current yield A bond's annual interest payment divided by its market price.

D

Date of record When a dividend is declared, it is paid to owners of record on the transfer agent's books as of the date record.

Debenture An unsecured bond.

Debt ratio Debt divided by total assets. A financial ratio measuring the degree to which the firm uses borrowed money.

Debt to equity ratio The relative amounts of debt and equity in a firm's capital structure.

Decision tree A timeline representation used in planning projects subject to multiple outcomes. Wherever an event has several outcomes, the timeline branches into as many paths, each with a probability. The result is a proliferation of possible paths to completion, each representing an outcome, its financial implication, and its probability. Hence the decision tree specifies a probability distribution for the project's overall financial outcome.

Declaration date The date on which a firm's board of directors declares a dividend.

Deductions Items of expenditure that the tax code allows taxpayers to deduct from income to arrive at taxable income.

Default risk The risk of loss to a lender from the borrower's failure to pay the full amount due including interest and principal.

Defensive tactics Actions taken by the management of a company to resist or avoid being acquired.

Depreciation The accounting entry allocating the cost of a long-lived asset against income over the asset's life. Depreciation is a *noncash charge,* so net income is generally less than true cash flow by at least the amount of depreciation.

Direct investment In international business, building facilities in another country.

Discount Generally a reduction in price or value. In finance, a reduction in the present value of a future sum due to the action of interest.

Discounted cash flow Calculations involving the present and future values of money under the action of compound interest. Also called the *time value of money.*

Diversification In finance, selecting a portfolio of different (diverse) investments to limit the overall risk borne by the investor.

Divestiture Getting rid of a business unit. The reverse of an acquisition.

Dividend The payment made by a corporation to an equity investor (stockholder).

Dividend decision The decision by management regarding the portion of earnings paid to shareholders as dividends. The alternative is to retain the money, investing it in the company for future growth.

Dividend theories: irrelevance, preference, and aversion Logical arguments that stockholders should be indifferent to, prefer, or be averse to the payment of dividends.

Dividend yield A stock's annual dividend divided by its current price.

Double taxation of corporate earnings The primary financial disadvantage of the corporate form. A corporation's earnings are subject to corporate tax when earned and personal tax when paid to stockholders as dividends.

Dunning Pursuing a customer for payment of an overdue receivable.

Du Pont equations A series of relationships between financial ratios that illustrates the inner workings of businesses and how performance in one area influences performance in others.

E

Earnings before interest and taxes. A measure of a firm's performance without regard to how it is financed.

Economic order quantity (EOQ) A technique for minimizing the sum of inventory ordering and carrying costs.

Economic value added (EVA) A measure of income that recognizes the cost of equity as well as debt. A positive EVA represents a contribution to shareholder wealth over that required by an equity investor, and is viewed as an increment to MVA. EVA is after-tax EBIT less the product of capital and the cost of capital. Also see *MVA.*

Efficient market hypothesis The assertion that information travels around the U.S. financial system so fast that stock prices virtually always reflect all available information. The concept implies that technical analysis is useless.

EPS Earnings per share. A firm's earnings stated on a per share outstanding basis. An important measure of business performance in the stock market.

Equity An ownership interest. The portion of a firm's capital representing funds belonging to its shareholders. An equity investment is an investment in stock.

Euro A common European currency adopted in January 2002 by most of the members of the European union.

Eurobond A bond denominated in a currency other than that of the country in which it is sold.

Eurodollars U.S. dollars deposited in banks in other countries.

Eurodollar market The debt market created when foreign banks with eurodollar deposits lend those funds.

Exchange rate In international finance, the rate at which one currency can be traded for another. *Spot* rates are available for current trades. *Forward* rates are available for currency to be delivered in a specified period of time.

Exchange rate risk The risk that international trade dealings will earn less than expected because of movement in exchange rates.

Ex-dividend date The date on which a stock trades without a declared dividend that has yet to be paid. Four days prior to the date of record.

Exemptions (personal and dependency) In personal taxes, an amount by which taxable income can be reduced for each person in a household.

Expectations theory With respect to dividends: a dividend that's lower than expected will be taken as a negative by investors even if it is larger than previous dividends. A variation on the signaling effect of dividends.

With respect to interest rates: A theory explaining the shape of the yield curve. The curve slopes up or down depending on whether expectations about future interest and inflation rates are increasing or decreasing.

Expected Return The return an investor believes is most likely on an investment—that is, the investor understands that the actual return may be somewhat different in certain investments like stocks. The mean of the probability distribution of returns.

Expense An item of expenditure not closely related to production. Contrast with *cost.*

Expropriate In international business, the seizure of assets held in a foreign country by the government of that country.

F

Factoring receivables Selling receivables to a financing source for an amount less than their face value.

Federal budget deficit The amount by which the government's spending exceeds its income in a year. A surplus implies income is greater. See *National Debt.*

Finance (noun) The art and science of handling money.

Finance (verb) To raise money to acquire an asset to do some project.

Financial analyst A person who studies the financial results of businesses and makes recommendations on their values as investments.

Financial assets Stocks and bonds. More generally a document giving its owner a claim to certain future cash flows. Stocks base that claim on ownership (equity), while bonds base it on debt. Also called a *security.*

Financial economics A somewhat archaic term for financial theory emphasizing the field's roots in economics.

Financial instrument A security or financial asset.

Financial intermediary An institution that pools investors' money and invests it on their behalf giving the investors shares of itself. Mutual funds are the primary example.

Financial markets Markets in which financial assets are traded—for example, the stock market.

Financial plan A projection of a company's financial statements into the future based on a series of assumptions about what the business and the environment will do. Part of a business plan.

Financial ratios See *Ratio analysis.*

Financial risk The variation in a firm's financial performance caused by using borrowed money (debt, leverage).

Financial statements Reports created from accounting records that summarize a firm's performance in money terms.

Fixed and total asset turnover Sales divided by fixed or total assets. Financial ratios that measure the firm's ability to generate revenue using its assets.

Fixed financial charge An expense item that must be paid regardless of how the firm is performing. Essentially, interest and lease payments.

Float Money tied up in the check-clearing process.

Floor broker A broker who buys and sells on the trading floor of a stock exchange.

Flotation costs The administrative cost of issuing new securities. Consists largely of commissions and marketing fees, but printing and engraving costs can also be significant.

Forecast A short-term projection of a company's financial results. For example, most firms do regular cash forecasts to predict their immediate funding needs.

Foreign bond A bond denominated in the currency of the country in which it is sold, but issued by a foreign borrower.

Foreign exchange A general term for the currency of foreign countries.

Foreign exchange market A financial market in which the currencies of different countries are traded.

Free cash flow Cash generated by a business above that needed for asset replacement and growth.

Fundamental analysis A systematic process in which a security is valued by estimating the performance of the underlying company and the future cash flows associated with owning the security. These are discounted to arrive at an *intrinsic value* for the security.

Funds Generally another term for cash.

Future value The amount a present sum will grow into at a specified interest rate over a specified period of time.

G

GAAP Generally accepted accounting principles. The general rules by which financial records are kept.

Going concern value The value of a firm as a profit earning business as opposed to as a collection of assets.

Gordon model A mathematical model for valuing stock based on an assumed constant growth rate into the indefinite future.

Greenmail To avoid an unfriendly acquisition, a firm may buy shares owned by a potential acquirer at a price above the market price of the stock. The above market payment is greenmail.

Gross margin Revenue less cost where cost is spending closely associated with production. Stated in dollars or as a percent of revenue. A fundamental measure of a business's strength.

H

Hedging A maneuver or contract that eliminates risk from a transaction. In international trade, eliminating exchange rate risk by purchasing a forward contract for delivery of foreign exchange at a specified rate at a specified time.

Holding company A company that owns other companies. A *parent* company.

Horizontal merger A merger between companies in the same line of business, usually as competitors.

I

Indenture Contractual agreements associated with bonds that limit the activities of the issuing companies. The limitations are designed to reduce the risk that the firm won't be able to pay the bond's interest and principal.

Independence hypothesis In capital structure theory, the original restrictive model by Modigliani and Miller that shows stock price to be independent of capital structure.

In play A company is in play when it is the object of an acquisition attempt.

Insider information Information about companies that can influence stock price that is available to insiders but not to the general public. It is illegal to make short-term profits using insider information.

Insolvent A firm is technically insolvent when it can't pay its short-term debts. Legal insolvency implies the firm's liabilities exceed its assets.

Institutional investor A business organization that buys and sells securities. Generally a fund of some kind such as a mutual fund or a pension fund that invests the pooled money of its clients.

Interest The return on a debt investment.

Interest rate risk The risk of loss to an investor from changes in the price of a bond that arise from changes in the market interest rate. Also called *price risk* and *maturity risk*.

International bond A bond sold outside the home country of the issuing organization (borrower).

Intrinsic value The value of a security calculated by discounting its estimated future cash flows. The result of fundamental analysis.

Invest (investing, investment) Using a resource (usually money) to improve the future rather than for current consumption. Investment by companies generally means buying assets to be used in their businesses. Investment by individuals usually means buying financial assets (stocks, bonds, savings accounts) that earn a return.

Investment bank An organization that assists companies in issuing securities and selling them to investors.

Investment grade bonds Bonds above a certain quality rating. Moody: Baa; S&P: BBB.

IOS Investment opportunity schedule. A schedule of capital budgeting projects arranged in decreasing order of IRR.

IPO Initial public offering. Stock in a new company offered to the public for the first time. Such stock tends make a volatile, high-risk investment.

IRR Internal rate of return. A capital budgeting technique that rates projects according to their expected return on invested funds. The higher the return the better.

J

Junk bonds Risky bonds issued by financially weak companies that pay high rates of interest. Also called *high yield bonds.*

Just in time (JIT) Just in time inventory systems. In theory, manufacturing parts arrive "just in time" to be used in production, eliminating the need for inventories.

L

LBO Leveraged buyout. A process in which an investor group buys up a company's stock using a small amount of equity and borrowing the rest of the money required. The debt is often secured by the firm's assets. The investor groups are often the firms' managements, and the company goes from being publicly held to being privately held.

Lease An agreement for the use of an asset in return for payments over a specified period. In recent years, long-term leases have been used to acquire assets rather than purchasing them with debt or equity capital. Lease payments then become fixed financial obligations similar to interest.

(Financial) Leverage The use of borrowed money to multiply financial performance in terms of ROE and EPS.

(Operating) Leverage The use of fixed as opposed to variable cost in a firm's cost structure.

Limited liability An advantage of the corporate form. Stockholder liability for the actions of a company is limited to the value of the stock. That is, a suit against the corporation cannot be made against a stockholder simply because the stockholder is an owner.

Line of credit A relatively informal, non-binding agreement with a bank as to the maximum amount a firm can borrow during a period of time.

Liquidation Ending a firm's life by selling off its assets.

Liquidity With respect to a company, the ability to pay its bills in the short run. With respect to an asset, the readiness with which it can be converted to cash.

Liquidity preference theory A theory of the shape of the yield curve. The curve slopes upward because, all other things equal, investors prefer shorter, more liquid investments. They must therefore be induced to lend longer with higher rates.

Liquidity risk The risk of loss to an investor from the inability to sell a security to another investor at a price close to its true value.

Listed company A firm that is traded on an organized exchange is "listed" on that exchange. Unlisted companies are traded, but not on the exchange.

M

Marginal tax rate The rate at which the next dollar of income will be taxed. Generally the taxpayer's bracket rate.

Marketable securities Highly liquid short-term debt investments held by companies instead of cash. Marketable securities provide nearly the liquidity of cash but earn a modest return.

Market risk Variation on the return on a stock investment caused by things that tend to affect all stocks.

Market segmentation theory A theory of the shape of the yield curve. The debt market is segmented by term, and each segment is independent of the others. Hence the curve slopes up or down depending on supply and demand conditions in the various market segments.

Market value added (MVA) The excess of market value measured by the product of stock price and the number of shares outstanding over the book value of equity. An indication of the effectiveness of management in contributing to shareholder wealth. Also see *EVA*.

Marriage penalty In the tax system, the phenomenon that a two-income married couple pays more tax than the sum of two single people making the same money.

Maturity The date on which the principal of a debt is due. Also the time from the present until that date.

Maturity matching The idea that the maturity of financing should match the duration of the project being financed.

Maturity risk The risk of loss to an investor from changes in the price of a bond that arise from changes in the market interest rate. Also called *price risk* and *interest rate risk*. The term *maturity risk* emphasizes the fact that interest-induced price changes are larger with longer maturities.

MCC schedule Marginal cost of capital schedule. A plot of the WACC (weighted average cost of capital) against the total amount of capital to be raised in a planning period. The MCC rises as more capital is raised and the costs of individual components experience step function increases.

Merger The combination of two or more businesses under one ownership in which all but one legal entity ceases to exist, and the combined organization continues under the name of the surviving firm. When the surviving firm acquires the stock of the other(s), the transaction can be called an acquisition. A merger is *friendly* if it has the approval and support of the acquired *(target)* firm's management. It is *unfriendly* if the target's management resists. The term *merger* tends to be used loosely to refer to any business combination.

Modified Accelerated Cost Recovery System (MACRS) The system of accelerated depreciation allowed for federal tax computations.

Money market A financial market in which short-term (less than one year) debt securities are traded.

Mortgage bond A bond secured by real estate.

Mortgage loan A loan secured by real estate. Commonly referred to simply as a *mortgage*.

Multinational corporation (MNC) A company with divisions or branches in several countries.

Municipal bond (Muni) A bond issued by a government unit below the federal level. The interest on municipal bonds is exempt from federal income tax.

Mutual fund An investment vehicle in which investors contribute to a fund that uses their pooled money to invest in stocks, bonds, and other financial assets. The fund owns the assets, while the investors own shares of the fund.

Mutually exclusive projects In capital budgeting, projects that automatically exclude one another. Projects are mutually exclusive either because they're different approaches to doing the same thing or because limited resources preclude doing more than one.

N

NASDAQ National Association of Securities Dealers Automated Quotation System. The electronic network on which the OTC market functions.

National debt The accumulated total of annual federal budget deficits funded by federal government borrowing.

Nominal interest rate The named or quoted rate usually stated on an annually compounded basis. May be different from the effective rate due to non-annual compounding.

Noncash charge An item of cost or expense in the Income Statement that doesn't require cash. The primary example is depreciation.

Normal growth In stock pricing models, growth at a rate less than the rate of return. Growth rates in excess of the rate of return are *super normal*.

Note A security reflecting an intermediate term debt relationship between the issuer and the holder.

NPV Net present value. A capital budgeting technique that rates projects according to the total present value of all their associated cash flows. The higher the total or net present value, the better.

O

Operating plan A short- to intermediate-term business plan addressing a firm's methods and goals over the period covered. Most companies have an annual operating plan.

Opportunity cost The benefit foregone by using an asset in a particular way. Usually the income or benefit it would produce in its next best use.

Option (financial) The contracted right to buy or sell a security at a fixed price within a predetermined period of time, usually three to nine months. Options give speculators the chance to profit on movements in securities' prices without actually owning those securities. For example, the owner of an option to buy will profit if the underlying security's market price rises substantially above the price specified in the option during the option period.

Option (real) See Real option.

OTC market Over the counter market. A network of securities dealers who trade unlisted (on an exchange) stocks for clients.

P

Payback period A capital budgeting technique that rates projects according to the speed with which they return invested money.

Payment date The date on which a dividend check is mailed.

Payout ratio The percentage of earnings paid to stockholders in dividends.

P/E ratio The ratio of a firm's stock price to its earnings per share (EPS). A measure of the value the stock market places on the company and its future prospects.

Perpetuity An infinite series of equal payments at equal intervals of time.

Personal guarantee Generally, a guarantee made by the owner of a small business when a loan is made to the business. The owner pledges his or her personal credit in addition to that of the company. Personal guarantees circumvent the limited liability feature of the corporate form in the context of lending to small businesses.

Planning assumption An assumption about the future on which a business plan is based. The assumption must be reflected in the firm's financial projections by calculating the specific financial statement figures it implies.

Planning horizon The time a business plan covers. Typically between a few months and five years.

Pledging receivables Borrowing money using receivables as collateral.

Poison pill A corporate tactic to avoid being acquired. A poison pill is a clause written into a firm's bylaws that makes it prohibitively expensive for an acquiring firm to take control.

Political risk In international business, the chance that the value of a firm's investment in a foreign country will be reduced by political actions of either the foreign government or terrorists.

Portfolio In finance, a collection of investments.

Portfolio investment In international finance, investment in the securities of a foreign company or government.

Portfolio theory A body of thought aimed at forming investment portfolios that minimize risk for a given return.

Preemptive rights A stockholder's right to maintain her proportionate ownership in a corporation. The stockholder has the right to buy a share of any newly issued stock that is proportionate to her fractional ownership of the company before the new issue. The right is not a matter of law but must be written into the corporation's bylaws.

Preferred stock A security that pays a constant dividend forever. A hybrid between debt and common equity.

Present value The value today of a sum promised at a specified time in the future given a rate of interest. The amount that would have to be deposited today at the specified interest rate to grow into the promised sum on the specified date.

Price risk The risk of loss to an investor from changes in the price of a bond that arise from changes in the market interest rate. Also called *interest rate risk* and *maturity risk*.

Primary market A subdivision of financial markets in which securities are sold for the first time. The sale is by the issuing company to investors. Compare with *Secondary market.*

Prime rate The interest rate banks charge their largest and best commercial customers.

Privately held company A company that is not registered with the SEC and whose securities therefore may not be sold to the general public. Also called a *closely held company.*

Profitability index (PI) A capital budget-ing technique that rates projects according to the ratio of the present value of cash inflows to the present value of cash outflows. Essentially a variation on the NPV technique. The higher the PI the better.

Progressive tax An income tax structure in which higher incomes are taxed at higher rates.

Promissory note A lending agreement in which the borrower promises to pay principal and interest in accordance with specific terms.

Prospectus A document disclosing the details of a security and the underlying business to prospective investors.

Proxy The right to act for another on a specific issue. In finance the right to cast another's vote in the election of corporate directors. Incumbent directors routinely solicit stockholders' proxies for reelection.

Proxy fight A fight for control of a corporation when two or more interests compete for the proxies of shareholders in the election of directors.

Publicly traded company A company that is registered with the SEC and whose se-

curities therefore may be sold to the general public.

Pure interest rate The earning power of money. An interest rate without an inflation component or premiums for risk.

Pure play company A firm in a single line of business, as opposed to a firm with divisions in several businesses.

Q

Quick ratio Current assets less inventories divided by current liabilities. A financial ratio that measures a firm's liquidity, the ability to pay its bills in the short run, without depending on converting inventory into cash. Also called the *Acid Test.*

R

Ratio analysis A technique of analyzing the strength of a company by forming (financial) ratios out of sets of numbers from the financial statements. Ratios are compared with the competition, recent history, and the firm's plan to assess the quality of its performance.

Real asset A tangible object with value derived from the service it provides such as a house or a car. Distinguish from a financial asset, which is a piece of paper giving its owner a claim to future cash flows.

Real option The ability to take a course of action that under certain circumstances leads to a benefit. The circumstances that make the action desirable are uncertain, and maintaining the ability to take it requires expenditures before that uncertainty is resolved. Hence bearing the preliminary cost gives one the option of taking an action in the future that may or may not turn out to be desirable.

Recourse In secured lending, if the asset collateralizing a loan proves not to have the value anticipated, recourse implies the borrower is still responsible for the debt. The lender is said to have recourse to the borrower.

Red herring A prospectus for the sale of a security not yet approved by the SEC. Stamped with the word *preliminary* in red letters.

Registered securities Securities with which the issuer or a *transfer agent* keeps a list of the names of owners. Dividends or interest payments are made to *owners of record* as of specified dates.

Reorganization In bankruptcy, a plan to restructure the failing company so that it may continue in business.

Required return The minimum return that keeps an investor in a particular stock. Generally a function of the risk perceived in the investment.

Residual claim Stockholders' claim to income and assets is the residual after all other claims are satisfied.

Residual dividend theory The idea that corporations pay dividends with whatever money is left over out of earnings after all projects with a positive NPV are undertaken.

(Debt) Restructuring A change in a bankrupt firm's debt obligations aimed at allowing it to continue in business. In an *extension* creditors agree to give the firm longer to pay. In a *composition* creditors agree to settle for less than the full amount owed.

Return The payment to an investor for the use of funds. Usually expressed as a percent of the investment.

Revolving credit agreement A formal, binding agreement with a bank as to the maximum amount a firm can borrow during a period of time. Interest is paid on the amount borrowed and a commitment fee is paid on the unused balance.

Risk (in finance) The probability that the return on an investment will be less than expected. The variability of the return on a particular investment. The variance of the probability distribution of return.

Risk-adjusted rate of return In capital budgeting, a rate used in place of the cost of capital to reflect especially risky projects.

Risk aversion The premise that most people prefer lower risk investments when expected returns are about equal.

Risk-free rate The interest rate excluding all risk premiums. The risk-free rate consists of the pure rate and an inflation adjustment. It is approximated by the three-month treasury bill rate. Written as k_{RF}.

Risk premium A component of a rate of interest or return that compensates the investor for bearing some kind of risk.

ROA Return on assets. Net income divided by total assets. A financial ratio measuring performance concentrating on profitability and asset utilization.

ROE Return on equity. Net income divided by equity. A financial ratio measuring performance concentrating on profitability, asset utilization, and the use of borrowed money.

ROS Return on sales. Net income divided by sales revenue. A financial ratio measuring performance concentrating on profitability.

S

Safety stock Extra inventory carried to prevent stockouts in the event of heavy use or delayed delivery.

Scenario analysis A business planning technique in which the implications of variations in planning assumptions are explored. Also known as "what-if-ing."

Seasoned issue An older bond.

Secondary market Sales of existing securities between investors. Compare with *Primary market.*

Secured debt Debt backed by specific assets (the security or collateral) that become the property of the lender in the event of default.

Securities analysis A systematic approach to valuing securities, especially stocks, by studying an issuing firm's business and industry. The *securities analyst* plays an important role in the financial industry.

Securities and Exchange Commission (SEC) The federal agency responsible for regulating securities dealings.

Security A financial asset. Commonly a stock or a bond. An asset pledged to guarantee the repayment of a loan.

Signaling effect of dividends The idea that dividends send a message about management's confidence in the future of the firm—that is, paying a regular or increased dividend signals that the firm is fundamentally sound even if it appears to be having problems. The signaling idea leads to the practice of holding dividends constant or raising them in the face of poor financial performance. Also known as the *information* effect of dividends.

Sinking fund An arrangement to guarantee that funds are available to pay off a bond's principal at maturity.

SML Security market line. The central element of the *CAPM.* The SML purports to explain how the market sets the required return on a stock investment.

Specialist An official in a stock exchange. The specialist is assigned the stocks of specific companies and is responsible for conducting an orderly market in those securities.

Spinoff A method of divesting a business unit by setting it up as a separate company and giving its shares to stockholders in proportion to their holdings of the original firm. After the spinoff stockholders can trade the two stocks separately.

Spontaneous financing Financing provided by current liabilities that arise automatically as a result of doing business.

Stable dividend A dividend that may remain constant or increase over time but that does not decrease.

Stand-alone project In capital budgeting, a project with no competition either for the task it is to accomplish or for resources.

Stand-alone risk The risk associated with investing in a stock that's held by itself, outside of a portfolio. Stand-alone risk depends on the volatility of a stock's own return rather than on the effect its inclusion has on the volatility of the return of a portfolio.

Stock A financial asset representing a share of ownership of a corporation. Entitles the owner to dividends if any are paid.

Stockbroker A person licensed to assist investors in buying and selling securities for a commission.

Stock dividend Essentially a stock split in which the number of new shares issued is less than or equal to 20% of the original number outstanding.

Stock exchange A physical place in which stocks are traded by brokers on behalf of their investor clients.

Stock market The network of exchanges, brokers, and investors that trade in stocks.

Stockout An inventory shortage.

Stock split A change in the number of shares outstanding by issuing new shares in proportion to those already owned. All stockholders' proportionate ownership is maintained, and no economic value is created. Used to keep stock prices within a desirable trading range.

Strategic plan A long-term business plan addressing broad issues of what a company's management wants it to become and how it is to do business.

Stretching payables Paying invoices after they're due according to the terms of sale. Also called *leaning on the trade.*

S-type corporation A corporate form in the tax code that gives small businesses some of the benefits of both the traditional corporation and the proprietorship. Most notably, S-type corporations escape the double taxation of earnings.

Subordinated debt Debt with a lower priority for the payment of interest and principal than other (senior) debt.

Sunk cost A cost associated with a project expended prior to making the decision to undertake that project (for example, the cost of research into the idea). Since sunk funds are already gone, they cannot alter future costs or benefits, and should not be included in the analysis leading to a decision.

Sustainable growth rate The rate at which a firm can grow if none of its financial ratios change and it doesn't raise any new equity by selling stock. The growth in equity created by earnings retained.

Synergy A situation in which two companies operating together under one ownership perform better than the sum of their separate performances. A popular reason claimed for mergers.

T

Takeover The transfer of control over a company from one group to another. The term generally has a hostile implication.

Target capital structure The capital structure that management strives to maintain as new capital is raised. An estimate of the structure that maximizes stock price.

Target company The object of a corporate acquisition or merger. See *Merger.*

Tax base The thing that is taxed. Generally income, wealth, or consumption.

Tax bracket A range of income over which the tax rate is constant.

Tax loss carry back (or forward) The allocation of losses in a year to previous or subsequent years for the purpose of calculating taxes in those years. Losses may be carried back 3 and forward 15 years.

Technical analysis An approach to valuing securities by examining past patterns of price and volume. The technique is based on the idea that such patterns repeat themselves.

Temporary working capital Working capital that supports seasonal peaks in business.

Tender offer A general offer to stockholders to purchase shares at a specified price, usually for the purpose of acquiring a company.

10-K Report A supplement to the annual report that public companies must file with the SEC.

Term The time until a debt security's principal is due to be repaid. Also called the debt's maturity or time until maturity.

Terms of sale The conditions under which a sale is made primarily with respect to payment. Terms include a date on which payment is due and often specify a *prompt payment discount* that may be taken if payment is made within a specified time.

TETR Total Effective Tax Rate. The combined income tax rate including federal and state tax. Less than the sum of the two because state tax is deductible from federal tax.

Time value of money Calculations involving the present and future values of money under the action of compound interest. Also called *discounted cash flow.*

Top-down planning Business planning based on a set of goals forced on the organization by senior management. Top-down planning has a tendency to lead to excessively optimistic plans.

Trade credit Credit granted in the normal course of business between companies. That is, vendors don't usually demand immediate payment for their products.

Trading range A price range in which stocks are thought to appeal to the widest variety of investors. Typically between $30 and $100. Stock splits function to keep prices within a trading range when the stock is appreciating.

Transaction gain or loss The difference between the net result of an international transaction and what was initially expected that arises from variation in exchange rates.

Transfer agent An organization that keeps records of the owners of a company's securities. When a security is sold by one investor or to another, ownership is transferred on the record by the transfer agent.

Translation risk The gain or loss on the value of assets and liabilities held in another country that results from variation in exchange rates. Generally relatively meaningless as long as the foreign operation is not liquidated or sold. Therefore not generally taxable.

Treasurer The executive in charge of external financing in most companies. The treasurer generally reports to the CFO.

Trustee With respect to bonds, an organization that ensures compliance with the conditions set forth in the indenture. With respect to bankruptcy, a person who administers the bankrupt organization to ensure funds are properly handled.

V

Valuation A systematic process to determine the price at which a security should sell in financial markets.

Vertical merger A merger between companies when one is a supplier or a customer of the other.

W

WACC See *Cost of capital.*

Warehousing In finance, a method of securing the lender's interest when borrowing is secured by inventories. The inventory is placed in a warehouse operated by a third party. When it is drawn out of the warehouse by the borrower, a pro rata share of payment on the loan is due.

What-if-ing See *Scenario analysis.*

White knight When a firm is an acquisition target by an unattractive suitor, a more desirable acquirer is known as a white knight. (The original suitor may be known for particularly ruthless treatment of acquired companies.)

Widely held company A corporation whose ownership is distributed over a large number of people with no single individual or group having a significant proportion.

Working capital The balance sheet accounts associated with day-to-day operating activities. *Gross working capital* is generally defined as current assets and *net working capital* as current assets minus current liabilities.

Y

Yield Return.

Yield curve The relationship between interest rates and the term of debt, generally expressed graphically. A *normal* yield curve is upsloping, reflecting rates that increase with increasing term. An *inverted* curve is downsloping.

YTC Yield to call. Bond pricing calculations assuming the bond will be called at the end of the protected period.

YTM Yield to maturity. Bond pricing calculations assuming the bond will pay interest until maturity at which time it will repay its principal (face value).

Z

Zero coupon bond A bond that pays no interest during its life. A "zero" sells for the present value of the principal repayment. However, the IRS imputes interest during the bond's life on which the bondholder must pay tax.

INDEX